HANDBOOK
OF
VISUAL COMMUNICA

THEORY, METHODS, AND

LEA'S Communication Series

Jennings Bryant/Dolf Zillmann, General Editors

Selected titles include:

Bryant/Zillmann · Media Effects: Advances in Theory and Research, Second Edition

Heath/Bryant · Human Communication Theory and Research: Concepts, Contexts, and Challenges, Second Edition

Newton · The Burden of Visual Truth: The Role of Photojournalism in Mediating Reality

Reichert/Lambiase · Sex in Advertising: Perspectives on The Erotic Appeal

Zillmann/Vorderer · Media Entertainment: The Psychology of Its Appeal

Riffe/Lacy/Fico · Analyzing Media Messages: Using Quantitative Content Analysis in Research

For a complete list of titles in LEA's Communication Series, please contact Lawrence Erlbaum Associates, Publishers, at www.erlbaum.com.

HANDBOOK
OF
VISUAL COMMUNICATION

THEORY, METHODS, AND MEDIA

Edited by

Ken Smith
University of Wyoming

Sandra Moriarty
University of Colorado

Gretchen Barbatsis
Michigan State University

Keith Kenney
University of South Carolina

LEA LAWRENCE ERLBAUM ASSOCIATES, PUBLISHERS
2005 Mahwah, New Jersey   London

Senior Acquisitions Editor:	Linda Bathgate
Editorial Assistant:	Karin Wittig Bates
Cover Design:	Kathryn Houghtaling Lacey
Textbook Production Manager:	Paul Smolenski
Full-Service Compositor:	TechBooks
Text and Cover Printer:	Hamilton Printing Company

This book was typeset in 11/13 pt. Dante Roman, Bold, Italic.
The heads were typeset in Franklin Gothic, Demi Bold, and Demi Bold Italic.

Lawrence Erlbaum Associates, Inc., Publishers
10 Industrial Avenue
Mahwah, New Jersey 07430
www.erlbaum.com

Library of Congress Cataloging-in-Publication Data

Handbook of visual communication research : theory, methods, and media / edited by
   Ken Smith . . . [et al.].
       p.   cm.—(LEA's communication series)
   Includes bibliographical references and indexes.
   ISBN 0-8058-4178-4 (alk. paper)—ISBN 0-8058-4179-2 (pbk.: alk. paper)
    1. Visual communication.   2. Visual communication—Methodology.   I. Smith, Ken
(Kenneth Louis), 1947–   II. Series.

  P93.5.H363   2005
    302.23—dc22
                                       2004018622

Contents

Preface

In his 1990 book, *Eye and Brain*, Richard Gregory wrote, "We are so familiar with seeing that it takes a leap of imagination to realize that there are problems to be solved (p. 17). While we humans had to learn how to walk, talk, and read, we never had to learn how to see. Thus, unlike walking or talking or reading, we are less cognizant of the many processes that contribute to what we see. Scholars in the rapidly evolving field of Visual Communication now attempt to identify and describe these many processes. Yet, the field is so new, so diverse, and evolving so rapidly that recognizing all the processes involved in seeing is difficult because few attempts have been made to compile the diverse and varied work of Visual Communication scholars.

This book represents one such attempt to bring this work together. In the process, it compiles the dominant theories used by scholars to explain the many processes that affect vision, and it demonstrates many of the methodologies utilized by Visual Communication researchers. The studies included in this volume relate to a wide scope of different media, so this book also contributes to the knowledge of how viewers utilize and perceive different media.

Although the book could be organized by methodology or by media type, it was instead organized by theoretical area. The fundamental processes of seeing were grouped into 12 theoretical areas (as conceived and explained in the introductory chapter). Each body of theory is then followed by exemplar studies that illustrate some of the types of research used in exploring each of these areas. In no case are these methodologies the only ones used to explore the theoretical area in question. Nor are studies of each specific medium limited to the methodologies presented in this volume. Rather, the intent is to display the wealth of methodologies available to visual communication scholars and to increase the body of knowledge about the media types that they examine. Just as researchers are beginning to discover evidence that relates to the way humans see, so also is this book a starting point—one that attempts to group together the theories and methodologies that aid in this understanding.

As a result this book is appropriate for the academic scholar, the visual communication student, and the media practitioner. For academics and students, it serves as a compilation for much of the theoretical background necessary to understand visual communication. It also serves as a methodological handbook, of sorts, for visual communication researchers. For the media practitioner, it aids in the understanding of how audiences use media, and it can contribute to more effective use of each specific medium.

Much of the work in this volume is an outgrowth of a number of organizations. Primary among these is the unaffiliated Annual Visual Communication Conference initially established by Robert Tiemens from the University of Utah and Herb Zettl from San Francisco State. The conference served as a focal point for nurturing the development of visual communication theory and research through the richness of interdisciplinary perspectives.

Many of these disciplinary areas are reflected in other academic conferences where visual communication scholarship was encouraged. These include the Association for Education in Journalism and Mass Communication, the National Communication Association, the International Communication Association, and the International Visual Literacy Association. Much of the work in this book was initially presented at the conferences for these organizations, and the editors would like to thank all of those who have worked in support of the visual communication divisions of these groups. They represent the primary formats for the presentation of visual communication research and without these venues, this book would not be possible.

The editors would also like to thank the editors at Lawrence Erlbaum who helped to bring this project to fruition, especially Linda Bathgate and Karin Wittig Bates. Most of all, the editors would like to thank the authors who were willing to endure the red ink and criticism that their chapters were required to suffer in order to make this volume possible.

From an Oak to a Stand of Aspen: Visual Communication Theory Mapped as Rhizome Analysis

SANDRA MORIARTY
University of Colorado

GRETCHEN BARBATSIS
Michigan State University

As with others interested in pictorial signification, Stafford (1996) found a significant historical link between the downgrading of visual sense making and an "aggressively linguistic" view of cognition (p. 7). Because this view dominates virtually every discipline, she argued the need to "forge an imaging field" that would be "focused on transdisciplinary problems and to which we as scholars, creators, and teachers of visual communication bring a distinctive, irreducible, and highly visible experience" (p. 10). The distinctiveness and explanatory mode of a field of imaging would be in a "deeply connected body of non-verbal knowledge with specific cognitive and formal properties, rules, and techniques" needed to "understand visuals and the intricate processes of imaging" (p. 127).

Identifying the transdisciplinary roots of any field calls for a different analytical approach. Investigations into the theory and philosophy of traditional academic fields often focus on determining the roots of the field using a tree of knowledge metaphor complete with a trunk, or central organizing theory, and branches, which are offshoots of the discipline. As illustrated in Fig. 1, the logic is hierarchical, linear, and fairly rigid. We argued in the past, however, that this approach is inappropriate for a field such as visual communication where the organization is scattered and fragmented (Barbatsis & Moriarty, 2000). Rather than an oak tree, a more appropriate metaphor might be the stand of aspen or clump of bamboo that grows and spreads through the type of rhizomatic

FIG. 1.   Oak tree.

FIG. 2.   Bamboo clump.

process illustrated in Fig. 2. A rhizome, then, is the metaphor we use in this chapter to map visual communication as a way to introduce both the complexity and the dynamics of this emerging field.

The challenge, however, is in defining the field of visual communication. To be a discipline, one expects to see one or several central or unifying theories that guide the development of the content area over time. In visual communication, however, there is no unifying theory, nor should there be, because the area represents the intersection of thought from many diverse traditions. In a discussion of whether semiotics qualifies as a field, Umberto Eco (1979) made the distinction between *a field of studies*, which he defined as a repertoire of interests that is not as yet completely unified, and *a discipline*, which is an area with its own method and a precise objective. Craig (1999) explained that a field will emerge to the extent that its scholars increasingly engage with theories and research questions that cut across various disciplinary traditions. In other words, if visual communication is emerging as a field, then there should be a sense of a repertoire of theories and research methods that scholars in that area find useful. The analysis in this chapter of the visual communication roots and offshoots is an attempt to determine if such a trend is observable for visual communication.

RHIZOME ANALYSIS

From botany we learn that a rhizome is a horizontal creeping stem lying on or under the ground from which shoots arise or spread and roots descend. Nodes are sometimes connected to a main stalk and they can be separated to create new plants. Strawberries, crabgrass, bamboo, and iris plants are common examples of rhizomes from nature. As Fig. 2 shows, the rhizome is a dynamic, decentered, system or network. It is a structure without any controlling center of hierarchy, a kind of self-reproducing multiplicity that cannot be understood as a single organization or localized in a particular territory. It's also generative in that the offshoots or runners become freestanding plants.

Deleuze and Guattari (1987) used the metaphor of the rhizome to distinguish between totalizing unities and nontotalizing multiplicities. They discuss traditional arborescent thought, or what we refer to as the tree of knowledge metaphor, as universalizing and essentializing knowledge of "systematic and hierarchical principles (branches) that are grounded in firm foundations (roots)." Rhizomes, on the other hand, are "nonhierarchical systems of deterritorialized lines that connect with other lines in random, unregulated relationships" (Best & Kellner, 1991, pp. 98–99).

Rhizomatic thought deconstructs the binary logic of arborescent thought, seeking to pluralize and disseminate its "roots and branches" so to produce "differences and multiplicities by making new connections" (Best & Kellner, 1991, p. 99). Importantly, the method of rhizomatic analysis is productive or generative of new forms through lines of thought or intersections of ideas. As Deleuze and Guattari (1987) stated, "In truth it is not enough to say, 'Long live the multiple,' difficult as it is to raise the cry. No typographical, lexical, or even syntactical cleverness is enough to make it heard. The multiple must be made" (p. 6).

The multiple is made, then, through rhizomatic analysis. The subject of rhizomatic analysis is conceptualized in terms of three basic kinds of lines, which explain the decentered nature of the system. These "lines" refer to a phenomenon's constituting or deconstituting components. As shown in Fig. 3, this triadic schema includes rigid lines,

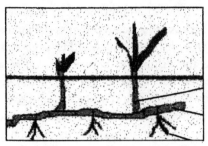

rigid lines (molar)

supple lines (molecular movements)

lines of escape (flight)

FIG. 3.   Rhizome structure.

supple lines, and lines of escape. The first, rigid segmentary lines, are molar lines that "construct fixed and normalized identities...by way of binary oppositions" (Best & Kellner, 1991, p. 99). Molar aggregates of a rhizomatic or decentered system are components that are characterized by "hierarchy, stratification, and structuration" (p. 91). The second kind of lines, supple segmentary lines, are "molecular movements away from molar rigidity," which disturb the "linearity and normalcy" of molar aggregates (p. 100). They represent "cracks" in their totalizing facades. Finally, there are lines of flight, which form the "plane of creativity" (p. 100). These lines are "the full-fledged deterritorializing movements away from molar identify where cracks become ruptures and the subject is shattered in a process of becoming multiple" (Best & Kellner, 1991, p. 100). As suggested earlier, Deleuze and Guattari characterized these lines of flight as "fundamentally positive and creative," rather than as lines of "resistance or counterattack" (1987, p. 531).

Lines of flight (runners) form the most interesting part of a rhizomatic map because they indicate arenas of dynamic creative activity. This generation of multiplicity differs from other forms of analysis that tend to manufacture hierarchies. Grounded theory analysis, for example, provides an approach for developing a model that is systematically derived from data, yet it also works toward the creation of a coherent theory. As with other traditional methods, its purpose is to discover categories from which to inductively build a hierarchically structured theoretical framework with structural cohesion. Methods such as this seek to generate a convergent, rather than divergent, conception of reality.

By contrast, positive and creative theorizing of the development of a rhizomatic field as following lines of flight is based on the notion that multiple paths of escape and transformation are possible because there is no system "that does not leak in all directions" (Deleuze & Guattari, 1987, p. 204). Accordingly, as represented schematically in Fig. 4, centers of power "are defined much more by what escapes them or by their zone of impotence than by their zone of power" (Deleuze & Guattari, 1987, p. 217).

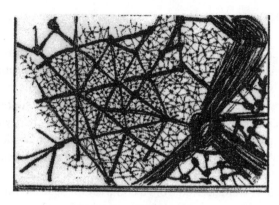

FIG. 4.   Rhizome map.

THEORIZING ABOUT VISUALS

As a method for theorizing visual signification, then, rhizomatic thought analyzes the various "flows" of theoretical activity and research associated with visual sense making. It looks for theoretical "lines of escape which can be further deterritorialized" as well as for "rigid or supple lines that stratify" theoretical struggles and "threaten their revolutionary character" (Deleuze & Guattari, 1987, p. 204). As a theoretical model that maps creative flows and combats "totalizing modes of thought" (Best & Kellner, 1991, p. 103), it seems particularly appropriate to productive theorizing about visual sensemaking.

DETERRITORIALIZED AND DECENTRALIZED FRAGMENTS

Our rhizomatic theorization of visual communication sought to map its planes of creativity by constituting its multiplicities. We deterritorialized visual communication theory by decentering it. Instead of looking for philosophical roots and foundational principles, the analysis theorized the field as random and unregulated fragments. We attempted to generate as uncolonized fragments the terms that constitute a discourse of visual communication.

Following several brainstorming sessions, we identified the terms listed in various conceptual organizations of visual communication (Moriarty, 1997; Moriarty & Kenney, 1995). The taxonomy and bibliography generated by Moriarty and Kenney (1995), for example, produced 102 concepts and topics. The intent in this step of the analysis was to avoid overarching philosophical schemas or unifying theories, thus terms such as *psychology, narrative, aesthetics, representation*, and *mass communication* sat comfortably along side one another in a nonhierarchical and unstructured plane. These fragments of the discourse made a long list of terms related to visual communication. Using a rhizomatic approach, we theorized that these terms could be organized (and understood) according to a decentered system of molar aggregates, molecular movements, and lines of flight.

MOLAR COMPONENTS: DISCIPLINES

The first step in the analysis involved identifying nodes of discourse, the relevant disciplines that contribute to the emerging field of visual communication. Intrinsic in the rhizomatic model is the notion that the lines flow from some point to some other point. At its base, then, are "centers of power," or nodes that attract and support theory building. These are characterized by their segmentation of organized theory as well as unifying methods. We began mapping the field of visual communication by identifying traditional academic centers of power in terms of disciplines that inform the field of visual communication. We refer to these aggregations as *Molar Disciplines*. These molar components, as presented in Table 1, were derived from a compilation of academic departments listed in a collection of typical university catalogs. Some, although not all, contribute to visual sense making. The extent of the contribution is determined by a later step in the analysis.

TABLE 1
Traditional Molar Disciplines

	Unifying Theories	*Unifying Methods*
SOCIAL SCIENCES		
Psychology	theories of the individual	experimental
Sociology	theories of social systems	survey / case study / ethnolography
Anthropology	theories of culture	ethnography
Political Science	theories of political behavior	survey
Speech / Comm Rhetoric	theories of human interaction	rhetorical analysis, criticism content analysis
Linguistics	theories of language	study of pronunciation, grammar, and syntax
HUMANITIES		

Philosophy
  a. Epistemology
  b. Aesthetics
  c. Ethics
	theories of knowledge	analytic, theory building

Art	theories of aesthetics	historical, performance criticism
Literature	theories of text and reader	historical, performance criticism, textual analysis, reader response
History	theories of the past	historical method, interviews
NATURAL SCIENCE		
Biology / Physiology	theories of living organisms	experimental
Physics	theories of matter and energy	experimental
Geology / Geography	theories of the earth	time series

TABLE 2
Emerging Molecular Fields

Field of Study	Referent Points and/or Focus
RELEVANT OFFSHOOT FIELDS	
Semiotics	epistemology, linguistics, and sign systems
Critical/cultural studies	literature, cultural studies
Neuroscience	biology, perceptual psychology
Information systems	engineering, computer science, and technology
PROFESSIONAL FIELDS	
Mass communication	media and human interaction
Education	learning
Business	commerce and exchange
Law	regulation and policy
Architecture	design of space
Archaeology	prehistory structures, artifacts, and art

MOLECULAR COMPONENTS: FIELDS

The next part of the analysis identified the molecular components, or fields of study, that also contribute to the theorizing of visual communication. There are two types of molecular units: (a) offshoots of the traditional disciplines and (b) professional fields. Unfixed and deterritorialized fields of study, such as education and mass communication, which are professionally oriented, as well as offshoot areas such as cultural studies and information systems, mix and match pieces that have disciplinary roots from other areas but have no unifying theory or methodologies of their own. In a postmodern fashion, they reflect movements away from molar rigidities and disturb the traditional linearity and rigid hierarchical model of knowledge with professional orientations and performance dimensions that often cross disciplinary lines.

This list is not conclusive, because movement is continuous and the fields may still be defining themselves. Visual communication could be located in the offshoot list, although the purpose of this chapter is to define its focus and referent point in order to substantiate such a conclusion. Table 2 represents the combined list of professional fields and their focus, as well as the offshoot fields and their referent points in terms of related disciplines and fields.[1] These supple segmentary lines of visual sense making are presented in Table 2.

REFERENT POINTS FOR VISUAL COMMUNICATION

After identifying traditional molar disciplines and emerging molecular fields, the next step was to relate these categories of study to visual communication to identify points

TABLE 3
Taxonomy of Visual Communication

VisCom Area	Referent Points	
ART AND DESIGN		13 total
Aesthetics, composition	Aes, Art, Psy	
Graphic design	Aes, Art, Mass Comm	
Art history	Aes, Art, Hist	
Creativity, imagination	Psy, Art, Edu, Mus	
COMMUNICATION		12 total
Rhetoric, myth, persuasion	Comm, Mass Comm	
Nonverbal, gestural	Comm, Anthro	
Literary/literature	Lit, Crit Stu	
Signs and symbols	Sem, Comm, Mass Comm, Ling	
Attitudes, beliefs	Psy	
Arousal, emotion	Psy	
PSYCHOLOGY		12 total
Perception	Psy, Phy, Bio	
Cognition, visual intelligence	Psy, Bio, Neu Sci, Epis	
Multiple coding	Psy, Comm, Sem	
Psychology of art	Psy, Art	
CULTURAL AND CRITICAL STUDIES		12 total
Sociology, anthropology	Soc, Anth	
Linguistics	Ling	
Cultural studies	Cult Stu, Eth, Pol Sci, Econ, Soc	
Critical studies	Crit Stu, Lit, Art, 8Aes	
VIS COM THEORY		10 total
Representation	Ethics, Crit Stud	
Mental imagery, visualization	Psy, Edu, Art	
Philosophy, epistemology	Epist, Psy	
Language metaphor	Comm, Ling, Lit	
EDUCATION		8 total
Learning	Edu, Psy	
Visual Literacy	Edu, Mass Comm, Comm	
Teaching of visual communication	Edu, Mass Comm, Comm	
HISTORY		6 total
	Hist, Art, Phil, Mass Comm, Archi, Arche	
LAW AND ETHICS		4 total
	Law, Mass Comm, Eth, Cult Stu	
PHYSICAL SCIENCES		3 total
Vision, physiology, optics	Bio, Phy	
Neural processing	Neu Sci	
PROFESSIONAL AREAS		27 total
TV/Film Studies	FS, Bio, Lit, Hist, Mus, Aes	
Photography	Photo, Aes, Bio	
Journalism	Mass Comm, Lit, Cult St, Crit St	
PR and advertising	Mass Comm, Pers, Lit, Cult Stu, Criti St	
Architecture	Archi, Aes, Art, Hist	
Archaeology	Arche, Hist, Geo, Bio, Phy	

of intersection where visual communication theory and research seem to be emerging by comparing these components with a Taxonomy of Visual Communication developed as an outline for a visual communication bibliography by Moriarty and Kenney and published in the *Journal of Visual Literacy* (1995). Table 3 represents the disciplines and fields identified as referent points for articles under the key headings from the taxonomy (left column). By counting the number of referent points represented by these articles, this analysis determined which of the disciplines and fields seem to be contributing the most conceptual thought to the development of visual communication.

To further analyze Table 3, we looked at the dominant referent points in terms of the frequency of mentions in the coding schema used to match the visual communication taxonomy with the molar disciplines and molecular fields in terms of the current visual communication literature. These are the nodes that act as starting points for the lines of movement. Clearly the professional areas and their focus on practice and performance drive the development of thought in the field of visual communication. Beyond professional areas, however, there are four areas that are making equivalent contributions—art is highest, followed closely by communication, psychology, and the combined topic of critical and cultural studies. Next come visual communication theory and education. The other areas from the taxonomy—history, law, and the physical sciences—are presently on the margins of the visual communication field.

A RHIZOME "MAP" OF VISUAL COMMUNICATION

The same information was then used to begin mapping the field of visual communication in terms of its referent points and intersections. Figure 5 illustrates the clusters of referent points, both molar (oblong) and molecular (oval) components, as well as the points of intersection (diamond) where the central components of visual communication seem to be emerging.

Figure 5 displays the molar and molecular components of visual communication as well as the emerging lines of flight that are beginning to define the field of visual communication. The lines of flight represent the areas of visual communication study lying on a plane of creativity between disciplines and fields contributing to the development of visual communication as a field. In some cases, they represent intersections; in other cases, they represent points of departure. They are the components that "deconstitute" or "leak" from the totalizing efforts of the more traditional disciplines and fields. This map demonstrates, in other words, the interconnectedness of the ideas that are evolving and becoming the field of visual communication.

The final part of the analysis identified the lines of flight in our theorizing of visual communication. These components—characterized as "ruptures"—are full-fledged deterritorializing movements away from molar identities. They are fundamentally positive and creative, and form a "plane of creativity" characterized by "birth and rebirth" (as well as death and destruction). Comprising new insights and possibilities as well as old notions and dead ends, lines of flight are the most visible signs of temporality and multiplicity in a dynamic rhizomatic system. In some cases, they are the nonterritorialized fragments from the initial list of terms; in most cases, however, they are the

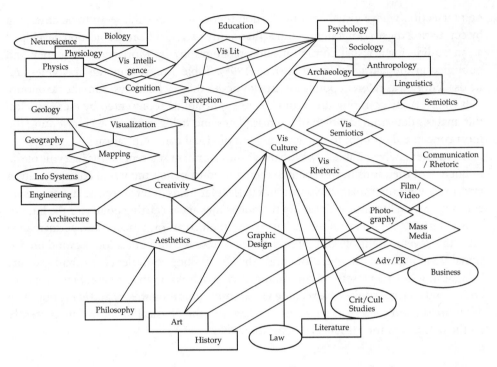

FIG. 5. A Rhizomatic Map of Visual Communication. (▢, Molar; ◯, Molecular; ◇, Intersections)

visual offshoots of the dominant referent point. Visual communication theory's plane of creativity and the primary nodes where various interests seem to cluster are presented below:

Visual Communication Nodes

- Visual intelligence / Cognition / Perception
- Visual literacy
- Graphic design / Aesthetics
- Visualization / Creativity
- Visual culture / Visual rhetoric / Visual semiotics
- Professional performance: Photography / Film / Video / Internet /
  Mass media / Advertising / PR

Such a list highlights the primary components of the emerging visual communication field. It is not, however, conclusive. Adjacent areas, for example, can be found in such fields as architecture, landscape architecture, archaeology, choreography, and costume design, among others. Because this is a dynamic system, some areas will become more central and dominant and others may shrink and even die.

A "NONTERRITORIALIZED" CONCLUSION

This chapter is a response to Stafford's invitation to begin the imaging of the field of visual communication. The metaphor that makes it possible to visualize this emerging field is a rhizome because it provides a method that is organic, dynamic, and decentered in order to identify the referent points, find the lines of flight, and plot the intersections of developing knowledge.

The plane of creativity constituted by the lines of flight in Fig. 5 is an area of difference that offers an opportunity to study visual sense making in its own terms. The multiplicity generated in lines of flight and their intersections is productive and creative. It does not operate in a traditional linear or language-centered reality. Rather it displays in the most exciting terms, a way of theorizing visual communication outside and beyond disciplinary boxes, an approach that is both organic and dynamic.

Issues to consider include how we apprehend the experience of visual communication with language that collapses and flattens the phenomenon in much the same manner as a cartographic projection. In familiar terms, the language map is simply not the pictorial territory. Language can be pushed, however. Narrative, analogy, metaphor, and poetic rhythms of harmony, counterpoint, variation, and accent all provide forms of language use that more closely resembles the nonlinear experience it attempts to describe (Stephens, 1998; Turkle & Papert, 1993). A new vocabulary of imaging and seeing—one of a show-er and show-ee—for example, can be developed and used to describe the communicating partners in a visual experience. Writing in a style of "thick description" can be encouraged in our portrayal of the visual encounters we observe. As we are able to use language in these and other ways that more authentically capture a visual sense-making experience, the plane of creativity generated by this rhizomatic analysis of visual communication theory and research could well be a guide map for this transdisciplinary territory.

ENDNOTE

[1] Although the term *root* would be appropriately used here, to avoid confusion between the concept of root in a rhizome structure and the concept of a central node in an arborescent structure, we are using the term *referent point* instead. Deleuze and Guattari pointed out, for example, that "arborescent structures have rhizome lines" and "rhizomes have points of arborescence that portend the emergence of hierarchy" (Best & Kellner, 1991, p. 102). Accordingly, the "distinction between arborescent and rhizomatic multiciplicities is not a rigid opposition" (p. 102).

REFERENCES

Barbatsis, G., & Moriarty, S. (2000, June). Strawberry fields forever. The 14th Annual Visual Communication Conference, Chico Hot Springs, MT.

Barry, A. M. (1997). *Visual intelligence: Perception, image, and manipulation in visual communication research.* Albany: State University of New York Press.

Best, S., & Kellner, D. (1991). *Postmodern theory: Critical interrogations.* New York: Guilford Press.

Craig, R. T. (1999, May). Communication theory as a field. *Communication Theory, 9*(2), 119–161.

Deleuze, G., & Guattari, F. (1977). *Anti-Oedipus* (R. Hurley, M. Seem, & H. Lane, Trans.). New York: Viking Press.

Deleuze, G., & Guattari, F. (1987). *A thousand plateaus* (B. Massumi, Trans.). Minneapolis: University of Minnesota Press.

Eco, U. (1979). *A theory of semiotics*. Bloomington: Indiana University Press.

Glick, J. (1987). *Chaos: Making a new science*. New York: Penguin Books.

Graber, D. (1990). Seeing is remembering: How visuals contribute to learning from television news. *Journal of Communication, 40*(3), 134–155.

Kosko, B. (1993). *Fuzzy thinking*. New York: Hyperion.

McCrone, J. (1994, August 20). Quantum states of mind. *New Scientist, 35–37*.

Messaris, P. (1994). *Visual "Literacy": Image, mind and reality*. Boulder, CO: Westview Press.

Moriarty, S. (1996). Abduction: A theory of visual interpretation. *Communication Theory, 6*(2), 167–187.

Moriarty, S. (1997). A conceptual map of visual communication. *Journal of Visual Literacy, 17*(2), 9–24.

Moriarty, S., & Kenney, K. (1995). Visual communication: A taxonomy and bibliography. *Journal of Visual Literacy, 15*(2), 7–156.

Neiva, E. (1999). Redefining the image: Mimesis, convention and semiotics. *Communication Theory, 9*(1), 75–91.

Stafford, B. (1996). *Good looking: Essays on the virtue of images*. Cambridge, MA: MIT Press.

Stephens, M. (1998). *The rise of the image the fall of the word*. New York: Oxford University Press.

Turkle, S., & Papert, S. (1993). Epistemological pluralism and the revaluation of the concrete. In I. Harel & S. Papert (Eds.), *Constructivism* (pp. 161–192). Norwood, NJ: Ablex Publishing.

Worth, S. (1981). *Studying visual communication*. Philadelphia: University of Pennsylvania Press.

Zettl, H. (1999). *Sight sound motion: Applied media aesthetics*. Belmont, CA: Wadsworth.

Aesthetics

1

Aesthetics Theory

DENNIS DAKE
Iowa State University

AN AESTHETIC THEORY OF VISUAL COMMUNICATION

One of the most important pieces of the visual communication puzzle is aesthetics. The nature of beauty and why it affects us so deeply is mysterious. Why do qualities so elusive to define (like a sunset or a half-opened rose) affect us so powerfully? This is an important question to consider in visual communication. It is suggested that, because of the essentially nonverbal nature of aesthetics, what can be written is only speculation "about" the nature of visual aesthetics and cannot therefore be "of" visual aesthetics itself.

The aesthetic aspects of communication are (a) visible, structural, and configurational in nature; (b) largely implicit in apprehension; (c) holistic in conveying meaning (not wholly translatable into parsed, discursive form); and (d) cognitive in a generative sense, based on a unique type of visual logic.

Three disciplines—philosophy, art, and science—have been used historically to study issues about visual aesthetics. Of these disciplines the visual arts offer the most complete and truly visual understanding. The sciences increasingly can, however, offer factual evidence for defining how aesthetic qualities play a foundational role in human communications.

THE PHILOSOPHIC PERSPECTIVE

Aesthetics is traditionally defined as "the study and theory of beauty and of the psychological responses to it" (Neufeldt & Guralnik D. E., 1998); the term specifically refers to the branch of philosophy dealing with art, its creative sources, forms, and effects. This definition forms a convenient launching point toward a much wider application of aesthetic phenomena to all visual communications, but it is only a starting point.

A brief historical review will outline the problem philosophers have had articulating a theory of beauty. Plato's analysis of beauty—in bodies, in souls, in knowledge—attempted to describe the affective dimensions (based on a "love" of something) of the aesthetic response. His approach became increasingly more abstract until it evolved as a Theory of Forms based on what he determined to be properties that beautiful things have in common (Dickie, 1971). Subsequent philosophers, such as Aristotle and St. Thomas Aquinas, continued the development of form theory in terms of an analysis of more practical objects from the world of experience. In the Renaissance, the evolving theory of art defined beauty in terms of a harmony of parts.

In the 18th century, however, philosophers added notions of the sublime and a philosophy of taste, which made notions of beauty more subjective and diffuse and contributed to the fragmentation of the theory of beauty. In other words, a useful theory of beauty based on proportion, unity, and other commonly considered dimensions could not be agreed upon. As Newton (1962, p. 11) observed, "Beauty could not be described, therefore it could not be defined." In response, British thinkers and the German philosopher Kant sought a unified theory in the realm of esthetic theory, in which cognitive and affective responses were recognized, but within a personal context that permitted individualistic appreciation of beauty. In more recent times, aesthetic theory has articulated two dimensions—the quality itself and the response to it. The aesthetic response, then, is the object of the search.

Aesthetics is a branch of philosophy that is rich in discursive theory and interpretative speculation, but not totally helpful in understanding the role aesthetic qualities play in visual communication. Visual aesthetics are visual in foundation and holistic in understanding. As the 19th-century artist Paul Cezanne observed, "Talking about art is almost useless" (Rewald, 1976, p. 303).

Philosophy is based on verbal discursive and parsed explication and follows logical, linear construction. The thousands of philosophical arguments for aesthetics advanced historically are based on thought and expression of a different order and character from visual creation and communication themselves. Thus, philosophical arguments may prove more of a distraction from exploration of aesthetic aspects of visual communication than an aid to understanding. A biologically based (from recent discoveries in neuroscience) understanding of aesthetics could encompass many diverse philosophical arguments and give a more stable foundation for understanding visual communication.

THE ARTISTIC PERSPECTIVE

Using visual and intuitive experimentation, artists provide a complementary body of knowledge and understanding on aesthetic visual communication. Although science provides explicit explanations of aesthetic response, the discipline of art provides a unique visually based perspective on the role of aesthetics in communication. Artists, as the makers of visual messages, are infinitely connected to subtle aesthetic clues, their selection, manipulation, and ultimate refinement. This knowledge of aesthetic relationships, gained through visual performance, provides a permanent visual record of decisions made and wordless aesthetic relationships established.

What is suggested (Dake, 1993, 1995, 1996, 2000) is a form of qualitative action research utilizing observed and expressed studio ideas of artists (artists' preparatory sketches, maquettes, diaries, letters, photographs of developing artworks) correlated with findings from the sciences. Analogical agreement from this perspective provides a critical, fact-based filter for expanding understanding of aesthetic communication. Where science and art provide compatible perspectives, there is hope for a more objective theory of visual aesthetic communication.

THE SCIENTIFIC PERSPECTIVE

Much scientific research on aesthetics has been generated in the biological and social sciences. One branch of knowledge yielding a promising perspective is experimental aesthetics (psychobiology). This approach to exploring aesthetic communication has generally focused on the responsiveness of individuals to aesthetic properties.

Over the past 40 years, most notably in Berlyne's ecological approach to responsiveness, a more precise understanding of aesthetic relationships has been generated. Berlyne coined the term "collative properties" to define stimulus qualities that depend on comparative apprehension with present or past stimuli. Collative variables such as complexity, ambiguity, incongruity, uncertainty, surprise, novelty, and indistinctness were shown to be critical to gaining and maintaining viewer attention critical to sustaining the aesthetic experience (Berlyne, 1974). By informed shaping of aesthetic relationships, visual communicators systematically study the capacities of the visual brain using a unique set of intuitive disciplinary tools.

Dr. Semir Zeki, of the International Institute of Neuroesthetics, in his book *Inner Vision: An Exploration of Art and the Brain*, discusses the primary importance of a brain-based disciplinary approach. "All visual art is expressed through the brain and must therefore obey the laws of the brain, whether in conception, execution, or appreciation; no theory of aesthetics that is not substantially based on the activity of the brain is ever likely to be complete, let alone profound" (1999, p. 1).

THE INTERDISCIPLINARY PERSPECTIVE

Studying all manner of visual communications media, not just those usually classified as art, makes it obvious that all visual communication must utilize the same human perception system as do art objects. There is no separate eye-to-brain connection for the processing of images labeled art. By looking at what is scientifically known about the way the brain processes visual information, one can learn more about the nature and functions of aesthetic aspects of perception and therefore the role that aesthetic phenomena play in visual communication. By studying art one can gain a deeper emotional and intuitive understanding of the multitude of sensitive aesthetic relationships involved in shaping an image of visual communication.

Establishing a physical basis for aesthetic expression by rigorous scientific exploration and object-based artistic observation promises to help the individual overcome the current confusing, subjective understanding of aesthetics. A common expression states,

"Beauty is in the eye of the beholder." Although it is true that subjectivity can enlighten the individual viewer's personal response, it also obscures deeper, more dependable, transpersonal contributions made by visual communication.

VISUAL AESTHETIC THOUGHT

Aesthetics is not about "things" but about systems of ecological relationships and the processes that create these relationships and aid in their interpretation. The three primary players in this ecological balancing act are: the visible object itself, the maker of this object, and the intended viewer. Figure 1.1 illustrates the interactive nature of these three elements.

The physical object itself contains observable relational properties among and between all the visible elements. Every line, shape, value, color, and so on, is related to the other visible elements. Creating meaningful connectedness between the developing visible form and a hoped for message is the goal of the maker. The physical, concrete nature is therefore vital to both the viewer and the maker, helping them connect and communicate.

As the image-maker engages in shaping the emerging system of phenomenological elements, an intimate relationship develops between object and maker. To fully participate in the creative process, the maker must focus on all emerging physical relationships, mental nonmaterial relationships, plus the relationship to personal intentions and goals. There must also be a concern for the potential response of the viewing audience.

While creating, the maker also serves as an initial viewer of the emerging image. Other viewers will also get visible information from the perception of the object. Short of explicit verbal statements of intention by the maker, the visually literate viewer needs to complete the maker's creative act by interpreting these relationships among visible relationships in the created object.

Aesthetics permeates all interactions between these three components of visual communication. Relationships may not immediately reveal the exact intentions of the creator or help the viewer discover any potential hidden interpretations; but intentions, of both the maker and the viewer can alter everyone's perspective on imagistic meaning. Knowledge of meaning can become clearer through a deliberate process of analysis and interpretation. Heightened awareness of one's own mental imagery is the first step to accessing this deeper aesthetic aspect of visual communication.

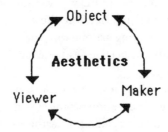

FIG. 1.1.   Diagram of aesthetic relationships.

PERCEPTION OF AESTHETIC RELATIONSHIPS

Visual Aesthetic Thought Is Configurational (Visibly Relational)

Aesthetic thought is first of all structural thought. Mental imagery (thought) is made manifest in the material world. In analyzing a work of aesthetic communication, Rudolf Arnheim has made this case: "What matters is that even at this abstract level the compositional structure is grasped as a whole, namely as a configuration of perceptual components symbolizing the psychological theme of the work by direct visual reflection. The example shows also what I meant when I said that basic perceptual features point directly to the deepest meanings of the artistic statement, even though to do so they need to be seen in the structural context of the whole" (1992, p. 33). Without a physical manifestation, aesthetic qualities would not be perceivable. Without a particular holistic configuration, an image / message would be different in its impact. The qualities of both the parts (details and separate visual elements) and of the whole structure of an image are simultaneously conveyed in a specific gestalt presentation. The aesthetics are embedded in the whole.

For visual communication to take place, both part (parsed and detailed) and whole (holistic and global) information need to be effectively mixed in the viewer's brain. Studies indicate that the local details of the image are processed in a module within the brain separate from the module for handling global information. A 1995 study by Heilman, Chatterjec, and Doty discovered that a global-local dichotomy "may be related to the manner in which the right and left hemispheres respond to spatial frequencies" (p. 60). Their data shows that the right hemisphere tends to direct attention toward visual extrapersonal space (far from the body). This makes right hemispheric processing more concerned with global matters of fuzzy, low spatial frequency. The left hemisphere, by contrast, directs attention to visual information taking place close to the body (peripersonal space with detailed, sharp, high spatial frequency). The shaping of successful aesthetic messages, therefore, must involve synchronization of two hemispheres through a process of creative visual thinking. Visual information that only considers individual parts rather than contextual relationships results in never seeing the forest for the trees. The perception and understanding of complex relationships are among the most basic contributions of aesthetic perception to visually based communication.

It appears that individuals trained in visual communication and aesthetic appreciation see more of the global, contextual information as well as more detailed nameable parts. Aesthetically trained brains take in more global structural information and balance it with a subtle perception of small detailed differences. Significant aesthetic perception begins, however, before conscious awareness processes can make reasoned decisions. Aesthetic perception precedes cortical information processing and therefore any conscious awareness of associative symbolic inferences. At a very basic level, visual-perceptual processing determines the type and amount of information that is sent to the brain for further thought.

Physiognomic Relationships

Aesthetic perception seems to utilize large-scale aspects of visual compositional structure. These complex relationships between visual elements are not easily comprehended in verbal terms. The designated term for these complex structural relationships is *physiognomics*.

In aesthetic communication, what is mentally compared and correlated are basic physiognomic structures supporting and composing each image. The contribution of aesthetic thought to the construction of meaning begins with a heightened sensitivity to this foundational aesthetic structure. Such aesthetic physiognomics are not household names for objects that can be easily grasped, named, and classified. Aesthetic physiognomics are largely overlooked by the naming functions of the brain's left hemisphere.

The sensitive perception of aesthetic/physiognomic qualities is present in both children and adults. According to a developmental study by Seitz and Beilin "Adults as well as children perceive category membership as a matter of degree" (1987, p. 324). Learning to deal constructively with the fuzzy boundaries is the mental space where visual appearance-based analogies begin to form and deep meaning is based.

Flexibility and Fluency

Creative thinking is closely related to aesthetic apprehension because both use similar areas of the human brain. Fluency and flexibility characterize all healthy and productive visual thought. From a variety of potential visual possibilities, the maker of an image can visually judge the most potentially potent and pertinent structural message. The aesthetic quality or spirit of a visual message can then best be understood as the embodiment of a certain quality of flexibility and fluidity of thought that offers new possibilities to the viewer's mind for consideration. During the graphic ideation of visual message, designers and artists leave an indelible structural mark on images, which then sets up a potentially equally creative outcome in the viewer's mind. The quality that makes for an effective visual message emerges from a visual comparison with a variety of knowable possibilities. This quality is directly perceivable by a trained individual who sees configurational relationships in their full meaningful context, including very personal and individual relationships to the image. A verbal analysis of aesthetics only deals with one part at a time and is therefore always incomplete in description and understanding.

In the creative design of visual messages, as well as in creative viewing and interpretation, flexibility of structural construction is vital. Flexibility provides for the purely perceptual apprehension of novelty, originality, and message integrity. Ritualized, stereotyped, and repetitive messages are not as likely to attract or sustain viewer attention. Therefore, the message's flexibility is crucial for discovering and imparting significant aesthetic aspects of meaning.

Implicit or Hidden Aesthetic Relationships

Not all perception of the visible world is explicitly available to the maker or the viewer. Neuroscientists theorize that the brain has dual memory systems, one explicit and one implicit. Visual message designers need access to the contents of implicit perception and memory to craft messages with communicative, experiential impact.

Current research tantalizingly suggests that the perception of aesthetics depends on a subconscious substrate that may not be totally a process of inductive (active) learning

FIG. 1.2. Untitled photograph, Stephen Herrnstadt, 1988 (used with permission of the artist).

or even based on enculturation. If this is true, then visual communications would not have to be learned as communication's conventions, but would be innate and support universal aspects of visual communications as is often proposed for the fine arts.

Do skilled visual communicators really see more of the contents of implicit perception as well as explicit configurations made up of lines, shapes, colors, values, and so on? A 1995 study by Liu found that experienced designers show greater awareness of implicit subshapes compared to inexperienced designers. Only experienced designers could lower their thresholds of recognition activation, which allowed them to discover implicit emergent subshapes. Seeing more aesthetic forces potentially opens up a whole world of "felt" holistic structural qualities. These intuitively felt qualities of orientation, implied spaces, and the essence of empty space add significantly to both the quality and quantity of visiospatial information available to the brain—things the viewer can explicitly see and name plus felt qualities of the image that convey more patterns of meaningful forces.

A comparison of three forest scene photographs by Stephen Herrnstadt in Figs. 1.2, 1.3, and 1.4 illustrates both the explicit perception of holistic configurational structure and the richness of implicit relationships. Although all of these images are of nameable forms called trees, this layer of meaning does little to help us understand the aesthetic dimension of communication.

FIG. 1.3.   Untitled photograph, Stephen Herrnstadt, 1988 (used with permission of the artist).

In the case of Fig. 1.2, there are several verticals that penetrate a textured ground in the left half of the photograph. The strongest structure is the widest with marginally more detail. The message of the verticals contrasts with the much looser and more dynamic forces of bramble of texture in the bottom half of the image, from which the verticals arise.

Figure 1.3 has a quite different aesthetic structure. The verticals here have a slight tilt, which makes them more dynamic. The widest and most dominant vertical is also the darkest. The middle linear form is lightest of the three verticals and bends most dramatically toward the third vertical on the right-hand side. This highly structured area relates to the lighter, bottom two thirds of the surface, which has a looser, more linear textural feel. There is a subtle curvature of ground/tree horizon line going from upper left to lower right. When combined with the strong spreading forces of the verticals, this curvature implies a kind of strong aesthetic energy emanating from the curvature of the earth itself.

Figure 1.4 also presents a dominant vertical, but in a central position. Because it is so detailed in texture compared to its surroundings, it becomes the commanding dominant focus. Some implicit relationships then create an even stronger contrast in meaning. In Fig. 1.4 the ground and horizon line are deemphasized in favor of a foggy atmospheric mist. The ambiguous depth of the background gives an otherworldly feel to

FIG. 1.4.   Untitled photograph, Stephen Herrnstadt, 1987 (used with permission of the artist).

the work. When combined with the strong backlit staging, it suggests a meaning more related to dematerialized spirit than earthly concerns. Together the explicit and implicit relationships create a fuller understanding of the visual message. A comparison of the aesthetic structure of these three photographs therefore yields a quite different aesthetic basis for communication of distinct visual messages.

Holistic Vision: Thinking by Appearance

How is it that the viewer is able to construct meaningful patterns out of an image's visible and hidden relationships? Could there be a visual semantic structure underlying visual communication? Dr. Betty Edwards first proposed a basic visual language structure in her book *Drawing on the Artist Within* (1986). Edwards described and demonstrated the expressive, communicative potential of an underlying nonobjective analog structure, visible in student exercises and works by historic artists.

Takahashi (1995) presented separate scientific collaboration of this universal semantic potential. By using similar visual analogs created by a group of art students, Takahashi showed the rich potential for visual communication in underlying visual holistic structure. Analysis of these analogs by an unrelated group of nonart students identified a remarkable degree of aesthetic communication. Takahashi concluded, "This finding suggests that a synergistic relation exists between some perceptual property and a specific word concept. The presence of specific visual structures may activate one's knowledge about kinds of affective categories" (1995, p. 681). Takahashi proposed a positive link between affective and aesthetic mental processes and later cognitive processes. The implication points to the existence of a purely visual aesthetic language based on holistic abstract structure, as revealed in outward appearance.

Thinking by appearance is a function of the right hemisphere of the brain. Levy and Trevarthen concluded in a 1976 study that "The right and left hemispheres are specialized for detecting structural and functional similarities, respectively" (p. 311). The left hemisphere makes logical connections between objects that fulfill similar functions within defined categorical boundaries. Associative reasoning seems to follow the same pattern. In contrast, the right hemisphere specializes in making comparisons based purely on structural appearance. Appearance-based reasoning in the right hemisphere is largely unknown to the left hemisphere. Perception of the same images presented to the left hemisphere yield logical and functional decisions. Thus words used to interpret meaning from images can, by their linear nature, distort and convert the information in the visual communication.

Reconstrual

Mary Peterson (1993) examined the multiple interpretive possibilities within shape memory and identified a foundational principle of aesthetic creativity she called reconstrual. She provided evidence of the vast potential for multiple mental reconstruals from a single geometric form. Instead of a singular visual recognition and categorization, Peterson suggested that in perception, "there exists a stage in which a structural description of a shape is not connected to an interpretation" (1993, p. 172). At this important stage of aesthetic perception there appears to be a rapid mental search through an imagistic mental lexicon for the best possible match with incoming visual stimuli. Awareness of the mind's ability to perform a multiple-layered search provides for imaginative perception and the discovery of possible multiple, meaningful interpretations.

Figure 1.5, "Self Portrait as Pagan Fire God" by Chuck Richards, presents a novel sense of multiple meanings to the traditional subject of self-portrayal. The representation is filtered through many layers of thinking by appearance. In addition to the symmetry of religious icons, appearance comparisons recall fabricated sets of old exotic movies (such as King Kong), sacrificial rituals of distant cultures, hedonistic masks of spring revels, mythic sculptural representations of gods who need to be fed (note the eating utensils), the manipulation behind the scenes (see small Wizard of Oz–like figure in lower-left-hand corner, and the showmanship of the circus). Rich and fluid appearance thinking endows the maker and viewer with the capability to stretch and break the tight conceptual boundaries of literal meaning. Once "outside the box," the multiple series of visual relationships and spatial associations lead inevitably to multiple analogies. These embedded analogies lead to a form of poetic "visual rhyming" and then as in the case of this example to new multiple-layered meanings for self-portraiture. Who is the person being portrayed? What is the individual's self-image and his in life? What personality characteristics define this person's life? The systematic analysis of analogies yielded by these reconstruals changes

FIG. 1.5. Self-portrait as pagan fire god, Chuck Richards, 24″ × 24″, colored pencil (used with permission of the artist).

the aesthetic tone of an actual scene and provides a charged series of potential metaphoric meanings. A self-portrait is more that the outward appearance of the individual.

Tolerance for multilevels of meaning occurring simultaneously is prerequisite to fully understanding meaning-making in visual communication. Logical, verbal reasoning is often not the best laboratory for discovering meaningful patterns. Arthur Koestler suggests the real basis for understanding visual meaning: "The mind is insatiable for meaning, drawn from, or projected into the world of appearances, for unearthing hidden analogies which connect the unknown with the familiar, and show the familiar in an unexpected light. It weaves the raw material of experience into patterns, and connects them with other patterns" (1975, p. 390).

Meaning in the world of the aesthetic visual communication can never be singular and literal because the viewer's brain will automatically make multiple connections through reconstrual. The attempt to impose singular meaning on images (through logical argument and discursive assertion) does not foreclose flexibility of appearance-based thinking.

Understanding how meaning arises from aesthetic qualities requires response-ability from individuals doing creative seeing. This implies not only the ability to respond to initial physiognomic phenomena, but also the obligation to pursue the universal implications

FIG. 1.6. Untitled photograph, Stephen Herrnstadt, 1988 (used with permission of the artist).

within individual responses. Painter Pablo Picasso comments on the subject: "Reality is more than the thing itself. I look always for the super reality. Reality lies in how you see things. A green parrot is also a green salad and a green parrot. He who makes it only a parrot diminishes its reality. A painter who copies a tree blinds himself to the real tree. I see things otherwise. A palm tree can become a horse" (July 10, 1950, *Sunday Observer*). Perceived meaningful information involving reconstrued aesthetic qualities becomes a creative mental action by the viewer.

Two photographic landscape images further demonstrate the diverse potential meanings generated by using thinking by appearance. The image shown in Fig. 1.6, Herrnstadt's untitled photographic work, has many possible reconstruals, new nonliteral connections beyond immediate associations. Could it be reminiscent of soldiers' corpses on a battlefield, for indeed the fallen, decaying trees on the forest probably resulted from destructive forces for organic life. The same configuration of fallen trees could also be analogous to the veins of Mother Earth herself. Through these veins would flow energy, creating further organic growth, much like decaying vegetable matter on the forest floor. The crystalline light shimmering on the organic forms transports the viewer to a transcendental and fantastic scene. None of these levels of meaning, however, forecloses a literal reading of the visible evidence. A forestry expert could make accurate scientific conclusions from the same visible evidence.

FIG. 1.7. Terminus, Mary Stieglitz, digital image, 2003 (used with permission of the artist).

Figure 1.7, Terminus, a digital print by Mary Stieglitz, presents nature up close in what appears to be the rotting carcass of an animal. The angular forms also resemble mountains rising from flat land. This relationship attaches a monumental importance to the message as a huge creature preys on the parched land. An altered sky area conjures up scenes of rusting metal, adding a decaying aesthetic. An organic beauty in this arrangement engages the viewer to carefully attend to the interplay of form and texture, as thinking by appearance lends deeper levels of meaning. Metaphoric thinking leads to far more significant meaning levels than a rotting carcass literally suggests. Visual meaning can certainly be understood through words (interpretation), deeds (visible attributes), or underlying tone (aesthetic qualities). The power of visual communication lies in relationships among these three aspects of understanding images.

THE LOGIC OF VISUAL AESTHETICS

How can the maker and viewer have faith and rely on a level of meaning embedded in an image? Why not opt for an imaginary construction in the mind? A central dilemma of aesthetic visual communication is whether visual images can provide evidence of important human cognitive activity or whether an image's communicative value is wholly dependent on discursive logic. Can one judge the quality, preciseness, and utility of communication by purely visual means? What makes a visual image "work" for maker and viewer alike?

The final part of this chapter's theoretical proposition speculates on the full cognitive import of aesthetic aspects of visual communication. The hypothesis is that effective communication depends on a unique visually based logic, created through visual modules and processes of the human brain. The order and patterns of neural brain structure determine visual communication effectiveness. Visual logic is defined here as a system of visual relationships that encourages a developed internal sense of image cohesiveness, integrity, and elegance necessary to attract attention and guide the viewer to a sense of aesthetic completion and comprehension.

Six individual, interlocking principles guide the development of this sense of visual logic. These six principles are (a) Ambiguity and Meaning, (b) Control of Direction, (c) Ecological Relationships, (d) Tensional, (e) Unity, and (f) Realism.

Ambiguity and Meaning

There are no "pictures" in the human brain, only individual neuronal responses to different elements in the image. The visual world is therefore always ambiguous (without a single level of meaning that can be clearly explained in words). Having accepted this, it is important for viewers to explore the "manner" in which meaning construction is taking place in their own brains. No amount of parsing with left hemispheric processes will alone suffice to comprehend meaning. The ambiguity and meaning principle suggests that, if aesthetic form and content are effectively related, the visually literate viewer is able to extract relevant information by concentrating on visible relationships and the nature of meaning-making in the human brain. Multiple meanings emerge later from the layered relationships with the other five principles.

Control of Direction

The control of direction principle suggests there are actions that the image-maker can control about the manner in which the image attains and maintains the viewer's attention and interest and elicits an aesthetic response. On the other hand, there are other aspects, such as arriving at a common uniform interpretation of meaning, that can't be dictated by the maker. Individual viewers will arrive at some degree of individual connection and relationship to the image based on their individual wants, needs, and expectations. The individual image-maker can control many aspects of "how" the viewer's perceptual system interacts with visible relationships but not the final interpretation. The maker can direct the viewer's eye throughout the image's significant areas through directional clues, groupings of elements, and tensions. The maker can also choose to emphasize certain aspects of the image and to subordinate others in order to direct the viewer's mind to significant matters. However, the sheer number of visible relationships will quickly overwhelm the parsing and decision-making functions of the brain. Intuition must therefore guide the image-maker and viewer in controlling the effect the image has on the brain.

Ecological Relationships

When interpreting the inherent visual logic imbedded in an image, the maker (during the act of ideation) and the viewer (in a process of perception) both become involved in an intimate reciprocal and ecological relationship with the image. The visual structure offers parameters for perception of possible multiple meaning levels, as well as the potential for fixation on one particular meaning or focused aesthetic response. The maker, through trial and error, shapes this image, and the viewer must empathize with this relationship while at the same time understanding his or her ecological interactions with the structure.

Gregory Bateson (1975) theorized that the human mind is essentially an ecological governor, controlling the body's processes to ensure that decisions are of maximal value. Because the body is part of the environment itself, appropriate mental interpretation cannot be totally fixed and objective. Through trial and error decision making, the brain compares visible structure to potential meanings. During this process, failures of judgment or aesthetic response (for example, an immediate "I don't like it," based on superficial viewing) could be viewed as positive experiences to be valued. Failures could indicate to the viewer that he or she has stretched interpretation beyond his or her past capabilities and is searching for less obvious relationships, analogies, and connections. The depth of visual logic is not always initially apparent.

Tensional

Illusionistic use of spatial clues adds an implied tension with the image's true flat surface. In addition, the visual elements on the picture plane's flat surface have tensional relationships with each other, with sides of the image, and with its center of the image. The sum total of all tensions, both explicitly perceived and implicitly apprehended, creates an aesthetic impression of mood and a visible foundation for the communicated message.

Generally, artists and image-makers intuitively and explicitly shape aesthetic elements to discover meaningful relationships and cause a specific brain response. Based then on the viewer's life experience with tensions in the environment, the message being communicated can be perceived as being more or less truthful. Important tensional relationships and their implied meanings are thus passed from message-maker to viewer based on normal human perceptual functions.

Unity

Because the brain's left hemisphere specializes in parsing information, rather than grasping it whole, the full cognitive and communicative potential of holistic gestalt forms of knowing is often overlooked (Bolles, 1991). Every effective visual message has cohesive visual forces that group visual elements (the gestalt grouping principles of similarity, proximity, closure, continuation, and common fate) into meaningful and aesthetically rewarding patterns. These underlying structures are not usually apparent to the untrained eye.

Unity of message implies a wholeness of spirit or purpose that give the visual sense trustworthiness. Without unity, the experience for the viewer lacks cohesion, making communicative interpretation less sure. With unity, the viewer's own natural perceptual abilities can interpret visual clues to determine the nature and type of visual message and its relationship to reality.

Realism

All imagery communicates some aspect of reality. That reality may not be a naturalistic illusion of optical conditions but conveys knowledge about aspects of reality not readily accessible to the unaided human eye (microscopic views, time-related processes, or energies outside the visible spectrum). To construct visual images, the maker has a series of clues to depth used that aid in communicating knowledge of reality. The knowledgeable viewer must be able to reinterpret these clues to meaning.

Gestalt psychology provides understanding of depth clues (overlap, shadow, color, gradients, and placement) that give the viewer clues to form and space. Motion clues in moving images also shape the nature of visual evidence. Awareness of complexity and arbitrary use of visual clues is necessary for viewers to independently evaluate the visual image for veracity and importance. Application of the realism principle provides a ground of information that is either believable and true or false and manipulative. Informed visual communication must consider the medium of realism selected by the message designer and its aesthetic and affective dimensions created within the viewer.

Layering

Visual elements never exist in isolation; they are always effected by what is around them. What is implicitly meaningful is the larger gestalt configuration. The philosopher John Dewey stated, "To think effectively in terms of relations of qualities is as severe a demand upon thought as to think in terms of symbols, verbal and mathematical" (Dewey, 1934, p. 46). For an effective visual message to be shaped, a composite, holistic gestalt must emerge from multiple types of separate aesthetic relationships, a layering of simultaneous events.

Each image contains forces and tensions; groupings; selections of depth clues; decisions made through trial, error, and reflection; and conscious design decisions directing the viewer's attention. Like geological stratum, each separate relationship represents a process of layered transparency, a unique type of visually based logic. This logic supports the process of visually based reasoning and the interpretation of the perceived message.

Visual logic is based on understanding of normal functions of perceptual processing of the human nervous system. Words can only speak of one thing at a time, but images arrive holistically, everything present simultaneously. Visual logic must be understood in a wordless way of speculating, considering, and eventually knowing.

SEEKING CONSILIENCE

Aesthetic exploration can lead to unique forms of knowing that are cognitive and affective at the same time. Zeki (1999) concluded that wordless modes of knowing can discover significant new knowledge, complementarily and sometimes foreshadowing science. Figure 1.8 is a painting by the author of this chapter entitled, "Thought Structure." Some years after its completion and titling, a chemist interpreted this image as an example of fractal geometry (the mathematics of asymmetry). As the artist, this was not my conscious

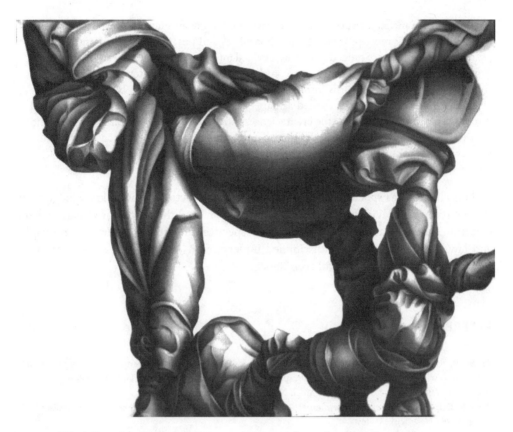

FIG. 1.8.   Thought structure, Dennis Dake, 22-1/2″ × 28″, airbrush/watercolor, 1977.

intention. My intention was to capture the structure of my thoughts: Mathematics as a subject had never entered my conscious thought. The visually logical resemblance to a representation of a fractal is, however, striking.

Aesthetics are the mute, unnamable aspects of visual communication that one could talk about forever. If visual communication is defined as only clarity and exactness in verbal interpretation, much potential power of visual imagery to connect human minds would be lost. Literary exactitude forces visual information through too narrow a funnel. Filtered out is some of visual language's richest potential for informational relationship.

In his 1998 book *Consilience: The Unity of Knowledge*, biologist Edward O. Wilson argued for the fundamental unity of all knowledge and the need to search for proof that everything is organized in terms of a small number of fundamental natural laws, underlying every branch of learning. The physical and biological sciences are now increasingly reaching such consilience, where new understandings can be based on common principles. Wilson saw the effort to bridge between the sciences and other disciplines as a great labyrinth, which must be negotiated. The greatest challenge Wilson foresaw was consilience between the sciences and the arts.

Interpretation has multiple dimensions, namely history, biography, linguistics, and aesthetic judgment. At the foundation of them all lie the material processes of the human mind.

Theoretically inclined critics of the past have tried many avenues into that subterranean realm, including most prominently psychoanalysis and post modernist solipsism. These approaches, which are guided largely by unaided intuition about the way the brain works, have fared badly. In the absence of a compass based on sound material knowledge, they make too many wrong turns into blind ends. If the brain is ever to be charted, and an enduring theory of the arts created as part of the enterprise, it will be by stepwise and consilient contributions from the brain sciences, psychology, and evolutionary biology. And if during this process the creative mind is to be understood, it will need collaboration between scientists and humanities scholars. (Wilson, 1998, p. 216)

This chapter has speculated on some possible connections among knowledge from the neurosciences, evidence from artistic expression, and the nature of visual aesthetic communication. Triangulation from these perspectives may generate verifiable principles and laws on which to base a disciplined understanding of aesthetic aspects of visual information exchange, a fruitful consilience.

REFERENCES

Arnheim, R. (1992). But is it science? In G. C. Cupchik & J. Laszlo (Eds.), *Emerging visions of the aesthetic process: Psychology, semiology and philosophy* (pp. 27–36). New York, Cambridge University Press.

Bateson, G. (1972). *Steps to an Ecology of Mind*. New York, Ballantine.

Berlyne, D. E. (1974). The new experimental aesthetics. In De. E. Berlyne (Ed.), *The new experimental aesthetics* (pp. 1–25). New York, Wiley.

Biederman, I. (1987). Recognition-by-components: A theory of human image understanding. *Psychological Review, 94*(2), 115–147.

Bolles, E. B. (1991). *A Second way of knowing: The riddle of human perception*. New York: Prentice Hall Press.

Buswell, G. T. (1937). *How people look at pictures—A study of the psychology of perception in art*. Chicago: University of Chicago Press.

Changeux, J. P. (1994). Art and neuroscience. *Leonardo, 27*(3), 189–201.

Dake, D. (1993). Visual Links: Discovery in Art and Science. In R. Braden, J. Baca, & D. Beauchamp (Eds.), *Art, Science, & Visual Literacy* (pp. 11–21). Blacksburg, VA: International Visual Literacy Association.

Dake, D. (1995). Process Issues in Visual Literacy. In D. Beauchamp, R. Braden, & R. Griffin (Eds.), *Imagery and Visual Literacy* (pp. 1–23). Blacksburg, VA: International Visual Literacy Association.

Dake, D. M. (1996). A Personal Vision Quest: Learning to Think Like an Artist (editer's choice award). In R. Griffin (Ed.), *Vision quest: Journey toward visual literacy—A Book of selected readings* (pp. 1–10). State College, PA: International Visual Literacy Association.

Dake, D. (2000). *Brain Compatible Visual Education: Part 1: A Knowledge Base for Improving Art Education*. Reston, VA: National Art Education Association.

Dake, D. (2000). *Brain Compatible Visual Education: Part 2: Some Promising Art/Science Connections*. Reston, VA: National Art Education Association.

Dake, D. (2000). *National Visual Mind: The Art and Science of Visual Literacy. Book of readings*, Natural Vistas in Visual Literacy & The Word Around Us.

Dewey, J. (1934). *Art as Experience*. New York, G. P. Putnam.

Dickie, G. (1971). *Aesthetics: An introduction*. New York, Pegasus Books.

Edwards, B. (1986). *Drawing on the artist within*. New York: Simon & Schuster.

Elliot, P. (1986). Right (or left) brain cognition, wrong metaphor or creative behavior. It is prefrontal lobe volition that makes the human difference in release of creative potential. *Journal of Creative Behavior, 20*(3), 203–214.

Fish, J., & Schivener, S. (1990). Amplifying the mind's eye: Sketching and visual cognition. *Leonardo, 23*(1), 117–126.

Goldschmidt, G. (1990). Linkography: Assessing design productivity. In Robert Troppl (Ed.), *Cybernetics and Systems* (pp. 291–298). Riveredge, NJ: World Scientific.

Goldschmidt, G. (1991). The dialectics of sketching. *Creativity Research Journal, 4*(2), 123–143.

Halbreich U., & Friendly, D. (1980). The characteristics of tension-provoking composition and lines as represented in Munch's paintings. *Confinia Psychiat, 23*, 1187–1192.

Heilman, K., Chatterjec, A., & Doty L. (1995). Hemispheric asymmetries of near-far spatial attention. *Neuropsychology, 9*(1), 58–61.

Humphreys, G. W., & Bruce, V. (1989). *Seeing static forms, in visual cognition: Computational, Experimental and Neuropsychological Perspectives* (pp. 9–21). Hillsdale, NJ: Lawrence Erlbaum Associates.

Jones-Gotman, M. (1986). Memory for designs: The hippocampal contribution. *Neuropsychologia, 24*(2), 193–203.

Jones-Gotman, M., & Milner, B. (1977). Design fluency: The invention of nonsense drawings after focal cortical lesions. *Neuropsychologia, 15*, 653–674.

Kitterle, F., Hellige, J. B., & Christman, S. (1992). Visual hemispheric asymmetries depend on which spatial frequencies are task relevant. *Brain and Cognition, 20*, 308–314.

Koestler, A. (1975). *The Act of Creation*. London: Pan Books, Ltd.

Kosslyn, S. (1994). *Image and Brain*. Cambridge, MA: MIT Press.

Kristjanson A., & Antes J. (1989). Eye movement analysis of artists and nonartists viewing paintings. *Visual Arts Research, 15*, 21–31.

Levy J., & Trevarthen C. (1976). Metacontrol of hemispheric function in human split-brain patients. *Journal of Experimental Psychology: Human Perception and Performance, 2*(3), 299–312.

Liu, Y. (1995). Some phenomena of seeing shapes in design. *Design Studies, 16*, 367–385.

Maar, D. (1982). *Vision: A computational investigation into human representation and processing of visual information*. New York: W. H. Freeman.

Mazrsolek, C. J., Squire, L., Kosslyn, S. M., & Lulenski, M. E. (1994). Form-specific explicit and implicit memory in the right cerebral hemisphere. *Neuropsychology, 8*(4), 588–597.

Miller, L., & Tippett, L., (1996). Effects of focal brain lesions on visual problem-solving. *Neuropsychologia, 34*(5), 387–398.

Nadaner, D. (1985). Mental imagery and art education. *Visual Arts Research, 11*(2), 84–89.

Nebes, R. D. (1972). Dominance of the minor hemisphere in commissurotomized man on a test of figural unification. *Brain, 95*, 633–638.

Neufeldt, V., & Guralnik, D. E. (Eds.). (1988). *Webster's New World Dictionary*, Third Edition (p. 21). New York: Simon & Schuster.

Newton, Eric (1962). *The meaning of beauty*. Hammondsworth, Middlesex, U.K: Penguin Books.

Nodine, C. F., & McGinnis, J. J. (1983). Artistic style, compositional design, and visual scanning. *Visual Arts Research, 9*(1), 1–9.

Peterson, M. A. (1993). The ambiguity of mental images: Insights regarding the structure of shape memory and its function in creativity. In B. Roskos-Ewoldsen, M. J. Itons-Peterson, & R. E. Anderson (Eds.), *Imagery, Creativity, and Discovery: A Cognitive Perspective*. Amsterdam: North-Holland.

Picasso, P. (1950). Quoted in *Sunday Observer*, July 10, 1950.

Pigott, S., & Milner, B. (1994). Capacity of visual short-term memory after unilateral frontal and anterior temporal-lobe resection. *Neuropshycologia, 32*(8), 969–981.

Rewald, J. (Ed.). (1976). *Cezanne Letters*, Paul Cezanne letter to Emile Bernard Aix, 26 May, 1904. New York, Hacker Art Books, Inc. NY.

Rosenblatt, E., & Winner, E. (1988). Is superior visual memory a component of superior drawing ability? In L. Obler & D. Fein (Eds.), *The exceptional brain—Neuropsychology of talent and special abilities* (pp. 341–363). New York: Guilford Press.

Rothenberg, A. (1986). Artistic creation as stimulated by superimposed versus combined-composite visual images. *Journal of Personality and Social Psychology, 50*(2), 370–381.

Ruff, R., Allen, C., Farrow, C., Niemann, H., & Wylie, T. (1994). Figural fluency: Differential impairment in patients with left versus right frontal lobe lesions. *Archives of clinical Neuropsychology, 9*, 41–55.

Samuels, M., & Samuels, N. (1975). *Seeing with the mind's eye: The history, techniques and uses of visualization.* New York: Random House.

Seitz, J., & Beilin, H. (1987). The development of comprehension of physiognomic metaphor in photographs. *British Journal of Developmental Psychology, 5,* 321–331.

Semmes, J. (1968). Hemispheric specialization: A possible clue to mechanism. *Neuropsychologia, 6,* 11–26.

Smolucha, L., & Smolucha, F. (1985). A fifth piagetian stage: The collaboration between analogical and logical thinking in artistic creativity. *Visual Arts Research, 11*(2), 91–99.

Sobel, R., & Rothenberg, A. (1980). Artistic creation as stimulated by superimposed versus separated visual images. *Journal of Personality and Social Psychology, 39*(5), 953–961.

Sperry, R. W. (1976). Lateral specialization in the surgically separated hemispheres. In F. O. Schmitt & F. G. Worden (Eds.). *The neurosciences: Third study program* (pp. 5–19). Cambridge, MA: MIT Press.

Springer S., & Deutsch, G. (1993). *Left brain, right brain.* New York: W. H. Freeman.

Staek, L., & Ellis, S. (1981). Scan paths revisited: Cognitive models direct active looking. In D. Fisher, R. Monty, & J. Senders (Eds.), *Eye Movements—Cognition and Visual Perception* (pp. 193–226). Hillsdale, NJ: Lawrence Erlbaum Associates.

Stein, M. I. (1975). *Physiognomic cue test manual.* New York: Behavioral Publications.

Sutherland, R. J., & Rudy, J. W. (1989). Configural association theory: The role of the hippocampal formation in learning, memory, and amnesia. *Psychobiology, 17*(2), 129–144.

Takahashi, S. (1995). Aesthetic properties of pictorial perception. *Psychological Review, 102*(4), 671–683.

Tucker, P., Rothwell, S., Armstrong, M., & McConaghy, N. (1982). Creativity, divergent, and allusive thinking in students and visual artists. *Psychological Medicine, 12,* 835–841.

Wilson, E. O. (1998). *Consilience: The Unity of Knowledge.* New York: Alfred A. Knopf Inc.

Yarbus, A. L. (1967). *Eye movements and vision.* New York: Plenum.

Zangmeister, W. H., Sherman, K., & Stark, L. (1995). Evidence for a global scanpath strategy in viewing abstract compared with realistic images. *Neuropsychologia, 33*(8), 1009–1025.

Zeki, S. (1993). *A Vision of the Brain.* Oxford, UK: Blackwell.

Zeki, S., & Lamb, M. (1994). The neurology of kinetic art. *Brain, 117,* 607–636.

Zeki, S. (1999). *Inner Vision: An Exploration of Art and The Brain.* Oxford: Oxford University Press.

2

Creative Visualization

DENNIS DAKE
Iowa State University

RESEARCH METHODS IN VISUAL COMMUNICATION AND AESTHETICS

Introduction to Method

A central dilemma of aesthetic visual communication is whether visual images can provide reliable evidence of important human cognitive activity and potentially meaningful affective responses or whether an image's communicative value is wholly dependent on what can be said about it; this would include discursive logic, applied subjectively, by each individual viewer. Is there communication if you can't seem to "put it into words"? Does the nature of visual information transmission, its accurate interpretation, and the meaningful importance of an image reside only in the *subjective* (inside the subject's head) processes of each individual viewer? Can there be a base of *objective* (based in a physical object) information on which multiple viewers can agree? Both the image-maker and all subsequent viewers must somehow have confidence in their ability to understand a level of meaning embedded in the image. If, as the subjective view holds, all interpretation is only a fanciful construction in the mind of each individual, how can any viewer judge the quality, precise meaning, and utility of the communication?

Research methods for the analysis of visual aesthetic relationships need to take both subjective and the objective perspectives into account. Before there can be any useful interpretation there needs to be solid agreement that there are, in fact, some actual, observable, and concrete phenomena present in the image on which multiple viewers will agree. Without this basis in observable fact, no method of analyzing visual communication can succeed. The methods of looking at the individual, subjective aspects of communication can be better understood if they are based on a common understanding of human perceptual functions, which all individual humans share.

Research in aesthetic aspects of visual communication must start with accurate and precise visual observations and not on propositional linguistic arguments. A predetermined propositional point of view threatens to use the visual image only to illustrate and not as a source for discovery of important cognitive and affective information. By starting with agreement on what visual elements and relationships are present in the object, both the original maker of the image and all subsequent viewers, who are visually literate, should have the potential to eventually experience some basic commonality of understanding.

To be successful, research methods must go beyond a discussion of formal elements and their interactions. Analysis methods must actively seek to reveal the cognitive and affective import of the visual communication. For this, the understanding must depend on a unique visually based logic, created through interactions between the visual elements and the processes of the human brain. Visual logic involves a developed internal sense of cohesiveness, comprehensibility, integrity, and elegance. Application of visual logic is necessary to guide viewers to a sense of adequate understanding.

Principles of Visual Logic

Six interrelated principles guide the development of this sense of visual logic. Three principles deal with objective observable relationships among visual elements. These three principles deal with (a) the visual *Tensions* within the work, (b) the type of and quality of visual *Unity* observable among visual elements, and (c) available clues to form and space that suggest to the viewer the nature of *Realism* (perception of "real" intended content) of the image. Three additional principles are based in the common processes that human perception confers on every individual. These principles deal with (a) relationship between *Ambiguity and Meaning,* (b) *Control of Direction* of the viewers' gaze and therefore their understanding of the image, and (c) the *Ecological Relationships* among visual elements and between the viewer and the embedded intentions of the maker of the image.

A visual description of these principles and their relational interactions are first defined and illustrated with examples from university art students who are beginning to develop their ability to produce images of visual logic. Researching (or teaching) aesthetic communication is aided by a focus on the process of visual formation during which the aesthetic relationships were created. Rather than treating the image as a static, set arrangement, it is more productive for understanding to view images as evidence of an ongoing process that is always completed in the viewer's mind. The process of image creation proceeds through extended visual-to-visual experimentation shaping relationships with aesthetic precision through extended visual exploration. Finally, the synergetic interactions between the six principles, called the **Layering** process, will be examined by comparing the highly developed aesthetics in two artworks by professional artist Chuck Richards.

TOOLS FOR RESEARCH INTO AND ANALYSIS
OF AESTHETIC RELATIONSHIPS

Tensional Principle

Tensions, physical, muscular, and psychological, are the very stuff of life experiences. This principle draws the image-maker's and the viewer's attention to the importance, meaningfulness, and interdependence of tensions within the image. Tensions are created within the human mind as it compares individual visual elements in one part of the image with all other elements in the composition. Every visual element is always in relationship to every other visual element (shapes seeming to move interactively with internal tensions, line dancing with line, colors pushing and pulling the eye, and illusionistic clues to space in tension with the flat surface of the paper); change one element and the whole image changes. Lines, shapes, or colors create tensions among themselves and within the whole field of existing gestalt forces. The image-maker must adjust and readjust individual elements attempting to create the best possible cognitive and affective tensions. The way the tensions are handled determines the mood, character, and communication of that visual configuration. It is the viewer's responsibility to focus on these tensions and interpret their role in communication.

Two pages (Figs. 2.1 and 2.2) from the graphic ideation sketchbook of student Paula Bolander vividly demonstrate the depth of rigorous experimentation necessary to develop the closest structural equivalent for the message content to be communicated. On these pages, tensions abstracted from architecture and nature yield plentiful elements for visual thought. For the image-maker these aesthetic relationships must be developed through flexible variations and seen. In this case the dynamics of dominant diagonals and a charged asymmetrical balance create a mood of excitement as a base of the visual message. These

FIG. 2.1. Study drawings, Paula Bolander, ink on paper (used with permission of the artist).

FIG. 2.2.   Study drawings, Paula Bolander, ink on paper (used with permission of the artist).

matters can't just be thought about in verbal terms. The most persuasive combinations that are "seen" can be combined and utilized for a final image of visual expression (Fig. 2.3). Even if the viewer does not see the preparatory visual thought, the aesthetic relationships embedded in the final image convey the mental effort and intentions that went into their construction.

These tensional relationships between visual elements hold fundamental importance for visual logic. Visual elements do not exists in isolation; they are always near or far from other elements. Spatial relationships among aesthetic elements are potentially meaningful in their implied interactions (for example, excited, distracted, attacking, sinuous, oppositional, and so on) and implicitly meaningful in their larger gestalt configurations. The large gestalt of tensions provides structural support for overall transmission of overt content and for a subliminal feeling-oriented structure underlying the outward messages.

Unity Principle

Tensions tend to tear the visual message apart into separate and competing elements for attracting the viewer's attention, conveying sense of chaos not choreography. Unity holds the message together in a cohesive and understandable order. The image-maker must learn to control the many levels of visual organization within a work of visual communication by the skillful use of grouping principles. (The gestalt grouping principles

FIG. 2.3.   Untitled painting, Paula Bolander, 24″ × 36″, acrylic on canvas (used with permission of the artist).

of similarity, proximity, closure, continuation, and common fate are the most commonly sited tools for producing this sensation of unity to the viewer's brain.) The goal is for each visual design to possess the maximum in purposeful organization related to its formal, psychic, and content information.

The search for visual unity can be observed in the two preparatory drawings of student David Ulch (Fig. 2.4) for a print on theme of the actual and implied motion of a motorcycle. At first (Fig. 2.4, top), in a very organic sketch the effect seems both more plantlike and chaotic than the subject seems to require. A more geometric and mechanical arrangement of circular forms, curved lines, and straight lines begins to develop in the second sketch (Fig. 2.4, bottom). In the final intaglio print (Fig. 2.5), the placement of light and dark values, as well as the other elements, are more unified in grouping, creating a meaningful arrangement of cohesive visual forces. As the motorcycle moves through space, it leaves memory traces of repeated forms and lines that convey the nature of mechanized energy. The type and strength of the visual groupings support this symbolic meaning. Purposeful use of gestalt-grouping tools brings pattern and order to the maker's efforts.

FIG. 2.4.   Study drawings, David Ulch, pencil on paper (used with permission of the artist).

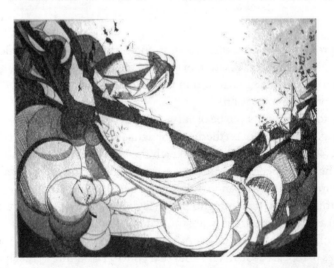

FIG. 2.5.   Untitled print, David Ulch, 6″ × 8″ (used with permission of the artist).

The viewer of the image can see a type of unity created by groupings of aesthetic elements, supporting either the overt message contextually or conveying other purely visual connotations. Paying attention to the multiple groupings that underlie the outward subject matter can reveal much of what aesthetics add to visual communication.

Realism Principle

This principle of aesthetic analysis holds that all styles of graphic communication (naturalistic to abstract to nonobjective) deal with some aspect of reality in one way or another. The disciplined graphic thinker who controls the visual tools (depth clues of overlap, shadow, color, gradients, and placement) can explore the nature of form and space for the nature of the real in experience. Mistaking optical naturalism, as the one and only form for communicating reality, is a common mistake of those unfamiliar with visual thinking and communication.

A comparison of two images of an artist's recently deceased father (Figs. 2.6 and 2.7) shows an interesting and flexible use of the depth clues for different but meaningful visual

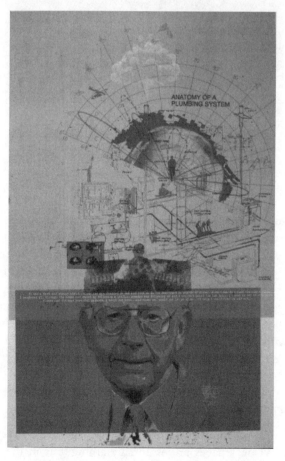

FIG. 2.6.   Portrait of My Father, Barbara Huisman, digital image (used with permission of the artist).

FIG. 2.7.   Do You See What I Mean? Barbara Huisman, digital image (used with permission of the artist).

statements. The student artist, Barbara Huisman, has skillfully given clues to the more naturalistic appearance of her father in Fig. 2.6 (lower 1/3) while using the upper 2/3 of the image to suggest diagrammatically and symbolically the engineering mentality and interests of the subject. The second version of this homage to a departed father (Fig. 2.7) plays more freely with the depth clues for more expressive, emotional messages, asking the question, "Do you see what I mean?" This second image conveys an affective message of a human reality far deeper emotionally than surface appearance—two images with the same subject but with far different aspects of reality communicated. The knowledgeable viewer must be able to interpret these clues for purposeful meaning.

Ambiguity and Meaning

This analysis tool draws the artist's attention to a provable characteristic of human perception; that all visual images are essentially ambiguous in the human brain and all configurations are therefore liable to more than one interpretation. During analysis

FIG. 2.8.   Student network, George Pritchard, 24″ × 30″, pencil on paper (used with permission of the artist).

of communication value, all configurations must be regarded as initially uncertain or indefinite in explicit meaning. The potential for communication is then carried forward by the observable visual elements, but the exactness of the target is not reducible to one set of words. Every image-maker knows this and every viewer needs to trust in the pattern-seeking forces in the brain and enter a process of lengthy pattern seeking.

Images often arise out of ambiguity. Figure 2.8, a drawing by student artist George Pritchard, shows a "network" of friends, the visual idea for which was discovered in a random scribble of lines (Fig. 2.9), which was then refined as a series of layered movements. Having arisen out of ambiguity, this image does not immediately give one definite interpretation of meaning to the viewer. Although the elaborate and dynamic depth clues suggest a message with important depth of meaning, no one interpretation comes readily to our attention as viewers. Perhaps the message is order even in the midst of chaos, or perhaps human interactions with complex electronic circuitry or, again, the dynamics of contemporary interpersonal human relationships. It is possible that all these interpretations or their combinations could require some hold on our attention when we consider the multilayered nature of meaning-making in this act of visual communication.

Can we trust a message that can be so differently interpreted? Ambiguity provides a vital function in aesthetic visual communication. Ambiguity slows the mind and suggests experiencing the image more fully in many dimensions. An idea is a temporary mental event; thus, words cannot always adequately convey the complex, structural, relational,

FIG. 2.9.   Source drawings (scribbles), George Pritchard, pencil on paper (used with permission of the artist).

and contextual nature of interrelationships among aesthetic phenomena. The image-maker's reasons and the viewer's mind can meet only after a period of critical viewing and extended analogical thinking.

Control of Direction

This principle holds that human beings are, on the one hand, able to make conscious decisions about the direction their designs will develop and also, to some extent about the way the viewer will process the visual clues. But also humans are a component part of nature and, therefore, must acknowledge that there are many aspects of their complex actions, consciously unknowable to the individual, which are best intuitively directed. These aspects require the image-maker to be skillful in inventing strategies for guiding the image-making process, particularly when the final visual goal cannot be known logically in advance.

Through preparatory drawings (Figs. 2.10 and 2.11 are selected examples), student artist Brian Roberts demonstrates the development of a successful strategy for integrating human and animal forms, vegetative patterns, and sharp, shattered, transparent planes. The final drawing (Fig. 2.12), a symbolic self-portrait, directs the viewer's eye by skillful use of high contrast in hair forms and hands while moving the eye sharply in sweeping arcs from side to side. Meanwhile the left shoulder and face of the subject are deemphasized with lower contrast of values. The intuitive decisions made as the image was developed cannot be explained as purely conscious actions but seem to have been generated through many, many trial-and-error sketches made to explore potential configurations and their effect on future viewers. In contemplating the interpretation of meaning conveyed by the image, the viewer would do well to consider why the image-maker might have used certain of these specific vision-controlling phenomena. Other more "mysterious" aspects of the message of which the artist himself may not have been consciously aware were probably decided on intuitively. This second group of phenomena reflects a visually

FIG. 2.10. Study drawings, Brian Roberts, pencil on paper (used with permission of the artist).

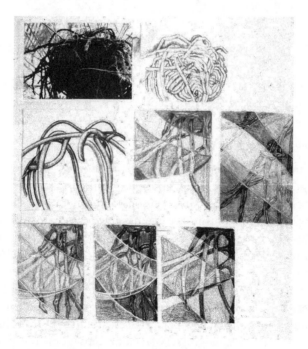

FIG. 2.11. Study drawings, Brian Roberts, pencil on paper (used with permission of the artist).

FIG. 2.12.   Self-Portrait, Brian Roberts, 20″ × 30″, pencil on paper (used with permission of the artist).

intuitive set of actions that can be fertile ground for both the image-maker and the viewer in discovering and growing new relationships.

Ecological Relationships

Images are not created all at once in the holistic fashion of human visual perception. Whether photographically captured or laboriously hand drawn, the image is the result of a long series of decisions, corrections, revisions, and generative explorations. Because of the fallibility of human thought and the complexity of the contextual relationships that need to be simultaneously developed, many tentative proposals must be worked through. Each small experiment used in generating a new image is only the best real-time projection of a possible solution. The image-maker must then deal with the incompleteness of any one image and try further experimentations to find a more complete solution. A sense of incompleteness or failure is in this case a positive spur to try again. Learning from mistakes and failures, integrating new perspectives, and then reprojecting through new configurations is the way a meaningful set of relationships within the image and between the image and the image-maker is worked out.

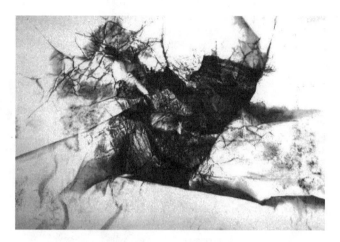

FIG. 2.13.   Source drawing (crumpled paper), Clint Hansen, pencil on paper (used with permission of the artist).

In interpreting the import of a visual message, it is appropriate to regard any interpretation as not totally fixed and objective. Perhaps the viewer would be best advised to use a more lengthy process of trail-and-error interpretations, the mirror image of the process the image-maker used in developing the image. This is the generation of an ecological relationship with both the image and with image-maker ideas of which the ecological relationship speaks. The viewer should search for less obvious analogies and associations, new layers of meaning waiting to be discovered.

Preparatory work (Figs. 2.13 through 2.17) by illustrator Clint Hanson shows a small part of the work by an artist shaping the ecological relationship with an image. This self-promotion image began with a crumpled piece of paper laid on a copy machine (Fig. 2.13). From the ambiguous gray shades, lines, and smudges, the artist perceived a mysterious face peering through a hole; this he enhanced. Moving forward, the artist explored the potential meaning in this imaginative invention in a page of sketches (Fig. 2.14), tried many flexible compositional and implicit shape studies (Figs. 2.15–2.16), and finally with overlaid tracing paper forms worked out some metaphoric meanings (Fig. 2.17). The final scratchboard self-portrait (Fig. 2.18) is far more than the simple physical appearance of the artist. The ecological relationship between the image and the viewer seems to convincingly convey the technical competence of the maker, several layers of meaning about his artistic skills and talents, a penetrating and focused observational ability, the mystery of creativity, and the ability to plunge below the level of consciousness to intuitively reach the viewer's mind. This is indeed a complex ecological relationship with the audience for this image.

DECIPHERING LAYERED AESTHETIC MEANING

Visual logic is finally holistic, uniquely applied in each specific instance. By layering the effects of the various analysis tools (as if they were individually and figuratively transparent), a more complex and complete understanding of the role of aesthetics in visual

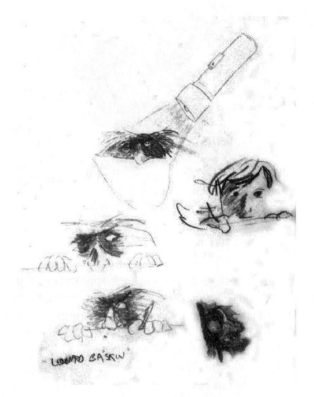

FIG. 2.14.   Study drawings, Clint Hansen, pencil on paper (used with permission of the artist).

FIG. 2.15.   Study drawings, Clint Hansen, pencil on paper (used with permission of the artist).

FIG. 2.16. Study drawings, Clint Hansen, pencil on paper (used with permission of the artist).

FIG. 2.17. Study drawing, Clint Hansen, pencil on tracing paper (used with permission of the artist).

communication can be seen. To demonstrate this most complex of aesthetic communication potentials, a comparison of two paintings by professional artist Chuck Richards provides an opportunity to appreciate how the careful and rigorous analysis of visual logic can result in a complex and nuanced appreciation of supported visual communication. Fig. 2.19, "Self-Portrait," is an oil painting of modest size but with a great complexity in the layering of visual logic principles. Figure 2.20, a much larger painting, "Man in Mayhem," has a remarkably different aesthetic structure, which creates a visually logical statement of a quite different type.

FIG. 2.18.   Self-Portrait, Clint Hansen, scratchboard, 24″ × 24″ (used with permission of the artist).

FIG. 2.19.   Self-Portrait, Chuck Richards, 30″ × 24″, oil on canvas, 1990 (used with permission of the artist).

FIG. 2.20. Man in Mayhem, Chuck Richards, 53″ × 44″, oil on paper, 1990 (used with permission of the artist).

Tensional Principle

In Fig. 2.19, "Self-Portrait," tensions circulate around the center of the image (the area of the artist's face) but in a more orderly and logically placed pattern when compared with the swirling forces within Fig. 2.20, "Man in Mayhem." The carefully placed and balanced tensions of "Self-Portrait," therefore, appear to reflect a more balanced and orderly mind than those in "Man in Mayhem." In traditional naturalistic terms, the space clues and spatial ordering of tensions in illusionistic space is also more consistent within "Self-Portrait." The space in "Man in Mayhem" fluctuates and spins, refusing to give the viewer's eye rest or a clear sense of spatial experience.

Unity Principle

Even in their black-and-white reproductions, "Self-Portrait" reveals a skillful grouping of light and dark values. Notice, for example, how the light of the table surface is repeated and grouped by similarity and continuity, presenting itself as a coherent whirl of energy around the image of the artist in the central mirror. The light band on the dark container on the left edge is picked up by the light edge around the reproduced drawing of snakes above. It is then passed along to highlights on the mask, the small reproduced child's drawing in the middle of the top, and the light on the electrical cord in the top right corner, and completes a cycle with the top of the animal skull at lower right. A unity of this carefully placed energy surrounds the artist in a meaningfully, loose and dynamic manner, perhaps reflecting the productive clutter of the artist's studio and flexible conditions of complex mind that characterize the artist. There is a visual rhyming in the grouping by similarity of the intertwined snakes at the left and the swirling of manmade electric cords on the far right side. The highlights in "Man in Mayhem" are more evenly and randomly distributed, although they are stronger toward the outer edges of composition. The light shapes are somewhat unpredictably but strategically placed to provide cohesion to an otherwise potentially chaotic visual display, a unity of message about the subject of disintegration.

Realism Principle

"Self-Portrait" gives a highly consistent set of depth clues as traditionally used in Western art. The pattern of light and dark, sense of overlap, placement of objects higher in the picture plane for depth, and gradients of value, size, and shape give a coordinated pattern that defines illusionistic space. Within this illusionistic system, however, some interesting complications are presented for the viewer's attention. Although the artist's central self-image gives clues indicating a solid object in space, the overlapping mirror frame reveals not a window but a reflective surface. The illusion of a mirror's cracked surface further complicates interpretation. Also, illusions of depth in the illustrated entwined snake refer to another layer of the artist's reality, because this is a reproduction of a previous artist's rendering of reality, a copy of a copy. The illusion of a childlike drawing at the top center shows another quite different use of depth clues but a child's honest approximation of reality quite different from naturalism. In many ways "Man in Mayhem" does not have as many levels of complexity. Depth clues are used more uniformly throughout the image for a shallow representation of space. Does this represent a shallower and more surfacelike frame of mind? The jumbled depth clues withhold an aesthetic sense of separate and well-formed objects instead favoring and being a swirling mass where individual items are subordinated to and overwhelmed by the whole. This difference in a sense of the real is vital to the emergence of levels of meaning in this work.

Ambiguity and Meaning

In viewing Richard's two images, "Self-Portrait" places the viewer's body in a more detached, observer position peering through a window at the illusions of space created. To perceive this visual message, the viewer stands in the position of the real artist reflected in the mirror. In "Man in Mayhem," the viewer gets a scene pressed against the paper surface and into the viewer's space. This forces the viewer mentally within the image, trapped within the Mayhem, along with the subject of the painting. In both cases the meaning the viewer can derive from this bodily perspective of the viewer determines the direction of interpretation. The viewer is relatively independent of the field of vision, in the prior case, and totally immersed and dependent on the swirling field in the latter.

Control of Direction

In "Self-Portrait," the artist gives a carefully constructed visual environment, both in surface organization and illusions of spatial depth. Each represented object is carefully placed so it produces a well-designed and ordered message for guiding the viewer's reconstruction in mind. The apparent strategy in the second painting, "Man in Mayhem," is aesthetically different. Although this artwork is also well structured and aesthetically consistent, its overall impact feels like shifting mental chaos of unsettling proportions. In both cases the artist/maker provides clues to help the viewer direct his or her interpretative processes. But the maker cannot control what exact discursive interpretative meaning the viewer will make of the aesthetic array. The strategies for viewing, which each image provides, give general direction to the viewer's mind but the individual relationships, which are suggested, leave the all-important connections to the viewer. Individual "hooks" to meaning provide control factors for deeper visual communication.

Ecological Relationships

The first impression of very orderly patterns in "Self-Portrait" alters slightly when small shifts of visual elements from a strict vertical and horizontal grid disturb the composition. The illusion of shattered cracks in the mirror gives an unsettling feeling that all is not as orderly as it first appears on the surface. The opposite is true in "Man in Mayhem." First impressions of near-total visual chaos change to a more studied awareness of subtle circular continuity relationships, lines of energy. These lines are reinforced by a swirling vortex of light areas. The viewer is placed on the verge of circulating destruction, struggling to maintain order. In either case, the artist has created a unity of message about eminent and impending chaos.

Layering

In summing up the previous analyses of our two painting examples (Figs. 2.19 and 2.20), a layering of the individual clues begins to yield deeper meaning. Although "Self-Portrait" reveals a young man with balanced, adult control of a complex mind, the "Man in Mayhem" shows wrinkled elderly skin and brain cortex in microscopic close-up, minus a whole human image. The unified chaos of tensions in "Man in Mayhem" reveals an individual in the grip of mental disintegration. Conversations with the artist disclosed that indeed the subject of "Man in Mayhem" was that of an older man, his father, with Alzheimer's disease, a series of in-depth meanings communicated effectively by visual means alone.

CONCLUSION: CHALLENGES FOR RESEARCH

The full impact of any group of aesthetic elements can only be understood through contextual and relational thinking. Because every aesthetic element in a visual design is relative to everything else in an image, the process is complex, with no simple route to a vital sense of internal integrity of its elements and accurately communicated meaning. Knowledge of the normal functions of perceptual processing of the human nervous system combined with critical analysis of the visible relationships among the elements of the image have the potential to yield creative discoveries of content not immediately apparent from surface appearance.

Words used to speak of what is communicated can only speak of one thing at a time, but images arrive holistically, everything present simultaneously. Visual logic must be understood in a wordless way of speculating, considering and eventually knowing.

Aesthetic aspects of visual communication are the mute and in many ways unnamable aspects that one could talk about forever. Literary exactitude forces visual information through too narrow a funnel. Filtered out is some of visual language's richest potential for informational relationship. The aesthetic aspects of visual communication lie in the conscious background and provide support for more explicit levels of associative and symbolic meaning through heightened viewer response. Effective research into aesthetic aspects of visual communication requires visual action, critical thought about visual relationships, and finally deep individual and personal participation in interpretation. The effort is worth it.

PART

II

Perception

3

Perception Theory

ANN MARIE BARRY
Boston College

How the brain enables the mind is *the* question to be answered in the twenty-first century.
—Michael Gazzaniga (1998, p. xii)

THEORETICAL PERSPECTIVES

Perception Theory is my own term for describing the application of neurological research and accepted psychological principles to the study of visual communication. By addressing how the mind/brain receives information, processes it, derives meaning from it, and uses it, this theoretical approach adds new medical information to the study of visual communication and helps us assess the efficacy of existing theories of communication derived from social research. Ultimately, in order to be useful, all communication theory and all assumptions about the way we process images and the impact they have on us must be compatible with neurological research.

Simply stated, this perceptual approach to communication theory acknowledges the primacy of emotions in processing all communication, and particularly targets visual communication as paralleling perceptual process dependent on primary emotion-based systems of response. In light of current neurological research, for example, we can no longer assume that a person's response to visual images will be conscious, or logical. Rather, neurological research reveals that visuals may be processed and form the basis of future action without passing through consciousness at all. Developmentally, too, we know that children and teenagers reason primarily through emotions, and are therefore highly susceptible to emotional appeals through visuals in the way they think and act. Every aspect of perception, therefore, has profound implications for all areas of communication, and none more than visual communication. Ultimately the key to understanding all visual communication lies in the neurological workings of the brain. We must therefore begin here.

The roots of this neurological approach go back a century and a half to the discovery of the connection between language and certain areas of the left cerebral hemisphere, and continuing through the work of William James and Gestalt psychologists Max Wertheimer, Wolfgang Kohler, and Kurt Koffka, and the ecological optics of J. J. Gibson. The major impetus for a neurological approach to communication, however, comes from the 1960s split-brain research of the late Roger Sperry at the California Institute of Technology and the visual-processing research of David Hubel and Torsten Wiesel of Harvard Medical School, for which the trio was awarded the Nobel Prize in Physiology and Medicine in 1981. The work of these men and of the subsequent generation of researchers who have continued their work on the organization of the human brain into the present—such as researchers like Michael Gazzaniga, Joseph LeDoux, Antonio Damasio, Semir Zeki, and Steven Pinker, among many others—is the basis of our expanding knowledge of the brain, and it is this knowledge that will drive visual communication study in the 21st century.

Because the history of the evolution of the brain's neurology is the also evolving story of human communication, as we trace the path of vision through the various visual-processing areas in the brain, we recognize at once how primitive and inaccurate is the idea, as Kepler suggested, that the eye is essentially a camera, passively recording an objective external reality. We also recognize just how inaccurate was Descartes' view of reason as the final arbiter of perception. What emerges instead from brain research is the awareness that although sight may indeed begin with light hitting the retina, vision occurs deep within the brain; and that perception, the process by which we derive meaning from what we see, is an elaborate symphony played first and foremost through the unconscious emotional system, with neural equipment evolved over millions of years. With our neural maps for the brain's development already in place, humans today advance according to the same principles by which their ancient ancestors developed.

As we learn to read this map, we find a variety of controversial questions in theory becoming resolved in interesting ways. These include the debate over nature versus nurture, over the relationship between language and thought, and most importantly, the primary relationship between reason and emotion, and between vision and memory. Although, for example, the debate between nature and nurture has raged from the mid-19th century when Darwin first published his *Origin of Species*, and neurological researchers today still argue forcefully that the key characteristics of mind are inherited (LeDoux, 2002; Pinker 1994, 1997; Dawkins, 1996; Wilson, 1999), the neural mechanics of the brain are far from reductive or deterministic. Joseph LeDoux, for example, estimated mind and behavior to be approximately 40% "nature" and 60% "nurture," but reminds us that "synapses are the key to the operations of both" and that these synapses are wired up in the brain by "one system that takes care of both situations" (2002, pp. 5–6). This system, prewired by evolution to detect and respond to danger, is thus built on and modified by perceptual experience.

Because visual experience is by far the most dominant learning mode, it is central to building synaptic connections in the brain. No other sensory system has been studied so completely as the visual, and no other has shown such promise in revealing the secrets of mind and therefore of behavior. Because much of our visual experience today comes vicariously through media, an understanding of how perception works is fundamental to ongoing communication research, particularly in terms of media effects. As media violence becomes the central focus of much social concern today, for example, it is important to note that much of the finger-pointing for assigning blame is beside the point: Whatever experience a child has will build the pattern of his or her future response. Family interaction, formal education, and media are all a part of the stream of influence that builds and reinforces certain brain synapses. If one influence is stronger, this will sway perception in a particular direction. If one is weaker, it will eventually go the route of all unreinforced and therefore ineffectual synapses and be reabsorbed into the system.

Because evolution is a slow process, our brains have not yet adapted to visual experience gained via media in any special way. Although biological evolution proceeds at a snail's pace, the technological revolution has sped by us at awesome speed. For the brain's perceptual system, visual experience in the form of the fine arts, mass media, virtual reality, or even video games is merely a new stimulus entering the same prewired circuits we have inherited as part of our brain potential and is processed in the same way. In other words, visual media is just as real to the emotional brain as any other visual experience, and it contributes just as much to the brain's synaptic wiring. In the same way that it can be argued that "we are what we eat," it can also be argued that how we see (and consequently how we behave) is primarily the sum of our perceptual experience. As Antonio Damasio (1994, 1999) observed, neurological research has shown us that we are not primarily thinking beings who also feel, but essentially feeling beings who also think.

Thus, neural research provides a rich heuristic for new insight into all aspects of existing visual communication theory. As the emerging picture becomes clearer of how the brain's learning and memory systems are fed by visual experience, and how its major pathways and modules work both independently of and in concert with one another to complete the process of perception, we find limitless opportunities for new research in visual studies. This chapter lays out some of the major concepts revealed through neurological research and explores the implications of these in terms of visual communication theory.

EVOLUTION AND THE MECHANICS OF VISION

Visual researcher R. L. Gregory and others suggested that visual perception first developed "in response to moving shadows on the surface of the skin—which would have given warning of near-by danger—to recognition patterns when eyes developed optical systems" (Gregory, 1998, p. 13). Richard Dawkins of Oxford University observed that it would not be surprising to find that all animals that have survived the process of natural selection possess some sort of "rudimentary eye," and he and others speculated that the eye most probably began as a patch of light-sensitive pigment that cued the animal to whether it was day or night (Dawkins, 1996; Gazzaniga, 1998, p. 11). The eye, a survival device that functions to detect change from nonchange, begins the process of making meaningful sense out of light from the external world. As the signal is carried via the optic nerve to the visual cortex, the internal brain takes control of the process.

The eyes are, in fact, a direct extension of the brain into the environment. The last and most sophisticated of our senses to evolve, our eyes send more data more quickly and efficiently through the nervous system than any other sense. Characterized by cells responsive to minute differences in shape, direction, degree of slant, and color, the eyes represent the first stage in a segmented sequential process that eventually results in meaning and all that is implied by "seeing." The *optical system*, an interface between the brain proper and the environment, is a synchrony of millions of nerve cells firing in particular patterns in parallel and sequential processing. Within the system, cells work separately and in concert with one another to activate and to inhibit certain responses, using continual feedback looping to hone the image that we see. *Perception*, the process by which we derive meaning through experience, is a dynamic, interactive system that utilizes built-in genetic programming to synthesize sensory input, memory, and individual needs. The eyes are only an initial part of the equation, and can, in fact, be bypassed altogether.

Experiments with blind people have shown, for example, that we actually do not need eyes to "see." Patients fitted with a device turning low-level video pictures (through a camera mounted next to the eyes) into vibrating pulses (fed to a patch of skin on their backs) have also learned to "see." The skin conducts the signals, which the brain can then convert into neural imagery—imagery that can then be interpreted as sight (Carter, 1999). This "vision" utilizes the rudimentary structures of perception, but does not result in understanding. Because it lacks the emotional processing through the limbic system that is essential for meaning, it gives us a clue as to how important emotional processing is to perception. Without it, we are in fact lost, and could not function adequately in everyday life.

As shown in Fig. 3. 1, perceptual process begins with ambient light that bounces off objects in the environment. This optic array is focused by the cornea and lens onto the 126 million receptors of the retina—120 million rods and 6 million cones—which line the back of the eye. As the visual system seeks and acts on information from the environment, retinal inputs lead to ocular adjustments and then to altered retinal inputs as the eyes actively engage the environment. Receptors in the retina then transform and reduce information from light into electrical impulses, which are then transmitted by the optic nerve from each eye to the brain's visual thalamus and onto the visual cortex where vision actually occurs.

In the thalamus, before conscious recognition of the object is achieved, the message is split into two processing routes (Fig. 3.2), which are key to the understanding of how perception works. The first route, the thalamo-amygdala pathway, is a crude network, which LeDoux (1994, pp. 50–57, 1998, pp. 163–167) described as "quick and dirty," that sends signals directly to the amygdala, the emotional center of the brain. In this part of process, the perceived shape of the situation is quickly matched to others stored in emotional memory and an emotional response then is framed that is in keeping with past positive or negative experience. Although we are not aware of the process, the end result is felt by us—most dramatically as "fight or flight" response in extreme situations, or in non life-threatening situations as a feeling or attitude that sets up our cognitive thinking, skewing it automatically toward a particular response. The second, slower route, the cortical pathway, transmits signals to the cortex where they are refined and

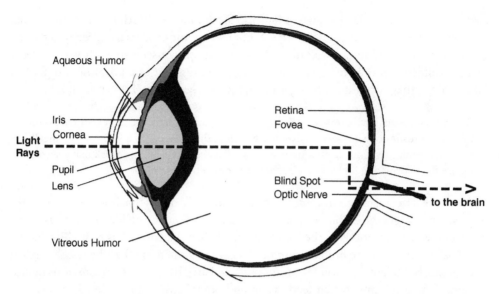

FIG. 3.1. Eye mechanics. When we see, light passes through the **cornea**, a tough membrane of four transparent layers, which reduces the speed of light and directs it toward the center of the eye; this light moves through the **pupil** and onto the **lens**, which focuses the light onto the **retina** at the back of the eye. The **optic nerve** then tranmits electrical signals from the retina to the brain, where vision occurs.

Mechanically, the retina is a complex network of neurons lining the back of the eye; it contains rods (that detect light and shape and are used in night vision) and cones (that detect color and are used in day vision). The area of clearest vision in the retina is the **fovea**, which consists only of cones. Where it leaves the retina, no rods or cones can exist, and we therefore have a **blind spot**. The **vitreous** and **aqueous humors** are fluids that maintain the shape of the eye and conduct light through them. The **iris** is a pigmented muscle that helps to protect the eye by changing the size of the pupil in response to varying degrees of light.

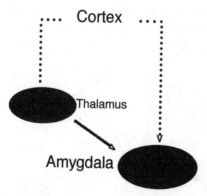

FIG. 3.2. Signals received by the thalamus are sent directly to the amygdala, the seat of our emotion, and also to the cortex, the seat of conscious processing. The signal sent through the thalamo-amygdala pathway is shorter and less complex than the signal sent through the cortical pathway. Emotional reactions are therefore faster than conscious ones, and emotional memory frames all conscious response. The cortex also sends a second signal to the amygdala, adding conscious input to emotional reaction and emotional response to thought. Emotional reaction is a survival-oriented unconscious response that can bypass conscious thought altogether.

again sent to the amygdala (shown in Fig. 3.2) for emotional coloring. It is in the cortex that we first become aware of what we see, but by then the process has already activated certain emotions and responses out of the range of our consciousness. It is this aspect that is so difficult for the average person to grasp, because our brain continues to fool us into thinking that our rational being is in charge. As Gazzaniga (1998) noted:

> By the time we think we know something—[i.e,] it is part of our conscious experience—the brain has already done its work . . . Systems built into the brain do their work automatically and largely outside of our conscious awareness. The brain finishes the work half a second before the information it processes reaches our consciousness. (p. 63)

Although it may seem counterintuitive, the "quick and dirty" thalamo-amygdala pathway, which engages the limbic system, still remains our first line of defense and has many more one-way connections to the thinking cortex than the cortex has to it. "Emotion," which is generated by the limbic system, refers not to something that the mind or brain does or has, but to different kinds of responses mediated by separate unconscious neural systems. These systems, which feed vision and other sensory processes, have evolved to accomplish behavioral goals associated primarily with survival and reproduction. They function unconsciously, and according to LeDoux, enter awareness only as "outcomes" and "only in some instances" (1998, p. 17). It is this emotional aspect of visual communication that is limited in patients fitted with the artificial tactile visual device described earlier: Even though male subjects tested had become practiced "viewers" and were able to accurately describe what they were seeing through the device, they remained emotionally unmoved by what they saw (Carter, 1999).

The cortical pathway, shown in Fig. 3.3, supplements and complements the emotional one and is slower and involves more evolutionarily developed structures. As the more refined signal progresses toward conscious recognition, it moves through separate brain areas in the visual cortex: In the area termed V1, general scanning is done in which points in the visual cortex match the external visual field. Here the picture is distorted, paralleling the foveal and peripheral vision fields of the eye (the fovea, the only part of the retina that sees with clarity, is more densely packed with neurons and so takes up a

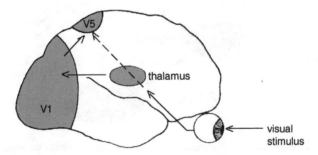

FIG. 3.3. Visual input travels through the eye, and via the optic nerve, to the thalamus and then to area V1, the primary visual cortex, where it is sent to other appropriate areas for processing. Area V5, which is geographically distinct and specialized for motion detection, receives signals directly from the retina and also through V1.

larger part of the V1 image). Area V5, a separate area specialized for detecting motion, receives signals from V1 and also directly from the retina. Because seeing change and the motion of a potential predator is one of the most important capabilities in survival, it is important that the brain receives this information as quickly as possible.

In the visual cortex, electrical signals sent from the retina are processed by thousands of specialized modules, each of which corresponds to a small area of the retina. When we ask the question "where?" for example, a pathway involving areas V1—>V2—>V3—>V5—>V6 is activated. When we ask "what?" a pathway from V1—>V2—>V4 is activated (Carter, 1999). There are four parallel systems involved in the different attributes of vision—one for motion, one for color, and two for form. Color is perceived when cells specialized to detect wavelength in V1 signal two other specialized areas in V4 and V2. Form in association with color is detected by a circuit of connections between V1, V2, and V4. Perception of motion and dynamic form occurs when cells in layer 4B of V1 send signals to areas V3 and V5 and through V2 (Zeki, 1992). Cells in V6 determine objective positioning. This symphony of intricate and delicate biochemical and electrical rhythms comes together as perception.

In the visual fine arts, neurologist Semir Zeki has used this knowledge to explore how artists have utilized the active process of vision as a means of gathering information to express a unified truth within an ephemeral world. Vision, Zeki commented, is "an active process in which the brain, in its quest for knowledge about the visual world, discards, selects, and, by comparing the selected information to its stored record, generates the visual image in the brain, a process remarkably similar to what an artist does" (1998, p. 21). The function of art and the function of the brain, he concluded, are both the same: to find and represent the constant, lasting, essential, and enduring features of objects, surfaces, faces, and situations. Zeki observed, for example, that the Fauvists, who tried to liberate color from form, faced an impossible task: Although color and form are processed separately by the brain, they are so intimately linked that only an extreme pathological condition could separate them (1998, pp. 197–204). Conversely, according to Zeki, Cubism's attempt to find the essence and permanence of things within changing views of it mimics the brain's ability to integrate successive views of objects and people as they move within the environment, or as we move around them within a given space, into a single image (1998, p. 54).

In the process of perception, data are reduced and compressed, and what was once a retinal image becomes not a cameralike picture of external reality, but rather a representative map of the visual field. In this way, light is transformed into meaning built from separate, specific functions in the brain. The eye—triggered by the attention system of the brain—is continually and automatically darting about to gather the specific information that will form the mental image. Both the eyes and the external world are in continuous motion; the brain creates from this motion a stable mental configuration that can be described as an "image."

An image, Damasio explained, consists of a neural pattern that represents the highest level of biological phenomenon (1999, p. 9). The ability to hold the image over time, a process described as "working memory," is ultimately the basis of extended consciousness. "All consciousness," Damasio explained, "operates on images" (1999, pp. 122–123).

TECHNOLOGY, THE BRAIN AT WORK, AND IMPLICATIONS FOR VISUAL COMMUNICATION

Within the past 30 years, primarily through the power of functional magnetic resonance imaging (fMRI), computerized tomography (CT), positron emission tomography (PET), and near-infra-red spectroscopy (NIRS), we can now view exquisitely detailed images of the brain and learn what parts are active in performing various visual, oral, and computative tasks. MRI works by magnetism, aligning atomic particles within body tissue and recording the feedback when these are bombarded with radio signals. CT, a sophisticated software system, then converts this information into a three-dimensional picture. Functional MRI adds to this picture, showing areas of greatest brain activity by revealing which parts are using the greatest amount of oxygen. By recording four images each second, fMRI provides a rapid scanning of the flow of activity in the brain as it undertakes various tasks. Although very expensive, fMRI provides the highest resolution image of brain activity to date. PET scans also show areas of activity in the brain, but without the high resolution of fMRI and with the additional drawback of requiring the injection of a radioactive marker through the bloodstream. NIRS also reveals active brain areas, but does so by bouncing light waves into the brain and measuring the reflection. Today, multimodal imaging that combines these techniques is becoming increasingly popular (Carter, 1999).

With the availability of such techniques, neuroscience has been able to build a map of how the brain's modules function and communicate with one another in solving particular problems and undertaking specific tasks. The image that we ultimately perceive is unified, not because the mind sees a picture of what is really "out there," but because the specialized areas in the visual cortex link four parallel systems into a vast network, a network in which reentrant connections allow information to flow both ways to resolve conflicts between cells. This network, neuroresearcher Zeki (1992, 1998) speculated, allows information processed in different places to be combined through synchronous firing, and this synchronicity yields perception and comprehension simultaneously. There is, many neurologists believe, no single area in the brain where all of the different sensory regions converge in such a way as to form the base for an "integrated mind." Instead, there is a system of modules, each with its own local attention and working memory devices. Our sense of ourselves as beings with a rational integrative mind in control is just an illusion. "Our strong sense of mind integration," Damasio explained, "is created from the concerted action of large-scale systems by synchronizing sets of neural activity in separate brain regions, in effect a trick of timing" (1994, p. 95).

This modular functioning also lends insight into the relationship between language and thought and, ultimately, to the efficacy of semiotic criticism in visual communication theory. Linguistic theoretician Ray Jackendoff observed, "language and thought, while related, are distinct forms of mental information." The answer to how thought can be different from language when we seem to think in words is that "the language we hear in our heads while thinking is a *conscious manifestation* of the thought—not the thought itself, which isn't present to consciousness" (1994, p. 187). Researcher Stephen Pinker, author of *The Language Instinct*, explained that the human brain utilizes at least four different formats in representing thought: (a) the visual image as a two-dimensional picturelike mosaic; (b) a phonological representation that runs like a tape loop; (c) grammatical representations of nouns and verbs, phrases and clauses, stems and roots, phonemes and syllables, arranged in hierarchical trees; and (d) "mentalese, the language of thought in which our conceptual knowledge is couched" (1997, pp. 89–90). This fourth format, "mentalese," Pinker explained, is the mind's "lingua franca," a medium in which gist is captured and concepts are stored; it is this format that is comparable to Damasio's concept of image as a biological cluster of neurons firing in synchronicity (1999, p. 9). "Mental imagery," Pinker stated, "is the engine that drives our thinking about objects in space. ... Images drive the emotions as well as the intellect" (1997, pp. 284–285).

Again and again, for example, great creative minds explain their creative thought generation in terms of visual imagery and their reliance on mental images as springboards for extending their understanding well beyond the parameters of verbal language. As Einstein observed of his own mental images to explain his theories, images lead to generative syntheses: "My particular ability does not lie in mathematical calculation, but rather in visualizing effects, possibilities and consequences" (Pinker, 1997, p. 285). Among other scientists Pinker describes as thinking in images are Faraday and Maxwell, Kekulé, Watson, and Crick. Cognitive psychologist Howard Gardner suggests that the creative mind works in images precisely because mental images allow us to understand one idea through another (1993, p. 365).

The format for all consciousness and all meaning, imagery thus appears to be a function quite separate from the processing of spoken language or grammar per se. More akin to the process of visual perception than to language processing, the imagery of consciousness consists in patterns of meaning in which neurons combine into gestalts with meaning greater than, and different from, the sum of individual parts.

Semiotic criticism or rhetorical criticism, like all verbal communication, therefore has the inherent weakness of using verbal grammar and expression to explain the inherently nonverbal. Because images are the basic communication medium of the brain, semiotics and rhetorical criticism come closest to understanding visual communication when they look at relationships and tropes. But even at this level, they are still a tier of understanding away from the "lingua franca" of the brain, and a whole system away from visual communication. When what we read, what we hear, and what we see reach the level of ideas, they all appear in a different format: the format of neural imagery. This neurological shift is what results in meaning, and it is this patterning of neurons that allows us to understand something about the impact of what we see.

In addition to modularity and synchronicity, another important aspect in understanding how perception works and its implications in terms of visual communication is the brain's basic hemispheric structure. The brain consists of two hemispheres, left and right, each a mirror image of the other with minor variations for specialization in each.

Each hemisphere directs the movements of the opposite side of the body, and coordination between the two hemispheres is made possible by the bridge of the corpus callosum, which connects them. Although the earliest biological research into the brain consisted mainly of postmortem examination of brain-injured patients, the work of Roger Sperry in the 1960s on split-brain patients with severe epilepsy showed that when the corpus callosum—the only informational conduit between the two hemispheres of the brain—is severed, the left and right hemispheres can no longer communicate thoughts or sophisticated emotions. Although each brain hemisphere is a mirror image of the other, each has its own strengths and weaknesses, ways of processing information, and special skills. Although subsequent research in the field has show this segmentation to be more complex than originally thought, we may still speak in general terms of left and right brain, although these two hemispheres maintain such a continuous and harmonious conversation so fully complementary and integrative that it appears to be a single stream of consciousness (Carter, 1999, p. 34).

In general, the left hemisphere can be said to be analytical, logical, abstract, and time-sensitive, while the right hemisphere is more holistic and emotional, as well as more fearful, sad, and pessimistic (Springer & Deutsch, 1993). Recognizing faces, finding your way around in space, discerning shapes in camouflage, and seeing patterns at a glance are right-brain activities; breaking down complex patterns into component parts, focusing on detail, and intense analysis are left-brain activities. In normal people, both sides of the brain continuously converse across the eight billion nerve fibers of the corpus callosum, but specialized tasks are directed to one side or the other.

In 95% of right-handed people, who themselves compose an estimated 90% of the world population, language facility is almost totally confined to the left hemisphere, which also houses the ability to recognize and imagine shapes according to the arrangement of parts. The right hemisphere, in contrast, is excellent at estimating measurements of whole shapes, can easily judge length and width, and processes information simultaneously and holistically. Most sensory input crosses from the incoming side to the opposite side of the brain (visual input from the right half of each eye, for example, goes to the left side of the brain for processing, and visual input from the left goes to the right).

In the science and the art of visual communication, these observations have enormous significance. Because images appeal to the right side of the brain, they are read in a different way from words, which appeal to the left for processing. In advertising, for example, Carter and Frith asserted that, much advertising "is designed to exploit the gap between the impressionable right brain and the critical left. Those adverts that use visual images rather than words to convey messages are particularly likely to impinge on the right hemisphere without necessarily being registered by the left" (Carter, 1999, p. 41). Zeki observed that "artists are in some sense neurologists, studying the brain with techniques that are unique to them, but studying unknowingly the brain and its organization nevertheless" (1998, p. 10), and certainly the same can be said of advertising moguls, who have long intuitively understood this hemispheric phenomenon. The Foote, Cone, & Belding (FCB) advertising agency, for example, developed an advertising planning model of purchase decision making well over 20 years ago that recognized feeling and thinking as distinctly separate parts within the same continuum and used this as the basis for developing effective creative strategies in ad campaigns.

As shown in Fig. 3.4 of the FCB Grid, on the left to right horizontal axis of the grid, consumers are seen as making decisions based on some relative degree of thinking and feeling, while on the top to bottom vertical axis, the relative importance of the decision is weighed from high to low. In this model, high-priced items, such as appliances for which consumers are likely to compare features and relative costs, would demand more rational reasons and fact content or "hard sell" arguments to persuade people to purchase. Products such as cigarettes, which suggest no logical reasons for purchase and

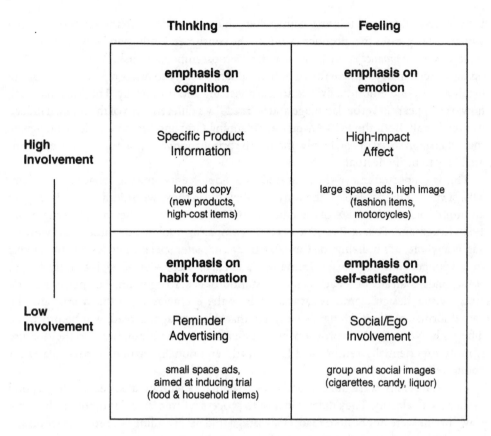

FIG. 3.4. Foote, Cone, & Belding's Advertising Planning Grid (after Vaughn, 1980). Horizontally, the sliding scale moves from the predominance of thought to feeling in terms of their relative influence on consumer behavior. Vertically, the grid moves from low to high involvement. All products and services can be placed on the grid through social and marketing research and subsequently positioned to determine the appropriate mix of cognitive and emotional appeals to sell them effectively.

which until very recently have been relatively inexpensive at the onset of a tobacco habit, however, demand a more "soft-sell" and "feeling" approach. The former lends itself to verbal argument, the latter to visual persuasion through images. As the late advertising guru David Ogilvy told us, "Writing advertising for any kind of liquor is an extremely subtle art. I once tried using rational facts to *argue* the consumer into choosing a brand of whiskey," he said. "It didn't work. You don't catch Coca Cola advertising that Coke contains 50 per cent more cola berries. . . . Next time an apostle of hard-sell questions the importance of brand images, ask him how Marlboro climbed from obscurity to become the biggest-selling cigarette in the world" (1985, pp. 15–16).

Leo Burnett, whose advertising agency is responsible for the Marlboro Man, explained that the most effective images resonate deep within the psyche: "The most powerful advertising ideas are non-verbal," he said, "and take the form of statements with visual qualities made by archetypes. Their true meanings lie too deep for words" (Broadbent, 1984, p. 3). "A strong man on horseback, a benevolent giant, a playful tiger. The richest source of these archetypes," Burnett believed, "is to be found at the roots of our culture—in history, mythology and folklore. Somewhere in every product are the seeds of a drama which best expresses that product's value to the consumer. Finding and staging this *inherent drama of the product* is the creative person's most important task." (Broadbent, 1984, pp. 3–4). Such images utilize the right hemisphere's ability to discern patterns, to ignore detail, to respond emotionally, and to learn visually and holistically. The warning label, however, appears in verbal language and is "read" by a different area of the brain, if indeed it is read at all. Both the FCB Advertising Planning Grid and brain neurology recognize that when high social or ego involvement is the prime motivating factor, cognitive appeals are likely to be ineffectual.

This is supported in eye-tracking studies of adolescents viewing tobacco ads, where 44% of viewers did not look at the warning label, and in those who did, average time spent amounted only to about 8% of their attention (Fischer, Richards, Berman, & Krugmann, 1989; Krugmann, Fox, & Fletcher, 1994). In comparing adolescents' time spent viewing ads as a whole, ads utilizing Joe Camel, a trade character specifically designed to appeal to a younger and cognitively immature audience, were viewed significantly longer (16 seconds) than any other ad, including Marlboro (Fox, Krugmann, Fletcher, & Fischer, 1998). Visual design elements invariably draw the eye away from the words; and the verbal format of the warning also ensures that the message, if read, will be processed differently. Not only are words processed differently by the brain, but also their nature is more experientially remote and less directly emotionally involving, particularly for youngsters.

Brains, it seems, were built to process visual images with great speed and to respond to them with alacrity. They did not evolve to process written verbal symbols in the same way. "Brains were not built to read," Gazzaniga told us. "Reading is a recent invention of human culture. That is why many people have trouble with the process and why modern brain imaging studies show that the brain areas involved with reading move around a bit. Our brains have no place dedicated to this new invention" (1998, p. 6).

In short, visual images have right-brain appeal, while verbal arguments are grabbed by the left brain for processing. This is why patients with damage to the left hemisphere may suffer speech problems, but those with damage to the right hemisphere are more likely to have perceptual and attentional problems (Springer & Deutsch, 1993). If the corpus collosum is severed, cognitive information from one side of the brain will remain trapped on that side. Emotional information, however, leaks easily across the hemispheres through the limbic system and is unconsciously shared and unconsciously learned. This realization should put emotional processing of visual messages at the forefront of all visual communication research.

EMOTIONAL AND COGNITIVE SYSTEMS

As stated earlier, there are fundamentally two information-processing systems in the brain—the cortical pathway and the thalamo-amygdala pathway. Until the mid-1980s, it was generally hypothesized that emotion had to come *after* conscious and unconscious thought processing. Richard Lazarus (1982), for example, argued that emotional reaction required cognitive appraisal as a precondition. It has now been shown, however, that the brain accomplishes its goals in an absence of awareness and that perception is not a system per se, but a description of what goes on in a number of specific neural systems (LeDoux, 1996, p. 16). In the amygdala—a subcortical region buried deep within the temporal lobe—emotional significance is attached to incoming data and readies the body to act before the mind makes the conscious decision to act. Sensory signals from the eye travel first to the thalamus and then, in a kind of short circuit, to the amygdala *before* a second signal reaches the neocortex. LeDoux explained: "The cortical systems that try to do the understanding are only involved in the emotional process after the fact" (1986, p. 241).

Beneath the cerebral cortex lies the anterior commissure, which connects deep, subcortical (nonthinking) regions of the brain, so that even if the left hemisphere of the split-brained person cannot name a stimulus, it is nevertheless capable of receiving emotional information about it. There exists in the brain, in fact, a "fundamental dichotomy—between thinking and feeling, between cognition and emotion" (LeDoux, 1998, p. 15), which runs deeper even than left/right brain asymmetry. The older emotional pathway, which allows raw emotions to connect with the thinking areas of the hemispheres, is that "quick and dirty" emotional route that connects the cortex and neocortex to the limbic system.

There is, in consequence, a measurable time gap between action and consciousness of action. As early as the 1950s, Libet (1996) demonstrated in experiments that the conscious will to act comes only *after* we initiate action, not *before*. Because of this delay, the mind is also geared to anticipate what is coming, which it does by calling up templates of past experience to predict the future. According to Gazzaniga, "what we see is not what is on the retina at any given instant, but is a prediction of what will be there. Some system in the brain takes old facts and makes predictions as if our perceptual system were a virtual and continuous movie in our mind" (1998, p. 75). LeDoux (1986) explained that this is truly advantageous to our survival, because in critical situations, instinctual responses must not only move rapidly through the limbic system but also must use emotional memory predictively if we are to survive.

Gazzaniga also suggested that although it is counterintuitive to our sense of rationality, one of the chief ways we use our cognitive faculties is to rationalize what has already been emotionally decided. Human beings, he explained, have a centric view of the world and like to think of ourselves as "directing the show most of the time." He argued, however, that the illusion that we are directing our actions "simply appears to be true because of a special device in our left brain called the *interpreter*. This device creates the illusion that we are in charge of our actions, and does so by interpreting our past—the prior actions of our nervous system. . . . Reconstruction of events starts with perception and goes all the way up to human reasoning. The mind is the last to know things" (1998, p. xiii). Gazzaniga's "interpreter," a special device in the left hemisphere of the brain, operates on the activities of other adaptations built into the brain through evolution and reconstructs the automatic activities of the brain in order to maintain an integrated view of the world and a holistic sense of self. Although these automatic activities are cortically based, they are nevertheless outside of our conscious awareness, and the role of the interpreter is to "construct theories to assimilate perceived information into a comprehensible whole. . . . We need something that expands the actual facts of our experience into an on-going narrative, the self-image we have been building in our mind for years. The spin doctoring that goes on keeps us believing we are good people, that we are in control and mean to do good. It is probably the most amazing mechanism the human being possesses" (Gazzaniga, 1998, pp. 26–27). Rationalization is not, therefore, a cognitive tool tied to logic so much as it is a process integral to perception itself.

A series of experiments in which identical stimuli produced a whole range of rationalizations may serve to illustrate. In one, a number of pairs of identical nylon stockings were laid out and women were asked to choose one. When asked the basis for their choices, each was able to cite reasons ranging from differences in color to texture and quality (Gazzaniga, 1992). Here rational cognition is used to justify an irrational choice. Ogilvy suggested an alternate experiment in which the emotional set-up can be used to overwhelm the cognitive beforehand: "Give people a taste of Old Crow, and *tell* them it's Old Crow. Then give them another taste of Old Crow *but tell them it's Jack Daniel's.* Ask them which they prefer. They'll think the two drinks are quite different. *They are tasting images*" (1985, p. 15). Just as we are prone to consciously rationalize unconscious emotional decisions after the fact, we are also prone to build preconceptions through images before the fact of rational cognition. But this weakness is also a perceptual strength. When everything functions appropriately, precognitive feelings point us in the right direction by tapping emotional learning and assisting the neocortex in its ability to make rational decisions. As Davidson and Irwin noted, "Emotion guides action and organizes behavior towards salient goals . . . The amygdala has been consistently identified as playing a crucial role in both the perception of emotional cues and the production of emotional responses" (1999, p. 11)

EMOTIONAL LEARNING

Our conscious mind and our emotional system usually work together smoothly, just as the complementary right and left hemispheres of the brain work together through a continuous dialogue across the corpus collosum. When they don't, however, the consequences can be catastrophic. In the process of developing a mature mind, several things can go wrong: Injury may prevent adequate emotional or cognitive abilites; deprivation or lack of use may prevent normal maturation during the evolutionary window of development that opens and closes according to a built-in genetic determinism; patterns of negative attitudes and behavior may prematurely close off broader choices or reinforce destructive habits of mind or action.

In his book *Descartes' Error*, for example, Damasio (1994) told the story of his patient, "Elliot," whose surgery to remove a fast-growing frontal lobe tumor severed the neural pathways from the amygdala, where emotions are generated, to the frontal cortex, where emotions are registered. The prefrontal cortex, a region of the frontal cortex behind the forehead, has also been identified as the site where decision making takes place (Carter, 1999). The surgery left Elliot without the capacity to feel emotion and therefore without the ability to reach decisions and make accurate judgments. Controlled, dispassionate, eminently rational, but without his emotional system to help, Elliot lost the ability to prioritize, to choose one path of action over another, and to accurately evaluate others' motivations and character.

Without a perspective on what was important and how much detail was sufficient, he was crippled in his decision making even though his base of knowledge and his intelligence remained intact. Ultimately, because of the surgical damage to the right frontal cortices, Elliot lost his family, his social acumen, his work, his wealth, and his former life. Damasio's patient reveals not only the interdependence of reason and emotion, but also the evolutionary wisdom in unconscious emotional processing to prepare the way for logic and reason.

Neurological research has also revealed the existence of genetic windows for development. From birth to age 3, for example, the brain is especially vulnerable. At this time, repeated abuse, neglect, or terror (from whatever source) causes a flood of stress-related chemical responses that reset the brain's fight-or-flight hormones and that make the child more or less reactive to stress throughout life. At this point, abusive parenting, or even repeated stressful media exposure, can change the way the brain responds in ordinary situations by hyperreacting to negative influences or by becoming totally unresponsive to them. Because the emotional system responds as automatically to a horror film as it does to the real thing, unconscious emotional memories are stored in the amygdala, and stressful events and traumatic memories may be burned into the system. Although cortical thinking can override the immediate influence of this visual experience, the emotional system continues working to get the body ready for fight or flight: The heartbeat quickens, breathing accelerates, pupils dilate, temperature drops, and blood is redirected to the muscles. Most importantly, as we physically experience the fight-or-flight response, an emotional memory is laid down to guide future action. The greater the impact of the emotional experience, the more deeply the emotional memory is etched. This memory, because it belongs to a survival-based system geared to learning from traumatic experience, may never be eradicated (LeDoux, 1998; Damasio, 1999).

When thematic activities and patterns of ideas and actions are repeated over and over again, they, too, become deeply embedded within the unconscious memory system, and are established as templates. In this way, emotional response to media becomes a permanent part of our response repertoire. Perhaps the most dramatic example of this has come from the long-term Cultural Indicators Project initiated in 1973 at the University of Pennsylvania. Cultivation Analysis Theory, which crystallized from the project, has concentrated on the storytelling function of media, and focused on the developing patterns of attitude that neurological researchers have found to be the basis of unconscious emotional learning. Correlating these with television viewing habits, they conclude that "the repetitive pattern of television's mass-produced messages and images forms the mainstream of the common symbolic environment that cultivates the most widely shared conceptions of reality. We live in terms of the stories we tell—stories about what things exist, stories about how things work, and stories about what to do—and television tells them all through news, drama, and advertising to almost everybody most of the time" (Gerbner Gross, Jackson-Beeck, Jeffries-Fox, & Signorelli, 1978, p. 178).

Because our mammalian brain interprets media images as reality and responds emotionally according to the circumstances presented to it, understanding perceptual processing has significant implications for media effects. Pinker explained: "When we watch TV, we stare at a shimmering piece of glass, but our surface-perception module tells the rest of the brain that we are seeing real people and places. . . . Even in a life-long couch potato, the visual system never 'learns' that television is a pane of glowing phosphor dots, and the person never loses the illusion that there is a world behind the pane" (1997, p. 29).

Although the intent of visual media directors and producers is often taken into account in the discussion of media effects, in terms of perception, the intention of the producer of the image is irrelevant. Neurological effects occur whether they are intended or not. When Gerbner and his associates argue that television exposure has both first- and second-order effects in which both facts and patterns of assumptions are learned, they are fully in tune with perceptual research. According to Gerbner's Mean World Index, for example, heavy viewers of television vastly overestimated the amount of actual violence in the real world and were more likely to see the world as fearful and to mistrust people in it (Gerbner et al. 1980). Because neurologically, continually stimulating groups of brain cells makes them more sensitive and easier to activate (Carter, 1999), repeated neural firings with the same thematic or emotional content increase the likelihood of attitudinal and behavioral repetition. Like traumatic exposure, this realization has profound implications in terms of habitual media use and recurrent patterns of attitude and behavior within media, especially in interactive media such as video games.

CONCLUSION

Neurologically, without our consciously realizing it, emotional learning occurs that pre-frames attitudes, thinking, and behavior. Emotional templates serve as a basis for perceptual anticipation of the future, and although reason and emotion both play crucial and inseparable roles in perception, at various times, emotion can and does function at the expense of reason. Whether we are continually bombarded with the same "mean world" pattern in media, or we select out and deliberately repeat specific movies or video games because they resonate with felt needs and realities, it is important to realize that the emotional learning that goes with media experience is both unconscious and peculiarly indelible.

Damasio explained that "images [i.e., mental patterns created through the senses] allow us to choose among repertoires of previously available patterns of action and [to] optimize the delivery of the chosen action" (1999, p. 24). Because the neurological maps that we use to navigate reality are drawn from the repetition of patterns of action provided by both direct experience and visual media, the parameters of our behavioral choices are determined by both, using the same underlying neural mechanisms.

In the words of Sperry in his 1981 Nobel lecture that initiated the neurological research that is the foundation for our new understandings in visual communication, "Where there used to be a chasm and irreconcilable conflict between the scientific and the traditional humanistic views of man and the world, we now perceive a continuum. A unifying new interpretative framework emerges with far reaching impact not only for science but for those ultimate value-belief guidelines by which mankind has tried to live and find meaning" (Sperry, 1981).

In the process of our becoming, visual communication plays a crucial role, one that is particularly vulnerable to emotional learning and to manipulation by political, economic and other vested interests. "Virtually every image, actually perceived or recalled," explained Damasio, "is accompanied by some reaction from the apparatus of emotion" and because "the engines of reason still require emotion . . . the controlling power of reason is often modest" (1999, p. 58). Pattern formation and repetition are the way in which the brain forms attitudes and ideas neurologically, and these repeated patterns create the templates that we use to map and to anticipate reality. Because neurons that "fire together wire together," these templates are peculiarly resistant to reason (LeDoux, 1998, p. 214).

Visual media with its frequently recurring patterns of action and thematic development are peculiarly well suited to emotional learning, as is the individual impact of specific paintings, drawing, and sculptures in the fine arts. In its "wisdom," Nazi propaganda in Germany in the era preceding World War II began not with control of the spoken word, but with a state art, architecture, and film initiative that captured people emotionally and intentionally bypassed reason. Today, remnants of the same visual techniques can be seen in entertainment from MTV to interactive video games to virtual reality. Because visual messages are mostly processed by unconscious regions of the brain that do not understand that art and mass media are not reality, their visual power can have enormous impact, unintended or not, on our emotional development. Through emotional templates, our attitudes, ideas, and actions are pushed in particular directions, positive or negative.

The neurological research that is currently mapping the mind thus can be seen to provide an invaluable framework for new research in visual studies that bridges the interdisciplinary chasm between the traditional "hard" and "soft" sciences, and for understanding the social implications of what it means to "see" and to "watch" in a visually dominated culture.

REFERENCES

Broadbent, S. (1984). *The Leo Burnett book of advertising*. London: Hutchinson.

Carter, R. (1999). *Mapping the mind*. Berkeley: University of California Press.

Crick, F. (1994). *The astonishing hypothesis*. New York: Touchstone.

Damasio, A. (1994). *Descartes' error: Emotion, reason and the human brain*. New York: Avon.

Damasio, A. (1999). *The feeling of what happens*. New York: Harcourt Brace.

Davidson, R. and Irwin, W. (1999). The functional neuroanatomy of emotion and affective style [Review]. *Trends in Cognitive Sciences, 3*(1), 11–21.

Dawkins, R. (1996). *The blind watchmaker*. New York: Norton.

Fischer, P., Richards, J. Jr., Berman, E., & Krugmann, D. (1989, January 6). Recall and eye tracking study of adolescents viewing tobacco advertisements. *Journal of the American Medical Association, 261*(1), 84–89.

Fox, R., Krugmann, D., Fletcher, J. & Fischer, P. (1998). Adolescents' attention to beer and cigarette print ads and associated product warnings. *Journal of Advertising, 27*(3).

Gardner, H. (1993). *Creating minds*. New York: HarperCollins.

Gazzaniga, M. (1992). *Nature's mind: The biological roots of thinking, emotions, sexuality, language and intelligence*. New York: Penguin Books.

Gazzaniga, M. (1998). *The mind's past*. Berkeley: University of California Press.

Gerbner, G., Gross, L., Jackson-Beeck, M., Jeffries-Fox, S., & Signorelli, N. (1978). Cultural indicators: Violence profile no. 9. *Journal of Communication, 28*, 176–206.

Gerbner, G., Gross, L., Morgan, M., & Signorelli, N. (1980). The mainstreaming of America: Violence profile no. 11. *Journal of Communication, 30*, 10–29.

Gregory, R. (Ed.). (1998). *The Oxford companion to the mind*. New York: Oxford University Press.

Jackendoff, R. (1994). *Patterns in the mind*. New York: Harper Collins/Basic Books.

Krugmann, D., Fox, R., & Fletcher, J. (1994, November/December). Do adolescents attend to warnings in cigarette advertising? An eye-tracking approach. *Journal of Advertising Research, 39–52*.

Lazarus, R. S. (1982). Thoughts on the relations between emotions and cognition. *American Psychologist, 37*, 1019–1024.

LeDoux, J. (1986). Sensory systems and emotion. *Integrative Psychiatry, 4*, 237–248.

LeDoux, J. (1994, June). Emotion, memory and the brain. *Scientific American, 270*(6), 50–57.

LeDoux, J. (1998). *The emotional brain*. New York: Simon & Schuster.

LeDoux, J. (2002). *Synaptic self*. New York: Viking/Penguin.

Libet, B. (1996). Neural time factors in conscious and unconscious mental functions. In S. R. Hameroff et al. (Eds.), *Toward a science of consciousness* (pp. 337–347). Cambridge, MA: MIT Press.

Ogilvy, D. (1985). *Ogilvy on advertising*. New York: Vintage Books.

Pinker, S. (1994). *The language instinct*. New York: William Morrow.

Pinker, S. (1997). *How the mind works*. New York: Norton.

Sperry, R. (1981, December 8). Nobel lecture: *Some effects of disconnecting the cerebral hemispheres*. Available at http://www.nobel.se/medicine/laureates/1981/sperry-lecture.html. Last date of acccess: June 3, 2004.

Springer, S., & Deutsch, G. (1993). *Left brain, right brain* (4th Ed). New York: W. H. Freeman.

Vaughn, R. (1980). "How advertising works: A planning model." *Journal of Advertising Research, 20*(5), 27–33.

Wilson, E. O. (1999). *Consilience*. New York: Random House.

Zeki, S. (1998). *Inner vision: An exploration of art and the brain*. New York: Oxford.

Zeki, S. (1992, September). The visual image in mind and brain. *Scientific American, 75–76*.

4

Eye Tracking Methodology and the Internet

SHEREE JOSEPHSON
Weber State University

The analogy between the eye and a camera is a false one. For the visual system, there is no fixed retinal image like a photograph. Instead, the image on the retina is in constant motion as the eyes continuously and automatically dart about gathering information in a world that is also in constant motion. The image that we perceive is a *mental* image, a stable configuration created by the brain.

The amount and speed of movement by the eyes is quite remarkable. The eyes move from two to five times every second. Eye movements are essential to vision because detailed visual information can only be obtained through the *fovea*, the small central area of the retina that has the highest number of photoreceptors. Visual acuity deteriorates rapidly outside the fovea.

To direct the fovea toward the visual scene, the eyes alternate between fixations, when they are aimed at a fixed point, and rapid movements called *saccades*. Fixations last between 200 and 500 milliseconds and 1 to 5 degrees of the visual angle of view is processed (Yarbus, 1967). They show where attention is being directed at a particular point in time. Fixations are separated by rapid, jerky movements, or saccades, during which the eyes' focus changes to a new location. Saccades are exceedingly quick and occupy only about 10 percent of the total time spent viewing information. Saccades rarely move the eyes more than 15 degrees of visual angle (Yarbus, 1967).

During a fixation, only a small area of the available visual information is selected at any time for intensive processing essential to processing clarity of detail. Levy-Schoen (1983) pointed out that this may have the functional value of protecting the central processors in the brain from overload. At the next instant, a new part of the available visual information can be selected for further intake and processing. She said:

> The way the visual system plays this role of a selective and active interface between the individual and his environment is very impressive. For the experimental psychologist, this natural device is also remarkable. Since oculomotor activity is an overt behavior that is

accessible to recording and measurement, it opens a door to the scientist interested in the organization of perceptual and cognitive processing. To the extent that eye movements are reliable correlates of the sequential centering of attention, we can observe and analyze them in order to understand how thinking goes on. (p. 66)

For more than 50 years, eye-tracking apparatuses have been available that precisely show what viewers are looking at and the order in which they are processing available visual information. The apparatuses record three main kinds of information: fixation frequency, fixation duration, and fixation sequence. *Fixation frequency* is the total number of fixations a viewer makes on an area of the visual field. *Fixation duration*, a related measure derived from summing the length of individual fixations, is how long—generally measured in milliseconds—a viewer looks at a specific visual area. *Fixation sequence* is a hierarchial mapping that records the order in which a viewer scans the visual information.

Corresponding to these three measurements are three critical assumptions: (a) the eyes fixate on the information currently being processed, (b) the fixation time of an item is directly proportional to the processing time, and (c) the eye-fixation sequence corresponds to the sequence of processing (Krause, 1982).

Numerous researchers agree that eye-tracking data provide one of the most valid measures of the acquisition of visual information, and volumes of research have accumulated in the last 50 years. Researchers attempting to summarize what has been learned in these 50 years cite three widely accepted propositions (Fisher, Karsh, Breitenbach, & Barnette, 1983): (a) fixations accumulate in locations judged to contain high semantic or visual information, (b) fixations are responsible for perception and are generally considered as a reflection of the individual's cognitive strategy, and (c) the fixation sequence allows for the encoding, storing, and subsequent reconstruction of the images.

ADVERTISING AND EYE-MOVEMENT RESEARCH

Despite hundreds or even thousands of published studies and the wide acceptance of fixation as a measure of visual attention in fields such as cognitive psychology and physiology, scholars studying advertising and marketing topics have only dabbled in the use of this research methodology. The cost and sophistication of the equipment and the complexity of the data analysis certainly have contributed to this situation. The proprietary nature of the findings for the few advertisers who have used this methodology has also probably contributed to the dearth of published research in this area.

Since the late 1970s, and until the writing of this article in 2000, only about 20 academic studies had been published using eye-tracking data as empirical evidence in the fields of advertising and marketing. Eye tracking has been used in consumer research to study how consumers look at print advertisements (Pieters, Rosbergen, & Wedel, 1999; Treistman & Gregg, 1979; Wedel & Pieters, 2000), tobacco (Fischer, Richards, Berman, & Krugman, 1989; Fox, Krugman, Fletcher, & Fischer, 1998; Krugman, Fox, Fletcher, & Rojas, 1994) and alcohol warning labels (Laughery, Young, Vaubel, & Brelsford, 1993), food nutrition labels (Goldberg, Probart, & Zak, 1999), yellow pages (Lohse, 1997), and television advertisements (d'Ydewalle & Tamsin, 1993; Janiszewski & Warlop, 1993). It has also been used to examine visual attention to products displayed on supermarket shelves (Russo & Leclerc, 1994) and point-of-purchase displays (Chandon, Hutchinson, & Young, 2001). Finally, the process of consumer choice in general (Janiszewski, 1998; Pieters & Warlop, 1999; Russo & Rosen, 1975) has been studied using this research methodology.

Now that the Internet is bursting with commercial messages, it seems logical to apply the eye-tracking research methodology to this medium. In a Poynter Institute study (2000) that focused on how consumers read Web newspapers, a secondary finding was that banner ads are seen 45% of the time. Poynter Institute fellow Andrew DeVigal found that the average fixation period on a banner was about 1 second, which he says is enough for the Web user to comprehend the brand message.

The lack of published eye-movement research on advertising and marketing in general, and the Internet in particular, cries out for research studies that "fixate" on online messages.

INTERNET BANNER ADS

Online advertising consists primarily of banner ads—flickering squares and rectangles that try to use just the right words or offers to convince Web surfers to "click here" to be transported to the advertiser's Web site where direct marketing can occur. "They're part billboard, part small-sized print ad, part direct mail, and part storefront, a strange combination that marketers are still struggling to understand" (Slater, 2000, p. 34).

This form of advertising, which didn't even exist until 1994, commanded about 5% of all U.S. advertising spending in 2000. One report estimated the annual run rate of online advertising spending at the end of 2000 was between $8 billion and $9 billion (Internet Advertising Bureau, 2000).

Despite this performance, a skepticism developed. Observers questioned whether banner ads actually work. Click-through rates (CTR) from banners to Web sites, a measure of audience response to banner advertising, declined steadily with growth in the volume of banner advertising, and ran at about 0.3% of impressions for Nielsen's sample of Web users in 2000 (Nielsen/Netratings, 2000).

Yet the Web's biggest advertisers continue to throw billions at banners. Some observers question why, believing that even a high CTR means nothing. They point to an online banner placed by WorldCom in 2000 with the provocative invitation, "Surf Naked." The ad received a huge number of click-throughs—but not a lot of new customers (informationweek.com, 2000). That goes to show that clicking doesn't necessarily translate into consideration of a product or service let alone a purchase decision.

Briggs and Hollis agreed that click-through rate may not be the best way to evaluate the effectiveness of Internet advertising. They said: "The practice of evaluating Web advertising on the basis of click-through is like evaluating television ads for automobiles on the basis of how many people visit a showroom the next day. A showroom visit is an ideal response, but hardly the most likely one, since relatively few people will be in the market for a new car on a particular day" (1997, pp. 33–34).

BANNER AD ANIMATION AND LOCATION

It didn't take long before the novelty of banners began to wear off, and marketers resorted to a number of techniques to try to draw attention to their advertising messages and get target audience members to click on the ad. In 2000, among the most widely used techniques were the use of animation and the demand for prominent placement on Web sites. At the time, much was said in the trade publications about the value of animation and placement, and marketing studies were commissioned to lend support for these widely held beliefs.

In 1996, a study by ZD Net (Business Marketing, 1996) found that animated ads generated click-through rates at least 15% higher than static ads, and in some cases as much as 40% higher. The study also found that people notice and pay attention to a banner if it has animation, even if they don't click on it. However, the researchers' conclusion was that even with animation, an ad must have a strong, well-crafted message and a clear call to action. A study by DoubleClick (DoubleClick.net, 1999) claimed that simple animation can increase response rates by 25%.

However, not all studies touted the advantages of animation. A study by Four Corners (1999) concluded that an animated "click here" button does not pull as well as a static "click here" button. A study by Millward Brown Interactive (1997) found little difference in the degree to which people thought animated and static banner ads were "eye-catching."

Complaints from Internet users about the pervasiveness of banners caused content providers—especially news sites—to have second thoughts about displaying advertising on top of news stories. Some news sites moved advertising copy to the bottom of the first view or to the bottom of the news story several screens of copy down. Obviously, many advertisers were not happy and studies were conducted to look at the effectiveness of ads appearing on the top of the page versus the bottom.

A study by DoubleClick (1999), a major ad-serving firm, found that banners at the top of the page are twice as effective as banners on the bottom of the page. In contrast, a study by Web page consultant Paul Lang (1999) claimed that banner ads at the bottom of the page perform better with a click-through rate of 2.1% compared to 1.5% for banner ads on the top of the page. That the location of a banner ad is an important variable is evidenced by the fact that marketers and content providers are using other locations for banners. However, a study reported in Web Week (1996) found that banners down the sides of Web pages don't do as well in terms of generating click-through.

In contrast, a University of Michigan study (Boyle, Minor, & Weyrich, 1999) showed that banners next to the right scroll bar (in the lower-right-hand corner of the first screen) generated a 228% higher click-through rate than ads at the top of the page.

RESEARCH QUESTIONS

Based on the discussions that were taking place in 1999 regarding Internet advertising, two independent variables of banner ads—motion and location—were selected for intensive study using eye-movement methodology. The research questions were:

1. Are viewers more likely to fixate on banner ads with animation as opposed to those without?
2. Are viewers more likely to fixate on banner ads on the top of a Web page as opposed to banner ads on the bottom of the page?

METHOD

Participants

The participants were 32 students (18 males and 14 females) recruited from communication classes at a large Western university. Their average age was 22 years. They were paid for participating in the study.

All participants were regular users of the Internet. All but three participants said they had been using the Web for more than a year. All but two said they use the Web more than 1 hour per week.

Apparatus

The RK-726PCI Pupil/Corneal Reflection Tracking System designed by ISCAN, Inc. of Burlington, Massachusetts, was used to record eye movements and fixations on the Web pages (see Fig. 4.1). The system is a PC card-sized, real-time digital image processor that automatically tracks the center of the pupil and the reflection from the corneal surface. The eye is illuminated with a low-level infrared source to allow the system to track exactly what an individual is looking at (ISCAN, Inc., 1998).

The processor operates at a sample rate of 60 Hz and the participant's eye position may be determined with an accuracy typically better than 0.3 degrees over a +/−20 degree horizontal and vertical range using the pupil/corneal reflection difference.

FIG. 4.1. Participant's eyes are being tracked using the corneal-reflection technique.

Stimulus Materials

Two Web pages published by Wired.com in 1999 were used in the study. Two Intel ads that were about to be published on the Web in 1999 were placed on the pages. The Web pages were current and the Intel ads were soon to be released.

Two versions of each banner ad were displayed. One version contained animation, while the other remained static. The banner ads were displayed in two locations on the page, on the top and on the bottom. When participants scrolled to view the content, the ads remained in their original positions on the screen.

The size of the banner ads was 468 pixels by 60 pixels. The ads were viewed with a browser size of 800 by 600 pixels.

Procedure

The Latin-square Design

The study employed the Latin-square Design, a protocol that provides for an efficient use of a limited number of participants (see Table 4.1). This protocol allowed for each of the participants to be exposed to both treatment conditions (moving or static banner ad and top or bottom display).

The 32 participants were divided into two groups of 16. Then one at a time, participants in each group were asked to look at two different Web pages. One of the Web sites had a banner ad on the top of the page, while the other had a banner ad on the bottom. Furthermore, one of the banner ads viewed by each participant used a moving image, while the other banner ad used a static image. Specifically, each member of Group 1 saw a Web site with a moving banner ad on the top of the page and a Web site with a static banner ad on the bottom of the page. Each member of Group 2 saw a Web site with a static banner ad on the top of the page and a Web site with a moving banner ad on the bottom of the page.

Instructions to Participants

On arriving at the eye-movement laboratory, participants were given an informed consent form explaining that the purpose of the study was to determine how people

TABLE 4.1
Latin-square Design

Animation		Location	
		Top	Bottom
	Animated	Group 1	Group 2
	Static	Group 2	Group 1

look at Web pages. The form stated: "The investigation uses eye-tracking information to determine what areas of the screen are attended to, and how the content on the screen attracts user's attention.... Most of the data will be collected using a standard eye-tracking apparatus. The apparatus will record the general area of the screen that the eye is focused on."

The differences in the display of the banner ads were not pointed out to the participants before the experiment was administered.

Recording Eye Movements

Participants entered the eye-movement laboratory separately. Before eye movements could be recorded, the eye-movement apparatus was calibrated to each participant by a procedure that requires the system operator to instruct the participant to fixate on five adjustable targets, one at a time. The targets were positioned in the center, the upper-left, upper-right, lower-left, and lower-right portions of the participant's field of view. The system calculates horizontal and vertical correlating factors for each of the four quadrants of the participant's field of view. After calibration, these correlating factors are used to compute the location of fixation for subsequent eye movements.

Data Collection

Eye movements were recorded while participants viewed two Wired.com Web sites containing Intel banner advertisements. The participants were allowed to look at the Web sites for as long as they chose. Data were recorded by the computer program, as well as captured on videotape.

Fixation Criterion

Before the eye-movement data were analyzed, the criterion for a fixation was specified. For the purpose of this study, a fixation was defined as a pause of at least 100 milliseconds within an area of 10 pixels by 6 pixels.

Software Analysis of Data

ISCAN, Inc. point-of-regard fixation analysis software Version 1.00A was used to analyze the data. The software displays the data in three main ways (ISCAN, Inc., 1998).

First, a list of fixations shows each fixation, its horizontal and vertical coordinates on the screen, and its starting time and duration in milliseconds (see Fig. 4.2). Second is a "raindrop fixation scanpath display" (see Fig. 4.3). This is a graphical display in which each fixation is represented as a circle on a simulated scene display. Each fixation circle center is connected to the next fixation chronologically. The diameter of each circle is proportional to the fixation duration. Third is a "raindrop fixation epoch coded display." This is similar to the scanpath display except that each fixation is color-coded within five time periods representing the order of the fixation, and the fixation circle centers are not connected.

Data may also be analyzed by correlating fixations to scene elements. To do this, the researcher must determine what areas of the screen are of particular interest (see Fig. 4.4).

```
PFA1_00                                                    _ □ ×

 Auto    ▾  ☐ 🗋 📷  ⊠  🖼🗗  A

* List of Fixations Data Display * .

Subject:      s31ad1_1                          Date:    031699
Description:                                    Sample Rate:  60 Hz

   Fix #          P-O-R H          P-O-R V          FixStart          FixTime

      96              225              368              14.367              0.233
      97              233              344              14.667              0.050
      98              287              381              14.817              0.083

      81               49              344              12.500              0.050
      82               57              356              12.503              0.050
      83              184              439              12.717              0.033
      84              206              368              12.967              0.033
      85              155              338              13.067              0.033
      86              199              327              13.200              0.083
      87              217              327              13.300              0.050
      88              226              330              13.350              0.050
      89              189              346              13.467              0.067
      90              210              353              13.503              0.067
      91              258              353              13.717              0.083
      92              302              357              13.883              0.067
      93              160              363              14.033              0.050
      94              160              370              14.083              0.100
      95              194              364              14.250              0.050

Press (a) to ABORT; (n) for NEXT data; (r) for new RANGE.
```

FIG. 4.2.   Data file lists the horizontal and vertical coordinates of fixations, as well as their starting times and lengths of duration.

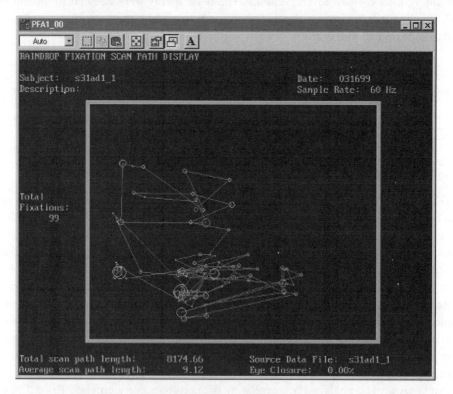

FIG. 4.3.   This display shows the path the eye followed as it scanned the Web page. The size of the raindrops is proportional to the length of fixation.

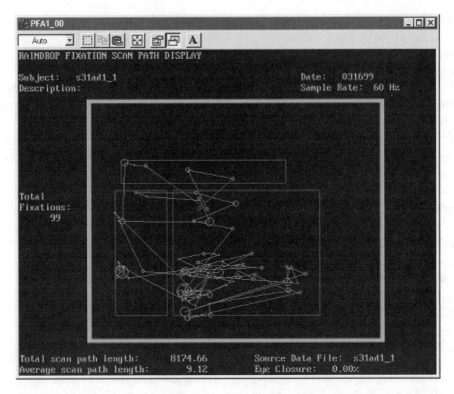

FIG. 4.4. Areas of interest on the Web page are defined. The top box indicates where the banner ad resided.

In this study, the researcher was interested in whether participants fixated on the banner ad or not. The banner ad was defined as the scene element of interest, and the data were analyzed accordingly.

Once scene elements are defined, the software allows the data to be displayed in the three main ways described earlier, along with a pie chart, a traditional bar chart, and a bar chart that tracks chronology. The pie chart displays the total number of fixations on particular areas of the screen and the total fixation time on particular areas of the screen as a percentage of the whole. Likewise, the bar chart can compare the number of fixations on particular areas of the screen as well as the total length of fixation on those areas. The chronological bar chart shows the fixation chronology along with total fixation time on a particular area at a particular point in time.

Statistical Method

Means were calculated and then the data on location and animation were analyzed using multiple analysis of variance (MANOVA). MANOVA is a statistical procedure that tests hypotheses about two or more interrelated dependent variables simultaneously. Dependent variables analyzed by the MANOVA procedure included: (a) total number of individual fixations on banner ad, (b) total number of seconds spent fixating on banner ad, and (c) the number of different times the banner was fixated on. To count as a different occurrence of fixation, participants had to look at the banner ad, then divert their attention to another area or areas of the Web page, then return to the banner ad. If participants made multiple fixations consecutively on a banner ad and never looked back after looking away, this measure of frequency was simply counted as one.

Descriptive statistics (percentages) were computed to show how many participants fixated at least once on the banner ad and how many participants clicked on the banner ad.

In addition, the scanpath—the order that individual elements were viewed on the page—was analyzed. To arrive at a number representing where the fixation on a banner ad occurred within the overall scanpath, the page was divided into logical areas—the banner ad, the nameplate or header, the navigation bars, and the text area. Then the number of areas a participant looked at until arriving at the banner ad was calculated. This procedure resulted in an ordinal number describing the location in the eye path in which the first fixation on a banner ad occurred. Means were calculated for this descriptor of the scanpath.

Finally, the amount of time that elapsed before participants fixated on the banner ad was recorded and the mean was computed.

RESULTS

A table of means shows that location is definitely more important than the use of animation in determining whether or not Web users will look at a banner advertisement. Placing the advertisement on the top of the page as opposed to the bottom dramatically increases the chances that a viewer will pay attention to the ad. Animation in the banner ad only slightly increases, but not to a statistically significant amount—the chances that it will be noticed. A table of means for the four treatments is included as Table 4.2.

One especially interesting finding noted in Table 4.2 is that overall participants fixated only 0.53 seconds on banner ads. This average was derived from the data of those participants who fixated on a banner ad, as well as those who didn't.

The importance of location is further manifested by the results from the MANOVA procedure, which yielded two significant F values on the factor of location (see Table 4.3). The significant F values turned up on the dependent variable of number of fixations on banner ads ($F[1, 30] = 11.206$, $p = .001$) and the related dependent variable of total duration of fixation on banner ads ($F[1, 30] = 4.696$, $p = .034$). The frequency of different times participants looked at a banner ad approached significance on the variable of location ($F[1, 30] = 3.628$, $p = .062$).

No significant F values turned up on the factor of use of animation (also see Table 4.3), although the variable of frequency of different times a participant looked at a banner ad with animation approached significance ($F[1, 30] = 3.628$, $p = .062$).

Overall, 44% of all banner ads were fixated on at least once in this study. This percentage is particularly interestingly because it is almost the same percentage derived from the study by the Poynter Institute (2000; 45%).

Again results show that location was the biggest determinant of whether an ad was fixated on at least once. Here are the results broken down according to the four treatments:

TABLE 4.2
Table of Means for Four Treatments

Treatment		Elapsed time until first fixation on banner	Order of first fixation on banner	Total duration of fixations on banner	Frequency of times subject looked at banner	Fixations on banner
				Report		
Animated banner on TOP	Mean	3.39	1.81	.84	1.25	2.00
	N	16	16	16	16	16
	Std. Deviation	6.96	2.23	1.26	1.06	2.28
Static banner on BOTTOM	Mean	4.20	1.38	.33	1.25	.75
	N	16	16	16	16	16
	Std. Deviation	9.67	1.75	.50	1.61	.86
Static banner on TOP	Mean	1.60	1.00	.92	1.69	1.56
	N	16	16	16	16	16
	Std. Deviation	3.70	1.21	2.21	1.62	2.06
Animated banner on BOTTOM	Mean	.58	.50	2.60E-02	.44	.13
	N	16	16	16	16	16
	Std. Deviation	1.64	1.37	7.41E-02	.73	.34
Total	Mean	2.44	1.77	.53	1.16	1.11
	N	64	64	64	64	64
	Std. Deviation	6.31	1.71	1.32	1.36	1.73

top with animation, 10 of the 16 participants looked at the banner ad; top static, 8 of 16; bottom with animation, 2 of 16; and bottom static, 8 of 16. When the data are consolidated, the impact of the variable of location becomes especially apparent. For a banner ad of any kind on the top of the page, 18 of 32 (56%) participants fixated on it least one time, while 10 of 32 (31%) participants fixated on a banner ad at least one time if it was on the bottom of the page. Interestingly, more participants fixated at least one time on a banner ad without animation. Specifically, for a banner without animation in any location, 16 of 32 (50%) of participants fixated on it, compared to 12 of 32 (38%) when the ad contained animation.

A further breakdown of the data from only those participants who fixated on the banner ads also shows some interesting results. The average number of fixations on a banner ad for those who made at least one fixation was as follows: top with animation, 3.2 fixations; top static, 3.13 fixations; bottom with animation, 1.0 fixations; and bottom static, 1.5. When the data are consolidated, the average number of fixations spent on a banner ad on the top of the page by those who fixated at least once was 3.17, compared to 1.40 fixations for banner ads on the bottom. For the variable of motion, participants

TABLE 4.3
MANOVA Tests of Between-Subjects Effects

Source	Dependent Variable	Type III Sum of Squares	df	Mean Square	F	Sig.
Corrected Model	Number of fixations on banner	299.063	3	11.182	4.337	.008
	Total duration of fixation on banner	8.689	3	2.896	1.719	.173
	Frequency of times subject looked at banner	13.062	3	4.354	2.527	.066
Intercept	Number of fixations on banner	78.766	1	78.766	30.552	.000
	Total duration of fixation on banner	17.804	1	17.804	10.563	.002
	Frequency of times subject looked at banner	85.563	1	85.563	49.661	.000
Animation	Number of fixations on banner	.141	1	.141	.055	.816
	Total duration of fixation on banner	.590	1	.590	.350	.556
	Frequency of times subject looked at banner	6.250	1	6.250	3.628	.062
Location	Number of fixations on banner	28.891	1	28.891	11.206	.001*
	Total duration of fixation on banner	7.914	1	7.914	4.696	.034*
	Frequency of times subject looked at banner	6.250	1	6.250	3.628	.062
Animation* Location	Number of fixations on banner	4.516	1	4.516	1.752	.191
	Total duration of fixation on banner	.185	1	.185	.110	.742
	Frequency of times subject looked at banner	.563	1	.563	.326	.570

*$p < .05$.

made an average of 2.83 fixations on an animated ad regardless of position, compared to 2.31 fixations for a static ad.

The related variable of the average amount of time spent on a banner ad for those who fixated was as follows: top with animation, 1.34 seconds; top static, 1.84 seconds; bottom with animation, 0.21 seconds; and bottom static, 0.65. When the data are further consolidated, it becomes evident for those who fixated that location was still the most important variable. For those participants who fixated on a banner ad, the average amount of time spent on an ad at the top of the page was 1.56 seconds, while the average amount of time spent on an ad at the bottom of the page was 0.56 seconds. For the variable of animation, 1.15 seconds was spent on a banner ad with animation, while slightly more time—1.25 seconds—was spent on a static ad. Overall, viewers who fixated at least once on any banner ad fixated for an average of 1.21 seconds.

The amount of time elapsed until the first fixation on a banner ad for those who fixated at least once was as follows: top with animation, 5.43 seconds; top static, 3.19 seconds; bottom with animation, 4.65 seconds; and bottom static, 8.40 seconds. For all ads on the top of the page, it took an average of 4.44 seconds for a participant to fixate the first time on a banner ad on the top of the page, compared to 7.65 seconds for an ad on the bottom of the page. For all ads with animation, it took participants 5.30 seconds until they fixated on a banner ad with animation, compared to 5.80 for a banner ad without animation. Thus, animation didn't dramatically affect how soon a participant looked at a banner ad in the overall process of looking at a Web page.

Finally, the scanpath was analyzed. These results represent the number of areas viewed before the banner was fixated for the first time. For those who fixated at least once, the results were as follows: top with animation, 2.9; top static, 2.0; bottom with animation, 4.0; and bottom static, 2.75. Participants who fixated at least once on a banner ad on the top of the page did so slightly earlier than those participants who fixated at least once on a banner ad on the bottom of the page. A banner ad on the top of the page was on average somewhere between the second and third (2.5) area viewed, compared to the third (3.0) area looked at when the banner ad was on the bottom of the page. As revealed by the scanpath data, participants surprisingly came to a static ad a little bit sooner than they came to a moving ad in their eye path across the Web page. Ads without animation were on average the second (2.38) area viewed, compared to the third (3.08) area viewed when they contained animation.

Click-through rates exhibited in this study were higher than those being reported by industry at the time of the experiment. The results are as follows: top with animation, 2 of 16 clicked (12.5%); top static, 4 of 16 clicked (25.0%); bottom with animation, 2 of 16 clicked (12.5%); and bottom static, 0 of 16 clicked (0%). In other words, the click-through rate for an ad on the top of the page was 18.75% compared to 6.25% for an ad on the bottom of the page. The click-through rate for a banner with animation was 12.5% compared to the exact percentage of 12.5% for a banner without animation. Overall, the CTR was 12.5%.

When participants were finished with the eye-tracking test, they were asked two questions about ad banner preference. Most participants, 22 of 32, reported they prefer ads on the top of the page. And most participants, 24 of 32, said they prefer banner ads with animation.

CONCLUSION

Location is definitely the strongest variable in determining whether viewers look at banner ads and affecting how long they look at them (see Figs. 4.5–4.8 for examples of

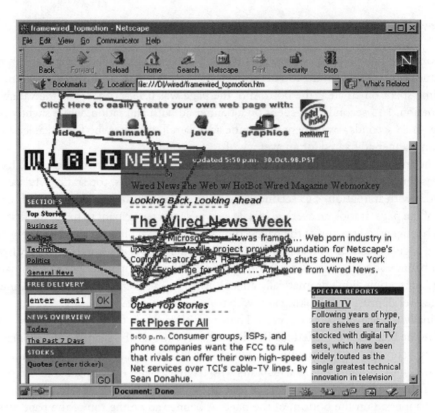

FIG. 4.5. Participants who looked at an animated banner on top of the page made an average of three fixations.

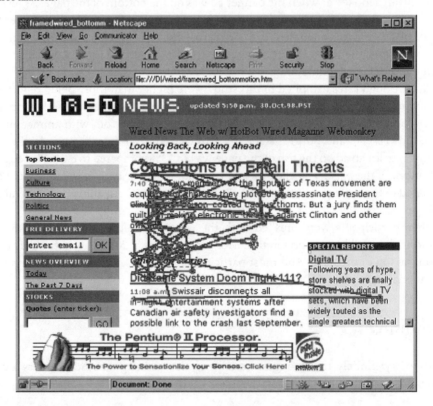

FIG. 4.6. This participant, like 29 others, did not look at the banner ad on the bottom of the page even when it contained animation.

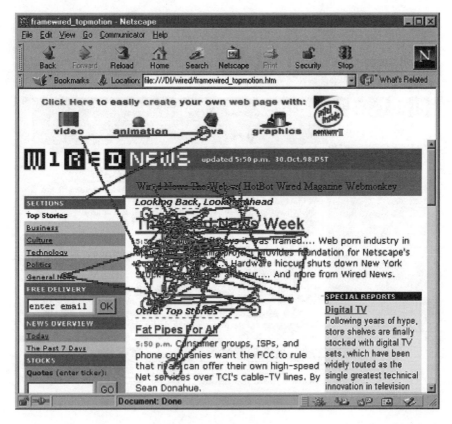

FIG. 4.7. Participants were likely to fixate on a banner ad on the top of the page, even though it did not contain animation.

scanpaths superimposed over Web pages). In this study, use of animation plays little or no significant role in whether viewers look at banner ads and for how long they look at them. In fact, there is almost no difference at all between the average number of fixations and the average length of time viewers spent looking at banner ads with animation or without. This is in stark contrast to the significant differences in the amount of time spent looking at banner ads on the top of the page versus those on the bottom. The importance of the variable of location holds up whether the results from all participants are taken into account or whether only the behavior of those participants who fixated on a banner ad at least once are analyzed.

Interestingly, in the analysis taking into effect only the data of those participants who fixated on the banner ads, ads without animation slightly outperformed those with animation in two respects—the amount of time spent fixating on a banner ad and the length of time that elapsed until participants looked at a banner ad. Overall, ads without animation were fixated on about one tenth of a second longer than those with animation, and it took about half a second more for participants to make their first fixation on an ad with animation. In addition, the eye path participants traveled until encountering a static ad was a little shorter than the one traveled to an animated ad.

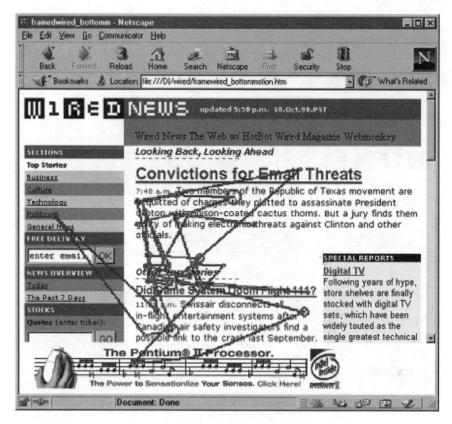

FIG. 4.8. Participants were more likely to look at banner ads on the bottom of the page without animation than at banners in the same location with animation.

Perhaps the amount of animation used in these particular ads impacted the results. The content of the banner ad remained consistent throughout the study whether the ads remained static or moved. Many Internet ads today contain dramatic amounts of animation with different content moving in and out. For example, the entire frame of the ad may be replaced by another frame of the ad. The amount of animation in a banner ad would be an interesting variable for a follow-up study.

But one thing seems apparent from the results of this study. Like they say in real estate, location is everything. When it comes to Internet property, advertisers on the Web should do everything they can to purchase ads on the top of the page.

Other important findings from this study are that on average fewer than half of the Web viewers looked at banner ads (44%), and these viewers who made at least one fixation only looked for 1.21 seconds on average at the banner ad. When all participants are taken into account, the average length of fixation on a banner ad was only 0.53 seconds. These findings are uncannily similar to those obtained by the Poynter Institute (2000). These findings should be taken into account as advertisers approach the messaging and design of banner ads.

However, as dismal as these viewership results might seem at first glance, they should hearten advertisers. They provide evidence that many more Web users are paying attention to banner ads than click-through rates in the industry show. Eye-movement data not only provide evidence of this response, they also provide a form of proof. In fact, eye-movement recording shows that click-through may dramatically underestimate the power of banner advertising. When looked at in this light, a relatively high percentage (44%) of Internet users look at ads. They may not take the time to carefully read them and to click on them, but they spend enough time to read a short message or see the advertiser's name.

REFERENCES

Boyle, K., Minor A., & Weyrich, C. (1999). Banner ad placement study. Retrieved June 10, 2004, from http://www.webreference.com/dev/banners/.

Briggs, R., & Hollis, N. (1997, March/April). Advertising on the web: Is there response before click-through? *Journal of Advertising Research, 37*(2), pp. 33–45.

Business Marketing. (1996, November 1). Study shows big lifts from animated ads. Retrieved May 31, 2000, from http://webreference.com/dev/banners/research.html.

Chandon, P., Hutchinson, J. W., & Young, S. H. (2001). Measuring the value of point-of-purchase marketing with commercial eye-tracking data. Insead R & D working papers.

d'Ydewalle, G., & Tamsin, F. (1993). On the visual processing and memory of incidental information: Advertising panels in soccer games. In D. Brogan, A. Gale, and K. Carr (Eds.), *Visual search 2,* (pp. 401–408). London: Taylor and Francis.

DoubleClick.net. (1999). Research findings: Banner effectiveness tips. Retrieved June 2, 1999, from http://studio.doubleclick.net/learning_center/research_findings/effectiveness.htm.

Fischer, P. M., Richards, J. W., Berman, E. J., & Krugman, D. M. (1989). Recall and eye tracking study of adolescents viewing tobacco advertisements. *Journal of the American Medical Association, 261*(1), 84–89.

Fisher, D. F., Karsh, R., Breitenbach, F., & Barnette, B. D. (1983). Eye movements and picture recognition: Contribution or embellishment. In R. Groner et al., (Eds.), *Eye movements and psychological functions: International views* (pp. 193–210). Hillsdale, NJ: Lawrence Erlbaum Associates.

Fox, R. J., Krugman, D. M., Fletcher, J. E., & Fischer, P. M. (1998). Adolescents' attention to beer and cigarette print ads and associated product warnings. *Journal of Advertising, 27*(3), 57–68.

Four Corners. (1999, April). Banner tips: Back issues: Issue #10. Retrieved June 2, 1999, from http://www.bannertips.combannerTips1999-04.shtml.

Goldberg, J. H., Probart, C. K., & Zak, R. E. (1999). Visual search of food nutrition labels. *Human Factors, 41*(3), 425–437.

informationweek.com. (2000, October 2). Advertisers seek more bang for their Web bucks: Agencies develop sophisticated ways to gauge an ad's success at brand building, driving sales. *informationweek.com,* 130–138.

Internet Advertising Bureau. (2000, December 20). Internet ad revenue report. Retrieved June 10, 2004, from http://www.iab.net/resources/adrevenue/archive_2000. asp#.

ISCAN, Inc. (1998, January). RK-726PCI pupil/corneal reflection tracking system (PCI card version). Operating Instructions. Burlington, MA.

Janiszewski, C. (1998, December). The influence of display characteristics on visual exploratory search behavior. *Journal of Consumer Research, 25,* 290–301.

Janiszewski, C., & Warlop, L. (1993). The influence of classical conditioning procedures on subsequent attention to the conditioned brand. *Journal of Consumer Research, 20,* 171–189.

Krause, W. (1982). Eye fixations and three-term series problems, or: Is there evidence for task independent information units: In R. Groner and P. Fraisse (Eds.), *Cognition and Eye movements* (pp. 122–138). Amsterdam/Berlin: North Holland/Deutscher Verlag der Wissesnschaften (joint edition).

Krugman, D. M., Fox, R. J., Fletcher, J. E., & Rojas, T. H. (1994, November/December). Do adolescents attend to warnings in cigarette advertising? An eye-tracking approach. *Journal of Advertising Research,* 39–52.

Lang, P. (1999, April). Banner Comparison: Top vs. Bottom. Retrieved June 17, 2004, from http://wilsonweb. com/webmarket/ad.htm.

Laughery, K. R., Young, S. L., Vaubel, K. P., & Brelsford Jr., J. W. (1993). The noticeability of warnings on alcoholic beverage containers. *Journal of Public Policy and Marketing, 12*(1), 38–56.

Levy-Schoen, A. (1983). Central and Peripheral Processing. In R. Groner, C. Menz, D. F. Fisher, and R. A. Monty (Eds.), *Eye movements and psychological functions: international views* (pp. 65–71). Hillsdale, NJ: Lawrence Erlbaum Associates.

Lohse, G. L. (1997). Consumer eye movement patterns on yellow pages advertising. *Journal of Advertising, 26*(1), 61–73.

Millward Brown Interactive. (1997). Interactive Advertising Bureau advertising effectiveness study. Available at: http://www.intelliquest.com/search/results.asp?v path = /resources/reports/mbi_report02.asp

Nielsen/Netratings. (2000, December 1). Nielsen/Netratings Reporter. Retrieved December 29, 2000, from http://209.249.142.22/weekly.asp#usage.

Pieters, R., Rosbergen, E., & Wedel, M. (1999, November). Visual attention to repeated print advertising: a test of scanpath theory. *Journal of Marketing Research, 36*, 424–438.

Pieters, R., & Warlop, L. (1999). Visual attention during brand choice: The impact of time pressure and task motivation. *International Journal of Research in Marketing, 16*, 1–16.

Poynter Institute. (2000). Stanford-Poynter Project/Eye tracking online news. Retrieved June 10, 2004, from www.poynterextra.org/et/i.htm.

Russo, J. E., & Leclerc, F. (1994). An eye-fixation analysis of choice processes for consumer nondurables. *Journal of Consumer Research, 21*, 274–290.

Russo, J. E., & Rosen, L. D. (1975). An eye fixation analysis of multialternative choice. *Memory & Cognition, 3*(3), 267–276.

Slater, J. (2000). Learning curve: Internet advertising yet to take off in Asia, but marketers are beginning to wise up to ways to tap the medium's true potential. *Far Eastern Economic Review, 163*(29), 34–36.

Treistman, J., & Gregg, J. P. (1979). Visual, verbal, and sales responses to print ads. *Journal of Advertising Research, 19*(4), 41–47.

Web Week. (1996, October 23). 5 tips for effective banner advertising. Retrieved June 10, 2004, from http://webreference.com/dev/banners/research.html.

Wedel, M., & Pieters, R. (2000). Eye fixations on advertisements and memory for brands: A model and findings. *Marketing Science, 19*(4), 297–312.

Yarbus, A. (1967). *Eye movements and vision.* New York: Plenum.

5

Perception and the Newspaper Page: A Critical Analysis

KEN SMITH
University of Wyoming

Throughout much of the history of newspapers, design had little to do with perception and was based primarily on two factors. The first was the technical constraints imposed by the methods of printing. The second was the nature of news. The philosophy of "getting it first and getting it right" (Utt & Pasternack, 1984, p. 15) affected the look of newspaper pages because design had to accommodate tight deadlines.

Technological advances during the later decades of the 20th century allowed newspapers to increase their use of color and graphics and also shortened production time, thereby easing the deadline pressure on news staffs. The result was a whole new look in newspaper layout. The use of these new design elements apparently met with the approval of readers (Pasternack & Utt, 1986; Click & Stempel, 1978; Garcia, Click, & Stempel, 1981; Bain & Weaver, 1979).

However, while researchers have found that readers like the design changes that have occurred in the past 30 years, not much research has examined if these changes are harmonious with perceptual processing by readers and actually facilitate reading. Even though newspapers today rely more on graphic specialists than on the back shop production personnel of the past for layout, an observation by Sissors in 1965 may still apply today. He said, "Changes being made today have been based on feeling rather than on objective evidence concerning which design is easier to read" (p. 237).

This chapter examines newspaper design and its relationship to human perception. More specifically, this chapter uses a critical method to examine how well newspaper design complies with the principles of visual organization known as *gestalts*.

THEORETICAL BACKGROUND

Gestalt theory suggests that humans have a subconscious tendency to combine diverse bits of information into organized "wholes." The basic law of gestalts describes a striving toward the simplest, most regular, most symmetrical structure that a person can perceive in a given situation (Arnheim, 1974). This tendency makes the processing of information more efficient because a person does not have to expend the effort necessary to attend to each of the individual parts. Instead, those parts are processed as a unified whole. As Kreitler and Kreitler (1972) said, "Organization in terms of gestalt laws makes for economy in the encoding of information, and allows us to grasp maximum information through a relative minimum of means and efforts" (p. 89).

As applied to vision, "gestalt refers to the observable fact that things are seen as relating to each other and not as discrete elements" (Stroebel, Todd, & Zakia, 1980, p. 164). In the process of observing a visual field, viewers do not devote time and energy to individual bits of information. Instead they conserve both by their tendency to group the minute elements together and attend to the whole.

Although the exact physiological process responsible for gestalt perception is not certain, a number of areas of the brain are probably involved. As Barry stated in Chapter 3, "perception is not a system per se, but a description of what goes on in a number of neural systems." Gestalt perception may be related to what Barry called the brain's tendency to "respond emotionally to situations before we can think them through." Just as this tendency allows humans to respond to stimuli more quickly, gestalt perception allows humans to respond to stimuli with an economy of effort. At the very least, the focus in studies of perception is not on individual parts of the brain, but on "how specialized areas of the visual cortex work together to create a unified perception" (Barry, 1997, p. 44).

Among the gestalt principles that help to explain visual organization are similarity, proximity, continuation, closure, figure-ground, and symmetry. A seventh principle, iso-morphism, was formerly considered a gestalt, but has since lost universal acceptance. It is included in this analysis because it remains useful in explaining visual associations (Stroebel et al., 1980; Kubovy & Pomerantz, 1981).

Similarity is the tendency to perceive objects that are similar in appearance as belonging together. In Fig. 5.1, the viewer perceives the white circles as belonging with each other

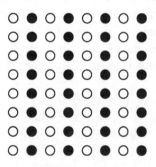

FIG. 5.1.   Similarity

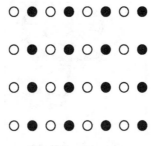

FIG. 5.2. Proximity.

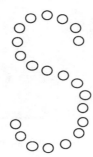

FIG. 5.3. Continuation.

and the black circles as also belonging together. The result is that the viewer organizes the circles into a series of vertical columns.

Proximity is the idea that objects will be grouped together based on their distance from each other. The closer two or more elements are, the greater the probability that they will be perceived as related. Figure 5.2 provides an example of proximity. Despite the similarity in appearance among the white versus the black circles, the viewer will now perceive a series of horizontal rows because of proximate relationships.

Continuation is based on the idea that viewers tend to close up spaces between objects and perceive them as continuous or as forming lines. Figure 5.3 contains 21 separate circles. Yet because viewers group the circles together rather than attend to the spaces between them, they tend to perceive a continuous line. By doing this, they see an "S" rather than a grouping of circles.

Closure is the principle that suggests shapes or lines that are nearly complete will be perceived and remembered as complete forms. Viewers have a strong ability to fill in missing information, which allows them to organize and make sense of the information that is present (Spoehr & Lehmkuhle, 1982). Figure 5.4 depicts an oval form that is interrupted by the frame. Even though the form is not complete, the viewer subconsciously fills in the missing information, makes sense of the form, and recognizes it as a depiction of an umbrella.

Figure-ground is based on the idea that when two figures overlap, the smaller of the two is more likely to be perceived as the figure and the larger as the background. The figure is the object to which the viewers tend to pay attention (oftentimes called the subject in

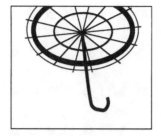

FIG. 5.4. Closure.

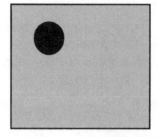

FIG. 5.5. Figure-ground.

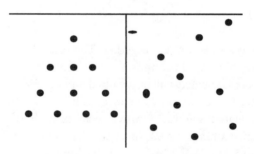

FIG. 5.6. Symmetry.

visual media such as photography). When a small black circle and a larger gray square overlap in Fig. 5.5, viewers have a tendency to perceive the circle as the figure and thus assign greater importance to it. The square is viewed as the background, an area whose role is secondary and supplemental to the figure.

With *symmetry*, diverse elements that are aligned in symmetrical shapes are likely to be seen as belonging together and perceived as a single entity. In Fig. 5.6, each side contains 11 dots, but the dots in the left side are more likely to be perceived as a single entity because they take the symmetrical shape of a triangle.

Isomorphism refers to a similarity between form and meaning—the idea that certain visual forms are associated with specific meanings and can even evoke feelings in the brain (Stroebel et al., 1980). Figure 5.7 provides an example. Visual media have no smell. Yet Fig. 5.7 conveys a sense of smell because of the association between a skunk and odor. Isomorphism was once considered a gestalt hypothesis because of the belief that

FIG. 5.7. Isomorphism.

"visual patterns are presented in the brain, not symbolically, but directly as corresponding points of excitation" (Stroebel et al., 1980, p. 176). Although isomorphism has now been discounted by many as a gestalt hypothesis, it can help to explain many of the associations that contribute to understanding in the visual media.

METHOD

In a critical analysis, a set of criteria are applied in the examination of a "text" in order to provide a distinct perspective for analyzing the text. The criteria used in the analysis are analogous to a "model" used in other types of research in that they provide a theoretical basis for examining the phenomenon in question. Critical analyses are frequently associated with the examination of rhetorical discourse, and they provide a tool in helping to break down a speech in order to gain a unique understanding of its content. However, the "text" does not necessarily need to be a written or spoken text. It can take the form of whatever the critic chooses to examine, as long as its parameters are well defined. Thus, critical analyses can be utilized in the examinations of media creations such as a television show, an advertisement, or a photograph. Rosenfeld suggested that the critic should have some expertise with the phenomenon under investigation so that the examination goes beyond mere observation. He called criticism, "Statements by an expert about the way things are" (1968, p. 52).

In this examination, the text will be newspaper front pages. The front pages representing three different styles of newspaper layout will be analyzed. (Note: Due to copyright concerns, actual front pages could not be used but model pages based on actual newspapers and typifying the different types of newspaper design are substituted instead.) They include a vertical-format newspaper, a horizontal-format newspaper, and a newspaper using a contemporary layout design. These three styles were chosen because the vertical format is the traditional design common to newspapers from a time when the technology constrained design. Many newspapers (including the *New York Times*) continue to use vertical formats. With the offset press, horizontal formats began to emerge because the newer method of setting type allowed for a more horizontal placement of stories on the page. One consideration in the emergence of horizontal design was that it accommodated a psychological tendency to organize information. The contemporary format, which to some degree was initiated and is typified by *USA Today*, brought what some felt was a more stimulating look to the front page. Unlike the symmetrical packages that often typified horizontal layouts, the contemporary design represented, in a sense, a return to vertical layouts, but did so by incorporating the color and graphic elements that newer technologies made possible.

The model that will be used to analyze the newspaper pages is gestalt theory. The pages will be examined to find instances where they display the gestalts of similarity, proximity, continuation, closure, symmetry, figure-ground, and isomorphism. As part of this analysis, gestalts that are common to newspaper design in general but may not be evident in these pages are also discussed.

This particular analysis looks for stylistic features contained in the text under examination. This is just one type of focus used in critical analysis. In other types, the focus includes but is not limited to an examination of themes, sources, subject matter, values, argument forms, psychological states, or political and power situations.

COMMON GRAPHIC ELEMENTS

Headlines

One gestalt observed in the headlines on these pages is similarity—or perhaps more appropriately, a lack of. The size and boldness of headlines are used to grade the news with larger or bolder headlines associated with more important news. When headlines are of equal size and weight, the reader is to assume the corresponding stories are of equal importance. The vertical format (Fig. 5.8) displays three headlines across the top of the page that are of equal size and weight, which sends a sign to the reader that the stories are of equal importance. Headlines lower on the page are smaller in size, indicating the news loses importance as it moves from the top of the page.

The horizontal format (Fig. 5.9) displays the largest and boldest headline at the upper right of the page (in newspapers, the traditional location of the most important story). Eye-tracking studies indicate the dominant photo is the main entry point into the page (Garcia & Stark, 1991), so if this large headline in the upper-right position indicates that the designers expect the reader to enter the page at this location, they may find it is a secondary point of eye movement after the reader is attracted to Photo No. 1.

The contemporary format (Fig. 5.10) uses headline size and weight to try and create a sense of importance throughout the entire page by utilizing the three largest and boldest headlines at lower points on the page. The variation in headlines displayed by the three formats indicates how designers can use differences in similarity to both move the eye around the page and to grade the importance of stories.

The gestalt of symmetry also comes into play in the use of headlines. When the headline and its accompanying story create a symmetrical (horizontal or square) package, the tendency of the reader is to perceive the two as belonging together. Vertical-format newspapers often violated the principle of symmetry as seen in Story No. 3 (Fig. 5.8) in which the headline covers an area that is not symmetrical as Story No. 3 wraps around

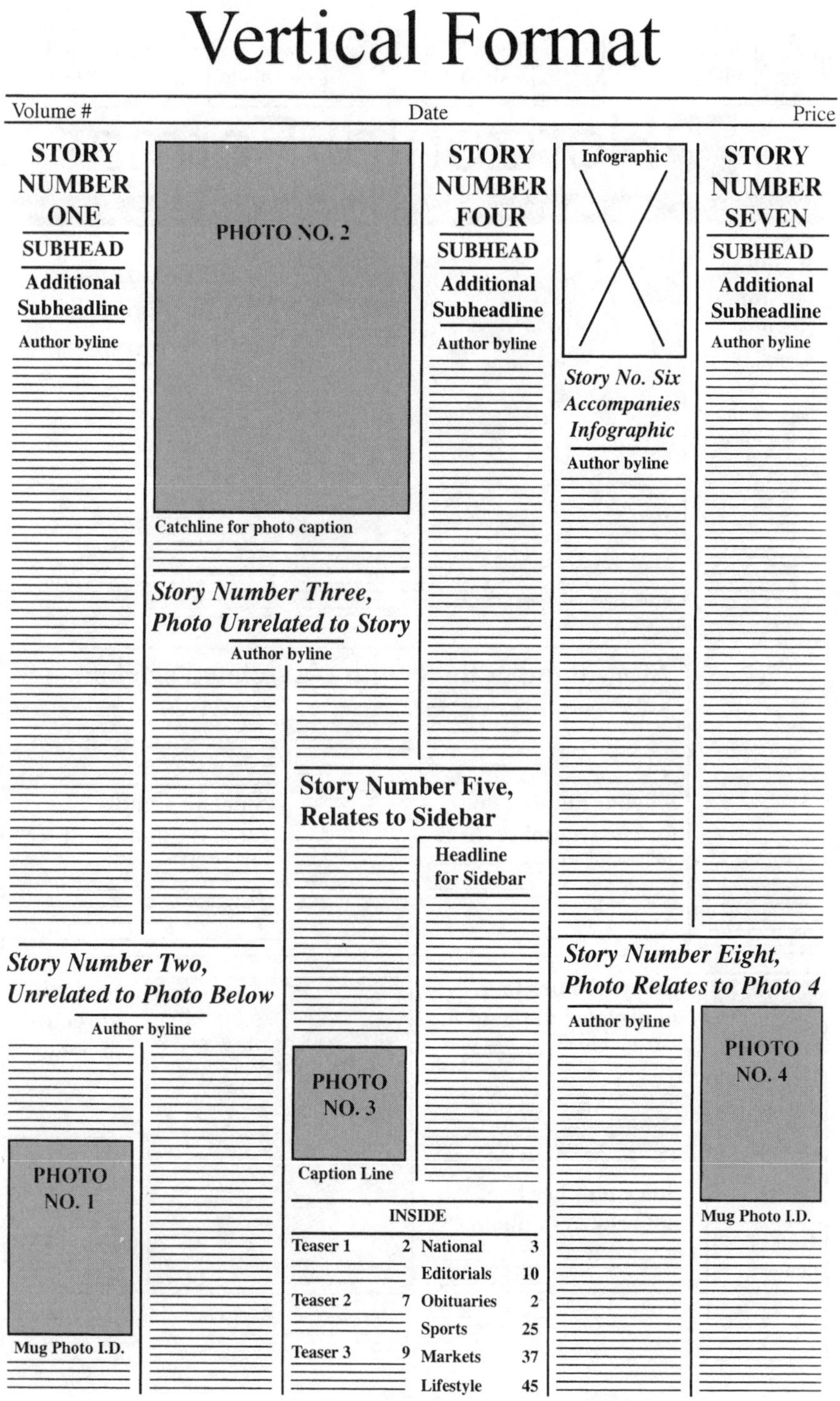

Vertical Format

Volume #	Date	Price

STORY NUMBER ONE
SUBHEAD
Additional Subheadline
Author byline

PHOTO NO. 2

Catchline for photo caption

Story Number Three, Photo Unrelated to Story
Author byline

STORY NUMBER FOUR
SUBHEAD
Additional Subheadline
Author byline

Infographic

Story No. Six Accompanies Infographic
Author byline

STORY NUMBER SEVEN
SUBHEAD
Additional Subheadline
Author byline

Story Number Five, Relates to Sidebar

Headline for Sidebar

Story Number Two, Unrelated to Photo Below
Author byline

Story Number Eight, Photo Relates to Photo 4
Author byline

PHOTO NO. 4

PHOTO NO. 3

Caption Line

PHOTO NO. 1

Mug Photo I.D.

Mug Photo I.D.

INSIDE

Teaser 1	2	National	3
		Editorials	10
Teaser 2	7	Obituaries	2
		Sports	25
Teaser 3	9	Markets	37
		Lifestyle	45

FIG. 5.8.

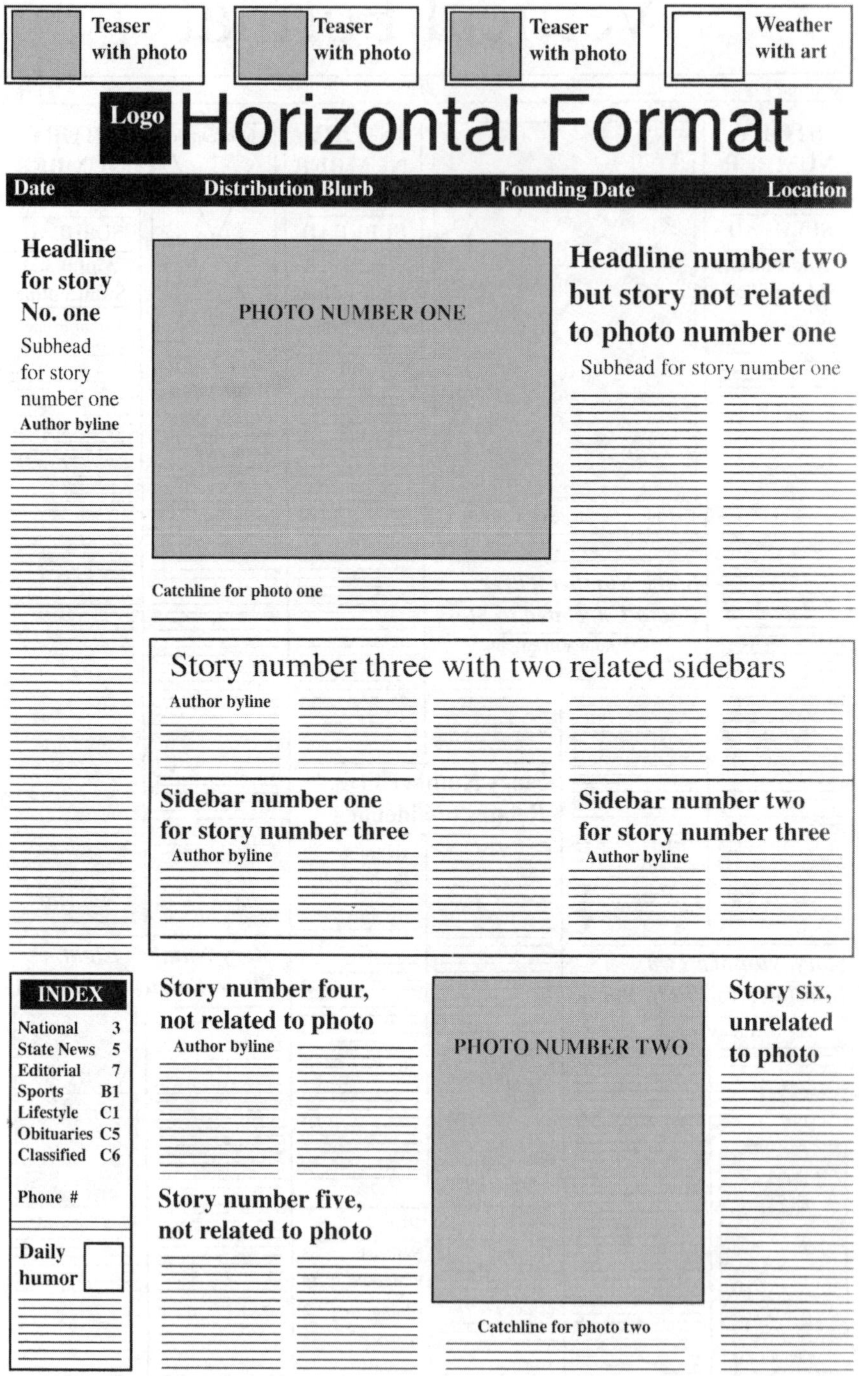
Teaser with photo
Teaser with photo
Teaser with photo
Weather with art
Logo
Horizontal Format
Date
Distribution Blurb
Founding Date
Location
Headline for story No. one
Subhead for story number one
Author byline
PHOTO NUMBER ONE
Catchline for photo one
Headline number two but story not related to photo number one
Subhead for story number one
Story number three with two related sidebars
Author byline
Sidebar number one for story number three
Author byline
Sidebar number two for story number three
Author byline
INDEX
National 3
State News 5
Editorial 7
Sports B1
Lifestyle C1
Obituaries C5
Classified C6
Phone #
Daily humor
Story number four, not related to photo
Author byline
Story number five, not related to photo
PHOTO NUMBER TWO
Catchline for photo two
Story six, unrelated to photo

FIG. 5.9.

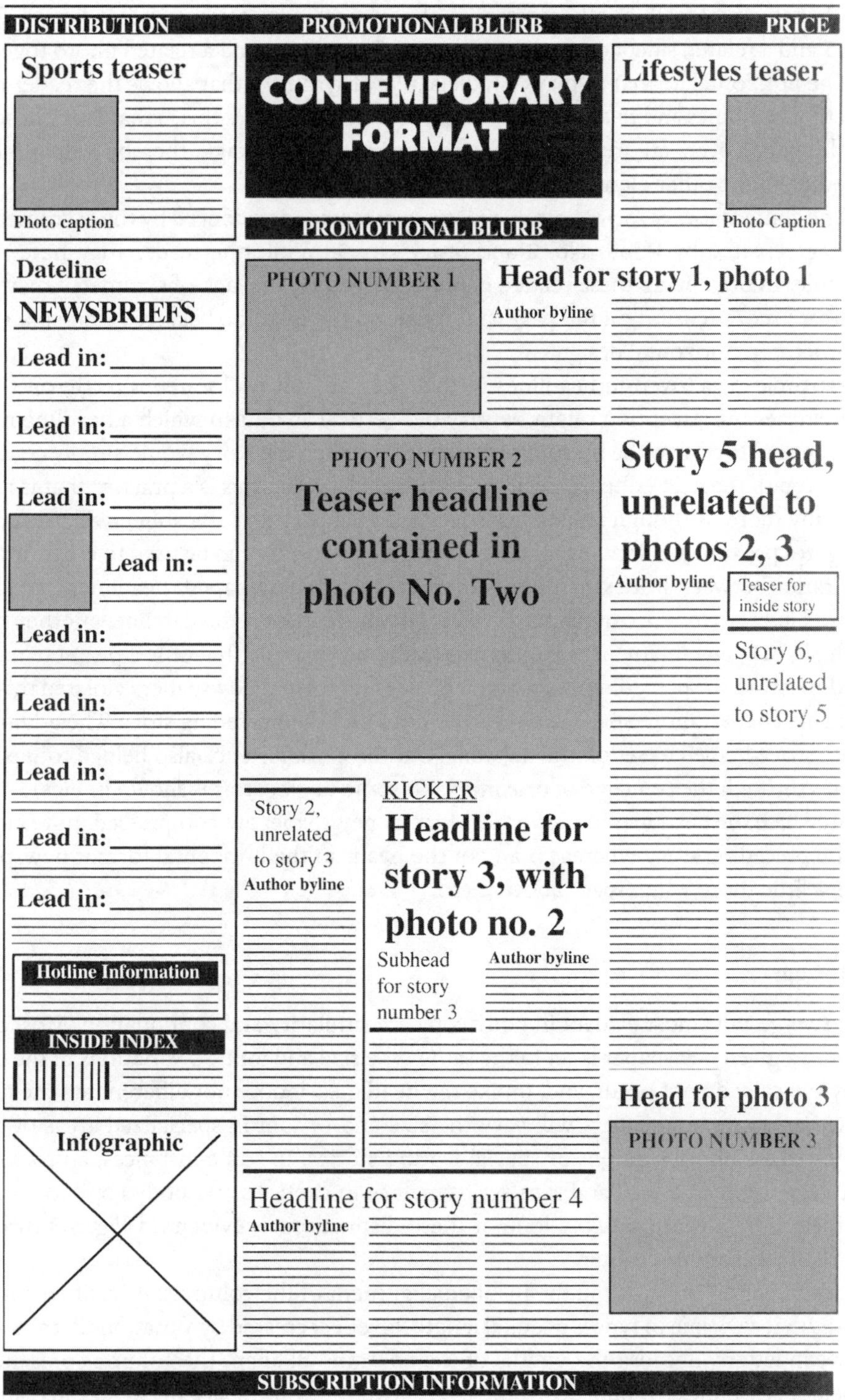

DISTRIBUTION **PROMOTIONAL BLURB** **PRICE**

Sports teaser

Photo caption

CONTEMPORARY FORMAT

PROMOTIONAL BLURB

Lifestyles teaser

Photo Caption

Dateline

NEWSBRIEFS

Lead in:_____

Lead in:_____

Lead in:_____

Lead in:___

Lead in:_____

Lead in:_____

Lead in:_____

Lead in:_____

Lead in:_____

Hotline Information

INSIDE INDEX

Infographic

PHOTO NUMBER 1

Head for story 1, photo 1

Author byline

PHOTO NUMBER 2

Teaser headline contained in photo No. Two

Story 5 head, unrelated to photos 2, 3

Author byline | Teaser for inside story

Story 6, unrelated to story 5

Story 2, unrelated to story 3

Author byline

KICKER

Headline for story 3, with photo no. 2

Subhead for story number 3

Author byline

Head for photo 3

PHOTO NUMBER 3

Headline for story number 4

Author byline

SUBSCRIPTION INFORMATION

FIG. 5.10.

another story below it. In other instances, the vertical format uses symmetry to tie Story No. 5 and a related sidebar together, and to tie Story No. 8 and a related photo together.

The horizontal format displays a judicial use of symmtry that allows the reader to tie together headlines and related stories. Figure 5.9 demonstrates this in that every headline on the page covers an area that creates a symmetrical package, thereby helping to tie together all the other elements that relate to the head.

The contemporary format often violates symmetry as evidenced by the asymmetrical package created by Photo No. 2 and Story No. 3. While the reader may have more difficulty in organizing these related elements together, the lack of symmetry may help to create more tension on the page and break up the extreme balance often created by symmetry in horizontal design.

Proximity is a given in headlines in that they are always located directly on top of their stories. An exception might be very old vertical layouts in which a headline might introduce a story near the bottom of the page, and then the story would simply continue at the top of the next column, far from its head. However, this is a practice that is rarely seen any more. Although readers have learned to expect that a headline will precede its story in a proximate relationship, to some degree proximity can be used to create a slight separation between stories. In tradional vertical-format newspapers, headlines were often located in very close proximity to the element above it, be it the dateline, another story, or the like. In fact, many newspapers even adhered to a rule that only a pica separated a headline from the preceding story. Some horizontal-format newspapers violated this one pica rule and left more space between the head and the preceding story. The additional white space helped to set off the headline, but the extra distance also helped to separate stories through the principle of proximity. To some degree, this is shown in Figs. 5.8 and 5.9 in which the headlines in the vertical-format newspaper are compressed more closely to the preceding story whereas many of the heads in the horizontal-format newspaper have a little more white space above them.

Body Copy

The two gestalts most evident in body copy are similarity and continuation. Most body copy in a given newspaper is set in the same type size and font, so variations in the body copy typically do not occur, and, unlike the headlines, it does not differentiate the news. However, some newspapers will vary the size and/or font in specialized areas of body copy such as photo captions or special feature stories. In some instances, a newspaper will vary between a serif and sans serif typeface in captions and body copy to create a distinction between the two. None of these distinctions is evident in Fig. 5.8 through Fig. 5.10 used in this chapter.

Continuation is evident in the justified alignment of the columns. A justified column means that each line of type is of equal length, an effect created by variations in the spaces between letters. Because the widths of the columns all align, the columns present the appearance of lines running down the page, with the white space between the columns creating what is known as *gutters*.

Traditionally, newspapers would not rely on the continuous lines of justified type to create gutters. This is evident in the vertical format (Fig. 5.8), which is a more traditional design. In the vertical format, lines are actually used inside the gutters to separate the columns. To some degree, this is counterproductive because the lines can create a slight block to the eye. Story No. 5 and its sidebar serve as an example. Even though the two are related, the line between them tends to create a slight sense of separation.

As the horizontal format evolved, designers recognized that they could rely on the principle of continuation by itself to separate columns. This is evident in Fig. 5.9 in which lines are used not to separate columns but are only used to create a box around related stories and tie them together. The contemporary format (Fig. 5.10) also uses continuation in the form of justified type to create columns and only uses lines to create borders that separate unrelated stories.

Flags

The flag is the area of the front page that includes and immediately surrounds the name of the newspaper. It may include such information as the date, price, edition number, location, and teasers that identify inside stories. Two gestalts, similarity and isomorphism, are most typically associated with newspaper flags. Although similarity is not apparent in the flags on these front pages, it is often observed on inside pages. Designers will reproduce the newspaper's name in the same distinctive typestyle that is used on the front as a heading for inside pages. The similar appearance of the newspaper's name as a title on inside pages—although in a much smaller type size—helps to create a visual association between these pages and the front page, one that helps to tie the entire newspaper together as a package.

Isomorphism is apparent in that certain devices are utilized in the flag whose meaning is independent of their forms. One example is the typestyle. In Fig. 5.8, the typestyle used on the flag of the vertical-format newspaper is a serif type. Serif types convey a more traditional mood, one that many vertical-format newspapers continue to use to create a harmonious appearance with their more traditional layout. Many vertical-format newspapers, including such famous ones as the *New York Times* use a very old-fashioned Old English type in their flags.

The horizontal-format newspaper in Fig. 5.9 displays a sans serif type in the flag, which is common in this type of layout because it conveys a more modern mood. Not all horizontal-format newspapers adopted sans serif type for their flags, but if not to convey a modern look, the choice of type might relate to other isomorphic properties. Often this choice might relate to the newspaper's editorial philosophy or the prevailing political mood in the community. In either case, a serif typestyle would convey a more conservative mood while a sans serif typestyle represents an outlook that is less traditional.

Newspapers often use a logo or other associated artwork as part of the flag. This artwork may be a depiction of a famous landmark in the community, but often it depicts an element that represents the mood of a community. For example, the newspaper with statewide distribution in Wyoming, contains a cowboy on a bucking horse, a symbol of the heritage on which the state prides itself.

Color in flags can also display isomorphism because of its symbolic use. For example, the now-famous colors that are used in the headings of the pages on *USA Today* are not coincidental. Red (representing excitement) is used for sports, purple (the color of Easter, one that represents life) is used for the lifestyle page, and the fact that green is used for the money page demands no explanation. Ironically, the use of blue in the flag of *USA Today* is not based on isomorphism but on the fact that it is the favorite color of more adults than any other single color.

Photos

Eye-tracking studies suggest that readers have certain tendencies in the way they move around a page, and one of these tendencies is that readers will enter the page at the dominant photo. To some degree, this tendency can be explained by the gestalt of figure-ground, which suggests that when viewers look at a visual field, they will subconsciously identify a figure and everything else becomes the ground. The largest element within the frame of the visual field is typically perceived as the figure, and there is a tendency on the part of viewers to believe that the figure is of some importance. By using a dominant photo, designers provide readers with the largest element in the visual field thereby creating a "figure." That readers would then tend to enter the page at this point makes sense.

The larger size and upper placement of Photo No. 2 in both the vertical-format and contemporary-format newspapers provides readers with a "figure" that creates a probable entry point on the page. The horizontal-format newspaper uses a larger photo at the top. However, the size of the Photo No. 2 at the bottom is large enough that it can compete with Photo No. 1 for reader attention and may prevent it from serving as a dominant photo.

The principle of closure is also most evident in photos in the form of cropping, although it is not evident on these pages without the use of actual photos. The principle of closure indicates that humans have a great ability to fill in missing information when given just a small piece of visual evidence. Thus, they can see just a set of legs and perceive the presence of a person. Cropping allows photographers to focus attention on the important elements in a scene by cropping in close. Readers can still make sense of the photo because they easily fill in the information excluded by the photographer and are able to do this without expending unnecessary mental energy.

GRAPHIC ELEMENTS IN SPECIFIC NEWSPAPER FORMATS

Because the preceding text centered on the gestalts common to all newspaper design, the discussion in this section focuses either on deviations from good gestalts common in each type of newspaper design or on the gestalts unique to that specific type of design.

Vertical Format

The vertical-format newspaper in Fig. 5.8 displays three deviations from good gestalts that are typical of this type of design. The first is the use of column rules, which are not a necessary layout device as discussed in the section under body copy.

A second is the use of jim dashes. Jim dashes are the horizontal lines that separate heads from subheads or bylines. Because of the principles of similarity, proximity, and symmetry, readers will naturally make the distinction between heads and subheads. Differences in type size and the varying use of upper- and lowercase indicate to the reader that the subheads are not competing heads. Their proximity to each other in symmetrical packages also conveys the idea that they are related. In a sense then, jim dashes are counterproductive. They serve as a minor block to the eye that breaks up the natural reading flow. If their purpose is to distinguish heads, subheads, and bylines from each other, the principle of similarity will already accomplish this.

A third is the asymmetrical layout of related elements and the symmetrical layout of unrelated elements. Gestalt principles suggest that viewers will tend to perceive symmetrical elements as belonging together. Thus, in the vertical-format newspaper (Fig. 5.8), readers will tend to see Story No. 8 as related to Photo No. 4, which is the case. However, readers will also tend to associate Story No. 2 with Photo No. 1 because of their symmetrical placement when they are not related. Good symmetry is also violated by the way that Story No. 3 "wraps" around Story No. 5, preventing Story No. 3 from becoming a symmetrical package in itself and creating some relationship, however slight, between Stories No. 3 and 5.

Horizontal Format

In a sense, the horizontal format could be called a textbook example of gestalt principles because it eliminates many of the violations of good gestalts that were found in the more traditional vertical format. As the horizontal-format newspaper in Fig. 5.9 shows, column rules are eliminated, but the principle of continuity in the justified type creates good columns. Jim dashes are absent, but readers have no trouble distinguishing the difference between heads, subheads, and bylines because of the lack of similarity in type size, case, and boldness. No asymmetrical packages exist on the page, and this is especially evident in the manner in which symmetry is used to tie Story No. 3 together with its related sidebars.

The only violation of good gestalts is evident in the border tape used to separate Story No. 3 from its two related sidebars. The dissimilarity in size between headlines and body copy allows the heads for Sidebars No. 1 and 2 and the white space above the heads to effectively separate the sidebars from the stories. Thus, the border tape once again becomes counterproductive because it creates a minor block to the eye while effectively serving no functional purpose.

The symmetrical placement of Photo No. 1 with Story No. 2 or of Photo No. 2 with Story No. 6 could also cause some confusion because in neither case are the photos and stories related. Both of these situations offer examples where border tape could serve a functional purpose because a box placed around either the photo and its caption or the story would help to separate the two and break up the association that naturally occurs between symmetrical elements.

Contemporary Format

In some ways, the contemporary format, as evidenced by the example in Fig. 5.10, represented a return to the vertical format in the way it violated good gestalts. This is most evident in its violations of symmetry. The asymmetrical packaging of related elements is seen in the layout of Photo No. 2 with Story No. 3. Conversely, Stories No. 5 and 6 are tied together in a symmetrical package when the two are unrelated.

One design element that is not limited to contemporary design but came into vogue at about the same time—primarily through its heavy use by *USA Today*, a contemporary-design newspaper—is the infographic. Although the limitations of Figs. 5.8–5.10 in this chapter do not allow the depiction of infographics, they typically rely on isomorphism through the use of symbolic elements to convey their message with a minimal amount of processing effort. If the infographic at the bottom left of the page in Fig. 5.10 related to a decline in student learning, for example, it might contain the stylized depiction of a book. Although the form of a book does not mean learning, it can represent the meaning of that concept, one that might otherwise be difficult to depict.

Contemporary-design newspapers also pioneered an innovative use of another gestalt—similarity—in their use of color (another concept that cannot be depicted in these figures because of their limitations). Many contemporary-design newspapers would take the color most evident in the dominant photo in the center of the page and reproduce it in the graphic elements at the corners of the page. For example, in Fig. 5.10, if red was the main color in Photo No. 2, it might also appear in the photos accompanying the Sports and Lifestyles teasers, in the infographic, or in Photo No. 3. The theory is that the viewer subconsciously notices the similarity of color, and that this helps to tie the page together.

DISCUSSION

As this analysis indicates, principles of visual organization as explained by gestalts are very evident in newspaper design, especially as it evolved. Although the vertical-format newspaper in this analysis is based on a more modern vertical design, it still displays many of the traditional elements that are a holdover from the days when when layout was more a function of press limitations than visual principles. One is the similarity evident in a tendency toward single-column headlines that use the same type size in the main stories, and thus do not differentiate the importance of the news. Another is the use of column rules that traditionally were needed to separate columns where not much white space existed.

With the horizontal format came the incorporation of a number of gestalts into design that are evident in this analysis. One is the grading of the news through a dissimilarity of headline size and weight. Another is the judicious use of symmetry to visually tie related elements together. A third is the elimination of column rules with the idea that the continuation created by justified lines of body type was in itself enough to create distinguishable columns.

The contemporary format both introduced the use of additional gestalts and violated some of the good gestalts introduced by the horizontal format. The asymmetrical packaging of some stories is a primary example of how the contemporary format violates good gestalts. Perhaps this is done in the name of balance under the assumption that when too much symmetry is employed, the page is too much in balance and thus not very stimulating.

Contemporary-format newspapers did pioneer the use of other gestalts primarily through their use of color. They would use similarities in color to help the reader perceive the page as a single entity. They would also use the psychological properties of color for isomorphic purposes. One example not evident on front pages is the weather map, where contemporary-format designers began using colors to represent temperatures with warm colors (red, yellow, and orange) indicating warmer temperatures and cooler colors (blue, green, and violet) indicating colder temperatures. The use of isomorphism also increased with the proliferation of infographics that were pioneered to a large extent by contemporary-design newspapers.

As this critical analysis shows, the application of gestalt principles to newspaper design does serve a useful function in helping to explain certain of the graphic elements used by designers. The analysis also indicates that as design evolved, it was not based solely on the whims of the designers, but incorporates new elements that do facilitate reading. Although this analysis certainly does not explain the function of all design elements appearing on the page, a critical analysis does not purport to do this.

Yet while many of the elements examined in the analysis are an everyday part of a newspaper designer's job, describing their function in terms of human-processing tendencies such as gestalts can shed a different light on their validity. This analysis serves that purpose and helps to explain why newspapers often appear the way that they do, even though formal gestalt terminology is not used by designers in laying out their pages.

REFERENCES

Arnheim, R. (1974). *Art and visual perception*. Berkeley: University of California Press.

Bain, C., & Weaver, D. (1979). Readers' reaction to newspaper design. *Newspaper Research Journal, 1*, 48–59.

Barry, A. M. (1997). *Visual intelligence*. Albany: State University of New York Press.

Click, J. W., & Stempel, G. H. (1978, September 28). Rate of adoption of modern format by daily newspapers. *ANPA News Research Report, 22*, 6–10.

Garcia, M., & Stark, P. (1991). *Eyes on the news*. St. Petersburg, FL: The Poynter Institute for Media Studies.

Garcia, M., Click, J. W., & Stempel, G. H. (1981, September 3). Subscribers reactions to redesign of the *St. Cloud Daily Times*. *ANPA News Research Report, 32*, 32.

Kreitler, H., & Kreitler, S. (1972). *Psychology of the arts*. Durham, NC: Duke University Press.

Kubovy, M., & Pomerantz, J. R. (1981). *Perceptual organization*. Hillsdale, NJ: Lawrence Erlbaum Associates.

Pasternack, S., & Utt, S. H. (1986). Subject perception of newspaper characteristics based on front page design. *Newspaper Research Journal, 8*(4), 29–35.

Rosenfield, L. (1968, March). Anatomy of critical discourse. *Speech Monographs, 35*, 50–69.

Sissors, J. (1965). Some new concepts of newspaper design. *Journalism Quarterly, 42*(2), 236–42.

Spoehr, K. T., & Lehmkuhle, S. W. (1982). *Visual information processing*. San Francisco: W. H. Freeman.

Stroebel, L., Todd, H., & Zakia, R. (1980). *Visual concepts for photographers*. London: Focal Press.

Utt, S. H., & Pasternack, S. (1984). Front pages of U.S. daily newspapers. *Journalism Quarterly, 61*(4), 879–884.

Representation

III

Representation

6

Representation Theory

KEITH KENNEY
University of South Carolina

REPRESENTATION: WHAT DO WE "SEE" WHEN WE LOOK AT A "PICTURE"?

Behaviorists attempt to observe and measure the real world directly. *Phenomenologists* are exclusively interested in a person's introspective experience. *Semioticians* and *rhetoricians* try to understand the linkages between our internal world and the external world, and that linkage is necessary, they believe, because the external world is always mediated by our senses and our mind. Whereas rhetoricians have investigated how humans create and manipulate symbols in order to persuade other humans, semioticians have been more interested in how humans (and other animals) interpret all kinds of signs, including symbols, that were created by other people, as well as natural signs that may have resulted from plants, animals, or inorganic matter. Both rhetoricians and semioticians, therefore, are concerned with how signs "mediate" between the external world and our internal "world," or how a sign "stands for" or "takes the place of" something from the real world in the mind of a person. What these scholars are concerned with is called *representation*. This chapter explains the strengths and weaknesses of four types of theories of how pictures represent.

The concept of representation has been thought of as a relationship with two, three, and four parts. The two-part model is associated with Saussure (among many others), who defined the *linguistic sign* as a "two-sided psychological entity" consisting of a sign vehicle and its meaning. He used the word *signifier* for the sign vehicle (the antecedent experience, or the word, or expression, or speech sound) and the word *signified* for the meaning of the sign (the consequent experience, or the thing, or the content, or the response in hearer).

The three-part model is associated with Peirce (among many others), who defined representation as a relationship among sign, object, and interpretant. For Peirce, *semiosis* occurs when an existing sign is connected with the object signified to produce meaning in the mind of the interpreter.

The four-part model is associated with Mitchell (1990). The additional dimension is the *maker* of the representation. Mitchell envisions representation as a quadrilateral with two diagonal axes, one connecting the representational object to that which it represents (like Saussure's dyadic model), and the other connecting the maker of the representation to the viewer. The lines connecting the signifier and object are called the *axis of representation*. The lines connecting the maker and the viewer are called the *axis of communication*. Peirce's triadic model omits the fourth dimension (maker) because it allows the possibility of natural signs, which do not have makers who intend to communicate. One advantage of Mitchell's model, therefore, is that it emphasizes communication, appropriate for the study of pictures, which presumably were created with the intention to communicate, or to express the creator's feeling, or to elicit an (intended) emotional response in viewers.

A crucial consideration for the analysis of representation is the relationship between the sign and the object. Semioticians distinguish three types of relationship: an *iconic* relationship that stresses resemblance, a *symbolic* relationship that is primarily arbitrary, and an *indexical* relationship that is based on cause and effect, or a relation such as physical proximity or connectedness. Most representations use more than one type of sign-object relationship.

The four types of theory of pictorial representation are directly connected to these three types of relationship between signs and their objects. Causal relation theories (including transparency theory and recognition theory) emphasize indexical and iconic relations. Resemblance theories (including nonperceptual and perceptual) emphasize iconic relations. Convention theories emphasize symbolic relations. Mental construction theories (including illusion, make-believe, and "seeing-in") emphasize iconic and symbolic relations. This chapter also relates the four types of theory to Mitchell's (1990) model of representation.

In order to begin to understand theories of pictorial representation, please think about what happens when YOU look at a photograph of a dancer stretching. Do you see a *real* dancer stretching? Are you *reminded* of a dancer stretching? Does the picture *look like* a dancer stretching? Or do you have an experience that is *just like the experience* of looking at a dancer stretching? Do you read the *language* of the photograph and realize it concerns a dancer stretching? Do you have the *illusion* you are in the presence of a dancer stretching? Do you *make believe* you see a dancer stretching? Do you *see* a dancer stretching *in* the picture and *also* see the surface of the picture? The sometimes subtle differences between these questions (and their answers) reflect key ideas in the various theories.

CAUSAL RELATION THEORIES

Transparency Theory: The Picture Is Made Automatically

Kendall Walton (1984) made the provocative statement that photographs (or films or videos) are *transparent*, and "we see the world *through* them" (p. 251). He considered camera pictures to be "aids to vision" just as we look "through" (transparent) eyeglasses, telescopes, and microscopes in order to see things we would not be able to see with just our eyes. We supposedly can see the real dancer stretching when we see a photograph of her stretching even though the dancer is not in our presence. Moreover, Walton claimed that camera pictures allow us to see into the past. He wrote that we *"see*, quite literally, our dead relatives themselves when we look at photographs of them" (1984, p. 252).

This power of photography, wrote Walton, comes from its "mechanical" or "automatic" origins (see also Arnheim, 1974; Bazin, 1967; Brubaker, 1993; Cavell, 1971). A photograph of a couple having a picnic on a grassy hill, for example, was *mechanically caused* by light reflecting off of the man and woman, bottles of soda and wine, blanket, plastic plates, and so on and onto a piece of light-sensitive film. The image also is mechanical because if someone placed a camera with the same film, lens, position, and so on as with the first photo, and if the picnickers and background elements and light never changed, then the same results would *automatically* occur. It seems, therefore, that we see things firsthand through the transparent photograph. "Handmade" pictures (i.e., drawings and paintings) would be considered secondhand information because a picture-maker's judgment intervenes between us and the picnickers, and because eye-hand coordination cannot make exact copies as a mechanical camera can.

Transparency theory states that a camera picture represents a phenomenon because it was automatically and mechanically caused by the existence of the phenomenon and because the picture looks like exactly like the phenomenon. In terms of Goodman's four-dimensional model of representation, it exclusively focuses on the vertical axis running from the object to its sign (1976). Transparency theory is silent about the communication axis running from maker to viewer because it ignores the viewer and the maker.

Transparency theory ignores the viewer because it assumes that viewers are so naive as to think they are actually seeing the objects themselves when looking at a camera picture. The theory ignores the fact that viewers interpret pictures. Transparency theory also pretends that a picture of a migrant worker stands for just that individual, when, in fact, it may stand for a whole group of migrant workers.

Transparency theory ignores the maker and his or her ability to control the taking, developing, and printing of film. When Walton tries to rebut arguments about the control of picture-makers (and, therefore, the lack of mechanical automaticity), he argued that just because we see things through a photographer's eyes doesn't mean that *we* don't really see them. "I do see those things myself," he wrote (1984, p. 262). In other words, the viewer has control over seeing, not the maker. This is an important philosophical point because whoever controls the "seeing" decides where attention and mind will be fixed. The controller *intends* the meaning.

If photographers control the seeing, as is generally believed, then we look at the results of their intentions. We can, of course, misinterpret their intentions, and we can see more or less than was intended. For example, we can draw on our background knowledge (or lack of knowledge) of dancing in general, or of this particular dancer, to "see" something more (or less) than was intended. But the photographer is in control.

If photography is an "aid to vision," as Walton wrote, then *we* should be able to control the seeing, just as if we used a telescope to see the dancer stretching; *we* could control the telescope and change what we see depending on our interest. We cannot, however, control the seeing with a camera picture, so Walton cannot see things himself.

In fact, the only time that *we as viewers* can control imagery is with virtual-reality equipment. If we had access to real-time, photographic-quality, three-dimensional imagery of the dancer stretching, and if the dancer took 10 seconds to hold a stretch and we saw her stretching for 10 seconds, and if we could control our angle and distance of viewpoint, *then* we might agree the medium is "transparent" and that we can see "through" the medium to the dancer, and there was no "intent" by the maker, and, essentially, the maker could be eliminated from the representation process (see Carroll, 1995; Currie, 1991; Martin, 1986; Warburton, 1988 for criticisms of the transparency theory).

If we reject the transparency theory and acknowledge that photographers communicate their intentions, then camera pictures seem kind of like paintings, yet because there is *some* causal connection between the film image and the subject, camera pictures also seem "special." Maynard (1989) used the concepts of depiction and detection to explain the special nature of camera pictures. To *depict* is to represent, which means "to stand for" or to communicate by signs or symbols. To *detect* is to discover something with certainty. Like paintings, camera pictures depict because they represent things that may be real or fiction. Unlike paintings, camera pictures detect because they are the results (or *traces*) of *photochemical actions*. Camera pictures used as detection have a similar *automatic* quality as sunburns (another example of a trace of photochemical action). Camera pictures also seem to give evidence of the *fact of* photochemical effects just like sunburns.

A "pure" photographic depiction would represent something, but not be a trace of that thing. A photograph of a fairy, an angel, or the Loch Ness monster would be a pure depiction because it would represent a fictional phenomenon and yet the fictional phenomenon would not have caused the photochemical action. For example, a photographic depiction of "blueberry ice cream" may actually be a photograph of mashed potatoes with blue food coloring.

A "pure" photographic detection would ascertain the presence of something but it would not represent, or be about, anything. Examples of photographs used purely for detection would include traces of light from stars and traces of radiation from X-rays. Another example of a nondepicting photograph would be any image that resulted from accidentally pressing the shutter. From viewing the resulting image we could discover what had been in front of the camera, but that scene would not represent anything.

When we say: "This is a photograph of a dancer stretching," we generally mean it is both a trace of the dancer and a depiction of the dancer. If everything that was depicted was also detected, then we would consider it to be a documentary photograph, with an aura of realism and objectivity. Pure documentary photographs and films, however, are impossible to make. If I wanted to shoot a pure documentary, I would have to exercise little or no control over the essential shots. The more I aimed my camera at subjects I believed would interest an audience, and the more I followed a "style," or concerned myself with aesthetics, including decisions about exposure, sharpness, composition, camera angle, and the like, and the more I tried to shoot pictures to fit a storyline, the less purely documentary the result. An ideal documentary would seem to be surveillance camera footage; each shot is a trace of its subject and is only connected to other subject traces.

Not only is it difficult to make a pure documentary, it is also difficult to view it. We understand photographs and films by fitting them into our prior knowledge of genres, schemas, and other preexisting categories. Viewing "traces" will inevitably be affected by our own expectations and background experiences. The moment shown in the picture will evoke many ideas that are not shown. It may seem "easy" to "perceive" the "traces" of photographs and film, but our minds do not stop at that point; we inevitably make connections, and those connections lead to narrative content.

A photographer who tried to take "pure" documentary photographs placed a camera on a tripod and aimed it outside the passenger window of his car. He used the camera's automatic features and he mechanically connected the camera to his odometer so the shutter automatically would be pressed each mile. After driving across the United States, he had 3,000 or so photographs that were traces lacking depictive qualities. He was dissatisfied with the results, however, because he had driven on interstate highways and many photos were too redundant, so he repeated the trip and this time took smaller roads. Apparently, however, he was still worried whether these "traces" would be sufficiently interesting. During a conference presentation, he admitted "cheating" by connecting a cable to the camera so he could manually override the automatic shutter release if he saw something particularly interesting right before or after the one-mile interval. His need to make the images appealing eventually overcame his need to follow his own procedure of eliminating the photographer (the "maker" in Mitchell's model). Even if he had followed procedure, however, he still would have selected a route across county and so would have played a role in the image-making.

In conclusion, transparency theory is important because many viewers, and some picture-makers, continue to implicitly, if not explicitly, believe that camera pictures are aids to vision that allow us to see the world directly. People enjoy looking at photographs of loved ones; they use photographs as evidence in courts of law, and news organizations use photographs to report on people and events. From a theoretical perspective, the idea that camera pictures have a (limited) indexical relationship to their objects and a (limited) iconic relationship is valid, but not new. The idea that camera pictures do not (yet) offer viewers control over what they see is more interesting because that fundamental idea may change with the development of virtual-reality equipment. The concepts of depiction and detection are useful for clarifying the nature of documentary pictures. Overall, however, the insufficient roles given to makers and viewers hurt this theory of pictorial representation.

Recognition Theory: The Picture Reminds You of the Object or Person

What if instead of claiming that we see the dancer *through* the photograph, we claim that we *recognize* the dancer in the picture because we can recognize Sandra face to face. In other words, the recognition skills we bring to pictures depend on and extend the recognition skills we use in ordinary perception. This theory states that a picture represents a phenomenon because the picture looks exactly like the phenomenon. It emphasizes the iconic relationship between sign and object and deemphasizes any symbolic relationship. In terms of Goodman's four-dimensional model of representation, recognition theory focuses both on the vertical axis running from the object to its sign and on the viewer (1976). It resembles Peirce's triadic model of the sign.

A key concept of recognition theory is *aspects*. Wilkerson (1991) suggested that *aspect-seeing* has five main features. One, seeing aspects involves noticing resemblances. We see a dancer-aspect in the picture of Sandra by consciously focusing attention on a resemblance between the picture and a dancer. Two, seeing aspects is an imaginative activity. We visualize the scene of a dancer stretching even if the dancer is not present. Three, seeing aspects is subject to the will. We can *try* to see an aspect, and others can guide our efforts by drawing our attention to crucial parts of the picture; whereas with ordinary seeing we do not make an attempt to see what is in front of us. Four, seeing an aspect is detached from belief. We may see a swan-aspect in a cloud (or picture), yet we won't believe that the cloud (or picture) is literally a swan. Five, seeing an aspect often involves definite experiences, and one of them, the experience of suddenly noticing an aspect, or a change of aspect, is akin to experiencing a sudden dawning of understanding. We look at the picture and think, "Aha, that must be Sandra at 16 because she has the same nose and chin as her mother."

Recognition theory deemphasizes the symbolic relationship between sign and object because it states that picturing is *generative*, which means we do not need to learn the meaning of unfamiliar pictures in the way we must learn the meaning of unfamiliar words. We can "generate" understanding of almost any picture of a familiar object at a glance provided we have mastered the pictorial system. When we encounter new pictorial systems, for example, cubism, we must first learn the system, and then we can again recognize any familiar objects. Pictorial competence, therefore, is system-relative, and pictorial recognition abilities can vary in speed and accuracy with the system of representation.

Conventionalists, who emphasize the symbolic relationship between sign and object, believe that first we learn the conventional codes, grammar, language, vocabulary, or other system based on social agreement, and then we can "read" pictures. Recognition theories, on the other hand, take almost the opposite approach. They believe we can see pictures and identify objects in pictures, and thereby learn about the world and real life. In a sense, the picture books of our youth become the socially agreed on conventions for understanding the world and real life.

Pictorial recognition theory differs from simplistic understandings of iconic relations, generally thought of as *resemblance* between sign and object, because recognition is *dynamic*. Whereas simple recognition ability would require an overwhelming similarity between incoming information and information stored from the past, dynamic recognition ability can link currently perceived objects (or pictures) with objects perceived in the past despite what may amount to radical changes in appearance. Face-recognition is especially dynamic. A face may be contorted by laughter or grief and other expressions, yet we can recognize it. To say that recognition is dynamic is to say that features can be recognized under different aspects (Lopes, 1996).

Wittgenstein (1953) considered whether noticing an aspect is *seeing* or *interpreting*. When we change from seeing something one way to seeing it another way and thereby notice an aspect of it, do we really see differently, or do we merely interpret what we see differently? Does our visual experience change, or does our visual experience remain constant and the interpretation that we place upon what we see alter? The answer probably is "both." The concept of seeing an aspect *lies between* the concept of seeing color or shape and the concept of interpreting: it resembles both of these concepts, but in different respects (Budd, 1987). This point is important for pictorial representation because if noticing an aspect was only *seeing*, then transparency theory would be supported, and if noticing an aspect was only *interpreting*, then convention theory would be supported. Instead, noticing an aspect is between seeing and interpreting, and recognition theory is between transparency and convention theory.

In conclusion, recognition theory is related to transparency theory because pictures and objects have the same properties. Even if the picture is a cubist painting, we could follow a circuitous route from the features of the painting to the features of the dancer stretching. Recognition theory also recalls Walton's idea that photographs are an aid to vision. About pictorial recognition, Lopes writes: "Pictures are visual prostheses; they extend the informational system by gathering, storing, and transmitting visual information about their subjects in ways that depend upon and also augment our ability to identify things by their appearance" (1996, p. 144). Instead of being limited to photographs, however, recognition theory can explain any type of picture. In addition, it recognizes the necessary role of the viewer to interpret the picture, and the sophisticated concept of aspects explains how that interpretation occurs. The theory, however, allows too much latitude to the spectator's imagination and does not explain how picture-makers limit our roving imaginations and constrain what we see as the representative features of the picture (Peetz, 2001). Another problem is that the theory cannot explain how pictures can misrepresent or be inaccurate (Rollins, 1999).

RESEMBLANCE THEORIES

There are two major types of resemblance theories. Both are based on the idea that pictures resemble their objects, which means that the iconic nature of a sign-object relationship is emphasized. In terms of Goodman's four-dimensional model of representation, resemblance theories exclusively focus upon the vertical axis running from the object to its sign (1976). They are silent about the communication axis running from maker to viewer because they ignore the viewer and the maker. Resemblance theories apply to pigeons as well as humans, so no higher-level thinking skills are required.

Nonperceptual Resemblance Theory: The Picture Looks Just Like My Aunt Hilda

A *nonperceptual theory* states that pictures represent by virtue of similarity with their subjects. This theory has intuitive appeal because when we look at pictures, we seem to see similarities between the picture and what it represents.

Goodman (1976) criticized this theory, writing that while a picture may resemble its subject in some respects, in many respects it does not. A two-dimensional, 4-inch-by-6-inch photograph of a dancer, for example, does not look like a 110-pound woman in most respects. To understand what someone means when she or he says this picture *looks like* that subject, we must know which kinds of similarity she or he is referring to, and knowing which kinds are pertinent would depend on the context of the picture and on custom (Black, 1972).

Hyman (2000) overcame this criticism by explaining that we are not comparing a flat object to a subject; instead we are comparing the marks of a picture to the marks of a subject. He wrote, there is a "strict and invariable relationship between the lines, shapes, and colours on a picture's surface and its *internal* subject" that can be defined without referring to the picture's psychological effect on a spectator (2000, p. 24).

Despite its appeal, nonperceptual resemblance theory has several problems. First, resemblance is a symmetrical relationship. If the color picture resembles the dancer stretching, then the dancer stretching must also resemble the color picture. Representation, however, is not symmetrical; we believe that the photo may represent the dancer, but the dancer cannot represent the photo (but see Files, 1996). Therefore, a resemblance relationship does not distinguish a representation from what it represents. Second, a picture resembles a copy of itself more than it resembles the dancer, but a picture cannot represent a picture; nor can it represent itself. Resemblance, therefore, is not sufficient for pictorial representation because resemblance exists without representation. Third, is the chicken-egg problem. Do we notice picture-subject similarities and then know what is represented, or do we first know what is represented and later notice similarities?

Perception-based Resemblance Theory: Pictures of Predators Can Be Recognized by Pigeons or People

The second type of resemblance theory, like recognition theory, is based on perception (see Budd, 1993; Hopkins, 1994; Manns, 1971; Neander, 1987; Novitz, 1975). A painting resembles its subject if the painting has the same power to affect our organs of sight as its subject. According to resemblance theory, at an early stage of vision, at least, we just receive visual information and what we see is not affected by our beliefs, values, or background knowledge (Rollins, 1999). This early visual information is segregated from higher cognitive processes. It also is separated from information from other senses (hearing, smelling, etc.). The process of acquiring this early visual information is the same whether we view pictures or real life; both lead to the same perceptual experience (Gilman, 1992). If this theory was correct, then we could initially view pictures with an "innocent eye." It also would mean that someone from a "primitive" culture, who had never seen a photograph before, but who was used to seeing elephants, should be able to recognize a photo of an elephant. Moreover, animals should be able to recognize pictures of predators. In fact Danto (1993) wrote about pigeons that were able to distinguish among pictures on the basis of their subject matter even though the pictures' settings, lighting, and viewpoints varied. Danto speculated that pigeons may even be able to appreciate stylistic differences in photographs as they recognize and classify pictures. If resemblance theory is true, then instead of noticing *aspects*, we recognize *objects* (Charlton, 2000).

Resemblance theory also may explain the appeal of Andreas Gursky's large photographs. Up to 16 feet across and full of detail, they seem to offer viewers an opportunity to recognize more objects per image than most other pictures. One picture, for example, shows eight crowded aisles of a grocery store and another shows tens of thousands of people at a rock concert. Another example of pictures that seem real because they look just like their subjects is IMAX films, which are shot with larger film stock so more detail can be captured. The films then are projected onto huge screens, so we cannot see the edges of the screen, and we feel immersed in the subject.

Perceptual resemblance theory, however, has problems. First, perceptual experience is not solely based on basic visual information. If it was, then we could not distinguish a picture of a dancer from the real dancer. Because we can (easily) distinguish, some higher-order processing, including culturally inculcated beliefs, must occur. Second, if pictures and reality affect our visual sense organs the same way, then the feelings we have in looking at pictures should be the same as those we have in viewing real scenes, but they are not. We might expect that viewing reality would arouse stronger emotions. Charlton, however, points out that pictures move us profoundly and that they have certain advantages over looking at things. He wrote: "The feelings we have in looking at pictures are likely to be much stronger than those we have in looking at real people, real animals, and even real inanimate objects that are useful or dangerous" (2000, p. 478). Three, resemblance theory could not allow for different marks, from different pictorial traditions, depicting the same things. Four, it could not allow for similar marks, with different provenances, differing in meaning.

Resemblance theory goes still further. Peacocke (1987) suggested that resemblance is not based on objective similarities between a picture and subject, but on *subjective* similarities between our experience of pictures and our experience of the subject. He distinguished "sensational" and "representational" properties of experience. When we draw a picture of the dancer's outstretched foot, we inevitably draw the foot the way we "know" a foot is shaped and colored, or its *representational content*. Depending on the angle we actually viewed her outstretched foot, however, the shape may be distorted, and the color may be affected by nearby objects, so we see its *sensational content*.

For any subject, there is a myriad of ways in which it can be seen, and to each of these ways there corresponds a different possible *visual field*, defined as an imaginary plane interposed between the scene and viewer. A picture's sensational content looks like its subject with respect to the properties of the spectator's visual field, not to some "objective" viewpoint. Because of the concept of visual fields, many pictures may resemble the same subject, yet those pictures may differ radically.

Peacocke's additional concepts offer the advantage of including the viewer in the representational process, at least to some extent. One problem with Peacocke's concept of the visual field is that it is closely tied to Alberti's use of a fixed frame in order to draw a scene with "normal" perspective. Resemblance theories based on the idea of a visual field, therefore, will "work" for photographs and other realistic pictures, but the theories don't work with cubist or split-style pictures or pictures with reversed perspective or pictures that distort their subjects to ridicule them. (For other criticisms, see Kemp, 1990.)

Some philosophers see a connection between recognition and resemblance theories. They believe that we notice a resemblance between a picture and its subject before we recognize the picture. Schier (1986) rejected this idea because it presupposes a homuncular theory of mind. In other words, some subcognitive part of the person would then have to "note" resemblances. Sartwell (1991), however, countered that there is no need for a recourse to homunculi. Similar properties, he wrote, are simply the immediate causal antecedent of recognition.

In conclusion, pictures resemble their subjects better than words, but pictures don't necessarily resemble their subjects in all ways, and trying to identify *which* ways is difficult. It really depends on the picture. Sometimes shapes may be important, but not always.

One must consider the context of the picture, and knowing about context means drawing on background knowledge, which of course differs depending on the viewer. There is no "innocent eye." Resemblance theories must take into account the viewer of pictures (and, perhaps, the maker too).

CONVENTION THEORY: YOU HAVE TO LEARN THE LANGUAGE

Convention theory holds that a picture represents whatever it does by virtue of belonging to a symbol system with rules or conventions that link marked surfaces of pictures with external things. Convention theory is much different than the other theories because, according to Goodman (1976), pictures do not copy, imitate, or resemble their subjects. Instead, the relationship between a picture and its subject is based upon custom and "almost any picture may *represent* almost anything" (Goodman, 1976, p. 38). This does not mean that almost any picture may *depict* almost anything. Recognizing at least some resemblance is necessary for depiction (see Drost, 1994).

But, someone might protest, some pictures are realistic and anyone looking at those realistic pictures would see the same subject. Goodman (1976) would respond that resemblance is just one of many possible conventional phenomena that *can* be used in representation. It is neither a sufficient nor a necessary condition for representation. Because we think that resemblance between a picture and its subject is natural (and, in the case of camera pictures, mechanical and automatic), we are tempted to draw the conclusion that resemblance is not a convention. Even filmic representations, however, are based on conventions; their power and immediacy comes from the easy sharing of conventions among creators and viewers. The content of pictures, Goodman wrote, is determined by its syntactical and semantic properties, and when those properties become familiar, or *entrenched,* the picture seems realistic. Moreover, the degree to which a picture *"looks like"* its subject may increase or diminish as customs change. There are no fixed criteria for realism, according to conventionalists. Instead, pictorial "reality" is shaped by a viewer's way of seeing, which is under the control of the conventions imposed by a culture.

With convention theory, the relationship between sign and object is predominantly symbolic. Moreover, Goodman's (1976) communication axis between maker and viewer is emphasized rather than the axis of representation.

One problem with convention theory is that pictorial systems are not as varied as we'd expect. If pictures are conventional, then the world's diverse cultures should produce diverse systems of pictorial representation and that has seldom happened. A second problem is that the relationship between a picture and its subject is not always based on convention. If it was, then I should be able to take a "realistic" picture of an unclothed man and travel to many diverse cultures and find varying understandings of the picture. Of course, it is possible that most cultures naturalize their conventions, and if so, it would be extremely difficult to recover those conventions even while they operate. A third problem with convention theory is that representational meaning would have to depend on pictorial structure in the same way that languages depend on grammatical structures. There is no nontrivial way of segmenting pictures into parts, however, so that those parts contribute to the meaning of the whole picture. A fourth problem is that Goodman's theory ignores perception. He proceeds from a critique of the resemblance theory to the claim that pictures symbolize according to their system. We don't know *how* they symbolize.

In conclusion, Goodman has made rules or conventions central to picture representation, but his theory been justly criticized as having the consequence that any picture can represent anything because resemblance between a picture and its object is rejected as a necessary condition for depicting. (For revisions of Goodman's theory of representation, see Arrell, 1987; Bach; 1970; Beardsley, 1978; Drost, 1994; Files, 1996; Lopes, 2000; Robinson, 1979, 2000; Savile, 1971; Wollheim, 1973.)

MENTAL CONSTRUCTION THEORIES

Three major theories explain pictorial representation in terms of mental states: illusion, make-believe, and seeing-in. With these theories, detailed, complete mental representations of a scene or object are constructed. Because generalizations about all three theories are difficult, their relationship to the Goodman's (1976) model of representation and to Peirce's typology of sign-object relations are discussed in each subsection.

Illusions: We're Only Fooling Ourselves

According to the illusion theory (Allen, 1993, 1995; Brinker, 1996; Gombrich, 1977, 1982; Wilson, 1982), pictures give us the false perceptual belief we are in the presence of the subject. It is the eye, not the mind, that is fooled. The picture triggers a nonveridical visual experience through the arousal of visual sensations. We look at the picture and see something that is not a dancer but that nevertheless causes us to have a visual experience of seeing a dancer.

Gombrich (1977, 1982) believed we fully participate in the game of illusion by intentionally ignoring nonmatching aspects of the representation and by concentrating on following the hints of the painter, who provides sufficient clues to allow our imaginative powers to *project* what is not there and to complete the representation. Because the illusion is coproduced, we cannot complain of falling into a delusional trap. Gombrich wrote that our experience of a picture alternates between a perception of the subject and a perception of a flat, object (painting, drawing, photograph). We could not have both experiences at the same time because then the illusion would be spoiled, he thought.

The history of Western art, Gombrich wrote (1977, 1982), is the story of how artists experimented with new methods and schemes in order to paint the appearance of people, objects, and scenes more naturalistically. Over time they abandoned old, entrenched habits (i.e., conventions) of representation. Aesthetic changes occurred by means of schema and correction (or "making and matching"). Artists started with an initial schema, and then gradually, step by step, they corrected and refined it until they arrived at something reasonably naturalistic. For example, they suggested three-dimensional space by diminution of background figures and exploitation of the fact that parallel lines appear to converge in the distance. These "schemas" are themselves conventions, and to "decode" "natural" pictures, we still must be acquainted with the symbol system in which the picture was composed. Gombrich, however, anticipates a gradual movement to an abso- lutely true (that is, more "correct") representation, one that requires fewer codes for us to see the subject. The ideal would be the disappearance of codes altogether, so that each vi- sual representation can become a trompe l'oeil (Feagin, 1998, distinguishes trompe l'oeil and pictorial representations). The sign-object relationship, therefore, is both iconic and symbolic. The model of pictorial representation includes all four of Goodman's (1976) dimensions.

Although the illusion view is a fair description of our experience of many realistic pictures, it shares a flaw with resemblance theories in not accounting for more stylized or abstract pictures, which could never trick the eye. Moreover, the surfaces of many paintings compel our attentions, so illusions would be impossible. Finally, it is not clear that all pictorial representation is actually based on conventions at the picture-making and picture-viewing stages, and if it isn't, then a major premise of illusion theory is undercut (Rollins, 1999).

Make-Believe: Just Pretend You're at the Eiffel Tower

According to make-believe theory, looking at handmade pictures is like playing children's games of make-believe because in both cases we exercise our imaginations in order to understand and appreciate *fictional worlds* (Walton 1973, 1990). To continue the analogy, children use dolls and toy trucks as props and we use pictures as props in make-believe games. When a girl holds a doll in her arms, her friends imagine that she is holding a baby. When we see the picture of the dancer stretching—we imagine a scene with the dancer stretching—the seeing and the imagining are integrated into a single complex phenomenological whole.

Some clarification is necessary. Walton is not saying that we imagine the masses of color to be a dancer. Instead, we imagine that our actual perceiving of the canvas is an act of perceiving a dancer. Again, clarification is needed. He is not saying that we are aware of perceiving *both* the canvas *and* the dancer. Instead we have a *single* experience that is both perceptual and imaginative. We do not deliberately imagine the dancer in the picture. Instead, we have a spontaneous response to the marks on the canvas. Our perception of the picture is colored by our imagining. It is colored by our imagining our perception to be of a dancer.

In this theory, the function of pictures may be independent of artists' intentions. Although sometimes artists create pictures in order to communicate a message to viewers, other times pictures are not vehicles of communication. We may not care what the painter meant by what she or he painted. Instead, we look at the picture and imagine our own fictional world. Pictures, unlike words, have a role in make-believe that is independent of, and prior to, communication (Walton, 1990), so Goodman's (1976) axis of representation is emphasized. The theory is based on iconic relations between sign and object.

One problem with the make-believe theory is that pictures often provide us with information and it seems unlikely that, in order to extract that information, we have to engage in a game of visual make-believe. Why can't pictures simply be used to refer to something? Another problem with this theory is the lack of psychological evidence of mental pretending in a gamelike, rule-governed way (Wollheim, 1986, 1991). Wollheim argued that we have a perfectly good explanation of how we look at pictures without invoking imagination, namely "seeing-in."

Seeing-in: What Do You See in Those Cloud Paintings?

According to seeing-in theory (Wollheim, 1980, 1986, 1988, 1993, 1998), we *see* pictures' subjects *in* the marks, colors, and textures of the pictures' surfaces. Of course, we also can see subjects in things other than pictures. We might see a dancer in a cloud formation or in the cracks of a wall. The difference between the two kinds of seeing-in, however, is that what we see in pictures was intended by a picture-maker and what we see in clouds was not. We do not deliberately see subjects in pictures; instead, seeing-in is spontaneous and involuntary. It also, Schmitter believed (2000), can be taught. Viewers may develop skills and knowledge enabling them to see a whole host of represented meanings in a work.

Wollheim denied that resemblance makes up part of the explanation for seeing-in (Budd, 1992). He also denied that theories of illusion and convention underlay seeing-in. Instead, he simply believed that if we see a subject in a picture and the artist marked the picture so that we should see it, then the picture represents the subject. For Wollheim, therefore, an explanation of seeing-in is unnecessary because it is an everyday experience that everyone will understand.

Wollheim called the experience of seeing-in "two-foldness." This concept means that we experience the surface of the two-dimensional picture and we experience the dancer in the picture—and these two experiences coincide. Actually, Wollheim's explanation of the concept is not that simple. Rather than two distinct experiences occurring simultaneously, Wollheim thought of pictorial representation as two aspects of a single experience. What is the difference between two experiences and two aspects of a single experience? The only difference seems to be that the two aspects are inseparable, but that doesn't seem to be true because, as Walton noted, we can be aware of the lines and texture of a painting without recognizing the subject.

One problem with seeing-in theory is that Wollheim doesn't explain how we can recognize or identify the subject in the picture. Instead of explaining seeing-in, Wollheim wrote that it doesn't need explaining because it is so natural that we all understand implicitly. Another problem is that trompe l'oeil art would not be considered representational because there would be no twofold experience (see Levinson, 1998; Maynard, 1994, for criticisms of twofoldness).

In conclusion, with the three mental construction theories, we perceive the picture and then we think about a scene, and our perceptions and thoughts become mixed together. With illusion theory, we don't notice the mixing. With make-believe theory, we understand that perceptions and cognitions have been mixed. With seeing-in theory, the mixing is not explained. With both seeing-in theory and illusion theory, the role of the maker of pictorial representations is acknowledged, but a greater role is given the maker in the seeing-in theory. With make-believe theory, the intentions of the maker are ignored.

CONCLUSION

This chapter reviews the advantages and disadvantages of four types of theory of pictorial representation and has related these theories both to Goodman's (1976) four-dimensional model of representation and to Peirce's three-part model of the relationship between signs and their objects. Any future theory that improves our understanding of pictorial representation will need to incorporate all seven concepts: viewer and maker; sign and object; icon, index, and symbol. The problems with existing theories generally stem from an overemphasis on some of these concepts and the exclusion of others.

Seeing-in theory seems to hold great promise. It utilizes all four dimensions of Goodman's model of representation. It also implies both the iconic and symbolic nature of pictorial signs. The indexical nature of pictures is not relevant because this theory focuses on communication intended by a maker and interpreted by a viewer. Seeing-in theory's weakness is that it does not address the concept of recognition, so some combination of seeing-in theory and recognition theory, including its concept of aspects, might benefit scholars of pictorial representation.

Representation is a key concept to semiotics, phenomenology, and rhetoric. In general, each of these fields has its own vocabulary, its own leaders, and its own assumptions, which together seem to lock scholars into a fixed and limited theoretical approach to investigating pictures. The three mental construction theories are closely tied with phenomenology, and the causal relations–resemblance–conventional theories are closely tied with semiotics. Rhetoric has a looser connection to conventional theory and the mental construction theories. Future theoretical work should attempt to facilitate communication and argumentation among these three competing, isolated fields in order to create a theoretical synthesis that would be useful to anyone studying pictures and how they represent.

REFERENCES

Allen, R. (1993). Representation, illusion and the cinema. *Cinema Journal, 32,* 21–48.

Allen, R. (1995). *Projecting illusion: Film spectatorship and the impression of reality.* New York: Cambridge University Press.

Allen, R. (1997). Looking at motion pictures. In R. Allen & M. Smith (Eds.), *Film theory and philosophy* (pp. 76–94). Oxford, UK: Clarendon Press.

Arnheim, R. (1974). On the nature of photography. *Critical Inquiry, 1,* 149–161.

Arrell, D. (1987). What Goodman should have said about representation. *Journal of Aesthetics and Art Criticism, 46,* 41–49.

Bach, K. W. (1970). Part of what a picture is. *British Journal of Aesthetics, 10,* 119–137.

Bazin, A. (1967). The ontology of the photographic image. In H. Gray (Trans.), *What is cinema?* (pp. 9–16). Berkeley: University of California Press.

Beardsley, M. (1978). Languages of art and art criticism. *Erkenntnis, 12,* 95–118.

Black, M. (1972). How do pictures represent? In M. Mandelbaum (Ed.), *Art, perception and reality* (pp. 95–130). Baltimore: Johns Hopkins University Press.

Blinder, D. (1986). In defense of pictorial mimesis. *Journal of Aesthetics and Art Criticism, 45,* 19–27.

Blocker, H. G. (1977). Pictures and photographs. *Journal of Aesthetics and Art Criticism, 36,* 155–162.

Brinker, M. (1996). *Art and illusion* and *the image and the eye:* Philosophical implications. In R. Woodfield (Ed.), *Gombrich on art and psychology* (pp. 42–59). Manchester, UK: Manchester University Press.

Brook, D. (1983). Painting, photography and representation. *Journal of Aesthetics and Art Criticism, 42,* 171–180.

Brubaker, D. (1993). Andre Bazin on automatically made images. *Journal of Aesthetics and Art Criticism, 51,* 59–67.

Bryson, N. (1983). *Vision and painting: The logic of the gaze.* New Haven CT: Yale University Press.

Budd, M. (1987). Wittgenstein on seeing aspects. *Mind, 96,* 1–17.

Budd, M. (1992). On looking at a picture. In J. Hopkins & A. Savile (Eds.), *Psychoanalysis, mind and art: Perspectives on Richard Wollheim* (pp. 266–280). Oxford, UK: Blackwell.

Budd, M. (1993). How pictures look. In D. Knowles & J. Skorupki (Eds.), *Virtue and taste: Essays on politics, ethics and aesthetics* (pp. 154–175). Oxford, UK: Blackwell.

Bull, M. (1994). Scheming schemata. *British Journal of Aesthetics, 34,* 207–217.

Carney, J. D. (1981). Wittgenstein's theory of picture representation. *Journal of Aesthetics and Art Criticism, 40,* 179–185.

Carney, J. D. (1993). Representation and style. *Philosophy and Phenomenological Research, 53,* 811–828.

Carroll, N. (1988). *Philosophical problems of classical film theory.* Princeton, NJ: Princeton University Press.

Carroll, N. (1995). Towards an ontology of the moving image. In C. A. Freeland & T. E. Wartenberg (Eds.), *Philosophy and Film* (p. 71). New York: Routledge.

Cavell, S. (1971). *The world viewed: Reflections of the ontology of film.* Cambridge: Harvard University Press.

Charlton, W. (2000). Pictorial likeness. *British Journal of Aesthetics, 40,* 467–478.

Currie, G. (1991). Photography, painting and perception. *Journal of Aesthetics and Art Criticism, 49,* 23–29.

Currie, G. (1995). *Image and mind: Film, philosophy and cognitive science.* Cambridge, UK: Cambridge University Press.

Currie, G. (1999). Visible traces: Documentary and the contents of photographs. *Journal of Aesthetics and Art Criticism, 57,* 285–297.

Danto, A. (1993). Animals as art historians. In A. Danto (Ed.), *Beyond the brillo box* (pp. 15–31). New York: Noonday Press.

Drost, M. P. (1994). Husserl and Goodman on the role of resemblance in pictorial representation. *International Studies in Philosophy, 26,* 17–27.

Elkins, J. (1998). *On pictures and the words that fail them.* Cambridge, UK: Cambridge University Press.

Elkins, J. (1999). *The domain of images.* Ithaca, NY: Cornell University Press.

Evans, D. (1978). Photographs and primitive signs. *Proceedings of the Aristolian Society, 79,* 213–238.

Feagin, S. L. (1998). Presentation and representation. *Journal of Aesthetics and Art Criticism, 56,* 234–240.

Files, C. (1996). Goodman's rejection of resemblance. *British Journal of Aesthetics, 36,* 398–412.

Friday, J. (1996). Transparency and the photographic image. *British Journal of Aesthetics, 36,* 30–42.

Gibson, J. J. (1954). A theory of pictorial perception. *Audio-Visual Communications Review, 1,* 3–23.

Gibson, J. J. (1971). The information contained in pictures. *Leonardo, 4,* 27–35.

Gibson, J. J. (1973). On the concept of "formless invariants" in visual perception. *Leonardo, 6,* 43–45.

Gibson, J. J. (1979). *The ecological approach to visual perception.* Boston: Houghton Mifflin.

Gilman, D. (1992). A new perspective on pictorial representation. *Australian Journal of Philosophy, 70,* 174–186.

Gombrich, E. H. (1977). *Art and illusion: A study in the psychology of pictorial representation.* London: Phaidon Press.

Gombrich, E. H. (1982). *The image and the eye: Further studies in the psychology of pictorial representation.* London: Phaidon Press.

Gombrich, E. H. (1984). Representation and misrepresentation. *Critical Inquiry, 11,* 195–201.

Goodman, N. (1976). *Languages of art: An approach to a theory of symbols.* Indianapolis: Hackett Publishing.

Goodman, N., & Elgin, C. Z. (1988). *Reconceptions in philosophy.* Indianapolis, IN: Hackett Publishing.

Harrison, A. (1991). A minimal syntax for the pictorial: The pictorial and the linguistic analogies and disanalogies. In I. Gaskell & S. Kamel (Eds.), *The language of art history* (pp. 213–239). Cambridge, UK: Cambridge University Press.

Harrison, A. (1997). *Philosophy and the arts: Seeing and believing.* Bristol: Thoemmes Press.

Hopkins, R. (1994). Resemblance and misrepresentation. *Mind, 103,* 421–438.

Hopkins, R. (1995). Explaining depiction. *The Philosophical Review, 104,* 425–455.

Hopkins, R. (1998). *Picture, image and experience: A philosophical inquiry.* Cambridge, UK: Cambridge University Press.

Howell, R. (1997). Review essay: Mimesis as make believe. *Synthese, 109,* 413–434.

Hyman, J. (1989). *The imitation of nature*. Oxford, UK: Blackwell.

Hyman, J. (2000). Pictorial art and visual experience. *British Journal of Aesthetics, 40*, 21–45.

Hyslop, A. (1986). Seeing through seeing-in. *British Journal of Aesthetics, 26*, 371–379.

Kemp, G. N. (1990). Pictures and depictions: A consideration of Peacocke's views. *British Journal of Aesthetics, 30*, 332–341.

King, W. L. (1992). Scruton and reasons for looking at photographs. *British Journal of Aesthetics, 32*, 258–265.

Kjorup, S. (1978). Pictorial speech acts. *Erkenntnis, 12*, 55–71.

Krieger, M. (1984). The ambiguities of representation and illusion: An E. H. Gombrich retrospective. *Critical Inquiry, 11*, 181–194.

Levinson, J. (1998). Wollheim on pictorial representation. *Journal of Aesthetics and Art Criticism, 56*, 227–233.

Lopes, D. (1996). *Understanding pictures*. Oxford, UK: Clarendon Press.

Lopes, D. (2000). From *Languages of art* to art in mind. *Journal of Aesthetics and Art Criticism, 58*, 227–231.

Manns, J. W. (1971). Representation, relativism and resemblance. *British Journal of Aesthetics, 11*, 281–287.

Martin, E. (1986). On seeing Walton's great-grandfather. *Critical Inquiry, 12*, 796–800.

Maynard, P. (1983). The secular icon: Photography and the functions of images. *Journal of Aesthetics and Art Criticism, 42*, 155–168.

Maynard, P. (1989). Talbot's technologies: Photographic depiction, detection, and reproduction. *Journal of Aesthetics and Art Criticism, 47*, 263–276.

Maynard, P. (1994). Seeing double. *Journal of Aesthetics and Art Criticism, 52*, 155–167.

McDonell, N. (1983). Are pictures unavoidably specific? *Synthese, 57*, 83–98.

Mitchell, W. J. T. (1986). Nature and convention: Gombrich's illusions. In W. J. T. (Ed.), *Iconology: Image, text, ideology* (pp. 75–94). Chicago: University of Chicago Press.

Mitchell, W. J. T. (1990). Representation. In F. Lentricchia & T. McLaughlin (Eds.), *Critical terms for literary study* (pp. 11–22). Chicago: University of Chicago Press.

Neander, K. (1987). Pictorial representation: A matter of resemblance. *British Journal of Aesthetics, 27*, 213–226.

Neiva, E. (1999). Redefining the image: Mimesis, convention, and semiotics. *Communication Theory, 1*, 75–91.

Novitz, D. (1975). Picturing. *Journal of Aesthetics and Art Criticism, 34*, 145–155.

Novitz, D. (1977). *Pictures and their use in communication: A philosophical essay*. Dordrecht, Netherlands: Martinus Nijhoff.

Peacocke, C. (1987). Depiction. *Philosophical Review, 3*, 383–410.

Peetz, D. (2001). Some current philosophical theories of pictorial representation. In A. Ch. Sukla (Ed.), *Art and representation: Contributions to contemporary aesthetic* (pp. 137–147). New York: Praeger.

Quigley, T. R. (2001). A causal theory of pictorial representation. In A. Ch. Sukla (Ed.), *Art and representation: Contributions to contemporary aesthetics* (pp. 148–162). New York: Praeger.

Reed, E., & Jones, R. (1982). *Reasons for realism: Selected essays by James J. Gibson*. Hillsdale, NJ: Lawrence Erlbaum Associates.

Robinson, J. (1978). Two theories of representation. *Erkenntnis, 12*, 37–53.

Robinson, J. (1979). Some remarks on Goodman's language theory of pictures. *British Journal of Aesthetics, 19*, 63–75.

Robinson, J. (2000). *Languages of art* at the turn of the century. *Journal of Aesthetics and Art Criticism, 58*, 213–218.

Rollins, M. (1999). Pictorial representation: When cognitive science meets aesthetics. *Philosophical Psychology, 12*, 387–413.

Ross, S. (1982). What photographs can't do. *Journal of Aesthetics and Art Criticism, 41*, 5–17.

Roupas, T. G. (1977). Information and pictorial representation. In D. Perkins & B. Leondar (Eds.), *The arts and cognition* (pp. 48–79). Baltimore: Johns Hopkins University Press.

Sartwell, C. (1991). Natural generativity and imitation. *British Journal of Aesthetics, 31*, 58–67.

Savedoff, B. E. (1992). Transforming images: Photographs of representations. *Journal of Aesthetics and Art Criticism, 50*, 93–106.

Savile, A. (1971). Nelson Goodman's 'languages of art': A study. *British Journal of Aesthetics, 11*, 33–27.

Savile, A. (1986). Imagination and pictorial understanding. *Aristotelian Society Supplementary Volume, 60*, 19–44.

Schier, F. (1986). *Deeper into pictures: An essay on pictorial representation*. Cambridge, UK: Cambridge University Press.

Schmitter, A. M. (2000). About representation; or, How to avoid being caught between animal perception and human language. *Journal of Aesthetics and Art Criticism, 58*, 255–272.

Scholz, O. R. (1993). When is a picture? *Synthese, 95*, 95–106.

Scruton, R. (1981). Photography and representation. *Critical Inquiry, 7*, 577–603.

Singer, I. (1977). Santayana and the ontology of the photographic image. *Journal of Aesthetics and Art Criticism, 36*, 29–44.

Snyder, J. (1980). Picturing vision. *Critical Inquiry, 6*, 499–526.

Snyder, J. (1984). Photography and ontology. In J. Margolis (Ed.), *The worlds of art and the world* (pp. 21–34). Amsterdam: Rodopi.

Snyder, J., & Allen, N. W. (1975). Photography, vision, and representation. *Critical Inquiry, 2*, 143–169.

Squires, R. (1969). Depicting. *Philosophy, 44*, 193–204.

Stampe, D. W. (1975). Show and tell. In B. Freed et al. (Eds.), *Forms of representation* (pp. 221–245). Amsterdam: North Holland.

Todd, J. (1980). The roots of pictorial reference. *Journal of Aesthetics and Art Criticism, 39*, 47–57.

Walton, K. L. (1973). Pictures and make-believe. *Philosophical Review, 82*, 283–319.

Walton, K. L. (1984). Transparent pictures: On the nature of photographic realism. *Critical Inquiry, 11*, 246–277.

Walton, K. L. (1986). Looking again through photographs: A response to Edwin Martin. *Critical Inquiry, 12*, 801–808.

Walton, K. L. (1990). *Mimesis as make-believe.* Cambridge: Harvard University Press.

Walton, K. L. (1991). Reply to reviewers. *Philosophy and Phenomenological Research, 51*, 413–431.

Walton, K. L. (1992). Seeing-in and seeing fictionally. In J. Hopkins & A. Saville (Eds.), *Psychoanalysis, mind and art: Perspectives on Richard Wollheim* (pp. 281–291). Oxford, UK: Blackwell.

Walton, K. L. (1997). On pictures and photographs: Objections answered. In R. Allen & M. Smith (Eds.), *Film theory and philosophy* (pp. 60–75). Oxford, UK: Clarendon Press.

Warburton, N. (1988). Seeing through "seeing through photographs." *Ratio (New Series), 1*, 64–74.

Wicks, R. (1989). Photography as a representational art. *British Journal of Aesthetics, 29*, 1–9.

Wilkerson, T. E. (1978). Representation, illusion and aspects. *British Journal of Aesthetics, 18*, 45–58.

Wilkerson, T. E. (1991). Pictorial representation: A defense of the aspect theory. In P. French, T. Vehling Jr. & H. Wettstein (Eds.), *Midwest studies in philosophy, xvi* (pp. 152–166). Nortre Dame, IN: University of Notre Dame Press.

Wilson, C. (1982). Illusion and representation. *British Journal of Aesthetics, 22*, 211–221.

Wittgenstein, L. (1953). *Philosophical investigations.* G. E. M. Anscombe (Ed.). Oxford, UK: Blackwell.

Wollheim, R. (1973a). Nelson Goodman's *languages of art.* In R. Wollheim (Ed.), *On art and the mind: Essays and lectures* (pp. 290–314). London: Allen Lane.

Wollheim, R. (1973b). Reflections on *art and illusion.* In R. Wollheim (Ed.), *On art and the mind: Essays and lectures* (pp. 261–289). London: Allen Lane.

Wollheim, R. (1980). Seeing-as, seeing-in, and pictorial representation. In R. Wollheim (Ed.), *Art and its objects* (pp. 205–226). Cambridge, UK: Cambridge University Press.

Wollheim, R. (1986). Imagination and pictorial understanding. *Aristotelian Society Supplementary Volume, 60*, 45–60.

Wollheim, R. (1988). What the spectator sees. In N. Bryson, M. A. Holly, & K. Moxey (Eds.), *Visual theory: Painting and interpretation* (pp. 101–150). New York: HarperCollins.

Wollheim, R. (1991). A note on *mimesis as make-believe. Philosophy and Phenomenological Research, 51*, 401–406.

Wollheim, R. (1993). *The mind and its depths.* Cambridge, MA: Harvard University Press.

Wollheim R. (1998). On pictorial representation. *Journal of Aesthetics and Art Criticism, 56*, 217–226.

Wolterstorff, N. (1980). *Work and worlds of art.* Oxford, UK: Clarendon Press.

Wolterstorff, N. (1991). Two approaches to representation—and then a third. In P. French, T. Vehling Jr., & H. Wettstein (Eds.), *Midwest studies in philosophy, xvi* (pp. 167–179). Notre Dame, IN: University of Notre Dame Press.

7

Cultural Palettes in Print Advertising: Formative Research Design Method

SANDRA MORIARTY
University of Colorado

LISA ROHE
Independent Scholar

A representation is something, usually an image (picture, photograph, drawing, diagram, etc.), that stands for, denotes, or symbolizes something else. The previous chapter by Keith Kenney described a number of different theories of how representation works. One factor that was mentioned in that chapter is the social or cultural aspect of representation. Kenney observes that the conventional theory of representation identifies a viewer's way of seeing as being under the control of the conventions imposed by culture. That is the focus of this chapter and the methodology it describes.

How people are represented is a particular concern in a cross-cultural communication situation where the choice of symbols must be culturally acceptable to the audience, as well as the designer. The problem is using imagery that advances cultural sensitivity rather than cultural stereotyping (Bhabha, 1999; Lippard, 1988). The most controversial example of that is the use of Native American symbols in sports, even when Native Americans protest the use (Buck, 1991).

In advertising and other areas of graphic design, designers are sometimes inclined to make decisions about illustrations based solely or primarily on their aesthetic judgment. They may find themselves proposing design solutions that reflect their own culture and personal taste, designs that exhibit little sensitivity to the nuances of symbols and colors used in other cultures.

In instrumental communication, such as advertising, designers must be aware of the appeal of their visual messages to the targeted audience and also consider the functional requirements of the message objectives. In cross-cultural communication, however, the aesthetic and functional decisions are further impacted by the cultural filters of the communicator, as well as the audience. Gombrich refers to this as the "beholders share," which he describes as the contribution we make to any representations from the stock of images stored in our mind, the "hidden assumptions" with which we approach an image (1972, p. 89; Moriarty & Kenney, 1997, p. 240).

Cross-cultural communication is commonly traced to the anthropologist Edward T. Hall and his work at the Foreign Service Institute in Washington, D.C., in the 1945–1955 period. As Rogers (1999) explained, Hall was one of the first to use the term *intercultural communication* and his book *The Silent Language* (Hall, 1959) established many of the concepts central to research in cross-cultural communication, such as the notion that cultural differences impact on the effectiveness of communication.

This chapter focuses, not on a particular study, but rather on a methodology—the cultural palette—that can be used to create more culturally sensitive images. The cultural palette uncovers the "hidden assumptions" and uses them in a positive way to help designers make creative decisions that reflect differing symbolic viewpoints and visual practices.

THE PROBLEM

This chapter begins with an example of how the methodology works and concludes with a review of multiple studies that have been conducted using the cultural palette methodology. In the initial study, one of the authors who is a designer was asked by a local fast-food restaurant owner to develop a poster and other visuals for a Hispanic Heritage program for that store. The store wanted to emphasize its sensitivity to the local Hispanic culture of both customers and employees who come from the surrounding neighborhood.

An all-too-common response would be for the designer to develop a design based on that person's personal sense of aesthetics and then present it to the manager. That approach precipitated this project: The designer developed a poster proposal featuring Picasso's Don Quixote and the manager questioned whether this was an appropriate symbol for the local Hispanic community, most of whom traced their roots to Mexico, rather than Spain.

The problem the designer faced was determining what symbols and colors could be used to communicate visually in a way that depicted the Hispanic community with sensitivity and at the same time communicated in an interesting way to non-Hispanic people about the culture.

Cross-cultural communication can be either one way or two way. In one-way communication, such as advertising, one culture, usually a dominant or majority one, communicates to another, which is a subculture. In the restaurant's case, a company run largely by white middle-class Anglos was attempting to develop a message for Hispanics with whom it does business.

In two-way cross-cultural communication, the symbols that are appropriate to use in communication *with* the subculture have to also communicate effectively *about* the subculture to the majority culture. In other words, the colors and symbols are appropriate and deliver meaning for both the subculture and the majority culture. In the restaurant example, this means that the design package must be appealing and communicate just as effectively to the Anglo employees and customers who will also see the poster.

It should also be noted that cross-cultural communication projects are sometimes location specific. A specific Korean American community, for example, may share a general set of culturally nuanced symbols with other Korean American communities, but it may also be different in its view of the appropriateness of specific symbols because of its history and traditions. That is particularly true for the tremendous variety of distinctive cultures loosely identified in the United States as Hispanic, which includes such cultural roots as Puerto Rican, Cuban, Mexican, and Spanish, among others. The confusion also lies in the terms we use for these groups such as Hispanic, Chicano, Latino, and Mexican American, terms that also carry nuanced meanings.

THE CONCEPT OF A CULTURAL PALETTE

In order to better assess the cultural acceptability of design symbols, the concept of a cultural palette has been developed to assist the designer in the development of culturally sensitive symbols. A palette is the board on which an artist mixes colors, but the word is also used to refer to the range of colors used in a particular painting.

A cultural palette (Moriarty & Rohe, 1992) was developed using a qualitative method to formulate a set of culturally sensitive symbols and colors, as well as other graphic elements such as layouts and artistic styles, that may reflect cultural nuances. The symbols are determined to be culturally sensitive as a result of a structured assessment process, which is the focus of this chapter.

THE ASSESSMENT PROCESS

In general, the procedure involves a series of interviews and the collection of visuals used in the compilation of an image bank. Next, a panel of experts is identified who will review the image bank and identify the ones that are good (appropriate and inoffensive) and poor (inappropriate and offensive) symbols and colors. The final step is to create the palette of colors and symbols that provides a range of culturally sensitive graphics at the same time identifying the insensitive or inappropriate colors and symbols that need to be avoided.

The following steps summarize the process of performing a visual cross-cultural analysis involving a complex two-way communication situation to create a cultural palette:

1. *Majority Culture Images*: Investigate the images of the subculture as seen and used by the source or dominant culture and the images currently used to communicate about the subculture *to* and *within* the dominant culture. These materials can be accumulated from books, magazines, brochures, advertising, packaging—or any other source of graphics that is targeted to that group.

2. *Subculture Images*: Investigate the images used by the subculture itself in its self-presentation. These can come from observational field research, subculture media, and interviews with local experts.
3. *Image Bank*: Develop an image bank combining all these symbols, as well as colors and design styles.
4. *Expert Panel Evaluation*: Establish a panel of experts for that culture and ask the experts to rate the images in terms of their appropriateness, representativeness, and potential for offensiveness and sort them into piles of sensitive or insensitive images. This sort can be conducted either through in-depth interviews or a focus group. The result is an image sort (similar to a photo sort as used by advertising planners to match message strategies to target audiences).
5. *Cultural Palette*: Sort the images into four piles representing acceptable and unacceptable symbols and colors according to the evaluations of the expert panel.
6. *Cross Cultural Palette*: Within the cultural palette, rank-order those colors and bias-free symbols that communicate best to the dominant culture, as well as the subculture.

APPLYING THE PROCEDURE

For the restaurant's Hispanic Heritage project, the designer first defined the subculture involved in the corporation's programs as being primarily of Mexican American background living in Denver. (Note: This investigation was aimed at Hispanics living in this particular area, and thus the conclusions may not be valid for other regions of the United States.) It is important that the procedure be applied to the appropriate local community.

Dominant Culture Images

To determine the images of the subculture as seen by the majority culture, the researcher collected travel brochures about Mexico and analyzed the visuals and colors used in these publications. This simply gives an indication of what symbols and colors are seen as communicating effectively about Mexican culture to American tourists, primarily affluent white Anglos. Other sources included Mexican-themed products and services marketed to the majority culture.

The first list of symbols from the majority culture included the tourist imagery of beaches, palm trees, sand, sun, parrots, tropical fish, tropical drinks by a pool, Mayan ruins, Mariachi bands, guitars, pinatas, sombreros, dancers in traditional dress, an open market (mercado) with symbols like hanging chili peppers, and colorful handwoven blankets and shawls. The most popular color was blue, ranging from turquoise to deep blue, which seemed to be used for water and sky imagery. One brochure used fluorescent day-glo pink as an accent with the blue.

The American brands in the Mexican food section used a color palette dominated by red, green, yellow, and brown. Other colors that occurred with some frequency included pink, turquoise, and orange. Symbols included chili peppers in both red and green, a piñata, a man wearing a sombrero sleeping under a cactus, a bull, a duck, a woman in a sombrero and Mexican costume, a mesa with a cactus, an Aztec sun, and a pueblo or adobe house. The Taco Bell restaurant chain also uses adobe-style architectural motifs and turquoise, purple, and pink colors.

Subculture Images

For the local part of the study, the research analyzed the packaging and merchandising of American products and products with Spanish-language labels in grocery stores in the Hispanic neighborhood. Other sources included Spanish-language publications available within the community, interviews with local Hispanic media representatives, Hispanic art in museums or books, and discussions of the subculture's graphic code in other articles and books.

The Spanish-labeled products used the same color palette as the American foods—red, green, yellow, and brown. Most of the designs were bands of color with type. Typically the packages used very little artwork and few symbols. One package used a green bowl with flames coming out of it.

Interviews were conducted with Hispanic community representatives, media executives, and university specialists. More specifically, the eight experts consulted for this study included a specialist in Latino culture at the Museum of Natural History, an advertising executive who owns an agency that specializes in Hispanic advertising, the editor of a Spanish-language newspaper, the owner of a Spanish-language radio station, the research director and a policy analyst for the Latin American Research and Service Agency, the research director at the Bueno Center for Multicultural Studies on campus, and the director of Chicano Studies.

From these interviews, a list of possible colors was developed that included the Mexican flag colors (green, white, red), yellow, brown, orange, black, traditional costume colors (brights), primary colors (red, yellow, blue), purple, turquoise, burgundy, gray, and sand. The symbols included chili and jalapeno peppers, families, pyramids, the Spanish language itself, Aztec and Mayan symbols, the sun, Southwest nature images, circles, sarape (shawl) designs, swords, folkloric stamps, century cactus, and santos (religious statues).

Image Bank Creation and Evaluation

These two sets of symbols and colors were compiled and presented visually as an image bank. The experts interviewed initially were again consulted this time as an expert panel to judge the appropriateness of the symbols in the image bank. They were asked in individual in-depth interviews to sort the symbols and colors according to cultural appropriateness and freedom from bias. (Note: in other studies, a focus group of "average" people from within the subculture was used for the image sort.) The image sort for the restaurant project resulted in the following cultural palette. The items marked with an asterisk identify the overlap with dominant culture imagery and indicate the cross-cultural palette

Most appropriate colors: green*, red*, and white (the colors of the Mexican flag), yellow*, brown*, and orange.

Least appropriate colors: black, purple, turquoise, burgundy, gray, sand, mauve, and pastels. Blue, the color that dominates most, appeals to Anglos, is rarely appropriate according to these experts. (Note that this group includes the Taco Bell color palette.) **Most appropriate symbols**: anything that says "familia" such as home and hearth, chili peppers* (symbols for traditional cooking but also the red and green relate back to the flag), circles (hands and arms interlinked reflect back to the family or home motif), and sarape designs*. Also the historical Aztec and Mayan symbols* were identified as appropriate. The Spanish language itself was identified as a positive symbol with suggestions that Spanish words can be used as graphic markers.

Least appropriate symbols: sombreros, cactus, donkeys, man sleeping against a cactus, Frito bandito and Juan Valdez (the experts did not approve of any symbol that signified peasants, bandits, or outlaws). Southwest images, such as pueblos, and Southwest colors were declared to be more representative of the American Southwest than of Mexican-based cultures.

OTHER STUDIES

In addition to this Hispanic study, additional studies have investigated culturally sensitive symbols for other ethnic groups using the cultural palette technique. A follow-up project compared the results of the original Denver Hispanics study with Tex-Mex communities in San Antonio. Additional work has been done with students of an Indian (Indian subcontinent) background, Korean students in the United States, a Navajo community in Arizona, and a more generalized analysis of Native American symbols and imagery to determine if there are any that are universal and less reflective of tribal specifics.

In a more instrumental communication situation, such as advertising and public relations for an information or marketing campaign, "target audiences" have been studied that are subgroups or market niches that may have culturally nuanced visual communication patterns. These studies are situated in a product or service marketing effort in terms of how a campaign could sensitively address their needs and interests. The groups we have studied include high school cheerleaders, snowboarders, vegetarians, lesbians and bisexual women, gay men, mothers of infants, young single women (ages 21 to 26), young children studying science, single mothers with young children, obese people, and handicapped people.

The results of various of these studies of both ethnic groups and market segments are summarized in the appendix that follows in terms of appropriate and inappropriate symbols and colors.

DECONSTRUCTING THE CROSS-CULTURAL COMMUNICATION PROCESS

Stepping back from the details of these various studies, we can see the outline of the process used in cross-cultural visual communication. The process involves both encoding, decoding, and sometimes recoding. An important part of the process is the recognition of the critical role played by cultural lenses and cultural filters.

Encoding, or message design, begins with the development of an intended visual message and the functional frame that surrounds it. In other words, who is it addressed to and what are its objectives? The message is also modified by the encoder's cultural lens that shapes and focuses the meaning of the message in terms of the encoder's cultural codes. An important dimension of the cultural lens, particularly for visual communication, is the aesthetic frame that is fitted around the visual message. The result of these functional, cultural, and aesthetic steps in the message design process is a set of symbols acceptable to the message designer through which the message is presented.

Decoding, or perception, begins with the confrontation of the message designer's set of symbols (symbolic elements, colors, layout, artistic styles, composition, graphic decisions, as well as the verbal elements), which are processed through the receiver's aesthetic frame and cultural filter. In addition to interpreting meaning, the cultural filter also identifies inappropriate symbols in the message as presented. Assuming the cultural fit is acceptable, then the interpretive process continues on through the decoder's functional frame (what is this message all about?) to arrive at a perceived message.

To analyze the complexity of such a process, let's return to the restaurant example. In this case, the *encoding* of the posters was driven by the company and its hired designer. As the designer finishes the Hispanic Heritage message design (poster, signage, other graphic materials), employees (both Anglos and Hispanics) *decode* the message as presented to create their own perceived messages, which may vary depending on their own experiences but more importantly may be modified or countered by their cultural filter. Employees may also *encode* a response message back to the company, which also will be affected by their cultural filter. In addition, employees may recode the message as they deliver it personally to customers. The customer (both Anglos and Hispanics) *decodes* messages about the Hispanic Festival both from the visual communication vehicles (posters, etc.) and from the interpersonal communication of the employees. The customer may also *encode* a response message back to the company as well as to the employee.

Note how many times in this cross-cultural communication situation the message is translated through a cultural lens or a cultural filter. At each of these points, a decision is being made about acceptability based on a fit with the individual's cultural code.

Notice also, that the corporate encoding is identified as coming through an Anglo cultural lens. The objective of the cultural palette research was to add a Hispanic viewpoint to the encoding process at this critical point in the message design process. It is hoped that this cultural palette assessment method will make it possible to better manage these cultural intersections in order to deliver visual messages that are more sensitive to cultural nuances.

REFERENCES

Bhabha, H. K. (1999). The other question: The stereotype and colonial discourse. In J. Vans & S. Hall (Eds.), *Visual culture: The reader* (pp. 370–378). London: Sage.

Buck, R. (1991, October 28). The last stereotype. *Adweek's Marketing Week*, 16.

Gombrich, E. H. (1972). The visual image. *Scientific American, 227*, 88.

Hall, E. T. (1959). *The silent language.* Garden City, NY: Doubleday.

Lippard, L. (1988, February 28). Laughing matters: Ethnic attitudes surface in a century of "The Funnies." *Boulder Daily Camera*, 1C, 5C.

Moriarty, S., & Kenney, K. (1997). A philosophical discussion of representation. In R. E. Griffin, J. M. Hunter, C. B. Schiffman, & W. J. Gibbs (Eds.), *IVLA Conference Proceedings* (pp. 235–242). University Park: Pennsylvania State University Press.

Moriarty, S. E., & Rohe, L. (1992, Winter). Cultural palettes: An exercise in sensitivity for designers. *Journalism Educator*, 32–37.

Rogers, E. M. (1999). Georg Simmel's concept of the stranger and intercultural communication research. *Communication Theory, 9*(1), 58–74.

APPENDIX

Part I: The Ethnic Studies

The Tex-Mex Study

Most-Appropriate Symbols: family scenes (in kitchen, at table, sitting on porch), children playing with handmade toys or family dog, cooking traditional foods (tortillas & tamales), the pinata.

Least-Appropriate Symbols: The Alamo, the Texas "Lone Star State" flag, sleepy Mexican leaning against cactus, authority figures (police, military), the serape, the sombrero, Mexican bandits and/or drug smugglers.

Most-Appropriate Colors: red, green, white (not because of the flag but because they are the colors of the main ingredients of salsa), blue and brown, yellow and orange.

Least-Appropriate Colors: fluorescent colors, Southwestern pastels (sand, mauve, aqua, turquoise).

The India (subcontinent) Study

Most-Appropriate Symbols: the rangoli pattern drawn on floors and entryways, a rangoli pattern with an image of the sun god, a rangoli pattern with an image of the bull, Nandi, a textile pattern featuring a mango leaf design, the symbol of creation and the first word (OM) in Hindu mythology (too sacred to be used in commercial communication), the symbol of Ganesh and his wife Paravati, another Ganesh symbol—the elephant boy, the conch shell symbol called Shenkh, the Hindu goddess of wealth—Lakshmi, a diya or small lamp made of red clay, the swastika, the peacock, the lotus flower, the rose, a flower garland, the cow, homemade earthenware pots and large brass containers.

Least-Appropriate Symbols: the half moon with stars (specific to the Muslim religion and a negative symbol for Hindus), nudity and blatant sexuality, an owl, cats.

Most-Appropriate Colors: red, maroon, yellow, dark green, saffron (dark yellow or orange).

Least-Appropriate Colors: white, black.

The Korean Student Study

Most-Appropriate Symbols: tiger, phoenix, dragon, magpie, lotus, bamboo, hawks, fish, flowers.

Least-Appropriate Symbols: cat, cow bird, snake.

Most-Appropriate Colors: white, red, blue, yellow, green, orange, magenta.

Least-Appropriate Colors: purple, pink, black, brown, pastels, gray.

The Navajo Study

Most-Appropriate Symbols: the loom and weaving patterns (swastika and the Greek cross), the eagle, the medicine man, water, clouds, the rainbow, corn.

Least-Appropriate Symbols: anything symbolizing death, Anasazi ruins (haunted), the owl, the snake, fish, the coyote (trickster, comes from some other tribe), any form of graphic self-representation, any representation of eye contact with strangers, alcohol and any suggestion of the drunk, lazy Indian.

Most-Appropriate Colors: four sacred colors—white (light shell color to beige), red (including shades from a deep maroon to orange), blue (turquoise or indigo), black (jet to gray).

Least-Appropriate Colors: gaudy colors.

The Native American Study

(this is a generalized investigation of tribal differences to determine commonalties, if any)

Most-Appropriate General Symbols: feathers, drum, flute, circle.

Tribal-Specific Appropriate Symbols: dwellings (adobe, teepee), pottery, buckskin clothing, turtle, moon, sun, eagle, moccasins, coyote, horse, papoose, buffalo, stars, art.

Least-Appropriate Symbols: war weapons that perpetuate the Indian stereotype as a savage warrior (tomahawk, bow and arrows), peace pipe, chief's feather headdress, anything that represents gambling or alcoholism, tribal specific symbols used inappropriately.

Most-Appropriate Colors: earth tones, red, blue, green, yellow, tan.

Least-Appropriate Colors: (too individualized by tribe to generalize).

Part II: The Market Segment Studies

The Study of Young Single Women (early 20s) for a Cosmetics Line

Most-Appropriate Symbols: flowers, jewels, circles and diamond shapes.

Least-Appropriate Symbols: a rose, exclamation points, squares and triangle shapes.

Most-Appropriate Colors: earth tone shades (peach, mauve, light brown, sea foam green, pale yellow, pale turquoise, soft pink, soft blue), royal blue.

Least-Appropriate Colors: bright reds, black, gold, burgundy, navy blue, bright yellow, kelly green, purple, hot pink.

The Study of Mothers of Young Children

Most-Appropriate Symbols: hearts, flowers, plants, circles, cute animals; shapes that are soft, rounded, and feeling oriented. (Note, pictures of cute kids and babies are not necessarily attention grabbers.)

Least-Appropriate Symbols: war, violence, sex, starvation, social discontent, anger, aggression (the Teenage Mutant Ninja Turtles, for example); harsh images with sharp edges.

Most-Appropriate Colors: yellow, purple, pastels (light blue, pink, mint green, lavender).

Least-Appropriate Colors: black, brown, neon colors.

The Study of Young Children and Science

Most-Appropriate Symbols: preferred stylized drawings over realistic photographs, animals, humorous images, gender role models (women for girls and men for boys).
Least-Appropriate Symbols: scary images (blow up of a fly).
Most-Appropriate Colors: preferred colorful images (green, orange, red), primary colors.
Least-Appropriate Colors: muted colors (white, brown, gray, silver).

The High School Cheerleader Study

Most-Appropriate Symbols: cars (sports cars, trucks), children, young animals (puppies, kittens), couples, attractive men, athletic women, medium to long length hair, baggy, faded and ripped jeans.
Least-Appropriate Symbols: lingerie, tampons, retro-fashions (black lipstick, white-powdered faces, bell-bottom pants), cigarettes (Joe Camel is OK), big hair, "girly" fashions (tight or spandex look, flowery, pastel colors), sexual imagery.
Most-Appropriate Colors: deep jewel tones—forest and kelly greens, sapphire and navy blues, amethyst and violet, mauve and burgundy, and sable and derby browns.
Least-Appropriate Colors: yellow and orange.

The Vegetarian Study

Most-Appropriate Symbols: rainbow, "mother earth," cornucopia (vegetables/grains), "v" for vegan, animals and people together, sun, scenery, tilled or planted soil, farmhouses and barns, old stoves, hearth, landscape, forest, old etchings, flowers, organic symbol (HM-Healthmark), old Native American women, cherubs.
Least-Appropriate Symbols: male and female bodies (no sex appeal), animal flesh, no bimbos/blondes.
Most-Appropriate Colors: primary colors, blues, greens, yellow, purple, bright red, white, rainbows of bright colors.
Least-Appropriate Colors: dark colors (grays, navy, brown, black), crimson red.

The Lesbian and Bisexual Women's Study

Most-Appropriate Symbols: the upside triangle (in pink), the double-sided axe or "labris," lambda, rainbow flag, an old surviving tree, water and earthen imagery, mystical and mythological symbols (sorceresses and goddesses), the snake, circles, black-and-white photography and line drawings, active woman acting assertively, women together (gentle and caring).
Least-Appropriate Symbols: passive or submissive women, solitary women, solitary assertive women, feminine imagery (makeup and cosmetics), provocative heterosexual imagery, black-and-white androgynous people, pornographic imagery, square shapes, playful erotic imagery with leather.
Most-Appropriate Colors: pink, purple, teal, green, white, blue, black.
Least-Appropriate Colors: neons, orange, brown.

8

Content Analysis of Representation: Photographic Coverage of Blacks by Nondaily Newspapers

KEN SMITH
CINDY PRICE
University of Wyoming

When reading a newspaper, normally the first thing that people notice is the photographs (McLellan & Steele, 2001). Photographs both catch readers' attention and are examined more often than the words on the pages (Wolf & Grotta, 1985). However, their influence extends beyond attracting the eye because photographs influence how people feel about the credibility of the paper (McLellan & Steele, 2001). This influence is so extensive that photojournalists often define to the public what is newsworthy (Miller, 1975).

In Chapter 6, Keith Kenney discussed the transparency theory of photography. Walton said that photographs are "transparent" because "we see the world through them" (1984, p. 251). Photographs allow us to see in the past and are more representative of the world than are drawings or paintings, which is why Walton indicated that photographs are used in courtrooms and by news media. As Kenney said in Chapter 6, we see things firsthand through the transparent photograph. Therefore, photojournalism has power because the viewers feel that they can see the event as it actually took place.

Because people experience reality based on what they see, hear, and experience (Berger & Luckmann, 1966), if people have no direct contact with those who are different, they often use media images to show them the "reality" of these other people. In this regard, photojournalism is especially powerful because, as W. Eugene Smith said, "Photographic journalism, because of the tremendous audience reached by publications using it, has more influence on public thinking and opinion than any other branch of photography" (Lyons, 1966, p. 103). Lewis (1995) said photojournalism is supposed to serve a social good.

"If done in the right spirit, photojournalism can be a powerful tool for explaining the larger world by conveying essential truths about the human condition" (p. 9). However, the media are not neutral because the reporters and photographers are the ones who decide what "mirror" to use for us to see the "truths" they are portraying (Martindale, 1986, pp. 40–41).

Photographs also have the ability to portray the roles that are appropriate for different types of people (Miller, 1975). The National Advisory Committee on Civil Disorders in 1968 reported: "If what the white American reads in the newspapers or sees on television conditions his expectations of what is ordinary and normal in the larger society, he will neither understand nor accept the black American" (Stempel, 1971, p. 337). Carby (1998) noted that the way African Americans are portrayed in the media gives society a stereotypical representation of the whole race.

Lester said media outlets were a contributing factor for some of the frustration in the African American community during the politically charged time of the mid-1960s because blacks were represented in the mass media only as "train porters, sports heroes, entertainers, or criminals" (1994, p. 380). Part of the problem with media coverage of African American issues is that those stories often are based on long-term events and unfold over several years. Unfortunately, they often do not get coverage until they become direct, visual confrontations (Martindale, 1986).

Several studies over the years have found that the number and percentage of pictures of African Americans has increased (Lester, 1994; Singletary, 1978; Stempel, 1971). Although some studies have shown fewer stereotypical images (crime, sports, and entertainment) (Stempel, 1971), others have some shown more of these pictures (Lester, 1994). However, all of these studies have focused on either magazines, such as *Life* and *Time*, or large, urban newspapers. Lester (1994) suggested that medium-sized and smaller newspaper should be examined to see if subject percentages are similar to daily papers. This chapter is an attempt to study the coverage of blacks by the community media because this type of newspaper is both a growing segment of the newspaper industry (Coulson, Lacy, & Wilson, 2000), and it covers the world at a more personal level than do metro newspapers or magazines. More specifically, this chapter uses a content analysis to examine photographic coverage of blacks in nondaily newspapers.

OBJECTIVITY OF PHOTOJOURNALISM

In deciding what content to put in a newspaper, news people use "news judgement" (Shoemaker & Reese, 1996, p. 110). The aspects that are used to decide what is news include prominence/importance, human interest, conflict/controversy, the unusual, timeliness, and proximity. Photojournalism answers the traditional journalistic questions of who, what, when, where, why, and how and must contain strong storytelling elements (Lewis, 1995). As reporters and photojournalists learn news routines and other technical aspects, they develop their professionalism because they are trained to become detached from the story and the conflicts of interest involved (Schudson, 1995). According to Soloski (1989), this objectivity is the most important professional norm for American journalists.

Because editors felt this news judging skill was so important, "a good technical photographer who lacks basic news evaluation ability might be more at home in a photo

studio than in a newsroom" (Pasternark & Martin, 1985, p. 135). When combined with
the story from the reporter and the reader's social and educational backgrounds, the
photojournalist's goal is to communicate a message so the reader can grasp right away
what the situation is (Hoy, 1993). The National Press Photographers Association (NPPA)
has a code of ethics that says that photojournalists should "strive for pictures that report
truthfully, honestly and objectively" (Lester, 1991, p. 163). The code continues, "(O)ur
chief thought shall be to fulfill that responsibility and discharge that duty so that when
each of us is finished we shall have endeavored to lift the level of human ideals and
achievement higher than we found it" (Lester, 1991, p. 163).

Photojournalist W. Eugene Smith said, "The photographer must bear the responsibility for his work and its effect.... Even on rather 'unimportant' stories, this attitude
must be taken—for photographs ... are molders of opinion. A little misinformation plus
a little more misinformation is the kindling from which destructive misunderstandings
flare" (Lyons, 1966, p. 104). To fulfill this responsibility, photographers need to study the
background of the people or places they picture, according to Smith. "The mind should
remain as open and free of prejudice as possible, and the photographer should never try
to force the subject matter into his or the editor's preconceived idea" (Lyons, 1966, p. 104).

However, this may be difficult when photojournalists cover people who are different
from themselves. Weaver and Wilhoit (1996) surveyed 1,156 journalists and photojournalists in the United States and found that regarding ethnicity, 87.1% (72.8%) were Caucasian
or other; 3.7% (12.1%), African American; 2.2% (9.0%), Hispanic; 1.0% (2.9%), Asian;
0.6% (0.8%), Native American; 5.4% (2.4%), Jewish. (The 1990 U.S. Census percentages
for these populations are in parentheses.) Newkirk (2000) wrote that even when African
American reporters are hired, they soon become conflicted and frustrated by their jobs.
She said of her first newspaper job: "(W)hen it came to writing about African Americans,
I often encountered difficulty filling out the puzzle that is race in this country because my
editors resisted perspectives that were foreign to the white cultural mainstream. They
found it easier to exclude or malign *alien* viewpoints then to attempt to understand ideas
that did not mesh with their own" (p. xvii).

PREVIOUS STUDIES OF NEWS PHOTOGRAPHS

A number of studies have examined photojournalistic coverage of blacks. Singletary and
Lamb (1984) examined 222 award-winning news photographs that were printed in the
monthly publication of the NPPA. They examined two overall categories: news and
feature. They found that an overwhelming number of news photos were negative in
tone; only 9 of 111 were positive or neutral. Because many of the prize-winning photos
were of extraordinary events, 81% of news photos involved accidents, disasters, crime,
and violence. "Disproportionately few of the award-winning news photos were taken
indoors (15.5%, despite the fact that so many of the significant and far-reaching events
of life occur indoors)" (Singletary & Lamb, 1984, p. 105). In news photos, blacks were in
19% (21 of 111). Of those, 11 showed blacks being arrested or in court, while 4 were of
black heroes and award winners. About half of feature photos related to "coping with
adversity," such as cancer, alcoholism, and other disabilities. Blacks were in 14% of feature

photos (16 of 111). Some were stereotypical (an unwed teenage mother, a wino, a security hospital inmate), but others were more ideal (a nurse, a drill sergeant, and a cheerleader). Overall, the authors concluded that few pictures depicted broad social issues or political events and were primarily taken indoors. "This further supported the argument that news photos should not be seen as an accurate reflection of life" (Singletary & Lamb, 1984, p. 233).

Stempel (1971) examined the percentages of news pictures with blacks and whites in five news magazines in 1960 and 1970. He found in 1960, 94.6% of pictures were "white only"; 2.8% were "black only"; and 2.5% included both races. In 1970, those numbers changed to 87.4% "white only"; 6.9% "black only"; and 5.6% included both races. Stempel concluded that there was room for improvement, but that the data showed marked increases in black visibility.

Trayes and Cook (1977) looked at the photographs in 16 major daily U.S. newspapers and examined how many people of different races appeared. When grouping all of the newspapers together, the authors found that 81% of all pictures with people in them were "white only" while 10% were "black only." In only 3% of the cases were those races shown together. When examining the front page, 91% of the people pictures were "white only"; 4%, "black only"; 3%, "mixed"; and 1%, "other" (Trayes & Cook, 1977, p. 597).

Singletary (1978) conducted a long-term analysis of page-one photographs from six newspapers in 1936, 1956, and 1976. As far as racial composition, in 1936, 94.9% were "white only"; 1%, "black only"; 0.8%, "white-black mixed"; and 3%, "white-other mixed." In 1956 these percentages had changed to: 91.5%, 1.5%, 2.1%, and 4.6%. In 1976, the percentages were: 80.1%, 3.8%, 9.2%, 6.5%. Categories of page-one photos also changed over the years. Crime and corruption photos went from 9.3% of coverage in 1936 to 7.1% in 1956 to 5.9% in 1976. Accident and disaster photos had a similar decline: 14.5% to 11.6% to 9.7%. Human-interest photos declined from 29% to 26.8% to 24.9%. Economic-related photos changed from 2.2% to 0.3% to 0.5%. Sports photos showed an increase in the three years: 1.1% to 3% to 5%. Public affairs and political photos were: 32.7%, 37.9%, and 36.5%. Violent photographs were: 6.3%, 5%, and 8%.

Lester (1994) analyzed more than 250,000 photographs from four urban daily newspapers from selected periods between 1937 and 1990. The *New York Times, Chicago Tribune, New Orleans Times-Picayune* and the *San Francisco Chronicle* were chosen because they were regionally or nationally important and had large populations of African Americans. He examined all pictures with people and divided the topics into stereotypical (crime, sports, and entertainment), race-blind (accident, war, human interest, science, and religion), special interest to African Americans (society news, politics, business, social problems, education, and health), and advertising images. In all of the years combined, he found that 5.7% of the pictures (16,008) showed African Americans. Of these pictures, 49.9% were stereotypical images; 13.2%, race-blind; 12.1%, special interest, and 24.4%, advertising. In the modern era (1978 to 1990), 52.3% of African American pictures were stereotypical with more than half of that percentage being sports pictures. The other percentages were 11.5%, race-blind; 11.9%, special interest; and 24.3%, advertising. He concluded that in the modern era, most pictures treat African Americans as equal, productive members of society compared to earlier images that either showed them in low-level jobs or as simpletons. However, the fact that in many images, African Americans are shown as sports stars still emphasizes the "hidden message that African Americans are primarily valued for agility and strength during sporting events" (Lester, 1994, p. 391).

METHOD

This study utilizes a content analysis to examine the representation of blacks in nondaily newspapers. Wimmer and Dominick listed eight steps through the data-collection process that should be considered in conducting content analyses:

1. Formulate the research question or hypotheses.
2. Define the population in question.
3. Select an appropriate sample from the population.
4. Select and define a unit of analysis.
5. Construct the categories of content to be analyzed.
6. Establish a quantification system.
7. Train coders and conduct a pilot study.
8. Code the content according to established definitions. (1997, p. 116)

This study utilizes research questions rather than hypotheses. The reason for this decision is that this study investigates a subject—the representation of race in nondaily newspapers—that has not received much attention from researchers. As a result, predictability about the relationships between variables is limited making hypotheses difficult to formulate. A set of research questions to examine general areas under investigation is more appropriate.

The research questions are:

1. How frequently are blacks depicted in photos that appear in nondaily newspapers, especially as compared to depictions of whites?
2. In what manner are blacks depicted in nondaily newspapers? Are these images stereotypical or do they relegate blacks to less-important roles?
3. How do depictions of blacks in nondaily newspapers compare to those appearing in daily newspapers?

The population to be examined in this study is general circulation nondaily newspapers in the United States. The term *non-daily* is used because many newspapers are published two or even three times a week rather than on a once-a-week basis. Yet the industry normally considers newspapers published at these spaced intervals as part of the same category. This population is important because nondailies are typically the only source of information about the specific communities—be they urban or rural—that they serve. Often they leave coverage of world and national events to dailies and highlight only stories of local importance on their front pages.

The sample for this study is all nondaily newspapers in the United States. However, since almost 10,000 nondailies are published in this country, examining all nondailies would be an overwhelming task. Thus it was decided to limit the study to a random sample of 500 newspapers drawn from this population. To obtain this sample, a random numbers table was used to select 500 newspapers from the 10,000 nondailies listed in the *1998 Editor & Publisher Yearbook*. A letter was sent to each selected newspaper asking for a copy of its most recent edition.

The unit of analysis is the photo. Every photo (including mug shots) appearing in the sample of newspapers that was not used for a commercial (advertising) purpose was included. The photos were examined to determine the races of the people depicted. Photos were also classified based on their location in the newspaper and on their subject matter.

In constructing these categories, the number of people in each photo was not counted. Each photo was merely categorized as containing Caucasians or blacks. Ideally, photos would be categorized based on all races, but this system might lack the necessary reliability because of problems in accurately coding races. Because the coding was based primarily on the images of the people contained in the photos, some confusion in identifying racial type could result. Thus, the coding scheme also included the "None" (no people depicted) or "Race Undetermined" categories. Seventeen categories of subject matter were created based on the 14 categories used in a previous study (Lester, 1994), but with three more added including History, Agriculture, and Scenic/Weather. The necessity of including these three categories probably demonstrates the differences in coverage by nondailies and the large metro dailies used in the Lester study. For example, in many smaller nondailies, agriculture may be central to many of their communities whereas in large metro dailies it may only make the news when some other aspect of news value, such as Accident/Disaster, is involved.

Photo type was also coded. This categorization included all photos, front-page photos, dominant front-page photos, and sports photos. This categorization was used under the assumption that the front page is the showcase of the newspaper and the most important photos would appear in this location. The dominant photo is the largest and thus the most important photo on the front making it even more significant. Sports photos were also specifically coded because sports could be considered a stereotypical role for blacks in society, and this category could indicate if nondailies are depicting blacks in this role in disproportionate numbers.

All the material was coded by an independent researcher. To determine the reliability of the coding, 10% of the sample was tested by the authors for intercoder reliability for the categories of racial type and subject matter. Using Holsti's measure, intercoder reliability was 99.1% for the race category and 93.9% for the subject matter category. Both these figures suggest reliability in coding since a Holsti of over 90% is normally desirable.

In order to compare coverage of blacks in nondaily and daily newspapers, two earlier studies were used to provide the statistics for dailies. One showed the frequency of appearance of blacks in front-page daily photos (Traynes and Cook, 1977) while the other listed the subject matter of the photos in which blacks were depicted (Lester, 1994). These comparisons are of limited usefulness, especially in showing the frequency of depiction of blacks, because the Trayes and Cook study was conducted in 1976.

The quantification system is based on nominal units since only categories were counted.

Of the 500 randomly selected newspapers, 260 submitted a copy for a response rate of 52%. All submitted issues were published in either July or August 1998. The sample

TABLE 8.1
Depictions of Race by Photo Type

	Photo type			
	All photos (%)	Front-page photos (%)	Dominant photos (%)	Sport photos (%)
Race or Gender				
White Only	74.7	66.3	61.9	77.3
White Inclusive	77.5	69.3	66.5	81.7
Blacks Only	2.5	3.3	4.6	2.6
Blacks Inclusive	5.3	6.3	9.2	7.0

of newspapers contained 2,264 photos that were suitable for analysis. Of these, 676 were front-page photos, 152 were dominant front-page photos, and 273 were sports photos.

RESULTS

If the communities that the nondailies serve contain the same racial proportions as the country as a whole, African Americans are underrepresented because blacks appear in only 5.3% of all photos when roughly 12.1% (the percentage of blacks in the general population) would be the expected figure (Table 8.1). If blacks are underrepresented, they are given a place of prominence when they are depicted because the more important photos tend to contain a higher percentage of blacks (6.3% of front-page photos and 9.2% of dominant photos). The percentage of front-page and dominant photos containing Caucasians are both lower than the percentage of all photos in which they are depicted. Blacks are depicted in a higher percentage of sports photos than of all photos, but so are whites.

When the subject matter of the photos is considered, nondailies do appear to consign blacks to stereotypical roles. The percentage of photos containing blacks is higher than the percentage containing whites in the three stereotypical categories of Crime, Sports, and Entertainment (Table 8.2). In the race-blind categories of Accident/Disaster, War, Human Interest, Science, and Religion, blacks and whites are depicted in almost equal proportions with the exception of the Human-Interest category in which whites were depicted more frequently. Whites were depicted much more frequently in the important Politics category while blacks were more frequently associated with social problems. Blacks were depicted more frequently than whites in the Education category, but apparently their social events drew less attention than those of whites. Based solely on the photos appearing in nondailies, apparently only whites are engaged in agriculture in those communities.

TABLE 8.2
Depictions of Race by Subject Matter

Subject Matter	White (%)	Black (%)
Politics	8.0	4.1
Education	7.6	13.7
Agriculture	4.8	0.0
Human Interest/Recreation	9.4	6.9
Business/Economy	3.4	5.5
Entertainment	4.9	6.9
Sports	33.7	43.8
Social Events	18.2	5.5
Accident/Disaster	1.6	1.4
Religion	0.9	0.0
History	0.7	0.0
Scenic/Weather	0.4	0.0
Crime	1.4	4.1
Science	0.0	0.0
Social Problems	3.0	6.9
Health	2.0	1.4
War	0.1	0.0
Total	100.1	100.2

The overall depiction of blacks in nondailies pales in comparison to that by dailies (Table 8.3). Although the percentage of whites depicted by nondailies is also lower, it is not nearly as proportionately low as that for blacks.

If blacks are depicted less frequently in nondailies, at least the subject matter of the photos in which blacks are depicted speaks better for nondailies than for dailies (Table 8.4). Nondailies depicted blacks much less frequently in stereotypical photos and much more frequently in special-interest images than did dailies. Of particular note are the special-interest categories of Social Events, Business/Economy, and Education in which blacks were shown much more frequently in nondailies than in dailies. However, nondailies also depicted blacks much more frequently in association with social problems.

DISCUSSION

If the manner in which a group is represented in the media helps to determine how that group will be perceived by society, then nondailies are doing a better job of serving Caucasians than African Americans. In terms of sheer numbers, blacks are depicted much less frequently than their proportion of roughly 12.1% in the population would warrant. In terms of the types of depictions, blacks are depicted in stereotypical roles more frequently than whites are depicted in those same roles. To their credit, when

TABLE 8.3

Depictions of Race in Front-Page Photos by
Dailies and Nondailies

	Dailies (1976) (%)	Nondailies (1998) (%)
Race or Gender		
White	95.8	80.3
Black	13.0	7.3
Other or Race Undetermined	15.9	0.4

TABLE 8.4

African American Photos in Dailies and Nondailies
by Subject Matter

Subject Matter	Dailies (1978–1990) (%)	Nondailies (1998) (%)
Stereotypical Images		
Crime	5.7	4.1
Sports	52.5	43.8
Entertainment	11.1	6.9
Total	69.3	51.8
Race-Blind Images		
Accident/Disaster	1.3	1.4
War	0.7	0.0
Human Interest	12.1	6.9
Science	0.3	0.0
Religion	0.5	0.0
Total	14.9	8.3
Special-Interest Images		
Social Events	1.6	5.5
Politics/Government	5.1	4.1
Business/Economy	1.6	5.5
Social Problems	3.5	6.9
Education	3.3	13.7
Health	0.6	1.4
Total	15.7	37.1

nondailies do depict blacks, they have a slight tendency to place them in the front page and dominant photos that are of greater importance.

In comparing photo coverage of blacks by dailies and nondailies, the amount of coverage would indicate that dailies are doing a better job. However, the overall amount of coverage might be misleading. While dailies do depict blacks more, they also have a greater tendency to depict them in stereotypical roles, which, as Lester (1994) said, would contribute to the type of perception of blacks that many are striving to overcome.

Regarding those larger dailies, although the cities that they serve may have a significant, sometimes a majority, population of blacks and other minorities, the number of photographs do not reflect that percentage because the editors and publishers feel it is economically more feasible to focus on the white population (Trayes & Cook, 1977) because newspaper publishers mostly cater to the affluent middle and upper classes for profitability (Martindale, 1986). Yet a newspaper should serve the needs not only of the subscribers, but also of the whole population, whether they subscribe or not, according to Lester (1994).

Crime, sports, and entertainment still remain the primary categories in which African American pictures are used in dailies. While nondailies used these categories less frequently than did dailies, they still depicted blacks in these categories more than they did whites.

Lester contended that daily newspaper editors need to consider philosophies in selecting photos other than those based on always using the most dramatic, the finest technically, or the best composed photograph. "Editors should make sure that the moment captured on film by a photographer during a breaking news story is an accurate representation. A photograph of a news event, like its word counterpart, should always be truthful, set within a broader context and not stereotypical" (Lester, 1994, pp. 392–393).

Nondaily editors may use a different set of criteria in selecting photos—one that is based somewhat less on breaking news and somewhat more on community activities. However, in their own way, they need to ensure that their photos represent a representative depiction of their communities.

Whether the level of newspaper be daily or nondaily, the manner in which they depict the world is important for, as Newkirk observed, "It should, by now, go without saying that the media's role in moving us to action and shaping our perceptions is profound, as is their potential for changing those perceptions" (2000, p. xviii).

In regards to the usefulness of a content analysis, Wimmer and Dominick called it, "a valuable tool in answering many mass media questions" (1997, p. 111). In examining the visual communication question of photo coverage of blacks in nondailies, a content analysis served three of the five purposes for which Wimmer and Dominick said it is typically used. First of all, it allowed for a description of communication content by providing the data that showed the frequency and types of coverage that blacks receive in nondaily newspapers. Second, it allowed for a comparison between media content and the real world. By showing how frequently blacks are depicted, the data could be compared to the overall number of blacks in society. Third, it allowed for an assessment of the image of particular groups in society. Categorizing the types of photos in which blacks appeared allowed for some inferences to be drawn about how well blacks are depicted.

Determining the manner in which the media contribute to society's perception of certain groups in society is an important question for visual communication researchers because if, as Kenney said in an earlier chapter, we "see" the world through transparent photographs, then it is important to know what the world is seeing. In this chapter, a content analysis served as a useful tool in helping to answer a small part of this larger question.

REFERENCES

Berger, P. L., & Luckmann, T. (1966). *The social construction of reality*. Garden City, NY: Doubleday.

Carby, H. V. (1998). *Race men*. Cambridge, MA: Harvard University Press.

Coulson, D., Lacy, S., & Wilson, J. (2000, August). Weekly newspaper industry: A baseline study. Paper presented at the Association for Education in Journalism and Mass Communication Convention, Phoenix, Arizona.

Hoy, F. P. (1993). *Photojournalism: The visual approach* (2nd Ed.). Englewood Cliffs, NJ: Prentice-Hall.

Lester, P. (1991). *Photojournalism: An ethical approach*. Hillsdale, NJ: Lawrence Erlbaum Associates.

Lester, P. M. (1994, Summer). African-American photo coverage in four U.S. newspapers, 1937–1990. *Journalism Quarterly, 71*, 380–394.

Lewis, G. (1995). *Photojournalism: Content & technique* (2nd Ed.). Dubuque, IA: Brown and Benchmark.

Lyons, N. (1966). *Photographers on photography*. Englewood Cliffs, NJ: Prentice-Hall.

Martindale, C. (1986). *The white press and black America*. Westport, CT: Greenwood.

McLellan, M., & Steele, B. (2001, August). Photography and the vulnerable. *The American Editor, 26*, 34.

Miller, S. H. (1975). The content of news photos: Women's and men's roles. *Journalism Quarterly, 52*, 70–75.

Newkirk, P. (2000). *Within the veil: Black journalists, white media*. New York: New York University.

Pasternack, S., & Martin, D. R. (1985, Spring). Daily newspaper photojournalism in the Rocky Mountain West. *Journalism Quarterly, 62*, 132–135, 222.

Schudson, M. (1995). *The power of news*. Cambridge, MA: Harvard University Press.

Shoemaker, P. J., & Reese, S. D. (1996). *Mediating the message: Theories of influences on mass media content* (2nd Ed.). White Plains, NY: Longman.

Singletary, M. W. (1978, Autumn). Newspaper photographs: A content analysis, 1936–1976. *Journalism Quarterly, 55*, 585–589.

Singletary, M. W., & Lamb, C. (1984, Spring). News values in award-winning photos. *Journalism Quarterly, 61*, 104–108, 233.

Soloski, J. (1989). News reporting and professionalism: Some constraints on the reporting of the news. *Media, Culture and Society, 11*, 207–228.

Stempel, G. H., III. (1971, Summer). Visibility of Blacks in news and news-picture magazines. *Journalism Quarterly, 48*, 337–339.

Trayes, E. J., & Cook, B. L. (1977, Autumn). Picture emphasis in final editions of 16 dailies. *Journalism Quarterly, 54*, 595–598.

Walton, K. L. (1984). Transparent pictures: On the nature of photographic realism. *Critical Inquiry, 11*, 246–277.

Weaver, D. H., & Wilhoit, G. C. (1996). *The American journalist: U.S. news people at the end of an era*. Mahwah, NJ: Lawrence Erlbaum Associates.

Wimmer, R. D., & Dominick, J. R. (1997). *Mass media research, An introduction (5th Ed.)*. Belmont, CA: Wadsworth.

Wolf, R., & Grotta, G. L. (1985). Images: A question of readership. *Newspaper Research Journal, 6*, 30–36.

PART
IV

Visual Rhetoric

9

Theory of Visual Rhetoric

SONJA K. FOSS
University of Colorado at Denver

Visual rhetoric is the term used to describe the study of visual imagery within the discipline of rhetoric. As a branch of knowledge, rhetoric dates back to classical Greece and is concerned with the study of the use of symbols to communicate; in the most basic sense, *rhetoric* is an ancient term for what now typically is called *communication*. Visual rhetoric is a very new area of study within this centuries-old discipline. Not until 1970 was the first formal call made to include visual images in the study of rhetoric, which until then had been conceived exclusively as verbal discourse. In that year, at the National Conference on Rhetoric, convened by the Speech Communication Association, a recommendation produced by the conference participants called for an expansion of the study of rhetoric "to include subjects which have not traditionally fallen within the critic's purview; the non-discursive as well as the discursive, the nonverbal as well as the verbal" (Sloan et al., 1971, p. 221). The participants went on to suggest that a rhetorical perspective "may be applied to any human act, process, product, or artifact" that "may formulate, sustain, or modify attention, perceptions, attitudes, or behavior" (Sloan et al., 1971, p. 220).

The embrace of Kenneth Burke as a rhetorical theorist by the discipline of rhetoric also contributed to the emergence of rhetorical scholarship on visual images. For Burke, symbolicity included not only talk but also all other human symbol systems, and he encouraged analysis of symbols in all of their forms, including "mathematics, music, sculpture, painting, dance, architectural styles, and so on" (1966, p. 28). The door to the rhetorical study of images swung open farther as rhetorical scholars such as Douglas Ehninger (1972), whose standing among traditional rhetoricians was undisputed, proposed a definition of rhetoric that did not privilege verbal symbols and was sufficiently broad to include the visual. He defined rhetoric as the ways in which humans "may influence each other's thinking and behavior through the strategic use of symbols" and suggested as appropriate subject matter for rhetorical study art, architecture, dance, and dress (p. 3). Current definitions of rhetoric continue to support the expansion of rhetorical study beyond its traditional concern for verbal texts. Definitions of rhetoric such as "the social function that influences and manages meanings" (Brummett, 1991, p. xiv) suggest the easy fit between the visual image and rhetoric.

Although a natural affinity appears to exist between rhetoric and visual symbols, the inclusion of visual imagery in rhetorical study has not been the seamless process that the above narrative suggests. Proposals to expand rhetoric to encompass the visual were met at first with vociferous objections. Such objections included the concern that rhetoricians lack knowledge about visual images. Waldo W. Braden, for example, suggested that rhetorical critics simply are not trained to deal with images or other forms of nondiscursive rhetoric: "I argue that by inclination and training most of us are best qualified to study the speech or rhetorical act" (1970, p. 105). Another reason cited for the reluctance of rhetorical scholars to tackle the study of visual images had less to do with personal competencies and more with their desire to accumulate theoretical insights into rhetoric. This was Roderick P. Hart's position: "To the extent that scholars deviate from traditional, commonly shared understandings of what rhetoric is—by including non-social, mechanically mediated, and nonverbal phenomena in the rhetorical mix—they are, to that extent, necessarily forsaking the *immediate* implementation of the theoretical threads derived in previous studies of human, non-mediated, problematic, verbal interchanges." He suggested that, by studying the visual, "the cogency with which we as a field make theoretical distinctions will be severely opened to question" (1976, pp. 71–72). John H. Patton's response to proposals to study visual symbols was similar, and he advocated "the centrality of language in rhetorical theory" (1979, p. 143). He suggested that a redefinition of rhetoric to include nonlinguistic symbols represented a kind of rhetorical dislocation and a break from clear connections with a central theoretical core.

Other scholars of rhetoric suggested that imagery as a rhetorical form is tainted when compared to discourse in terms of its impact on public communication. Although these rhetoricians did not oppose the study of visual imagery, they privileged the study of discourse over the visual because of what they saw as the superior properties of discourse. Neil Postman, for example, argued that the visual epistemology of television "pollutes public communication" (1985, p. 28) and contributes to a decline in "the seriousness, clarity and, above all, value of public discourse" (1985, p. 29). Similarly, David Zarefsky suggested that rhetorical forms such as visual images "stand in for a more complex reality" (1992, p. 412), contributing to the deterioration of "a rich and vibrant concept of *argument*, of public deliberation" (p. 414). Kathleen Hall Jamieson asserted that images are particularly susceptible to a truncation of argument (1988, p. 240) and that the cognitive processing of images is less conscious and critical than the processing that occurs in the assignment of meaning to verbal discourse (Jamieson, 1992, p. 60).

That the study of visual images continued and, indeed, now flourishes in rhetorical studies is because of a number of factors. Primary among them is the pervasiveness of the visual image and its impact on contemporary culture. Images in the form of advertisements, television, film, architecture, interior design, and dress constitute a major part of the rhetorical environment, and such images now have the significance for contemporary culture that speeches once did. As much as rhetorical scholars may feel nostalgia for a culture in which public speeches were the symbols that had primary impact, that culture is gone. To restrict the study of symbol use only to verbal discourse means studying a miniscule portion of the symbols that affect individuals daily.

The study of visual imagery from a rhetorical perspective also has grown with the emerging recognition that visual images provide access to a range of human experience not always available through the study of discourse. Because theories of rhetoric have focused on and have been developed from the study of discursive symbols, they feature the dimensions of rhetorical processes that can be captured through discourse. Many human experiences, however, are unlike those captured by discursive symbols. Jean Y. Audigier explains that

> discursive language has definite limits to its usefulness. Because it employs conventional meaningful units according to rules of grammar and syntax, because each word has a relatively fixed meaning and the total meaning of this type of discourse is built up along a linear and logical pattern, it can only refer to the neutral aspects of our world of observation and thought. But there is another side of existence which escapes the control of discursive language. (1991, p. 4)

Human experiences that are spatially oriented, nonlinear, multidimensional, and dynamic often can be communicated only through visual imagery or other nondiscursive symbols. To understand and articulate such experiences require attention to these kinds of symbols.

Another force prompting the rhetorical study of visual imagery is the desire for greater comprehensiveness and inclusiveness in rhetorical theory. Hart (1976) was correct in suggesting that rhetorical theory has been created almost exclusively from the study of discourse. As a result, rhetoricians lack understanding of the conventions through which meaning is created in visual images and the processes by which images influence viewers. By situating visual imagery at the periphery of their rhetorical theories, rhetorical scholars have overlooked information about important communicative processes, resulting in inadequate, incomplete, and distorted understandings of symbols. Attention to visual symbols provides a more holistic picture of symbol use.

As a result of nascent efforts to explore visual phenomena rhetorically, the term *visual rhetoric* now has two meanings in the discipline of rhetoric. It is used to mean both a visual object or artifact and a perspective on the study of visual data. In the first sense, visual rhetoric is a product individuals create as they use visual symbols for the purpose of communicating. In the second, it is a perspective scholars apply that focuses on the symbolic processes by which images perform communication.

VISUAL RHETORIC AS A COMMUNICATIVE ARTIFACT

Conceptualized as a communicative artifact, visual rhetoric is the actual image rhetors generate when they use visual symbols for the purpose of communicating. It is the tangible evidence or product of the creative act, such as a painting, an advertisement, or a building and constitutes the data of study for rhetorical scholars interested in visual symbols. Visual rhetoric as an artifact is conceptualized broadly to include both two- and three-dimensional images such as paintings, sculpture, furniture, architecture, and interior design. The images included under the rubric of visual rhetoric are equally broad in terms of their functions. Both aesthetic and utilitarian images constitute visual rhetoric—works of art as well as advertisements, for example.

Not every visual object is visual rhetoric. What turns a visual object into a communicative artifact—a symbol that communicates and can be studied as rhetoric—is the presence of three characteristics. In other words, three markers must be evident for a visual image to qualify as visual rhetoric. The image must be symbolic, involve human intervention, and be presented to an audience for the purpose of communicating with that audience.

Symbolic Action

Visual rhetoric, like all communication, is a system of signs. In the simplest sense, a sign communicates when it is connected to another object, as the changing of the leaves in autumn is connected to a change in temperature or a stop sign is connected to the act of stopping a car while driving. To qualify as visual rhetoric, an image must go beyond serving as a sign, however, and be symbolic, with that image only indirectly connected to its referent. The shape and color of the stop sign, for example, have no natural relationship to the act of stopping a car as it is being driven; these dimensions of the sign were invented arbitrarily by someone who needed a way to regulate traffic. A stop sign, then, counts as visual rhetoric because it involves the use of arbitrary symbols to communicate.

Human Intervention

Visual rhetoric involves human action of some kind. Humans are involved in the generation of visual rhetoric when they engage in the process of image creation—painting a watercolor or taking a photograph, for example. The process involves the conscious decision to communicate as well as conscious choices about the strategies to employ in areas such as color, form, media, and size. Human intervention in visual rhetoric also may assume the form of transforming nonrhetorical visual images into visual rhetoric. For example, trees are not inherently visual rhetoric. They become so only when human beings decide to use them as rhetoric, as when they are brought into homes to symbolize the Christmas holiday or when they are used on brochures by environmentalists to create appeal for environmental causes. Visual rhetoric, then, requires human action either in the process of creation or in the process of interpretation.

Presence of an Audience

Visual rhetoric implies an audience and is concerned with an appeal either to a real or an ideal audience. Visual elements are arranged and modified by a rhetor not simply for self-expression—although that may constitute a major motive for the creator of an image—but also for communication with an audience. The creator of an image can serve as that audience; the audience need not be external to the rhetor. As Burke suggested, "A man can be his own audience, insofar as he, even in his secret thoughts, cultivates certain ideas or images for the effect he hopes they may have upon him; he is here what Mead would call 'an "I" addressing its "me"'; and in this respect he is being rhetorical quite as though he were using pleasant imagery to influence an outside audience rather than one within" (1974, p. 38). Even if the only audience for an image is its creator, some audience—and thus the implied act of communication—is present in visual rhetoric.

Visual rhetoric as artifact, then, is the purposive production or arrangement of colors, forms, and other elements to communicate with an audience. It is symbolic action in that the relationship it designates between image and referent is arbitrary, it involves human action in some part of the visual communication process, and it is communicative in its address to an audience. As a tangible artistic product, such a visual artifact can be received by viewers and studied by scholars as a communicative message.

VISUAL RHETORIC AS A PERSPECTIVE

The term *visual rhetoric* is used in the discipline of rhetoric to refer not only to the visual object as a communicative artifact. It also refers to a perspective scholars may take on a visual image or visual data. In this meaning of the term, *visual rhetoric* constitutes a theoretical perspective that involves the analysis of the symbolic or communicative aspects of visual rhetoric. Visual rhetoric as a theoretical perspective—or what might be called a *rhetorical perspective on visual imagery* to distinguish it from the other sense of *visual rhetoric*—is a critical-analytical tool or a way of approaching and analyzing visual data that highlights the communicative dimensions of images. It is a particular way of viewing images—a set of conceptual lenses through which visual images become knowable as communicative or rhetorical phenomena.

Visual rhetoric as a perspective is not a theory with constructs and axioms that describe specific rhetorical components of visual imagery; it is not composed of certain kinds of content or knowledge about visual imagery. In fact, the content that emerges from the application of the perspective is virtually limitless, bound only by the perspective's focus on how visual artifacts function communicatively. Because the perspective of visual rhetoric is relatively new in the discipline of rhetoric, the knowledge the perspective is beginning to produce about how visual images operate symbolically does not yet constitute a coherent theory. Relatively few studies have been done in which a rhetorical perspective has been applied to visual imagery, and it has been applied to such widely diverse and dispersed rhetorical dimensions, ranging from metaphor to ambiguity to argumentation, that identification of key constructs has not yet been undertaken. Neither have connections begun to be made among the key constructs as a result of the insights produced by the application of the perspective.

Key to a rhetorical perspective on images and what makes the perspective a rhetorical one is its focus on a rhetorical response to an image rather than an aesthetic one. An aesthetic response consists of a viewer's direct perceptual encounter with the sensory aspects of the image. Experience of a work at an aesthetic level might mean enjoying its color, sensing its form, or valuing its texture. There is no purpose governing the experience other than simply having the experience. In a rhetorical response, in contrast, meaning is attributed to the image. Colors, lines, textures, and rhythms in an image provide a basis for the viewer to infer the existence of images, emotions, and ideas. The visual rhetoric perspective's focus is on understanding rhetorical responses to images.

Another major feature of the rhetorical perspective on visual imagery is a particular conception of the audience for the images studied. Scholars who apply the perspective generally conceptualize the audience for the images they study as lay viewers. These scholars are interested in the impact of visual symbols on viewers who do not have technical knowledge in areas such as design, art history, aesthetics, or art education. They assume that viewers are individuals whose responses to images are not developed on the basis of art protocols or frameworks that privilege the art expert's knowledge of art traditions and conventions in attributing meaning to images. Lay viewers' responses to images are assumed to be constructed on the basis of viewers' own experiences and knowledge, developed from living and looking in the world. Scholars who adopt a perspective of visual rhetoric are most interested, then, in the ways in which visual symbols communicate to these lay audiences.

A rhetorical perspective on visual imagery also is characterized by specific attention to one or more of three aspects of visual images—their nature, function, and evaluation. The study of the nature of visual imagery is primary; to explicate function or to evaluate visual images requires an understanding of the substantive and stylistic nature of those images.

Nature of the Image

Essential to an application of a rhetorical perspective is explication of the distinguishing features of the visual image. Description of the nature of the visual rhetoric involves attention to two components—presented elements and suggested elements. Identification of the presented elements of an image involves naming the major physical features of the image. At this stage, the scholar describes such presented elements as space, which concerns the mass or size of the image; media, the materials of which the image is constructed; and shapes, the forms featured in the image. The scholar then identifies suggested elements, which are the concepts, ideas, themes, and allusions that a viewer is likely to infer from the presented elements, as, for example, the ornate gold leafing found on Baroque buildings might suggest wealth, privilege, and power (Kanengieter, 1990, pp. 12–13). Analysis of the presented and suggested elements allows the scholar to understand the primary communicative elements of an image and, consequently, to develop a meaning the image is likely to have for an audience.

Function of the Image

A second focus for scholars who take a rhetorical perspective on visual imagery can be the function or functions the visual rhetoric serves for an audience. Scholars who focus on function attempt to discover how the image operates for its viewers. *Function*, as it is used in this perspective, is not synonymous with *purpose*, which involves an effect that is intended or desired by the creator of the image. Scholars who adopt a rhetorical perspective on visual images do not see the creator's intentions as determining the correct interpretation of a work. Not only may the scholar not have access to biographical or historical evidence about the intentions of the creators of images, but the creators may not be able to give clear verbal accounts of their intentions and even may be mistaken about what motivated them. In addition, a privileging of creators' interpretations over the interpretations of viewers closes off possibilities for new ways of experiencing the image. Once an image is created, scholars who adopt a rhetorical perspective on imagery believe, it stands independent of its creator's intention.

The function of an image from a rhetorical perspective is the action the image communicates (Foss, 1994). The function that a painting of Elvis on velvet serves for an audience, for example, may be to memorialize the late singer. The interior design of a living room may function to create a feeling of warmth and coziness. The function of an abstract sculpture may be to encourage viewers to explore self-imposed limitations. These are the kinds of functions that scholars who adopt a rhetorical perspective on visual imagery seek to discover and explore.

Evaluation of the Image

A third area in which scholars may focus as they apply a perspective of visual rhetoric is evaluation. They may be interested in assessing an image, which can be done in a number of ways. Some scholars choose to evaluate an image using the criterion of whether it accomplishes the functions suggested by the image itself. If an image functions to memorialize someone, for example, such an evaluation would involve discovery of whether its media, colors, forms, and content actually accomplish that function. Other scholars choose to evaluate images by scrutinizing their functions, reflecting on their legitimacy or soundness determined largely by the implications and consequences of the functions. Such an assessment is made according to scholars' reasons for analyzing an image—to discover whether the image is congruent with a particular ethical system or whether it offers emancipatory potential, for example. A scholar analyzing a trailer house covered with a siding of plastic "rock," for example, might suggest that it mocks nature and encourages a disconnection from it, functions inexcusable in a world where this kind of disconnection is severely damaging the earth's resources. Whatever criteria are used, scholars who adopt a rhetorical perspective on images and choose to focus on evaluation are interested in improving the quality of the rhetorical environment by discriminating among images.

Studies of images from a rhetorical perspective—whether focused on nature, function, or evaluation—assume one of two forms. Some scholars deductively apply rhetorical theories and constructs to visual imagery to investigate questions about rhetoric and to contribute to existing rhetorical theories generated from the study of discourse. A second approach involves an inductive investigation of visual images designed to highlight features of the visual images themselves as a means to generate rhetorical theory that is expanded to include the visual.

DEDUCTIVE APPLICATION OF THE RHETORICAL
TO THE VISUAL

Scholars who apply a rhetorical perspective to visual imagery deductively use visual imagery to illustrate, explain, or investigate rhetorical constructs and theories formulated from the study of discourse. They begin with rhetorical constructs and theories and use them to guide them through the visual artifact. Underlying this approach is the assumption that visual images possess essentially the same characteristics that discursive symbols do. Consequently, the visual image is treated as a language-like symbol, and, in most of the deductive studies, discursive artifacts could have been used just as well as visual ones to investigate the rhetorical processes being explored and with similar outcomes. The result of these studies is a contribution to a rhetorical theory focused on verbal discourse. The influence between artifact and theory in these studies is unidirectional; the theory affects the understanding of the artifact, but what is discovered in the artifact has little effect on the nature of the theory. It remains a theory that describes symbolicity discursively, and analysis of the visual artifact largely affirms the discursive features of the theory.

Virtually any theory or construct from rhetorical theory can serve as a guiding analytical tool in the deductive analysis of images. Lester C. Olson (1990), for example, studied Benjamin Franklin's commemorative medal *Libertas Americana* as epideictic, deliberative, and apologetic rhetoric, while David S. Kaufer and Brian S. Butler (1996) applied the rhetorical canons of invention, organization, style, delivery, and memory to image design. Greg Dickinson (1997) analyzed the town of Old Pasadena using the construct of memory; Janis L. Edwards and Carol K. Winkler (1997) explored editorial cartoons of the photograph of the flag raising at Iwo Jima using the construct of appropriation; and Carole Blair, Marsha S. Jeppeson, and Enrico Pucci, Jr. (1991) used the concept of public memorializing to explicate the Vietnam Veterans Memorial. Electronic media, in which visual images often predominate, also have been the subject of studies designed to explore rhetorical theories or constructs in visual data. Janice Hocker Rushing (1986) analyzed space fiction films using the concept of myth; Kathleen Campbell (1988) applied the strategy of enactment to her analysis of the film *The Year of Living Dangerously*; and Karen Rasmussen and Sharon D. Downey (1991) used dialectical disorientation to explore Vietnam War films. In all of these studies, scholars applied a rhetorical theory or construct generated from discourse to visual data to generate insights into that rhetorical theory.

A more detailed example of the deductive application of a rhetorical perspective on visual images illustrates such an approach. Lawrence W. Rosenfield (1989) analyzed New York City's Central Park using the rhetorical construct of epideictic rhetoric. He applied features of epideictic rhetoric to the park such as repose, rhetorical sensibility, emblem and allegory, and ornamentation. Despite his focus on a visual artifact, the language in his analysis remained strikingly rooted in the discursive, a characteristic feature of the deductive approach to a rhetorical perspective on images. His discussion of repose included the statement, for example, that "[o]rators needed temporary respite from the cares of events, not to rest but to rejuvenate themselves. . . . The garden revitalized its user for a return to public activity" (1989, p. 239). His analysis of rhetorical sensibility included an exploration of the paradox of rhetorical sensibility that involves mutual influence: "the orator influences the audience by adapting to it. The Renaissance garden also fostered mutual dependence" (1989, p. 241). In epideictic rhetoric, he continued, the "rhetorician must capture the topic's essentials in a few instantly recognizable, highly suggestive strokes. . . . Likewise, the garden dweller was expected to move among and pause to gaze at a series of scenes whose mimetic features and continually altered aspects would bring vividly to mind ancient legends and reminders of noble deeds" (1989, p. 246). Rosenfield's application of the concept of epideictic rhetoric, a type of discursive rhetoric, to the visual artifact of Central Park produced results typical of deductive studies of images: Affirmation of the features of epideictic rhetoric and an understanding of the park very much in line with a discursive conception of the construct.

INDUCTIVE EXPLORATION OF THE VISUAL TO GENERATE THE RHETORICAL

A second approach to the application of a rhetorical perspective on visual imagery is the investigation of the features of visual images to generate rhetorical theory that takes into account the distinct characteristics of the visual symbol. Scholars who pursue this route begin with an exploration of visual images and operate inductively, generating rhetorical theories that are articulate about visual symbols. An assumption of scholars who proceed inductively from visual images is that visual images are different in significant ways from discursive symbols, and they are cautious about importing rhetorical theory developed from the study of discourse into the realm of the visual because of these differences. As Haynes suggested, "the fundamental conceptualizations of rhetorical process are dominated by the thought patterns and belief systems of literate culture" (1988, p. 72), and he reminds rhetorical theorists of the cognitive biases underlying rhetoric's focus on discourse.

Although debates continue about the precise ways in which visual images differ from discourse, some features of visual images clearly require attention to different elements and a different treatment of those elements from what discourse does. For example, images do not express a thesis or proposition in the way that verbal messages do; they appear to do so only because viewers attribute propositions to them. Images also lack the denotative vocabulary that characterizes visual imagery. To identify the smallest independent units of a visual image that would correspond to words is difficult, if not impossible. Even if agreement were reached on the definition of the minimal units within one image, these minimal units do not have the independent meanings and are not the uniquely differentiated characters that words are. Another difference between verbal and visual symbols is that language is general and abstract, while images are concrete and specific. Verbal discourse is able to deal with *book*, for example, as an abstract and not simply a unique concept, while images are tied to a physical form that requires them to deal in particularities.

As a result of such differences between visual images and discourse, scholars who take an inductive approach to the study of images focus on the qualities and functions of images to develop explanations of how visual symbols operate. They assume that these differences make enough difference so that rhetorical theory has to be developed anew from visual symbols if it is to be relevant to and take into account the dimensions of visual forms of rhetoric. Examples of this approach to the study of visual imagery include Kanengieter's (1990) exploration of the process by which messages are formulated from architecture; Kaplan's (1992) work on visual metaphors to distinguish visual from language-based metaphors; Foss's (1993) exploration of the construction of appeal in visual images; Chryslee's (1995) analysis of the process of viewership by which a rhetorical response to nonrepresentational art is developed; and Lancioni's (1996) discovery of techniques by which visual argument is created in archival photographs. Some scholars who employ the inductive approach seek to discern the meaning of particular visual symbols in an effort to discover how the process of meaning construction works in visual imagery. Foss's (1987) analysis of body art was an effort to discover how audience members organize and interpret the works to make them meaningful, and Reid (1990) analyzed Hieronymus Bosch's painting *The Hay-Wain* in an effort to derive meaning from the idiosyncratic work.

A study by Chryslee, Foss, and Ranney (1996) provides a detailed example of an inductive, image-based approach to the rhetorical analysis of images. Their objective in the study was to discover key elements of the process of visual argumentation. They began with the premise that although rhetorical theorists know a great deal about the process of argumentation as it occurs in discourse, virtually none of this knowledge is applicable to visual argumentation because of the properties that distinguish visual imagery from discursive symbols. They analyzed three images—the Eames shell chair; the Central Police Headquarters building in Columbus, Ohio; and a photograph of a dead German soldier from World War I—as data from which to begin to describe steps in the inferential process of using reasons to arrive at claims. Their analyses of the images revealed four elements involved in the process of developing a claim from an image. Presented facts are the physical data and features of an image and include design elements such as form, style, and medium. Feelings are affective states evoked in the viewer by an image. Knowledge is technical, cultural, or historical information accumulated by the viewer through experience or learning. Function is the use for which an image is employed outside of its form as an image. The argumentation process in each of the images makes use of these elements in different ways, and the authors suggested factors that may account for these variations.

As a perspective, visual rhetoric constitutes an approach to the analysis of visual artifacts. Its focus is on understanding the communicative dimensions of images through attention to their nature, function, or evaluation. The deductive and inductive approaches that are options in the perspective produce equally useful but different kinds of results. The deductive, rhetoric-based approach offers ease of connection to rhetorical theory. Because it begins with rhetorical theory and applies existing theory to visual data, theoretical connections are easily made between the visual and the verbal in the development and elaboration of rhetorical theory. The inductive, image-based approach, on the other hand, offers rhetorical expansion. Because it begins with the characteristics of images and builds rhetorical theory on the basis of those characteristics, this approach has the potential to expand rhetorical theory beyond the boundaries of discourse and to open up possibilities for recognizing the different kinds of epistemologies that underlie different kinds of symbolicity.

CONCLUSION

Visual rhetoric, as it is employed in the discipline of rhetoric, has two meanings. One refers to visual images themselves—visual communication that constitutes the object of study. The second meaning references a perspective or approach rhetorical scholars adopt as they study visual rhetoric. Together, these two senses of the term point to the need to understand how the visual operates rhetorically in contemporary culture. Visual rhetoric, as communication data to be studied and as an approach to those data, suggests the need to expand understanding of the multivarious ways in which symbols inform and define human experience and constitutes a call to expand rhetorical theory, making it more inclusive in its encompassing of visual as well as verbal symbols.

REFERENCES

Audigier, J. Y. (1991). *Connections*. New York: Lanham.

Blair, C., Jeppeson, M. S., & Pucci, E., Jr. (1991). Public memorializing in postmodernity: The Vietnam Veterans Memorial as prototype. *Quarterly Journal of Speech, 77*, 263–288.

Braden, W. W. (1970). Rhetorical criticism: Prognoses for the Seventies—A symposium: A prognosis by Waldo W. Braden. *Southern Speech Journal, 36*, 104–107.

Brummett, B. (1991). *Rhetorical dimensions of popular culture*. Tuscaloosa: University of Alabama Press.

Burke, K. (1966). *Language as symbolic action: Essays on life, literature, and method*. Berkeley: University of California Press.

Burke, K. (1974). *A rhetoric of motives*. Berkeley: University of California Press.

Campbell, K. (1988). Enactment as a rhetorical strategy in *The Year of Living Dangerously*. *Central States Speech Journal, 39*, 258–268.

Chryslee, G. J. (1995). The construction of a rhetorical response to visual art: A case study of *Brushstrokes in Flight*. Unpublished doctoral dissertation, Ohio State University.

Chryslee, G. J., Foss, S. K., & Ranney, A. L. (1996). The construction of claims in visual argumentation: An exploration. *Visual Communication Quarterly, 3*, 9–13.

Dickinson, G. (1997). Memories for sale: Nostalgia and the construction of identity in Old Pasadena. *Quarterly Journal of Speech, 83*, 1–27.

Edwards, J. L., & Winkler, C. K. (1997). Representative form and the visual ideograph: The Iwo Jima image in editorial cartoons. *Quarterly Journal of Speech, 83*, 289–310.

Ehninger, D. (1972). *Contemporary rhetoric: A reader's coursebook*. Glenview, IL: Scott, Foresman.

Foss, S. K. (1987). Body art: Insanity as communication. *Central States Speech Journal, 38*, 122–131.

Foss, S. K. (1993). The construction of appeal in visual images: A hypothesis. In D. Zarefsky (Ed.), *Rhetorical movement: Essays in honor of Leland M. Griffin* (pp. 210–224). Evanston, IL: Northwestern University Press.

Foss, S. K. (1994). A rhetorical schema for the evaluation of visual imagery. *Communication Studies, 45*, 213–224.

Hart, R. P. (1976). Forum: Theory-building and rhetorical criticism: An informal statement of opinion. *Central States Speech Journal, 27*, 70–77.

Haynes, W. L. (1988). Of that which we cannot write: Some notes on the phenomenology of media. *Quarterly Journal of Speech, 74*, 71–101.

Jamieson, K. H. (1988). *Eloquence in an electronic age: The transformation of political speechmaking*. New York: Oxford University Press.

Jamieson, K. H. (1992). *Dirty politics: Deception, distraction, and democracy*. New York: Oxford University Press.

Kanengieter, M. R. (1990). Message formation from architecture: A rhetorical analysis. Unpublished doctoral dissertation, University of Oregon.

Kaplan, S. J. (1992). A conceptual analysis of form and content in visual metaphors. *Communication, 13*, 197–209.

Kaufer, D. S., & Butler, B. S. (1996). *Rhetoric and the arts of design*. Mahwah, NJ: Lawrence Erlbaum Associates.

Lancioni, J. (1996). The rhetoric of the frame revisioning archival photographs in *The Civil War*. *Western Journal of Communication, 60*, 397–414.

Olson, L. C. (1990). Benjamin Franklin's commemorative medal, *Libertas Americana*: A study in rhetorical iconology. *Quarterly Journal of Speech, 76*, 23–45.

Patton, J. H. (1979). Permanence and change in rhetorical theory. *Central States Speech Journal, 30*, 134–143.

Postman, N. (1985). *Amusing ourselves to death: Public discourse in the age of show business.* New York: Penguin.

Rasmussen, K., & Downey, S. D. (1991). Dialectical disorientation in Vietnam War films: Subversion of the mythology of war. *Quarterly Journal of Speech, 77,* 176–195.

Reid, K. (1990). *The Hay-Wain:* Cluster analysis in visual communication. *Journal of Communication Inquiry, 14,* 40–54.

Rosenfield, L. W. (1989). Central Park and the celebration of civic virtue. In T. H. Benson (Ed.), *American Rhetoric: Context and Criticism* (pp. 221–265). Carbondale: Southern Illinois University Press.

Rushing, J. H. (1986). Mythic evolution of "the new frontier" in mass mediated rhetoric. *Critical Studies in Mass Communication, 3,* 265–296.

Sloan, T. O., Gregg, R. B., Nilsen, T. R., Rein, I. J., Simons, H. W., Stelzner, H. G., & Zacharias, D. W. (1971). Report of the Committee of the Advancement and Refinement of Rhetorical Criticism. In L. F. Bitzer & E. Black (Eds.), *The prospect of rhetoric: Report of the National Developmental Project* (pp. 220–227). Englewood Cliffs, NJ: Prentice-Hall.

Zarefsky, D. (1992). Spectator politics and the revival of public argument. *Communication Monographs, 52* 411–414.

10

A Visual Rhetorical Study of a Virtual University's Promotional Efforts

KEITH KENNEY

University of South Carolina

In the theory chapter, Sonja Foss generally defined visual rhetoric as the study of the use of visual symbols to influence and manage meanings. This chapter explains how visuals can be analyzed as rhetorical phenomenon (rather than as aesthetic ones).

Visual rhetoric does not follow the social scientific model of research, so essays do not follow the format of literature review, then methods section, followed by findings and conclusions. Instead, visual rhetoric follows the interpretive paradigm, and the end product is a critical analytical essay in which authors state a thesis and then provide support for their arguments.

The format of these essays may vary, but the components of rhetorical criticism are consistent. They include analysis of historical context, formal description of the visuals, identification of the function of the visuals, and evaluation of the function. These four components of criticism are not distinguishable in the final essay. Instead, critics integrate all the material into a unified essay according to whatever format they believe is most suitable. This chapter maintains the distinct stages of rhetorical criticism in order to demonstrate how the process of rhetorical criticism can be applied to visuals.

Rhetorical criticism may be confused with formal criticism in the field of aesthetics because both discuss some stylistic aspect of pictures (such as metaphor) or attempt to categorize the picture according to form (as in genre criticism). The basic distinction between a rhetorical approach and a formalist-aesthetic one is probably the attention given to intent and effect. For instance, identifying an advertising picture as a "trope" (which is simply rhetorical terminology for *metaphor*) and perhaps going further to categorize the trope as a "metonymy" (in which juxtaposition alone points to similarities) would be a typical formalist-aesthetic approach. By stopping there, the analysis would be rhetorical only in terminology—it is essentially a formalist exercise. If, however, critics continue and use historical context to argue about the intentions behind the use of a trope, then the analysis has started to become rhetorical.

Rhetorical criticism assumes that each aspect of the picture was intentionally selected in order to try to get someone else to think, feel, or something. To that end, the rhetor will select from among a range of options the tone, color, perspective, moment, subject matter, and so on that he or she feels is most likely to have the desired effect among the intended audience.

All pictures, including documentary photographs, are unavoidably selective and, therefore, rhetorical. When describing a picture and inferring intent, the critic considers not only what has been selected, but also what is not shown. Further, it is axiomatic that how something is shown is as important as what is shown. Rhetorical critics also consult external sources in search of information about the rhetor, the audiences exposed to the visual, and the persuasive forces, including other rhetorical messages, operating on the visual. Only then can critics begin to determine why the rhetor made particular artistic and strategic choices when creating the visual.

Historically, critics considered the function of a message from the sender's perspective; they wanted to evaluate how well the message conveyed the rhetor's intentions. Today, however, the function of a visual is considered to be determined by the audience rather than the creator because a message, once completed, stands independent of its production. After identifying the function of a visual, one must then assess how well that function is fulfilled. Connections are made between the identified function and the means used to achieve that function. The critic again looks at subject matter, medium, forms, colors, organization, craftsmanship, and context, and the picture is compared to other images with the same or a similar function to evaluate its success. Attempting to gauge an actual effect of some sort, however, is better than merely speculating about audience response. In addition to effects, critics also evaluate a visual's success in terms of truth criteria, ethical criteria, and artistic criteria.

Rhetorical critics have developed a number of perspectives for examining a text, but in general, these tools have been applied to written texts rather than visual texts. Traditionally, critics evaluated speeches in terms of the rhetor's "invention," "arrangement," "style," "delivery," and "memory." This rationalistic perspective has occasionally been adapted and applied to visuals. Medhurst and DeSousa (1981), for example, applied this perspective to the study of political cartoons. Many others have applied part of the perspective, in general "style," to the study of visuals, but in this author's opinion, a rationalistic perspective is not useful for analyzing visuals (see Kenney & Scott, 2002). Other perspectives are psychosocial criticism and dramatistic criticism, which includes the analysis of symbols, identification, structure, and Burke's pentad. Other tools for analysis include the study of narratives, fantasy themes, myths, ideographs, representative forms, metaphors, and genres. Unlike research in the social science paradigm, where agreed on methodological procedures must be followed in a strict manner, rhetorical critics are encouraged to mix-and-match analytical tools and even to invent new ones for analyzing their texts. The final essay is judged on its effectiveness in helping readers understand and appreciate the text, and to make informed judgments about about how well the rhetor succeeded in communicating his or her intentions and about how the phenomenon affected an audience. The means to the end are not so important.

Rhetorical essays generally focus on a single speech, painting, monument, or other "discourse" or "text." An example is selected because it has been involved in controversy and/or because of its potential impact and consequences. Because the essay focuses on a single example, no attempt is made to generalize to a larger group of the phenomena. Rhetorical criticism does, however, help us understand how people use symbols to influence one another.

The remainder of this chapter describes the marketing materials of a virtual university and evaluates the presumed effects of the university's Web site and its viewbooks given the rhetors' intentions of persuading students to enroll at the school. The first section puts the marketing goals of the virtual university within the historical context of marketing higher education in general. It also provides background information about the school, its owner and president. The second section describes the visuals in the viewbooks and on the Web site(s). This description follows the spirit of both Aristotle and Burke. Aristotle defined rhetoric as "the faculty wherein one discovers the available means of persuasion in any case whatsoever" (1991, p. 36). Kenneth Burke defined rhetoric as the use of symbols to persuade creatures who by their nature respond to symbols. The description, therefore, refers to metaphors and symbols selected by the rhetors, as well as the use of myths, cliches, identification, and arguments in the visuals and the design of the materials. The final section evaluates the visuals in terms of the rhetors' intentions as well as in comparison with promotional materials used by other virtual universities. Some evaluation in terms of "truthfulness" are "art" also are made.

HISTORICAL CONTEXT

Online education and virtual universities have had an increasing impact on the huge market of higher education. Some people have predicted that one third of the existing independent U.S. colleges and universities will close in the next 10 years because of increased competition for tuition dollars and because of declining support for traditional schools from state legislators (Dunn, 2000). Controversy over the quality of education at virtual universities is partly because of suspicion of the new and unknown, but concerns are legitimate because many of the schools are not yet accredited and they have not yet established a history of good job placements. Some people are concerned about the quality of instruction and the lack of an immersive experience where people interact face to face.

Virtual universities are defined as schools whose physical location is of secondary importance or nonexistent. They provide educational certificates and degrees via distance learning, and increasingly their preferred method of delivery is the Web. Virtual universities may be publicly funded, private, or they may be associated with corporations or publishers. They are important because they provide a less expensive alternate to traditional brick-and-mortar schools, and many "nontraditional" students have begun to choose virtual universities. Unlike residential colleges, there are no costs associated with building maintenance, and class sizes (and tuition dollars) can grow with few negative consequences. Virtual universities appeal to people who cannot commute to the educational institution of their choice and who cannot attend classes at the times classes are scheduled. With asynchronous delivery on the Web, virtual university students can take classes and interact with classmates and professors at any time. They can live any-where and move as often as they need (or like) without concern. Virtual universities are particularly useful for people in rural areas who need to satisfy states' requirements for certification or annual continuing professional education courses. Most students at virtual universities are less interested in athletic and social programs and more interested in improving a skill or receiving certification.

Marketing a virtual university differs from marketing traditional schools. Brick-and-mortar schools generally use viewbooks to distinguish themselves from other college options, while virtual universities generally rely on their Web sites. Traditional schools brag about the following, which are seldom relevant to virtual universities:

- Historical traditions of the college
- Campus location
- Campus safety
- Success of athletic teams
- State-of-the-art facilities
- Opportunities to study abroad

Brick-and-mortar schools also brag about the following assets, for which virtual universities could be highly competitive:

- Innovative approaches to learning
- Leadership of administrators
- Accessibility of professors
- Strength of the academic program
- Affordable and/or availability of financial aid
- Job placement of graduates

(See Durgin, 1998; Kealy & Rockel, 1987; Wright, 1995; Braxton, 1990.)

In viewbooks of brick-and-mortar schools, the "purpose" of photographs is to show what the campus looks like and answer questions such as "Where will I live?" and "Where can I eat?" Photographs of ivy-covered brick buildings with white columns serve as metaphors for the "ivory tower." Photographs of large old trees on open grass-covered areas help perpetuate the agrarian myth that pastoral settings nurture young minds and develop students' morals away from the temptations of the city (Severino, 1995). Viewbook pictures commonly show interpersonal relationships among students and between students and professors, and in these pictures, professors seem like parents, friends seem like siblings, and the campus seems to offer the comforts and resources of home (Miller, 2000). Some viewbooks have a unifying visual symbol (a globe in every photo at Mansfield University), a common analogy (college is an intellectual safari at MIT), or a theme (preparation for the fast-paced future at ITT Technical Institute).

The "purpose" of visuals marketing virtual universities remains the same as for marketing traditional schools—to give prospective students a "feeling" for the educational experience. Although with virtual universities there is no place to describe, virtual universities still publish pictures that resemble the images of brick-and-mortar schools. Virtual university pictures commonly show the base of a column, teacher-student interaction, or student-student interaction even though such things may not exist. Virtual universities also use generic stock photographs, such as a picture of a keyboard, mouse, or globe.

Jones International University (JIU) was selected as an exemplar of virtual universities because it is the first "fully online, fully accredited" university. Other colleges or universities may have been "fully online" earlier, but without accreditation they have less credibility and therefore pose less competition to location-based schools. JIU received accreditation in March 1999 from the North Central Association of Colleges and Schools, which is the same accreditation organization that sanctions traditional schools in that region, such as Northwestern and the University of Chicago. Accreditation is important because it means that a school has been recognized by the U.S. Department of Education, that the program has integrity, and that course units can be transferred. Prospective students can assume that minimum-quality standards of education are met and they are more likely to qualify for employer-tuition-reimbursement plans.

The number of educational programs as well as the number of students at JIU have risen dramatically since accreditation. In March 1999, JIU offered a bachelor's and a master's degree program in business communications with a total of 74 degree students. Two years later, it offers 15 degree programs (7 MBA; 6 MEd; 1 MA, and 1 BA in business communication) and 43 professional education certificate programs (Business Wire, March 5, 2001). As of June 2001, it had enrolled a total of 5,000 students (Curtin, 2001). Since accreditation, tuition also has risen substantially. In March 1999, students paid $600 for a three-credit bachelor's degree course and $700 for a master's course (Stern, 1999). In March 2001, the numbers were $690 and $825, respectively, plus additional fees.

JIU is a for-profit institution launched in 1995 by Glenn Jones with startup capital he earned in the cable TV industry. The son of a Pennsylvania coal miner, Jones founded Jones Intercable in 1967 with $400 borrowed against his Volkswagen (jonesinternational.edu) and went on to build the nation's third largest cable operator, putting cable TV in more than 1 million homes in 17 states. Over the past 30 years, Jones has created more than 20 technology companies in the Internet, e-commerce, software, education, entertainment, radio and cable television programming industries. He is a successful entrepreneur "who knows how to deliver customer service, market his ideas, and target an audience" (Stern, 1999, p. 16).

Pease, the president of JIU, has a Ph.D. from the Annenberg School of Communication at USC, but her only teaching experience was as an adjunct lecturer at various schools (Stern, 1999).

Pease said that JIU had spent more than $2.5 million developing its courses and much of that went to paying content experts (Blumenstyk, 1999). Courses run eight weeks and generally have 25 students.

DESCRIPTION OF VISUALS AND IDENTIFICATION OF FUNCTION

Unlike other virtual universities, whose marketing materials were examined for this essay, Jones International University mails prospective students one of several viewbooks, with the thickest one being about 40 pages. The viewbook photographs are discussed in terms of visual theme, audience, tone and structure.

The most recurring visual theme in these viewbooks is the value of computers. Pictures show people with portable computers at the kitchen table, on a boat, in bed, outside while planting seeds, at an outdoor cafe, and so on, as they stay "wired" to the world, including JIU classes. It seems that all good things, such as education, socialization, and discussion with classmates and teachers, comes from computers, so JIU is implying that one must have a computer to be effective in today's society, and what better way to utilize a computer than to help build your education and professional capabilities through JIU? The visual message of convenience is reinforced with the following text (from JIU's Web site):

> At Jones International University®, Ltd., we understand you have a busy life. That's why JIU is dedicated to giving adult learners, whose lives can't always accommodate a classroom schedule, the same access to education as more traditional students. JIU provides vast educational opportunities by delivering our curriculum via the Internet. Whether it's three o'clock in the morning or eight o'clock at night, when you're online, class is "in session." Welcome to Jones International University®, Ltd.!

The audience for JIU can be seen in viewbook examples of visual "identification," commonly defined by rhetorical critics as the symbolic process that allows us to recognize and acknowledge our shared experiences. In one image, a woman in her 30s sits at her kitchen table in a T-shirt and unbuttoned flannel shirt, alone and totally relaxed with a cup of coffee on the table. Ever diligent, she is reading a book with her left hand, and her right hand is touching her laptop keyboard. A bowl of fruit, a vase of purple Iris, and a cup of coffee make it seem like everyone's home. In another photo, a man with a receding hairline eats a bowl of cereal as he concentrates on a computer monitor next to file folders on a desk in his living room. They seem like middle-class people, not models. Viewbook photos also show well-groomed people in their late 20s in tailored suits at corporate meetings, which reinforces the message of "success." Men and women appear equally, and African Americans, Asians, and Hispanics are well represented, which reinforces the message of "diversity."

The tone of the viewbook photos is direct. They are not "personal" because we seldom make eye contact, yet they are not "distant" because most people's upper bodies fill the frame—an example of a medium shot and "normal" interpersonal space. They are not truly "elegant" because they are supposed to have a spontaneous feel, but neither are they "realistic" because the background objects are too perfect.

The design of the viewbooks seems unified, consistent, and coherent because all viewbook photos have a consistent style. On the other hand, the style was unremarkable, except for the fact that several images had tilted horizons, which normally is considered a "mistake," but also can be viewed as more "hip," "artistic," or "energetic." Text and photos were not integrated well, so it seems the design was determined more by the art director's need for a picture to break the monotony of text than by any urgency to communicate a specific message. "Patriotic" colors are used for the viewbook headlines. Main headlines are red, important subheads are blue, the next level of subheadings are red again, so red and blue stand out on the white page.

In addition to the viewbooks, every "page" of the JIU Web site was examined in February, March, and August 2001. The importance of the Web as a source of information for high school students was underscored by a recent *Newsweek* article, which stated that "The Net is one of the most pervasive—if not *the* most pervasive—tools for college information" (Begun, 2000, p. 97).

FEBRUARY 2001 SITE

The JIU logo is the first thing that appears as the Web site is loading. The circular design in strong colors simply states "Jones International University" along the top arc and "University of the Web" on the bottom arc. In the purple middle of the circle is the word "JONES" (black text on white field) and a white, elongated "J" that covers the entire depth of the circle, off-center to the right. The logo lacks traditional "crest" qualities (shields, mythological symbols, Latin text, etc.) that usually symbolize humankind's quest for knowledge in higher education. It is more of a corporate logo that gives a crisp, sharp, and efficient image, which serves as a metaphor for JIU's educational philosophy: no-nonsense, professional education for adult students. This logo remains in the upper left corner of every page that one visits on the site.

The first sentence of the homepage states that you don't need ivy-covered walls or cheerleaders to be credible. The statement is deceiving, clever, and effective. Of course you don't need CHEERLEADERS to be credible. Nor do ivy-covered walls mean a quality education will be gained. The statement cleverly disparages the credibility of brick-and-mortar schools while implying the credibility of virtual schools.

On the right-hand side of the homepage are four pictures, each in different duotones (gray, blue, green, and yellow). Each provides a link to a particular topic—MBA Programs, Masters of Education in e-learning, Bachelor of Arts, and Professional and Executive Certificates.

The "MBA Programs" link portrays a 30-something-year-old black man in a suit (presumably at work) involved in a serious face-to-face discussion with a white, female coworker against a backdrop of a blue wall that features window frame shadows (presumably, a corporate office setting). This image is obviously a staged shot, but it relays to the viewer the program's purpose, which is to help you achieve professional success and put you in a position to be involved in serious business matters.

The "Masters of Education in e-learning" photo is simply a head-and-shoulders shot of a 30-something white female looking into the camera, slightly smiling and slightly resting her chin on her hand. The woman appears confident, and her short brown hair gives the viewer the impression of an executive in the office, not an educator. JIU more than likely did not have any "education" photos to use, so they used an image of someone that could look like a school teacher in order to be consistent with the text.

The next photo, "Bachelor of Arts," shows a white male with a laptop and a female discussing something they are obviously viewing on his computer's screen. They are sitting on the steps of a gray and white building with Greek columns, similar to buildings on traditional campuses. In emphasizing the column, which has come to symbolize the concepts of "knowledge" or "university," the photograph shows that JIU still holds traditional academic values in high esteem, which might reassure prospective students and employers. The image, however, also contradicts what JIU previously asserted—that "ivy-covered walls" and face-to-face interaction are not necessary to acquire a rewarding experience in higher education.

The fourth visual, "Professional and Executive Certificates," displays a close-up of hands using a computer keyboard. It implies that JIU can offer you (or your employees) the best possible professional skills and training in today's competitive world. As an employee, these skills will advance your career. As an employer, your staff will receive the latest training, keeping you one step ahead of the competition.

With these four photos, JIU tries to stress diversity among its students (as do most college recruiting materials). The viewer sees two males (one black, one white), three females (white), and what appear to be black female hands.

Photos of the nine students (six women and three men) on other Web pages were duotones with a blue-black ink, so they had a kind of old-fashioned feeling. Two of the images lacked resolution, probably because they were enlargements of one small section of larger photographs. Two showed 1950s-type mothers who get their hair styled every Friday. Two of the three men were dressed formally—either a suit or a tuxedo—and seemed as if they would make serious accountants. In contrast, two images showed self-confident younger people who seemed quite pleased with their appearance and future prospects.

On the "alumni" pages of the Web site, photographs generally showed older women in casual clothes with too much makeup, who looked like housewives getting a degree in their spare time. These photos were probably taken in students' homes by family and friends because the backgrounds are cluttered with home furnishings. Quality control was low as one image was out of focus and dark, while another was too small. Sometimes harsh shadows appeared on the walls behind students' heads from the use of direct flash, or no light reached students' eyes because no flash was used. Sometimes the camera was too close to the student (leading to uncomfortable interpersonal distance) and sometimes too far away (leading to low legibility of facial details). Sometimes students had a greenish tint because they were underneath fluorescent lights. Patti, the first graduate, had an extra-large image that obviously was taken by a professional. She stood in a cap-and-gown next to a computer monitor displaying a different image of someone in graduation garb.

JIU's art directors use a restrained, functional design. Some Web sites seem over-crowded with hyperlinks and animated text that give the same impression as discount retailers with their crowded newspaper ads, or pushy car dealers with their spinning, "exploding" sales-type on television. The pace of Jones' site is slower, and a visual impression of sincerity is created by avoiding the gimmicky use of animated text.

MARCH 2001 SITE

This version of JIU's Web site gives a "strictly business" message. Gone are all photos of students and alumni, professors and administrators and staff, which made JIU's site seem more personal and more "real" than sites of other online universities. No more pictures of keyboards, "mice," globes, clocks, or diplomas as only five photos remain (four on the homepage). The video of President Pease delivering a graduation speech also has been deleted. The almost text-only Web site now closely resembles JIU's competitors, although a couple of new animations appear under "demo."

"Demo" shows what the "reality" of interacting with other students, professors, and advisors would be like via the computer. These pages are mostly animation, but some show headshots of "students" and "faculty" or "administrators," as they "converse" via the laptop, discussing things like homework assignments and degree guidance, or using the library and bookstore services, and the like. The demo uses many moving arrows and other animated visuals to show "motion" and "interaction" between headshots of people and to reiterate how technology is of utmost importance.

The main visual that "leads" the viewer through the demo is the ubiquitous "white hand with index finger extended" icon that in so many ways symbolizes computer technology, especially the Internet. This icon takes the viewer through the demo, showing how easy it is to earn a degree via the Internet. The icon "clicks" so the student can hand in and discuss her homework, ask questions of faculty and counselors, buy books, "go to" the library, and so on. In the "graduation" portion, the white hand icon clicks onto an animated scrolled-up diploma tied with a ribbon. With JIU, you can "click your way to your future."

The "buy books" animation consists of the following animated sequence:

1. A simple drawing of portable computer appears and on its monitor is the heading: JIU Bookstore. Next to the portable is a box.
2. A moving cursor then drags a book icon from the monitor window and places it in the box. This action repeats twice more.
3. Then a mailbox appears and the (book) box is placed into the mailbox. The red flag goes up.

This "explanation" of how one may order books from JIU's online bookstore is not helpful; even if the necessary information was provided, it would be insulting because of its kindergarten nature.

In the "world map" section of the demo, "students" of different ethnic backgrounds (white woman, black male, Asian male) pop up on the screen from different locations around the page, thereby demonstrating JIU's accessibility from anywhere. Although each student is of a different ethnicity, all the models portray an image of "American" citizens. For example, the Asian student looks like an Asian American, not someone taking the class from his home in Japan, Korea, or wherever, and there are no visual signs that the student lives abroad. As each student submits his or her work and thoughts on a project, a digital "clock" rolls (like a stopwatch) to the time when, presumably, each student submitted his or her message. Unfortunately, JIU makes each student's clock stop on the same date and time, which does not promote each student's choice in "attending" class. This message would have been much better had the times been different; after all, each student makes his or her own schedule.

An interesting metaphor appears on many Web "pages." In elongated, thin white type, "JIU" appears in front of an orange color that was animated to resemble daybreak, with an orange sky getting brighter as the "sun" rises. The message of this revised logo appears to be that JIU marks the dawn of a new era of education—online universities.

AUGUST 2001 SITE

On the "virtual graduation" pages, the illustrated scrolled diploma and mortarboard symbols are ubiquitous as JIU constantly reminds visitors of the ultimate goal: graduation and celebration. This is similar to the marketing efforts of many traditional schools that highlight graduation by showing photos of happy graduates posing with family or fellow students, mortarboards thrown in the air, and so on. JIU tries its best to conjure the notion of a gala, but falls short. There is at least one photo of a graduate holding a diploma with (what appears to be) an ex-teacher, but the "graduation party" is merely an hour-long chat session on a discussion board. Visitors who click on the "faculty" link will see photos of professors in full regalia. Such symbols of traditional universities appear to contradict JIU's symbols of today's high-tech, fast-paced educational environment.

Erin Brockovich was the "guest speaker" at JIU's 2001 virtual graduation. She was a low-income mother who took a secretarial job at a law office and eventually "cracked" a multimillion-dollar case against a chemical company that was polluting public water in a California town. She was financially rewarded for her heroic deeds, and, because of the film, has become a guest speaker on a national scale. She is described on the Web site as understanding what it takes to "overcome adversity" and to find the time to balance "work, family and lifelong learning." In other words, JIU has spun her celebrity status to appeal to prospective students, implicitly saying, "Here is someone that has a family and understands the value of learning. If she can do it, so can you." Interestingly, it does not say if she has ever graduated from a college, let alone a virtual one.

Another noteworthy item is the pair of cartoon feet that "walk" us through the steps of "virtual graduation." The cartoon feet are similar to those used on Hang Ten™ merchandise, and as they "walk" from one link to another, they remind us of the paths that used to decorate children's cereal boxes. They are meant to to show graduation is a fun and easy event, but they trivialize the entire "tradition" of graduation.

A visual symbol that is encountered throughout many pages of the site is the globe. On the calendar page, a horizontal banner appears at the top that shows a close-up of a hand on a mouse at far left, which fades into a computer keyboard at the center, which fades into a globe image at far right. JIU is visually saying that the "world is at your fingertips" if you choose to attend its school. As part of the library pages, the globe and/or map image is used repeatedly to remind visitors that they are "connected to the world" (and any books or sources in the world) if they use JIU's library.

EVALUATION OF THE FUNCTION OF VISUALS

For established brick-and-mortar schools, many people can influence prospective students—high school teachers, university students and alumni, and other high school students (Kealy & Rockel, 1987)—but given the newness of virtual universities, such sources are likely to be silent about online education. Other activities are also impossible or unlikely, including campus visits and meetings with faculty members. Nor are virtual universities likely to be mentioned in guidebooks and reference books. Viewbooks and Web sites, including photos, therefore, take on increased importance.

JIU's viewbook pictures of portable computers do a good job of visually persuading potential students that JIU provides convenience and innovative approaches to learning. Photos are better than words at saying online education makes you powerful, connected, and free. The Web sites, however, do not support this message, which presumably was intended by JIU owners/administrators. The Web sites lack pictures of people using portable computers in varied settings as well as pictures of people interacting.

JIU's logo reminds viewers of a profit-generating corporation rather than a public-serving school. A direct competitor, Capella University, uses a purple and gold crest, which is constant on all pages, and resembles crests of traditional colleges. It features a winged, robed woman with arms raised (to signify triumph, "breaking out," etc.). It also contains the phrase, "Petere sapientium," Latin for "to seek knowledge." Capella also incorporated an effective marketing tactic at the bottom of the crest, where the words "Accredited by the Higher Learning Commission (NCA)" constantly remind visitors that Capella has been accredited (at least by one organization).

Even a cursory comparison of the pictures of students in the JIU viewbook and on its Web sites would lead one to conclude that willful misrepresentations occurred. The viewbook images show African American and Asian people, yet all of the students or alumni appear to be Caucasian. The viewbook images also show younger, more glamorous people in positions of greater responsibility and power than the students we get to know by reading their profiles on the Web site. On the other hand, when one looks at the Web photographs of alumni, one thinks, "If they can do it, so can I!" Even though many of the Web photographs of students and alumni were poorly executed, they probably were more persuasive than professionally taken images would have been because they seemed "real."

If you compare JIU's marketing to the marketing of more traditional universities, it seems to rely heavily on a few selling points, such as "accessibility from anywhere," "scheduling flexibility," and accreditation. Missed opportunities include showcasing successful alumni and featuring current students. Capella University, for example, has a "featured learners" section that offers black-and-white headshots of students with brief testimonials about their experiences at the school. This section would help prospective students see and relate to other students. The marketing materials also could include video press releases about the school, such as the ones available at the web site for Capella University from its "in the news" link. In addition to stories and press releases like those found in JIU's newsletter, Capella's site lets visitors download and view actual TV news clips about the university.

Although its tuition seems high, JIU could easily argue that its programs are a bargain. A *USA Today* article linked to its Web site says: "Jones International University offers a degree at about half the cost of a traditional college, when living and transportation expenses are factored in." The article also points out that accreditation opens the way for JIU students to apply for federal aid not available at unaccredited colleges. Saving money and finding financial aid are major concerns for many students, yet JIU has hidden these selling points under a minor link. Nor did the university brag much about its $5 million scholarship program for students transferring to its BA program from a partner community college. Illustrations could be used to visually tell these stories.

One of the controversies surrounding virtual universities is the quality of its teachers and of the courses students take. Many of JIU's faculty are moonlighting from their regular jobs at prestigious universities, but that information is not highlighted and not depicted visually. Cardean University, another competitor, features logos of several traditional, high-profile educational institutions, including Columbia Business School, Stanford University, the University of Chicago Graduate School of Business, Carnegie-Mellon University, and the London School for Economics and Political Science. By viewing these logos, visitors know that the courses they will take are challenging and rewarding. Cardean immediately acquires an aura of respectability and leaves the dirty work of looking up courses and seeing that are "co-op'ed" with which schools for later.

Because JIU's Web pages are almost exclusively text, the school has not taken advantage of the Web's multimedia, interactive recruiting potential. The Web site for ECPI College of Technology, a traditional college, offers a startling contrast. It utilizes virtual-reality technology to give you a complete view of its classrooms and laboratories, as well as animation to capture and keep your attention and brief videos to demonstrate teaching techniques.

JIU also doesn't use visual media to demonstrate how courses are taught. When JIU uses animation, such as the sequence about how to buy books using the postal system, both the idea that help is needed and the simplistic animated instructions are insulting to viewers. Cardean University's multimedia demonstration of an actual course uses a pleasant female voice, graphics, and photos to give an overall feeling of "moving forward," which is perfect for a business atmosphere. Visitors see how communication occurs between students and professors, where to hand in assignments, how talk to the professor, how to get notes, and so on.

Simply relying on text not only is a waste of the potential of the Web, but also may be ineffective. Based on my observations, university students scan material on the Web, but if they want to read-study-think-learn text, then they print the material. Perhaps JIU is appealing to "scanners" rather than "readers" with both its marketing and also its curriculum. Visual material, such as photographs, animations, video, virtual reality, and the like, would help by capturing viewers' attention, and then if real content was provided, learning would occur.

In conclusion, if projections hold true, the competition for students at virtual universities will increase. One marketing strategy has been to either partner with prestigious traditional universities or with corporations that can offer employment on graduation. Virtual universities have been using symbols of the future, of convenience, and of international connections to sell their programs and degrees. Accreditation already seems to have become necessary for survival. One can expect that future marketing strategies will include multimedia learning opportunities, lower prices, broader curricula, and prestige, which will be based on placement of schools' alumni.

REFERENCES

Aristotle. (1991). *On rhetoric: A theory of civil discourse*. George A. Kennedy (Ed. and Trans.). New York: Oxford University Press.

Begun, B. (2000, October 30). Campus Tours 1. *Newsweek*, 97–98.

Blumenstyk, G. (1999, March 19). In a first, the North Central Association accredits an on-line university. *Chronicle of Higher Education*, p. A27.

Braxton, J. M. (1990). How students choose colleges. In J. Hossler & J. P. Bean (Eds.), *The Strategic Management of College Enrollments* (pp. 57–67). San Francisco: Jossey-Bass.

Business/Technology Editors. (2001, March 5). Jones International University launches first ever Master of Education in e-learning. *Business Wire*, p. 2143.

Curtin, D. (2001, June 18). Colorado cable TV magnate blazes new trail: Cyber education. *KRT Business News*.

Dunn, S. L. (2000, March). The virtualizing of education. *The Futurist*, pp. 34–38.

Durgin, K. L. (1998). Is it worth it?: Viewbooks as communication between colleges and prospective students. *Journal of College Admission, 159*, 22–29.

Kealy, M. J., & Rockel, M. (1987). Student perceptions of college quality. *Journal of Higher Education, 58*, 683–703.

Kenney, K., & Scott, L. (2002). A review of the visual rhetoric literature. In L. Scott & R. Batra (Eds.), *Persuasive imagery: A consumer response perspective* (pp. 17–56). Hillsdale: Lawrence Erlbaum Associates.

Medhurst, M. J., & DeSousa, M. A. (1981). Political cartoons as rhetorical form: A taxonomy of graphic discourse. *Communication Monographs, 48*, 197–237.

Miller, C. M. (2000). "Aim high": Toward an analytical schema for visual rhetoric. Advertising and Consumer Psychology Conference, Ann Arbor, Michigan.

Severino, C. (1995). The urban mission in the groves of academe. AAHE paper cited in Miller.

Stern, G. (1999). "Jones International: An exclusively online university. *Link-Up, 16*, 16. (linkup@optonline.net).

Wright, A. B. (1995). Admissions recruitment: The first step. *New Directions for Student Services, 71*, 11–23.

11

Visual Metaphors in Print Advertising for Fashion Products

STUART KAPLAN
Lewis & Clark College

In Chapter 9, Theory of Visual Rhetoric, Sonja Foss calls attention to the benefits of visual communication studies for the extension and further development of rhetorical theory. Because visual images play an increasingly important role in all types of discourse and argumentation, the study of visual rhetoric in contemporary culture should assume a more central role in rhetorical scholarship than has traditionally been the case. This chapter is intended to contribute to that effort by focusing on the communicative functions of a particular class of nonlinguistic symbol, the visual metaphor. I examine the features of visual metaphors in a sample of advertisements taken from selected popular magazines. Thus, this study is an example of what Foss has characterized as "inductive exploration of the visual to generate the rhetorical."

A substantial body of metaphor research has developed during the last three decades. In addition to the many essays that are concerned primarily with developing metaphor theory (for a recent example, see Engstrom, 1999), numerous researchers have investigated the nature and function of actual metaphors used in particular situations or types of discourse. Topics covered in these studies include, for example, the role of metaphors in public opinion theory (Back, 1988), metaphorical thinking in organizational change (Smith & Eisenberg, 1987), figures of speech in the text accompanying advertising images (Leigh, 1994), and metaphors in judicial discourse (Bosmajian, 1992).

Nonlinguistic metaphors have also been a focus of this effort. Two primary emphases in the literature are metaphors in artistic presentations and metaphors used for rhetorical purposes. Examples in the first category include metaphors in painting, sculpture, and graphic design (Aldrich, 1971; Hausman, 1989; Johns, 1984) and metaphors in movies (Whittock, 1990). Studies of visual metaphors used for rhetorical purposes generally concentrate on advertising. A familiar example is the technique of juxtaposing a picture of a sports car (in an ad for that type of vehicle) with the image of a panther, suggesting that the product has comparable qualities of speed, power, and endurance. A variation on this common technique is to merge elements of the car and the wild animal, creating a composite image. Kaplan (1990) investigated images of technology in commercial advertising and metaphors used in public service ads that promote civil liberties (1993). Meister's (1997) study of advertising for a popular sports utility vehicle contextualizes a visual metaphor in those ads within contemporary political discourse regarding environmental policy. Other studies have examined visual metaphors in a broad range of advertising for products and services and classified them according to their formal features (Forceville, 1996; Leigh, 1994).

The effort to develop and test theories of visual metaphor has been an interdisciplinary one, engaging the participation of scholars in a broad range of fields, including cognitive psychology, linguistics, communication, and the fine arts. The practical benefit of gaining a better understanding of the rhetorical functions of visual metaphors has also attracted the attention of academic researchers in advertising and marketing. This broad participation in visual metaphor studies represents a convergence of interest in nonverbal language and rhetoric. Of special note is the issue on "Metaphor and Visual Rhetoric" published by the influential journal *Metaphor and Symbolic Activity* (Kennedy & Kennedy, 1993).

Relatively few studies of visual metaphors have operated inductively. More typically, researchers select examples of visual metaphors to illustrate specified characteristics or to support an argument about the nature of a particular text or a body of discourse. One benefit of the inductive approach is that it allows for conclusions regarding the prevalence of metaphors in various forms of discourse, thus facilitating comparisons both within and across texts. This chapter outlines a method for analyzing metaphors in visual modes of communication and applies the procedure in an exemplar study. The goal is to facilitate further research on the occurrence and nature of visual metaphors in rhetorical texts. Before describing the method and example study, a brief review of some leading theoretical perspectives on metaphors, the visual form in particular, is helpful.

LINGUISTIC AND VISUAL METAPHORS: SIMILARITIES AND DIFFERENCES

Metaphors present two ideas or terms in relationship to one another such that one is used to organize or conceptualize the other (see Kittay, 1987; Lakoff & Johnson, 1980). For example, the statement "Encyclopedias are Gold Mines" uses the idea of gold mines to clarify or modify the reader's conception of encyclopedias. Various names have been given to the two terms that are combined in a metaphor. In the example just given, the subject of the metaphor, encyclopedias, is often called the *topic* or *target*. The idea that is used to transfer new meaning to the topic (e.g., that encyclopedias store riches) is often called the *vehicle* or *metaphor source*. These two essential components of metaphors apply to both the linguistic and nonlinguistic type. However, the task of identifying the two metaphor terms may be more difficult when they are presented in pictorial form.

For a metaphor to accomplish its work, there are two additional conditions that must be met. First, the two terms must share some properties and those common properties need to be at least minimally relevant to the claim made by the metaphor (i.e., A is B). Otherwise, the attempt at creating an analogy will seem implausible to the reader. Some metaphor theorists refer to the process of transferring the properties of the source to the target (for the sake of consistency, the terms *source* and *target* will be used to refer to the two components of a metaphor) as one of "mapping" relevant aspects of the source on to the target (Lakoff & Johnson, 1980). In this view of metaphor effects, the source transfers both some of its properties to the target and a structure for articulating the relationships among those properties. A somewhat different theoretical perspective is called *conceptual blending* (Turner & Fauconnier, 1995; Veale, 1998). There, the metaphor is said to create a unique conceptual structure in which selected aspects of the source and target are combined.

The second essential condition for a metaphor to work is that the attempt to combine properties of the source and target must seem at least mildly incongruous or initially nonsensical to the reader or viewer. That is, the proposition that A is B cannot be literally true. McQuarrie and Mick (1996) referred to this phenomenon in the context of advertising as an "artful deviation." An effective metaphor creates tension by intentionally violating norms of language use or the reader's beliefs about the world. Nilsen (1986) identified three types of metaphoric tension: linguistic, pragmatic, and hermeneutic. In the context of visual metaphors, linguistic tension might result from a violation of conventions regarding the medium's syntax (e.g., not following the rules for framing a shot). Pragmatic tension might result when objects in a picture are distorted or greatly exaggerated. Hermeneutic tension results from a challenge to the viewer's beliefs about the true abstract qualities of the target of a metaphor.

The interplay of simultaneous similarity and incongruity in an effective metaphor stimulates a problem-solving response in the reader or viewer (Phillips, 1997). Brown emphasized the literal absurdity of a good metaphor:

> The logical, empirical, or psychological absurdity of metaphor thus has a specifically cognitive function: it makes us stop in our tracks and examine it. It offers us a new awareness. The arresting vividness and tensions set off by the conjunction of contraries forces us to make our own interpretation, to see for ourselves (1976, p. 173)

Empirical evidence for the psychological response suggested by metaphor theories comes from a study by Tourangeau and Sternberg (1981) in which the participants were presented with metaphors that varied as to the proportion of shared and incongruous features and asked to rate the appeal of each example. The researchers found, for example, that the metaphor "A wildcat is an ICBM among mammals" received a higher rating than "A wildcat is a hawk among mammals," presumably because it possessed a substantial amount of incongruity in combination with sufficient similarity of features (both wildcats and ICBMs can be considered aggressors within their respective semantic domains) as to make the combination comprehensible. Some additional empirical evidence regarding metaphor effects is presented later in the section on their use in advertising.

Metaphor form will also affect the amount of tension or perceived incongruity in a metaphorical statement. The major formal distinction in this regard is between metaphors and similes. The proposition that "encyclopedias are *like* gold mines" (a simile) is a plausible analogy, whereas the metaphor "encyclopedias *are* gold mines" cannot be literally true. Thus, one would expect metaphors to stimulate greater engagement and problem-solving activity than might be the case with the equivalent simile. Support for this prediction is found in an experiment by Verbrugge (1980), in which the subjects gave more imaginative and fanciful written interpretations to sentences like "skyscrapers are giraffes" than to the equivalent simile "skyscrapers are like giraffes." In a test of this effect involving visual metaphors, Kaplan (1992b) found that subjects judged the metaphor version to be more imaginative than its simile equivalent and also attributed greater tension to the former.

Many metaphor theorists consider linguistic and visual metaphors to be essentially similar in most respects (see Dent & Rosenberg, 1990). Both types are based on two interacting terms, the source and the target, and a transfer of properties takes place either because the combination invites a direct analogy (i.e., in the case of similes) or because the presence of incongruity stimulates the reader or viewer to posit a provisional explanation or interpretation based on known or depicted similarities.

Other theorists call attention to the differences between words and images. For example, Whittock (1990) posited that visual images are inherently more specific than words because the underlying meaning category is made manifest through the artist's choice of a particular image. In Gibson's theory of pictorial perception, information is conveyed through an "informative structure of ambient light that is richer and more inexhaustible than the informative structure of language" (1971, p. 34). Thus, to Gibson, "visual thinking is freer and less stereotyped than verbal thinking" (p. 34). These observations on the symbols used to create linguistic and visual metaphors suggest that the latter type may allow for greater range of treatments and variations.

Another characteristic that may distinguish visual from linguistic metaphors concerns the directionality of a metaphoric combination. In common usage, linguistic metaphors are rarely reversible. Thus, it usually doesn't make sense to say "gold mines are encyclopedias." Asymmetry is a principle of linguistic metaphors that has been observed by a number of theorists (see Indurkhya, 1990; Verbrugge, 1980). It is reflected in the use of terminology like "source" and "target." However, some theorists suggest that metaphors in visual form are more likely to be multidirectional. Hausman made the case for reversibility in the context of visual metaphors in painting and sculpture, using the example of a painting in which houses with angular roofs are shown in front of angular mountains (1989, p. 149). Thus, the juxtaposition causes the mountains to be domesticated and the houses to become mountainous in character. Forceville (2002) responded to this argument regarding reversibility by noting that visual metaphors are typically associated with contextual cues that leave little doubt as to the intended direction of a metaphoric effect. According to him, this is particularly the case in advertising because the advertiser's goal is usually to invest the product (i.e., the metaphor target) with favorable properties borrowed from the metaphor source.

Although the perspectives and theoretical arguments of scholars in this field differ on some points, there is widespread agreement on the fundamental role that metaphors play in thinking, behavior, and a range of aesthetic activities. Once considered little more than stylistic embellishment, metaphors are now broadly viewed as basic interpretive frameworks for organizing information about the world and making sense of experience:

> Accordingly, metaphor is neither an unusual use of language nor a special type of mental construction; rather, it is a form of resonating to the world, which is the source and the goal of metaphors. Thus, individual metaphors, and metaphors as such, come from perceiving the world, and they change one's perceiving of the world. (Dent-Read & Szokolszky, 1993, p. 240)

As basic interpretive frameworks, metaphors can possess considerable creative power, shaping how people come to understand unfamiliar or new ideas, products, and political issues (Gozzi, 1999). Schon (1979) noted the generative power of metaphors for suggesting novel solutions to difficult problems. He gave a number of actual examples of this phenomenon, including one where the metaphor of a paint brush was the key to solving a difficult engineering problem in the design of a new pump.

VISUAL METAPHORS IN ADVERTISING

Given the ability of metaphors to influence how people perceive and understand something, it is not surprising that they are a staple in advertising. The widespread use of metaphors and similes in advertising images, as well as text, has motivated a number of studies regarding the function and effects of metaphors in commercial persuasion. Advertising studies now constitute a major subject in the research literature on visual metaphors. Leiss, Kline, and Jhally (1986) found research evidence suggesting that the visual modality and metaphorical techniques dominate modern advertising. They contend the "metaphor is the very heart of the basic communication form used in modern advertising" (p. 181).

In addition to the studies concerning types of visual metaphors in advertising that are cited earlier, several researchers have also investigated the effects of using visual metaphors in ads. In a study reported by Phillips (1997), there was general agreement among a group of respondents on the meaning of the metaphors in a sample of print ads. Furthermore the interpretations made by her respondents matched the intent of the ads' producers as ascertained through interviews with the art directors who created those particular ads. McQuarrie and Mick (1999) presented subjects in two experiments with a variety of print ads, some of which contained figures of speech in visual form, including metaphors. They found that subjects who viewed the ads containing figures of speech paid more attention to those materials, produced a more elaborate interpretation of their meaning, and reported a more positive opinion regarding the ad.

A METHOD FOR ANALYZING VISUAL METAPHORS

The following outline of a process for identifying and analyzing visual metaphors sets out the basic steps that might be usefully applied to a variety of visual texts, including advertising. It is based on theoretical concepts and definitions from the research reviewed earlier, as well as specific procedural suggestions by Gozzi (1999) and Forceville (1996, 2002). Portions of this procedure were also employed in this author's earlier studies of visual metaphors in advertising (Kaplan, 1990, 1992a). Although the method described here is intended to be general, the emphasis is on visual metaphors in advertising.

Note the Presence of a Metaphor

The first hint that some feature (or combination of features) is intended to evoke a metaphorical response in the viewer is the presence of images or pictorial elements that seem distorted or out of place. Often, the cue is a violation of the viewer's understanding of physical reality. McGuire noted that the deviation from the viewer's expectations touches off an attempt at interpretation:

> In the case of pictorial metaphor, the artist succeeds in getting his or her audience to appreciate some point or to think about one thing by means of presenting a picture that is about something utterly different. The picture itself will typically involve distorted representations or other fictitious features, which are what prompt the viewer to search for an additional reference. (1999, p. 299)

For a metaphorical interpretation to occur, the deviation from the viewer's expectations has to be perceived as intentional and not simply a mistake (McQuarrie & Mick, 1996; Phillips, 1997).

Although the viewer's expectations might be challenged in a variety of ways, the following list seems to encompass the techniques used most frequently in advertising. Accordingly, the examples are actual print advertisements—from the study reported here or from prior research on metaphors in advertising.

1. *Modification of physical characteristics*: The visible physical properties of one pictorial element are modified through distortion, superimposition, or blending of features from another element, or through changes in scale. For example, in an ad for Boucheron's "Le Parfum Perle," small white pearllike drops are depicted flowing down a woman's face and collecting around her neck in the shape of a necklace. The drops represent particles of perfume that morph into pearls.

2. *Inappropriate setting or depicted function*: In this type of metaphor, incongruity may be achieved by showing a significant pictorial element in an unexpected or inappropriate location. For example, an ad for a moisturizer crème shows the jar in the hands of a member of a primitive tribe in an exotic desert setting. In advertising metaphors, the incongruity necessary to mark the picture as metaphorical is sometimes attained by suggesting an inappropriate or unexpected function for the pictorial element. An athletic footwear ad in which a man is shown licking the shoe provides an example of this technique. Here the depicted function of the product as an object of desire for a foot fetishist is (at least mildly) unexpected. In both of these examples, the pictorial element that is the primary subject of the metaphor is physically integrated with the other pictorial element. That distinguishes this metaphor type from the one where the two elements are juxtaposed in the picture but not integrated.

3. *Juxtaposition*: Two pictorial elements are shown side by side (or arranged as fore-ground and background) in a manner that cues the viewer that the artist intends for them to be compared. In an ad for a Seiko watch called "Spoon," the watch is shown against a background of eating utensils and the text statement "Essential Utensil" is incorporated in the ad copy. This approach to creating a metaphorical effect corresponds to the lin-guistic simile, in which term A is said to be like term B (Forceville, 1996, pp. 152–162).

Designate the Two Terms of the Metaphor

The target of the metaphor is the pictorial element that is changed or reconceptualized as a result of the action of the metaphor source. Thus, the target is understood or experienced in terms of the metaphor source (Lakoff & Johnson, 1980). In the case of linguistic metaphors, identifying source and target tends to be a fairly unambiguous task, because the sentence usually makes the relationship between the two terms clear. For example, the metaphorical statement "my job is a jail" contains a proposition about the relationship between the metaphor source (jail) and its target term (my job). As I noted in an earlier section of the chapter, distinguishing between source and target in visual metaphors may be less clear in some instances.

To make that determination, it is usually necessary to consider the context for the picture. Often, the intent of the creator of the picture is obvious or can be inferred from various contextual cues. When metaphors are used as persuasive devices, they are designed to lead the reader or viewer to certain conclusions and that purpose is generally well understood (Gozzi, 1999). This is particularly the case with advertising, where the metaphor target tends to be either the product or service being advertised or some pictorial element that is metonymically related to that product or service (Forceville, 1996, p. 137). Thus, it should be generally clear which is the target and which is the source when visual metaphors are encountered in advertising.

When the pictorial elements alone are insufficient to unambiguously establish the metaphor source and target, the advertiser is likely to include text that helps the viewer make that determination. After all, the point of most advertising is to make claims about the thing being advertised. In an ad for Canadian Furs, a female model wearing a fur coat is posed and made up in a way that is slightly suggestive of a wild animal. To leave little doubt as to the intended meaning of the visual metaphor (or simply to reinforce the message), the advertiser has superimposed the phrase "get wild" over her image.

Identify the Properties That Are Transferred to the Product

Both verbal and visual metaphors involve a transfer of meaning from source to target. By identifying the properties of the source that are transferred to the target, the researcher can gain a better understanding of the artist's intended meaning and rhetorical tactics. At the next level of analysis, properties that are frequently observed in a sample of persuasive texts can provide insight into the cultural values that underlie rhetorical efforts. This step requires that the researcher create categories for describing and labeling source properties. For example, in a study of visual metaphors in print advertising for communications technology products, the author found that the properties of "lever" and "synthesis of old and new values" were the most frequently encountered features of metaphor sources that were being mapped on to the advertised products (Kaplan, 1990).

The Question of Threshold or Baseline

Messaris (1997, p. 10) noted that visual analogies are a ubiquitous phenomenon in advertising. Artists regularly incorporate objects, colors, and the like, that represent qualities of the advertised product or service. It is a staple of advertising to pose automobiles outside of expensive homes and juxtapose a picture of a skin moisturizer jar with the face of a woman who has a flawless complexion. This common practice in advertising production poses a problem for metaphor research because an overly broad definition of visual metaphor (or simile) would yield too many cases for meaningful analysis. The threshold question is fairly easily resolved for those metaphors where there is physical distortion or transformation of the target element because of the action of the metaphor source. That kind of obvious violation of physical reality seems most likely to engage the viewer in a process of interpretation.

The threshold question is more difficult in the case of metaphors that involve an inappropriate setting or function for the advertised product or that are established through juxtaposition. To address that methodological issue, the following coding rule can be used: To classify a picture as metaphorical there should be enough similarities between the two elements with respect to physical form or abstract qualities as to permit a tentative analogy, yet enough differences between them to cue the viewer that the artist did not intend the depiction or representation to be taken as literally true. This is offered as a general coding rule for studies of visual metaphors. For specific kinds of visual texts (architecture as compared with advertising, for example), it may be necessary to modify the rule somewhat to accommodate unique characteristics of the genre or form.

AN EXEMPLAR STUDY OF VISUAL METAPHORS IN ADVERTISING

The procedure outlined earlier was applied to a sample of print advertising for clothing and other fashion products. The choice of product type was dictated by a desire to compare the results with a previous study of visual metaphors in print advertising for automobiles and alcoholic beverages (Kaplan, 1990).

Sample

A sample of full-page ads for clothing, grooming products (e.g., lipstick), jewelry, and fragrances was obtained from three mass-circulation magazines that typically carry advertising for these products, primarily directed at a female readership. Sixteen issues randomly selected from *Elle*, *Vogue*, and *W* magazines published during 2001 and 2002 were examined, resulting in a total of 432 ads for these products.

Coding Procedure

The coding method for analyzing visual metaphors described earlier was applied for the purpose of (a) identifying those ads that contained a visual metaphor as defined

TABLE 11.1
Two Main Types of Visual Metaphors

Type of Visual Metaphor	Linguistic Equivalent	Underlying Psychological Process	Advertising Example
Identity Metaphor	Metaphor	Integration of Source and Target (A is B)	Diamond brooches are grafted onto the stems of a plant suggesting that the jewelry is a flower.
Juxtaposition Metaphor	Simile	Explicit Comparison between Source and Target (A is like B)	The image of a pair of "Royal Elastic" shoes is placed next to a picture of a young man using a slingshot made from a large rubber band.

in the method, (b) designating the source and target of the metaphor most closely related to the selling purpose of the ad, and (c) analyzing the presentation technique for transferring properties of the source to the target. In addition, a distinction was made between identity metaphors and juxtaposition metaphors as these types are specified in Table 11.1.

The aspect of presentation technique that was analyzed for this study was the directness of the implied linkage between the metaphor source and the target. To this end, a distinction was made between ads in which the properties of the metaphor source are directly presented and those in which an additional interpretive step was needed to understand the meaning. An example of direct presentation is an ad for a brand of fur coats in which a female model wearing one of the coats is made up to look a little bit like a cat. This approach can be contrasted with an ad for a skin moisturizing cream in which the product is shown next to a flower that has been modified such that half of it is depicted as a fractal structure, similar to what one might see if examining the flower through a microscope. The ad copy touts the extensive scientific research that went into the development of the product. Thus, the second ad is an example of one in which an additional interpretive step is needed to make sense of the metaphor.

Results

A total of 188 full-page ads (43% of the total ad sample) for the designated fashion products met the criteria for containing visual metaphors. Identity metaphors accounted for nearly two thirds of the visual metaphors. The remaining cases were the juxtaposition type. In 63% of the ads with visual metaphors, the properties of the source that were applied to the target were directly presented, whereas the other ads required an additional interpretive step.

DISCUSSION

Studies of visual metaphors in advertising typically use selected examples to illustrate metaphor types or other theoretical constructs. Although that approach is useful for clarifying a theoretical argument, inductive research provides a basis for claims about actual advertising practices, including the extent of visual metaphors of various kinds in advertising for particular product types. Thus, comparisons can be made across product categories, intended audiences, etc.

In one of my previous studies with advertising images for alcoholic beverages and automobiles (Kaplan, 1992a), visual metaphors appeared in 31% of the sample. The juxtaposition type of visual metaphor accounted for 71% of the cases. This compares with the overall frequency of 43% for visual metaphors in this product sample and the 63:37 ratio of identity metaphors to the juxtaposition type. A possible explanation for these differences is the more abstract nature of the appeals used to promote fashion products as contrasted with automobiles. In the latter product type, concrete features such as fuel economy and engine power are more likely to be incorporated in the advertising. Thus, according to this analysis, visual metaphors, particularly those in which the source and target are visually blended in some way (i.e., identity metaphors), are considered more apt for promoting the abstract qualities of fashion goods. Further research testing this supposition should hold the type of magazine constant.

This chapter was limited to print advertising. Although print ads are a convenient source for developing theoretical concepts and procedures for research on visual metaphors, it cannot be assumed that the same principles apply to visual metaphors in moving image media, such as television. For this reason, it is important to extend this line of research by also examining other presentation formats. Extant theoretical works on cinematic metaphors (Whittock, 1990; Forceville, 2002) together with the concepts outlined in this chapter may provide a useful foundation for developing principles and operational definitions for research on visual metaphors in television advertising. Another important area for future research is visual metaphors in multimedia presentations, including those where some degree of interactivity is possible. What happens, for example, when the viewer has a measure of control over the timing and order of a visual presentation?

REFERENCES

Aldrich, V. C. (1971). Form in the visual arts. *British Journal of Aesthetics, 11*, 215–226.

Back, K. W. (1988). Metaphors for public opinion. *Public Opinion Quarterly, 52*, 278–288.

Bosmajian, H. (1992). *Metaphor and reason in judicial opinions.* Carbondale: Southern Illinois University Press.

Brown, R. H. (1976). Social theory as metaphor: On the logic of discovery for the sciences of conduct. *Theory and Society, 3*, 169–197.

Dent, C., & Rosenberg, L. (1990). Visual and verbal metaphors: Developmental interactions. *Child Development, 61*, 983–994.

Dent-Read, C. H., & Szokolszky, A. (1993). Where do metaphors come from? *Metaphor and Symbolic Activity, 8*, 227–242.

Engstrom, A. (1999). The contemporary theory of metaphor revisited. *Metaphor and Symbol, 14*, 53–61.

Forceville, C. (1996). *Pictorial metaphor in advertising.* New York: Routledge.

Forceville, C. (2002). The identification of target and source in pictorial metaphors. *Journal of Pragmatics, 34*, 1–14.

Gibson, J. J. (1971). The information available in pictures. *Leonardo, 4*, 27–35.

Gozzi, R. (1999). The power of metaphor: In the age of electronic media. *ETC: A Review of General Semantics, 56*, 380–389.

Hausman, C. R. (1989). *Metaphor and art: Interactionism and reference in verbal and nonverbal arts.* Cambridge, UK: Cambridge University Press.

Indurkhya, B. (1990). Modes of metaphor. *Metaphor and Symbolic Activity, 6*, 1–27.

Johns, B. (1984). Visual metaphor: Lost and found. *Semiotica, 52*, 291–333.

Kaplan, S. J. (1990). Visual metaphors in the representation of communication technology. *Critical Studies in Mass Communication, 7*, 37–47.

Kaplan, S. J. (1992a). A conceptual analysis of form and content in visual metaphors. *Communication, 13*, 197–209.

Kaplan, S. J. (1992b, June). *An empirical investigation of tension in visual metaphors.* Paper presented at the Sixth Annual Visual Communication Conference, Flagstaff, Arizona.

Kaplan, S. J. (1993, June). *Visualizing a civil liberty: Graphic representations of censorship and free expression.* Paper presented at the Seventh Annual Visual Communication Conference, Jackson Hole, Wyoming.

Kennedy, V., & Kennedy, J. (1993). A special issue: Metaphor and visual rhetoric. *Metaphor and Symbolic Activity, 8*, 149–151.

Kittay, E. F. (1987). *Metaphor: Its cognitive force and linguistic structure.* New York: Oxford University Press.

Lakoff, G., & Johnson, M. (1980). *Metphors we live by.* Chicago: University of Chicago Press.

Leigh, J. H. (1994). The use of figures of speech in print ad headlines. *Journal of Advertising, 23*, 17–33.

Leiss, W., Kline, S., & Jhally, S. (1986). *Social communication in advertising.* Toronto, Canada: Methuen.

McGuire, J. M. (1999). Pictorial metaphors: A reply to Sedivy. *Metaphor and Symbol, 14*, 293–302.

McQuarrie, E. F., & Mick, D. G. (1996). Figures of rhetoric in advertising language. *Journal of Consumer Research, 22*, 424–438.

McQuarrie, E. F., & Mick, D. G. (1999). Visual rhetoric in advertising: Text-interpretive, experimental, and reader-response analyses. *Journal of Consumer Research, 26*, 37–54.

Meister, M. (1997). "Sustainable development" in visual imagery: Rhetorical function in the Jeep Cherokee. *Communication Quarterly, 45*, 223–234.

Messaris, P. (1997). *Visual persuasion: The role of images in advertising.* Thousand Oaks, CA: Sage.

Nilsen, D. L. F. (1986). The nature of ground in farfetched metaphors. *Metaphor and Symbolic Activity, 1*, 127–138.

Phillips, B. J. (1997). Thinking into it: Consumer interpretation of complex advertising images. *The Journal of Advertising, 26*, 77–87.

Schon, D. A. (1979). Generative metaphor: A perspective on problem-setting in social policy. In A. Ortony (Ed.), *Metaphor and thought* (pp. 254–283). Cambridge, UK: Cambridge University Press.

Smith, R. C., & Eisenberg, E. M. (1987). Conflict at Disneyland: A root-metaphor analysis. *Communication Monographs, 54*, 367–380.

Tourangeau, R., & Sternberg, R. (1981). Aptness in metaphor. *Cognitive Psychology, 13*, 27–55.

Turner, M., & Fauconnier, G. (1995). Conceptual integration and formal expression. *Metaphor and Symbolic Activity, 10*, 183–204.

Veale, T. (1998). *Pragmatic forces in metaphor appreciation: The mechanics of blend recruitment in visual metaphor.* Paper presented at the CMA2, An International Workshop on Computation for Metaphors, Agents and Analogy, Aizu, Japan.

Verbrugge, R. R. (1980). Transformation in knowing: A realist view of metaphor. In R. P. Honeck & R. R. Hoffman (Eds.), *Cognition and figurative language* (pp. 87–125). Hillsdale, NJ: Lawrence Erlbaum Associates.

Whittock, T. (1990). *Metaphor and film.* Cambridge, UK: Cambridge University Press.

12

Empowerment Through Shifting Agents: The Rhetoric of the Clothesline Project

Trischa Goodnow
Oregon State University

Until late in the 20th century, rhetoric was the domain of men and verbal words. Denied access to standard channels of public communication, women often resorted to covert forms of persuasion to effect change in the public atmosphere. For example, during the early days of the Suffrage movement, women would embroider pro–Women's Rights messages into the parasols displayed in public (Parker, 1989, p. 198). At the close of the last century women still resorted to displays deemed "appropriate" to their gender.

To those ends, the Cape Cod Women's Agenda developed a public project, the Clothesline Project, designed to educate, break the silence, and bear witness to violence against women. This project, a public installation of visual images, displays T-shirts with messages of domestic abuse in the public arena. The individual images are created by women survivors of violence or the families of victims of gender-based violence.[1] The clothesline was thought to be an appropriate choice for the installation because "doing the laundry has always been considered women's work; and in the days of close-knit neighborhoods, women often exchanged information over backyard fences while hanging their clothes out to dry" (Chitchetto, 1994, p. 2). Accordingly, the founders of the project set forth four purposes for the Clothesline:

1. To bear witness to the survivors as well as the victims of the war against women.
2. To help with the healing process for people who have lost a loved one or are survivors of this violence.
3. To educate, document, and raise society's awareness of the extent of the problem of violence against women.
4. To provide a nationwide network of support, encouragement, and information for other communities starting their own Clothesline Project.

The idea of using the visual image as a source of persuasion began to be considered by rhetorical scholars in the late 1960s. In this vein, Paul Lester (1996), in his book *Images that Injure*, examined the role of the visual image in creating and maintaining cultural stereotypes, and Paul Messaris (1997) put forward a theory in *Visual Persuasion* of visual argument in advertising. Most significantly to our consideration of the Clothsline Project, Edelman (1995) in *From Art to Politics* drew a connection between arguments evident in the visual image and constructions of political and social argument. It is the purpose of this chapter to examine the Clothsline Project as visual rhetoric.

Most arresting about the rhetorical characteristics of the installation is a shift that takes place involving the agents of action portrayed in the individually designed T-shirts that make up a display. Despite the fact that creators are limited by only two restrictions— first, if a T-shirt is made for someone, permission must be obtained from her or his family and second, perpetrators may not be named in full unless they have been convicted of the crime—the narratives contain two similar stories, the tale of the abuse and the tale of where the survivor is now. I argue that these narratives, despite their various authors, are consistent in the two narratives that the shirts tell: the first, a tale of abuse focusing on the abuser and the second a tale focusing on the survivor. Thus, the agent of action shifts as women continue through the healing process and regain a healthy self. In exploring this shift in agents to articulate how women gain empowerment through the transformative nature of the Project, I argue further that the rhetoric empowers the survivors to move through the various stages in the healing process. Creating a T-shirt "gives each woman a new voice with which to expose an often horrific and unspeakable experience that has dramatically altered the course of her life" (Chichetto, 1994, p. 1). Chichetto, the national coordinator for the Clothesline Project, suggested that "the hanging of her shirt gives her the opportunity to leave behind some of the pain of her experience and move on to the next phase of her life" (1994, p. 2).

At the same time that the T-shirts function for individuals, the installation of T-shirts as a whole creates a powerful rhetorical message for the public at large. Though each shirt is a unique piece of rhetoric, the content among them is remarkably similar. This visual image generally displays two plot lines: an account of the abusive situation or a narrative of the current situation with a projection to the future. An analysis of the Clothesline Project installation using Kenneth Burke's dramatistic pentad reveals that there are two contemporaneous pentads that allow a woman to regain control of situational constraints that have led to the abuse and thus to reclaim her life. In this analysis we see how the women's narratives shift the agent from the abuser to the survivor, thereby aiding the recovery process by transforming perceptions of the here and now.

THE CLOTHESLINE PROJECT AS VISUAL RHETORIC

That the Clothesline Project is visual is obvious: The messages of the project are delivered through decorated T-shirts hung in a public place. Certainly, discussions raised by the T-shirt display among viewers and organizers help to advance the message, but it is the T-shirts themselves that are the primary site of rhetoric. Messages on the T-shirts are delivered through two means, words and images. All T-shirts have some words, and many have accompanying images. To understand the visual nature of this project, we can discuss both the words and the images to uncover the rhetorical role that they play in the Clothesline Project.

Although the history of rhetoric has been most concerned with verbal manifestations of language and their influence, the written word has also been an area of interest, most notably in English studies. Dondis (1973) argued that the capacity to use language is inherent in the human being. We have to learn the rules and the specific language. Literacy, however, refers to an individual's ability to actually interpret visual symbols as a means of communication. Consequently, Dondis argued that at least one aspect of verbal language is visual. To exclude the written word from a study of visual communication would ignore a primary means of visually communicating. There are several potential areas of study within the written word. For example, graphic designers are interested in the typography with which words are printed. Indeed, the script on the shirts is revealing as any handwriting analyst can tell. However, my interest lies elsewhere. My argument is such: Space on T-shirts is limited so the words that are printed there are particularly revealing. Because of the brief messages displayed the words of the T-shirt creators are unusually stark with little padding to ease the viewer into their ultimate meaning. Were these same messages to be delivered verbally, the stories would be eased into, given greater detail, and supplied a beginning, middle, and end. However, with limited space the rhetor chooses to highlight certain segments of the story. It is in this highlighting that I am interested. Indeed, in the choice of words we can discover the rhetor's view of the world they wish the audience to adopt. Burke's pentad will help us to discover those views. Because the narratives are told with the written word in limited space, this study provides a unique opportunity to discover the power of the written word as visual image observed in the public sphere.

The majority of images created by the shirts are made with words, though some also include pictorial illustrations. These are not complex illustrations. Rather they are simple, minimalistic explanations of the words. Yet perhaps it is in their stark depiction of the creator's attitude that they find their power. It should be remembered, though, that it is the visual installation as a whole, with the many, many shirts that confront viewers with stories of abuse and survival that the genius of the project is realized. This visual image invades the public space of public places. In its images, narratives and numbers, the Clothesline Project provides the audience with a rhetoric that the viewer must physically avoid to ignore.

KENNETH BURKE AND THE DRAMATISTIC PENTAD

In *A Grammar of Motives*, Kenneth Burke (1955) articulated his concern with uncovering human motives. He stated, "any complete statement about motives will offer *some kind of* answers to these five questions: what was done (act), when or where it was done (scene), who did it (agent), how he did it (agency), and why (purpose)" (emphasis original, p. xv). Burke also contends that the "act" is always the central component of any pentadic analysis. However, the "act" may be reinterpreted given a dominant term in a dramatistic ratio. Consequently, by determining which term the rhetor emphasizes, the audience can determine the motive of the speaker. Perhaps Ling summed up the application of the pentad best when he wrote, "it is possible to examine a speaker's discourse to determine what view of the world he [sic] would have an audience accept" (1970, p. 83). Indeed, as Foss suggested in regard to the pentad, "How we describe a situation indicates how we are perceiving it, the choices we see available to us, and the action we are likely to take in that situation" (1996, p. 456). These ideas are particularly relevant to our explaination of the healing process as seen in the Clothesline Project.

In the case of the Clothesline Project, the rhetors have vested interest in exposing the agent of the act so as to relinquish guilt and reclaim their lives. Vardi cited one T-shirt creator as saying, "By doing this you get rid of the guilt and shame, and place it back on the perpetrator's shoulders. It makes you feel stronger. It doesn't heal everything, nothing does, but this is powerful" (1998, p. C3). To understand the rhetors' motives in going public with their personal pain, we can analyze the dramatistic elements of the project rhetoric.

THE CLOTHESLINE PROJECT

Designed as both an outlet for survivors of abuse to tell their stories and as a means for raising public awareness about domestic abuse, women's organizations in cities and towns invite women from their communities to create a shirt. Organizers provide materials for survivors to create a T-shirt at the site of the installation. Consequently, no two Clotheslines are alike. To date, Clotheline installations have been seen in most communities in the United States and in over 40 countries throughout the world. The T-shirts examined for this project are from three of these installations, one in Ashland, Oregon, one in Corvallis, Oregon, and one in Fairfax, Virginia. In addition, T-shirts displayed on numerous Web sites have also been examined.[2]

As communities organize Clothesline displays, organizers establish few if any guidelines for the creation of T-shirts. Those guidelines given, aside from the two rules cited above, are mostly about materials, for example, sewing instead of gluing. Survivors are given guidelines to the symbolism behind the shirts: red, pink, or orange for women who have been battered or assaulted; yellow or beige for women who have been battered; blue or green for women who are survivors of incest or child sexual abuse; purple or lavender for women attacked because of their sexual orientation; and white for women who have died of violence. Women are counseled that the T-shirt need not follow this color scheme if a color or particular shirt has special meaning for the woman.

These color choices for the T-shirts have important rhetorical value for both maker and viewer of the display. For example, a purple or lavender shirt represents women who were attacked because of their sexual orientation. Purple and lavender have long been associated with gay and lesbian causes. Consequently, the use of this color T-shirt serves two purposes. First, it readily identifies the reason for the shirt. If one sees purple shirts, one can absorb the nature of the abuse as having to do with sexuality. Second, the use of the color to indicate sexual orientation reinforces the association of the color with that cause. Because the color is already associated with gay and lesbian causes, the use in the Clothesline Project reinforces that color association.

The actual content of the images and words is left solely to the survivor, though most follow one of the two narratives revealing a survival strategy. By applying Burke's pentad we can see the importance of this strategy. That there are two contemporaneous pentads is important in establishing a before and after chronology. Before "he" was in charge. His acts were abuse, either physical or psychological. After, "she" is in control. Her acts are regaining self-esteem, growing strong, and surviving. A closer examination of these pentads will allow us to see the transformative nature of the narratives.

THE BEFORE NARRATIVE

The before narrative relates stories of the abuse and can be analyzed by its pentadic terms:

act: the abuse
agent: the perpetrator
agency: dependent on act
scene: places of previous safe harbor
purpose: to expose the abuse

The narrative of the abusive episodes is consistent in its agent—him or the perpetrator of the abuse. Rarely does the women name herself as responsible for the abuse. Instead, the woman relinquishes responsibility to "him" and a situation she deems out of her control. Because the agent is the root term in this pentad, we can spend considerable time analyzing this aspect. The naming and importance of agent serve two purposes: assigning responsibility and altering the relationship of the perpetrator to society.

Perhaps most important to the healing process is the naming of the perpetrator (Chichetto, 1994, p. 2). Wood argued that "naming is perhaps the fundamental symbolic act" (1992, p. 2). It allows the namer to define a reality. Men often disregard abuse of women as "not serious, not meant, not abusive." Some T-shirts express the frustrations of these excuses, "If nothing happened, then why does it hurt so much?" By including the name of the perpetrator, the survivor both relates what was done to her and assigns responsibility to the perpetrator.

Sometimes, just naming is enough because the naming changes the relationship of the perpetrator to the survivor as well as the relationship of the perpetrator to society at large. For example, one T-shirt simply said, "He was the sheriff." A sheriff's position is one of trust and esteem to the community; by naming the sheriff, both esteem and trust are minimized. As such, the woman can reduce the power of the position and put herself on equal footing with the sheriff. Another T-shirt proclaimed, "To Brooklyn's father: NewsFlash! You're Not Supposed to Have Sex with 8-Month-Old Babies." The father / child relationship is supposed to be one of love and support. However, by naming the father, the survivor can redefine the parent/child relationship and the perpetrator/society relationship. One T-shirt seemed to sum up the position of agent in this first pentad, "All along I thought it was me. Now I am understanding that it was you."

The act in this before pentad is important in terms of establishing the evil perpetrated by the abuser. Naming the act allows the survivor to reveal the pain and horrors suffered at the hands of the abuser. Acts such as rape, sodomy, ritual abuse, molestation, and misogyny are common on the T-shirts of the Clothesline Project. Perhaps most persuasive and poignant on the shirts are drawings that depict the act. Many reveal the perpetrator in superior positions over the victim, inflicting pain with some type of weapon. These weapons are evident in the element of agency.

Agency in these shirts is wrapped in the idea of act (implied). Indeed, part of the transformation of the relationship as discussed earlier is in naming the act that the abuser conducted. As in the Brooklyn T-shirt, fathers don't have sex with their children. Thus, the T-shirt creator cements the idea that the perpetrator has conducted himself inappropriately, calling down the wrath of society.

Scenes are important in the stripping of innocence. When the scene is mentioned, either verbally or through images, it is mentioned in passing to illustrate the seemingly normal situation into which the abuse was brought. So, a bedroom, closet, or girl's bathroom are often mentioned or drawn as the scene. These are places that each of us visit daily, without fear of abuse. But for a survivor of domestic abuse these places are places of fear. Perhaps the perpetrator uses these comfortable places to inflict abuse so as to make the woman ill at ease in the very places she should feel safe. If abuse is about control, then an easy way to control is to manipulate the places where one should feel safe.

These narratives are illustrated with images. The most common image on the shirts is the figure of a person, usually drawn as a stick figure or as a cartoon. The figure is of one of two characters, the victim—usually depicted bleeding—or the perpetrator engaging in an act of abuse—usually yelling, hitting, or shooting a gun. These images accentuate the powerlessness of the victim or the power of the perpetrator. In these simple drawings, the pain of the abuse is blatant. Further, the feelings of the abuse, helplessness, and powerlessness become immediately available to the viewer. Because the images are simple, the audience can easily interpret who has the power in the subject of the T-shirt. Often the perpetrator is seen as being larger than or above the survivor or victim, thereby having control of the situation.

In discussing the pentadic analysis of the T-shirts, the critic must uncover the purpose as articulated by the rhetor. Yet the purpose for the abuse is conspicuously absent unless to blame the survivor or to remove blame from the perpetrator. For those shirts that talk about blaming the survivor, it's not the survivor who blames herself, rather it is the perpetrator blaming the survivor. We see this in the following examples, "He said I hurt him because my unhealed stitches scratched his penis. I spent a week in the hospital"; "I was only being friendly—he said I was being a flirt." These T-shirts illustrate how the perpetrators blame the survivors without taking on responsibility themselves. In addition, some shirts will attempt to take blame from the perpetrator. For example, one shirt explains the abuse with the following, "For my daughter, molested in infancy by a woman who was molested in infancy."

This discussion of the before narrative assumes that something will follow, namely acceptance, reclamation, and survival. As part of the healing process, survivors need to go through stages of blame, disbelief, and even justification. Once these stages are experienced, however, the survivor moves to stages of acceptance and empowerment. We see this process in the after narrative.

AFTER NARRATIVE

Unlike the before narrative where the agent was often the perpetrator who seemed to control not only the survivor but also the situation, the after narrative has the survivor taking control of herself and her situation. The elements of the pentad can be summarized as such:

act: surviving
agent: survivor
agency: empowerment
scene: any place
purpose: to reclaim control of the survivor's life

In this pentad, the survivor reclaims herself and her life with the abundant identification of herself as agent: "I am a person who counts"; " I am a survivor"; "I will come strong." These T-shirts illustrate the reclamation survivors embody when they take responsibility and, thus, control of their lives.

The shift in agents is in conjunction with the shift in acts. Although the before narrative had the perpetrator acting in hideous ways, the after narrative shows the survivor taking positive action to reclaim her life. T-shirts illustrate this, "Courage to remember"; "I take my life back. I am being myself"; "I am better than your beer"; "I survive. I thrive." These T-shirts imply action on the part of the survivor but also counsel for action on the part of the viewer for one of the benefits of empowerment is in bringing strength to others.

In telling how the work must be done, survivors counsel others how to empower themselves: "tell your story—work for change"; "We can fight back. Learn to protect yourself" (this was printed on the back of a karate jacket); "Transform anger. Reclaim power." All of these T-shirts express methods of empowering the survivor. By using these and similar methods survivors in the early stages of recovery can move toward the healthy survivor.

Like the before narrative the scene is conspicuously absent. Perhaps this is because the abuse can never be forgotten. Survival means surviving in every place the person is. Yet memories linger. Some shirts illustrate this, "I still can't walk or even be at home without fear"; "As I sit in the sun darkness devoures [sic] me. I am haunted by him . . ." Perhaps the women who created these shirts have not completely reclaimed their lives, perhaps they never will. However, as other T-shirts illustrate, there is hope for survival.

The image that most often illustrates the after narrative is that of the heart. When one normally thinks of the icon of the heart, one is reminded of Valentine's Day, romance, and love—warm issues. The most frequent image on the after shirts is that of the heart. When the survivor's life is back on track, the portrayal of this image confirms her newfound hope in all of the romanticism of the heart icon. Although I don't mean to suggest here that the creator views life as all better and full of roses and romance, there is a promise of love and fulfillment in the survival of the abuse. These images, although simple, enable the maker of the shirt to assert some control over the situation. Because she is no longer under the control of the abuser, the survivor can imagine life as positive with potential.

These after images are broader images that encompass all the possible outcomes of surviving. The before images are finite in that they tell of one aspect of life, the abuse. In the after images, life is not controlled by that one aspect. Rather life is about a myriad of options that these positive images signify. The rhetorical analysis of these images reveals this shift in attitude that reinforces and expands the verbal narratives the T-shirts tell. Words tell of detail while images convey an overall attitude of the creator.

The purpose behind this after pentad is perhaps best expressed by the T-shirt that says, "Be human again." As illustrated in the act, the purpose in this pentad is empowerment. By remaining strong and moving on, women can reclaim their lives. Further, this reclamation provides models for other women recovering from abuse. As one T-shirt creator suggests, "such projects are important to create a sense of solidarity among victims and to raise awareness of domestic violence" (Abdullah, 2000, p. A19).

TRANSFORMATION

As Davis and Bass (2000) discussed, healing occurs in stages. As women move through these stages, they must break the silence. Davis and Bass articulated the four stages of healing as remembering, admitting the abuse occurred, placing blame, and resolution and moving on. Many of these stages can be witnessed in the rhetoric of the Clothesline Project. The early stages of remembering and admitting the abuse, which occurred along with placing blame, are countered with women's voices who have moved further along the healing path. Sometimes the whole process is recounted on a single T-shirt:

> I wish that you could understand how I felt when you seered [sic] me with your harsh words. Hands that could be so gentle lashed out to bruise me. I wanted so much to love. Why did you choose to hurt me when you claimed to love me? All along I thought it was me. Now I am understanding that it was you. 4 1/2 years we were together and I had to take myself away to survive. I am sad. I am angry.

The public enunciation of healing has an internal rhetorical power. The public admission confirms both the experiences and the woman's newly held esteem. This public affirmation assures the survivor that she is on the right track.

The controlling term in these two pentadic narratives is the agent. That the agent shifts in the contemporaneous pentads illustrates the transforming nature of the rhetoric in the Clotheslines. Women are able to articulate and recognize in the first narrative the domination of the abuser and then relinquish this domination to reclaim control of their lives. This, then, leads to empowerment. Indeed, Honora Goldstein, one of the Project's founders, suggests that one of the purposes of the Project was about "the transformation from being a victim to being a survivor" (Reynolds, 1995).

That a single woman does not create T-shirts does not negate the transformative power of the narratives. Because bearing witness to the abuse is part of the healing process, merely creating a shirt opens the rhetor survivor to the possibility of transformation. Indeed, as a woman sees her story next to the story of a woman who may be in the latter stages of healing, she witnesses hope of her own transformation. Conversely, the woman who is in the latter stages of healing can view those shirts of early healing and see how far she has come.

In addition to the personal transformations evidenced in the Clothesline Project, there is an additional public transformation. Domestic abuse has too often remained society's dirty laundry, to be hidden from public view. By displaying these T-shirts in public, with the ugly stories of abuse as well as the stories of hope and survival, the problem is aired in the public sphere, forcing an admission on the viewer's part that the problem exists. Hence, a public transformation is precipitated.

IMPLICATIONS

This analysis of the Clothesline Project allows several implications about the Project itself, Burke's pentad, and visual rhetoric as a persuasive form. Following in the footsteps of previous minority movements, the Clothesline Project sheds light on a societal problem in a manner that gains public attention while using alternative means of public communication.

In considering the Clothesline Project as a rhetorical device, we must consider its audiences to uncover its power. There are two audiences, first, the T-shirt creators themselves and, second, the viewing public. For the survivors of domestic abuse, creating something that confirms their experiences is empowering because it proclaims to the world that the abuse happened. This proclamation forces the public to admit that the abuse happened. In addition, seeing her shirt next to others who have experienced similar pain reinforces the idea that the survivor is not alone. The visual nature of the display allows for more permanence and a broader audience.

For the viewing public, the Clothesline Project is often a wake-up call to domestic abuse. Too often, issues such as domestic abuse are pushed off as something that "other people" experience. With the visual display housed in town squares and other unavoidable places, the public is often forced to confront the issue. By viewing the stories of domestic abuse survivors, the public is forced to admit that the problem exists, and, often, not just to the anonymous "other." Because perpetrators are often named and the stories tell of danger in the everyday details of all of our lives, viewers have to rethink their own situations. For example, one T-shirt proclaimed that the perpetrator was the local karate instructor. Does the viewer or someone the viewer knows take karate? It makes the viewer think.

In Ling's (1990) summation of the pentad, he stated that we can uncover the rhetor's view of the world that the audience is to accept. What is the view of the world that the two narratives reveal? The before narrative asks the audience to alter its worldview that domestic abuse does not happen or that it's not important to them. To go through the healing process, the survivor must admit or acknowledge that the abuse occurred. This process is eased when the public also admits that the abuse happened. The after narrative asks the audience to believe that there is hope, that there is life after abuse. Because these narratives focus on the success of the survivors in moving on and future plans and hope for the survivors, these narratives ask the viewers to perceive the world as a place that can improve, especially with their help.

That there is no single rhetor does not dim the worldviews offered by these pentads. Across T-shirts and different Project displays, the same two stories are repeated again and again. This makes sense because survivors are going through a healing process that takes the same steps. Perhaps because the stories are so similar, additional power is granted to the Project; although each story is different, the process is the same. If a survivor starts caught in the grips of the perpetrator, she can know that eventually she will reclaim herself as well as control over her own life.

Were a town to hold a public meeting where survivors of domestic abuse told their stories, the narratives would necessarily be very short to allow as many women to speak as tell their stories in the Clothesline Project. Although the stories on T-shirts aren't long, the handwriting and accompanying visual images add poignancy to often overlooked stories. Consequently, the verbal telling of abuse stories often has power because of the detail that the speaker can reveal. However, the visual recounting of such narratives gains power and emotive responses because of the lack of detail. The short, to the point summations of abuse are often all the audience needs to know. In addition, that the T-shirts invade a public space that often can't be avoided ensures that the T-shirts aren't just available to interested parties, as a public speech might be.

The visual clearly has dimensions that verbal speech does not for both audiences of the Clothesline Project, the creator and public viewer. The invasive and more permanent nature of the installation allows both of these audiences to experience the rhetoric in a more reflective manner. One can contemplate the shirts, experience the emotion of the shirts, and, in turn, hope to do something about the situation.

CONCLUSION

The Clothesline Project is a rhetorical device in the long tradition of marginalized groups, namely, a visual device. Recognizing the potential of the visual image to move audiences, women have chosen to take their stories of domestic abuse to the public sphere for both their own benefit and the benefit of the public at large. The narratives tell two stories that resonate with survivors and the public at large. The first narrative illustrates the perpetrator of the crime as having control of the situation. The second narrative shifts control to the survivor as she reclaims her life and projects a positive future. The Clothesline Project offers hope to survivors and forces society to acknowledge the problem of domestic abuse. Through this installation we learn about the power of the visual to transform not only survivors of domestic abuse but also society at large.

ENDNOTES

[1] The Clothesline Project makes a distinction between *survivors*, those who live through the abuse, and *victims*, those who die at the hands of their abuser.

[2] Websites with multiple photos can be found at: http://www.sa.psu.edu/cws/images/clothesline/photopage.html, http://www.utoronto.ca/health/programs/info/clthslne.htm. There are a great variety of websites.

REFERENCES

Abdullah, H. (2000, April 3). "Clothesline airs abuse issues." *Newsday*, A19.

Burke, K. (1955). *A grammar of motives*. New York: Prentice-Hall.

Campbell, K. K. (1999, Summer). "The rhetoric of women's liberation: An oxymoron." *Communication Studies*, 125–138.

Chicetto, C. A. (1994, October). "The Clothesline Project." Pamphlet. The Clothesline Project National Network.

Davis, L., & Bass, E. (2000). *The courage to heal: A guide for women survivors of child sexual abuse*. New York: Harper & Row.

Dondis, D. A. (1973). *A primer of visual literacy*. Cambridge, MA: MIT Press.

Edelman, M. (1995). *From art to politics: How artistic creations shape political conceptions*. Chicago: University of Chicago Press.

Foss, S. K. (1996). *Rhetorical criticism: Exploration and practice*. Prospect Heights, IL: Waveland Press.

Lester, P. M. (1996). *Images that injure: Pictorial stereotypes in the media*. Westport, CT: Praeger.

Ling, D. A. (1970, Summer). "A pentadic analysis of Senator Edward Kennedy's address to the people of Massachusetts July 25 1969." *Central States Speech Journal*, 81–86.

Messaris, P. (1997). *Visual persuasion: The role of images in advertising*. Thousand Oaks, CA: Sage.

Parker, R. (1996). *The subversive stitch: Embroidery and the making of the feminine*. London: Women's Press.

Reynolds, K. M. (1995, August–September). "The Clothesline Project." [electronic version] *Canadian Dimension*, 35–36.

Vardi, N. (1998, May 18). "Project suits survivors to a T." *Ottawa Citizen*, p. C3.

Wood, J. T. (1992, November). "Telling our stories: Narratives as a basis for theorizing sexual harassment. *Journal of Applied Communication Research, 20*(4), 349–362.

Cognition

13

Cognitive Theory

RICK WILLIAMS
Independent Scholar

Visual cognitive theory is an exciting, complex, and rapidly developing field of study that integrates work from a number of distinct disciplines including neurobiology, cognitive science, psychology, education, art, and communication. Because of its interdisciplinary nature, visual theory is approached from various perspectives by different scholars in different fields. The purpose of this chapter is twofold: first, to review significant theories that contribute to the understanding and intelligent use of visual cognition as a process of knowing; and, second, to integrate these diverse ideas into a unified system that is more easily understood and applied in the classroom and in the world beyond academia.

In order to organize and understand this ever-changing and diverse field, we must start with theories of cognition, or knowing, and then integrate and apply them to visual cognition. To accomplish this, I have integrated my own work with the research of scholars in related fields to develop a theory of cognitive balance I call *omniphasism*, which means "all in balance." This refers to the need to balance the development and use of the two primary cognitive processing systems and the multiple intelligences that human minds use to know, understand, and respond to the world and the self in relation to the world.

Omniphasism calls these two primary cognitive systems *rational* and *intuitive* and organizes their respective intelligences as either rational or intuitive on primary cognitive levels. Application of the theory helps develop techniques to teach and use intuitive and rational cognitive abilities as equally significant and complementary components of an integrated model of cognition in which visual cognition and learning are the basis of a primary intuitive intelligence.

I discuss omniphasism in detail after we review the various theories that will help the reader understand visual cognition. But I have already referred to several ideas that are new to many readers and I want to explain these concepts before moving on to the review and integration of the other visual, cognitive theories that support the omniphasic organizational model.

For instance, cognition and intelligence are related but are not the same. Cognition refers to the mental processes of knowing or understanding. Intelligence is the ability to know and understand. Although all people have some ability to know or understand both intuitively and rationally, one individual might have a more highly developed linguistic intelligence while another has a more highly developed visual intelligence. One would use his or her linguistic intelligence to activate cognitive processes in the brain that allow one to use language and to know or learn from language.

Even though the concept of left and right brain is generally known in our educational system, the concepts of rational and intuitive cognitive modalities and of multiple intelligences (Gardner, 1993) are relatively new. The research that we review does show that the human mind uses two primary cognitive processing systems to know and understand and that these cognitive processes are supported by a number of distinct intelligences. One of these cognitive systems is analytical in nature and relies on reason as a means of knowing. I call this the *rational cognitive system* and it is the cognitive basis for mathematical and linguistic intelligences. The other cognitive system is synthesistic in nature and allows one to attain to knowledge directly without the need for reason. For instance, one sees and instantly knows. I call this the *intuitive cognitive system* and it is the cognitive basis for visual and musical intelligences, among others.

These distinct cognitive systems operate independently but also have the ability to work together. For instance, visual intelligence is intuitive at its cognitive base. We most often see, know, and respond to visual stimuli without applying rational cognitive processes. However, information gained from intuitive, visual cognition can subsequently be considered using rational processes to develop a reasonable response. In this way the independent intuitive and rational processes are integrated or balanced from an omniphasic perspective.

Another important theme that is central to all of the research that we review in this chapter is that there is a significant bias toward the development and use of rational intelligences and away from the teaching and use of intuitive intelligences in our culture. Since visual intelligence is the primary intuitive intelligence, this bias is significant to the study of visual cognition. This bias is also the basis for the omniphasic premise that there is a need to balance the use of rational and intuitive intelligences through development and integration of the two primary cognitive processing systems.

Visual knowing uses complex and multifaceted cognitive processes that draw on perception, memory, imagination, and logic. Visual knowing can involve both intuitive and rational intelligences that are processed by both the unconscious and the conscious mind. In fact, neuroscientists have proven that primary visual cognition happens on unconscious cognitive levels and guides behavior before the rational mind is aware that information has been received and processed.

The visual information that stimulates these processes can be generated by the physical eyes and by the imagination or the mind's eye. For instance, beyond seeing with the eyes, visual knowing can be stimulated by thought, music, words, memories, color, light and darkness, meditation, dreams, scent, and touch. We can see into the past as well as the present. Some even claim to see the future. We can know visually as well with our eyes closed as we can with them open. It is believed that only about 10% of the processes of visual knowing actually occur in the eyes. The remainder is cognitive. So pervasive and profound are our visual intelligences that "I see" commonly means "I know." Historically language, both written and spoken, evolved from seeing and thus did logic and reason, which are language-based, rational cognitive processes. Even today the majority of information that our brains process every moment is visual. Ancient people's, as well as many cultures today, rely on visions and dreams to define reality and to guide their lives.

Similarly, I would suggest that the 3,000–4,000 mediated images that the average U.S. citizen sees every day are part of today's dreamscape. Much like the dreams and visions of ancient times, mediated visual images are cognitively processed by the same unconscious pathways and memory systems as nonmediated visual information. The unconsciousness mind does not distinguish between real and mediated images as it commits them to memory. Thus, they play profound roles in developing perceptions of reality and normalcy and thus in creating values and in guiding behavior. The success of mediated imagery as a tool of information and persuasion exemplifies the unique character of visual cognition to synthesize information in preconscious formats that transcend logic and that guide and generate behavior prior to the cognitive use of reason. Yet as significant as visual communication is to our personal and cultural identities and our behavior, few consumers of visual information understand even this most basic concept of visual cognition as intuitive intelligence.

Because of recent discoveries in cognitive neuroscience, this intuitive phenomenon can now be explained from a neurobiological perspective. Visual information, generated by the activities of the mind or by the perceptions of the physical eye, follows neurological pathways that initially bypass the neocortex, the cognitive center of logic and reason. It travels first to the thalamus and then to the amygdala and on to the prefrontal lobes, a primary repository of unconscious memory. In the prefrontal lobes visual information is synthesized with other unconscious cognitive information to form unconscious biases that guide and generate behavior before a second signal is processed by the neocortex where a rational response can be formulated (Wolfe, 1983; LeDoux, 1986; Goleman, 1995; Bechara, Damasio, Tranel, Damasio, 1997).

This suggests that we may not be the rationally motivated beings that we believe ourselves to be. In fact, it may suggest that our reason is a secondary response to our intuitive cognitive processes. It may also suggest that our behavior is driven, on primary cognitive levels, by unconscious cognitive processes and intuitive intelligences that are strongly visual.

With these provocative ideas and this brief overview of visual cognition as background, I want to move on to a deeper exploration of the theories that explain visual cognition and to the concept of Omniphasic cognitive balance.

UNDERSTANDING COGNITION AS INTUITIVE AND RATIONAL

The first step to understanding visual knowing and cognitive theory is to explore the concept of balancing independent but complementary rational and intuitive cognitive systems from a historical context. This illustrates that modern culture is not the first to recognize the significance of verbal/analytical and visual/intuitive intelligences to human behavior. It will also show how rational thinking might have grown out of intuitive knowing in history and provide a historical context for the beginning of the rational bias in culture. The correlation between Julian Jaynes' ([1976], 1990) work on the bicameral mind of the ancient Greeks and the hemispheric specialization, or right and left brain theory, work by Joseph Bogen (1969, 1975) and Roger Sperry (1968, 1973) in the late 1960s and early 1970s provides a basis for historical support of a rational/intuitive cognitive model.

Then, I integrate this omniphasic concept of rational and intuitive cognitive balance into today's culture through modern science. This correlates contemporary research in several diverse areas of science with the historical research to support a modern model of cognition and visual knowing that is based on rational and intuitive intelligences. The integration of contemporary studies will include Howard Gardner's *Multiple Intelligences* (1993) work in education and psychology, the work of cognitive neuroscientists Joseph LeDoux (1986) and Bechara, Damasio et al. (1997) on the unconscious mind, and the works of other leading scholars in education, cognition, visual literacy, psychology, and physics.

Finally, I integrate the historical and contemporary cognitive theories with my own work to explain the omniphasic theory in greater detail. In doing so, I outline a cognitive organizational model for diverse visual theories in postulates 1–3 and propose new correlations and research ideas in postulates 4–6. I close the chapter by suggesting how the omniphasic theory might be used in visual education and in culture to balance the study and application of rational and intuitive cognition and intelligences.

I want to note that the omniphasic separation of cognitive processes and intelligences into intuitive and rational is a conceptual device to aid in the understanding of the independently functional, though integrated, primary cognitive systems. It is important to keep in mind that all are part of our one brain and that Omniphasism is about learning to use the integrated processes of the whole brain.

Visual Knowing from a Historical Perspective:
Jaynes' Bicameral Mind and the Evolution of Reason

Evidence of the two major cognitive processing systems of the human brain, operating in tandem, but in separate and distinct ways, is recorded in written language as far back as 1000 BCE, the approximate time of the first written version of the *Iliad*. According to psychologist Julian Jaynes, the Greeks of the *Iliad* operated from a cognitive arena where human nature was split in two and the mind of the Mycenaean was bicameral (Jaynes [1976], 1990).

The bicameral mind, meaning two legislatures, operated in a way so that one half was directly connected, through visions and hallucinatory voices, to the divine source (gods and goddesses in this instance) and served as the admonitory guide and director of all human activities. The other half was connected to the corporal world and directed activities to carry out the guidance of the admonitory (visual, divine) mind. Jaynes reasons that this left humankind without consciousness, or conscious decision-making abilities, because the gods directed all decisions and there was no need or process for conscious introspection. Though Jaynes cites numerous early cultures throughout the early world that probably exhibited the same intuitive cognitive base as the Greeks, he focuses on Homer's *Ulysses* because it is the only written work from that time that is in a language that can be clearly interpreted.

Jaynes' other significant contribution that is relevant to our rational/intuitive concept is in his assertion that the evolution of the rational, reasoned, conscious mind, as evidenced in the writings developed just prior to the Greek Golden Age of Reason, led to the origin of consciousness in humankind and, subsequently, to the demise of the bicameral mind. Thus, when humankind began to apply the rational mind and reason to move toward introspection, self-determination, and consciousness, reason began to dominate the guidance of the visual, divine mind, initiating the development of a disabling bias against visual/synthesistic intelligences in society.

In the most recent revision of *The Origin of Consciousness in the Breakdown of the Bicameral Mind* (1990), Jaynes asserted that the results of research in asymmetrical hemispheric function, "even conservatively treated, are in agreement with what we might expect to find in the right hemisphere on the basis of the bicameral hypothesis" (pp. 455–456). He pointed out that the superior ability of the right (visual) hemisphere to process information in a synthesistic manner and in a way that uses visual intelligence to add clarity to cognition is, indeed, the same synthesistic process that provided the visions and admonitory voices perceived as the divine voice of the gods to provide clarity of direction in the early bicameral mind. Jaynes further suggested a relationship between asymmetrical hemispheric function and the bicameral mind, stating that hemispheric specialization of the brain is the contemporary neurological model of the bicameral mind.

I want to suggest a correlation between Jaynes' explanation of the reason-generated demise of the visual/synthesistic dominance in the 10th century BCE bicameral mind and the subjugation of the synthesistic, right-hemisphere processes to the logical, left-hemisphere processes of the human mind described in the 20th-century research of neuropsychologist Roger Sperry (1968, 1973) and neurosurgeon Joseph Bogen (1969, 1975). This correlation provides historical context for the visual/synthesistic and verbal/rational cognitive model and places the beginning of the development of a cultural bias in favor of reason around 1000 BCE with the advent of the Greek Golden Age of Reason.

The Right and Left Brain: Bogen and Sperry and Distinct Cognitive Systems

I believe it is important to note that, although some current research challenges parts of the hemispheric specialization theory, it does not challenge the critical idea of the distinct visual/synthesistic and verbal/analytical cognitive processes described by Bogen and Sperry. Though the hemispheric specialization theory predates Bogen and Sperry and is controversial, with respected researchers on either side of the argument, the Bogen and Sperry works do provide empirical evidence of different and independent cognitive systems. This evidence has kindled the explosion of more than 45,000 publications on the subject since 1970 (Ornstein, 1997). Further, it is the *character* and *function* of the processes, *not their locations* in the brain, that are significant to omniphasic theory (Barry, 1997;

Bechara, Damasio, Tranel, & Damasio, 1997; Ornstein, 1997; Gardner, 1993; Edwards, 1989; Erdmann & Stover, 1991; Springer & Deutsch, 1989). In order to maintain the integrity of the original research and theory, in this section only, I use the terms *divine* (Jaynes), *visual, synthesistic, global, right hemisphere* and *r-mode* (Bogen & Sperry) to refer to the cognitive processes and intelligences that I have renamed intuitive/synthesistic. Similarly, I use the terms *verbal, logical, analytical, left hemisphere,* and *l-mode* (Bogen & Sperry) to indicate the processes that I characterize as rational/analytical. Beyond this section, right- and left-hemisphere references should be understood as metaphors for intuitive/synthesistic processes and rational/analytical processes, respectively.

In order to understand the significance of the Bogen and Sperry research to this study, it is necessary to be familiar with only the very basic structure of the human brain as being physically divided into two major halves, the right and left hemispheres, that are connected by the corpus callosum. When Bogen and Sperry began their research in the early 1960s, it was generally hypothesized that the left hemisphere processed verbal information and the right hemisphere processed visual information. The two hemispheres are connected by the corpus callosum, which serves as an integrative communication device between them.

Until the late 1960s and early 1970s, the left hemisphere, the seat of language that we link to logical thinking and reasoning, was considered to be the dominant or major hemisphere. The right hemisphere was thought to be the subordinate or minor hemisphere, both in terms of complexity and function.

In the 1960s, neurosurgeon Bogen performed a series of innovative neurosurgical procedures at The University of California at Los Angeles to sever the corpus callosum, the communication connector between the two hemispheres, in a number of individuals. This procedure relieved patients suffering from incapacitating chronic epileptic seizures and allowed them to live a basically normal life by all appearances. Because, after the operation, these patient's hemispheres operated independently and were no longer integrated by the corpus callosum, they were the perfect "split-brain" subjects for Dr. Roger Sperry and his student, Jerre Levy, to use in studies of hemispheric specialization at California Institute of Technology (Bogen, 1969).

By administering a series of tests to these patients in the 1970s, Dr. Sperry and his colleagues were able to determine that each hemisphere experiences reality in its own way and each has its own way of experiencing and processing information. He also discovered that the processes of the right hemisphere were as complex as the processes of the left hemisphere (Sperry, 1968). Dr. Sperry was awarded the Nobel Prize for his groundbreaking work.

Most significant to our omniphasic concept of rational and intuitive cognitive systems is the Bogen and Sperry characterization of the processes of the left brain as verbal, analytical, logical, linear, and the processes of the right brain as visual, synthesistic, global, perceptual, and metaphorical (Sperry, 1973).

Jerre Levy, one of Sperry's doctoral students who worked and published with Sperry on the experiments, discovered that the mode of processing used by the right brain is rapid, complex, whole pattern, spatial, and perceptual and is comparable in complexity to the left brain's verbal, analytical mode. Levy, in fact, suggested that the language of the left, logical hemisphere was inadequate for the rapid complex synthesis achieved by the right hemisphere. Levy described the left hemisphere as analyzing over time and the right hemisphere as synthesizing over space (Levy, 1968, 1974).

In addition to these findings, Sperry's own comments on his research indicated that he clearly recognized both a societal and an educational bias against right-hemisphere processes. These biases are significant to our understanding of contemporary assumptions that reason dominates our cognitive processes and the subsequent visual illiteracy of our culture. Sperry wrote:

> The main theme to emerge . . . is that there appear to be two modes of thinking, verbal and nonverbal, represented rather separately in left and right hemispheres, respectively, and that our educational system, as well as science in general, tends to neglect the nonverbal form of intellect. What it comes down to is that modern society discriminates against the right hemisphere. (1973, pp. 209–229)

Contemporary brain research has focused on locating the site of specific cognitive processes within each hemisphere and has challenged Sperry's assertion of strictly left/right hemispherical specialization (Bechara, Damasio, Tranel, & Damasio, 1997; Edwards, 1989). However, as noted earlier, this challenge does not alter the concept of distinct cognitive processes, a concept that has been extensively corroborated since Sperry's original work (Ornstein, 1997). Our omniphasic model is concerned with the distinct processing systems and not with the location of each cognitive process.

Thus, it is the very early recognition of a dual brain—half visual/synthesistic, half verbal/analytical—and the dominance of the visual/synthesistic brain prior to the Greek Golden Age of Reason that is of interest in Jaynes' work. And it is the Bogen and Sperry descriptions of a local versus global, verbal/analytical versus visual/synthesistic perspective in cognitive processes, each functioning with equal intelligence and significance to inform the whole individual, that forms the correlation and provides the basis for an omniphasic perspective of rational and intuitive cognitive systems.

Further, Jaynes' recognition of the beginning of the demise of the visual/synthesistic in favor of the verbal/analytical during the Age of Reason, and Sperry's recognition of a societal bias against the visual/synthesistic supports the need to balance the teaching and application of our cognitive modalities.

Cognition and Intelligence in Contemporary Science: Parallel/Dualistic Organizational Models and Gardner's Multiple Intelligences

In some ways, a parallel/dualistic system such as verbal and visual, rational and intuitive is too simplistic to define the complex cognitive patterns of the human mind. Certainly, in terms of identifying specific locations of the numerous processes in the brain, or of mapping the interaction of verbal and visual processes and intelligences, a dualistic system of this nature cannot tell the whole story. However, some kind of organizing framework is necessary to our discussion. Defining the nature of the two primary cognitive systems as rational and intuitive organizes their respective processes as predominantly analytical (rational) or synthesistic (intuitive). In other words, intuitive and rational cognitive processes that work independently but are integrated support the idea of complementary intuitive and rational intelligences such as visual and verbal in a way that correlates with Jaynes' bicameral mind and Bogen's and Sperry's right/left hemisphere work. As we shall see, this organization also provides a framework or model that integrates Howard Gardner's (1993) mulitiple intelligence theory into the rational/intuitive paradigm.

Gardner's theory of multiple intelligences (MI) suggested that all humans use a variety of intelligences such as verbal, mathematical, visual, and musical instead of one primary intelligence. Gardner said that, "except for abnormal individuals, intelligences always work in concert, and any sophisticated adult role will involve a melding of several of them" (1993, pp. 15, 17). Remember that cognition refers to the mental processes that create knowing or understanding. Intelligence is the ability to understand. One uses specific intelligences, such as visual or verbal, to activate cognitive processes related to seeing or speaking. The greater one's visual intelligence, the greater his or her ability to use the processes of cognition to understand and respond to what he or she sees.

Gardner used a parallel/dualistic organizational model to amplify and simplify a complex, integrated system for the purpose of discussion and analysis. He listed and described eight independent intelligences and separated them into two distinct categories, those that are testable by logical, linguistic tests such as the SAT and those that are not testable by these methods. The two intelligences Gardner listed as logically/linguistically testable are similar to those cited by Bogan and Sperry as verbal/analytical cognitive processes, and those he designated as nonlogically/linguistically testable appear to correlate with their designation of visual/systheistic cognitive processes. Gardner's noting of strong cultural/educational biases against the development of those intelligences that are not testable by logical, linguistic instruments also parallels the bias cited by Jaynes, Bogen, and Sperry against systhesistic cognitive processes.

These similarities form the basis of a model of visual communication that reflects the omniphasic principle of complementary and balanced cognitive modalities organized under rational and intuitive cognitive systems. This suggests that, if an intelligence that one uses to understand what one sees is based in cognitive processes that are intuitive and synthesistic rather than rational and analytical, then one can infer that the basic ability or intelligence to understand what one sees is also intuitive and synthesistic. Because of the integrated aspects of our cognitive systems, a primary intuitive intelligence, like visual intelligence, can subsequently be integrated with rational intelligences, such as verbal or mathematical intelligences, and provide information for rational analysis and response. It might also integrate only with other intuitive intelligences, such as music or bodily kinesthetic intelligence, and never be rationally considered in a conscious' cognitive format.

Though I cannot definitively assign all of the intelligences Gardner defines as predominantly rationally/analytically or intuitively/synthesistically based on primary cognitive levels, his own definitions support the type of omniphasic cognitive organizational model suggested in Table 13.1. Gardner's mathematical/logical and linguistic intelligences fit the concept of rational/analytical intelligences. Gardner's visual, musical, bodily kinesthetic, and intra/interpersonal intelligences fit the concept of intuitive/synthesistic intelligences. Though Gardner's spatial intelligence does not fully incorporate the concept of visual intelligence as I have suggested in Table 13.1, recent studies of visual intelligence (Barry, 1997; Hoffman, 1997; Williams, 1999; Newton, 2000) suggest that it is an appropriate

TABLE 13.1
Multiple Intelligences and Omniphasic Orgnizational Model

Omniphasic Model	Rational Intelligences	Intuitive Intelligences
Gardner's MI Model	Logically Testable Int.	Nonlogically Testable Int.
	Mathematical	Logical/Spatial/Visual*
	Linguistic	Musical
		Bodily Kinesthetic
		Intrapersonal
		Interpersonal
		Naturalistic

and critical addition though it need not always be linked with spatial (see Table 13.1). Gardner has recently added Naturalistic, which seems to relate most closely to the processes of synthesis.

This omniphasic model provides a basic format that places the concept of independent but integrated cognitive modalities within a historical framework of dualistic, rational/intuitive cognitive processes. It also correlates that organizational model to Gardner's contemporary MI theory and provides groups of specific intelligences that support the omniphasic cognitive organization. The remaining step needed to support the rational/intuitive model as a holistic cognitive system involves an exploration of how the actual cognitive modalities work within the brain. Does contemporary neuroscience, with its ability to map mental processes, support the omniphasic, rational/intuitive model, and what role does visual cognition play in this paradigm? How does visual cognition lead to understanding and how does it effect behavior?

Visual Cognition, the Unconscious Mind, and Behavior: LeDoux, Damasio, Barry, Goleman, Ornstein, Capra

Working from a neurobiological perspective in his book *Decartes' Error* (1994), Antonio Damasio pairs emotion and reason as complementary aspects of cognition. Damasio asserted that, "even after reasoning strategies become established in the formative years, their effective deployment probably depends, to a considerable extent, on a continued ability to experience feelings . . . certain aspects of the process of emotion and feelings are indispensable for rationality" (1994, pp. xii and xiii).

In later research (Bechara, Damasio et. al., 1997; Damasio, 1999), Damasio and his team suggested that the prefrontal lobes of our brains are the repository for a memory system that is developed and used unconsciously, synthesistically, to develop unconscious biases that generate advantageous, rational behavior. Further, they suggested that it is possible that rational behavior is dependent upon access to unconscious biases.

Bechara's and Damasio's work supports the proposition that synthesistic intelligences attain to direct knowledge before reason and without evidence of reason and operate in complementary, parallel processes to both guide and support rational decisions. Though Damasio's experiment did not isolate visual cognition, Wolfe suggested a similar scenario for visual processes as early as 1983 (Wolfe, 1983, pp. 94–98).

Later, LeDoux (1986) described this complex visual process from a cognitive perspective that suggests a similarity between Damasio's unconscious biases and preconscious visual processes.

> The newer research contradicts earlier thought and reveals how sensory signals from the eye travel first to the thalamus and then, in a kind of short circuit, to the amygdala before a second signal is sent to the neocortex. (pp. 237–248)

Simply put, the eyes see and, from a preconscious mode using the amygdala in concert with the prefrontal lobes, motivate behavior before the rational mind is activated. By integrating the work of LeDoux and Damasio, we discover a potential correlation between the synthesistic, neurobiological processes between the eye and the brain and the type of cognitive processes that characterize the unconscious memory of our prefrontal lobes, Both processes operate on preconscious cognitive levels to process information into knowledge and to motivate behavior before the conscious, analytical processes of the neocortex receive the information.

If this is true, visual communication, including the messages of persuasion imbedded in visual media imagery, operate both spontaneously as preconscious motivators of behavior and subsequently as they become part of the unconscious memory that forms the biases that later guide our decisions and our behavior. This supports the postulate suggested in the introduction of this chapter that visual intelligence operates as a highly synthesistic process that motivates behavior both before and beyond reason.

In *Visual Intelligence* (1997), Ann Marie Barry addresses LeDoux's work and this preconscious visual phenomenon, suggesting that visual processes, not rational, are the primary motivators of behavior. Barry explained:

> The implication of this is that we begin to respond emotionally to situations before we can think them through. The ramifications of this fact are significant, suggesting that we are not the fully rational beings we might like to think we are. What this second emotional route signals, in fact, is the likelihood that much of cognition is merely rationalization to make unconscious emotional response acceptable to the conscious mind. (p. 18)

Both Damasio and Barry suggested that emotions are the primary cognitive complement to reason. Goleman (1995) offered compelling evidence that emotional intelligence is more significant to decision making and behavior than rational intelligences. Goleman also correlates emotional intelligence with Gardner's personal intelligences (1995, pp. 40–43). From the perspective proposed in this chapter, this correlation and the preconscious character of emotion place emotional intelligence within the omniphasic framework of intra/interpersonal intuitive intelligences.

Further, drawing on the work of LeDoux and Damasio, Goleman describes a relationship between the amygdala and prefrontal lobes suggesting that they work together to mediate and guide preconscious behavioral motivations. He explained that the amygdala provides the more spontaneous, rudimentary response and the prefrontal lobes the more sophisticated, synthesistic response, both in preconscious formats (Goleman, 1995, pp. 17–21). This develops the correlation between LeDoux's preconscious motivations from the amygdala and Damasio's unconscious biases and supports the concept that visual intelligence is a primary intuitive intelligence that guides and motivates behavior prior to reasoned considerations.

Robert Ornstein (1997), approaching the subject from a psychological background, reviewed the major literature of the hemispheric specialization debate from the 1970s to the present in *The Right Mind: Making Sense of the Hemispheres*. He concluded his exhaustive survey of psychological, psychiatric, and biological literature on cerebral asymmetry, encountering more than 45,000 publications, with a statement similar to, though perhaps more metaphorical than, Damasio's:

> I'd say that there exists in the right side a capacity that updates the different possibilities for action at any time. It's necessary, for the brain to guide us through this complex world, for the different centers of the brain to be put on-line when it is time to analyze sounds, update memory, or decode a new dish of food. So one aspect of the right side's overall or higher view of events is that it may well have a measure of influence over which mental module gets activated. Context, in our life, trumps text, not the other way around. "Higher consciousness" is another way of putting it. (1997, p. 159)

In another realm of science, physicist Fritjof Capra (1991), in *The Tao of Physics*, uses a dualistic model of parallel perspectives to address the need to develop a more holistic scientific worldview. His work supports the concept that visual/synthesistic cognitive processes are as critical to science as verbal/analytical cognitive processes are. Capra cited such scientific luminaries as Neils Bohr and Werner Heisenberg in quantum physics as he described a contemporary, ongoing paradigm shift in scientific vision that leads away from the concepts and values of an outdated rational, technological worldview (Capra, 1991, p. 325). Capra's paradigm embraces an organic, holistic view of the world, recognizes the limitations of all rational approaches to reality, and accepts intuition as a valid way of knowledge (Capra, 1991, p. 325). Capra's "ecological worldview" is dualistic in that it recognizes two guiding principles, rational and intuitive thought, and is parallel in that it recognizes the interdependence of the two principles.

The dualistic approach embraced in this chapter draws from centuries of cross-cultural traditions that have explored and defined aspects of everything from human psychology (conscious/unconscious), neuropsychology (left/right brain), and mythology (masculine/feminine archetypes) to academia (qualitative/quantitative), philosophy (yin/yang), and physiology (male/female). To emphasize this dualistic, interdisciplinary perspective, I want to close this part of the discussion of visual cognitive theory with a comparison of ancient and contemporary parallel ways of knowing. This comparison visually and analytically illustrates the basic premise that underlies all of the theories and ideas that I have presented. Thus, Table 13.2 compares Bogen's *Parallel Ways of Knowing*

TABLE 13.2
Parallel Ways of Knowing

Parallel		Duality	
L-Mode	R-Mode	L-Mode	R-Mode
(Rational)	**(Intuitive)**	**(Rational)**	**(Intuitive)**
intellect	intuition	yang	yin
convergent	divergent	masculine	feminine
digital	analogic	positive	negative
secondary	primary	sun	moon
abstract	concrete	light	darkness
propositional	imaginative	right side	left side
analytic	relational	cold	warm
lineal	nonlineal	spring	autumn
rational	intuitive	summer	winter
sequential	multiple	conscious	unconscious
analytic	holistic	left brain	right brain
objective	subjective	reason	emotion

Source: Bogen, 1975, pp. 24–32.
(Based on *I Ching*, ancient Chinese Taoist work.)

(1975) with the ancient Chinese model of duality from the *I Ching* (1950). This graphically and conceptually illustrates the concept of complementary, parallel dualities, in both historical and contemporary formats. I have added the bold headings to show the relationship between these earlier ideas and the omniphasic concepts of rational and intuitive cognitive systems.

OMNIPHASISM: BALANCING VISUAL KNOWING AND COGNITIVE THEORY

A Visual Theory of Cognitive Balance

The omniphasic theory integrates and organizes the work already described in this chapter with the author's original work. The first postulate of omniphasism suggests that *human intuitive and rational intelligences complement one another as equal and parallel cognitive processes that operate independently, but are integrated.* This concept is grounded in the historical framework of Jaynes' bicameral theory and Bogen and Sperry's hemispheric specialization research. It suggests that the human mind utilizes two primary cognitive-processing systems. The theory transcends the semantic and neurotechnical problems associated with historical right- and left-hemisphere research by focusing on function rather than location and by redefining the cognitive modalities as functionally rational and intuitive. Rational intelligence is the ability to attain to knowledge through cognition based on reason. Intuitive intelligence is the ability to attain to knowledge directly, through cognition, without evidence of reason.

Further, the theory draws support from contemporary researchers in communication, education, art, neuroscience, psychology, visual studies, and physics to suggest, in postulate 2, that the *intuitive and rational systems are equally complex and equally significant to balanced, whole-brain functions of a human being.* The theory also notes, in postulate 3, that *a significant bias exists against the development and maintenance of intuitive intelligences throughout our scientific, economic, educational, and cultural systems.*

In addition to the historical perspective, these postulates are grounded in an interdisciplinary synthesis of contemporary work that specifically includes the multiple intelligence theory of Howard Gardner; Antonio Demasio's theory of unconscious biases;

TABLE 13.3
Key Postulates of the Omniphasic Theory

Postulate 1

- Human intuitive and rational intelligences complement one another as equal and parallel cognitive processes that operate independently but are integrated.

Postulate 2

- Rational and intuitive intelligences are equally complex and equally significant to the balanced, whole-brain functions of a human being.

Postulate 3

- A significant bias exists against the development and maintenance of intuitive intelligences throughout our scientific, economic, educational, and cultural systems.

Postulate 4

- This bias has created an experiential and psychological *intuitive intelligence void* in our culture that promotes *intuitive illiteracy* and leaves us cognitively unbalanced, lacking and longing for completion as whole beings.

Postulate 5

- This intuitive illiteracy has opened the door for the media to be used as the educational/exploitation system for intuitive intelligences. The power of the media to persuade and shape lives and cultures lies in their ability to develop intuitive communication processes that effectively fill this intuitive void.

Postulate 6

- The development of a holistic educational model that embraces a balanced curriculum, developing both intuitive and rational intelligences as equivalent and complementary, has the potential to prepare a more balanced, fully educated, self-determining individual, less susceptible to manipulative media influences and better prepared to apply classroom experiences to life experiences in ways that generate balance within the individual and thus within the cultural systems subsequently developed.

TABLE 13.4
Summary of Theories Relevant to Omniphasism

Omniphasism	Rational Intelligence	Intuitive Intelligence
Williams	The ability to learn or understand through a process relating to, based on, or agreeable to reason.	The ability to learn or understand through a process based on the power or faculty to attain to direct knowledge or cognition without evident rational thought or inference.
Bicameral Mind Jaynes	*Corporeal Function Brain* Conceptual	*Admonitory Brain* Perceptual
Hemispheric Spec. Bogen/Sperry	*Left Brain/L-Mode* Rational, verbal, logical, analytical	*Right Brain/R-Mode* Intuitive, visual, synthesistic, gestalt
Multiple Intelligence Gardner/Walters	*Logical Intelligences* Logical/Mathematical Linguistic	*Nonlogical Intelligences* Spatial/Visual Musical Personal Interior Personal Exterior Bodily Kinesthetic Naturalistic
Unconscious Memory Damasio	*Logical Intelligence* Reason	*Synthesistic Intelligence* Unconscious Bias
Visual Intelligence Barry	*Associative Logic* Visual Mosaic Logic	*Unconscious Memory* Perception
The Right Mind Ornstein	*Left Hemisphere* Text	*Right Hemisphere* Context
Science/Paradigm Shift Capra	*Technology/Mechanical* Rational Knowledge	*Ecological/World View* Intuitive Knowledge

Joseph LeDoux's research on visual cognition; Carl Jung's theory of the unconscious mind; Ann Marie Barry's theory of visual intelligence; Daniel Goleman's theory of emotional intelligence; Robert Ornstein's concept of text and context; and Fritjof Capra's theory of an ecological worldview.

The omniphasic integration of the work of the scholars presented in this chapter with the author's original work also suggests that most, if not all, intelligences and cognitive processes have strong visual components. For instance, the written formats of both math and linguistics are visual. Many mathematical concepts, such as fractals, have significant visual expressions in both the digital and biological worlds. Literature, voice, and music use visual notation and generate mind's-eye visual imagery that draw on conscious and unconscious imaginative and psychological intelligences. Intrapersonal and interpersonal intelligences rely heavily on both physical seeing and on mind's-eye visions in dreams and meditations. These interdisciplinary visual components suggest that the study of visual cognition and visual literacy provide a unified format for the study of certain areas of both intelligence and cognition.

In Table 13.3 I listed, in addition to the three postulates that are directly supported by the theories and scientific data explored in this chapter, three additional postulates that I suggest can be projected from that data. Postulates 4, 5, and 6 draw on original experiments in visual and media literacy that I have developed over the last 14 years. They also suggest why and how the omniphasic theory might be used to integrate visual learning, intuitive intelligence and cognitive balance into the educational system. Table 13.4 provides a summary that organizes all of the theories and data discussed in this chapter under the classifications of rational and intuitive intelligences and cognitive processes.

CONCLUSION

I believe that the sound quantitative data and science that support the first three postulates lead naturally to the theory proposed by the last three postulates. Together they generate a number of significant ideas and research questions for further study in terms of advancing omniphasic visual communication education and practices toward balanced visual and intuitive cognition. Some of the questions include the following:

- If the visual/synthesistic and verbal/analytical processes of the brain are equally complex and significant in their cognitive abilities to inform and establish the whole individual, and if there is an economic, educational, and scientific bias against the visual/synthesistic processes, then what is the effect of this bias on the individual and on society?
- If the effect is significantly negative, why do we continue to support it?
- What can be done to rectify the problems generated by this bias?

It appears that, as individuals, we are equipped with minds that, as a society, we are half-educating at best. We are leaving a major portion of our cognitive abilities out of the equation of cognition and education. We have created a society that wonders (with our verbal/analytical half-mind):

- Why is society so out of balance and out of control in terms of ecology, violence, war, starvation, distribution of wealth and goods, poverty, equality of gender and race, economies, greed, and peace?
- Why do so many seem to struggle to resolve such personal and public problems— often with the aid of a rapidly growing, quick-fix, self-help industry—as if toward some reasoned solution that remains just out of grasp.

I want to suggest that perhaps the emptiness and longing that so many feel in their lives is directly derived, at least partially, from our half-headed educational and cultural systems that ignore the growth toward individual and cultural wholeness that educating the whole mind, all of our cognitive abilities, could provide. Perhaps the void that many individuals experience and express, as well as unsolved answers to many personal and cultural problems, resides, to a significant degree, in the empty spaces of the untapped potential that balancing the use of our visual/synthesistic and rational/analytical intelligences and cognitive abilities would realize.

Omniphasism supports the idea that mass-communication media are rapidly becoming less verbally dominant and increasingly visually dominant. Because visual intelligence is a primary intuitive intelligence, visual and intuitive cognitive and communication skills then become requisite of this and future generations of citizens of visual cultures as well as communication professionals and scholars. Because of this, and because of the visual components of most intelligences, visual education provides a particularly significant arena for the study of the questions asked earlier and of the broader applications of intuitive intelligence and the application of the omniphasic theory. This paradigm shift toward an omniphasic cognitive and intelligence learning model is critical because visualization and other synthesistic cognitive abilities are supported by primary intuitive intelligences that, historically, have been studied predominantly from a rationally biased, educational perspective (Williams, 1999).

Omniphasism explores the rational biases of traditional visual education and suggests ways that we can build on the foundation of those approaches and expand them to embrace an omniphasic curriculum based on visual and media literacy (Williams, 2003; Ryan, 2004). I suggest that these rational biases contribute *to visual and intuitive illiteracy* and thus to the effective proliferation of persuasive, intuitive, media-generated communication. Thus, the rational bias perpetuates the power of the media to exploit intuitive illiteracy by using intuitive persuasion techniques to create perceptions of reality that, through conscious and preconscious cognitive processes, guide our behavior, including our personal and corporate development, on virtually all levels toward a consumer-consumed culture (Williams, 2000a).

In traditional theory development, a theory must be testable. Although the very nature of omniphasism rejects societal insistence on linear data support, I nevertheless have offered both historical and contemporary interdisciplinary, quantitative, and theoretical evidence to support my ideas by building on neurobiological, educational, communication, and psychological experiments on cognitive processing. I also offer qualitative evidence obtained through application of omniphasic techniques in the classroom over 14 semesters.

The omniphasic theory draws on the results of an omniphasic visual literacy class that I have taught to nearly 500 students each semester for 14 semesters. For this class I have developed 14 creative and cognitive exercises that use visual cognition to help students develop both intuitive and rational intelligences and cognitive processes. From this very successful experiment and experience I suggest, in other publications, (Williams, 2003), how one might begin to develop a new educational model that initiates the teaching of rational and intuitive intelligences as equal and complementary cognitive processes through omniphasic visual literacy. I also explore, from that base, how the development of intuitive intelligence can be integrated into other areas of our educational system (Williams, 2000b).

This holistic omniphasic approach to visual cognition and intelligence has the potential to teach students to use their whole minds to replace invasive and oppressive intuitive media experiences with self-directed intuitive experiences. The subsequent development of whole-mind processes fosters greater creativity, more powerful problem-solving abilities and balance between the desire for quantity and the nurturing quality of relationships and integrated life experiences. A more fully educated, self-determining individual who is less susceptible to manipulative media influences is also better prepared to apply classroom experiences to life experiences in ways that generate balance within the individual and thus within the cultural, economic, educational, and scientific systems subsequently developed.

REFERENCES

Barry, A. M. (1997). *Visual intelligence: Perception, image, and manipulation in visual communication.* New York: State University of New York.

Bechara, A., Damasio, H., Tranel, D., & Damasio, A. (1997). *Deciding advantageously before knowing the advantageous strategy. Science, 275,* 1293–1295.

Berger, A. A. (1998). *Seeing is believing: An introduction to visual communication.* Mountain View, CA: Mayfield Publishing.

Bogen, J. E. (1969). *The other side of the brain. Bulletin of the Los Angeles Neurological Societies, 34,* pp. 73–105.

Bogen, J. E. (1975). *Some educational aspects of hemispheric specialization. U.C.L.A. Educator, 17,* pp. 24–32.

Capra, F. (1991). *The tao of physics.* Boston: Shambhala.

Capra, F. (1996). *The web of life.* New York: Anchor.

Damasio, A. (1994). *Descarte's error.* New York: Putnam.

Damasio, A. (1999). *The feeling of what happens.* New York: Harcourt Brace.

Debord, G. (1983). *Society of the spectacle.* Detroit, MI: Black and Red.

Edwards, B. (1989). *Drawing on the right side of the brain* (Rev. Ed.). New York: Putnam.

Erdmann, E., & Stover, D. (1991). *Beyond a world divided.* London: Shambhala.

Gardner, H. (1985). *Frames of mind: The theory of multiple intelligences.* New York: HarperCollins.

Gardner, H. (1993). *Multiple intelligences: The theory in practice.* New York: HarperCollins.

Goleman, D. (1995). *Emotional intelligence.* New York: Bantam.

Hoffman, D. (1997). *Visual intelligence: How we create what we see.* New York: Norton.

I Ching or book of changes. (1950) (R. Wilhelm, Trans.). Princeton, NJ: Princeton University Press.

Jung, C. (1964). *Man and his symbols.* Garden City, NY: Doubleday.

Jaynes, J. ([1976], 1990). *The origin of consciousness in the breakdown of the bicameral mind.* Boston; Houghton Mifflin.

LeDoux, J. (1986). Sensory systems and emotion. *Integrative Psychiatry, 4,* 237–243.

Levy, J. (1968). Differential perceptual capacities in major and minor hemispheres. *Proceedings of the National Academy of Science, 61,* 1151.

Levy, J. (1974). Psychobiological implications of bilateral asymmetry. In S. J. Dimond and J. G. Beaumont (Eds.), *Hemisphere function in the human brain,* 121–183. New York: Wiley.

Newton, J. (2000). *The burden of visual truth; the role of photojournalism in mediating reality.* Mahwah, NJ: Lawrence Erlbaum Associates.

Ornstein, R. (1997). *The right mind: Making sense of the hemispheres.* New York: Harcourt Brace.

Ryan, W., & Conover, T. (2004). *Graphic communications today, 4th Ed.* (pp. 32–35). New York, NY: Thompson/Delmor.

Sperry, R. W. (1968). Hemisphere disconnection and unity in conscious awareness. *American Psychologist, 23,* 723–733.

Sperry, R. W. (1973). Lateral specialization of cerebral function in the surgically separated hemispheres. In F. J. McGuigan & R. A. Schoonover (Eds.), *The psychophysiology of thinking* (pp. 209–229). New York: Academic Press.

Sperry, R. W., Gazzaniga, M. S., & Bogen, J. E. (1969). Interhemispheric relationships: The neocortical commissures; syndromes of hemisphere disconnection. In P. J. Vinken & G. W. Bruyn (Eds.), *Handbook of Clinical Neurology* (pp. 273–89). Amsterdam: North Holland.

Springer, S. P., & Deutsch, G. (1989). *Left brain, right brain* (3rd. Ed.). New York: W.H. Freeman.

Williams, R. (1999, Autumn). Beyond visual literacy: Omnipahsism, A theory of cognitive balance, Part I. In N. Nelson Knupfer (Ed.), *Journal of Visual Literacy*, *19*(2), 159–178.

Williams, R. (2000a, Spring). Visual illiteracy and intuitive visual persuasion, Part II. In N. Nelson Knupfer (Ed.), *Journal of Visual Literacy*, *20*(1), 111–124.

Williams, R. (2000b, Autumn). Omniphasic visual-media literacy in the classroom part III. In N. Nelson Knupfer (Ed.), *Journal of Visual Literacy*, *20*(2), 219–242.

Williams, R. (2003). Transforming intuitive illiteracy: Understanding the effects of the unconscious mind on image meaning, image consumption, and behavior. In J. Yaross Lee & L. Strait (Eds.), *Explorations in Media Psychology*, *2*(2), 119–134.

Wolfe, J. (1983). Hidden visual processes. *Scientific American, 248*(2), 94–103.

14

Children's Comprehension of Visual Images in Television

GEORGETTE COMMUNTZIZ-PAGE
Independent Scholar

It's bedtime. A 3-year-old sits in a comfortable chair with his mother as she reads aloud. Typically, the two engage in an interesting discussion about the pictures and the story. In one of the illustrations, a cow is portrayed jumping over a crescent-shaped moon. "Oh, look at that moon!" she exclaims to her son, who has a disconcerted look on his face. When she asks her 3-year-old what is wrong, he tells her that the moon is "broken." "Yes, I guess it does look that way," says the mother, realizing that a crescent-shaped moon is not yet part of her preschooler's visual vocabulary.

This storybook scene is an example of the way young children make sense of visual conventions, which producers assume hold the same meaning for all viewers. Television is full of instances wherein portrayed images are presumed to be understood by everyone in the same way; however, sometimes producers miss the mark in creating clear visual messages for their viewers, particularly those who are less sophisticated. Take, for instance, a child who is watching the news and sees two persons engaged in a conversation, framed in boxes in a space that viewers are to assume is different from that of the news anchors. Although these two people are presumably talking to each other, they are depicted side by side, looking straight into the camera, without any semblance of convergence or connection that is apparent in other instances when the camera cuts back and forth from one person to the other. How would most viewers interpret this visual? Would the more unsophisticated audience "get" that these two people are engaged in conversation? What would a child think? I would argue that on seeing the two people talking in boxed spaces on the news, a child might ask, "Who are they talking to?"

Following a brief discussion of the pertinent theories of child development and visual communication, this chapter highlights a study that examines children's interpretations of a production technique used in television news formats. This technique utilizes first- and second-order space. Zettl defined first-order space as "the space of the television as defined by the borders and perceived depth of the TV picture" (Zettl & Communtziz-Page, 1998, p. 3); second-order space is "clearly defined space within the first-order space of the television screen such as the box over the newscaster's shoulder" (p. 3). Findings from the study reveal that producers' intentions of depicting two people who are talking to each other in boxed or framed, second-order space may present problems to viewers, especially those who have not yet acquired the necessary cognitive skills within the spatial realm of intelligence that support their comprehension of such a technique. By integrating theories in the fields of child development and visual communication, the study exemplifies a method that is useful in determining what child viewers understand about visual presentations.

CHILD DEVELOPMENT

The field of child development offers a pool of literature that may be used in studies that examine young children's understandings of visual media. In studying how children develop, theorists have taken many different perspectives; however, those who have recognized the importance of the interaction between internal and external factors are most conducive to the study of children's perceptions of visual messages. The seminal work of the renowned developmentalist Jean Piaget emphasized the interactions between children and their physical worlds in learning to understand basic concepts. His stage theory presumes that children go through predictable stages in reaching the ultimate goal of learning how to think logically and hypothetically by the time they are young adults (Boden, 1979; Bybee & Sund, 1982; Piaget, 1954, 1955; Sugarman, 1987).

Other basic theories that provide a strong foundation for explaining various phenomena of children's development include those of Lev Vygotsky (1978) and Jerome Bruner (1966). Both emphasized the importance of interactions between the individual child and the environment; however, Vygotsky's emphasis is on culture and how it shapes thinking. Bruner's theory highlights the reciprocal interaction among internal and external elements as he asserts that the children learn to think by first acting directly on objects, then picturing them in their heads, and finally representing them symbolically.

Multiple Intelligences

These seminal theorists have provided scholars with a firm ground for studying children's comprehension of visual media. A more complete interactive theory that emerged in 1983 and finding its place in many developmental "camps" is that of Howard Gardner. In his theory of multiple intelligences, Gardner (1983, 1993) incorporated the best aspects of Piaget's stages of cognitive development, Vygotsky's emphasis on culture as the predominant force in learning how to think, and Bruner's focus on the reciprocity between internal and external aspects of developing the ability to think symbolically.

Gardner (1983, 1993) examined many different populations, including individuals who were prodigies, brain injured, gifted, savants, normal, and experts in different fields, and those from various cultures in order to affirm that at least seven areas of intelligence exist: logical-mathematical, linguistic, spatial, musical, bodily kinesthetic, inter- and intrapersonal. More recently, he illuminated an eighth realm, naturalist, which includes skills in observing, understanding, and organizing patterns in the natural environment (Campbell, 1996).

Spatial Intelligence and Perspective Taking

An important area of cognitive development is children's concepts of space (e.g., Siegler, 1998). Within the theory of multiple intelligences, spatial knowledge is one of the most relevant to the study of visual media because this intelligence is concerned with the three-dimensional world and how it is represented two-dimensionally. Spatial intelligence involves objects in space and transforming mental images of three-dimensional reality; it is demonstrated in navigators, expert chess players, sculptors, and engineers. According to the theory, spatial intelligence skills center around three-dimensional thinking: recognizing the qualities of an object, perceiving the changes in that object, mentally rotating the object in space, and reproducing it by drawings, paintings, and other graphic depictions (Gardner, 1983, 1993). When viewers comprehend what is presented on television or film, they must interpret visual conventions such as cuts, zooms, dollying, split screens, and mats. How young children understand the conventions depends to a large extent on their cognitive abilities within the spatial realm.

Understanding different points of view and manipulating objects in space is an aspect of spatial intelligence that developmental psychologists have examined in perspective-taking studies. These studies have found that children represent space in ways that are fundamentally different from that of adults. Beginning with the seminal three mountains study of Piaget and Inhelder (1956), results in subsequent studies show that children who are around 4 years of age begin to understand that what one person sees in one viewing position may be different from what another person sees in another viewing position. Before acquiring this ability, young children indicate that what they see is what everyone else sees, regardless of the viewing position. Scholars at first attributed this deficiency to young children's egocentricity which inhibits them from seeing beyond their own point of view; however, in subsequent studies, researchers have varied their form of questioning and have found that children as young as 3 years of age are able to understand different points of view. (Newcombe & Huttenlocher, 1992, 2000; see also Newcombe, 1989, for a complete review of subsequent studies.) These scholars argued that when children are asked questions by picking from a set of alternative viewpoints or by constructing a model, they must understand two frames of reference. Others found that when children can trace a line between the dolls to see if the dolls can see each other or if the dolls can see different objects, then children performed well on the perspective-taking tasks (Hughes & Donaldson, 1979; Yaniv & Shatz, 1990).

Scholars who study perspective taking have taken many different approaches and have still yet to agree on the developmental aspects of such phenomena. The controversy seems to lie in the type of tasks that are administered to the child subjects. Newcombe and Huttenlocher addressed the discrepancies of results in perspective-taking studies by concluding, "what develops is a strategy or set of strategies for dealing with a cognitive situation challenging to individuals of all ages: the situation in which two or more frames of reference must be maintained at once, yet distinguished from each other and interrelated. The advent of success on such tasks in late childhood is a functionally significant transformation of cognitive ability" (2000, p. 125). Although these scholars of perspective taking have used many different means of testing children, few have investigated young children's understanding of the various viewpoints that are portrayed on television (Comuntzis, 1987; Communtziz-Page, 1997; Page, 1997; Smith, Anderson, & Fischer, 1985).

Children's Televiewing Experience

In the literature from the fields of child development, scholars have continued to study the relationship between mass media, particularly television, and young viewers (e.g., Huston, Wright, Rice, Kerkman, & St. Peters, 1990; Kunkel, 1992). Consequently, there is a preponderance of evidence showing that children's viewing experience is often different from that of adults. These scholars used variables such as age, sex, attention, and elements of the viewing situation in order to understand how children interpret televised material. As well, the majority of studies concentrate on the *content* of the presentation (e.g., Paik and Comstock, 1994; Sawin, 1990; Wiegman, Kuttschreuter, & Baarda, 1992). Some scholars looked at the *form* of the medium in relation to young children's comprehension (e.g., Calvert, 1988; Smith et al., 1985; Wright & Huston, 1983). Others argued that both content and form are inseparable in interpreting televised material (Wartella, 1986). These studies demonstrate that young viewers often have different interpretations of what they see on television than do adults, yet there are only a few studies that incorporate spatial intelligence as a way to explain differences in children's interpretations.

In several studies that I have done, I have articulated an important relationship between children's comprehension of visual media and their spatial intelligence. (See Page, 1997, for a review.) One study shows that young children have difficulty in interpreting the convention of changing viewpoints on television as the camera cuts from longshot to over-the-shoulder shot to close-up while two actors playing a game of checkers (Comuntzis, 1987). I found in this study that a close relationship exists between children's understanding of changing viewpoints depicted in a televised scene and their performances on a three-dimensional perspective-taking task (described in the next section), which was developed from other studies on perspective-taking ability. This unique approach to studying children's understanding of the forms of visual presentations that are depicted on television incorporates Gardner's spatial realm and minimally relies on the children's verbal responses to find out what young children are comprehending from the visual information that is presented to them.

By using such a method, which is grounded in theories of child development, investigators can gain more insight into young children's televiewing experiences. When producers depict characters simultaneously in two different spaces through matted images or split screens, cut from one shot to another within the same scene, or have cameras dolly around objects in a scene, viewers' spatial intelligence determines, to some extent, how they make sense of these commonly used techniques. Young viewers in particular may be confused by these conventions depending on their abilities within the spatial realm as well as the extent to which these production techniques are isomorphic with naturally occurring events in the world.

THE STUDY: ARE THEY TALKING TO ME?—A PROBLEM IN VIDEO PROXEMICS

Visual communication theory also plays a significant role in a study I did in collaboration with Herbert Zettl, who has developed many theories about television aesthetics and production techniques (e.g., 1989, 1997, 1999). The study investigates a problem in *video proxemics*, which Zettl defines as the screen space and the people who are portrayed as operating within that space (Zettl & Communtziz-Page, 1998). In this study, I took an approach that focuses on children's spatial ability as a major determinant in how they interpret various manipulations of televised space and empirically tested Zettl's arguments and assumptions about how viewers perceive a visual used by producers of television news wherein actors are portrayed in first- and second-order space. Zettl defined first-order space as that in which the borders and depth are defined by the television picture; second-order space occurs within first-order space in a clearly defined area such as a boxed frame. He argued that when producers depict two people, who are talking to each other, converging (cuts from one actor to another, creating Z-axis index vectors), not continuing, lines (actors side by side, looking straight into the camera) need to be used in order to effectively depict a conversation between the two people; otherwise, viewers do not perceive the two actors as being directly connected to each other.

As a first step in understanding how viewers' perceptions are established and how they work in relation to this news format, I studied children 3 to 6 years of age (Zettl & Communtziz-Page, 1998). By looking at young children's responses to questions about first- and second-order space depicted on a videotape, it is possible to see how viewers first begin to understand this type of video space. The study answered the following questions: How will young children interpret a conversation of two people who are shown "boxed" into separate side-by-side frames while looking at the child viewers rather than at each other? Will they readily understand that the two conversation partners, who both look at the children, are supposed to be looking at each other? The basic assumption is that such video proxemics will not facilitate the children's perception of these two people talking to each other and will leave the children confused.

Other variables in this study include age, sex, and children's performance on a perspective-taking task. Perspective-taking ability is one indication of a child's spatial knowledge and pertains to understanding that someone situated in a different viewing position sees things differently from another person in another position. Perspective taking is also relevant to this study because viewers must know about the performers' different points of view in order to determine where the actors are and to whom they are talking in second-order space.

Subjects

Fifty-six children (19 girls, 37 boys) were drawn from preschools and child care centers in or near a small university town. Their ages ranged from 3 to 6 years, with a mean age of 4 years, 6 months. They were tested separately in a room in their center or school with the researcher, who introduced herself and talked to them about what they were going to do. If any child refused to participate, he or she went back to regular activities. (Only three children refused.)

Materials

All children were given two tasks. In the first task, the child sat in front of a TV monitor and watched one of the versions of a videotaped conversation between two actors (Joey and Bayley) involving conventional or digitally structured video space. In order to preserve ecological validity for televised images viewed by children, I let them see the segment all the way through one time before they watched it with paused frames to answer questions about the frozen image. (See Figs. 14.1–14.5.)

The first version depicts two actors talking to each other sequentially in first-order space: Joey and Bayley greet each other and then proceed to talk to each other in sequential Z-axis close-ups (Fig. 14.1). The second version uses digitally produced frames around Joey and Bayley, who are side by side, looking straight into the camera (Fig. 14.2). The third type of visual incorporates another use of second-order space in which Joey and Bayley are angled toward each other in three-dimensional (trapezoid) frames (Fig. 14.3). The fourth and fifth versions of the conversation use profiles of Joey and Bayley in first-order and second-order space respectively (Figs. 14.4 & 14.5).

Procedure

Children were initially shown one of the five versions of Joey and Bayley talking to each other and then were asked four questions, requiring simple, one-word answers, revealing the child's interpretations of Joey and Bayley's conversation. Their answers show whether the viewers "buy into" the notion that the two performers are talking to each other and whether the performers see each other.

The questions asked to the children are similar to the type used by developmental psychologists (e.g., Flavell, Flavell, & Green, 1983, 1986; Flavell, Flavell, Green, & Kormacher, 1990; Gopnik & Astington, 1988): "When you look at this with your eyes,

FIG. 14.1. Sequential Z-axis close-ups.

FIG. 14.2.   Continuous close-ups.

FIG. 14.3.   Trapezoid frames.

FIG. 14.4.   Profile—First-order space.

FIG. 14.5.   Profile—Second-order space.

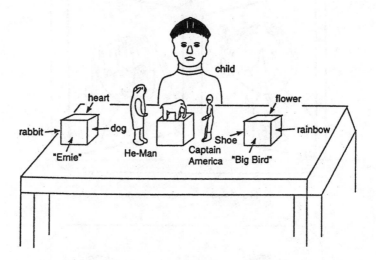

FIG. 14.6.   Three-dimensional perspective-taking task.

does it look like Joey's/Bayley's talking to someone? For real, who is he/she really and truly talking to? When you look at this with your eyes, does it look like Joey's/Bayley's really and truly looking at someone? For real, who's Joey/Bayley really and truly talking to?" These questions require only one-word answers, thereby reducing any dependence on the children's verbal abilities.

The second task included the table task that I have used in previous studies (Communtziz-Page, 1997). In this study, children sat in chairs across from me at a table that displays dolls situated near blocks with stickers of familiar objects on the sides. As shown in Fig. 14.6, the two characters look at a middle block on which a toy elephant faces one of them.

The children and I first talked awhile about the objects (the names of the characters, the objects portrayed in the stickers on the sides of the blocks, and the parts of the elephant) in order to become more comfortable with each other and to make sure that the children understood all of the terms used in the questioning. The display was fixed so that children saw one side of the blocks and one side of the elephant. They never had to remember what objects were not within view because I reminded them where the objects were.

The questions I asked determined the level of perspective taking for each child. Level I is characterized by children knowing that what they see is different from what another person in a different position sees. "Do you see the elephant?" and "Does Zack see the elephant?" are questions that test this first level. Children are at Level II when they know that a person may see the object differently than they do. For instance, "Does Kimberly see the sides of the blocks that you see?" is a question that reveals whether children are at the second level. The third level of ability is reached when children know what an imagined viewpoint is like: "Let's pretend that Kimberly sits down on the table right where she is. Does she see the heart sticker?"

I finished the perspective-taking task by bringing out two finger puppets placed on pencils and asked the children to "fix the two puppets to make them look like they're talking to each other." I then allowed the children to turn the puppets any way they wished in order to show them "talking" to each other. Finally, I took back the puppets and had them face the children, not each other, and asked, "What if I do this" (fixing the puppets next to each other, facing outward to the child). "Can Jason and Zack talk to each other now?" After the children answered this last question, the task ended.

Results

Subjects were given scores (1–4) for their responses to questions about the TV performers depicted in one of the five configurations using first- or second-order space. They received one point for each question they answered correctly on the video task. Scores on the perspective-taking task were determined by answering questions correctly within each level of ability (1–3). If they missed more than one question within a level, they were designated to be at the next lower level of ability.

I also noted how the children responded to the questions about the finger puppets talking to each other, whether they put the puppets facing each other and if they answered "yes" or "no" when I asked if the puppets could talk to each other when facing outwardly.

Mean scores on the video task were compared between and among the five conditions. The visual that elicited the most correct responses from the children in this study used profiles in first-order space (Fig. 14.4), having a mean score of 3.5.

In this visual, Joey and Bayley faced each other and were depicted in cuts from one to the other as they conversed. The version that had the next highest average score (3.4) on the video task was the one in which Joey and Bayley were shown talking to each other and facing the camera as the image cut from one to the other in first-order space (Fig. 14.1).

Low scores on the video task were a result of children viewing those versions using second-order space. The visual having the lowest mean score (2.6) on the video task depicted Joey and Bayley talking to each other in trapezoidal frames, which gives an illusion of three-dimensionality (Fig. 14.3).

The next lowest scores on the video task (2.7) resulted from the children watching the profiled (boxed) conversation in second-order space (Fig. 14.5). The version in which Joey and Bayley were shown conversing in boxes next to each other and looking straight at the camera (Fig. 14.2) resulted in lower scores (3.0) than those from the nonboxed versions.

The most significant difference in scores on the video task was between the groups of children watching the visuals using performers in second-order, boxed space and those watching the performers in first-order space ($t = 1.88$, $p < .05$). Interestingly, when the scores on the perspective-taking tasks from the same groups were compared, a significant difference was also found ($t = 2.36$, $p < .01$).

When responding to the question of how the finger puppets should be facing when talking to each other, 94% (45/48) of the children made the puppets face each other. When asked if the puppets could still converse when they were facing forward and not at each other, 67% (30/45) said that the puppets could not talk to each other if they faced outward.

Discussion

This study was done to examine the questions asked about the use of second-order space in television. According to the data from this study, when any kind of graphication is used to depict two performers engaging in conversation, young viewers are not convinced that the performers are talking to each other.

There were no significant differences between and among the ages and sex in each group of children watching the five versions of the video used in this study, which indicates that other factors are contributing to the confusion. Judging from the results of this study, the type of visual used to depict a conversation on TV is important to a young viewer's interpretation of that dialogue. Because there was a significant difference found between scores on the perspective-taking tasks in the group who saw the boxed versions and those who saw the unboxed versions, the spatial ability of the viewer (demonstrated by their performance on a perspective-taking task) may be a factor in how well they understand the graphications used in second-order space.

The use of computer-generated visuals that frame performers as they presumably carry on a conversation present problems for young viewers, particularly those who have fewer spatial abilities. In answering the specific question as to whether viewers perceive the z-axis index vectors as converging or continuing when two people pretend to talk to each other in second-order space, this study shows that young viewers are generally unable or unwilling to change their mental maps to accommodate the continuing vectors as converging ones. An explanation for their confusion may be found in their inability to make the frames transparent and to perceive them as connected video space. That is, children may see the frames, particularly where the performers face each other, as barriers. The index vectors in this type of visual are stopped by the frames, hence, inhibit the visual connection between the performers.

The use of the boxes portrayed as trapezoids, giving the illusion of three-dimensionality, also presented problems to young viewers in this study. Regardless of the angled intention of the frames, young viewers did not think that the performers were talking to each other.

CONCLUSION

Children in this study were confused when we made them interpret a conversation between two people in second-order space, even if their index vectors are converging rather than continuing. The results clearly call for additional testing. There is, as in other such studies, the possibility that the children's confusion was triggered by a lack of spatial intelligence or by a misunderstanding of just what the computer-generated effects had to do with their viewing task. These results, however tentative, seem to support the original hypothesis—that perceiving the continuing index vectors as converging does not happen when two people pretend to talk to each other while being stuck in two side-by-side, second-order screen boxes. As adults, we may make the connection of the two people talking to each other through audio rather than video. The children, however, were obviously less persuaded to substitute the audio track for the video problems. Children in this study were confused when they interpreted a conversation between two people in second-order space. Findings from the study warrant further inquiry into this problem of video proxemics. Nevertheless, results supported the assumption that children's interpretations of such a production technique are dependent on the their spatial abilities, defined by their performances on a perspective-taking task. Children in this study, especially those who did not demonstrate their spatial abilities on a three-dimensional perspective-taking task, were not convinced that the two actors were talking to each other, particularly when the actors were depicted in framed, second-order space.

The study exemplifies an approach that I took in order to investigate children's interpretations of a production technique used in television news. I considered findings from previous studies of children's spatial abilities in order to establish a theoretical framework and method for this particular investigation. I also based this preliminary study on Zettl's arguments and assumptions about how viewers perceive a visual used by producers of television news wherein actors are portrayed in first- and second-order space. Thus, the research is theoretically grounded within the fields of child development as well as visual communication. I used a method that incorporated tasks and questions that required children to rely mostly on their visual-spatial skills and less on their verbal abilities. Findings, albeit tentative, indicate that there may be a relationship between young viewers' spatial knowledge and their skills in interpreting a visual used in television. With few exceptions, this relationship has rarely been explored by those studying children's comprehension of televised events.

REFERENCES

Boden, M. (1979). *Jean Piaget*. New York: Viking.

Borke, H. (1975). Piaget's mountains revisited: Changes in the egocentric landscape. *Developmental Psychology*, 11(2), 240–243.

Bruner, J. (1966). Studies in cognitive growth. New York: Wiley.

Bybee, R., & Sund, R. (1982). *Piaget for educators*. Prospect Heights, IL: Waveland Press.

Calvert, S. (1988). Television production feature effects on children's comprehension of time. *Journal of Applied Developmental Psychology*, 9(3), 263–273.

Campbell, B. (1996). *Teaching and learning through multiple intelligences*. New York: Allyn & Bacon.

Communtziz, G. (1987). Young children's understanding of changing viewpoints in a televised scene (Doctoral dissertation, University of Utah, 1987). *Dissertation Abstracts International,* 48/04-A, 771.

Communtziz-Page, G. (1997). A preliminary study on children's understanding of the conventions used in television interviews. In R. Griffin, J. Hunter, C. Schiffman, & W. Gibbs (Eds.), *Vision-quest: Journeys toward visual literacy* (pp. 411–419). Visual Literacy Association. State College, PA.

Flavell, J., Flavell, E., & Green, F. (1983). Development of the appearance-reality distinction. *Cognitive Psychology, 15,* 95–120.

Flavell, J., Flavell, E., & Green, F. (1986). Development of knowledge about the appearance-reality distinction. *Monographs of the Society for Research in Child Development, 51* (Serial No. 212).

Flavell, J., Flavell, E., Green, F., & Kormacher, J. (1990). Do young children think of television images as pictures or as real objects? *Journal of Broadcasting and Electronic Media, 34,* 399–417.

Flavell, J., Green, F., & Flavell, E. (1989). Young children's ability to differentiate appearance-reality and level 2 perspectives in tactile modality. *Child Development, 60,* 201–213.

Gardner, H. (1983). *Frames of mind: The theory of multiple intelligences.* New York: Basic Books.

Gardner, H. (1993). *Multiple intelligences: The theory in practice.* New York: Basic Books.

Gopnik, A., & Astington, J. (1988). Children's understanding of representational change and its relation to the understanding of false belief and the appearance-reality distinction. *Child Development, 59,* 26–37.

Hughes, M., & Donaldson, M. (1979). The use of hiding games for studying the coordination of viewpoints. *Educational Review, 31,* 133–140.

Huston, A., Wright, J., Rice, M., Kerkman, D., & St. Peters, M. (1990). Development of television viewing patterns in early childhood: A longitudinal investigation. *Development Psychology, 26,* 409–420.

Kunkel, D. (1992). Children's television advertising in the multichannel environment. *Journal of Communication, 42*(3), 134–152.

Newcombe, N. (1989). Development of spatial perspective taking. In H. W. Reese (Ed.), *Advances in child development and behavior,* vol. 22 (pp. 203–247). San Diego: Academic Press.

Newcombe, N., & Huttenlocher, J. (1992). Children's early ability to solve perspective-taking problems. *Developmental Psychology, 28,* 635–643.

Newcombe, N., & Huttenlocher, J. (2000). *Making space.* Cambridge, MA: MIT Press.

Page, G. C. (1997). Visual intelligence and spatial aptitudes. In J. Flood, D. Lapp, & S. Heath (Eds.), *A handbook for visual literacy educators: Research on teaching the communicative and visual arts* (pp. 55–61). New York: Macmillan.

Paik, H., & Comstock, G. (1994). The effects of television violence on antisocial behavior: A meta-analysis. *Communication Research, 21*(4), S516–546.

Piaget, J. (1954). *The construction of reality in the child.* New York: Ballantine.

Piaget, J. (1955). *The language and thought of the child.* New York: Meridian.

Piaget, J., & Inhelder, B. (1956). *The child's conception of space* (F. Langdon and J Lunzen, Trans.). London: Routledge & Kegan Paul.

Sawin, D. (1990). Aggressive behavior among children in small playground group settings with violent television. In K. D. Gadow (Ed.), *Advances in learning and behavioral disabilities, 6* (pp. 157–177). Greenwich, CT: JAI.

Siegler, R. (1998). *Children's thinking.* Upper Saddle River, NJ: Prentice-Hall.

Smith, R., Anderson, D., & Fischer, C. (1985). Young children's comprehension of montage. *Child Development, 56,* 962–971.

Sugarman, S. (1987). *Piaget's construction of the child's reality.* Cambridge, UK: Cambridge University Press.

Vygotsky, L. (1978). *Mind and society.* Cambridge, MA: Harvard University Press.

Wartella, E. (1986). Getting to know you: How children make sense of television. In G. Gumpert & R. Cathcart (Eds.), *Inter/media: Interpersonal communication in a media world* (3rd Ed., pp. 537–549). New York: Oxford University Press.

Wiegman, O., Kuttschreuter, M., & Baarda, B. (1992). A longitudinal study of the effects of television viewing on aggressive and prosocial behaviors. *British Journal of social Psychology, 31,* 147–164.

Wright, J., & Huston, A. (1983). A matter of form: Potentials of television for young viewers. *American Psychologist, 38,* 835–843.

Yaniv, I., & Shatz, M. (1990). Hueristics of reasoning and analogy in children's visual perspective taking. *Child Development, 61,* 1491–1501.

Zettl, H. (1989) The graphication and personification of television news. In G. Burns & R. J. Thompson (Eds.), *Television studies: Textual analysis* (pp. 137–163). New York: Oxford University Press.

Zettl, H. (1997). *Television production handbook.* Belmont, CA: Wadsworth.

Zettl, H. (1999). *Sight sound motion: Applied media aesthetics.* Belmont, CA: Wadsworth.

Zettl, H., & Communtziz-Page, G. (1998). *Are they talking to me? A problem in video proxemics.* Unpublished manuscript.

Semiotics

15

Visual Semiotics Theory

SANDRA MORIARTY
University of Colorado

In the movie *13 Days*, a chronicle of the Cuban missile crisis, there is a scene in which Bob McNamara tries to explain to an admiral, who is in the process of escalating the military response, why his orders are wrong-headed. McNamara says that military options are a language and the Kennedy administration is trying to teach the Russians a new language. He was referring to military actions as the communication of subtle diplomatic messages, rather than as a series of predictable military escalations. In other words, a bombing raid is a message with a number of meanings, just as the absence of a bombing raid is another type of message.

This riveting movie scene demonstrates how and why semiotics is an important tool to use in the process of excavating meanings in messages. *Semiotics* is the study of signs and codes, signs that are used in producing, conveying, and interpreting messages and the codes that govern their use. Jakobson used a broad definition when he says that semiotics is the communication of any messages whatever (1974, p. 32); however, Sebeok defined semiotics more tightly as the exchange of any messages whatever and the system of signs, or codes, which underlie them (1991, p. 60). Fiske added the idea of the generation of meaning to this definition (1990, p. 42). Messages, therefore, can be seen as made of signs and conveyed through sign systems called codes—in communication, meaning is derived only to the degree that the receiver of the message understands the code. In the scene quoted above, the admiral understands the military response code but McNamara understands the code of military response as a set of signs, or cues, used in the larger code system of Cold War negotiation.

Semiotics and semiology are two different but related approaches to a theory of signification—how these sign systems and codes work. Researchers in semiotics come from varied areas, such as communication, linguistics, anthropology, film study, literature, and marketing, as well as the natural sciences, where sign systems are studied in such areas as cellular biology and zoology. The focus of our concern is on the communication aspects of a sign, and particularly the communication of nonverbal signs and the role of nonverbal signs in communication.

WHAT IS A SIGN

In semiotic theory, a sign is anything that stands for something else—that is, a sign stands for an object or concept (Hoopes, 1991, p. 141; Eco, 1986, p. 15). The Swiss linguist Ferdinand de Saussure, who is known as the father of European semiology, expressed this relationship in his *Course in General Linguistics* (1966) as the marriage between a sound or an image—called a signifier (Sr)—and the concept for which it stands (or content)—called the signified (Sd). The signifier is the form in which the content is expressed—the word, sound, picture, smell, or gesture. In explaining his theory of how the sign relationship works, Saussure used a tree and a drawing of a tree to both function as signifiers for the concept of "treeness," which he referred to as "arbor." (See Fig. 15.1.)

Saussure explained the closeness, or coherence, of these relationships with the metaphor of a sheet of paper as Fig. 15.2 illustrates. He said the paper itself was like the sign—one side of the sheet being the signified and the other side being the signifier. Note that in his model both visual and verbal communication are equally represented as signifiers. As he develops his theories further, as we will see later in this discussion, his work becomes more highly logocentric and he uses language as a preferred model for sign systems, a viewpoint that privileges language at the expense of other sign systems, particularly visual perception and communication.

At the same time, around the beginning of the 20th century, as Saussure was developing his ideas of semiosis, American Charles S. Peirce was working on his model of knowledge and the way reality is represented in mind and thought. Peirce concluded in *The Collected Papers* that reality (and thoughts) can only be known through representation via signs, further that this signifying activity can best be explained through a three-part model of sign, interpretant, and object (1931, II, p. 135). The *sign* is equivalent to Saussure's signifier and the *object* is similar to Saussure's concept (see Fig. 15.3). The *interpretant* is the idea evoked in a person's mind by the sign. An association or personal experience, for example, contributes to my interpretation of the word *tree*—I see aspens in the fall turning gold. Someone else might see a new spring green seedling being planted, a brilliant red/orange maple in the fall, or a stand of evergreens against a backdrop of snow. These personal

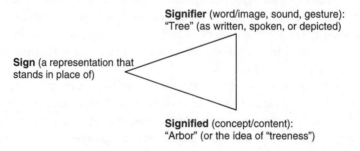

Signifier (word/image, sound, gesture):
"Tree" (as written, spoken, or depicted)

Sign (a representation that stands in place of)

Signified (concept/content):
"Arbor" (or the idea of "treeness")

FIG. 15.1.   Saussure's sign relationships.

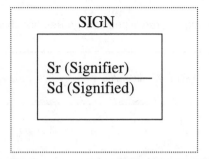

FIG. 15.2.   The relationships of signification.

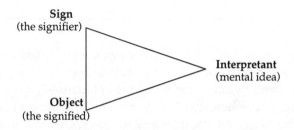

FIG. 15.3.   Peirce's model of a sign.

responses affect our interpretation of the sign and its object and lead to individualized interpretations.

Saussure's work was based in linguistics and his semiological contributions are important to critical analyses of how meaning operates in texts. Peirce's work, which became known as *semiotics* (although he never used that term), is even broader because of its epistomological focus. When Terence Hawkes in his analysis of the theory of signs declared that "Logic is only another name for semiotic, the formal doctrine of signs," (1977, p. 123) he reflected Peirce's larger concern for the important role signs play in the way we know things and think about things, rather than just talk about them. And because of Peirce's emphasis on representation as a key element in how a sign "stands for" its object, semiotics has become particularly useful to visual communication scholars who are, by definition, scholars and students of representation.

THE SIGN RELATIONSHIP

Important to both Saussure and Peirce is the notion of a relationship between the sign and object or signifier and signified. The question is, how does something come to stand for something else or how is the signifier connected to the signified? Different scholars have described this relationship in different ways.

Peirce, for example, used another triad—iconic, indexical, and symbolic—to explain the nature of the relationships he identified for signs (1931, II, p. 157, IV, p. 359,

TABLE 15.1
Peirce's Three Types of Sign Relationships

	Nature of Relationship	*Example*
Iconic	Resembles by mimesis—i.e., "looks like"	A photograph; a portrait
Indexical	An indicator of the existence of something	Smoke to fire; sympton to disease
Symbolic	"Stands for" is understood through convention	A flag for a country; a mascot for a team

II 143–144). As depicted in Table 15.1, an iconic sign is mimetic and resembles its object as a photograph does; it can be an indicator or material trace of its object (indexical) such as smoke indicates fire; or it can be connected to its object solely by convention as a flag symbolizes a country. Note how easy it is to analyze visuals using a Percian approach.

These three types of sign relationships lend themselves so easily to an explanation of how visual signs operate that Peirce's explanations of sign relationships are essentially all visual. One might conclude that for Peirce, visual communication is the underlying or master model for thought, rather than verbal language.

It is important to note that a sign can have various facets of these three types of meaning relationships. For example, when Sinead O'Connor tore up the photo of the Pope on a television show, the photo was iconic in that it looked like the person; it was indexical in that it indicated that the man actually exists; and, most importantly, the photo symbolized the institution of the Catholic Church with all its strictures and traditions. As Shaw pointed out, viewers responded with horror, but it wasn't because O'Connor destroyed an iconic image but rather because the photo—and the act of its destruction—carried such an overload of symbolic meaning (Shaw, 1994).

In addition to analyzing the type of sign relationship, semiotic scholars also consider several other important aspects of the sign relationship. At the heart of a theory of signs is the notion of oppositions and their role in creating meaning. The difference between motivated and unmotivated relationships and the difference between connotative and denotative meanings are also important points of analysis in semiotic theory.

Oppositions

At its most basic, the logic of a sign relationship, from a Saussurean or structuralist perspective, is based on a pattern of oppositions. As Muffoletto explained, meaning is derived in terms of "this is not that" (1994, p. 301). This is also the logic behind meaning, as well as formal definition with its structure of similarity and difference (Barthes, 1968, pp. 71–82); that is, to define something you state what category it belongs to, and then you delimit the definition by indicating what isn't included. The oppositional structures contribute to meaning based on the same logic—you can understand "pretty" only by understanding "ugly." So a sign, particularly a visual sign, defines what something is, but also what it isn't. This relational structure is what makes it possible to communicate "rich" (relative to "poor") with a simple picture of a status item such as a mansion. Meaning emerges through the play of difference between these oppositions.

Motivated and Unmotivated

Saussure, in his *Course in General Linguistics,* saw the relationship between signifier and signified as arbitrary and motivated—motivated meaning that there is no natural connection between the two linguistics (Saussre, 1966, pp. 67–68). A word, for example (except perhaps for onomotopeia), has no connection with its concept. It is an arbitrary assignment that has to be learned. In visual communication, only symbolic visual signs would meet Saussure's criteria for signification—the way the mythical figure of the Jayhawk, for example, has come to stand for the University of Kansas.

Because he privileges language with its inherent arbitrariness as his model sign system, Saussure's logocentricity (Silverman, 1983, p. 5) limits the usefulness of his approach for visual communication scholars because so many visual signs are unmotivated, that is, natural and similar to their object. As Russian scholar Jakobson admitted in his critique of Saussure's approach (1985, p. 28), Peirce's schema is more flexible because it allows for unmotivated signification, such as that conveyed in iconic and indexical sign relationships.

Connotation and Denotation

Semiologist Roland Barthes (1968) and cultural studies theorist Stuart Hall (1999) have extended the concepts of signified (Sd) and signifier (Sr) to include connotation and denotation. Denotation is the direct, specific, or literal meaning we get from a sign. It is a description or representation of the signified—that is, language (or visual) specifically about the object. Connotation is meaning that is evoked by the object, that is, what it symbolizes on a subjective level. In Barthes' work, connotation reflects cultural meanings, mythologies, and ideologies. A connotative meaning is the "cultural baggage" attached to or associated with the object. It is derived from past experiences or repeated associations between a sign and its object. Barthes' theory is that there is a first and second level of meaning. Denotation is the starting point; meaning making then shifts to the second level where connotation takes over and delivers a richer experience of the meaning by engaging Peirce's interpretants.

Denotation and connotation are both used in visual communication. Clearly an iconic image, such as a portrait, is denotative. Lifestyle advertising, however, is an example of an arena where visual association is used to rapidly convey connotations. A product such as a car is first of all of the denotative level, a certain make of car with certain specific features. On the second or connotative level, it is depicted as associated with a big house, elegant clothes, or an expensive meal to connote such things as quality, good taste, premium price, status. Another product, a soft drink, is a particular type of beverage with a specific type of flavor. However, in the advertising it is associated with young teen boys having fun at a swimming hole or skateboard rink to connote such things as cool, not adult, but more importantly, an escape from work and responsibility. In advertising, a huge part of message is conveyed through connotations that are delivered visually in subtle ways to extend what, on its face, appears to be a simple delivery of a simple message. Most of these connotative meanings operate in the nonverbal mode.

THE THEORY OF SIGNIFICATION

The objective of analyzing signification is to determine meaning—or a set of meanings. The process of creating meaning is essentially that of locating or identifying the signified, that is, the concept, based on the cues given by the signifier, the sign. In a deterministic philosophy, the encoding is a process of "reading" sense data, a set of natural signs that represent "true conditions." In these empiricist traditions, language and other mediated signs can be literally true and the observer of the sign simply reacts to it (Anderson, 1993). But the meaning-making process is more complex than the simple definition of a word or decipherment of a code, particularly for visual signs.

The concept of a process of perception adds points where individual factors, such as relevance, operate on the intended meaning. This subjectivity is further affected by social conditioning. Signification, then, is a complex process with various steps and levels, all of which offer points for individual personalization of meaning by the receiver. Signification, then, can be analyzed initially as a process of chains and shifts.

Chains

One charactertistic of the signification process is its ability to extend meaning either through the notion of the interpretant (Peirce) or the play of connotation (Barthes). Typically what results from signification is a plurality of meanings. There may be one preferred reading—that is, that intended by the creator of the message, but there are often other meanings and levels of meaning that are created as the message is decoded by a recipient. That occurs for two reasons: either through the multiplication of signifiers or signifieds. Barthes referred to one type of plurality of signs as signifiers ($Sr^{1,2,3}$) that "float above" the signified (Sd) with the concept refusing to be anchored or constrained (Silverman, 1983, p. 32). In other words, there are a lot of ways to express an idea or depict something. Likewise, signifieds can also be interpreted in multiple ways. An example explained by Berger (1984, p. 15) are "Droodles," which are simple drawings (Sr) that can be read to mean many different things ($Sd^{1,2,3}$).

The notion of plurality also suggests a chain of signification, the means by which these multiple signifieds and signifiers come to exist. Deeley describes meaning making as "a dynamic view of signification as a process" (1990, p. 23). Peirce explained that the meaning-making process is an infinite process of interpretation, what Eco called endless or "unlimited semiosis." Eco explained that because of similarities and resemblances "everything can be connected with everything else, so that everything can be in turn either the expression or the content of any other thing." He also called this interpretive approach "Hermetic drift" (Deely, 1990, p. 24).

Variously called *transactions* or *commutations* by other scholars, this notion of chains is similar to how free association works. In this process a sign that functions as a signified then becomes a signifier that leads to other signifieds. This continues in an endless process of associational shifts. Derrida described the process of signification as leading from a signified that turns out to be another signifier in a process of endless chaining (Silverman, 1983).

$$Sr \rightarrow Sd \rightarrow Sr \rightarrow Sd \rightarrow Sr, \text{etc.}$$

Shifts

In addition to pluralities and chains, the process of signification also involves mental shift of several kinds. The first, as can be seen in the chain above, is a shift of focus from a signifier to its signified as the recipient of a message searches for meaning. However, that can also involve a shift of form, say from an image to a word to the underlying concept, idea, or thought. Meaning-making also involves a shift between the signified (Sd) and the interpretant as the interpreter searches for the meaning of a sign. According to Barthes, these shifts occur at a denotative level; however, as the interpretant process begins, then a more complex series of connotative shifts take over.

As mentioned earlier, in Barthes' original writings on connotation and denotation, most signs are thought to begin at the denotative level where the denotative signifier (DSr) and the denotative signified (DSd) combine as a sign unit to form the connotative signifier (CSr). Connotation, the second level, begins the process of generating additional meanings (CSd) and represents a paradigmatic shift. This is modeled in Fig. 15.4 and is similar to the way the interpretant functions in Peirce's model of a sign. For example, a photo of a house's elaborately carved wooden door may evoke not only an entry (the denotative meaning), but also wealth and art (CSd)—that is, people who can afford to own such an elaborate door probably live in fancy houses and appreciate "good" art.

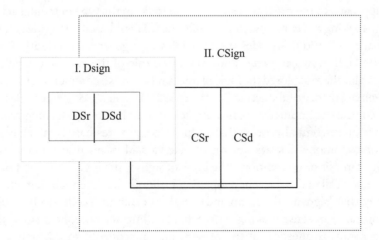

FIG. 15.4. The relationship of denotation to connotation.

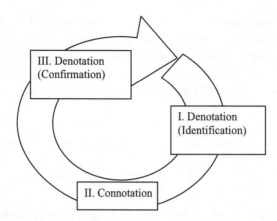

FIG. 15.5.   The circular nature of denotation and connotation.

Perhaps it also symbolizes the door to such aspirations (CSr) for people who dream of such a lifestyle with all its attendant symbols and associations—fancy car, Rolex watch, designer clothes, servants, travel, and so on.

In later work, Barthes rejects the notion that denotation always comes first and, instead, sees denotation as both establishing and closing the reading (1974, p. 9). Another way to express the relationship between denotative and connotative is to begin with denotation—by asking, what is it?—as Barthes did initially, then move to connotation—by asking, what does it suggest?—and finally wind up back at the beginning with confirmation of the denotation. In other words, using this adapted model of Barthes' work, the process of shifts, as depicted in Fig. 15.5, may be circular with denotation both beginning and ending the process.

Abduction

Another approach to the process of signification looks at the type of mental act involved in meaning-making as a complex effort of inference. This is based on the idea that logic, in its most basic definition, provides the principles that govern the validity of inference (Houser, 1991). In trying to better understand the role of the interpretant in meaning-making, scholars have explored the logic of interpretation as a complex inferential process based on Peirce's theory of abduction (Moriarty, 1996; Buchler, 1955, Peirce, 1931; Hoopes, 1991). In contrast to inductive (reasoning to) and deduction (reasoning from) logic, abduction is an inferential process that fashions conjectures based on "clues" that are available or conditions that are known. As Neiva said in his discussion of semiotics, rather than mimesis or convention, "the logic of signs is the logic of possibilities" (1999, p. 76). Anderson called this the "encyclopedic," rather than referential, character of signs. He explained that "signs are the command to make meaning in a collectively recognizable, local performance of sense making" (1993, p. 212). Furthermore, he insisted that what something means is question of the present and appropriate to ask only at the site of considerable efforts and that must be answered anew at the next act of meaning construction (1993, p. 216).

In order to accumulate clues, the abductive process begins with observation, the bits and bytes of perception. It's similar to the way a doctor accumulates symptoms until he or she arrives at a diagnosis. Peirce described the formation of an abductive hypothesis as "act of insight," the idea coming "like a flash"—the proverbial light bulb. In a more formal statement, abductive reasoning assembles the observations and attributes a variety of characteristics or conditions to a subject (the conjecture process) until a match is made and a conclusion can be stated. Another metaphor for abductive thinking is the semiotician as a detective, which Eco and Sebeok (1983) presented in their book, *The Sign of Three*. Beyond the linear forms of deductive and inductive logic, abductive reasoning more closely resembles massive parallel processing by computers, one that is not at all like language processing. The processing, however, is close to the nonlinear pattern used in perceptual processing, as Barry (1997) has explained in her book, *Visual Intelligence*.

Visual interpretation, however, involves more than simple inference. From semiotics we know that what is missing is sometimes as important as what is there. Eco (1979) suggested that a viewer goes through a process of "synthetic" inference that involves both denotative (realism, representation) and connotative (associations, attitudes, emotions) processes. Association unlocks this chaining process by deconstructing and unpacking the chains and shifts of signification. In this complex inferential process where information is being actively synthesized, an involved audience extends and fills in meaning, as well as decodes the meaning (Fry & Fry, 1983).

CODES: SYSTEMS OF SIGNS

A code is a set of rules (formula, ritual, genre) for usage or behavior, either stated or unstated. Eco suggested that it is not true that a code organizes signs but rather it is more correct to say that codes provide the rules that generate the signs (1979, p. 49). Language, for example, is governed by grammar and syntax. Other codes that have a more restricted language base include the Morse code and codes for flying and sailing. Driving has a set of rules of the road that a novice must master in order to get a driver's license. Every religion is a code for belief, as well as behavior. There is a code for dating that regulates acceptable and unacceptable behavior. Myths are considered by anthropologist Levi-Strauss (1967) to be a set of "coded" messages from a culture to its individuals. Parables operate the same way, particularly in a religious or ethical context. Myths and parables, in addition to manners and fashion, are examples of "cultural codes," which Silverman (1983, p. 36) defined as a conceptual system organized around key oppositions and equations that provide a basis for connotation. Approaching culture from the social perspective, Berger (1984, pp. 156–157) defines culture-codes as the secret structures that shape our behavior, or at least influence it. Culture itself is a code for human socializing.

Codes can be visual (road signs, sign language, Renaissance art), verbal (the alphabet, the Pledge of Allegiance), kinetic (cheerleading), tactile (Braille), and auditory (musical notation, Morse code), as well as use other senses. The importance of a code is that it contributes meaning to a sign, as Muffoletto explained, "because of its historical uses in practice resulting in a seemingly fixed meaning, which has become part of a system of signs, or codes" (1994, p. 301). The code fixes the meaning of a sign.

A code can also be hidden or largely unnoticed, even by the people using the code. That's how grammar operates as the background of language. Another example of a hidden code in a visual area is the film code that governs shots, camera direction, movement, and editing. Different kinds of shots (close-ups, reaction shots, etc.) have different meanings. Photographers and film and TV directors intuitively understand this "language of film" and use it deliberately to convey meanings separate from the words. A similar code governs the design principles used in graphic arts. The conventions of a genre—soap opera, documentary, Western, science fiction—are also codes that define a type of communication. Semiotics scholars analyze these codes, as a way of "foregrounding the surreptitious signifying event" (Silverman, 1983, pp. 238–239), which brings the unnoticed code to the surface adding another layer of meaning to the interpretation of the passage.

Sorting Out the Language

This discussion of codes as sets of signs brings us to a problem in the discussion of semiotics, particularly visual semiotics, and that is the tangle of language-based terminology needed to express ideas and theories about how signification works. Signs are variously referred to as words, visuals, or images. And, although we recognize that a complex set of signs make up a sentence, photograph, painting, drawing, or movie scene, we lack the language to clearly articulate between and among these various types and levels of message carriers. Muffelotto, for example, described a picture as a collection of signs placed in relationship to each other (1994, p. 302). Film scholar Gretchen Barbatsis (1998) has been laboring with this problem and has recommended using the word "passsage" (as in an earlier paragraph) for the complex constructions, be they verbal, visual, or moving images. A schema, then, for the language of semiotics, one that also separates the basic units of analysis, is as follows (see Table 15.2).

Types of Sign Systems

There are numerous ways to classify codes in addition to the elaborated/restricted distinction. Berger, for example, identified five levels of codes in terms of their origin: universal,

TABLE 15.2
The Language of Signification

Sign or Sign Unit	Passage	Code
A word (verbal cue)	A sentence, paragraph	Grammar/syntax
A visual element (visual cue)	An image, picture, or composition (drawing, photo)	Layout, design principles
A shot (visual cue)	A scene (film, TV)	Film/video conventions or "grammar" of film

national, regional, local, and individual (1984, p. 158). Barthes' five levels of connotation—semic (defines person or place), hermeneutic (sets up enigmas), proairetic (analyzes actions), symbolic (creates oppositional patterns), and cultural (identifies "truth")—creates a kind of code for the structural analysis of connotation (see Silverman, 1983, p. 241). French semiologist Pierre Guiraud identified three kinds of sign systems: social, aesthetic, and logical (Barthes, 1982, p. 158).

In Saussure's approach to semiological theory, codes are analyzed in terms of meaning structures—paradigmatic or syntagmatic—using either synchronic or diachronic approaches or methods of analysis (Berger, 1982, pp. 23–32; Berger, 1984, p. 173; Silverman, 1983, pp. 10–11, 17). Although his approach is basically linguistic and only looks at how words and sentences are structured, this analytical schema has been broadened by other scholars to use with various types of meaning structures. A paradigmatic structure is the latent or hidden patterns that contribute to meaning usually focusing on similarity or difference (oppositions and associations) or subcodes (the conventions or "grammar" of film). A syntagmatic structure is the chain of events, actions, or signs that lead to an understanding of how meaning is built up, such as words in a sentence or shots in a scene. The meaning structure and its method of analysis can be paired. A synchronic analysis of the system of meaning looks at the similarities or oppositions in a paradigmatic structure. A diachronic analysis is more historical in approach and looks at the way meaning unfolds over time in a syntagmatic structure through the sequencing of signs or events.

But Saussure also made the distinction between synchronic and diachronic meanings. He explained that synchronic linguistics was concerned with the logical, psychological, and associational relationhips that bind together items and form a meaning system; diachronic linguistics studies relationships that bind together successive terms in sequence without forming a system (Saussure, 1966, pp. 99–100). It would seem, then, that paradigmatic meanings (latent, hidden) can be analyzed using a synchronic approach (logical, oppositional, and associational relationships), and sytagmatic meanings (chains and shifts) might best be analyzed using a diachronic approach (history, sequence). These relationships are depicted in Table 15.3.

A good example of visual research that analyzes both paradigmatic and syntagmatic structures using both synchonic and diachronic analysis is a study by Barbatsis of a

TABLE 15.3
The Structure of Meaning Relationships

	Meaning Relationships	*Analytical Approach*
Logic	Paradigmatic Structures: latent, hidden systems, and codes	Synchronic Analysis: oppositions, associations
History & Sequence	Syntagmatic Structures: events, actions, evolution	Diachronic Analysis: chains, shifts, successivity, how things unfold over time

television commercial called *The Harbor*. Barbatsis looked at the structure of oppositions embedded in the design of the visual message, as well as the way they are sequenced, to determine the propositions behind this essentially nonverbal commercial.
(See Chapter 19) The point is that an understanding of these types of structures and methods of analyzing them provides another method for unpacking the levels of meaning in
a sign or passage.

INTERPRETATION: CRACKING THE CODE

Semiotic meaning is complicated by the fact that, as Jakobson noted, "Language is a
system of systems, an overall code which includes various subcodes" (1985, p. 30). That's
true as well for visual messages, which are also composed of sets of signs and these sign
sets are presented according to one or more sign systems, or codes. A house, for example,
is a sign system. It has such elements as a kitchen, living room, bedrooms, bathroom,
kitchen, garage, and basement. The kitchen, for example, encompasses various sets of
codes that govern cooking, hygiene, food presentation, eating patterns, and storage.
Westerners, particularly Americans, understand this schema. However, a hundred years
ago, an America would have a hard time understanding a garage and contemporary
Americans may not have a clue about the purpose and function of a parlor. Asians may
find some of these elements just as puzzling, and no one has clearly articulated the use
of a kiva in the homes and villages of the ancestral puebloan peoples. One of Barthes'
most respected books, *The Empire of Signs* (1982), documents Japanese culture from a
semiotic viewpoint analyzing the meaning of practices, activities, and other forms that
have almost unintelligble meanings for Westerners.

   The goal of a semiotic analysis of sign systems is focused on interpreting the interplay of a multiplicity of codes. In other words, the process of signification, or semiotic
interpretation, involves the deconstruction of the various sign systems and layers of
codes that are operating in a passage (picture, image, etc.). Like peeling an onion, one
sign system is studied, then another, then another, until reaching the essence of the
sign—a process of unlayering, or working backward from the sign units to the sign's
position in the various systems, to analyze how meanings are built up by the multiplication of signs and codes. This is the classic approach to art appreciation, which
looks at, among other things, the figures and settings, the foregrounding and backgrounding of elements, the aesthetic cues, the perceptual cues (such as perspective), the
lighting, the colors, the historical cues, as well as the mythical or allegorical associated
meanings.

Structure

The notion of a code as a system of signs reflects a structuralist view of culture. Crack-
ing the code, from a structuralist perspective, means deconstructing the pattern of the
underlying rules that govern the system. An example from the verbal arena is the analysis of speech as elaborated or restricted—elaborated being more complex and open to
interpretation while restricted is more simple and predictable.

In an open system the meaning is less structured and codified. Visuals are more susceptible to varied interpretations because of their open systems of meaning; more so
than are words whose meaning is more likely to be fixed through dictionaries and conventional, agreed on uses. Because of the openness of visual communication structures,
there are also more opportunities for chains and shifts. An example is an advertisement
for a lifestyle product, such as an exotic vacation, which invites the viewers to project
themselves and their lives into the ad situation in the visual and make it their own. In
contrast, an ad for a cold medicine will typically use visual and verbal elements to spell
out exactly when and how the product is to be used.

Likewise, deduction and induction are more closed because of the rigid structure
of the underlying logic; abduction, in contrast, is more open to interpretation. Such
personalized interpretation is invited in art, particularly abstract and modern art, where
viewers are invited to create their own meanings. Renaissance painting, however, may be
more closed because the composition can be more accurately interpreted if the viewer
is trained in deconstructing the code.

ISSUE: THE BOUNDARIES OF VISUAL COMMUNICATION

This discussion has focused on signs and sign systems; however, there is another term
that generates a critical issue in understanding visual semiotics, and that is the word
signal. A signal, such as a stoplight, is a message communicated through signs that incite
action. The process of signaling is used to relate or make something known. Consider
a red blinking light at a train crossing where viewers of the signal know from previous
experience that the red blinking light warns of an oncoming train. The question is: Is that
communication and can it logically be approached through semiotic analysis? The reason
this question arises is because the signifying process is based on recognition, rather than
interpretation.

In analyzing the scope and breadth of semiotics Eco (1979) and Sebeok (1991) both
identified different types of natural semiotic systems that function in a communicative
way as signaling systems. For example, *zoosemiosis* includes animal communication—
all those puzzling questions we ask about how bats fly, how flocks of birds turn syn-
chronously, the meaning of dolphin and whale sounds, and the mapping communicated
by the honeybee's dance. In the more general area of *biosemiosis*, a biological theory
of communication operates through the signaling process of cells. A particular kind of
biocommunication called *endosemiotics* studies communication at the molecular level.
One might ask how cells can be described as communicating organisms. Molecular and
cellular biologists, however, are involved in puzzling out signaling systems used both
inside a cell as proteins and acids are moved around, and between cells as they create
complex molecular and cellular structures. But is such signaling truly communication?

As mentioned earlier in the section on definitions of signs and semiotics, Jakobson uses
a broad definition when he said that semiotics is the communication of any messages
whatever. Using that approach, nature can be seen as a system of coded signs. Eco made
the argument that the roots of semiotics lie far back in time with hunters and trackers
who could read the signs of nature. More recently, Bill McKibbon in his book *The Age of*

Missing Information (1992) made the point that our ancestors were much more attuned to the land, to weather, to animal behavior, and to nature than we are now. They knew how to read the cues and clues (Perice's indexical signs) much better than we can because most of us are not familiar any more with these code systems.

Other scholars, however, make a distinction between human communication and other forms of what is essentially signaling based on recognition. University of Pennsylvania scholars Sol Worth and Larry Gross (1981) analyzed communication in terms of what they call "interpretive strategies." In other words, signaling that does not call for interpretation is of less interest to them as a communicative behavior. They make a distinction between *sign events*, events that generate an interpretive response, and *nonsign events*, events that are latent, hidden, or coded transparently. Then they distinguish between natural sign events (Peirce's indexical signs and Eco and Sebeok's zoosemiosis) and symbolic sign events, such as words. Natural sign events, such as a footprint, can be interpreted as a sign of something but it does not necessarily represent an intentional piece of communication. In other words, communication is grounded in intended meanings that need to be interpreted. Communication, then, requires an interpretive strategy on the part of both the sender and the receiver. A stoplight, then, is communication, but a footprint or signaling processes at the cellular level aren't.

Obviously this issue is important to visual communication scholars because it defines the boundaries of their investigations. Is intention a requirement for a communication to occur? In spite of Peirce's argument in support of the importance of indexical signs, are they to be ignored by visual communication scholars because some, if not most, are natural signs and lack intention? Or is the communication in the mind of the receiver—that is, if a sign generates meaning, isn't that communication? The purpose of this chapter is more to raise such issues than to resolve them. Further theory-building will help set the parameters for better informed research in this area.

REFERENCES

Anderson, J. A. (1993). The role of interpretation in communication theory. In Nikos Metallinos (Ed.), *Verbovisual literacy: Understanding and applying new educational communication media technologies* (pp. 211–222). IVLA International Symposium, Delphi, Greece.

Barbatsis, G. (1998, June). *Analyzing meaning in form: Domestic comedy's angle of refraction.* Paper presented at the Visual Communication Conference, Winter Park, Colorado.

Barry, A. M. (1997). *Visual intelligence.* Albany: State University of New York Press.

Barthes, R. (1968). *Elements of semiology.* Annette Lavers & Colin Smith (Trans.). New York: Hill and Wang.

Barthes, R. (1974). *S/Z.* Richard Miller (Trans.). New York: Hill and Wang.

Barthes, R. (1982). *The empire of signs.* New York: Hill and Wang.

Berger, A. A. (1982). *Media analysis techniques.* Newbury Park, CA: Sage.

Berger, A. A. (1984). *Signs in contemporary culture.* New York: Longman.

Buchler, J. (Ed.). (1955). *Philosophial writings of perice.* New York: Dover.

Deeley, J. (1990). *Basics of semiotics.* Bloomington: Indiana University Press.

Eco, U. (1979). *A theory of semiotics.* Bloomington: Indiana University Press.

Eco, U. (1986). *Semiotics and the philosophy of language.* Bloomington: Indiana University Press, Midland Book Edition.

Eco, U. (1990). *The limits of interpretation.* Bloomington: Indiana University Press.

Eco, U., & Sebeok, T. A. (Eds.). (1983). *The sign of three.* Bloomington: Indiana University Press.

Fiske, J. (1990). *Introduction to communication* (2nd ed.). London: Routledge.

Fry, D. L., & Fry, V. H. (1983). A semiotic model for the study of mass communication. *Communication Yearbook, 9,* 443–462.

Griffin, M. (1999). Camera as witness, image as sign: The study of visual communication. *Communication Yearbook, 24,* 433–463.

Hall, S. (1993). Encoding, decoding. In Simon During (Ed.), *The cultural studies reader* (pp. 90–103). New York and London: Routledge.

Hall, S. (1999). Introduction to Part III: Looking and subjectivity. In Jessica Evans & Stuart Hall (Eds.), *Visual culture: the reader.* London: Sage Publications.

Hawkes, T. (1977). *Structuralism and semiotics.* Berkeley: University of California Press.

Hoopes, J. (1991). *Peirce on signs.* Chapel Hill, NC: The University of North Carolina Press.

Houser, N. (1991). Competing icons. In John Deely & Terry Prewitt (Eds.), *Semiotics 1991* (pp. 20–26). New York: University Press of America.

Jakobson, R. (1974). *Main trends in the science of language.* New York: Harper & Row.

Jakobson, R. (1985). *Verbal art, verbal sign, verbal time.* Minneapolis: University of Minnesota Press.

Levi-Strauss, C. (1967). *Structural anthropology.* Garden City, NY: Doubleday.

McKibbon, B. (1993). *The age of missing information.* New York: Dutton.

Moriarty, S. (1996). Abduction: A theory of visual interpretation." *Communication Theory, 6*(2), 167–187.

Muffoletto, R. (1994). Representations: You, me, and them. In David (Mike) Moore & Francis Dwyer (Eds.), *Visual literacy* (pp. 295–312). Englewood Cliffs, NJ: Educational Technology Publications.

Neiva, E. (1999). Redefining the image: Mimesis, convention, and semiotics. *Communication theory, 9*(1) 75–91.

Peirce, C. S. (1931). *Collected papers.* Vols I–VIII. Charles Hartshorne & Paul Weiss (Eds.). Cambridge, MA: Harvard University Press.

Saussure, F. de. (1966). *Course in general linguistics.* Wade Baskin (Trans.). New York: McGraw-Hill.

Sebeok, T. A. (1991). *A sign is just a sign.* Bloomington: Indiana University Press.

Shaw, D. (1994). *Getting to the pulp of it: Sinead O'Connor and the iconoclastic pulpit.* Paper presented at the Speech Communication Association Conference, New Orleans.

Silverman, K. (1983). *The subject of semiotics.* New York and Oxford: Oxford University Press.

Worth, S., & Gross L. (1981). Symbolic strategies. In Larry Gross (Ed.), *Studying visual communication* (pp. 134–147). Philadelphia: University of Pennsylvania Press.

16

An Intended-Perceived Study Using Visual Semiotics

SANDRA MORIARTY
University of Colorado

SHAY SAYRE
California State University–Fullerton

As millions of viewers paused for half-time on Super Bowl Sunday, a 60-second drama unfolded on their television screens. Here's how it played out:

> Faceless masses, their complexions and uniforms a cool blue gray, march into a room to hear the words of Big Brother on the screen. While the image on the screen drones on, there is a burst of color and commotion. A young woman, clad in red jogging shorts and carrying a sledgehammer, races into the hall pursued by visored, helmeted storm troopers. As she throws her hammer into the screen, smashing it, a cold wind blows across the vacant-eyed masses. The commercial's tagline: "On Jan. 24, Apple will introduce the Macintosh. And you'll see why 1984 won't be like *1984*." (Kindel, 1984, p. 40)

The first American commercial to win the Grand Prix at Cannes and recipient of 34 national and international advertising awards, *1984* is recognized as the commercial that out-played the game.[1] Football excitement did not deter the audience from understanding the message intended by the sponsor: "The Macintosh is now available at your local computer store and you should rush out tomorrow and buy one." The drama moved over 200,000 of those viewers to purchase a Macintosh the next day, its first day on the market (Scott, 1991). But did viewers also receive the implied meaning that suggested a battle between David (Apple) and Goliath (IBM)? Did they understand what Apple's announcer meant when he said, "1984 wouldn't be like *1984?*"

The purpose of this chapter is to demonstrate how visual semiotics can be used to deconstruct meaning in advertising visuals. The commercial *1984* provides a good example and is the text that is deconstructed in this examination.

THE PRODUCTION OF VISUAL MEANING

How is meaning perceived in messages that are primarily visual? This question is particularly relevant when the message is one that relies almost exclusively on visual communication cues. The production of meaning from visual messages in such visually intensive areas as advertising has been largely uninvestigated even though the question is of tremendous importance to designers of advertising messages. The reason is because of the difficulty of capturing visual meaning and the lack of structured research approaches to code and categorize such information. This study investigates the meanings of the images in the commercial as produced by a group of viewers in terms of a semiotics analysis of the visual aspects of the text. "Expert readings" by two researchers—Arthur Asa Berger (1989) and Linda Scott (1991)—using semiotic interpretation will be used to develop the categories of meaning analyzed on the coding sheet.

Admittedly 1984 is in the past and that unique Super Bowl viewing situation cannot be re-created, but this particular commercial is still an ideal tool for analyzing meaning production because of its message structure and complexity and because of the extensive interpretive analysis it has received since its airing. This study is an exploratory effort that attempts to analyze the different readings in terms of types of visual meaning and clusters of meaning cues. It focuses primarily on developing techniques and tools of meaning analysis and does not intend to make scientific claims about the commercial's effectiveness.

SEMIOTIC ANALYSIS

Most semiotic scholars do "expert readings" to unpack the levels of meaning in a message. As Sturken and Cartwright explained in *Practices of Looking*, "We decode images by interpreting clues to intended, unintended, and even merely suggested meanings" (2001, p. 26). As discussed in Chapter 15 on visual semiotics theory, semiotic scholars find these clues using the analytical tools of either Saussure (image = signifier; meaning = sign) or Peirce (image = signifier; object or referent = signified; thought = interpretant). For example, a picture of a stop sign provides a number of formal clues that help in the interpretation of the sign's meaning—the eight-sided shape, the color red, the four block letters that spell out the word *Stop*. Using Peirce's schema, the image signifies the concept of stopping—that is, motion is to cease—and the subsequent thought is that the viewer needs to apply the brake, which is the way the interpretant manifests itself, in this case, as a thought leading to direct action. We are all semiotic scholars in that we respond to the common sign systems that make up our environment without even thinking about the process of interpretation.

Semiotic scholars, however, move beyond the common and obvious meaning of well-codified signs, such as street signs, to interpret levels of meaning and, sometimes, hidden meanings in their expert readings of complex messages. Denotation and connotation are literary tools that can be used to unpack various types of meanings in more complex visuals that are less rigidly codified than a stop sign. Most pictures are filled with cues, multiple signs that can be interpreted in different ways. A semiotic technique that leads to this deeper analysis of more complex imagery is to analyze the types of relationships signs have with their signifieds. As was explained in Chapter 15, Peirce distinguished between three kinds of signs: iconic (representation through mimesis—it resembles what it represents); indexical (a trace or track that represents the existence or occurrence of something); and symbolic (representation through convention, an arbitrary connection). For example, the Marlboro Man is a cowboy usually seen with a horse—and that is an iconic image central to the famous advertising campaign. The surrounding landscape with its trees, mountains, streams, snow, and other indexical clues suggest the untamed West. At the symbolic level, however, the cowboy and the Western landscape represent independence and rugged male individualism. On a more global plane, the imagery suggests America through its celebration of the freedom and individualism of the Western mythology.

So how does semiotic analysis work? Berger in his book *Seeing Is Believing* said that meaning is determined not by content but by relationships (1998, p. 37). A semiotician, then, unpacks the meaning by looking at the relationship of the signs to their signifieds, but also at the relationship among the signs in a complex message. In other words, what does it mean to locate a man on a horse in front of a mountain? The two cues together suggest the West. Without the mountain, the man could be a farmer in Iowa. Roland Barthes (1973), a French scholar, used semiotics to analyze the cultural meaning of ordinary objects in French life as "texts" (i.e., an object that operates as a message because of its signification function). Elli Lester described his work as using "semiotics to reveal the structural relationships within sign systems and how those relationships generate meanings" (Frith, 1997, p. 21). Much of semiotic analysis, therefore, owes its interpretive focus to structuralism.

However, other scholars have approached semiotic analysis from a receiver viewpoint with an emphasis not on the linkages in the message, but rather on the connections in the mind of the viewer. Reception studies scholars work from the viewpoint of the receiver of the message—the reader/viewer of the text—and try to analyze the cues in the message, not so much as the message presents them, but rather as the viewer interprets them. These two approaches to the meaning of a text could also be expressed as a search for the *intended* meaning—the structural logic of the text as it is composed—versus the *perceived* meaning as received and interpreted by reader/viewers.

In addition to questions about the levels of meaning in this complex metaphoric visual message, a semiotician might wonder how the various cues effectively performed as signifiers. Also, because the crux of the comparison of intended versus perceived messages seems to lie with the symbolic roles of the woman and big brother, a semiotic analysis might also consider their relationship to IBM and Apple to determine whether the presentation of the oblique competitive message was successful. This study was undertaken to further investigate these relationships.

METHODOLOGY

This study moved beyond the single "expert-reading" approach of traditional semiotic analysis. It triangulated the interpretations of the expert readers against the stated intentions of the producers, as well as the thoughts of real viewers. The introduction of real viewers as a source of information about the signification process provides a check on the sense-making process elicited by the *1984* commercial so the "reading" represents the views not only of expert readers, but also of lay viewers.

Any discussion of the innovative *1984* commercial leads to several interesting research questions about how meaning is produced in an advertisement, particularly in a visually complex nonverbal message like the *1984* commercial. In general, this study was undertaken to find out what meanings an audience can derive from a single showing of a very complex television commercial text, which is also a metaphorical story based on George Orwell's novel *1984*. The study was designed to test the level of agreement that exists among authors' intention, the analysis of semiotic experts, and the responses of viewers (Moriarty & Sayre, 1995).

- What are the dominant visual images? How are they described and what do they symbolize?
- How do message elements carrying the various types of semiotic meanings differ in their frequency of mentions and the type of impact they create on viewers perceptions?
- What is the difference between the intended and the perceived meanings?

Various Analyses of *1984*

Two scholars who have used these semiotic and literary tools to explain the complex meanings in the *1984* commercial are Berger and Scott. Both provide semiotic interpretations of the commercial using the "expert-reader" approach by which they unpack the various meanings using their expertise in semiotic and literary analysis to make sense of the signification processes operating in the text. They are experts in the sense that they are able to look at the decoding process through the eyes of a learned viewer who understands the intricacies of signification. Sometimes this interpretation is also informed by a knowledge of the goals and objectives of the creator of the message, as well, which makes it possible for these expert readers to also compare their perception of the message to the intended meanings of the message producers. Although a highly subjective and interpretive process, the expert reading is a traditional approach used in semiotic analysis.

Berger's (1989) detailed semiotic analysis of the *1984* commercial in "1984—The Commercial" provides a synopsis, background, and interpretation of the main images found in the ad, as well as his speculations about how the images generate meaning. Berger describes the commercial as a 60-second microdrama and as "a condensed form of aversion therapy" for consumers who can avoid the pain of Big Brother and its symbolic manifestation as IBM by choosing Apple who would liberate. Scott described the spot as breaking every rule of the advertising genre (1991, p. 185). There were no product shots, no on-camera demonstrations, no litanies of product specs, and only minimal corporate identification. She described the unorthodox commercial as a concentrated, metaphorical presentation of a quick series of cryptic images and sounds. Its theme and symbolic meaning is one of radical, individual action to prevent a homogenizing tyranny from imposing a collective mentality on society. The gladiator image is assigned to a young woman and linked through association to the upstart new Macintosh, and only by implication is the Big Brother role assigned to the dominant computer maker IBM.

To further anchor the analysis of the *1984* commercial's intended message, secondary research uncovered statements about the objectives of the advertiser and producers of the commercial. Film director Ridley Scott (*Alien* and *Blade Runner*) produced the *1984* commercial with his unique aesthetic approach to narrative and message, resulting in a $1.6 million micro–art film. Lee Clow, creative director for the Chiat/Day advertising agency that developed the idea for the commercial, claimed that the commercial was a daring departure from typical product introduction advertising because the product was not shown during the commercial.

> We placed our audience within the context of Orwell's view of society, a place where the dominant computer technology held consumers captive. The intended message was that Mac would set consumers free from the unfriendly technology of the competition. We gave the message impact with bold imagery designed to contrast Apple with the competition. (1987)

Although Clow claimed the commercial was not overtly aimed at IBM, he has also described the competitive situation in which the commercial appeared in this way: "All you have to do is look at IBM's historic approach to computers as something for the few, where they might let you in if you conformed and learned their language, programming. Then look at how Apple makes computers accessible to people" (Kindel, 1984, p. 40).

Viewers' Responses

Some 200 viewers enrolled in two introductory mass-communication courses were shown the *1984* commercial and asked to reflect on the meaning of the commercial. This study was conducted some years after the original showing of the commercial and no one in the respondent pool had seen the commercial. This audience was further determined to be in the market for the product as they were in a demographic group targeted by Apple for its Macintosh computers. The survey instrument contained a set of open-ended questions that sought to probe the types of meanings the viewers derived from the commercial using a technique called *thought listing*, which asks respondents to record their thoughts on significant points under investigation. In the *1984* project, the respondents were asked to give their thoughts about the point of the message intended by the makers of the commercial. They were also asked to cite the visuals they remembered seeing and describe the thoughts about these images that they deemed critical to the commercial.

The Semiotic Analysis

This study used Peircian semiotics to identify the iconic, indexical, and symbolic imagery in the 1984 commercial as reported first in the words of the producers of the commercial, and then in the expert readings. These two sources of interpretation provided clues about the general categories of signification operating in the commercial. These signification patterns were then compared with the thoughts and words of real viewers.

A content analysis of the viewers' thought listings was conducted to analyze their responses. A code sheet was developed based on an analysis of the key cues or meaning elements observed in the commercial. First, the authors determined the key images and listed them on the form. The thoughts of the viewers were then coded in terms of whether the mentions were phrases that were iconic, indexical, or symbolic in meaning. Then the layers of meaning as they were expressed by the viewers were identified. These meanings were coded as superficial—a simple retelling of the story—or interpretive, which involved some transformation of the meaning from the iconic to the symbolic. Finally the intended meanings, as derived from the creators' discussions and the informed readings, were compared with the perceived meanings as expressed in the viewers' comments. Thoughts were noted that related to meanings intended by the creators—taken from interviews with Clow, the agency creative director, and Ridley Scott, the director—as well as the intended meanings suggested by the two expert readings by Berger and Scott. Aberrant meanings that were not intended by the creators were also tracked.

This content-analysis form was used to deconstruct and categorize the meanings and meaning clusters found in the viewer responses. This approach is basically qualitative although it uses content-analysis methodology to bring structure to the compilation of the 200 responses. This is similar to the approach reported by Leiss, Kline, and Jhally, which they described as a semiological/content analysis combining a sensitivity to layers and patterns of meaning with the more systematic strategies of quantitative content analysis (Leiss et al., 1990).

FINDINGS

The following is a compilation of the dominant elements based on the number of respondents who referred to that element. Note that the highest number of mentions was for a character—the woman runner—followed by two objects—the sledgehammer and the TV screen. If the various actions were compiled, then action would also be a dominant element as at least 92% referred in some way to an action. (See Table 16.1.)

In terms of other elements, the Apple logo was only mentioned by 12% of the viewers; however, the "won't be like 1984" phrase was noted by 69% and the "We shall prevail" line was noted by 9%. Other verbal elements include Big Brother's spoken ideological rhetoric (70%) and his words on screen (9%).

Color

In addition to the message elements in Table 16.1, there were some other categories of symbolic elements that clearly were important to the viewers. Color, for example, was

TABLE 16.1
Dominant Elements and Their Meanings

% (n)	Element	Type of Representation	
92% (n = 184)	*Characters:* The woman	Iconic:	athlete, runner (22%)
		Symbolic:	heroine, liberator, rebel (41%)
			the future, innovator (23%)
			Apple (26%)
		Idiosyncratic:	Hooter's chick, David (as in David and Goliath), Eve, feminist symbol
69 (138)	*Objects:* TV screen	Iconic:	large screen/projection TV (14%)
		Symbolic:	computers/terminals/old technology (3%)
			mind/media control, brainwashing (23%)
69 (138)	*Objects:* Sledgehammer	Iconic:	hammer, mallet (69%)
		Symbolic:	destroyer/breaker/bringer of change (36%)
			the Macintosh (7%)
61 (122)	*Characters:* The drones	Iconic:	people (61%), bald/shaved heads (26%) prisoners (23%)
		Symbolic:	zombies, mind controlled (45%)
			modern society (8%)
			IBM users (2%)
51 (102)	*Characters:* Big Brother	Iconic:	the man, old guy, talking head (11%)
		Symbolic:	leader, boss, controller (45%)
			evil, despot (13%)
			bureaucrat (7%), IBM (7%)
		Idiosyncratic:	Hitler
37 (73)	*Objects:* Clothing	Iconic:	drone's grey, dark uniforms (46%) red shorts (39%)
		Symbolic:	Drone's concentration camp garb woman's clothes look like Apple logo
35 (69)	*Characters:* Police	Iconic:	cops, riot police, mind police, military army, SWAT team, troops, guards (35%)
		Symbolic:	bad guys controlling/restrictive authority resistance to innovation; conservatism, big companies resisting change
		Idiosyncratic:	Nazis, storm troopers, anti-women
17 (33)	*Setting:* Tunnel	Iconic:	environmental structure; tubular, metal, steel, concrete, enclosed walks, grated floor (17%)
		Symbolic:	control, conformity, Orwellian (11%)
7 (14)	*Action/Sound:* Explosion	Indexical:	explosion sounds, hissing wind; flash of light (7%)
		Symbolic:	freeing, revitalizing, cleansing the drones (2%)
	General Actions:	Iconic:	woman running, jogging (92%)
			drones sitting, staring at screen (47%)
			hammer smashing/shattering/destroying the screen (48.3%)
			Big Brother lecturing, preaching (48%)
			police running (35%)
			drones marching (33%)
		Symbolic:	(drones marching)—depersonalized automatons (19%) (smashing the screen)—the destruction of a totalitarian order (48%)

TABLE 16.2
Color Imagery

Color Notation	Idosyncatic
dark/gray	Red, white, and blue
white/bright	
colorful	
red	

mentioned by many people in a variety of different ways. Table 16.2 summarizes the color imagery used in the viewers' responses.

Usually the color was associated with either the woman, the men, or the surroundings. Overall, 59% of the viewers mentioned the colors associated with the woman and 46% mentioned either dark or gray, the color scheme associated with the men and the surroundings. In other words, half of the viewers were sensitive to the impact of the color—or lack of it—in terms of cueing the commercial's message.

Colorful and *colorless* were the primary terms used to describe the woman. Other descriptive phrases relating to color were *contrast, vibrant,* and *monotone.* Several people also saw the woman as wearing the colors of Apple. It is interesting that several viewers noted the woman as wearing red, white, and blue, which is a clear association with American symbolism. It also didn't appear in the commercial, so this is an example of the operation of an idiosyncratic symbolic system that overrides the actual presentation and creates imagery that didn't exist in order to make it fit into the person's schema.

ANALYSIS

The findings were summarized in terms of the percentage of the viewers giving certain categories of responses. For an analysis of the intricacies of the semiotic meanings, a different type of compilation will be created based on the various phrases used to identify message elements. In other words, for each message element, all of the phrases used to note, describe and explain their meanings, were compiled. Because one viewer may refer to a message element several times in different ways, the base for constructing percentages will be the number of mentions, rather than the number of viewers.

Dominance

In terms of the first research question about the dominant elements, Table 16.2 identifies the element mentioned by the greatest number of viewers as the woman runner, followed by the TV screen and the hammer, then the drones. In an inspection of the raw mentions in Table 16.3, however, the powerful impact of the action in the commercial is apparent

TABLE 16.3
Dominant Elements Based on
Frequency of Mentions

Message Element	Total Mentions
actions	242
drones	212
woman runner	205
total color mentions	185
woman's colors	94
men's colors	91
hammer	138
TV screen	138
1984 tagline	137
Big Brother	104
clothing	73
police	69
other words	69
tunnel	36
other sounds	26
Apple logo	24

as action (of various kinds) is most frequently mentioned. In terms of sheer mentions, the action elements were followed by the drones, the woman runner, and then references to color.

Semiotic Meanings

As we have seen, a variety of message elements were embedded in the 1984 commercial and they also carry different levels of semiotic meaning, which is the point of the second research question. For example, the woman runner is an iconographic element at the simplest level of reference (as woman / lady / girl runner, etc.), but at a more complex level she carries a rich variety of symbolic meanings (change agent, revolution or rebellion, metaphor for Apple or Macintosh, feminist symbol, etc.). For this analysis, the phrases used to note the various message elements were categorized as being iconic (mostly representational such as a label or description), indexical (a signal of the presence or existence of something), or symbolic (something that stands for something else—a meaning assigned by convention). Table 16.4 summarizes the number of viewers noting the various message elements and the level of semiotic meaning associated with each element.

In terms of sheer quantity, there were more iconic message elements noted than symbolic. The most frequently mentioned message element was action, an iconic element, which attests to the power of dynamic elements to create memorability. In general, one might conclude from inspecting such an array that the iconic meanings tended to be

TABLE 16.4
Semiotic Meanings

Message Element	Symbolic n/%	Indexical n/%	Iconic n/%
actions	4/2	3/1	235/97
inmates	109/51	0/0	103/49
woman runner	173/84	0/0	32/16
total color mentions	16/9	0/0	169/91
woman's colors	11/12	0/0	83/88
men's colors	5/5	0/0	86/95
hammer	63/46	0/0	75/54
TV screen	30/22	0/0	108/78
1984 tagline	137/100	0/0	0/0
Big Brother	46/44	0/0	58/56
police	32/46	0/0	37/54
clothing	4/5	0/0	69/95
other words	38/55	0/0	31/45
tunnel	21/58	0/0	15/42
other sounds	0/0	3/12	23/88
Apple logo	24/100	0/0	0/0

noted more because nine of the message elements were identified predominately as iconic in meaning and only five were identified as primarily symbolic. By this we mean that the phrases used to note the iconic elements in the viewers' responses were either obvious labels, or more descriptive than symbolic in their meaning construction. Certain message elements—actions, colors, clothing, and sound—were treated predominantly as iconic signs in the viewers' responses. The TV screen was also recognized as having a high level of iconic meaning, although not as high as the other four.

It should also be noted that there were few mentions of indexical signs and where they were mentioned, they were used to refer to sounds and actions signaling the explosion. Some scholars, such as Goran Sonesson (2002), believed that photography is primarily indexical because the referent is always pointing out something in reality. As this study suggests, it could be that at the level of indexical signaling, the meaning is so transparent that it doesn't call attention to itself and thus receives few mentions in a thought listing exercise.

Several other elements—Big Brother, the hammer, and the police—tended to be more iconic than symbolic in the viewer's interpretations, although the difference was not as great. In fact, one might conclude that a range of interpretive levels are operating with these elements and that meaning construction might be at both the iconic and symbolic levels. For example, a viewer might note the hammer, in one comment, simply as a hammer and then in another comment refer to it as a tool of change. One might conclude that these message elements are less rigidly structured in their presentations, which allows for more ambiguity and idiosyncratic interpretations.

Six message elements were found to be predominately symbolic signs—the drones, the woman runner, the tunnel, the *1984* verbal tagline, other words (such as Big Brother's rhetoric), and the Apple logo. It should also be noted that of the three elements receiving the most mentions on the list, two of them—drones and woman runner—are heavily symbolic in meaning. In other words, although more message elements may have operated at the iconic level, the ones that had the most impact were more likely to be symbolic in focus.

Although it seems clear from the thought listing that the iconic elements of the messages were mentioned most frequently, the elements with symbolic meaning—fewer though they may be—created great impact and were mentioned first—the young woman, Big Brother, the hammer, the drones. One might speculate that because the symbolic meanings of these message elements are more unrestricted and less predictable, they are more interesting and mentally engaging. These symbolic elements are also more complex and demand more involvement by the viewers to interpret the meanings. Their frequent mentions suggest the power of abduction and the impact of elaboration as a mental engagement strategy in visual interpretation. This could be a dangerous strategy because too much symbolism and ambiguity might just as easily turn off the attention of viewers. But at least in this one example, the creators of the commercial were able to maintain engagement without being overly ambiguous.

Why would the symbolic meanings noted in reference to the drones and woman runner tend to carry this much impact? The answer to such a question, of course, demands more qualitative investigation than this study provides. One might speculate, however, that the symbolic meanings of these message elements are more ambiguous and less predictable than the iconic elements and could be seen as more interesting. They are also more complex and demand more involvement of the audience to interpret the meanings; therefore, they may need a more emphatic presentation, and at the same time they stimulate more effort in interpretation.

Intended and Perceived Meanings

In terms of layers of meaning, 10% gave a superficial reading and primarily retold the story. At a deeper level, 37% of the responses were judged to be equally focused on the story and on some aspect of the sales message. Another 48% primarily focused on the sales message, which means they understood the code of advertising even in such an ambiguous format.

In other words, as the creators hoped, these viewers were able to make the metaphoric leap in their interpretation. Given the lack of verbal explanation within the commercial, this finding demonstrates the ability of "noninformed" viewers to get the point of a complex, metaphoric, visual message. In terms of the nature of this message, 44% were aware of the intended meaning about competition in the computer market dominated by one player, and 7% specifically mentioned IBM. The characterization of IBM as gigantic, super-powerful, bureaucratic, or a monolithic monster, corporation was expressed by

6% of the viewers who were able to make this very oblique association. Even though the sponsorship line at the end was oblique, 85% of the viewers mentioned Apple or Mac in their responses.

CONCLUSION

This study demonstrates that a semiotic analysis of visuals can be tested against viewer responses and the message intended by the creators to identify key patterns of meaning reception and construction. The design, in other words, evaluates whether the message got interpreted as intended. The concept of signification, as explained by C. S. Peirce, sets up three categories of meaning—iconic, indexical, and symbolic—that are helpful in deconstructing how visuals work and whether they deliver the intended message.

The study found that visuals carrying different types of semiotic meanings elicit different levels of response from viewers. In general, more viewers note iconic message elements than symbolic or indexical elements. In terms of sheer frequency of mentions, there were more iconic message elements on the list than symbolic, at least in terms of this particular commercial—and it should be remembered that this advertisement has generally been described as being a highly symbolic commercial. However, those elements with symbolic meaning—fewer though they may be—can create great impact. In other words, several of the elements with high levels of symbolic meaning came to mind first rather than other elements that were higher in iconic meanings, perhaps attesting to the power of ambiguity to create interest and memorability.

All of these semiotic tools were brought to the analysis of the 1984 commercial, a particularly complex visual message that uses a metaphoric narrative to represent the introduction of a new computer product. The highly symbolic story was presented as a nonverbal message using words, not to explain the selling point, but rather to reinforce the association between George Orwell's novel and a new product launch by Apple—a connection that delivers a strong, although oblique, competitive message against IBM.

To answer the original research question, this semiotic analysis determined that the viewers were able to understand the symbolism and connect the context of the story to the idea of unfriendly technology. Further, they understood that the fictionalized narrative was a metaphor for the launch of the new Macintosh computer, which would liberate its users and unleash a new creative future. Although the metaphoric 1984 story line was extremely powerful, the Macintosh introduction message was still the focus of the viewer interpretations. Although a replication of the actual viewing situation was impossible, this study as conducted supports the notion that a well-crafted text has a high probability of achieving agreement among the commercial's critic, creator, and reader, even when it uses a complex unconventional message that operates largely without words.

ENDNOTE

[1] Lee Clow's actual words were: "The next day, a news announcer said to me, 'The game wasn't much, but did you see the commercial?'" From *The Fastest Game in Town*, a videotape from the *Marketing Series* produced by Holt, Rinehart, Winston, 1987.

REFERENCES

Barthes, R. (1973). Mythologies. St. Albans, UK: Paladin.

Berger, A. A. (1989). 1984—The commercial. In Arthur A. Berger (Ed.), *Political culture and public opinion* (pp. 175–186). New York: Transaction.

Berger, A. A. (1998). *Seeing is believing* (2nd ed.). Mountain View, CA: Mayfield Publishing.

Clow, L. (1987). *The fastest game in town*. Videotape from the *Marketing Series* produced by Holt, Rinehart, Winston.

Kindel, S. (1984, February 13). Lifestyle wars. Forbes, p. 40.

Leiss, W., Kline, S., & Jhally, S. (1990). *Social communication in advertising*. Scarborough Ontario: Nelson Canada.

Lester, E. P. (1997). Finding the path to signification: Undressing a Nissan Pathfinder direct mail package. In Katherine Toland Frith (Ed.), *Undressing the ad* (Chapter 2). New York: Peter Lang.

Moriarty, S., & Sayre, S. (1995, August). *Visual semiotics and the production of meaning in advertising*. Paper presented at the meeting of the Association for Education in Journalism and Mass Communication, Washington.

Scott, L. M. (1991, Summer). For the rest of us: A reader-oriented interpretation of Apple's "1984" commercial. *Journal of Popular Culture, 68*.

Sonesson, G. (2002, April 17–18). Beyond indexicality in the semiotics of photography. *Proceedings of Analytic Approaches to Visual Communication, An International Symposium* (pp. 7–67). Izmir, Turkey: Ege University.

Sturken, M., & Cartwright, L. (2001). *Practices of looking*. Oxford: Oxford University Press.

17

The Image and the Archive:
A Semiotic Approach

DENNIS DUNLEAVY
San Jose State University

Over the centuries people have made sense of history and human experience through collecting and preserving for posterity their words and images. Today, much of what is known about the past is conserved in archives belonging to public and university libraries, museums, and social and government institutions, as well as in private collections. It is suggested in this chapter that an archived image constitutes a ritualized representation of the past through the selective process of collecting, cataloging, and conserving. From a semiotic perspective, this study explores how meaning is imposed on archived images through C. S. Peirce's trichotomy of signs (Noth, 1990). Further, the cultural function of archives is examined to provide a richer context for understanding the transient nature of historical meaning as it is constructed through the accumulation and commodification of social artifacts.

In this analysis, archived images are understood in a *Peircian* sense[1] to (a) resemble other objects (icon), (b) be causally and logically connected to other objects (index), and (c) be conventionally associated with other objects (symbol). The interpretant, or the meanings generated, as is shown, are therefore created through the interrelatedness of these sign functions.[2] To explore the layers of signification, this chapter engages, as Goran Sonesson suggested, a concern for "The different forms and conformations given to the means through which humankind believes itself to have access to "the world." The first section of this chapter offers a brief description of how the archive and the image function as signs in society through the triad of index, icon, and symbol. In the second part, the analysis moves from theory to practice by evaluating two historic images from the Clarence Leroy Andrews photographic collection at the University of Oregon Division for Special Collections and University Archives.[3] To link this investigation of the social and cultural function of archived images with Peirce's theory of signification, two research questions emerge:

R-1: To what extent do archived images act as persuasive visual warrants for declarative and faithful documents of historical truth?

R-2: How do images, once fixed within the space of an archive, function to shape a society's socialized knowledge and collective memory of the past?

Peirce observed that meanings are determined through signification—a process where one object is thought to represent another (Greenlee, 1973, p. 22). More concisely, signification is a relation between something that signifies and something that is signified. By using Peirce's basic categories of signs, index, icon, and symbol, the archive as a social institution as well as the images stored in it are introduced as the semiotic *representamen*[4] of complex constructs of socialized knowledge. It is presumed, then, that the signification of archived images, once exhumed and appropriated from the original context, go beyond the historic contingencies of occurrence, object or personality. To summarize, value and meaning are conveyed through archived images as historical evidence, be it for economic, cultural, political, or emotional reasons.

ARCHIVE/IMAGE INTERRELATE AS INDEXICAL SIGNS

The etymological root of the word *archive* as a place for preserving historical material is drawn from the Greek *archeion* or official documents from a government house.[5] The authority of the archive resides in the power of signification relating to a system of signs that communicate an aura of immutable facts concealing larger social, cultural, political, economic, and historic contingencies. Further, the archive as a source of social knowledge also mediates experience, rarifies representations, and extenuates interpretants. At the same time, historic images hold semiotic value because they have been appropriated as objects of cultural significance. In the process of collecting and conserving objects, the curator often acts as the custodian and agent of interpretants. With some level of confidence, semiotics offers a systematic approach toward reading the layers of signification in an archived image as they function to intermediate the causal connection between institution and artifact. According to Peirce's schema, historic images as indexical signs correlate a causal connection to a hierarchical social order by virtue of value exchange placed on them through collecting and conservation.[6] The archived image, as an indexical sign of a semiotic object, that is, the archive, indicates or points toward an actual or imagined causal connection.[7] Therefore, without considering the interrelation of objects and the existential connection of how the historic image "points-to" the archive as a source of socialized knowledge, only a superficial illusion of the past may be achieved (Zeman, 1977, pp. 36–37).

ARCHIVE/IMAGE INTERRELATE AS ICONIC SIGNS

Semioticians have long argued over Peirce's division of signs; however, the notion of an icon, something that "partakes of the life of its object," has been the most problematic (Zeman, 1977, p. 37). As Moriarty observed, sign systems are "grounded in perception, extended internally through cognition and language, and modified through social and cultural frames."[8] The archived image intrinsically resembles the similarities and properties of an object and therefore leads the viewer to believe it to be an immutable and objective representation of that which has been captured by the camera. In this way, the signifier and the signified become inextricably linked (Carter, 1998). In an archive, signification operates through the transient process of encoding and decoding meanings. As researchers sift through historic material, images act as visual clues whereby knowledge of a specific historic contingency is decoded through interplay of emotional and intellectual appeals. For Pink (2001), "Any experience, action, artifact, image or idea is never definitively just one thing but may be redefined differently in different situations, by different individuals and in terms of different discourse."[9] The archived image, as a sign within a series of signs, that is, the collection, infers meaning through associations and interrelations between signifier and signified. This process becomes abductive when the viewer uses observation or visual cues to make sense of a scene in order to construct a logical hypothesis about the subject, relationships, or patterns. Further, this is why as Moriarty noted "Semiotics and the notion of abduction can be such a useful tool in visual communication research and theory building."[10]

ARCHIVE/IMAGE INTERRELATE AS SYMBOLIC SIGNS

The symbolic signification of images resonates from the conventional associations to which they are anchored with a particular context. The meaning of an archived image begins with the researcher's experience with the conventional relation between object and sign (Greenlee, 1973, p. 93). In one respect, the sign system of index and icon is brought together through the conventional explanations of agreed on meanings. For Zeman, "The employment of icons and indexes is a necessary condition of communication but the conceptualization that is so essential a part of human interaction with the environment rests directly on symbols" (1977, p. 38). The researcher approaches the archive with a set of assumptions, expectations, and problems to solve. Meanings grow through experience with other signs, especially icons. As a sign, a symbol is not naturally or universally linked to the semiotic object, but is bound by the intellectual and emotional associations made through the social conventions used. In Moriarty's analysis of the power of advertising images, she concluded that what is visually communicated and mediated for us is often associated with "lived experience."[11]

ANALYSIS

In this section, Peirce's theory of signs is applied to archival images to illustrate the interrelatedness and interdependence of icons, indexes, and symbols. It is also an opportunity to address how images fixed within the space of an archive function to shape a society's socialized knowledge and collective memory of the past. However, to discuss the function of signs without recognizing another mediating element, the interpreter, is shortsighted. The semiotic object, that which is signified and interpreted in the archive, is brought into the world and actualized through the historian's experiences with it.

FIG. 17.1.   Clarence Leroy Andrews (1862–1948), possibly from a time (1885) when he served as
a county clerk in Eastern Oregon before leaving for the Alaskan territory and Washington state
where he worked at a variety of jobs. Used with permission University of Oregon Division of Special
Collections and University Archives.

Only 2 of the 1,843 images comprising the Clarence Leroy Andrews Photographic
Collection at the University of Oregon's Division for Special Collections and University
Archives are examined in this chapter. Clarence Leroy Andrews (1862–1948) spent most
of his life in Alaskan territory and Washington state working at a variety of jobs, including postal clerk, customs agent, marine insurance agent, journalist, and schoolteacher
(see Fig. 17.1). Among his passions, however, were historical writing (Andrews is the
author of several books on Alaska) and photography. Although much of Andrews' work
can also be found at archives in Alaska and Washington, the Oregon collection is significant in that he was still working with the material at the time of his death. Andrews'
experiences, those left behind in the form of photographs and writing, came at a time
of intense cultural change for Native Alaskans.[12] After its purchase in 1867, the colonization of Alaska coincided not only with the peak of the Indian wars in the American
West, but also with the rise of the white supremacist movement in the southern states.[13]
During this period, racial discrimination against the native peoples by whites, as well
as exploitative practices by large corporations, left many Native Alaskan villages on the
brink of starvation.[14] In this context, historic documents such as Andrews' contribute to
an understanding of the cultural other as depicted in representations of native peoples
during Alaska's territorial period.[15]

"MADONNA AND THE FLOURSACK"

Andrews' 1925 portrait depicting a Native Alaskan child wearing a kerchief made from a discarded floursack illustrates the complexities of Peirce's sign classes: icon, index, and symbol. Further, the image is selected for close reading because it shows the interrelatedness of representational signs of a semiotic system of socialized knowledge (see Fig. 17.2). First, as an icon, the image is a resemblance of a child posing for the camera. Second, as an index, the image indicates the cultural and social importance of an archive. Ultimately, as a symbol, the image, titled "Madonna and the Floursack" by the author, adds a layer of social convention to the experience of viewing.

The first task of the interpreter is to authenticate the signification of an archived image as a cultural and historical artifact. Following the archive's research protocol, the interpreter must first requisition a cataloged item, wear white cotton gloves when handling images, and be supervised by archive staff during the viewing. The signification process, in this case, starts with the causal and physical interrelation between the archived

FIG. 17.2.   As a schoolteacher for the Bureau of Indian Affairs, C. L. Andrews made this portrait of a Native Alaskan child wearing a kerchief made from a discarded floursack in Wainwright, Alaska (1925). Used with permission University of Oregon Division for Special Collections and University Archives.

image and a social institution, which conserves the documents for prosperity. The semiotic object, in this case, is a faded six by seven inch silver gelatin photograph indicating or pointing toward a larger collection. The photograph is also indexical in that its values are concomitant with a form of communication, a large-format black-and-white print, indicating a specific period in American history.

The denotative and connotative aspects of the image as icon take on distinct meanings. The interpreter's eye is drawn to the light and dark values of the print, the implicit and explicit lines of compositional design and unity, as well as conventional meanings associated with the child's pose, expression, and gaze. Denotative and connotative meanings are conveyed to the interpreter through a variety of signifying visual clues, such as the cloth floursack used as a kerchief or the infant riding on the young girl's back dressed in a traditional parka. However, there are always limits to an analysis of this kind without knowing the social and political context in which the event occurred. Can iconic, indexical, and symbolic signs contribute to understanding the photographer's motive for making the image or speculating about the child's social economic status? The most immediate answer is, most likely not. The best that can be hoped for, however, is that by carefully noting the interplay and interrelation of signs in an image, some insight into an otherwise forgotten moment in history may be obtained.

Language is a symbolic system that shapes and mediates experience by rhetorically transporting the viewer to another way of knowing. The process of signification is extenuated as the interpreter consigns a particular meaning and value to the image without fully knowing the context in which it was created. According to Scott, "With the passage of time, photographs gradually lose their indexical reliability—we cannot say exactly what the circumstances of their taking were—and thus are compelled to fulfill a representative role."[16] Andrews' image can be interpreted as symbolic when the expressions used to describe it move beyond resemblance toward mental conventions. The juxtaposition of such terms as *Madonna* and *floursack* convey conventional meanings, which evoke imagined notions of the sacred or domestic. In this case, the photographer provides the viewer with a "value-added" symbolism that extends the meaning of signs beyond the original occurrence by attaching an emotional expression to it. In this instance, the iconic characteristics of the image are subsumed by symbolic meanings. The viewer's visual encounter with the semiotic object is mediated by the author's metaphoric language. Therefore, how this image is interpreted historically may persuade its interpreter to consider more than simply a Native Alaskan child posing for the camera. From a rhetorical perspective, the moral agency of the image-maker is inextricably bound to aspects of the signification process, especially when metaphoric language is encoded with the persuasive force of cultural and political meaning. The interrelations between image and experience, expression, and content are socially constructed and reinforced ultimately as a form of socialized knowledge. Andrews' image and words shape the viewer's aesthetic and historic experience. The interdependence and interrelationship between the signifying properties of icon, index, and symbol are complex and transient when considering the confluence of visual and linguistic shifts. At the same time, the historic context embodying the image's significance leaves the researcher with a dynamic array of meanings to experience and interpret for future generations.

GRAVEYARD, POINT HOPE

Introducing a second example, Andrews' image of a graveyard, demonstrates how signs communicate through context and relationship to other signs. Ultimately, it is expression and content that contribute to some form of mediated understanding. In 1925, Andrews photographed a whalebone fence encircling a cemetery in the arctic community of Point Hope, Alaska (see Fig. 17.3). As he approached the graveyard with his heavy large-format camera, what Andrews perceived constitutes a series of signs that held physical and imagined meaning for him, that is, the cross, frozen tundra, icy fog, whalebones, and the cemetery. Skillfully, Andrews positioned his camera to interpret the scene compositionally, reflecting knowledge and training in the art of photography. Just below the horizon, the wooden cross was centered within a portico of bleached whalebones jutting out into a frozen gray arctic sky. On various levels, the image Andrews produced suggests varying levels of meaning from the perspective of index, icon, and symbol. Denotatively, the simplicity of the composition, vantage point, proportion, and contrast moves the eye across the frame from bones to cross in rapid and continuous motion. Connotatively, the socialized knowledge represented by the predominant symbols

FIG. 17.3.   C. L. Andrews' image depicting a whalebone fence encircling a cemetery in the arctic community of Point Hope, Alaska (1925). Used with permission University of Oregon Division for Special Collections and University Archives.

in the image, whalebones and cross, suggests the imposition of Western death rituals on an indigenous culture. The symbolism of the image for Native Alaskans looking on the enclosed space of the graveyard represents a break from cultural rituals, which allowed them to roam free across the tundra until they returned to the earth at death. The signification in the graveyard image, then, may be interpreted as an instance of colonization through the Christian rite of burial. From a critical perspective, the image symbolically communicates the ordained, sacred, and orderly space of a Western cemetery in an alien landscape. For Huhndorf, "These images of the frontier, which implied that westward expansion and conquest were both natural and inevitable, reframed American history" (2001, p. 58). In other words, beneath the surface of the iconic and indexical interrelation of the image resides the symbol for providing a richer historical, cultural, and social context. Again language comes into play in the symbol represented through Andrews' caption. As the process of signification unfolds, the author's anecdote on the back of the image serves as a personal and historical reference of interpretation:

> When the Episcopal missionary went to Pt. Hope (Tigara mission) he gathered the skulls, numbering many hundreds, dug a hole—buried them—raised the cross over them—then finished the cemetery with jawbones and ribs of whales that had been taken at that whalery.[17]

As a conventional sign, Andrews' writing signifies a clue for understanding the underlying tensions contrasting cultural belief systems. In this context, one possible reading might suggest that the framing of the bones around the cross is designed to signify the demise of a culture—one way of ritualized experience and socialized knowledge supplanted by a more pervasive and dominant form. At the same time, another reading might simply convey Andrew's compositional style, which is consistent with the aesthetic traditions of the times in which it was made. In terms of signification, however, whatever the interpretation, the archived image awaits decoding—one that may only contribute to a fragmented picture of the past. As Nordstrom (1991) contended, photographs are "documents of culture contact. They are a product of interaction between subject and photographer which hold a variety of meanings to subsequent consumers in which we may find sources of contemporary understanding, practice and ways of seeing."[18]

DISCUSSION

Removed from the context of historic specificity, the archived image mediates the interpretative process. Considering the process of selecting, accumulating, and conserving the archived image, as well as the successive signifying practices inherent in the encoding and decoding process, meaning appears transient and inextricably tied to the context of interpretants. For example, in this chapter the two images chosen for analysis resonate meaning through "lived experience" and are a link to a particularized social knowledge. It has been argued here that Peirce's trichotomy not only may deliberate on denotative and connotative meaning, but also may reveal, to various degrees, the political, social, economic, and cultural contexts affixed to the imagery. This point is illustrated in evaluating Andrews' graveyard image where a confluence of signs, denotative and connotative, resonate meanings. Furthermore, this proposition treats the archived image as a visual trope, that is, a visually persuasive determinant susceptible to the ideologically encoded determinants of a society's moral and political value system.

Examined holistically, through the interstice of culture and ideology, the archived image signifies a frame of moral adjustment or correction within society. Without attaching motive to the making of the image, this notion appears valid when considering such images as Andrews' "Madonna and the Floursack" and the "Graveyard." A frame, in this instance, is an ideological benchmark of an image's function and provides what Wolfgang Kemp observed as a prerequisite condition for structural perception.[19] Reading the social and historical specificity of the archived image in terms of how it is explained and described by the photographer through anecdotes, titles, and captions reveals the function of a socially constructed frame. Through labeling Andrew's image the "Madonna," the intrepretant becomes extenuated by the author to convey an emotional attachment. The archived image provides the topographic features of a mental map of the world that is socially constructed and presented to us through a highly selective processes. Like a map, the archived image encompasses a larger universe of relations between signs as things, places, and ideas embedded within the social, political, historical, and economic pathways of culture. Wood (1992) contended, the function of a map is to "present us not with the world we can see, but to point toward a world we might know."[20] Andrews' work serves as a reminder of the elasticity of meaning consolidated between the denotative and connotative characteristics of an image. In the "Graveyard" image, the researcher is offered a fragment of reality that is subject to signification far removed from the original context in which the image was produced.

Central to this study, and related to research questions 1 and 2, is the arbitrary nature of the paradigmatic shift between index, icon, and symbol meaning. How are we to interpret the past through the filter of archived material? Therefore, how the researcher acquires the skills to decode the ambiguity of meaning embedded within the image is problematic when considering the polysemic qualities of the interpretants. Reconstructing a reliable and comprehensive history, chronologically or thematically, presents a challenge to the researcher seeking a broader ideological context for the encoding and decoding of cultural and social meaning. However, when the process is treated as a gestalt—something that recognizes that archived images cannot be analyzed singularly—the researcher is rewarded with a more complete understanding of the world in which the images were created. First and foremost, this analysis points toward the tensions (objective and subjective/intellectual and emotional) that produce meanings through a system of sign relations. Turning to semiotic analysis, the process of interpretation requires an orderly explication of the social and cultural frames constituting any given historic account. As illustrated in the analysis of Andrews' imagery, archived images can be evaluated as mediating signs of power and knowledge in society. Evaluating the socialized knowledge of archived images, as well as their aesthetic value, proposes another way to explore the social, economic, political, and cultural conditions in which visual imagery as historic artifacts resides.

ENDNOTES

[1] See Arthur Asa Berger (1984).

[2] Peirce's model of sign function emphasizes the role of the triad in so far as *firstness* (the representamen) is represented by the archive; *secondness* (the object) is represented by the image; and *thirdness* (the interpretative process) by the historian. It is helpful to read David Scott's essay "Representing Chaos" for clarification on Peirce's function of signs. Available at: http://www.pucsp.br/pos/cos/face/chaos.htm.

[3] Andrews, C. L. Collection. University of Oregon Division for Special Collections and University Archives.

[4] Merrell, F. (2000). *Change through signs of body, mind and language.* Prospect Heights, IL: Waveland Press. Merrell noted, "A representamen is Peirce's term for a sign when it is interrelated with its semiotic object and its interpretant" (130).

[5] Merriam-Webster Online. (2002). Available at: http://www.m-w.com/cgi-bin/dictionary.

[6] Peirce, C. S. (1931). Collected papers of Charles Sanders Peirce. In C. Hartshorne & P. Weiss (Eds.), *Principles of philosophy, 1.* Cambridge: Harvard University Press, p. 51.

[7] See Berger, A. A. (1998). *Seeing is believing: An introduction to visual communication* (pp. 38–39). Mountain View, CA: Mayfield Publishing.

[8] Moriarty, S. (1996). Abduction. A theory of visual interpretation. *Communication theory, 6*(2), p. 168.

[9] Pink, S. (2001). *Doing visual ethnography* (p. 19). London: Sage.

[10] Moriarty, 1996, p. 168.

[11] Moriarty, S. (2002, December 23). Personal communication.

[12] In this chapter the term *Native Alaskan* refers to the indigenous peoples of the northern district of Alaska.

[13] Cole, T. M. (1996). Jim Crow in Alaska. In S. W. Haycox & M. Childers Mangusso (Eds.), *An Alaska anthology: Interpreting the past.* Seattle and London: University of Washington Press.

[14] Trover, E. L. (1972). *Chronologies and documentary handbook of the state of Alaska* (p. 53). Dobbs Ferry: Oceana Publication.

[15] Historians suggest that Alaska's territorial period existed between purchase and statehood (1867–1950).

[16] Scott, C. (1999). *The spoken image: Photography and language* (p. 33). London: Reaktion Books.

[17] Andrews, C.L. Graveyard, Pt. Hope. In *Clarence Leroy Andrews Photographic Collection.* University of Oregon Division for Special Collections and University Archives. AX67/PH 1/Box 11. No. 1259. BW, Paper, 8_ × 6_.

[18] Nordstrom, A. D. (1991). Persistent images: photographic archives in ethnographic collections. In J. Richardson (Ed.), *Continuum: The Australian Journal of Media & Culture, 6*(2). Online. *Photogenic Papers.* June 1996. Accessed July 10, 2001. Available at: http://wwwmcc.murdoch.edu.au/ReadingRoom/6.2/Nordstrom.html.

[19] Kemp, W. (1996). The narrativity of the frame. In P. Duro (Ed.), *The rhetoric of the frame: Essays on the boundaries of artwork* (pp. 11–23). New York: Cambridge University Press.

[20] Wood, D. (1992). *The power of maps.* New York: Guildford Press.

REFERENCES

Andrews, C. L. (undated). *Biographical notes.* In P. C. W. Smith (Ed.), University of Oregon. Accession, No. AX67/Box 1.

Andrews, C. L. (1925a). *Madonna of the Floursack.* Wainwright, Alaska: University of Oregon Division for Special Collections and University Archives.

Andrews, C. L. (1925b). *Graveyard, Pt. Hope.* Tigara, Alaska: University of Oregon Division for Special Collections and University Archives.

Andrews, C. L. (1936, November). The Eskimo. *The Eskimo, 3*(8).

Andrews, C. L. (1937, October). The authorization of two million dollars. *The Eskimo, 4*(1).

Andrews, C. L. (1939a, April). Aggression on native industry. *The Eskimo, 6*(2).

Andrews, C. L. (1939b). *The Eskimo and his reindeer in Alaska*. Caldwell, ID: Caxton Printers.

Baudrillard, J. (1981). *For a critique of the political economy of the sign*. St. Louis, MO: Telos Press.

Barthes, R. (1981). *Mythologies*. (A. Lavers, Trans. 12th ed., pp. 70–73). New York: Hill and Wang.

Barthes, R. (1998). Rethoric of the image. In N. Mirzoeff (Ed.), *The visual culture reader*. London: Routledge.

Benjamin, W. (1968). The work of art in the age of mechanical reproduction. In H. Arendt (Ed.), *Walter Benjamin: Illuminations, essays and reflections* (pp. 217–251). New York: Schocken Books.

Berger, A. A. (1984). *Signs in contemporary culture*. New York: Longman.

Berger, A. A. (1998). *Seeing is believing*. Mountain View, CA: Mayfield Publishing.

Carter, P. (1998). A semiotic analysis of newspaper front-page photographs. Retrieved from: http://www.aber.ac.uk/media/Functions/mcs.html

Cole, T. M. (1992). Jim Crow in Alaska: The passage of the Alaska Equal Rights Act of 1945. *The Western Historical Quarterly, XXIII*, pp. 429–450.

Dunleavy, D. (2001). *Images of war: A rhetorical analysis*. Paper presented at the International Communication Association, Washington, DC.

Dunleavy, D. (2001a, June). *The image and the archive: A semiotic analysis of photographs, commodification and the implications on historic research*. Paper presented at Visual Communication Conference, Yamhill, Oregon.

Dunleavy, D. (2001b, October). *The reformist journalism of C.L. Andrews and the Eskimo Newsletter*. Paper presented at the American Journalism History Association Conference, San Diego, California.

Greenlee, D. (1973). *Peirce's concept of sign* (pp. 44–45). The Hague: Mouton and Company.

Godzich, W. (1985). The semiotics of semiotics. In M. Blonsky (Ed.), *On signs* (pp. 421–447). Baltimore: Johns Hopkins University Press.

Haycox, S. W., & Childers Mangusso, M. (Eds.). (1996). *An Alaska anthology: Interpreting the past*. Seattle and London: University of Washington Press.

Hinckley, T. C. (1972). *The Americanization of Alaska 1867–1897*. Palo Alto, CA: Pacific Book.

Hinckley, T. C. (1989). Missionaries, Indians and politics. In M. Childers Mangusso & S. W. Haycox (Eds.), *Interpreting Alaska's history: An anthology*. Anchorage: Alaska Pacific University Press.

Huhndorf, S. M. (2001). *Going Native: Indians in the American cultural imagination*. Ithaca, NY: Cornell University Press.

Kemp, W. (1996). The narrativity of the frame. In P. Duro (Ed.), *The rhetoric of the frame: Essays on the boundaries of artwork*. New York: Cambridge University Press.

Manning, P. K., & Cullum-Swan, B. (1998). Narrative, content, and semiotic analysis. In N. Denzin & Y. S. Lincoln (Eds.), *Collecting and interperting qualitative materials*. London: Sage.

Marcuse, H. (1969). *An essay on liberation* (5th ed.). Boston: Beacon Press.

Mitchell, W. J. T. (1987). *Iconology, image, text, ideology*. London: University of Chicago Press.

Moriarty, S. (1996). Abduction: A theory of visual interpretation. *Communication Theory, 6*(2), 167–187.

Noth, Winfried. (1990). Handbook of semiotics. In T. Sebeok (Ed.), *Series advances in semiotics* (pp. 39–47). Bloomington: Indiana University Press.

Nordstrom, A. D. (1991). Persistent images: Photographic archives in ethnographic collections. In J. Richardson (Ed.), *Continuum: The Australian Journal of Media & Culture, 6*(2). Online: *Photogenic Papers*. June 1996. Retrieved from: http://wwwmcc.murdoch.edu.au/ReadingRoom/6.2/Nordstrom.html.

Olson, D. F. (1969). *Alaska reindeer herdsmen: A study of native management in transition*. Online: Institute of Social, Economic and Government Research University of Alaska. Retrieved from: http://www.alaskool.org/projects/reindeer/history/iser1969/RDEER_1.html.

Peirce, C. S. *Collected papers*. (Vol. 1). Cambridge: Harvard University Press. p. 540.

Pink, S. (2001). *Doing visual ethnography: Images, media and representation in research*. London: Sage.

Schiller, D. (1988). How to think about information. In V. Mosco & J. Wasko (Eds.), *The political economy of information* (pp. 27–43). Madison: University of Wisconsin Press.

Scott, C. (1999). *The spoken image: Photography & language*. London: Reaktion Books.

Sekula, A. (1983). Reading an archive: Photography between labour and capital. In J. Evans & S. Hall (Eds.), *Visual culture: The reader* (pp. 125–127). London: Sage.

Solomon, J. (1988). *The signs of our time: The secret meaning of everyday life*. New York: Harper & Row.

Sonesson G. (2002). *The Internet semiotics encyclopedia*. Online. Retrieved from: http://www.arthist.lu.se/kultsem/encyclo/icon.html.

Trover, E. L. (Ed.). (1972). *Chronologies and documentary handbook of the state of Alaska*, Vol. 2. Dobbs Ferry, NY: Oceana Publications.

Wolkomir, R. (1993). Trying to decipher those inscrutable signs of our times. *Smithsonian, 24*(6), 64–71.

Wood, D. (1992). *The power of maps*. New York: Guilford.

Zeman, J. J. (1977). Peirce's theory of signs. In T. Sebok (Ed.). *A perfusion of signs* (pp. 27–39). Bloomington: Indiana University Press.

Reception Theory

Reception Theory

GRETCHEN BARBATSIS
Michigan State University

Reception theorists direct attention to the interaction that takes place in what they call a text-reader or medium-audience nexus. For our purposes, it is a picture-viewer engagement that creates this nexus. This space, which is marked by the hyphen, is considered a site of meaning production and it is the process that occurs here that reception theorists mark out as their object of study. With philosophical underpinnings in phenomenology, a reception perspective asks "how" rather than "what" something like a painting or a photograph or a film "means." In focusing on the meaning-making process, this approach to understanding mediated communication works with the notion that a text—such as a picture—does not live in isolation from a context of "reading" and "response" (Freund, 1987). Accordingly, a reception perspective conceptualizes audiences as active and texts as indeterminate, and meaning is viewed as belonging to neither a text nor a reader. The notion that meaning is something that is made—or constituted—in a text-reader (picture-viewer) interaction has important implications for how we conceptualize visuals and visual communication as well as how we study them.

If you have ever found yourself in an art gallery wondering what a picture means—or put another way, what an artist is trying to say—you have had the experience of the picture-viewer nexus and the act of meaning making. Theorizing this experience, a reception perspective begins by acknowledging that for mediated communication encounters— such as we experience in visual communication—a mediated text is separated in its production from its reception. This has led scholars to take two different, though complementary, approaches to the role that readers (or viewers) play in the determination of meaning. On the one had, scholars taking a reader-oriented approach have focuses on how a media text structures a viewer's active participation in the production of meaning. Robert Allen's (1992) discussion of television soap opera, for example, focused on how the structure of serial narrative accounts for the soap opera viewing process, and my (1996) analysis of negative campaign commercials explained how their persuasive effectiveness is accomplished through visual compositional form. Fixing their gaze on the production side of the picture-viewer interaction, studies of this sort consider how a media text implies and guides an act of meaning making. Reception analysis, on the other hand, fixes its gaze on the reception side and focuses on audience sense making. In this approach, scholars focus more on media audiences, seeking to understand both how audiences make sense of a media text and how this sense making contributes to the social construction of reality (Jensen, 1987, 1990).

To highlight the contribution of a reception perspective for visual communication theory, this chapter is organized by consideration of these two approaches to the text-reader nexus. A discussion of reader-response emphasizes its significance in the theorizing of pictures as "text," and a discussion of reception analysis identifies its contribution to opening up new ways of understanding viewers as visual meaning-makers. The two methods chapters that follow illustrate research done in each of these domains. Using close analysis, one study looks at how the ideational production of a political argument on the part of a viewer is inscribed in the pictorial compositional structure of a negative campaign commercial; the other uses the principles of the "new historicism" to explore the reception of a 1908 magazine illustration within the sense-making context of that visual culture and the visual interpreting communities of the time. In asking how rather than what a visual text means, both studies reflect reception theory's philosophical underpinnings in phenomenology. After a brief discussion of terms, it is there that we turn first.

INTRODUCTORY TERMS: THE "RETURN OF THE READER"

As with any theoretical area, there are terms that are important and need to be understood with respect to how they are defined and used by scholars in that arena. I have used the term *reading*, for example, which may seem odd when considering a picture; we do not commonly talk about reading a painting or a photograph, a film, or a television commercial. References such as reader, the reading process, and reader-response—rather than viewer, viewing process, and viewer-response—occur, however, because this area of inquiry, with beginnings in the 1970s, grew out of issues concerning the nature of the literary text (Ingarden,1973; Iser, 1978; Jauss, 1970; Poulet, 1972). Literary critics would naturally think and speak of readers and not viewers or listeners, and as the arena of reader-response and reception studies expanded to include media studies, many writers continued to use the term reader even though it was with an understanding that reading includes viewing as well as listening. As used by reception theorists, the notion of reader—or viewing-reader—refers, moreover, to more than we are accustomed to associating with the term. Although it includes the idea of deciphering symbols such as words, its reference is more broadly to something akin to an act of interpretation, and it includes a variety of symbolic materials beyond the printed word as well as a diversity of the symbol systems with which they are formed (Goodman, 1976).[1] A reception theorist might consider the pictorial symbol systems of African fabric, for example, as well as the gestural symbols systems of hip-hop dance. Accordingly, scholars would speak of a viewer reading the fabric or reading the dance, and this would include the notion of interpretive meaning making on the part of a viewing-reader.

It might also seem odd to have encountered my use of the term *text* in reference to a picture. We are, after all, accustomed to thinking of a text as a book, and for literary scholars this is the case. As reception theory has been appropriated in other areas of the arts and humanities as well as by the social sciences, however, the term is applied to just about any kind of symbolic composition. Reception theorists speak of televisual and filmic texts, pictorial texts, dance texts, fabric texts, soap opera texts, and so on. One might also refer to an installation, a building, and a city as text. In the spirit of a recent car commercial, in the arena of reception theory, that of which we speak is not just your "English teacher's text" anymore.

In general, it is these terms—reader, reading process, response—as they relate to the notion of a text-reader interaction that distinguish reader-response or reception theory as well as reader-oriented criticism and reception analysis. They are at the heart of a theoretical endeavor that creates, as Jane Tompkins described, "a way of conceiving of texts and readers that reorganizes the distinctions between them" (1980, p. x). The endeavor refers to a general shift in concern, as Robert Holub described, from the "author and the work to the text and the reader" (1984, p. xii), which, in "acknowledging the significant and active role of the reader" (Karolides, 2000, p. ix), is marked by a set of common concerns centering on the interaction between a text and a reader (or "reading audience"). Another way to put the significance of this "return of the reader" (Freund, 1987) is to say that texts are meant to have meaning by readers as they are read. This is a phenomenological orientation, which views meaning as the outcome of an action. It shifts the question of meaning from one that is concerned with what a text means, to one that considers, instead, how a text means, and it indicates that the object of study for reception theorists is not a work or even an author, but the act of meaning making occasioned in a text-reader interaction. It is to a discussion of the philosophical orientation that provides the underpinnings of a reception perspective, then, that we turn next.

PHENOMENOLOGY: "HOW" A TEXT MEANS

Asking or wondering "what" something means, as we did at the beginning of this chapter by recalling interpretive experiences in an art gallery, makes an assumption about meaning that is quite different from what it would be had we said to a companion, " 'How' does this painting mean?" The notion of investigating meaning from the perspective of how rather than what is a distinction in kind that shifts one's understanding of meaning away from that of an essence or thing that an articulated object—such as a painting or illustration or television commercial—might contain. A question of how something means implies, instead, recognition that there is an intention on the part of a producing agent—a painter, a director, a photographer—about how she wants a text—her painting, film, photograph—to be read and, further, that reading-viewers would approach these pictures "expecting to find out," as Steven Mailloux suggested, "how authors want their texts to be read" (1982, p. 9). In other words, if I asked a viewing companion not what a painting means but, rather, how a painting means, I might expect my friend to talk about choices that are exemplified in the colors of the pigment, the dominant shapes in the structure of the content, the angle and field of view, and so on, which I might expect to be followed by an explanation of how these choices on the part of its painter suggest the presence of viewers such as we who would be making meaning from these clues.

It is significant to our understanding of reception theory to see that an explanation such as this describes the selection of pictorial elements by a picture-maker *as the reason for* interpretation (Grice, 1957). As distinct from asking what a picture means—which implies that encoded clues are the *cause of* interpretation, asking how a picture means implies that meaning is produced—that it is an achievement of meaning *making* rather than a response—and, further, that the intention encoded in a visual text is to create the occasion for this meaning-making work on the part of a viewing-reader. This view, arising as it did in theorizing about literature and literary works, shifted the concept of a literary work as something that exists apart from its producer and consumer, to a notion of its being something that is "actualized"—or brought into being—"only through the convergence of reader and text" (Tompkins, 1980, p. xv). The phenomenological perspective of reception theorists is, in short, that meaning arises from and is constituted by contingency; it is what is knowable and created by one's interactive experience with a phenomena. To say it another way, meaning is something that is made, not something that exists outside of one's experiencing of a phenomenon.

Although we have been concerned with mediated phenomena in this discussion, as a philosophical system, phenomenology's orientation to meaning is not limited to things that are made with symbol systems—be they pictures, passages, dance or musical performances—nor, for that matter to things that are humanmade—bridges, buildings, or cities, for example. We also *make* meaning of things that occur in nature–such as the Grand Canyon or a flower growing alongside a country road—in terms of our interaction or experience with them. At the same time, however, we do not presume that these things in nature exist with an intention of our interacting with and interpreting them. Unlike mediated things, their existence is *not* the reason for interpretation. They do not implicate us in a communication relationship as the things made with a symbol system—such as pictorial—and a medium—such as film—do (Worth, 1981).[2] Although I may read a wild flower by the side of a country road as a sign of summer, for example, I am not likely to interpret its appearance as having anything to do with a flower-maker's intention regarding an experience for me, the flower-beholder. Instead, I am likely to *make* meaning of my experience of the flower by attributing what I know of flowers and of seasons from previous experience to what I have encountered and chosen to notice on the side of a country road.

Once that flower is pictured, however, I should recognize it as a different kind of phenomenological encounter. Perhaps it is the painting we have been considering, or a photograph on the cover of *Scientific American*, or the focus of someone's gaze in a cutaway sequence of a movie. Unlike the growing flower, where the encounter is with an existential phenomenon, with any of these picture-flower texts, where the encounter is with a symbolic phenomenon, there is an intention of meaning making on the part of a maker for a beholder. Although I also *make* meaning of these images through my experience with them, I understand, or should—from a phenomenological point of view—that my comprehension of the picture-text is "not through a ruinous comparison with reality," as Iser (1978, p. 181) puts it. Instead, even if it is a photographic image, I should recognize it as a fiction or simulated reality.[3] Goodman's (1976) term *representation-as* further elaborates, indicating that the nonexistent world referenced by a mediated object is intentionally organized and, thus, an inferential structure. In other words, although this picture-text does not represent an actual, existing flower by the side of a country road, the fiction—or nonexistent reality—it creates, *-as* a particularly formed (e.g., close-up, high angle, full chroma, flat light) flower-by-the-side-of-the-road representation, is understood to function representationally. It's purpose, which reception theorists recognize as the communicative function of fiction, is to enable us to see reality with new eyes. As Iser described, the text performs its function of insight—or seeing with new eyes—by communicating "a reality which it has itself organized" (1978, p. 181).

Reception theorists' view of the text as a communicative structure is inextricably tied to a phenomenological notion of communication as *dialogue or experience of otherness*, which, as Robert Craig described, is "founded on the experience of direct, unmediated contact with others" (1999, p. 138).[4] The experience of *otherness*—"not only the other as other to me but myself as other to the other"—arises in this encounter (Craig, 1999, p. 138). Accordingly, the process of communication arises from and is constituted by the contingency of two partners involved in a process going on between them in which the "field of experience" for each of the partners in the interaction includes one's direct view of oneself and one's direct view of the other as well as one's *metaperspective* of the other's view of oneself. The constituency arises because neither partner is actually able to see herself as the other sees her, so each is "constantly supposing" that the other sees her in a particular way, and each is "constantly acting in light of the supposed attitudes, opinions, needs" the other has in respect to her (Laing, Phillipson, and Lee, 1966, p. 4). It is with respect to this sense of being in a relationship in which one experiences the "otherness" of a partner and of oneself that Iser spoke of in text when he said that we comprehend or know it "through the experience it makes us undergo" (1978, p. 189). Reception theorists, in short, understand the text as a communication structure that inscribes this dyadic process of "constant supposing" and "constant acting in light of."

Iser (1978) described how one particular contingent structure of communication is useful for understanding how this joint effort is possible when the interaction is a technologically mediated one. With reference to reading a written work, he considered the partners in the dyadic process as the text and the reader. As with face-to-face communication, a contingency or gap is constituted by the competing behavioral plans of a reader and of a text along with the inability of both text and reader to experience how the other experiences them. Because the text itself cannot change, the process of the two partners mutually working within this contingency is characterized as asymmetrical. That is, as Iser described, "a successful relationship between text and reader can only come through changes in the reader's projections" and these projections "must be controlled in some way by the text" (1978, p. 167). With reference to this contingency structure in a face-to-face interaction, Iser described the asymmetry as: "Partner A gives up trying to implement his own behavioral plan and without resistance follows that of Partner B. He adapts himself to and is absorbed by the behavioral strategy of B" (1978, p. 164). Although there are other kinds of communication contingencies available in face-to-face dialogue, it is this one that characterizes the communication relationship of a "mediated" dialogue. It is from this perspective, then, that the concept of dialogue is extended to mediated communication. The convergence of text and reader is viewed as an asymmetrical communication contingency in which Partner A—the reader—recognizes that Partner B—the text—has an experience it intends her to know and a strategy for initiating and guiding her production of that experience. Accordingly, as in a face-to-face encounter, one *makes* or produces or constitutes textual meaning through acts of interpretation—"supposing" and "acting as if"—which are initiated and regulated by the way textual content is structured.

The section titled Visual Text as Discourse explains how reception theorists' notion of a text as a compositional structure of given and not-given information functions to initiate and guide these acts of meaning *making*. First we must turn, however, to a consideration of the different context of meaning making that is presented when the face-to-face communication relationship is transposed through a medium and neither Partner A nor Partner B is present for the other (Giddens, 1987; Mitchell, 1994).

ASYMMETRICAL CONTINGENCY: MEDIATED TRANSFORMATION

Just as a phenomenology of reading theorizes a text in terms of its similarity with the experience of a dyadic relationship, it also provides the underpinning for theorizing a mediated *dialogue or experience of otherness*. Clearly, a viewer's encounter with a painting or a Web site or a billboard is not with the flesh-and-blood partner of a face-to-face encounter, and just as clearly, neither is a creator's. For the experience of otherness, each must constitute the existence of the other, though this does not mean in terms of a literal person. Rather, to understand a mediated encounter as a discursive encounter, one must imagine that a creator and a viewer who separately engage in a meaning-making process do so with a sense that each has been the subject of the thought of the other. Accordingly, if I were to read a film, I would engage it with a view of myself, with a view of a creating entity that is other than me, *and* with a sense that the creating-other has a view of me. Or, from the other side, if I were the filmmaker composing the film, I would engage the text making with a view of myself, with a view of a viewing entity that is other than me, *and* with a sense that a viewing-other will have a view of me. Because it is possible to mentally image or constitute this "field of experience" defining the dialogic process going on between two partners, phenomenology further theorizes the text in terms of two "quasi-independent" meaning-making activities (Traudt, Anderson, & Meyer, 1987). These constituent practices include the activity of producing a mediated text, on the one hand, and the activity of interpreting a text on the other. Although it is true, as James Anderson reminded us, that "neither producers nor auditors need enter a communication relationship to do their work" (1998, p. 211), when they do, it is in terms of this dialogic experience of *otherness*.

Because the two partners in the process are neither in the presence of each other nor usually even known by the other, the experience of otherness must be achieved by production or encoding practices that project the construction of a viewer and reception or decoding practices that envision the intentions of a maker. In the field of visual communication, reception theory and research seek to illuminate the phenomenon of the visual text—be it a photograph or a video, a painting or a Web site—through attention to and faithful description of these structures of experience. On the encoding side of a text, reader-oriented criticism provides a particularly useful approach for theorizing and attending to how structures of experiential otherness make a dialogic partner *available*, if not physically present, in a text-reader interaction.

VISUAL TEXT AS DISCOURSE: READER-ORIENTED CRITICISM

Reception theorists' notion of the text as an asymmetrical dyadic interaction also recognizes that the text-reader relationship is, as Holub stated, "two deviations from the norm" (1984, p. 92) of a face-to-face situation. A reader, unlike a participant in a real-time interaction, is neither able to test whether or not her understanding is correct nor to clarify what the other person intended something to mean. Like this situation, however, the asymmetrical text-reader encounter is concerned with a process of correcting and overcoming the not knowings that arise because, whether face-to-face or not, neither partner in a dyadic process is able to see herself as the other sees her. As with an interpersonal encounter, a regulatory context of give and take between the two partners is necessary for meaning making. Because a picture—or a book, or a musical score—cannot change, it falls to the viewer—or reader or listener—side of the interaction to do all of the "correcting and overcoming." In other words, as Iser pointed out, "a successful relationship between text and reader can only come through changes in the reader's projections" and these projections "must be controlled in some way by the text" (1978, p. 167).

Iser (1978) described how a text achieves this necessary regulatory process of give and take—of correcting and overcoming—through its structural arrangement of given and not-given information. It is in such a structural arrangement, one recalls, that we look for clues as to how a text means. Interestingly, it is the not-given part of a textual composition that is significant. This probably seems odd to the many of us who, in the process of analyzing a pictorial expression—a television show, movie, news photo, cartoon, and so on—most likely were focused on what we could *see*—its given information—and probably did not give conscious thought to what was left out of a frame or the spaces between frames.[5] As Iser described this relationship, however, the given or "what *is* said only appears to take on significance *as a reference to what is not said.*" This pertains because a reader is "drawn into the "events" or givens of a text and "made to supply what is meant from what is *not* [emphasis mine] said, or "not given" (1978, p. 168).

The notion that a structure of not-givens or blanks chart a course for meaning making relates to the conception of the blank as a unit of communication that initiates and guides an ideational process on the part of the reader. As Iser explained:

> [Blanks] are the hollow form into which meaning is to be poured, and as such, they bring about the process . . . whereby knowledge is offered or invoked by the text in such a way that it can undergo guided transformation in and through the reader's mind. (1978, p. 217)

This process of invoking and guiding ideations on the part of a reader is fundamental to reception theory's notion of the text as "a reality that it has organized itself" (Iser, 1978,

p. 181). To understand this notion, it is important to differentiate between the text in its material manifestation—such as words and pages of a book—and the text—or literary work—as it is actualized in and through the mind of a reader.

The text that we might hold in our hands is, literally, a compositional structure of given and not-given information. It is words on a page, organized into a structure of sentences, paragraphs, and chapters. The not-given space between one sentence and the next, one paragraph and the next, or one chapter and the next simultaneously creates these structures and points to a need to connect them. Encountering the end of a chapter, for example, a reader is directed to make some sense of its intent in terms of the story it is meaning to tell or the argument it is intending to make. This sense making is an ideation. In addition, because this blank space occurs at the beginning of the next chapter, it also directs a reader to make sense of the juxtaposition created between the given information on this side of the blank with the ideation it stimulated on the other side. In this sort of give and take with the textual blank, readers work with material that they, themselves, generate. That is, they adjust, change, correct, and expand on the ideations that they have been stimulated to produce by a structure of given and not-given information. Although it might seem odd to think of places that interrupt the flow of given information as productive, it is precisely because they do impede textual coherence that the meaning of a text can be *made*, because blanks transform themselves into stimuli for acts of ideation (Iser, 1978). This is the process by which reception theorists explain the notion that meaning is "not something that one extracts, but an experience one has in the course of reading" (Tompkins, 1980, p. xvi).

The sum of the experience that one has in the course of reading is understood as an ideational object that has been produced by and exists in the reader's mind. It is the realization, for that reader, of the intention of the material text. In this sense, reception theorists think of the material text as a set of instructions and the literary text as the ideational object that can only be produced as a co-creative act with an ideating reader.

Although reception theorists endow this process of reading the text with literary value, they differ in their notions about the role of the reader's activity as a source of that value. Because Iser's (1978) focus is on the active reader who constitutes meaning under the guidance of textual instructions, his interest is with how a structure of blanks exerts control in the text-reader "dialogue." He identified two ways in which suspended connectability in a text regulates an ideational process. One, which he called a blank or gap, denotes omissions or missing links and stimulates ideational connections between previous ideations. The other, which he called a negation, denotes deficiency and stimulates ideational cancellations of previous ideations. In terms of the text-reader dialogue, it is through this process of regulating the ideational process that a metaperspective view of other is experienced. In the asymmetrical contingency arising out of a text-reader interaction, this experience of otherness is inscribed in a structure of givens and not-givens that invites an absent reader to "adapt to . . . and be absorbed by the behavioral strategy" of an absent, though *available*, maker (Iser, 1978, p. 64).

The attention that Iser (1978) and other reception theorists such as Stanley Fish (1976, 1980) give to this process of meaning making provides a particularly useful set of analytic tools for theorizing visual communication. As we recall, a phenomenological orientation that approaches the mediated encounter as practice centered directs our attention to how meaning is made in the practices of pictorial encoding and pictorial decoding. Among the outcomes of encoding work are the pictorial media expressions we know as our films, television programs, photographs, video games, and Web sites, to name a few. Reception studies that approach the text as a site of production shape the assumptions we make about a picture by theorizing these media materials as a compositional structure of given and not-given information that pictorially stimulates and guides the production of meaning making.

The significance of theorizing pictures as texts is that it places pictorial expression and our ongoing efforts to sort out differences between it and other symbolic forms—such as a linguistic expression—within a common framework. Approaching pictures as structures of discourse between picture-text and viewer-reader allows us to consider how a picture-text means in conceptually similar ways to how a linguistic-text means, and, at the same time, does not arbitrarily impose verbal constructs on visual ones. Theorizing textual structures from the perspective of intersubjectivity directs attention to questions of how a picture-text means in terms of its pictorial inscriptions of interaction with a viewer-reader. Moreover, the analytic tools of reader-oriented criticism direct attention to the manner in which a picture-text organizes and guides a reading-viewer's acts of ideation through its structure of pictorial blanks and pictorial negations. Working from this perspective, the formal compositional features of pictorial expression—such as a wide-view or a close-up, a high angle, flat lighting, and so on—are contextualized as structures of dialogue that invests them with the quality of intentionality necessary for an act of communication (Worth, 1981). This is significant for theorizing visual *communication* because, as we recall the separate activities of production and reception characterizing a mediated encounter, a communication relationship must be empirically demonstrated, not merely presumed (Anderson, 1998). Theorizing the picture as text—whether it is a photograph or a film, a painting or a Web site—provides a new repertoire of interpretive devices for thinking about pictorial expression in terms of its pictorial means of sense making.

One immediate consequence of this way of thinking about pictorial expression is to discard the notion flowing from language-based assumptions that commonly equates a "picture" with a "word." Familiar examples abound, particularly when the semiotic concepts of Saussure's notions of signifier and signified are introduced. Though we know better, at least theoretically, it is still all too common to see references in our work that reveal this categorical mistake (Mitchell, 1994).[6] As a practical matter, a reception approach to the text provides a useful model for grounding theory about pictorial compositions in terms that more appropriately equate "picture" with "passage." Freed from assumptions arbitrarily imposed by verbal constructs—such as equating a picture with the qualities of a word—it gives us the tools to ask of a picture as we do of a passage: What is its pictorial "voice"? What is its pictorial point of view? What are its compositional patterns of pictorial statements and vacancies? What are its patterns of pictorial connectability? What is its propositional logic? Framing these questions in terms of the text gets us to the heart of differences between pictorial and other forms of representational communication without the implication that both a pictorial and a written text organize meaning in the same way. Within a common theoretical notion of text, greater understanding of a perceptual or pictorial means of representing holds the promise of integrating, as a matter of process, encoding, decoding, and textual considerations of sense making to productively frame investigation among pictorial forms of communication as well as between pictures and other symbolic forms. This is particularly consequential for research with a medium such as television or film, and will become increasing so for multimedia, where it is important to differentiate pictorial and linguistic (as well as gestural and musical) structures and patterns if one is to understand how they work together.

Theorizing the picture as text is, in short, a significant perspective shift in that it orients us toward understanding the outcomes of encoding work—such as films, photographs, paintings, and video games, to name a few—as achievements of meaning in relationship to a pictorial dialogue. It supports research questions that approach the text as a site of production and puts the focus on how a joint effort at meaning making is achieved. Research questions addressing practices of pictorial textual coding as well as pictorial media production have begun to illuminate how an experience of other is achieved by production practices that project the construction of a viewer. (This is not possible, of course, when the notion of a picture is equated with the notion of a word.) In describing how the "the patterns of collective activity we... call an art world" are the achievements of an effort at joint meaning making, for example, Howard Becker (1982, p. 1) approaches art—with a capital A—as a text-(viewing) reader achievement. The "collective activity" of which he spoke is an intersubjective one and the "patterns" he described are the terms or conventions that make "art possible."[7] As his work shows, conventions "make art possible" because they provide the terms for "easy and efficient coordination of activity among artists and support personnel" (p. 30) and because they are the various levels of distributed knowledge that "regulate the relations between artists and audience" (p. 29). With a more specific focus, Donald Schwartz and Michael Griffin (1987) described how knowledge of pictorial conventions regulates a process of intersubjectivity among amateur photographers. Approaching "images as components of *communication processes,*" their work identified a joint effort at meaning making embodied in a "camera club aesthetic," which includes a set of shared conventions as well as an organization of collective activity maintaining them. In the sense of an intersubjective text-viewer relationship, the structures of conventions examined in both of these studies are "sets of instructions" (p. 215).

Other studies focus on how a joint effort at meaning making is achieved in practices of textual coding. In an historical reconstruction, for example, Paddy Scannell described how the encoding of program formats and programming schedules incorporates an experience of "conversation" (1995, p. 10). In this research, which returns conceptually to a moment in time when "how to do broadcasting" had to be discovered, Scannell identified how textual structures of format and schedule incorporate the "discovery of audiences"— though not in the sense of a "collective" (1995, p. 10). He provided an example of "how meaningfulness of programs is organized by those who make them as there-to-be-found by those for whom they are made" in the analysis of a televisual news text (1995, p. 12). The study of a political campaign commercial presented in Chapter 19 of this volume provides an example of a close textual analysis that addresses how the elements of pictorial composition—or form—encode a discursive—or intersubjective—meaning-making process. As with other studies of the encoding process that approach mediated expression as a text-viewer interaction of sense making, it discusses how, as Scannell (1995) said, the experience of other is both unobtrusively and pervasively embedded in the pictorial text.

Theorizing textual structures from the perspective of intersubjectivity also opens new possibilities for linking studies of encoding with studies of decoding as viewers in their encounters with pictorial materials exhibit them. The interpretive reading of a pictorial text for example, draws inferences based on perceptual principles as well as an assumption that they are organized with an inferential sense making intent in mind.[8] A different viewer-reader than the author might concentrate on the content of this pictorial text rather than on its compositional structure, however, and might make sense of the commercial by attributing meaning to it from his or her personal experience with similar objects rather than through an inferential strategy of meaning making.[9] Theorizing the commercial as text provides a productive framework for examining how it is that a picture might mean differently for either of these viewer-readers, however. At one and the same time, this theoretical perspective allows that the outcomes of decoding work are performances of meaning constituted by a text-(reading) viewer relationship *and* provides a means for locating and examining the evidence of an engagement in one interpretive strategy or another within the compositional structure of the picture-text itself. Studies such as this have, however, been more typical of the audiencing research that investigates reception rather than production as the site of meaning making.

Although the movement in literary theory and criticism acknowledges the significant and active role of the reader in the production of meaning, its focus remains primarily on the status of the literary text. As Tompkins described, it is because a "work's fate or mode of experience" depends on the reader that reader-response critics attend to the reader's experience (1980, p. xiv). The reader is, for the most part, a speculative construct critically deduced from the text and only rarely examined in any empirical sense (Jensen, 1987). Still, this movement is a direct antecedent to the work of communication scholars who, in theorizing mass communication as reception, center their inquiry on the audience and on empirically studying how audiences make sense of media content. Similar to the movement in literary study, theorizing mass communication as reception makes a significant shift in thinking about media and the notion of audience.

VIEWERS AS MEANING-MAKERS: RECEPTION AS A DISCURSIVE PRACTICE

Quite differently from traditional understandings of media and audiences, works theorizing mass communication as reception conceptualize media content and media audiences as an interactive medium-audience nexus of sense making (Jensen, 1987). With similarity to the interactive and interpretive notion of reading introduced by reader-oriented criticism, communication scholars conceive of media audiences as audiencing or actively producing meaning. Empirical audience studies that began to emerge in the decade of the 1980s focused on these meaning-making encounters as the object of their investigation and provide a body of evidence that testifies to the complex and unexpected ways that audiences make sense of media content (Ang, 1985; Jensen, 1986; Katz & Liebes, 1984; Lindlof, 1987; Lull, 1988; Morley, 1980, 1986; Radway, 1984).

The notion of audiences as active meaning-makers in relation to media content rests on a phenomenological assumption about meaning that places it in the everyday world of experience. That is, as we discussed earlier, meaning arises from and is constituted by contingency; it is what is knowable and created by one's experience with a phenomenon. Moreover, because media content is a mediated or semiotic phenomenon, meaning is understood as simultaneously social and discursive. It is, as Klaus Jensen described, "the outcome of an interest-driven situated act of interpretation performed by a social agent" (1990, p. 4). This notion locates the meaning of media content in the real world of people living their lives, rather than in a particular media text, and focuses attention, as discussed with reader-oriented criticism, on the issue of how rather than what something means. Interestingly, however, when the question of how a media text means is posed from an audiencing or decoding perspective, it is not only the "fate of the work" as an ideational object that is of interest. Indeed, much of the early audiencing work in reception was framed from a perspective that assumed many social roles for media other than that of the aesthetic response investigated by literary scholars.

Typical of a style of qualitative audience research that Lindlof (1991) characterized as social-phenomenological,[10] for example, television viewing itself was the subject of a number of studies. This work is illustrated by James Lull's (1982) ethnographic work that looked at the role of television viewing as a socially constructed experience within the family as well as Wolf, Meyer, and White's (1982) focus on the role of viewing in a longitudinal study of a married couple. Dorothy Hobson's (1980) early investigation of English housewives and mass media also examined the social role of television viewing. Other studies framed from the perspective of how media content means, examined the role of the medium-audience nexus in the construction of social reality. Traudt and Lont made reference to how "conventional forms" found in the composition of media content become part of "everyday social actions" (1987, p. 142), for example, and Pacanowsky and Anderson described how police officers use television portrayals of law enforcement roles to describe how they feel about "themselves and their colleagues in relation to the larger social universe" (1982, p. 753). Other audiencing studies identified how compositional characteristics of form played a role in audience interaction with televisual texts. Reid and Frazer observed, for instance, how children were "aware of programming cues and employ them to keep 'in tune' with the television screen" (1980, p. 68).

Reader-response or reception analysis is distinguished from this social-phenomeno-logical "style" of audience study, however, because of its focus on the text-audience encounter (Lindlof, 1991). Typically, with reception analysis the interpretations produced in acts of viewing or reading or listening are compared to the media text with which viewers, listeners, or readers interact to provide insights about how audiences construct its meaning. As Jensen and Rosengren described this scholarship:

> Audience discourses are generated within small-scale empirical designs relying particularly on indepth interviewing and participant observation. Comparing these discourses with the structure of media content, reception studies have indicated how particular genres and themes may be assimilated by specific audiences. (1990, p. 222)

John Fiske provided an illustration of this kind of work in an observational study of the television program *Married . . . With Children* and an audience of teenage students who gathered to watch it regularly (1994, p. 189).

Beginning with a description of the media text, Fiske noted that "the normative family in which gender and age differences are contained within a consensual harmony is simultaneously mocked and inverted by the show" (1994, p. 191), and then centered his analysis on its "carnivalesque offence" in which "offensive bodies extend into offensive family relationships and thence into offensive social relations" (1994, p. 190). At the same time, he noted that many student viewers "called it the most 'realistic' show on television and used its carnivalesque elements as ways of expressing the difference between their experience of family life and that proposed for them by dominant social norms" (Fiske, 1994, p. 191). Importantly, and with reference to the role of given and not-given information discussed earlier, these differences were not shown in the content available for viewing, but were constructed in the ideational process of audiencing. The complexity of this construction is apparent in Fiske's description of how this audience of regular teenage viewers made sense of the text:

> The Bundys did not represent the teenagers' parents, but the teenagers' view of the Bundys and the comedy lay in the difference between parents-as-seen-by-teenagers (represented on the screen) and parents-as-seen-by-themselves (known by the audience, and brought to the screen by them, but never shown on it). (1994, p. 191)

This meaning of *Married . . . With Children* was, in short, what was knowable and created by the teenage viewer's experience with the show. Moreover, it was quite different from meanings recoverable in the discourses of other socially situated audiences, such as those who organized an advertiser boycott to protest their sense of the text as an anti-family discourse.

The notion that these meanings are simultaneously social and discursive carries with it particular ideas about methods of studying the phenomenon of a text as it is experienced by an audience as well as a reappraisal of what audiences are. Both are integral to theorizing mass communication as reception, and distinguish this approach to audience research from that derived from a traditional sender-message-receiver model.[11] It is to the methodological considerations of qualitative audience study that we turn first.

RECOVERING AUDIENCING DISCOURSE: QUALITATIVE RESEARCH

Reception analysis takes as its object of study the meaning-making process of an interactive medium-audience relationship. With similarity to the position of reader-oriented critics, scholars theorize reception as ideational work on the part of viewers, readers, and listeners who interact with media texts. This discursive work on the part of respondents is often referred to as *audiencing*. Reception analysis, which Jensen characterized as a "qualitative form of audience-cum-content-analysis," seeks to understand how discourses of audiences compare with discourses of media texts (1993, p. 21).

The discourse of media content is recoverable, as we recall from discussion of reader-oriented criticism, through interpretive analysis of a textual structure—such as a television program, a Web site, or a magazine ad. An analysis of this sort provides us with a sense of the world—or insight into reality—that any one of these media text's might intend us to make. Still, as we similarly recall, because a "Work's fate or mode of experience" depends on a viewing-reader (Tompkins, 1980), it is also necessary to recover the ideational discourse that occurs in a reader's mind. Qualitative audience studies that investigate processes of audiencing a media text take on this task. Although reception theorists in communication studies are similarly focused on the discursive nature of an interactive medium-audience relationship, the scope of audiencing studies also includes, as Jensen said, "the contribution of the media audience to the social construction of reality" (1987, p. 22).

Audiencing studies that theorize mass communication as reception generally follow a social-constructionist position on the audience (Lindlof, 1991). Inquiry is based on an ontological notion of relativism, which Egon Guba and Yvonna Lincoln (1994) characterized as the "break away" assumption of constructionism. Accordingly, a social-constructionist position on the audience comes with the assumption that:

> Realities are apprehendable in the form of multiple, intangible mental constructions, socially and experientially based, local and specific in nature (although elements are often shared among many individuals and even across cultures), and dependent for their form and content on the individual persons or groups holding the construction. (Guba and Lincoln, 1994, p. 110)

Moreover, the "constructions" or ideations that one studies when the object of study is an audiencing interaction with a media text" are not more or less 'true,' in any absolute sense, but simply more or less informed and/or sophisticated. Constructions are alterable, as are their associated 'realities' (Guba and Lincoln, 1994, p. 111). Importantly, meaning is viewed as not only constructed, but also as socially based.

Theorizing the social characteristic of sense making highlights the importance of studying the processes of decoding in contexts of social interaction and with methodological assumptions appropriate for apprehending the processes of meaning production at work in these sites of reception. Although reception is the "meeting of a medium and an audience," as Jensen said, the "nature of the reception is also an important concern" (1987, p. 25). Again, as Guba and Lincoln described methodology within a constructionism paradigm:

> The variable and personal (intramental) nature of social constructions suggests that individual constructions can be elicited and refined only through interaction *between and among* investigator and respondents. These varying constructions are interpreted using conventional hermeneutical techniques, and are compared and contrasted through a dialectical interchange. The final aim is to distill a consensus construction that is more informed and sophisticated than any of the predecessor constructions. (1994, p. 111)

For reception theorists, the contingent nature of meaning places an emphasis on situational factors or the contexts in which media texts are used. This places researchers in the real world of people living their lives with the central task of explaining this social action in a way that preserves the integrity of sense-making practices. Accordingly, various qualitative strategies are used to generate, and thus recover, these situated audience discourses. Reception study has included such ethnographic methods as participant observation and indepth informant interviewing as well as strategies such as the focus group interview, which creates sites of social interaction.

Michelle Wolf's (1987) work with children's audiencing of television is of particular interest as a methodological example here because it specifically addressed the visual communication features of a televisual text. To generate and recover the discursive practices of audiencing, Wolf engaged her subjects in a video production project. The children's discourse as audience to their own media discourse indicated that they made sense of television as an intersubjective experience. In talk about a superimposition, for example, one child explained: "He's seeing things in his mind. . . . See that little picture? It's like a picture of ideas in his mind. You can tell, see? They're just showing it to the people watching TV, but not the people on the show" (Wolf, 1987, p. 89). Similarly, with reference to camera shots, editing, and special effects, the children "consistently voiced their opinions on how 'things' on television were 'done'" (1987, p. 87). By providing a context within which these young viewers could verbalize their sense making of a mediated interaction, then, the researcher uncovered the children's interpretive experience of how a creator and receiver are available to each other through the discursive structure of a text.

The methodologies of audiencing studies such as this seek to preserve the form, content, and context of social phenomena. With an analytical emphasis on processes of interpretation, researchers look for meaningful patterns in the expressions that occur in the audiencing of a media text, turning to these discursive materials as exemplifications of sense making. With an accent on the process of sense making, the focus of inquiry is necessarily local and particularistic (Lindlof, 1991). At the same time, however, reception theorists are also interested in the notion that audiences act as cultural agents, particularly in relationship to the construction of social structures. Horace Newcomb and Paul Hirsch (1983) discussed television as a social resource of meaning, for example, and as such, characterize the medium-audience nexus as a "cultural forum." This larger social perspective suggests, as Jensen pointed out, the opportunity for organizing and analyzing locally generated audiencing discourses "with reference to a metadiscourse" (1990, p. 28), including television audience perceptions of genres—such as family sitcoms and medical or crime dramas—which deal with significant social institutions (Lindlof, 1988).

To link the social dimension of these audience discourses to the idea of cultural agency, reception theorists turn to the notion of audiences as "interpretive communities." This concept provides a framework for probing the social relations at play in an audiencing encounter as well as the connection of this discursive activity to the construction of social realities. It is to this concept, then, and its contribution to a reevaluation of what audiences are, that we turn next.

AUDIENCES AS MEANING-MAKERS: RECEPTION AS
A SOCIAL PRACTICE

Within literary studies, American reader-response theorist Stanley Fish (1980) created the concept of "interpretive communities" to account for the social context of meaning production. This was a move away from what he called the "tyranny of the text"—even in the framework of a "set of instructions"—for guiding the production of meaning (1980, p. 7). Although giving the reader a central role in the production of meaning, though, Fish turned to the shared interests defining a socially constructed community of readers to replace the guiding role that other theorists had placed in the text. He proposed, as Tompkins explained, that a reader's interpretations are neither a response to what an author meant nor to the content and form of an expression, but are, rather, "the result of the interpretive strategies one possesses" (1980, p. xxiii). These interpretive strategies are theorized as existing prior to engagement with a text, though as Fish states, they:

> proceed not from [the reader] but from the interpretive community of which [the reader] is a member; they are, in effect, community property, and in so far as they enable and limit the operations of [the reader's] consciousness, [the reader] is [community property]. (1980, p. 14).

As with others in this literary movement, Fish's interest was with the reader insofar as it defined the status of the text. His conception of interpretive communities had to do with preserving the concept of literature by locating the meanings and texts produced by his interpretive model of the reader in something other than idiosyncratic and irresponsible interpretations. Accordingly, the concept of interpretive communities locates the interpretive strategies—or social relations—that a reader brings to a text-reader interaction in a "public and conventional point of view" (Fish, 1980, p. 14).

Mass communication theorists working with an interpretive model of the audience find the notion of interpretive communities appealing because it accounts for how audience interpretations of content can vary, as Liebes and Katz (1990) observed in their cross-cultural audiencing study of *Dallas*, yet still be socially intelligible (Lindlof, 1991). With similarity to Fish, reception theorists in media studies conceive of interpretive communities as affiliations that generate "communities of meaning" (Jensen, 1987, p. 28). One might view the classroom as one interpretive community (Karolides, 2000, p. 312), for example, or readers of popular romance novels (Radway, 1984), trade union viewers of a news magazine (Morley, 1980), and teenage viewers of *Married . . . With Children* (Fiske, 1994) as another. Each is a community of meaning to the extent that its shared interests and experiences of everyday life make a difference in how meanings are produced when reading or audiencing a media text.

This notion of interpretive communities or communities of meaning conceptualizes audiences in the terms of "discourses" rather than in the terms of traditional socioeconomic categories (Jensen, 1987, p. 28). It argues, in fact, that the idea of socioeconomic categories such as race, gender, or class are themselves the socially constructed reality of a discourse that has an interest in an essentialized notion of knowledge. Reception theorists, having an interest in a relativistic notion of knowledge, ask instead how language works to produce knowledge and turn to the discourses produced in the audiencing of a media text to capture an audience's social construction of itself. Because meaning is viewed as indeterminate, and constructed "by persons by means of unique meaning matrices" (Lindlof, 1988, p. 87), the notion of some sort of shared meaning or consensus is necessary if one is to entertain the concept of audience in relationship to a particular media text. In work that argued for understanding media audiences as interpretive communities, Lindlof (1988) discussed how audiencing studies of a television show provide evidence of the notion empirically. As he described:

> There is actually a great deal of variation [in how meaning is constructed] once an effort is undertaken to inventory from a variety of persons the actual expressions and attendant meanings about [what elements make up the show] (p. 87).

At the same time, Lindlof noted, there is among these persons "a consistency of agreement on . . . conceptual categories[s]" (p. 87). As he suggested:

> The existence of agreement . . . indicates a high frequency of communication on the subject, exposure to the same types of verbal and nonverbal performance, and enactments in roughly similar media use situations for the persons that are sampled (p. 87).

Although Lindlof was referring specifically to consensus about the elements that make up a realistic cop show, the concept of an interpretive community was evidenced in Radway's readers of romance novels and Morley's viewers of *Nationwide*, to name two of the pioneering studies in reception analysis of media audiences.

As Lindlof's description suggested, the notion of interpretive communities contributed to a significant shift in how we think about what audiences are. Understanding audiences as discourses implies a social formation, which is identified by what its members do rather than what they are (Fiske, 1994). Moreover, this way of thinking about audiences locates the source of meaning-making practices in the "commonalities of purpose or practice," which define a particular socially constructed formation, such as the teenage viewers of *Married . . . With Children*. Jensen (1987) referred to these strategies as "codes of understanding" and, for analytical purposes, suggests that audiences be understood not as members of a demographic category—such as teenagers and young adults—but as codes of understanding—which, in this example, had to do with using the carnivalesque elements of the show to make sense of the social experience of family from a sensemaking place where there was a "difference between their experience of family life and that proposed to them by the dominant social norms" (Fiske, 1994, p. 191). Another audiencing formation was identified in codes of understanding that had to do with using the carnivalesque elements of the show to make sense of the social experience of television from a sense-making place where there was a difference between this audience group's experience of the show as offensive and antifamily and their expectation that its role as a socializing institution implied providing positive images of the family. In other words, shared interests and experiences of everyday life served to unite each audience group as a "community of meanings" in a way that made a difference in their audiencing of this media text (Jensen, 1987). At the same time, there might be other interests and experiences for which there is a consensus among the persons in both of the audience groups relative to their audiencing of a different media text. Hypothetically, they might employ a similar strategy of understanding for television news, as an example, based on the level of reality and relevance they find in the genre (Jensen, 1987).

Because interpretive strategies are related to the notion of a text-reader or medium-audience interaction and draw from various interests and experiences of everyday life, it is important to think of the consensus in strategies of understanding that indicates an interpretive community as relative. In other words, as Lindlof stated:

> from the socially constructed meaning approach, . . . consensus does not advance the warrant for objectified reality. It only indicates trace evidence for widespread social practices that have culminated in a relatively high degree of intersubjective agreement. (1988, p. 87)

Consensus includes, then, the notion that sense-making achievements are more than idiosyncratic and irresponsible interpretations as well as that they are variable. Accordingly, as Jensen (1990) pointed out, interpretive communities are multiple, overlapping, and potentially contradictory.

First, different audience groups may apply *multiple* interpretive strategies to the same media discourse and still make sense of it . . . Second, interpretive communities [are] *overlapping* . . . in that a group of recipients may share some by not all interpretive strategies with other groups . . . Third, and perhaps the most important, interpretive strategies that are employed by the same individual or group may be mutually inconsistent, or *contradictory*, because they derive from different contexts or represent the orientations of different social formations that may be in conflict.

Fish (1980) provided the theoretical explanation that underpins this position when he introduced the interpretive community conception of reading. As he stated:

> An interpretive community is not objective because as a bundle of interests, of particular purposes and goals, its perspective is interested rather than neutral; but, by the very same reasoning, the meanings and texts produced by an interpretive community are not subjective because they do not proceed from an isolated individual but from a public and conventional point of view. (1980, p. 14)

Just as reader-oriented critics theorized the text as actualized only through the convergence of reader and text (or audience and medium), so scholars employing reception analysis theorized the audience as actualized through, and only through, the convergence. In conceptualizing audiences as discursive, this perspective shift takes audiencing—rather than audiences—as its object of study.

The attention that reception theorists give to the notion of interpretive strategies provides a useful orientation for theorizing a pictorial mode of audiencing. A number of different approaches to pictorial representation, if not communication, describe a wholly different mode of sense making at work from that of a linguistically organized representation, and yet, as Ann Marie Barry suggested, "the attempt to understand visual constructions . . . as systems of meaning that can be used to communicate" almost always "begins problematically with the imposition of arbitrary verbal constructs on visual ones" (1997, p. 108). Reception analysis focused on visual achievements of meaning making has a significant contribution to make in identifying strategies of visual understanding.

The work of scholars in a number of disciplines, from art to psychology and engineering to philosophy as well as communication, suggests the notion of "holistic logic" as fertile ground for reception analysis. The notion of "holistic logic," which "acknowledges relationships that are not strictly proportional" (Barry, 1997, p. 100), emerges from work with the gestalt concept of nonlinear and dynamical systems (Gleik, 1987; Kosko, 1993; McCrone, 1994). Barry (1997) argued that a holistic logic is associated with "visual intelligence" and in a very similar approach, Stafford discussed "intelligence of sight " as a rich "modality for configuring and conveying ideas" (1996, p. 4). As alternative to linear thinking, she characterized this organizational logic as "mosaic presentation" (1996, p. 16). Turkle and Papert (1993) described a similar notion in their use of the term *bricolage* to differentiate a cognitive style of organizing work from that of a canonical analytical approach. They characterize this style as one of negotiation and rearrangement where the sensemaking activity is patterned by working with bits and pieces, "feeling ones way from one . . . to another," building them up, sculpting a whole (Turkle & Papert, 1993, p. 172). This idea of working from bits and pieces to "fashion a hypothesis" also parallels Moriarty's discussion of "abductive reasoning," which emerges in semiotics as alternative to the "traditional analysis of logic . . . based on inductive and deductive forms" (1996, p. 180). With similarity to the gestalt, she described "the formation of an abductive hypothesis" in Peirce's words as "an act of insight" where an idea comes "like a flash" (1996, p. 181). Edwardo Neiva's discussion of a sign's triadic structure in terms of a "may-be, can-be, and would-be" further suggested how a process of negotiation and rearrangement, whether referred to as abductive or bricolage, might be accounted for as a holistic sense-making logic (1999, p. 82).

Complementary to these propositions about audience sense making are parallel notions defining pictorial or "spatializing media" as holistically composed. Stafford (1996) conceptualized the "new media" of digital picturization—including the bricolages of video, film, and computer screens, as well as such multidimensional imaging as one finds in the presentations of PET, MRI, and CT scans—as a "mosaic," and Mitchell Stephens extended the idea by describing "fourth motion logic" collisions. In contrast to the "one word-follows-another, one-thing-at-a time logic" of print, a logic of collision "[chops] the world into fragments, . . . [layers] on words and graphics" and "[arranges] those fragments in new and meaningful patterns" (Stephens, 1998, pp. 182, 193, 208). The result is an experience of "complex seeing" not only apparent in the editing style celebrated on MTV but also exploited as well by cubist, surrealists, abstract impressionists and pop art (Stephens, 1998, pp. 112–123). Herbert Zettl (1999) used the term *complexity editing* to describe this way of organizing reality.

But is this how a viewer experiences a media text? Do viewers engage pictorial texts as spatial rather than linear ways of knowing about the world? Do they make sense of the text as a "mosaic," a "collision" of fragments and layers? Is this the discourse of the visual text? Does the audiencing discourse provide evidence of holistic strategies of interpretation? Are these strategies characterized by "bricolage" and "abductive" reasoning? These and any number of other questions can and should be fruitfully explored. Though we need no longer justify the importance of visual communication research, the fact that we now live in a preponderantly visual symbolic environment mandates that we understand the social construction of reality in *pictorial* as well as linguistic terms. Audiencing studies should identify, for example, how strategies of visual interpretation might differ for social groups who have been closely identified with print media, as well as for those who have been on its margins (Jensen, 1987). By locating viewer's visual strategies of interpretation in the practices of their everyday life, reception analysis provides a significant tool for understanding both the discursive and social phenomenon of visual meaning.

In summary, the contribution of reception theory to visual meaning making is to theorize the picture as text and to theorize viewing audiences as communities of visual meaning. The two studies that follow in Chapters 19 and 20 illustrate the fruitfulness of this contribution.

ENDNOTES

[1] References such as this to symbol systems and symbolic materials is informed by the philosophical work of Nelson Goodman (1976) with symbol systems as well as the framework of symbol systems proposed by Larry Gross (1974). Goodman's work with a general theory of symbols is significant for its articulation of nonlinguistic reference—such as pictorial—in terms of syntactic and semantic properties. Gross' work with forms of expression distinguishes five primary modes of communication in terms of the symbol systems used. He identifies them as pictorial, linguistic, gestural, musical, and mathematical.

[2] Sol Worth (1981) discusses the differences between a natural and a symbolic sign event, as well as the interpretive strategies appropriate to each. In this scheme, any articulated or mediated event—such as a picture—is a symbolic event, though this does not mean that it will be interpreted as such. He distinguishes between attribution—which assigns meaning by attributing characteristics to a sign that come from the beholder—and inference—that assigns meaning by inferring from the structural characteristics of the composition itself. Interpretation of a natural sign event is usually made on the basis of what we perceive to be a resemblance between what is being referred to by a sign and our knowledge or direct experience of the world. Interpretation of a symbolic event, on the other hand, requires "subordinating what one knows experientially" to one's knowledge of the rules and conventions referred to or represented by the sign.

[3] Iser's (1978) notion of fiction is in the sense, not of something false or unreal, but, rather of a reality that is organized by a text, and that is a "rival" to the world not organized by a text. This notion is particularly important for understanding pictorially constructed fictions. As Iser stated, "the literary text [or pictorial text] is like the world in so far as it outlines a rival world. But it differs from existing ideas of the world in that it cannot be completely deduced from prevailing concepts of reality. If criteria of fiction and reality consist in the extent to which they deal with the given, it will be seen that fiction is almost totally nongiven . . . it possesses none of the criteria of reality and yet it pretends that it does." The literary text, like the picture, "performs its function by communicating a reality which it has organized itself" (p. 181).

[4] This notion is the subject of an essay (Barbatsis, 2002) that explores the issues for theorizing visual communication from a phenomenological understanding of communication as a dyadic encounter with language as the primary medium of a meaning-making experience. The discussion considers the issue of extending the idea of dialogue to a pictorially mediated encounter between makers and beholders not present to each other as well as the issue of pictorial codes in describing the meaning-making practices of production (encoding) and interpretation (decoding).

[5] *Not* focusing on content is probably harder with pictorial than with linguistic signs, because pictures prominently present properties of both iconic reference and indexical relationship. In fact, it is these characteristics that we encounter first as beholders of pictorial representations. Gardner discussed this kind of representational relationship as "object related," noting that it is "subject to the kind of control exerted by the structure and function of the particular objects with which individuals come into contact." By contrast, a linguistic expression exhibits neither an iconic resemblance nor an indexical relationship to what it represents. As a sign, it is not physically "fashioned or channeled by the physical world" (1993, p. 276).

[6] Research often slides into assumptions that pictures are categorically equivalent to words in comparisons of visual and verbal of journalistic material. A range of choices is assumed when it comes to written words, but constrained with relationship to pictures and video. Mitchell (1994) uses examples of Kjorup's (1978) formal analytic work that equates the picture to a speech act to illustrate his argument about this assumption.

[7] The art made possible here is clearly not accounted for in the sense of a material object such as a painting or a television program. Rather, like the dyad, it is useful to think of it as a process that goes on between a virtual text—or encoding instructions for experiencing an ideational object—and a performed text—or actualizing of an ideational object. The two ideational objects, of course, may or may not bear much resemblance to each other.

[8] Barnhurst took a similar approach in his interpretation of the newspaper page as a pictorial text whose content is graphics. He focused on the structure of spatial relations made by the "blacks and whites in different textures and shades of gray" as they form shapes and resonate with meaning (1994, p. 7). His interpretative distinctions among graphic arrangements of spatial relations also focus on the sense making characteristics of compositional structure. In another example, Yan Ma (1995) took this approach to the study of postmodern Chinese visual art.

[9] Although a communication relationship is based on intention, which calls for an inferential strategy of interpretation, as Anderson (1998) reminded us, neither a producer nor an auditor need enter a communication relationship to do his or her work. Because of its iconic properties, a pictorial expression is often interpreted attributionally rather than inferentially, and the more "realistic" a pictorial text seems, such as through the "mechanical naturalization" of photography, and the less aware one is of the picture-making processes, the more likely this is to happen (Gross, 1985). This tendency to interpret through attribution rather than implication might even be purposely manipulated as a strategy of persuasion (Barbatsis, 1996).

[10] Lindlof made the point that each of the various approaches to qualitative audience study is itself a "scholarly discourse that engages its object of inquiry in distinctive ways" (1991, p. 25). He uses the term *style* of qualitative audience study to emphasize this point.

[11] The traditional sender-message-receiver model proposes a linear relationship between the medium and an audience and characterizes the content of communication as delimited units of information that can be transferred from a sender to a receiver. A text-reader model, on the other hand, implies a dialectic relationship between the medium and an audience, and characterizes communication as a contingent experience in which meaning is created intersubjectively.

REFERENCES

Allen, R. (1992). Audience-oriented criticism and television. In R. Allen (Ed.), *Channels of discourse, reassembled* (pp. 101–137). Chapel Hill: University of North Carolina Press.

Anderson, J. (1998). Qualitative approaches to the study of media: Theory and methods of hermeneutic empiricism. In J. Asamen & G. Berry (Eds.), *Research paradigms, television, and social behavior* (pp. 206–236). Thousand Oaks, CA: Sage.

Ang, I. (1985). *Watching "Dallas": Soap opera and the melodramatic imagination.* D. Couling (Trans). New York: Methuen.

Barbatsis, G. (1996). "Look and I will show you something you will want to see": Viewer engagement with negative campaign commercials. *Journal of Argumentation and Advocacy, 32*(2), 69–80.

Barbatsis, G. (2002). Toward a phenomenological understanding of visual communication. *Journal of Visual Literacy, 22*(1), 1–18.

Barnhurst, K. (1994). *Seeing the newspaper.* New York: St. Martin's Press.

Barry, A. (1997). *Visual intelligence.* Albany: State University of New York Press.

Becker, H. (1982). *Art worlds.* Berkeley: University of California Press.

Craig, R. T. (1999). Communication theory as a field. *Communication Theory, 9*(2), 119–161.

Fish, S. (1976, Spring). Interpreting the *Valiorum. Critical Inquiry, 2,* 465–485.

Fish, S. (1980). *Is there a text in this class? The authority of interpretive communities.* Cambridge, MA: Harvard University Press.

Fiske, J. (1994). Audiencing: Cultural practice and cultural studies. In N. Denzin & Y. Lincoln (Eds.), *Handbook of qualitative research* (pp. 189–198). Thousand Oaks, CA: Sage.

Freund, E. (1987). *The return of the reader, reader-response criticism.* London: Methuen.

Gardner, H. (1993). *Frames of mind.* New York: Basic Books.

Giddens, A. (1987). Structuralism, post-structuralism and the production of culture. In A. Giddens & J. Turner (Eds.), *Social theory today* (pp. 195–223). Stanford, CA: Stanford University Press.

Gleik, J. (1987). *Chaos: Making a new science.* New York: Penguin.

Goodman, N. (1976). *Languages of art: An approach to the theory of symbols.* Indianapolis, IN: Hackett Publishing Company.

Grice, H. (1957). Meaning. *The Philosophical Review, 66*(3), 377–388.

Gross, L. (1974). Modes of communication and the acquisition of symbolic competence. In D. Olsen (Ed.), *Media and symbols: The forms of expression, communication and education* (pp. 56–80). National Society for the Study of Education. Chicago: University of Chicago Press.

Gross, L. (1985). Life vs. Art: The interpretation of visual narratives. *Studies in Visual Communication, 4,* 2–11.

Guba, E., & Lincoln, Y. (1994). Competing paradigms in qualitative research. In N. Denzin & Y. Lincoln (Eds.), *Handbook of Qualitative Research* (pp. 105–117). Thousand Oaks, CA: Sage.

Hobson, D. (1980). Housewives and the mass media. In S. Hall, D. Hobson, A. Lowe & P. Willis (Eds.), *Culture, media, language: Working papers in cultural studies, 1972–1979* (pp. 105–116). London: Hutchinson.

Holub, Robert S. (1984). *Reception theory: A critical introduction.* London: Methuen.

Ingarden, R. (1973). *The cognition of the literary work of art* (R. A. Crowley & K. Olsen, Trans.). Evanston, IL: Northwestern University Press.

Iser, W. (1978). *The act of reading: A theory of aesthetic response.* Baltimore: Johns Hopkins University Press.

Jauss, H. (1970). *Literaturgeschichte als Provokokation.* Frankfort, Germany: Suhrkamp.

Jensen, K. (1986). *Making sense of the news: Towards a theory and an empirical model of reception for the study of mass communication.* Aarhus, Denmark: Aarhus University Press.

Jensen, K. (1987). Qualitative audience research: Toward an integrative approach to reception. *Critical Studies in Mass Communication, 4,* 21–36.

Jensen, K. (1990). When is meaning? Communication theory, pragmatism, and mass media reception. In J. Anderson (Ed.), *Communication yearbook 14* (pp. 3–32). New Brunswick, NJ: International Communication Association.

Jensen, K. (1993). The past in the future: Problems and potentials of historical reception studies. *Journal of Communication, 13*(4), 20–27.

Jensen, K., & Rosengren, K. (1990). Five traditions in search of the audience. *European Journal of Communication, 5,* 207–238.

Karolides, N. (2000). *Reader response in secondary and college classrooms.* Mahwah, NJ: Lawrence Erlbaum Associates.

Katz, E., & Liebes, T. (1984). Once upon a time, in Dallas. *Intermedia, 12,* 28–32.

Kjorup, S. (1978). Pictorial speech acts. *Erkenntnis, 12*(1), 55–71.

Kosko, B. (1993). *Fuzzy thinking.* New York: Hyperion.

Liebes, T., & Katz, G. (1990). *The export of meaning: Cross cultural readings of Dallas.* New York: Oxford University Press.

Laing, R., Phillipson, H., & Lee, A. (1966). *Interpersonal perception.* New York: Springer.

Lindlof, T. (1987). Ideology and pragmatics of media access in prison. In T. R. Lindlof (Ed.), *Natural audiences: Qualitative research of media uses and effects* (pp. 175–197). Norwood, NJ: Ablex.

Lindlof, T. (1988). Media audiences as interpretive communities. In J. Anderson (Ed.), *Communication yearbook 11* (pp. 81–107). Newbury Park, CA: Sage.

Lindlof, T. (1991). The qualitative study of media audiences. *Journal of Broadcasting and Electronic Media, 35*(1), 23–42.

Lull, J. (1982). The social uses of television. In E. Wartella & D. Whitney (Eds.), *Mass communication review yearbook* (Vol. 3, pp. 397–409). Beverly Hills, CA: Sage.

Lull, J. (Ed.) (1988). *World families watch television.* Beverly Hills, CA: Sage.

Ma, Y. (1995). Reader-response theory: An analysis of a work of Chinese post modern art. *Journal of Visual Literacy, 15*(1), 39–72.

Mailloux, S. (1982). *Interpretive conventions, the reader in the study of American fiction.* Ithaca, NY: Cornell University Press.

McCrone, J. (1994, 20 August). Quantum states of mind. *New Scientist, 35–37.*

Mitchell, D. (1994). Distinctions between everyday and representational communication. *Communication Theory, 4*(2), 111–131.

Moriarty, S. (1996). Abduction: A theory of visual interpretation. *Communication Theory, 6*(2), 167–187.

Morley, D. (1980). *The 'Nationwide' audience.* London: British Film Institute.

Morley, D. (1986). *Family television: Culture, power and domestic leisure.* London: Comedia.

Neiva, E. (1999). Redefining the image: Mimesis, convention, and semiotics. *Communication Theory, 9*(1), 75–91.

Newcomb, H., & Hirsch, P. (1983). Television as a cultural forum: Implications for research. In W. Rowland and B. Watkins (Eds.), *Interpreting television* (pp. 58–73). Beverly Hills, CA: Sage.

Pacanowsky, M., & Anderson J. (1982). Cop talk and media use. *Journal of Broadcasting, 26,* 741–756.

Poulet, G. (1972). Criticism and the experience of interiority. In R. Macksey & E. Donato (Eds.), *The structuralist controversy: The language of criticism and the sciences of man* (pp. 56–72). Baltimore: Johns Hopkins University Press.

Radway, J. (1984). Reading the romance: Women as interpretive communities. In J. A. Anderson (Ed.), *Communication yearbook 11* (pp. 81–107). Newbury Park, CA: Sage.

Reid, L., & Frazer, C. (1980). Television at play. *Journal of Communication, 30*(4), 66–73.

Scannell, P. (1995). For a phenomenology of radio and television. *Journal of Communication, 30,* 66–73.

Schwartz, D., & Griffin, M. (1987). Amateur photography: The organizational maintenance of an aesthetic code. In T. Lindlof (Ed.), *Natural audiences: Qualitative research of media uses and effects* (pp. 198–224). Norwood, NJ: Ablex.

Stafford, B. (1996). *Good looking: Essays on the virtue of images.* Cambridge, MA: MIT Press.

Stephens, M. (1998). *The rise of the image the fall of the word.* New York: Oxford University Press.

Tompkins, J. (1980). *Reader-response criticism, from formalism to post-structuralism.* Baltimore: Johns Hopkins University Press.

Traudt, P., Anderson, J., & Meyer, T. (1987). Phenomenology, empiricism and media experience. *Critical Studies in Mass Communication, 4,* 302–310.

Traudt, P., & Lont, C. (1987). Media logic-in-use: The family as locus of study. In T. Lindlof (Ed.), *Natural audiences: Qualitative research of media uses and effects* (pp. 139–160). Norwood, NJ: Ablex.

Turkle, S., & Papert, S. (1993). Epistemological pluralism and the revaluation of the concrete. In I. Harel & S. Papert (Eds.), *Constructionism* (pp. 161–192). Norwood, NJ: Ablex.

Willliams, R. (1974). *Television: Technology and cultural form.* London: Fontana.

Wolf, M. (1987). How children negotiate television. In T. Lindlof (Ed.), *Natural audiences: Qualitative research of media uses and effects* (pp. 58–94). Norwood, NJ: Ablex.

Wolf, M., Meyer, T., & White, C. (1982). A rules based study of television's role in the construction of social reality. *Journal of Broadcasting, 26,* 813–829.

Worth, S. (1981). *Studying visual communication* (L. Gross, Ed.). Philadelphia: University of Pennsylvania Press.

Zettl, H. (1999). *Sight, sound, motion: Applied media aesthetics.* Belmont, CA: Wadsworth.

19

A Textual Analysis of Political Television Ads

GRETCHEN BARBATSIS
Michigan State University

Each new election cycle brings its inevitable bombardment of political advertising and, as sure as day follows night, scholars and commentators address issues of political discourse carried out through 30-second spots. What seemed unthinkable over half a century ago when Eisenhower's presidential campaign introduced television commercials into the political scene, soon became a mainstay of political campaigns. Though critics in 1952 were astounded at the idea of selling a political product in the same creative manner as soap or toothpaste (Wood, 1982), today it would be a political campaign *without* television commercials that many would find odd.

Within this now commonplace environment of political advertising, the negative campaign ad continues to captivate and confound political analysis. The attack ad made a powerful debut with the now infamous *Daisy* commercial used in the presidential campaign of Lyndon Johnson (Kaid & Johnson, 1991). Although previous campaign commercials had employed such traditional advertising strategies as bolstering and "product" comparison to show their candidates or issues in a favorable light, the attack ad introduced a dimension into political advertising that was not used for products like soap or toothpaste because of its potential backlash effect. Its purpose, which viewers have consistently found to be distasteful (Ansolabehere & Lyengar, 1995; Garramone, 1984; Merritt, 1984; Stewart, 1975), is to build a degrading image of a rival candidate. Apparently the advertisers got it right, however. Despite the decrying of critics and the disdain of a voting public, negative campaign commercials continue to increase with each new election cycle.

Why they got it right, both in introducing the televisual spot to political discourse and in shaping that discourse with the negative attack ad, is an open question, however. Conventional wisdom concerning the efficacy of negative political commercials argues simply, that "they work." Using the often cited 1988 presidential campaign image of Michael Dukakis taking a tank ride used in an attack ad by the Bush campaign, creators and critics alike credit them with causing doubt about a candidate's veracity, potency, or trustworthiness. Measured in gross terms, they work not because voters necessarily turn to the other candidate, but because the doubts the commercials create depress the vote of the candidate whose image has been degraded. Clearly this form of political discourse works because it engages viewers in some meaningful way, but identifying how attack ads do that has been anything but a straightforward task. In particular there has been little work with the pictorial characteristics of this engagement, despite the fact that political wisdom holds to the image as critical to its persuasive process. Significantly for our work in visual communication, Kathleen Jamieson (1992) emphasized the role of visualization tactics in the complex and interactive engagement created by political commercials. As she states, "what is shown is not necessarily what is seen, and what is said is not always what is heard" (pp. 9, 43–101).[1]

Whereas much of the research examining negative campaign commercials has focused on its verbal content, our task as visual communication scholars is to understand how this discursive engagement is constructed visually. I argued elsewhere, for example, that an analysis of negative campaign commercials produced by the 1988 presidential campaign of George Bush helps us to understand how visual direct address as well as visual narrative is used to construct a political argument (Barbatsis, 1996). Quite apart from the words used in these commercials, close textual analysis of their visual structures shows how they intentionally manipulate the natural versus symbolic ambiguity of pictorial expression by converging these strategies: Although pictorial narrative engages the viewer in acts of ideation that construct the fictional world of their texts, pictorial direct address engages the viewer as a participant in photographing a seemingly "real" world. By way of extending this work, I argue here that these visual texts are also characterized by a propositional syntax that engages viewers in a holistically structured logic.

In making distinctions between the meaning-making characteristics of pictorial and linguistic structures, notions of propositional logic have generally been reserved for the linear properties of verbal language. Unlike the "explicit syntax expressing analogies, contrasts, causal claims and other kinds of propositions" in linguistic structures, pictorial compositions have been thought of as limited to an associational logic of spatial and temporal relationships (Messaris, 1997, p. xi). The idea of a nonlinear or holistic logic untangles some of the confusions about logical structures that flow from strictly language-based syntax, however, and opens the door to investigating the characteristics of pictorially composed propositional logic. In the analysis of a negative campaign commercial discussed here, I demonstrate how the visual text engages viewers by carefully guiding them through a visual syntax of four propositional statements. The analysis, which theorizes the picture as a text, uses reader-response theory, and particularly the work of Wolfgang Iser (1978), to examine this visual meaning-making engagement. The notion of textuality and of reader response has a significance specific to reception theory and deserves particular attention for the framing of this analysis. I do this with reference to the visual text of THE HARBOR, a negative attack ad produced for the 1988 Bush presidential campaign.[2] A storyboard of this visual text is presented in Fig. 19.1.

As seen in Fig. 19.1, the visual text begins as a title THE HARBOR fades onto a black screen. The black is replaced by an image of the skyline around a harbor as seen from the water in a moving boat; the first image at high tide and with a recreational feel, is replaced

THE HARBOR

FIG. 19.1. Pictorial story sequence.

by an inactive image of a weather beaten pier at low tide, and then a series of dark and dirty images of sewer pipes, an open culvert, and contaminated, polluted water. Toxic, bubbling foam then fills the screen, forming a skull shape, and floating over a submerged sign with the words "danger, radiation hazard, no swimming." A final foamy skull is replaced by images of dark, oily, stagnant water, heavily moving in a counterclockwise direction and then a shore line with water lapping on the lid of a garbage bin, beer cans, and dead fish.

Analysis and interpretation of the ways that meanings are composed visually in *THE HARBOR* are informed by reception theory's notion of a text. As will become clear in the next section, this means that the analysis of this commercial is not of the visual text per se but, rather, of a kind of text-reader interaction that is implied by the way the text is composed. This structure of interaction is identified by examining the visual content of the text in relationship to its compositional form. This close visual reading provides the evidence with which to proceed with an interpretation of how a viewer was intended to engage (or see) the world of the text.

TEXTUALITY AND THE READER'S RESPONSE

Reception theory, with its roots in literature and literary theory, developed because of an interest in how and under what conditions a text has meaning (Holub, 1984). Rather than focus on either the text or the reader as an object of study, the approach looks at the act of reading—that is, the interaction between a text and a reader—to understand how meaning is produced. Meaning—and ultimately the literary work—is conceived of as neither completely a property of the text nor as completely the subjectivity of the reader. Rather, it is conceptualized as a merger of the two—a transient ideation produced by an engagement between text and reader. From this perspective, it is important to understand that the analysis of *THE HARBOR* undertaken here is not of the visual text per se, but rather, of the structure of engagement with an intended viewer that its composition of visual elements implies.

In the approach taken by Iser, reader-response theory conceives of the text as having an "inner structure" of given and not-given information that, when engaged by the reader, activates a performance. Accordingly, the material text that one encounters when opening a book or picking up a newspaper is understood as a schemata of given information or manifest content and silent spaces or blanks. In the relationship between them, it is not what is said per se that is important, but rather, how this manifest content structures a reference to what is not said. The blanks created by what is not said initiate and guide acts of ideation by the reader, which in turn brings forth the world of the text. As Iser (1978) explained:

> [Blanks] are the hollow form into which meaning is to be poured, and as such, they bring about the process . . . whereby knowledge is offered or invoked by the text in such a way that it can undergo guided transformation in and through the reader's mind. (p. 217)

Rather than merely internalizing positions given in a text, the reader is induced, through the structure of given information and blanks, to "imagine something which would have appeared unimaginable" and in so doing to actually bring *into being* the fictive world of the text (Iser, 1978, p. 189). Because reception theory ties the performance of meaning to specific compositional schema or patterns of syntax, it offers a useful analytic tool for investigating how a negative political commercial works to engage its viewers. Accordingly, the method used in this analysis involved first identifying a compositional structure of vacancies or gaps in THE HARBOR, and then analyzing the gaps to identify the ways they structured the meaning of given information or image content.

Although Iser's work is with a text constructed linguistically, his concern for the details of interaction marked out in a textual schema makes his approach particularly useful for pictorial analysis. Iser identified statements made with words as the given information of a textual structure and the not given or vacant spaces in the schema as gaps.[3] In a parallel way, the schema of a pictorial text is composed of statements made with images that, like verbal statements, are characterized by both content and form (or syntax). Spaces outside and between an image or series of images compose textual vacancies or gaps. In other words, the given material of an image structure is what is there to be seen, and the not given is what has been left outside the frame, whether it be in the single-frame schemata of paintings and photographs or in the multiple-frame structures of film, video, and multimedia texts. The compositional pattern of content and form of any particular pictorial text can be described in terms of its pictorially given and pictorially not-given information, and this inner structure can be examined for the ways that it initiates and guides the ideations of a viewing-reader. A close reading begins by identifying this inner structure of given and not-given information.

Accordingly, the inner structure of THE HARBOR, as presented in Fig. 19.1, consists of the 15 visual statements identified in screens 1–15 and the 14 visually constructed vacancies identified in gaps a–n. Visual statements reflected in this storyboard are begun and ended with cuts, dissolves, fades, superimpositions, and wipes. By simultaneously marking where content is selected in as well as selected out, these compositional elements indicate that a text is composed of both its manifest content and the content selected to remain on "a cutting-room floor." Accordingly, the function of a pictorially structured gap is theoretically the same as one in a verbal composition: By using what is edited in (i.e., a given) to refer to what is edited out (i.e., a not given), it invites a projection about both the "what" and the "why" of material left on an image-maker's hypothetical cutting-room floor.

From the perspective of reception theory, these projections are ideations created in the mind of the reader-viewer, and it is the compositional structure of a text that guides this ideational process of meaning making. An analysis of these gaps seeks, then, to identify what kinds of ideations the text implies. Analyzing the gaps involves the generation of a textual schema, which describes the visual text in two ways. First, it describes the image or images of a visual text in terms that distinguish analytically between visual content and elements of visual form. Second, it describes the function of not-given information or gaps syntactically in terms of blanks and negations. The analysis involved in generating a textual schema also produces a pattern of ideational clusters, each of which is composed of images connected through the work of blanks and separated from one another through the work of negations. The textual schema produced for a close reading of THE HARBOR is discussed in the next section and presented in Fig. 19.2. A discussion of the ideational clusters identified follows the discussion of the textual schema.

Screen/Gap	DESCRIPTIVE Structure (image content)	LITERAL Structure (image form)			
		MOTION: TIME	MOTION: DIRECTION	ANGLE	SCALE
1	black	fade-in			
a		*blank: and*			
2	Title: The Harbor.	key-in		eye-level	full-shot
b		*blank: and*			
3	high-tide view of harbor skykine from position on the water	fade-in	pan: left-to-right	eye-level	long-shot
c		*blank: and*			
4	buoy prominent in foreground	key-out	pan: continues	eye-level	(close-up of buoy)
d		*negation: BUT...*			
5	low-tide view of weather-beaten and broken pier	dissolve	pan: right-to-left	eye-level	medium-shot
e		*blank: and*			
6	strong water flow from sewer pipe; mud in foreground	dissolve	pan: right-to-left; slight zoom-in	eye-level	medium-shot
f		*blank: and*			
7	large, open culvert; stagnant, polluted water in foreground	dissolve		eye-level	close-up
g		*blank: and*			
8	dirty, foamy water; floating rusty orange object	dissolve	slight zoom-out	eye-level	extreme close-up
h		*negation: ON the OTHER HAND*			
9	trash can lid, dead fish, bottles, plastic containers moving in counter-clockwise direction	dissolve		high angle	long-shot
i		*negation: ACTUALLY*			
10	abstract skull shape in frothing foam; submerged sigh: HAZARD	dissolve		from above	extreme close-up
j		*blank: and*			
11	submerged sign: DANGER Radiation Hazard No Swimming; rusty object; foam	super-imposition-in		from above	extreme close-up
k		*blank: and*			
12	abstract skull shape in frothing foam; rusty object exits	super-imposition-out		from above	extreme close-up
l		*negation: THEREFORE . . . BECAUSE*			
13	stagnant, oily, heavy water (slime)	dissolve		from above	close-up
m		*blank: and*			
14	water lapping on trash littered shoreline (beer cans, dead fish)	dissolve	slight zoom-out; tilt down, slight zoom-in	from above	medium-shot
n		*blank: and*			
15	small picture of Bush with disclaimer	key-in			

FIG. 19.2. Textual schema of *The Harbor*.

ANALYZING THE GAP: A TEXTUAL SCHEMA

Reception theory tells us that there is more to a performance of meaning than merely filling structural vacancies, however. Although gaps require that a viewing-reader supply the not-given information to determine the significance of the given information, they do not leave it wholly to an interpreter to select a projected meaning. Gaps also work within a syntagmatic and paradigmatic arrangement to guide the meaning-making process that they initiate. As Iser described these arrangements, in a syntagmatic pattern gaps acting as "blanks" open up connections between elements of the text, and in a paradigmatic pattern they act as "negations" to shift the reader from one perspective to another (1978, p. 216). An arrangement of blanks and negations in a textual schema provides a pattern of interaction that initiates and guides an ideational process. The ideations occur as a viewer-reader of the text is guided by the not-given space of a blank or negation to make sense of the image content that is presented as well as of the way the content is formed. In the textual schema of *THE HARBOR*, for example, the cut-vacancy marking the end of the second image statement (screen 2) indicates that there is some meaning to be made both of the two words making up its visual content (The Harbor) and of the eye-level angle and full-screen scale of this content, as well as of its appearance as a key-in to a previously empty, black space. Accordingly, to examine the details of interaction initiated by these vacancies of not-given information, it is useful to mark them in a schema that also makes an analytical distinction between the descriptive elements of an image's content and the compositional elements of its form. Though an artificial separation, the move is useful as a way to focus one's attention on the compositional syntax of an image or sequence of images.

The textual schema of *THE HARBOR* presented in Fig. 19.2 reflects such a move. Using terms introduced by Northrup Frye (1957), the visual content of an image is characterized as a "descriptive structure" while the elements of its form (or formal features) are characterized as a "literal (or syntactical) structure."[4] The elements of form selected for this analysis include angle of view, scale, and motion. These structures of "given" information are identified as screens 1–15. Structural vacancies (or not givens) in this textual schema are characterized functionally as either a blank or a negation and are designated by the letters a–n. With reference to this schematic analysis, then, I turn first to a discussion of how these gaps work to guide an ideational process of meaning making, and then to a description of how the sense making associated with a blank or a negation is located within the formal features that generate the form or literal structure of a pictorial text.[5]

ANALYZING THE GAP: IDEATIONAL CLUSTERS

The four negations identified in the textual schema mark out five ideational clusters in this negative campaign commercial. With regard to the visual content of each, they were labeled "Harbor-at-high-tide," "Harbor-at-low-tide," "Outside-seeing," "Inside-seeing," and "Truthful-seeing." As these labels suggest, the compositional structure of negations shifts the subject matter of ideation from an object (the harbor) first to the notion of seeing and then to a concept (the truth). The discussion that follows demonstrates the method of close reading that integrates image content and image form in an analysis of meaning potential.

Ideational Cluster: Harbor-at-High-Tide

The first details of interaction marked out in the textual schema of *THE HARBOR* are the three vacancies identified as gaps a, b, and c. They occur between the first four image statements of the text, identified as screens 1, 2, 3, and 4. These silent spaces of not-given information function syntagmatically, additively connecting the four images into a meaningful ideational cluster. Operating much as the "ands" of a verbal composition, they open up *connections* between elements of the composition by inviting the viewing-reader to link the sequential image statements of an empty, black space (image content: screen 1) first, to a graphic, *THE HARBOR* (image content: screen 2) then, to a picture of a harbor with the same word graphic (image content: screen 3), and, finally, to a picture of the harbor without a title (image content: screen 4). This structure of image statements related to each other with connecting ands implies an ideational cluster that represents a harbor "-as"[6] viewed from an eye-level angle, at the surface of the water and with a symmetrically balancing horizon line. Because it occurs at the beginning of *THE HARBOR* text, it is an implied frame of reference.[7] With the next vacancy (gap d), however, there is a shift from this perspective to a different one.

Ideational Cluster: Harbor-at-Low-Tide

A second ideational cluster emerges in the pattern of *THE HARBOR* schema's succeeding five vacancies indicated by gaps d, e, f, g, h and the four image statements represented by screens 5, 6, 7, and 8. As with the first sequence, the gaps *within* this series of images operate much as ands, opening up *connections* by inviting a viewing-reader to link the image statement of a pier at low tide (image content: screen 5) first, to a sewer pipe (image content: screen 6), then to an open culvert at low tide (image content: screen 7), and, finally, to dirty, foaming water (image content: screen 8). In contrast to the ideation of a harbor-at-high-tide provided by the first cluster, this cluster *shifts* to an ideation of a harbor-at-low-tide. The shift in perspective is structured by the vacancy (gap d) that occurs *between* the end of the first cluster (screen 4) and the beginning of the second cluster (screen 5). This gap terminates the sequence-building process of connections occurring with the first three vacancies, by shifting to a contrasting perspective that is composed by a second sequence-building set of connections. Acting much as the "but" of a verbal composition, rather than an "and," this vacancy (gap d) creates a reevaluation of preceding interpretations. It negates the previous implication that the represented or implied ideational object of this composition (as a whole) is a harbor "-as" viewed from the perspective of the water's *surface* at high tide.

The vacancy (gap d) composed by a juxtaposition of the "harbor-at-high-tide" cluster (screens 1–4) with the "harbor-at-low-tide" cluster (screens 5–8) is a negation. As described by Iser (1978), it acts paradigmatically because it structures ideation in both a forward and a backward direction. Ideation framed in a forward direction, by shifting the perspective to a low-water view with accompanying sewer imagery, invites an additive projection that might be stated: *"but, there is more to this picture-story."* Accordingly, the picture-story now has two parts instead of one, and they are in a relationship of contrast: a harbor "-as" represented at high tide and a harbor "-as" represented at low tide. A differing interpretation of this juxtaposition is simultaneously introduced, however, through a backward direction of ideation. Looking back on the initial high-water representation of this harbor *from the perspective of* a low-water representation forces a *reevaluation* of the role (or meaning) of the high-water representation in terms of the whole composition. Ideation that evaluates a previous ideation might interpret this juxtaposition to mean: *"but, this is not the* real *story."* Because one recognizes that the apparently "not real" story was constructed from a position on the surface of the water, the invitation of the juxtaposition "to mean" might be further elaborated as: *"surface appearances are deceiving."* There is, then, more than the shift in degree that is invited by the introduction of a contrasting perspective. By introducing an evaluation, it creates instead a distinction in kind.

This pattern of pictorial givens and not givens is meaningful, of course, because it is simultaneously an arrangement of both content and form. Yet as the foregoing analysis suggests, the source of meaning is, to use Northrop Frye's distinction, in the "literal" or syntactical structure of the image (Frye, 1957, p. 73). In other words, meaning is made in the way that elements of *form* bring content forth rather than in the imaged objects themselves (or content). If the preliminary sense to be made of THE HARBOR text is that the images we have been seeing of a harbor "are not the real story," the basis of that meaning must lie with the composition of the negating "but," which is found in the structuring elements or formal features of the image statements. With reference to Fig. 19.2, then, we can locate the literal meaning of this paradigmatic shift (gap g) by examining how a viewing-reader develops—from the space-time relationships within the syntax of the images—a meaning-making "sense of the larger [pictorial] pattern they make" (Frye, 1957, p. 73).

It is primarily in their arrangements of scale and of motion (direction) that the images on either side of the compositional vacancy labeled gap d compose a paradigmatic shift. The composition of screen 5, for example, organizes motion from a right-to-left direction (pan), which is in significant contrast to the left-to-right direction of motion composing screen 4. This arrangement literally brings one pattern of motion to a halt. In addition, it does so with an oppositional, high-energy, converging motion vector (Zettl, 1999). Another and complementary pattern of contrast in the structural form of these images occurs in their arrangements of scale. Screen 5 is composed with a medium field of view, which is a change from the long and full-scale arrangements of the previous screens. It is literally a transitional, moderating change between long and close fields of view (Zettl, 1999). Working experientially (Barry, 1997), then, these pictorial arrangements perceptually compose a pragmatic but by visually "pulling the viewer back" (with the pan) for what would appear to be movement toward "a closer look" (with the medium scale). This pattern is further developed by the compositional arrangements of the remaining three visual statements of this second cluster. A second right-to-left pan (screen 6) reinforces the "backward pull" (of screen 5) and a slight zoom-in points the transitional scale (of screen 5) in the direction of a "closer look." The next two image structures complete the ideation by literally delivering (screen 7, close-up) and then reinforcing (screen 8, extreme close-up) the intended "closer look." In other words, at the same time that compositional vacancies, such as gap d, induce a process of meaning making by indicating "that a combination is required," the structural form composing the gap indicates a particular kind of combination (i.e., a negating but) for its "necessary coherence" (Iser, 1978, pp. 185–186). Here, a pattern of converging motion vectors (left-to-right and right-to-left) indicates a two-part contrast (*but, there is* more *to this story*) and a pattern of transition from a contextual to an intimate view indicates a potential difference in kind (*but, this is not the* real *story*).

Further ideational clusters initiated and guided by textual vacancies complete the text. Unlike the first two ideations—*harbor-at-high-tide* and *harbor-at-low tide*—those that follow shift the subject of the ideation from an object—the harbor—first to a notion of "seeing" and finally to the concept of "truth." An ideation of *outside-seeing* emerges as a pattern created by a dissolve (gap h: negation) that juxtaposes a high-angle, long-shot view of beach trash (screen 9) with the previous eye-level, close-up image of dirty foam (screen 8). This is followed by an ideation of *inside-seeing* that emerges in a pattern of three intricately integrated high-angle, extreme close-up views (screens 10, 11, 12) created by dissolving (gap I: negation) and then superimposing (gaps j and k) images of foaming, toxic water. Finally, an ideation of *truthful-seeing* emerges in a pattern of three high-angle close-up and then medium-scale images of pollution (screens 13, 14, 15) similarly integrated by dissolving (gap l and m) and keying (gap n). (An analysis of the literal structure of these three ideational clusters similar to that discussed for the first two ideational structures can be found in Fig. 19.3.)

As the analysis thus far demonstrates, these elements of syntax create interactive patterns, which initiate and guide an ideational production of meaning by a viewing-reader. Although I have illustrated this process by separating the textual schema into five paradigm shifts, the foregoing discussion should also indicate that each of the ideational clusters is an interactive and indivisible part of a meaning-making whole. Not unlike a gestalt, a textural pattern of blanks and negations provides an ideated whole that is more than the sum of its meaning-making parts.[8]

Theories of the text describe various kinds of reader-text engagements based on distinctions made among differing ways that patterns of blanks and negations regulate patterns of connectability. Iser described an expository structure, for example, as a pattern of connectability in which "a multiplicity of meanings is constantly narrowed down" (1978, p. 184). As described by gestalt theory, its regulatory pattern is a system of "rigid connections . . . governed by constraints" (Kohler, 1938, p. 61). By contrast, a fictional structure exhibits a pattern of connectability more akin to a system where the "inner dynamics" are "freely . . . left to regulate themselves" (Kohler, 1938, p. 61). As Iser described this pattern of connectability, details of interaction in a fictional text-viewer engagement are distinguished by negations that "open up an increasing number of possibilities" (1978, p. 184). The analysis provided in Fig. 19.2 shows the dynamics of a fictional rather than an expository structure: THE HARBOR's syntax of blanks and negations works from beginning to end to open up rather than narrow down meaning possibilities. Its pattern of blanks guides the formation of ideational clusters and, at the same time, its pattern of negations continually reveals alternative sense-making possibilities by invoking perspective shifts. These perspective shifts are reflected in the nature of the ideational clusters, which move in subject matter from a descriptive *harbor-at-high tide* and *harbor-at-low-tide* through a

Frame of Reference

The frame of reference established in the first four images of this televisual text (screens 1–4) suggests that it intends to tell a story about a harbor. A title, *THE HARBOR*, signals the idea of a story, and the appearance of a harbor image provides a pictorial thematic referent. Visual image content establishes a familiar perspective. There is a shift in perspective, however, as the negation that occurs between the image of a harbor at high tide (in screen 4) and the image of a weather-beaten pier at low tide (in screen 5) simultaneously decontextualizes the normative image of a harbor and makes it a theme to be examined.

Perspective Shift: "But"

This first negation, functioning much as a "but" in linguistic syntax, is composed pictorially through screen movement and image scale. In concert with a change in scale from a contextual long-shot (of screens 3 and 4) to a transitional medium-shot, a pan moving from screen right-to-left halts the previous direction of left-to-right motion. This converging motion vector has the effect of "stopping, and pulling the reader back" at the same time that the medium scale provides a more close-up view. A second pan moving from screen-right-to-left (in screen 6) reinforces this "backward pull," and though the image scale remains transitional, a slight zoom-in suggests that the pattern of converging vectors intends a "closer-look." Punctuated by a cessation of the pans in a screen-right-to-left direction, screen 7 delivers that closer view, which is then reinforced with an extremely close-view (screen 8). The closer look constructed by this cluster begins with low-tide, as evidenced by the water marks on a disintegrating pier (in screen 5). Moving through a broken section of the pier (in screen 6), one finds a leaking sewer pipe defining a new horizon-line below the surface, and is then confronted full frame, first by a gaping culvert (in screen 7) and then by contaminated, foaming water in (screen 8).

Structurally, the first sequence (screens 1–4, gaps a–d) of this narrative incorporates into the text an external reality of a normative, high-water view of a harbor. The negation that follows (gap d), however, opens up the meaning potentials of this picture-world fiction by shifting the reader's perspective to consideration of sewer imagery with a low-water view. In a forward direction, the act of shifting to a low-water view puts this second perspective in a position of textual theme and moves the high-water perspective to a position of textual horizon. Accordingly, ideation framed in a forward direction might interpret this negating but to mean: "*but, there is* more *to this story.*" Characteristic of a literary text, however, the negation also opens up other meaning possibilities. By directing ideation backward, it structures a reevaluation of the interpretations one has already made. Thus, from the vantage point of a low-water perspective, ideation framed in a backward direction might interpret the juxtaposition to mean "*but, is this the* real *story?*" Unlike the theme of a forward framing, this ideation introduces a theme about the deception of "surface views."

For either interpretation, the iconic properties of the sign, apparent in its *descriptive structure*, foreshadow the two perspectives: an image of a buoy (screens 3 and 4) reveals a below-surface water line while it floats on the surface of the water. It is also important to recognize that both interpretations are valid. The negation does not pose a blanket rejection of the high-water perspective established in the framing reference. By expanding the story of the harbor to include a low-tide perspective, it only negates the assumption that the story is limited to one perspective. In addition, connecting the two textual segments with a dissolve serves to blend, rather than contrast, the differing perspectives.

FIG. 19.3.   Propositional syntax of *The Harbor: A discourse about "Seeing"*.

Perspective Shift: "On the Other Hand"

A second negation (gap h), functioning-as would an "on the other hand" in linguistic syntax, is composed pictorially through scale and angle of view. A shift from an eye-level angle and an extreme close-up scale (screen 8) to a high-angle, long-shot scale (screen 9) breaks the blending connections of the previous two sequences. The high-angle (screen 9) shifts the perspective of viewing from "on" (screens 1–4) and "below" (screens 5–8) the water's surface to "above" it and, along with a change in scale (screen 9), to a contextualizing long-shot, guides a reevaluation of everything that has gone before by simultaneously halting the progression of "closer and deeper looking" (developed in screens 5–8) and shifting from an immersed to an omniscient or "objective" vantage point. This opens up the picture-world fiction to consideration of an "alternative" (on the other hand) to the sense of "surface" initially invoked. In addition this alternative is constructed from an "objective" (high angle) rather than an "involved" (eye level; screens 1–8) point of view. In a forward direction of ideation, this "on the other hand" alternative suggests that if one takes an *objective* look, the story of the harbor is the same from both above and below the surface: it is a sewer. Accordingly, the harbor-as-sewer theme (developed in screens 1–8) shifts from being only one part of the story, to being *the* story. In a backward direction, this on the other hand alternative opens up another meaning possibility between the two preceding thematic clusters (screens 1–4 and screens 5–8): Perhaps the function of a low-tide perspective (screens 5–8) is not so much meant to cast the high-tide perspective as a surface view (screens 1–4) as it is to reveal the "surface-ness" or superficiality of such a view.

On the one hand, then, this negation answers one of the issues raised by the first negation: the conventional, framing image of a harbor is not the *real* story. Although the negating on the other hand offers a possibility that the real story is one of a sewer, however, it also opens the possibility that this story isn't really even about a harbor. Whatever its subject, though, the next image, containing the word "hazard," signals that the real story is a frightening one.

Perspective Shift: "Actually"

A third structural cluster (screens 10–12) is the crux of the story and the point of no return in the pictorial narrative. A third textual negation (gap h), functioning much as an "actually" in verbal syntax, is composed pictorially through operations of scale and special effect. In a complex construction incorporating a superimposition, this sequence changes the meaning of "normal" seeing by revealing relationships that are not normally visible to the (mind's) eye. Accordingly, a superimposition (screen 11) enables us to *look through to* the previous image (screen 10), to see the warning: DANGER Radiation Hazard No Swimming. This literal, visual experience of "extra-ordinary" or "super" seeing, along with an extremely close-up scale and an above-angle of view, opens up a further meaning possibility: "actually," the theme of this picture-world fiction might have to do with *how* we see. In the context of the "objectivity" within which the "super seeing" takes place, then, "normal" human seeing, when contrasted with "technological seeing," becomes subjective. Accordingly, in a backward direction, a shift in textual perspective here suggests that "*actually,*" what *we see has to do with* how *we see.*

Perspective Shift: "Therefore . . . Because"

The fourth negation (gap 1) is causal. In relationship to what has gone before, the juxtaposition created by the final structural cluster (in screens 13–15) shifts the perspective as

FIG. 19.3.   (Continued)

would a "therefore ... because" in verbal syntax. This final structural cluster, although re-taining an "objective" above-angle of view, reverses a progression of "closer-looking" (begun with screens 5–8; emphasized with screens 10–12) by widening the field-of-view, first to a close-up (screen 13) and then to a medium scale (screens 14–15). In concert with the pre-vious experience of having "seen-through" (screen 11), this negation guides a concluding ideation: *therefore, it does not matter what you* think *you are seeing*.

This perspective shift structures a cluster of causal relationships that clarify that what this picture-world fiction is about may not have to do primarily with harbors or with pollution at all, but, rather, that the *real* story here is about "seeing." The propositional statement "*Therefore, it does not matter what you think you see*" is the same for all four relationships in this negating cluster, as each explanatory "*because ...*" addresses the openings created by the three previous plus this fourth paradigmatic textual shift. Accordingly, addressing the meaning possibilities opened by the first textual shift ("but"), *it does not matter what you think you see,* because the harbor is a sewer; for the second ("on the other hand"), because surfaces are deceiving; for the third ("actually"), because human seeing is subjective; and for the fourth ("therefore, because"), because the "truth" is always hidden. By giving the "reader" the experience of "superhuman seeing," the text has revealed that when things are looked at "objectively," via the "special lens" of visual technology, the *real* truth, although not available through the "subjectivity" of normal seeing, can be seen.

FIG. 19.3.   (Continued)

notion of *outside-seeing* and *inside-seeing* to a concept of *truthful-seeing.* In concluding this analysis, then, I examine the pictorial pattern of connectability in this visual text as a propositional syntax of holistic logic.

PROPOSITIONAL SYNTAX: HOLISTIC LOGIC

The notion of holistic logic as a mode of sense making emerges from the gestalt concept of nonlinear and dynamical systems (Gleik, 1987; McCrone, 1994; Kosko, 1993). It is tied to perceptual rather than language (or postperceptual) principles and is typically associated with images (Arnheim, 1969; Gombrich, 1960; Gibson, 1979). As a non-linear system of meaning making, holistic logic "acknowledges relationships that are not strictly proportional," that is, as gestalts that "cannot be mathematically solved and ... cannot be added together" (Barry, 1997, p. 100). Reception theory's notion of distinctly different patterns of connectability based on the way that they guide ideation is helpful for describing how the syntax of a holistic system, while not a quantitative linear one, is nonetheless propositional. Accordingly, it allows us to untangle confu-sions about logical structures flowing from strictly language-based assumptions that have limited the sense-making properties of images to drawing spatial and temporal re-lationships while reserving "explicit syntax expressing analogies, contrasts, causal claims and other kinds of propositions" to the quantitative linear properties of verbal language (Messaris, 1997, p. xi). Analysis of patterns of connectability in the holistic syntax of *THE HARBOR* is provided in Fig. 19.3. It shows a compositional structure of four proposi-tional statements emerging from a pattern of four paradigmatic shifts (or negations) in the pictorial syntax. As we see, these propositions lead us to a conclusion that this pictorial text is about more than a harbor. Although its *descriptive* structure is made up of harbor imagery (Fig. 19.1), its *literal* structure fashions a claim about the nature of "truth." That claim is developed by a pictorial logic of contrast, alternative, existence, and consequence.

Contrast

The first negation is one of contrast. It links two textual segments in the propositional terms of a *but*, releasing meaning potentials created by a syntax of contrast (Fig. 19.3). One potential interpretation implied by juxtaposing two contrasting views of this harbor is that "there may be more to the story" than was presented by the first, and framing, perspective. At the same time, this juxtaposition also offers an interpretive possibility by directing us to reevaluate the thematic sense we made of the first and framing cluster. In this sense-making move, the *but* suggests that it "may not, in fact, be the real theme." In other words, in an evaluating shift, the *but* recasts the first thematic cluster, suggesting that its high-tide-view of a harbor is meant to denote a "surface" view. Although the first proposition in the contrast is one of degree, then, the second recasts the theme in a way that makes it a distinction of kind.

Alternative

The second perspective shift works with these two interpretive perspectives, both of which have been generated by the text, by fashioning an alternative (Fig. 19.3). Taking an "objective view" (i.e., a high-angle perspective) of the interpretative possibility that the "real theme may not be of a harbor," this negation opens up alternative sense-making possibilities by linking textual segments in the propositional terms of an "on the other hand." One implication is fashioned by posing an alternative that a "low-tide" view of the harbor is linked to the "real theme" of this story, rather than to a "high-tide" view of the harbor. This suggests, in other words, a possibility that the "real theme" is a "polluted" harbor. At the same time, a different kind of alternative is generated by a shift that evaluates the previously introduced notion that a high-tide view denotes a surface view. The "other hand" in this sense-making move releases a possibility that this story is not about a surface view of a harbor, but about surface views. Although the first proposition in this alternative is a shift in degree, the second one, which introduces the notion of metaphor, recasts the theme in a way that is a distinction of kind.

Existence

The third negation, composed by a superimposition, links textual segments in the propositional terms of an *actually*, releasing meaning potentials created by a syntax of existence (Fig. 19.3). As a matter of fact and in synchronous time, this multilayered linkage collapses the thematic notions of pollution and surface views into a spatial paradox of figure-ground relations (Zettl, 1999). By actually shifting the conditions of what is perceivable perceptually, it provides a technologically enhanced experience of seeing that absorbs previous meaning potentials into a proposition of their existence. In this distinction of kind, there is a twofold reevaluation of heretofore only conditionally entertained propositions. The first, implied by the technological act of actually physically overlapping two separately existing images, releases the possibility that the "real theme" of this narrative is about *"how* we see." At the same time, a second implication is released by the actual fact of the double exposure. Its properties being a spatial paradox, this introduces a distinction in kind that marks a point of no return in the sensemaking structure. At this culminating point of the propositional syntax, the "actually" proposes that *"how* we see determines *what* we see."

Consequence

The fourth and final negation lays out the consequences of this argument in the propositional syntax of a causal relationship. With a general widening of the field-of-view (zoom-out to medium scale), previous views are now "contextualized" (Zettl, 1999) in the propositional terms of "therefore" leading to "because." Drawing out the consequence of "super seeing," a "therefore" perspective concludes by releasing the sense-making possibility that "it does not matter what you *think* you see." Then, in an evaluating shift, it links this implication to all previous thematic shifts: first, "it does not matter what you think you see, *because the harbor is a sewer*"; second, "it does not matter what you think you see, *because surfaces are deceiving*"; third, "it does not matter what you think you see, *because 'normal' seeing is subjective.*" This evaluating perspective releases a final, causal implication in terms of the whole text: "it does not matter what you think you see, *because the real truth is always hidden.*" In other words, through a propositional syntax of perception principles, this pictorial text fashions a claim about "truth" that includes both its existence and its apprehension.

Typical of the observational reasoning discussed by Sandra Moriarty (1996), this pictorial syntax of spatial elements (such as angle, perspective, and field of view) and its pattern of connectability (such as clusters and perspective shifts) generates an ideational process of conjecture and educated guesses that moves back and forth, developing hypotheses, assessing their credibility, and reevaluating until a critical match is made. Syntactically characteristic of a holistic system, each negating perspective shift reveals meanings that "seem to move in every which way" and without resolution. In a slight shift of spatial relations from an extremely close (screen 12) to a close (screen 13) field of view, though, one finds the "internal attractor," as Barry described, that "pulls [the system] into a discernable shape" (1996, p. 102). This (apparently) "spontaneous emergence of self-organization" occurs as the "collective power of the whole" comes forth through the syntax of a culminating negation ("therefore, because") and its final causal implication which integrates all previous "hypotheses" (Gleik, 1987, p. 339). At the same time, the nature of this integration is so inherently unified that its meaning cannot be derived from the properties of these individual hypotheses. These meaning-making potentials are created by and apprehended through the propositional syntax of holistic logic found in the *literal* structure (or image form) of this text. Understanding the sense-making characteristics of this structure, especially as it induces viewing-readers to produce its ideation of "truth" in their minds, should go a long way to explain why the engagement of negative campaign commercials can be so compelling, even if distasteful.

SEEING STORIES, NOT "WORDS"

The significance of theorizing *THE HARBOR* or any pictorial event as text is that it places pictorial expression and our ongoing efforts to sort out differences between it and other symbolic forms within the defining terms of representational communication. One immediate consequence is to discard the notion flowing from language-based assumptions that commonly equates "picture" with "word." Though we know better, at least theoretically, it is still all too common to see references in our work that reveals this categorical mistake (Mitchell, 1994).[9] As a practical matter, theories of the text provide a useful model for grounding theory about pictorial representation in terms that more appropriately equate picture with "passage" and, at the same time, do not arbitrarily impose verbal constructs on visual ones. By describing textual structures from the perspective of communication, theories of reader-response provide practical tools for looking at a pictorial text as an intersubjective relationship between a picture-maker and a picture-viewer involving a pictorially expressed concept. The notion of a text as a discursive structure directs us to look for meaning in the interactive text-reader relationship, and the notion of a text as a *literal* and *descriptive* structure of sense making guides us to questions of how such a text-viewer discourse is inscribed though pictorial means. As tools for grounding our understanding of pictorial expression in principles of perception, it is important that these two notions work in concert. We understand theoretically that the content of a picture is meaningful *in terms of its means* of expression, and many have taken care to investigate the relationship between a pictorial sign and pictorial meaning in terms of formal or compositional features (such as field, angle, or perspective of view). Without the intersecting notion of intersubjectivity introduced by reader-response analysis, however, interpretation of these meaning-making structures remains arbitrary. How does one interpret a close field of view here and a wide view there? A high angle here, and a low angle there? An objective look here, a subjective look there? Although the notion of a *literal* structure guides us to these formal features, then, the notion of a discursive structure guides us to their quality of intentionality. It reminds us that "a means of representing" always has to do with a picture-maker's subjectivity "speaking" to a viewing-reader's subjectivity.

Theories of the text frame the assumptions we make about a picture in qualitatively different terms from those imposed by verbal constructs (equating picture with "word"). Whether we are viewing a photograph, a painting, a television show, or a Web site, they give us the tools to ask of a picture as we do of a passage: What are its compositional patterns of (pictorial) statements and vacancies? What are its patterns of (pictorial) connectability? What is its propositional logic? Framing these questions in terms of the text gets us to the heart of differences between pictorial and other forms of representational communication by requiring that the answers be found in a specifically perceptual or pictorial "means of representing." In other words, they direct inquiry in visual communication to focus on the intersubjective relationship of a picture-maker and a viewing-reader in terms of pictorial structures and compositional patterns of spatial relations that compose a pictorial expression.

These textual perspectives also open new possibilities for posing questions about the sense-making processes of interactants on either side of a pictorial text—its real-life producer and its real-life viewer. I have presented an interpretive reading of a pictorial text in this chapter, for example, that draws inferences based on my knowledge of perceptual principles and an assumption that they are organized with a particular sense-making intent in mind.[10] Although I have looked to the compositional form and pattern of this pictorial text to find meaning, however, another viewer might concentrate on its content and attribute meanings from his or her personal experience with harbors, dirty shore-lines, and polluted water. Because both strategies of interpretation are possible,[11] what is interesting and useful to visual communication research is the different patterns of sense making that they display. Importantly, each of these descriptions presents an opportunity to investigate and differentiate interpretive strategies in the same terms as those of the text, that is, in terms of what each implies about the viewer's conception of a picture-maker, a viewing-reader, an ideational concept and the means of representation. Theorizing the text as a discourse that foregrounds interpretation holds the promise of integrating, as a matter of process, encoding, decoding, and textual considerations of sense mak-ing to productively frame investigation among pictorial forms of communication as well as between pictures and other symbolic forms. This is particularly consequential for research with a medium such as television or film and will become increasingly salient for multimedia, where it is important to differentiate pictorial and linguistic (as well as ges-tural and musical) structures and patterns if one is to understand how they work together.

Theorizing the picture as text is a significant perspective shift. The notion of a picture as passage (rather than as word) provides a common framework of symbolic expression for sorting out differences between pictorial and other forms of sense making without the implication that both a pictorial and a written text organize meaning in the same way. Reader-response theory offers a viewpoint for seeing pictorial expression through a lens of nonlanguage-based assumptions, which allows nonlanguage-based questions to be asked and answers to be found in visual communication research. With reference to previous assumptions that pictures could only construct associational relationships of logic, the analysis discussed here that demonstrates a pictorial syntax of propositional logic is an important example.

ENDNOTES

[1] Jamieson's (1992) work with visual imagery in negative campaign commercials underscores the im-portance of understanding visual persuasion in its own terms. She found that impressions created by visual associations were only effectively countered by a visually constructed response (pp. 64–230, 281–288).

[2] THE HARBOR was the first in a series of negative political commercials developed by the 1988 Bush presidential campaign and is available from the Political Commercial Archive at the University of Oklahoma.

[3] Interestingly, Iser refers to the space between shots in a filmic sequence to describe how a gap functions in a textual schema. He explained by quoting Balaz: "Even the most meaningful take is not sufficient to give the picture its total meaning. This is ultimately decided by the position of the picture between other pictures" (as cited in Iser, 1978, p. 195).

[4] Frye (1957) described the descriptive structure of a text as an imitation (though not a recording) of real-world events and the literal structure as a "flow of significant sounds" (1957, p. 104). The content or descriptive structure directs attention outward as, with a linguistically formed text, "we keep going outside our reading, from individual words to the things they mean." At the same time, its literal structure directs our attention inward as "we try to develop from the words a sense of the larger verbal pattern they make" (1957, p. 73). In applying this notion to a pictorial composition, one sees that the content or descriptive structure

of a picture does, indeed, direct our attention outward from the individual objects to the things they mean. In fact, because an image is perceptually processed in the same way as direct experience (Barry, 1997), the symbols of an image are directly expressive of meaning in a way that the symbols (words) of a passage are not. The literal structure of an image, on the other hand, directs our attention inward to the sense making of its spatial elements (such as angle, perspective, field of view) and the larger pictorial patterns they make.

[5] Interpretation of pictorial structures and patterns throughout this analysis is drawn from work in contextual media aesthetics, particularly as it is informed by perception theory and discussed by Herbert Zettl (1999). The interpretive claims made, in the spirit suggested by Anderson, are meant to be taken as what "ought to be" intended and not what is (1993, p. 216). Semantic or meaning-making properties are discussed by indicating a pictorial referent or "quality" as well as a literal and a figurative property associated with a structure of spatial relations (Barbatsis & Kenney, 1987). For example, the referent (or pictorial quality) of "scale" is "field-of-view" and it is capable of composing various spatial relations of "distance." It can show (or literally inscribe) spatial relations of "closeness," which are meant to be seen as (or metaphorically inscribe) "intimacy." This approach is influenced by Goodman's (1976) work with a general theory of symbols and Gross' (1974) work with symbolic competence.

[6] This expression refers to Nelson Goodman's (1976) argument that representation is best understood in terms of its interpretive essence, which he expressed by the notion of "representation-as."

[7] As Iser (1978) explained, it is important that the initiating imbalance (or gap) between the world of a text and the world of a reader is constructed in such a way that its uncommonness of situation and frame of reference poses only a partial and not a "blanket rejection of the . . . norms" of its reader's external reality. Accordingly, the repertoire of a text must "incorporate a specific external reality into the text . . . to offer its reader a definite frame of reference or invoke a definite range of past experience" (1978, pp. 212–213).

[8] Barry's (1997) discussion of visual sense making brings early gestalt theory together with recent work in neurology and chaos theory. This reference to the gestalt recognizes her point that the implication of a gestalt is of a configuration "so inherently unified that its properties cannot be derived from the individual properties of its parts" rather than simply to the idea of a whole being more than the sum of its parts (p. 42).

[9] Research often slides into assumptions that pictures are categorically equivalent to words in comparisons of visual and verbal journalistic material. A range of choices is assumed when it comes to written words, but constrained with relationship to pictures and video available to journalists for creating news stories.

[10] Barnhurst took a similar approach in his interpretation of the newspaper page as a pictorial text whose content is graphics. He focused on the structure of spatial relations made by the "blacks and whites in different textures and shades of gray" as they form shapes and resonate with meaning (1994, p. 7). His interpretative distinctions among graphic arrangements of spatial relations also focus on the sense-making characteristics of literal structure.

[11] Although a communication relationship is based on intention, which calls for an inferential strategy of interpretation, as Anderson (1998) reminded us, neither a producer nor an auditor need enter a communication relationship to do their work. Because of its iconic properties, a pictorial expression is often interpreted attributionally rather than inferentially, and the more "realistic" a pictorial text seems, such as through the "mechanical naturalization" of photography, and the less aware one is of picture-making processes, the more likely this is to happen (Gross, 1985). This tendency to interpret through attribution rather than implication might even be purposely manipulated as a strategy of persuasion (Barbatsis, 1996).

REFERENCES

Anderson, J. (1993). The role of interpretation in communication theory. In N. Metallinos (Ed.), *Verbo-visual literacy: Understanding and applying new educational communication media technologies* (pp. 211–222). Delphi, Greece: International Symposium of International Visual Literacy Association.

Anderson, J. (1998). Qualitative approaches to the study of media: Theory and methods of hermeneutic empiricism. In J. Asamen & G. Berry (Eds.), *Research paradigms, television, and social Behavior* (pp. 205–236). Thousand Oaks, CA: Sage.

Ansolabehere, S., & Lyengar, S. (1995). *Going negative: How attack ads shrink and polarize the electorate.* New York: The Free Press.

Arnheim, R. (1969). *Visual thinking.* Berkeley: University of California Press.

Barbatsis, G. (1996). Look and I will show you something you will want to see: Viewer engagement with negative campaign commercials. *Journal of Argumentation and Advocacy, 32*(2), 69–80.

Barbatsis, G., & Kenney, K. (1987). *Pictorial language: Explorations of a universal or culturally bound code.* Paper presented at the Speech Communication Association, New York.

Barnhurst, K. (1994). *Seeing the newspaper.* New York: St. Martin's Press.

Barry, A. M. (1997). *Visual intelligence: Perception, image, and manipulation in visual communication.* Albany: State University of New York.

Frye, N. (1957). *Anatomy of criticism.* Princeton, NJ: Princeton University Press.

Garramone, G. (1984). Voter responses to negative political ads. *Journalism Quarterly, 61,* 250–259.

Gibson, J. (1979). *The ecological approach to visual perception.* Boston: Houghton Mifflin.

Gleik, J. (1987). *Chaos: Making a new science.* New York: Penguin.

Gombrich. E. (1960). *Art and illusion: A study in the psychology of pictorial representation.* Princeton, NJ: Princeton University Press.

Goodman, N. (1976). *Languages of art: An approach to the theory of symbols.* Indianapolis, IN: Hackett Publishing Company.

Gross, L. (1974). Modes of communication and the acquisition of symbolic competence. In D. Olsen (Ed.), *Media and symbols: The forms of expression, communication and education* (pp. 56–80). National Society for the Study of Education. Chicago: University of Chicago Press.

Gross, L. (1985). Life vs. art: The interpretation of visual narratives. *Studies in Visual Communication, 4*(11), 2–11.

Holub, R. (1984). *Reception theory: A critical introduction.* London: Methuen.

Iser, W. (1978). *The act of reading: A theory of aesthetic response.* Baltimore: Johns Hopkins Press.

Jamieson, K. (1992). *Dirty politics: Deception, distraction, and democracy.* New York: Oxford University Press.

Kaid, L., & Johnson, A. (1991). Negative versus positive television advertising in U.S. presidential campaigns, 1960–1988. *Journal of Communication, 41*(3), 53–64.

Kohler, W. (1938). Some gestalt problems. In W. Ellis (Ed.), *A source book of gestalt psychology.* New York: Harcourt Brace.

Kosko, B. (1993). *Fuzzy thinking.* New York: Hyperion.

McCrone, J. (1994, August 20). Quantum states of mind. *New Scientist,* 35–37.

Merritt, S. (1984). Negative political advertising: Some empirical findings. *Journal of Advertising, 13*(3), 27–38.

Messaris, P. (1997). *Visual persuasion: The role of images in advertising.* Thousand Oaks, CA: Sage.

Mitchell, D. (1994). Distinctions between everyday and representational communication. *Communication Theory, 4*(2), 111–131.

Moriarty, S. (1996). Abduction: A theory of visual interpretation. *Communication Theory, 6*(2), 167–187.

Stewart, C. (1975). Voter perception of mud-slinging in political communication. *Central States Speech Journal, 26,* 279–286.

Wood, S. (1982, November). *Eisenhower answers America: A critical history.* Paper presented at the meeting of the Speech Communication Association, Louisville, KY.

Zettl, H. (1999). *Sight, sound, motion: Applied media aesthetics.* Belmont, CA: Wadsworth.

20

Phenomenology and Historical Research

MICHAEL BROWN
University of Wyoming

Readers who opened the March 1908 issue of *Cosmopolitan* (Wells, 1908) viewed a frontispiece illustration of a family of Martians with one of them staring back at the viewers (see Fig. 20.1). The caption read:

> There are certain features in which they are likely to resemble us. And as likely as not they will be covered with feathers or fur. It is no less reasonable to suppose instead of a hand, a group of tentacles or proboscis-like organs.

The illustration was one of four featured in the article, titled "The Things That Live on Mars." The article featured a summary of the latest scientific beliefs about the "flora and fauna" of the planet Mars. As the frontispiece, the illustration was given a position of prominence and was the first item seen as readers engaged the editorial content of the magazine. What did such a strange image mean? How did viewers make sense of the illustration? Did viewers believe they were seeing accurate representations of Martians or simply an artist's imagination and fantasy? Was the illustration science, art, or simply a way to sell magazines?

The question of what this image might mean to viewers in 1908 is difficult to answer because "eyewitnesses" are not available to share their experiences and testify to the significance of the illustration. The illustration and the textual records that address it are the primary resources available to the scholar. The only way to understand how audiences might have interpreted the illustration is to examine these textual records.

This particular "question of meaning" is directed toward the domain of reception identified in the phenomenology chapter. The chapter also provides a methodological entry point by linking pictorial images, or in this case an illustration, to the concept of a "text." The methodological strategy is to treat the illustration as a text that is "read" by a popular audience and by a scholar. The purpose of this chapter is to demonstrate how phenomenological theory can direct historical research that reads or interprets visual

FIG. 20.1.   The things that live on Mars.

texts. Our primary interest concerns understanding how viewers make sense of visual images, so the discussion begins with a brief overview of key concepts used to direct the inquiry. The theoretical frame for this particular discussion emerges from an area of phenomenology that focuses on reader responses (or in this case viewer responses) to texts. Some basic principles of historical methods will be discussed, including the "new historicism" that emerged from literary criticism as a way for scholars to analyze historical texts. These principles will then be used to guide a scholarly reading of the

Martian illustration and offer some insights into questions raised in the phenomenological theory chapter.

COMBINING THEORY AND METHOD

Reader-response studies, sometimes grouped as reception theory, do not represent a unified, well-defined theoretical position apart from phenomenology (McQuillan, 1999; Crane, 1992; Allen, 1987). In general, reception theory reflects a common interest among researchers concerning the interaction between a reader and a text. From the phenomenological perspective the focus is on the decoding activity of the receiver. Reception theory and phenomenology share the common assumption that texts are indeterminate and incomplete, and readers actively create meaning from them (Crane, 1992). Wolfgang Iser (1999, 1978), one of the primary scholars associated with reception theory, suggested that readers fill in gaps when reading a text. The text provides an outside stimulus that engages the reader's imagination. The reader draws from personal experience and social context to make the text a relevant experience. Reception scholars have examined such areas as the historical circumstances of interactions, reading positions available to readers and the personal experiences of audience members. For visual representations the process is similar. The image is viewed and understood from a personal and social context that is meaningful.

Another assumption of reception studies is that multiple readings are possible with a single text. Different readings are made by different individuals and audiences, but also by different scholars who may analyze the same text. This approach assumes the researcher plays an active role when interpreting a visual text as part of the research process. Iser (2000) used the term *translate* to describe the work of a scholar analyzing a text. Translation implies that the researcher, in analyzing a text, actively shapes the meaning created from the research.

One important direction reception research has taken is the examination of the context of interaction between the text and the reader, or the visual image and the viewer. Examining interpretive contexts can provide insight into the social resources audiences used in order to make sense of pictorial images. The "new historicism" that emerged in the late 1980s offers a useful and valuable perspective for examining historical contexts (Veeser, 1989). New historicism treats the text as a material product of specific historical conditions. New historicism provides additional focus on historical context and has proven particularly successful in demonstrating that text and context are inseparable (Berkhofer Jr., 1997). According to new historicism, texts can only be understood by relocating them within their particular historical context.

There are several assumptions made by new historicists that provide methodological guidance for this research (Veeser, 1989). Texts are strongly interconnected to a variety of other texts and contexts, a concept generally referred to as intertextuality. This implies that the Martian illustration is connected to other elements in our culture. The illustration becomes what Bakhtin calls a chronotope, "an optic for reading texts as x-rays of the forces at work in the cultural system from which they spring" (Holquist, 1981, pp. 425–426). New historicists also suggest that the cultural forces at work represent powerful elements that are competing for dominance. This assumption suggests that competing power structures are evident in the text.

This review of reception theory and new historicism shapes the central direction of the research. Reception studies suggest that individual receivers have a great deal of freedom to interpret texts, but new historicism reminds us that there are powerful forces working to constrain those possibilities. By examining the Martian illustration as a text and placing it within the interpretive contexts available in 1908, we can begin to understand what an illustration of Martians might have meant to those who viewed it and identify what power structures are competing to influence its interpretation. Because there is no access to original viewers from 1908, examining the social context through which the Martian illustration was viewed becomes the primary focus of this research. These contexts help us identify the dominant "others" whose views were available to the general public and who competed to influence viewers' perceptions of the Martian illustrations.

HISTORICAL EVIDENCE

Not all historians agree that the methods of literary criticism produce good historical research. There is concern that shallow and poorly represented histories are being created, justified by the "interpretive freedom" allowed through some uses of literary criticism (Fox-Genovese and Lasch-Quinn, 1999). However, when combined with the rigors of traditional historical research, literary criticism has produced valuable research. Traditionally, historians have valued a deep emersion into historical documents and historical contexts in order to create an accurate, if not "truthful," account of the past. Regardless of specific theoretical and methodological choices made by individual researchers, a meticulous and thorough review of historical documents remains a principle of good historical research. The purpose of this emersion is to understand historical context, which is critical when making historical translations. In this sense, historical research is quite compatible with the research goals directed through phenomenology, particularly when the interest concerns interpretive contexts.

The evidential documents chosen for historical analyses are loosely divided into two categories: primary and secondary sources. Primary sources are those closest to the time period and context being studied, while secondary sources are those produced by other historians who have examined the same or similar topics from the time period being studied (Furay and Salevouris, 1988). The primary and secondary sources chosen by the researcher are based on the research question, the theoretical frame, and the methodological direction. In the case of the Martian illustration, the primary sources include the illustrated *Cosmopolitan* article and other texts from the late 1800s and early 1900s that provide relevant information. Identifying relevant primary texts can be an overwhelming task. Because this is an examination of interpretive contexts that were available to the general reading public, primary sources can be narrowed to those that were the most widely circulated to the general public. For the purposes of this chapter we can limit our sources to magazine articles. Magazines were the only true national media in 1908, they published a vast number of illustrations, and they provided a variety of perspectives and voices about American visual culture. These characteristics make magazines a valuable primary resource for understanding popular and public positions concerning visual images.

The secondary sources appropriate for examining our illustration come from two areas. One set of secondary sources direct the theoretical frame. In this chapter, the sources come from the body of literature that addresses phenomenology. The phenomenology chapter outlines basic theoretical positions that are further refined for this specific study through a focus on reception and new historicism. Another set of secondary sources discusses the state of American visual culture in the late 1800s and early 1900s. Both sets of secondary sources are needed to understand the primary data and direct a translation of the Martian illustration.

As a primary source, the Martian illustration suggests several directions to begin looking for interpretive contexts appropriate for understanding this particular visual expression. At least three visual communities were represented in illustration: magazines, art, and astronomy. The illustration appeared in a popular nationally distributed magazine, was drawn by a formally trained artist, and was an attempt to represent the latest views of astronomy concerning life on Mars. By focusing on these three visual communities, the researcher can begin to understand how each community affected the context that directed viewer's interpretations of the illustration.

All three of these visual communities were part of a dramatic change in American visual culture during the late 1800s and early 1900s. At least one historian suggested that, "The single generation of Americans living between 1885 and 1910 went through an experience of visual reorientation that had few precedents" (Harris, 1990, p. 307). Looking at images in the press provided a new way to experience the world that was mediated and vicarious (Crary, 1990; Tagg, 1988). The publishing industry, and magazines in particular, were intimately involved in this reorientation by providing American readers with thousands of images (Mott, 1954a). By the time the Martians appeared in *Cosmopolitan*, illustration had emerged as a significant form of visual communication presenting large numbers of both photographs and hand-drawn images. As early as 1885, Mason Jackson predicted that illustrations would provide an inexhaustible storehouse for the historian.

ILLUSTRATION AS ART

By 1908 audiences were accustomed to large numbers of images. Publishers found that illustrations helped to sell magazines. Factual articles used photographs and realistic drawings, while much of the fiction was accompanied by more artistic hand-drawn images (Brown, 2000a). Magazines were a powerful modern visual force because they were viewed in comfortable and familiar surroundings of the home. The American public was offered a new and unique opportunity to view American art. However, the art in magazines was produced and consumed outside of the traditional world of art. The result was a controversy over what constituted good and bad art, and who gets to decide (Brown, 1998).

At the turn of the century no public art galleries existed that allowed "common folk" to view art. As a consequence many homes were decorated with images taken from popular magazines (Larson, 1986). An illustration textbook published in 1896 by Joseph Pennell claimed that illustration was an important fine art produced by the most skilled artists. The magazines served as a gallery where artists could show their work (Mott, 1954b). By 1908 illustration was a lucrative profession (Stote, 1908), and some art schools specifically trained illustrators (Pyle, 1897). The work of illustration provided a unique opportunity for artists not available within the traditional world of art. Magazines promoted the aesthetic worth of illustration, provided a gallery and audiences, offered institutional and organizational support, and paid artists for their work. Magazines provided a modern new context for viewing and appreciating art that was beyond the control of traditional art.

W. R. Leigh, the artist responsible for the Martian illustration, was a formally trained American artist who developed a successful career as an illustrator. He was a child prodigy who studied realism in Munich. He was an accomplished, award-winning artist by the time he returned to the United States in the 1890s. Because of his skill and training, he was hired by the Scribner publishing house to produce illustrations. He developed into a popular and prolific illustrator who produced thousands of illustrations for a number of popular magazines. By 1910 he quit illustrating to become a full-time artist. Admirers and scholars claim his work depicting Native Americans of the Southwest places him in the same class as American West artists Frederick Remington and Charles Russell (Cummings, 1980; Carrington, 1899).

The art of illustration challenged the traditional world of art by creating a new artistic community anchored in the media. Although many talented and formally trained artists worked as illustrators, some art critics claimed that illustrations were not true works of art and were judged to be "aboriginal" with the character of "irritating comments" (Congdon, 1884). Critics believed that the economics of the publishing industry lured unqualified artists and allowed lazy artwork to be produced ("Decay," 1907; "Book and magazine," 1903; Coffin, 1896). To make matters worse, the text, not the artist, was the dominant creative force. The unique inner creative force that defined an artist was missing. In spite of those who believed illustration was a fine art, traditional art critics argued that illustration was not art.

ILLUSTRATION AS ASTRONOMY

The illustration of Martians was not only bad art but questionable astronomy as well. Like most other visual communities during this period, astronomy was experiencing the effects of modernization and struggling to become a modern visual science. Photographs were replacing drawings produced from direct observation and providing images superior to those that were hand-drawn. Coronas of the sun, nebulae, comets, and asteroids, as well as other objects in the sky, were photographed, producing a level of accuracy superior to the eye. However, planetary photography was the one area of astronomy where the promise of photography to deliver superior images failed, and hand-drawn illustrations continued to dominate.

The public fascination with Mars started in the early 1890s and was intensified in 1895 when Percival Lowell of the Lowell Observatory in Flagstaff, Arizona, published a book proclaiming that Mars was inhabited by intelligent beings desperately digging canals in order to distribute the planet's meager water supply (1895a). Lowell observed Mars during a "favorable opposition" in 1894, an opportunity that would not return until 1907, and reported seeing the canals. According to Lowell, as Mars approached the sun the ice caps melted and the Martians distributed the water through a system of canals that were used to irrigate crops. The discussion was generated and maintained through the prolific writings of Lowell. In addition to two books and several annals published by the Lowell Observatory, Lowell published magazine articles in *Atlantic Monthly, Scientific American, Popular Science, Outlook, Nature, Century, McClure's*, and others. Lowell's ideas generated a variety of responses; between 1895 and 1908, when the Martian illustration was drawn, hundreds of articles discussed the canals of Mars and the implications of their existence as astronomy struggled to understand the canals and offer an explanation for their presence.

Magazine readers were introduced to Lowell's ideas through a series of four articles in *Atlantic Monthly*. The first article discussed the atmosphere of Mars, which Lowell (1895b) described as a thin veil with a small amount of water vapor. The second article discussed the water problems on Mars. Lowell (1895c) claimed the "seas" that appeared to exist on Mars were actually vast dry plains and water was scarce. Lowell's (1895d) third article discussed the presence of canals. Previous observers of Mars had recorded canals that became more clearly visible and well defined through Lowell's observations. The artificial, systematic appearance of the canals was more evident with the improved scientific methods of modern astronomy. The canals also suggested the presence of intelligent life. The fourth article discussed dark circular spots on Mars that Lowell (1895e) identified as "oases." The oases formed "so many hubs to which the canals make spokes" (p. 223), and could only be "the effects of local intelligence" (p. 231). By the end of the last article, Lowell had placed intelligent beings on Mars engineering a massive irrigation project in order to maintain the last threads of life on an old planet dying of thirst. In 1907 Lowell repeated his argument in a series of seven articles in *Century Illustrated* titled "Mars as the Abode of Life" (1907a), and in another article for *Outlook* he concluded, "That life now habits Mars is the only rational deduction from the observations in our possession; the only one warranted by the facts. As to what the life habitant there may be like I should not pretend to say" (Lowell, 1907b, p. 848).

Lowell's work drew the attention of a broad spectrum of American culture as reviews of his work circulated through the popular magazines. One mathematician calculated the probability that canals and oases would intersect with such precision at "one to sixteen with 259 ciphers after it!" (Mathematician, 1907). The figure clearly indicated that the markings on Mars were not random, but the work of intelligent beings. Some scientists and observers even speculated about the character of Martian life.

One of the strongest arguments supporting the theory of life on Mars was evolution. Lowell (1895a) argued that Mars was in a slightly advanced evolutionary state and would produce intelligent life that was slightly more advanced than humans, although their physical characteristics would reflect the physical conditions found on Mars. The rare atmosphere of Mars would require relatively slight adaptations, most likely increasing the size of the lungs (Serviss, 1895; "Edinburgh Review," 1896). The lower gravity might produce Martians 19 feet tall with great physical power, "fifty-fold more efficient than a man" (Lowell, 1895e, p. 223). The lighter gravity would allow structures built by Martians to be four times as tall as those on earth (Delboeuf, 1897–1898). The famous French astronomer Camille Flammarion suggested that the lower amount of light reaching Mars would influence the eyes. He also speculated that the intelligent Martian might be able to fly, "To have wings, that is a very great advantage. . . . If birds had been worked out to perfection in this progression the human soul would have dwelt in some winged form" (1896, p. 546). There was speculation that an advanced civilization might exist on Mars (Gregory, 1900) that "outstripped us in intellectual achievement" (Kaempffert, 1907, p. 481) and was "possessed of inventions of which we have not dreamed" (Lowell, 1895e, p. 223). The scientists who supported the idea of life on Mars speculated that Martians would be physically different, more intelligent, and less imperfect than people on earth.

The different observations about life on Mars were consolidated in the article "The Things That Live on Mars," and readers were given the opportunity to see the first scientifically reasoned Martians by viewing the illustration (see Fig. 20.1) that accompanied the article (Wells, 1908). H. G. Wells, a skilled and popular writer with scientific training in biology and an interest in Mars, wrote *War of the Worlds* in 1895 and published it as a serial in *Cosmopolitan* in 1896. Wells acknowledged Lowell's help preparing "The Things That Live on Mars," and he drew heavily from discussions among astronomers and the theory of evolution to craft his argument. *Cosmopolitan* claimed the article represented the latest scientific discussions about life on Mars. Wells claimed that current scientific knowledge of Mars precluded the creation of "any foolish fantastic hobgoblin or any artistic ideal"; (p. 335) instead the Martians would have evolved from the "natural history of Mars (p. 336)." Wells described seasonal changes on Mars that indicated a cycle of plant life. The low gravity would produce long and slender growth in both plants and animals, and the lower levels of light would likely increase the size of a creature's eyes. The lack of water meant that land creatures would be the most successful life forms and the low levels of atmosphere would lead to big-chested creatures. Wells believed intelligent life on Mars would have evolved from a basic air-breathing land creature and could have a quasi-human appearance although it would be unique to Mars. Wells speculated that Martians had heads, eyes, backboned bodies, big brains, and big shapely skulls. They had large bodies, about 10 feet tall, covered with feathers or fur to insulate against the cold, and a "prehensile organ" to perform their feats of engineering. After years of discussing the possible character of life on Mars, audiences were finally given an opportunity to view a Martian for themselves.

The article immediately following "The Things That Live on Mars" was a report by Professor David Todd (1908) of the Amherst Observatory concerning the latest photographs taken of Mars during an expedition, sponsored by the Lowell Observatory, to the Andes Mountains. Todd claimed that the photographs did not capture the full intricacies of the canals as he had hoped, but they were clearly evident in telescopic observations. He stated, "Nearly everybody who went to the eyepiece saw canals; and once I fancied I heard even the bats, as they winged their flight down the pampa, crying, 'canali, canali, canali!'" (p. 349). Readers of the March 1908 issue of *Cosmopolitan* saw scientifically based Martians followed by an experienced astronomer's eyewitness account of the canals.

Although Lowell presented a powerful and public argument about life on Mars, many scientists disagreed with his vision. The immediate reaction to the illustration was not particularly positive. An editorial in *Scientific American* ("Red God") stated that, "Mr. Wells and his school have accepted the man of Mars, and a fine mess they have made of him" (1909, p. 270). A later editorial identified the Martians as "more or less transmogrified human beings" ("Perennial Martians," 1916, p. 172). There were many astronomers who reported seeing canals on Mars, and most believed some form of life was present, but many doubted the canals were a sign of intelligent engineering.

There were numerous explanations for the appearance of canals. Most of them assumed that the great distance between Mars and Earth meant that fine details on the planet's surface were obscured. Therefore, it was suggested the canals could be fissures in the surface, tidal channels, mountain ranges, or any number of natural features (Serviss, 1897). Some astronomers hypothesized that "optical delusions" ("Are Martian," 1903) or characteristics of the human visual system created the canals and suggested that the intelligent engineering was taking place on the terrestrial side of the telescope ("Evidence," 1903). The belief that intelligent engineers were at work on Mars was based on the assumption that the canals were engineered waterways; an alternate explanation would undermine Lowell's argument about intelligent engineers.

In 1901 an alternative hypothesis emerged: When numerous small objects are grouped together the visual system sees them as a single mass (Orr, 1901). The canals could be explained as a characteristic of the visual system rather than actual features on the surface of Mars. Through the early 1900s this became known as the "visual integration hypothesis" and developed into the dominant alternate explanation for canals (Pickering, 1908; Newcomb, 1908). Arguments between the "illusionists" and the "Lowellians" intensified in 1907 as the latest observations of Mars were published. Both sides agreed that a clear photograph would provide the solid evidence needed to settle the dispute, but photographic technology failed to produce a clear detailed image of Mars (Brown, 2000b). Mars remained at the threshold of our ability to gather accurate, detailed visual information, its image remained open for interpretation, and the existence of intelligent Martians remained a possibility.

DISCUSSION

Generally it would be desirable to go into more depth concerning the primary discussions generated by the three visual communities addressed in this chapter. It is through "thick description" that the full complexity of the sense-making process is revealed. Even within the limited discussion presented here, it is clear that making sense of the illustration of Martians is not a simple task and demonstrates what Stephen Greenblatt (1990) described as the cultural forces of mobility and constraint. Mobility is found in the freedom of interpretation that exists in the different arguments. Constraint is imposed by the specific institutional positions adopted by traditional art, astronomy, and popular magazines. The traditional world of art told viewers to judge the Martian illustration as a typical example of art corrupted by text, commerce, and popular taste. Therefore it was bad art. However, most viewers were seeing the form of art most familiar to them and, with little direct experience or contact with traditional art, were making their own judgments. If viewers rejected the illustration on artistic merit, they could justify its presence as astronomical evidence. However, professional astronomers tried to convince viewers the illustration was based on sensational and irresponsible speculation with no factual support.

The presence of "the other" that is suggested by phenomenology is evident in the illustration. The physical appearance of the Martians was created from ongoing discussions by "others" interested in speculation about life on Mars and how the characteristics of the planet would yield an intelligent life form. The illustration also reflected the immediate text of the article written by Wells. In addition, the illustration was hand-drawn by an accomplished artist who signed the work, an indication that the illustration was a work of art. In this particular case there were multiple "others" implicated in the illustration.

If a phenomenon is illuminated through "structures of experience," then the three visual communities were not given an equal chance to influence viewers. For viewers, their direct experience was with the magazines, not with art or astronomy, in part because the magazines were used within the fabric of everyday life. The visual context of modern magazine illustration was powerful in 1908. The primary goal of the magazine was the economic success generated by appealing to popular audiences, and illustration was a key part of that success. Magazines presented readers with a diversity of content and perspectives that allowed readers to draw from a variety of interpretive contexts to shape their understanding of the Martians. With little closure concerning whether illustration was art, or whether Martians were digging canals, viewers found a great deal of freedom to interpret the illustration. Viewers' direct and personal experience with magazines told them the illustration was drawn by a popular and talented artist, it was desirable to have illustrations accompany the text, and intelligent life could be present on Mars. The Martian illustration was offered in an immediate interpretive context that was shaped primarily by the magazine. If, as the phenomenology chapter suggests, visual images are processed in a holistic way that has more immediate impact than language, it would have been easy for viewers to accept, at face value, the claim represented by the illustration that intelligent life existed on Mars.

REFERENCES

Primary Sources

Are Martian canals a myth? (1903, January). *Current Literature, 34*, 79.
Book and magazine illustration. (1903, August). *Bookman, 17*, 651.
Carrington, J. (1899). W. R. Leigh. *Bookbuyer, 19*, 596.
Coffin, W. (1896, January). American illustrations of to-day. *Scribner's, 11*, 106.
Congdon, C. (1884, November). Over-illustration. *North American Review, 139*, 480.
The decay of illustration. (1907, February 2). *Littel's Living Age, 252*, 317.
Delboeuf, M. J. (1897–1898). In a world half as large. *Popular Science Monthly, 52*, 678.
"Edinburgh Review" on Mars (1896). *Living Age, 211*, 732. (The article was reprinted from *Spectator*)
Evidence of life on Mars. (1903). *Current Literature, 35*, 67.
Flammarion, C. (1896). Mars and its inhabitants. *North American Review, 162*, 546.
Gregory, R. A. (1900, April 7). Mars as a world. *Living Age, 225*, 21.
Jackson, Mason (1885j). *Pictorial journalism*. New York: Burt Franklin. (Reprinted 1969)
Kaempffert, W. (1907, March). What we know about Mars. *McClure's, 28*, 481.
Lowell, P. (1895a). *Mars*. New York: Macmillan.

Lowell, P. (1895b, May). Mars. I. Atmosphere. *Atlantic Monthly, 75*, 594.

Lowell, P. (1895c, June). Mars. II. The water problem. *Atlantic Monthly, 75*, 749.

Lowell, P. (1895d, July). Mars. III. Canals. *Atlantic Monthly, 76*, 106.

Lowell, P. (1895e, August). Mars. IV. Oases. *Atlantic Monthly, 76*, 223.

Lowell, P. (1907a, November). Mars as the abode of life. *Century Illustrated, 75*, 113.

Lowell, P. (1907b, April 13). Is Mars inhabited? *Outlook, 85*, 844.

Mathematician. (1907, October 26). The evidence of life on Mars. *Scientific American, 97*, 287.

Newcomb, S. (1908, July). Fallacies about Mars. *Harper's Weekly, 52*, 11.

Orr, M. A. (1901, March 30). The canals of Mars. *Scientific American Supplement, 51*, 21108. (The article was reprinted from *Knowledge*)

Pennell, J. (1896j). *The illustration of books*. Ann Arbor: Gryphon Books. (Reprinted 1971)

Perennial Martians (1916, February 12). *Scientific American, 114*, 172.

Pickering, W. (1908, January). Different explanations of the canals of Mars. *Harper's Magazine, 116*, 192.

Pyle, H. (1897, July 17). A small school of art. *Harper's Weekly, 41*, 710.

The red god of the sky. (1909, October 23). *Scientific American, 68*, 270.

Serviss, G. (1895, June 27). Is Mars inhabited? *Harper's Weekly, 39*, 712.

Serviss, G. (1897, May 22). Another theory about Mars. *Harper's Weekly, 41*, 518.

Stote, A. (1908, September). The illustrator and his income. *Bookman, 28*, 21.

Todd, D. (1908, March). Professor Todd's own story of the Mars expedition. *Cosmopolitan, 44*, 343.

Wells, H. G. (1908, March). The things that live on Mars. *Cosmopolitan, 44*, 335.

Wells, H. G. (1896). The war of the worlds, I. The eve of war. *Cosmopolitan, 22*, 615.

Secondary Sources

Allen, R. (1987). Reader-oriented criticism and television. In Robert Allen (Ed.), *Channels of discourse* (pp. 74–112). Chapel Hill: University of North Carolina Press.

Berkhofer, Jr., R. (1997). *Beyond the great story: History as text and discourse*. Belknap Press of Harvard University Press.

Best, J. (1984). *American popular illustration*. Westport, CT: Greenwood.

Brannigan, J. (1999). New historicism. In Julian Wolfreys (Ed.), *Literary theories* (pp. 417–428). New York: New York University Press.

Brown, M. (1998, autumn). The popular art of American magazine illustration, 1885–1917. *Journalism History, 24*, 94–103.

Brown, M. (2000a, summer). Discriminating photographs from hand-drawn illustrations in popular magazines, 1895–1904. *American Journalism, 17*, 15–30.

Brown, M. (2000b, winter). Imagining Mars: A case study in photographic realism. *American Journalism, 17*, 17–34.

Crane, D. (1992). Approaches to the analysis of meaning. In *The Production of Culture* (pp. 77–108). Newbury Park, CA: Sage.

Crary, J. (1990). *Techniques of the observer*. Cambridge, MA: MIT Press.

Cummings, D. (1980). *William Robinson Leigh: Western artist*. Norman, OK: University of Oklahoma Press.

Fox-Genovese, E., & Lasch-Quinn, E. (1999). *Reconstructing history*. New York: Routledge.

Furay, C., & Salevouris, M. (1988). Evidence. In *The methods and skills of history* (pp. 137–167). Arlington Heights, IL: Harlan Davidson, Inc.

Green, W. (1993). *History, historians, and the dynamics of change*. New York: Praeger.

Greenblatt, S. (1990). Culture. In Frank Lentricchia & Thomas McLaughlin (Eds.), *Critical terms for literary study* (p. 225). Chicago: University of Chicago Press.

Harris, N. (1990). Iconography and intellectual history. In *Cultural excursions* (pp. 304–317). Chicago: University of Chicago Press.

Holquist, M. (1981). *The dialogic imagination*. Austin: University of Texas Press.

Iser, W. (1978). *The act of reading*. Baltimore: Johns Hopkins University Press.

Iser, W. (1999). The imaginary. In Julian Wolfreys (Ed.), *Literary Theories* (pp. 179–195). New York: New York University Press.

Iser, W. (2000). *The range of interpretation*. New York: Columbia University Press.

Larson, J. (1986). *American illustration, 1890–1925*. Calgary: Glenbow Museum.

McQuillan, M. (1999). Reader-response theories. In Julian Wolfreys (Ed.), *Literary theories* (pp. 139–149). New York: New York University Press.

Mott, F. L. (1954a, December). The magazine revolution and popular ideas in the nineties. *American Antiquarian Society*.

Mott, F. L. (1954b). *A history of American magazines, 1885–1905*. Cambridge, MA: Harvard University Press.

Munslow, A. (1997). *Deconstructing history*. London: Routledge.

Tagg, J. (1988). *The burden of representation*. Amherst: University of Massachusetts Press.

Veeser, A. (Ed.) (1989). *The new historicism*. New York: Routledge.

VIII

Narrative

21

Narrative Theory

GRETCHEN BARBATSIS
Michigan State University

For many of us the word narrative probably sounds much too formal and literary to capture the familiarity we feel for stories and storytelling. What child does not know the enchantment promised by "once upon a time"? And who can resist the invitation from an eager listener to "tell me, what happened"? We tell stories of pregnancies and births, we grapple with a death by finding the story that makes sense of a life. With each returning autumn, school children know well how to craft the stories of a summer's vacation, and those of athletic challenge, worldly adventure, and teen romance. The list goes on; no mater what our age or where we are from, we live our lives telling and listening to stories. Some are rendered with words, others we experience in tales told through dance, pictures, or music. Some are made for television and film, others for the stage. But what is this disarmingly familiar thing we call a story? What is it that we recognize as similar in so many variations: the story told through mime and a children's book, ballet and a novel, the short story and a symphony, television news and situation comedy, the newspaper and a movie, the comic strip and a photo documentary?

The answer to this question lies in the secrets held by the characteristic way a narrative is made. Stories have a beginning, a middle, and an end, as Aristotle observed in *Poetics* (Fergusson, 1961). They arrange their elements in a particular kind of causal sequence that increases in intensity to a point of crisis and change. This form of arranging material is, as Northrup Frye suggested, "a way of structuring thought" (1957, p. 83). In other words, when we encounter a story, we experience a world that is formed or organized in this particular way. As Walter Fisher put it, a story sees the world as "sequence with meaning" (1984, p. 2). For the characters in a story, be they imaginary or real, the reality crafted by narrative is one of transformations. With narrative, sequences of events have meaning because they are related to a change or "point" from which there is "no return" to being what was. Both formal stories and personal narratives promise this experience. Whether the events of a story are authored by our lives or invented by someone else, it is this experience that we expect when we hear the words "once upon a time."

Importantly for our work as visual communication practitioners and scholars, we must also ask how this storytelling experience is crafted pictorially. How does one recognize a pictorial form composed of beginning, middle, and end, for example? How does one craft a causal sequence of crisis and change visually? Though Aristotle used pictorial characteristics to develop this notion of plot,[1] much, if not all, of the theorizing about narrative assumes a verbally constituted form of expression and mode of thought. As with so many of the theoretical perspectives we examine in this volume, pictorial expression has not been central in the theorizing of human storytelling behavior. Yet pictorial stories carved into the walls of caves thousands of years ago provide us with rich evidence of narrative in a pictorial form (White, 1989; Wartofsky, 1980). Their predating of verbal language further suggests a connection between a narrative and a pictorial "way of structuring thought."

This chapter reviews aspects of theorizing about the narrative form that hold promise for understanding and theorizing visual narrative. The discussion is meant to expand the meaning of narrative in terms that account for its way of rendering the world in visual as well as verbal forms. This approach, although perhaps challenging the notion of some that narrative must be a linguistically formed entity, makes the assumption that pictorial expressions are not qualitatively different from verbal ones. Instead, it considers pictorial storytelling as an alternative or variety of the narrative form, and it maintains that there is no "privileged" form. In other words, what ever it is that makes us know that we "are in the presence of a story" should be discernable in the gestural composition of a mime or a ballet, as well as in the musical composition of a symphony or the pictorial composition of photomontage (Berger & Mohr, 1982). By expanding the notion of narrative to include all symbolic forms of expression, visual communication scholars gain a valuable set of critical tools for examining this pictorial mode of sense making as a theoretical model for understanding visual communication.

The scope of work defining narrative theory and narrative analysis encompasses diverse interdisciplinary interests and applications. Some of the narrative theories that were developed in literary studies incorporate communication theory, for example, and some of the media theories in communication studies integrate literary perspectives. Scholars interested in finding out why it is that we seem to need stories ask questions about the function of such a universal and apparently natural human behavior. Those interested in understanding what kind of experience a story creates ask questions about its particular discursive form. Studies using narrative analysis to understand human behavior broaden the scope even more. In addition to applications with traditional literary forms, one finds the method used to interpret such diverse cultural "texts" as medical interviews, personal narratives, television programs, movies, cultural institutions, and historical events (Manning & Cullum-Swan, 1994). This chapter approaches narrative theory with these three interests in mind. It begins with a discussion of narrative as a way of making sense of the world, which Walter Fisher (1987) called "narrative logic," and in this section explores the similarities of a narrative and a visual logic. The discussion then turns to considerations of how a story is made. It focuses on Northrup Frye's (1957) distinction between what a story says, or its content, and how it says it, or its form, as an entree to theoretical understanding of the distinctions between the meaning-making roles of an image's pictorial content and its pictorial form or syntax. With this critical tool we locate and describe a picture's visual syntax in its compositional structure of spatial relationships. This allows consideration of a specifically narrative or pictorial storytelling syntax. Using Seymour Chatman's (1978) theorizing of narrative discourse, the discussion then turns to a description of how the storytelling relationships of an "implied author" and "implied reader" as well as a "narrator" and a "narratee" are visually inscribed in the pictorial syntax of an image. Expanding these theoretical notions of narrative to such pictorial expression as our television programs, films, photographic essays, Web sites, and comic strips, to name a few, provides analytic tools for examining how these cultural forms use a narrative rendering of reality to make their point. Finally, the discussion turns to consideration of personal narrative and how the storytelling form becomes a useful tool for interpreting individual subjectivity as well as to social, institutional, and cultural identity. This section concludes with suggestions for how to expand some of the analytic structures currently used for examining the conversational content of personal narratives to include consideration of their visually as well as verbally embodied stories.

MAKING SENSE OF OUR WORLD: A NARRATIVE LOGIC

Storytelling is such a universal human behavior that Walter Fisher (1984, 1987) proposed we should conceptualize ourselves as *Homo narrens*. People the world over tell stories. We create fictional accounts, and we tell about things that really occurred. We listen to the personal stories of lives lived, and we read imaginary tales crafted by gifted writers. We experience stories "told" visually, musically and through gesture and movement as well as with words. In a silent, internal form, stories are also a way we talk to ourselves. As human beings we apparently need to create and behold stories, and we have done so throughout our history on the planet (Campbell, 1949; Frazier, 1922; Boas, 1911). Scholars from a wide diversity of experience provide testimony to the notion that we are a storytelling species. Anthropologist Victor Turner concluded, for example, that "we must concede [narrative] to be a universal cultural activity, embedded in the very center of the social drama" (1980, p. 167), while psychologist Gregory Bateson asserted that "thinking in terms of stories must be shared by all . . . minds" (1979, p. 14). Alasdair MacIntyre claimed that we "understand our lives in terms of narrative" (1991, p. 197), and, according to Hayden White, "the absence of narrative capacity or a refusal of narrative indicates an absence or refusal of meaning itself" (1973, p. 6). But why this universality? What purpose does this mode of human thought and behavior serve?

Different disciplinary perspectives work with various forms of storytelling to answer this question. Literary and media scholars, for example, take formal texts as their object of study. They examine stories that are articulated through some form of mass medium such as television, print, film, and, more recently, hypermedia. With a slightly different focus, communication scholars take the speech act as their object of study. They are interested in the narrative modes of thought that emerge in conversational talk as well as in the telling of personal narrative (Langlellier, 1999; Riessman, 1993). These stories are told interpersonally, and as such, they are experienced as a performance and as particular to an interactional situation. As Catherine Riessman (1993) related, we experience narratives expressed conversationally as emerging and without clearly bounded beginnings and endings. With formal texts, on the other hand, we experience narratives as "discrete units, with clear beginnings and endings . . . [which are] detachable from the surrounding discourse" (1993, p. 17). We encounter them with an expectation that their internal coherence of plot structure, characterization, motivation, and so on is defined in advance (Miller, 1990). We anticipate, in other words, that mediated stories will hang together, and we judge them accordingly (Fisher, 1987). Even across such a broad range of storytelling behavior, however, scholars find that people use narrative to make sense of disordered, raw experience. As Cronon suggested, it gives reality a unity "that neither nature nor the past possesses so clearly" (1992, p. 1349). A good story makes good sense of the world. Put another way, storytelling makes "arguments" about the nature of reality. It poses and tests "hypotheses" about the way things are or how they could be. It functions as a powerful method of meaning making and a primary way of defining the world (Bruner, 1990; Fisher, 1984, 1987; Gee, 1985; MacIntyre, 1981; Mishler, 1986).

Narrative theorist Walter Fisher (1984, 1987) proposed that we think about this particular way of making sense of the world as a "narrative logic." His operationalization of the concept in terms of narrative probability and narrative fidelity as well as his theorization of a narrative mode of discourse provide a particularly useful approach to theorizing visual narrative. Before proceeding to that discussion, however, it is important to acknowledge other theoretical entrees.

There is a diverse body of theory investigating the narrative as a "way structuring thought" that provides a number of particular, though often overlapping, perspectives and considerations. Though none of these theorists base their work on the storytelling characteristics of visual narrative, each offers a potentially fertile approach to understanding visual sense making. The Slavic formalist approach of Vladimir Propp (1970) explained narrative sense making as a function of plot structures, while the reader-response perspective of Wolfgang Iser (1978) described a process stimulated and guided by textual structures of given and not-given information. Chapter 19 in this volume provides an example of narrative analysis that uses this theoretical approach. Other perspectives and the major figures associated with them include dialogic theories of narrative sense making (Bakhtin, 1981), new critical theories (Blackmur, 1975), Chicago School or neo-Aristotelian theories (Crane, 1952; Booth, 1961), psychoanalytic theories (Freud, 1999; Burke, 1970; Lacan, 1977; Abraham, 1995), hermeneutic and phenomenological theories (Ingarden, 1973; Ricoeur, 1984–88; Poulet, 1996), structuralists, semiotic and topological theories (Levi-Strauss, 1976–83; Barthes, 1974; Todorov, 1977; Greimas, 1987; White, 1973), Marxist and sociological theories (Lukacs, 1971; Jameson, 1981), as well as post-structuralist and deconstructionist theories (Derrida, 1980, de Man, 1979; Miller, 1990), although it is beyond the scope of this chapter to illustrate how each is useful as a structure for analyzing visual texts. One should be aware, as well, that these various ways of crafting an inquiry about the narrative form rest on choices that also profoundly affect their arguments about storytelling and narrative sense making. Neither the narrative "way of structuring thought," which comprehends reality as "sequence with meaning," nor the theories that explain it take things as they are. Each begins with a different set of assumptions, and each defines the reality of narrative sensemaking differently. A narrative analysis, in turn, will always proceed from a distinct theoretical perspective about narrative sensemaking when it takes a particular story or stories as its object of study.

As with all of these approaches, Walter Fisher's notion of narrative logic is a way to conceptualize the narrative form as a mode of sense making. Fisher's proposal tackled the issue of sense making directly, however, by proposing an alternative to the traditional logic of a "rational-world paradigm," which features "inferential and implicative structures" (1987, p. 59). Taking the perspective that humans "experience and comprehend life as a series of ongoing narratives, as conflicts, as chapters, beginnings, middles, and ends" (Fisher, 1987, p. 24), he maintains that we use a narrative logic of "good reasons" to craft and test this experience. He identifies the basic principles of this logic as coherence, which he characterizes as "narrative probability" and fidelity or truthfulness, which he characterizes as "narrative fidelity" (1987, p. 47). Narrative fidelity, as Fisher (1985) stated, "concerns the 'truth' qualities of a story" (pp. 349–350) and is a test of "whether the individual components represent accurate assertions about social reality and thereby constitute good reasons for belief or action" (1987, p. 47). As the analysis of news photos in Chapter 12 (Goodnow) shows, narrative fidelity is assessed by reference to what we know about the world. In other words, a good story makes good sense of the world if its argument fits what we know of experience. It provides a good argument if, in all probability, things could happen in life the way that they do in a narrative.[2] A good sense-making argument also fits with what we know of storytelling; a good story resonates with other stories that we have accepted as true (Fisher, 1984, 1987; Schrag, 1991).

Although narrative fidelity has to do with the reliability of the world a story creates, narrative probability is concerned with its internal coherence or "integrity . . . as a whole" (Fisher, 1985, p. 47). It is a test, as Fisher stated, of "whether or not a story coheres or 'hangs together,' whether or not a story is free of contradiction" (1985, pp. 349–350). As Fisher located the attributes of narrative probability in a story's formal features, this concept lays the foundation for distinguishing between what Frye (1957) described as the "literal" and "descriptive" structures of narrative. This is important for theorizing pictorial narrative because, as we see later in this discussion, it provides a theoretical entree that allows us to differentiate between an image's content and its syntactical structure. This distinction leads us to an identification of how a narrative discursive mode is inscribed in the formal features of an image. Fisher also characterized the kind of sense that a narrative logic makes of the world, and it is its similarities to what others have proposed as a "visual logic" that we turn next.

MAKING SENSE OF OUR WORLD VISUALLY: NARRATIVE AND PICTORIAL "LOGIC"

Although narrative scholars have not developed their theories from questions that begin with pictorial expression, and Fisher's proposal of "narrative as a paradigm for the general study of communication" was not prompted by an interest in visual communication (1987, p. 59), there are significant similarities in the notion of narrative logic with characteristics that scholars in other theoretical areas connect with a visual or "holistic" logic. As

Fisher described, narrative's mode of thought "simultaneously [appeals] to the various senses, to reason and emotion, to intellect and imagination, and to fact and value. It does not presume intellectual contact only" (1987, p. 75). Working with visual media, Mitchel Stephens (1998) described with similarity a "complex" mode of "seeing" that is exploited in the editing style of MTV as well as in the work of cubists, surrealists, abstract impressionists, and pop art. As he described the experience, it is a logic of collision that "[chops] the world into fragments, . . . [Layers] on words and graphics" and "[arranges] those fragments in new and meaningful patterns" (1998, pp. 182, 193, 208). Herbert Zettl (1999) used the term *complexity editing* to describe this mode of visual discourse.

In a similar vein, theorists working with the gestalt concept of nonlinear and dynamical systems observe a holistic mode of thought that "acknowledges relationships that are not strictly proportional" (Barry, 1997, p. 100; see also Gleik, 1987; Kosko, 1993; McCrone, 1994). Through work that links this body of material to research in visual information processing, visual communication scholar Ann Marie Barry (1997) proposed the notion of visual intelligence as a mode of holistic logic. In a complementary approach, Stafford conceptualized "an intelligence of sight," or "mosaic presentation," which she characterizes as a logic for "configuring and conveying ideas" (1996, p. 4). Turkel and Papert (1993), whose work is in cognition, described a pattern of working with bits and pieces, a way of thinking by "feeling one's way from one. . . to another," building up, sculpting a whole. They use use the term *bricolage* to describe the logic of this cognitive style that is marked by negotiation and rearrangement. The notion of working from bits and pieces to "fashion a hypotheses" also parallels Sandra Moriarty's discussion in this volume of "abductive reasoning" as an explanation of visual information processing (see also Moriarty, 1996). With similarity to the gestalt, she describes "the formation of an abductive hypothesis" as an "act of insight" where an idea comes "like a flash" (1996, p. 181). Edward Neiva's (1999) discussion of a sign's triadic structure further suggested how a process of negotiation and rearrangement, whether referred to as abductive or bricolage, might be accounted for as a holistic mode of thought.

These and other similarities between characteristics of a narrative logic and a visual logic theoretically underscore the notion of pictorial narrative. They also suggest a route for pursing questions of how it is that images make the sense they do of "disordered, raw experience." We can now turn, then, to a discussion of how a story is made, and with this critical tool, locate the syntactical structures that will lead us to an understanding of how a pictorial story is made.

MAKING NARRATIVE SENSE OF THE WORLD: NARRATIVE STRUCTURE

Once theorists conceptualize storytelling as a sense-making strategy, their interests understandably turn to investigating the character of the sense it makes. Theoretical inquiries focus on such questions about narrative structure as: How do we know when we are in the presence of a narrative rendering of reality? What is it about the phenomenon of a narrative that makes it a story rather than an essay or a poem? What are the necessary components of narrative? What must be there—and only there—to have this form of sense-making? Attempts to answer these questions define much of the work in narrative theory.

An early approach to narrative form comes from Aristotle's focus on plot as a story's "first principle." He characterizes it as a "whole" composed of causal relationships comprising a beginning, a middle, and an end.[3] We often speak of this "whole" as the dramatic curve or causal structure made up of an initial situation, including an introduction or exposition and inciting moment, followed by a sequence of rising action and complication leading to an apex or crisis point. The apex marks a "point of no return" in the causal sequence, forming the beginning of the end. Here a change or reversal of the situation resulting from a final confrontation leads to an irreversible change. Finally, in the descending arc of this storytelling sequence, revelation or resolution comes about through the consequences of the reversal (Miller, 1990; Rabiger, 1998).

In a similar respect, a dramaturgical approach appreciates this "sequence of meaning" as a process of stages that Kenneth Burke (1970) characterized as pollution, guilt, purification, and redemption. A story begins with actions that violate the rules or values of a system, or pollution. The dramatic process continues with actions that establish guilt by assigning blame to the person or thing that is responsible for the polluting violation. In the third, or purification stage, a search is undertaken to get rid of the problem and its cause, and in the final or redemption stage, a resolution occurs as the system is put back in order. Because the narrative form pivots on a "point of no return"—or transformation—the return of order to a system will always be different from the one that existed prior to its being upset by a violation of its norms. The characters may simply be "wiser for the experience," for example, or the "irreversible change" might also initiate a totally new social system, as is the case with myth. In its most basic sense, then, it is this "sequence" with the "meaning" of transformation that tells us we are in the presence of a storytelling experience or narrative "way of thinking."

Of course a story requires more than a sequence of incidents or plot. Although we anticipate a structure of inciting conditions and culminating events, for these actions to take place there must be some agents as well as some sort of pattern or narrative rhythm (Miller, 1990). Aristotle did not leave them out. In *Poetics* he proposed that every story "must have six parts: Plot, Character, Diction, Thought, Spectacle and Song" (Fergusson, 1961, p. 62). Accordingly, although the elements of plot, character, and thought constitute the "objects" of a story, the elements of diction and song, being language into which "rhythm, harmony, and song enter," constitute the "medium" in Aristotle's typology (Fergusson, 1961, pp. 61–62). It is the plot or "wholeness" of causal relationships forming a beginning, a middle, and an end, however, that makes a story a story and not something else. In other words, plot—or a sequence of incidents with meaning—is the "first principle" of narrative, and everything else is story "stuff." Characters and setting may change, various mediums may be used, and styles of telling will differ, yet we will recognize a story as a story because the narrative sequence with meaning is transposable from one set of this story stuff to another.

This notion of plot as a compositional form that is detachable from the content and texture of a story led theorists to inquiry about the "deep structure" of narrative form. Both Seymour Chatman and Northrup Frye work with this notion of form in a way that is quite valuable for theorizing visual narrative. Frye makes a distinction between

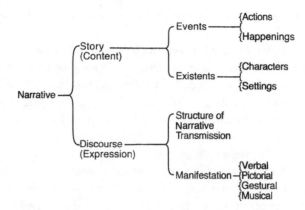

FIG. 21.1.   Narrative structure: Elements of story and discourse.

descriptive and literal structure that helps to theorize an image in terms of its pictorial syntax, and Chatman provides an approach to discourse structure that helps theorize pictorial narrative syntax. Structuralists make a theoretical distinction between the story (*historie*) and discourse (*discours*) of a narrative arguing that the narrative discourse or form is itself a semiotic structure that is independently meaningful. Although a story, according to Chatman, is "the content or chain of events (actions and happenings) plus . . . the existents (characters, items of settings)" of a narrative, the discourse is its "expression, the means by which the content is communicated" (1978, p. 19). French structuralists make similar distinctions as do Russian formalists who use the term *fable* (*fabula*) for *what* is depicted in a story and the term *plot* (*sjuzet*) for *how* it is told. (Chatman, 1978, pp. 19–20). The general form of this argument is illustrated in Fig. 21.1. This distinction between what constitutes the story or content of a narrative and what constitutes the discourse or expression of a narrative provides a theoretical entree to understanding distinctions between the meaning-making roles of an image's pictorial content and its pictorial form or syntax. Building on this, we can move to consideration of a pictorial inscription of discourse as well as an examination of how a sequence with meaning is constituted in patterns of pictorial diction. We turn first to theorizing an image in terms of Frye's (1957) distinction of descriptive and literal structures.

VISUAL NARRATIVE: DESCRIPTIVE AND LITERAL STRUCTURE

Fry (1957) discriminated between *what* a story says, or its content, and *how* it says it, or its form, by what he called the *descriptive* and the *literal* structures of a narrative. This distinction is useful for locating how meaning is made in an image and for appreciating visual representation as a two-part sign structure. Frye discusses a story's descriptive structure as the part that imitates (though does not record) real-world events. For most of us the part of a story that simulates real-world events probably encompasses our notion of narrative. It is the part we know as a storyworld of characters, settings, and actions whether encountered through the images we make or the images we see. Because this is the case, it is especially important to note that literary theorists' use of the notion of imitation is with a reference to the simulated or fictional reality of a literary text. As Iser explained, "The literary text is like the world in so far as it outlines a rival world. . . . Fiction possesses none of the criteria of reality, and yet it pretends that it does " (1978, p. 181). This is, of course, particularly relevant when considering cinematic and photographic expressions. In their descriptive structure they present an iconic simulation (though not a recording) of reality.

A story's literal structure, on the other hand, is not something that we can either image or see because it is syntax, or as Frye described, "a flow of significant sounds" (1957, p. 104). Of course narrative does not exist except as an integrated structure of the two, and so whenever we read or hear a story "we find our attention moving in two directions at once" (Frye, 1957, p. 73). The *descriptive* structure directs our attention outward in that "we keep going outside our reading, from individual words to the things they mean," and, at the same time the *literal* structure directs our attention inward as "we try to develop from the words a sense of the larger verbal pattern they make" (Frye, 1957, p. 73).

When we apply this way of thinking to visual narrative, we see how a language bias has influenced our conceptions of the image and of how we think about visual storytelling. In film and television studies, for example, scholars often focus on the visual content or descriptive structure of images, with little consideration given to the notion of pictorial syntax. In fact, because these narrative forms incorporate both images and words, considerations of a syntactical structure almost automatically fall to the verbal script. Of course, the visual part of a film or a television program is compelling and, because images are perceptually processed in the same way as direct experience (Barry, 1997), the visual part is immediately expressive of meaning in a way that the words are not. Images show their meaning, words do not. Even so, as we can understand from the distinction made in narrative theory, the meaning-making function of *how* a story's visual content or descriptive structure is formed is integral to the meaning of that content. Its descriptive structure, as Frye reminds us, imitates real-world events, it does not record them. Although the spatially rendered content of a film's images directs our attention outward, the compositional form of this content directs our attention inward to the sense-making relationships configured by angle, perspective, field of view, and the like.

We can appreciate this two-part relationship of pictorial form and pictorial content by considering the image depicted in Fig. 21.2. How would you describe it? Some might focus on its descriptive structure, characterizing it as a flower, perhaps a lily, growing beside a country road. Others might portray it as a literal structure whose compositional patterns of spatial relations incorporate a close-up with a low angle and a narrow field of view. Either depicts it correctly, of course, but neither does it completely because an interpretative act moves in both of these directions simultaneously. To capture this meaning-making process, one might try describing it as an intimate-(close-up)-larger-than-life-(low-angled)-spatially compressed-(narrowed depth-of-view)-lily-by-a-country-road-(a lily by a country road)-experience, though the linear and sequential requirements of language make such an attempt awkward. Nonetheless, by theorizing a visual expression in terms of a descriptive *and* literal structure, we more fully understand the image as a

FIG. 21.2.   Descriptive and literal image structure. (Photo Credit: Lauren Petrovich)

representation (of something) *in the terms of* its compositional (or literal) structure. As Nelson Goodman (1976) discussed this relationship, we more properly understand that a representation is always a "representation-*as*." With this in mind, an act of reading the two-part semiotic structure imaged in Fig. 21.2 is an interpretative act of *subordinating* what one knows experientially (or as simulated in the descriptive structure) to one's knowledge of the rules and conventions used to do its semiotic work (Worth, 1981).

Theorizing the image in this way as a two-part semiotic structure allows consideration of an independently meaningful pictorial syntax, which we can locate in the spatially rendered relationships that compose a picture's underlying structure (or form). What makes this structure independently meaningful as narrative, however, are the characteristics of a specifically storytelling form. For visual storytelling this means theorizing a *syntax of pictorial narrative*. For this we turn, finally, to a discussion of pictorially inscribed properties of narrative discourse and the work of narrative theorist Seymour Chatman.

VISUAL NARRATIVE: DISCURSIVE STRUCTURE

Though a literary scholar, Chatman (1978) works from a communication perspective to theorize meaning-making properties of narrative. He begins with the notion that storytelling presupposes the encounter of a teller and a listener, although the properties of this communication relationship are complex even when telling and listening take place face to face. With a teller-listener relationship in mind, Chatman proposes a framework of discursive "personages" as a way of talking about the abstract properties or underlying structure of narrative syntax. As shown in Fig. 21.3, Chatman proposes that in the telling of a story, "each party" to the encounter "entails three different personages," only one of which, you should notice, refers to the actual persons doing the telling and the listening

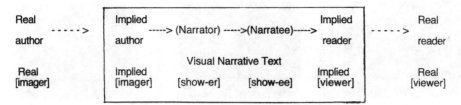

FIG. 21.3. Narrative communication structure.

(1978, p. 28). This means that the discursive structure pertains to whether a story is told in person or through a text, even though when stories are told through a text, the real-life author and the real-life audience can only communicate through their implied counterparts. In either case, though, the narrative form or compositional structure of the story is understood in terms of the inscription of an implied teller and an implied audience as well as that of a narrator and a narratee. As Fig. 21.3 shows, storytelling through the medium of a text makes it a little easier to see that the author of a story is neither the author implied in the text nor the narrator, and similarly, the audience is neither the audience implied in the text nor the narratee. Instead, these discursive "personages" refer to the perspective that a story takes toward the "events and exigents" of its storyworld, and the evaluation it makes of them. This framework of discursive "personages" is, in short, a way of talking about the abstract properties or compositional structure of narrative syntax. The framework is useful as an analytic tool to examine how a narrative rendering of reality—or, in Fisher's terms, a "narrative logic"—is implied through the syntax or "way" that a story is told. Furthermore, when casting these properties in pictorial terms, the framework is useful for theorizing and understanding a pictorially rendered narrative sense of the world. (See Barbatsis, 1996) With reference to Fig. 21.3, let us turn, then, to a description of these discursive properties of the narrative form and a discussion of how they are exemplified pictorially.

In the framework of discursive "personages" presented in Fig. 21.3, an implied teller is a story's point of view. As Chatman put it, "point of view is the physical place or ideological situation or practical life-orientation to which the narrative events stand in relation" (1978, p. 152). Its counterpart, an implied listener, is the perspective or vantage point from which one engages the narrative events. An image composed by an objective point of view, for example, places its narrative events in a reportive relationship to the camera or other composing instrument. At the same time, this compositional structure of spatial relations creates a reportive vantage point for engaging the events of an image. In distinguishing between the structures of implied author and narrator, Chatman emphasized that "point of view does not mean expression; it only means the perspective in terms of which the expression is made" (1978, p. 153). In other words, an objective point of view creates the terms of a reportive perspective as the frame within which one views the story elements. The same story elements might also be viewed in terms of a participatory perspective, for example, if they were framed from a subjective point of view. Within this framework of discursive "personages," then, it is the expression itself that is characterized as a narrator or narrating presence. Accordingly, a narrating presence is the particular way that the

THE HARBOR

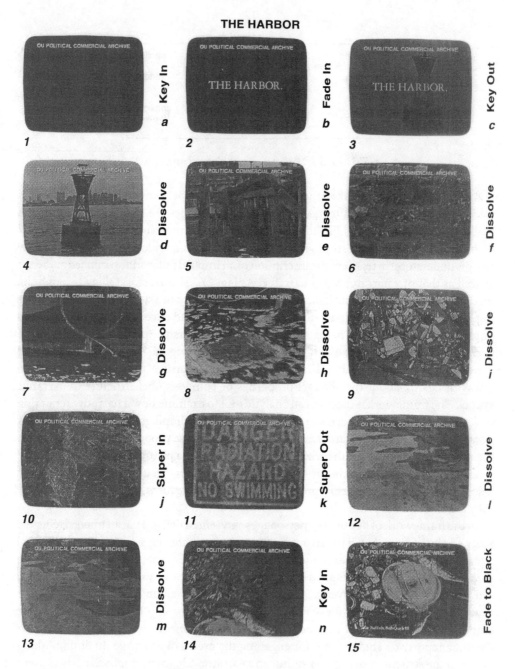

FIG. 21.4.   Pictorial story sequence.

material of a story is organized and its counterpart, a narratee or listening presence, is implied in the appraisal that one is meant to make of its particular compositional patterns. Though a narrating presence can take the form of a character in the story, it is not a person and certainly should not be confused with the author of a story. As Chatman stated, "it should mean only the . . . presence actually telling the story to an audience" (1978, p. 33). In other words, a narrating *presence* comes from an audience's sense that it is being told something. Sometimes characterized as a story's narrating voice, it "refers to the speech or other overt means through which events and existents are communicated to the audience" (p. 153). With an image, an audience's sense of being told something comes from the way the picture is made—through a close-up scale, from a high-angle, with high-contrast lighting, in a narrow field of view, and so on. In other words, these elements of spatial organization are the "overt means" through which the events and exigents (or content) of a pictorial story are 'expressed' and communicated to an audience (Chatman, 1978, p. 153). With reference to these terms, then, we can turn to a discussion of pictorial narrative syntax by casting these properties in pictorial terms, and we begin by generating a version of these terms that is more descriptive of image making.

With reference to Fig. 21.3, we might first recognize that the process of visual "authoring" involves creators who "image." They are painters, photographers, illustrators, graphic and multimedia designers, as well as film and video directors. Some image with a camera, others with pen and pencil, some with computer software programs, and still others with a brush. Their counterparts in the visual storytelling relationship are audiences who view. When picturing is done with a camera, for example, the imager is a real person who directs what the camera will see (typically a director) and the viewer is a real person who sees on a screen the results of this imaging. In a visual discourse, then, the notion of author is recast as imager and the notion of reader is recast as viewer. In this same mode, the textual properties that inscribe a visual point of view are recast as implied imager and implied viewer. Finally, the textual properties that inscribe a sense of being told something are recast in terms of being shown something, which can be thought of as the showing presence or "show-er" and "show-ee" positions of a visually composed discourse. The terms of a visual narrative syntax can be identified, then, as the inscription of a pictorial point of view (implied imager) along with a pictorial vantage point from which to view the imaged storyworld (implied viewer) as well as the organization of picturing elements (show-er) with an implication of the way this organization is meant to be seen (show-ee).

With the analytic framework cast in visual terms, we turn to a discussion of how a narrative rendering of reality occurs in pictorial forms. The sequence of images from a political campaign commercial shown in Fig. 21.4 will be used to illustrate the meaning-making properties of a picture's storytelling form. (The sense-making characteristics of this narrative syntax are fully analyzed in a close-reading of this pictorial text in Chapter 19.)

NARRATING "EYE": SHOW-ER TO SHOW-EE

A story to be a story has to be *told*. Although the content of a story is necessary, it is its discursive structure of *telling* that interests narrative theorists, and a syntactically inscribed narrator-narratee relationship is at the heart of this discourse. In a pictorial story structure the notion of this narrative presence is found in the way that images and sequences of images are composed by an imaginary show-er for an imaginary show-ee. In other words, a narrating "eye" leaves its trace in an image's organization of space and time (show-er) and in the meaning-making implications of these organizing qualities (show-ee). This relationship is at the heart of the discourse because these inscriptions form the fundamental sign-meaning relationships of visual representation (Metallinos, 1996; Zettl, 1999).

A narrating presence is inscribed, then, by such meaning-making elements of spatial organization as field of view (scale), level of view (angle), depth of view (perspective), and contrast of view (light and shadow) as well as temporal elements of motion (movement within a frame and between frames). In the terms used by Frye, these pictorial inscriptions make up the "flow of significant *sights*" or discursive (literal) syntax of an image (1957, p. 104). The syntax, we remember, directs our sense-making work inward to the meanings implied in the "way" that material is formed. Drawing on work in contextual media aesthetics (Zettl, 1999) we can identify an image's narrating presence by a close reading of its syntax of spatial and temporal elements.[4] With reference to Fig. 21.4, for example, let us consider the how the presence of a show-er is implied in the close-ups composing screens 7 and 13. Because objects in these screens are within touching distance, these compositions of space "show" (or literally inscribe) spatial relationships of "closeness." Furthermore, because touching distances are experienced perceptually as personal and intimate (Hall, 1982), the spatial relationships in these images are potentially meant to be "seen" as (i.e., metaphorically inscribe) "internalness" or intimacy (Zettl, 1999). In addition, though, spatial relations of angle are also at play in the syntax. An eye-level angle of view in screen 7 (literally) couples the spatial relationship of closeness with one of "normalness" (or normal eye-level seeing) and (metaphorically) couples its perceptual experience of intimacy with "naturalness." In other words, a narrating eye "shows" (literally) closeness and normalness with an implication that it be seen (metaphorically) as intimate and natural. By contrast, with a high-angle view in screen 13, the narrating eye shows (literally) closeness and highness with an implication that it be seen (metaphorically) as intimate and diminished.

Fundamentally, a narrating eye is the means by which space and time are organized. In addition, though, the narrating eye has to do this organizing work from some position in space and time. For example, it might be pictorially telling the tale as a participant within the world of the story, or as an omniscient observer. As an omniscient observer, the narrating eye organizes what it shows to an imaginary see-er as if both are outside of the pictorial story and looking in on it. In this kind of structure, the presence of a shower in the organization of an image remains hidden. The narrating eye (literally) reports what it shows, implying that it be seen (metaphorically) as "objectiveness." We find an example of this kind of structure in the first four screens in Fig. 21.4 where neither an imaginary show-er nor show-ee is acknowledged in any of the pictorial arrangements. By contrast, there is a composition of motion between screens 5 and 6 that self-consciously reveals the workings of a narrating eye. Here a left-to-right screen pan draws attention to the presence of a see-er in an abrupt reversal of direction in the organizational flow of space and time. In this discursive structure of pictorial direct address, an imaginary show-er addresses an imaginary see-er as if the two of them are involved in (rather than observing) a pictorial event. The show-er (literally) identifies its "participation" in the showing with the implication that it be seen (metaphorically) as "subjectiveness." To summarize, theorizing the narrative discursive syntax of an image includes these characteristics of a pictorially structured narrating presence and, to what we turn next, a pictorially composed point of view.

PICTORIAL POINT-OF-VIEW: IMPLED IMAGER
AND IMPLIED VIEWER

In the telling, a story also has to be *told* from a particular point of view. Although the spatial relations organized by a narrating eye create a pictorial storyworld, the spatial relations organized by a pictorial point of view create a position for viewing it. These spatial relations might be composed (literally) from an "observing" position, for example, with an implication that the view be seen (metaphorically) as "looking at" a picture world. Or they might be composed (literally) from an "involving" or a "participatory" position, implying that the view be seen (metaphorically) as "looking into" or "being in" a pictured world (Zettl, 1999, pp. 186–188). These spatial relations inscribe the textual positions of an implied imager and an implied viewer in the discursive syntax of a pictorial narrative.

We find all three variations of an implied imager and implied viewer interaction illustrated in the image structures of the first eight screens of Fig. 21.4. The first three screens are composed from an "observing" point of view, as if one were looking at the scene somewhat omnisciently from outside. In screen 4, however, the spatial relations created with a prominent foreground object suggest a point of view that is more involved in the events of the pictured world, as if seeing (perhaps over the shoulder) along with an imager and looking into, rather than just at, the way things are organized. Finally, in screens 5–8 the spatial relations of almost perfect symmetry suggest a participating point of view as if, in being addressed, one were part of being in this pictorial reality. In the short span of just eight screens, these images shift the point of view from a position of looking at to looking in and then to being in this storyworld.[5]

In summary, then, this discussion of a narrating eye and a pictorial point of view shows the utility of narrative theory to theorize a pictorial narrative syntax. Discursive structures of shower-er to show-ee create a pictorial storyworld and those of implied imager to implied viewer structure various subject positions for viewing it. These pictorial structures of spatial relations—such as an eye level, close-up from an observational point of view—are structures of syntax. They are the compositional structures that give form to the objects (or content) of an image, and that when analyzed, reveal how their arrangements create meanings according to the logic of a beginning, a middle, and an end. Chapter 19 illustrates, for example, how analysis based on an understanding of pictorial narrative voice—or the sense of being spoken to visually—is useful in describing how pictorial narrative logic structures the argument of a political campaign commercial. The notion of pictorial syntax is also useful for understanding the role of pictorial conventions in creating the specific experiences associated with various genres of storytelling.

PICTORIAL NARRATIVE SYNTAX: PICTORIAL CONVENTIONS
OF STORYTELLING GENRES

Narrative scholars find an answer to the question about why we need and enjoy stories in the notion of "narrative rationality." Narrative, it seems, is a powerful sense-making mode. If this explains why we need stories, however, it does not explain why we seem to need the same stories over and over again. Children, for example, love to have the same story told over and over, and they often insist that it be told exactly the same way each time. In an evening of television viewing, we are also likely to watch and enjoy the same story told over and over if we indulge in more than one situation comedy or catch more than one news program. Certainly a week's worth of viewing will find many variations on the theme of the crime story. We watch it from the perspective of the cops and from the perspective of the attorneys, from the perspective of the individual criminals and the perspective of international syndicates. Though the story "stuff" of these examples is not the same, like the children's book that is read over and over again, they have a similar story form that is both recognizable and distinct from that of a situation comedy or a news narrative. They are specific generic structures that are detachable from the narrative "stuff" of a story. Each of these forms follows a distinct transformational structure of crisis and resolution that we come to recognize as the kind of story it tells, or more significantly, the kind of argument it makes about the nature of the world. At a very general level, for example, the transformational structure of comedy affirms an idealistic point of view about the universe whereas the transformational structure of tragedy affirms a realistic perspective, the melodrama an optimistic point of view, and irony a pessimistic one (Frye, 1957; White, 1973). Experiencing one of these story structures over and over again is one way of engaging and reaffirming the values asserted through its transformational form. Situation comedies give us the opportunity to "know" the world as an idealistic place, for example, whereas with the melodramatic structures of news narrative we make a more optimistic sense of things. We usually refer to these structural sense-making forms as genres of storytelling.

By distinguishing between genres we appreciate that the shape of a sense-making structure is a "fundamental carrier of the sense" that the structure makes (Miller, 1990, p. 70). Scholars interested in how visual conventions carry this sense of meaning look for distinctive recurring or conventional patterns of visual composition within a generic form. In a close analysis of the visual texts of soap opera narrative, for example, Barbatsis and Guy (1991) identified a number of compositional conventions of the visual narrative, and in analyzing their aesthetic properties found that they created an experiential sense of reportiveness and realness associated with soap opera's other generic conventions. Studies such as this that investigate narrative structure as a fundamental carrier of cultural meaning answer the question of why we need the same stories over and over by demonstrating how narrative sense-making structures are "very powerful ways of asserting the basic ideology of a culture" (Miller, 1990, p. 71).

NARRATIVE ANALYSIS: STORY AS OBJECT OF STUDY

This chapter began with a discussion of narrative as a particular way of "structuring thought" (Frye, 1957), which Fisher (1987) termed *narrative logic*. Much of what we have considered thus far has concerned theorizing about what narrative is, as well as how we can apply this theorizing to pictorial expressions. Hopefully we have answered the theoretical question of whether or not there is such a thing as visual narrative with a resounding "yes!" That being the case, we can employ the method of narrative analysis to interpret the ways in which visual materials use a narrative way of "structuring thought" to make sense of the world.

Because we make our way in the world by structuring our experiences into stories, narrative structures are deeply revealing of how we think, what we value, and why we act (Schrag, 1991). Whether in the form of anecdotes, case studies, dialogue, role-play, parables and fables, a journal, a joke, a news item, or a novel (Polking, Bloss, & Cannon, 1983), storytelling behavior provides an entree to individual subjectivity and identity as well as social and institutional sense making (Riessman, 1993). Narrative analysis is the methodology used for studying the narrative logic of this human storytelling behavior.

Not surprisingly, narrative analysis is found across a broad interdisciplinary spectrum of interpretive research including formal literary studies in the humanities, personal narrative in contemporary anthropology and feminist studies, news, advertising and entertainment in mass media and cultural studies, as well as societal level analyses of public-service campaigns, public policy making, and institutional processes in political and social studies (Alasuutari, 1995; Manning & Cullum-Swan, 1994; Griffin, 1991).[6] Although a government report or a medical interview might not seem to have much in common with a work of fiction or even a documentary, each has a narrative logic of sense making embedded in a plot structure. Each and all of these sense-making structures has to do with "how protagonists interpret things," as Bruner stated, and it is for this that we engage in narrative analysis (1990, p. 51).

Alasuutari explained, for example, how the ideological undercurrents of policy and legislation can be identified in government committee reports by analyzing their narrative logic: how they "define the present situation," how they "describe the inherent problems, then present possible solutions," and how they "justify the rationale of the solutions" (1995, p. 78). Although less formally defined than a television drama or a novel, these government committee reports are similar to them in exhibiting a causal sequence or plot structure of problem, complication, crisis and resolution. And, as with formal literary works, this structure is itself infused with meaning because it is one of any number of ways this story could be told and as such can be appreciated as an ideologically located way of making sense of the world.

The embodied stories of personal narrative which are concerned with lives and lived experience present yet another different level of formality because they are generated in conversation.[7] Still, these stories have a narrative logic or plot line in the way that they tell what happened, where and when it happened, who did it, how, and why. In addition, even though less formally defined, personal narrative plot structures allow comparison and interpretation across a number of cases. Ginzberg (1989) generalized, for example, about the "place of reproductive experience in the life stories of contrasting groups of women" (Riessman, 1993, p. 33). Studying the life stories generated with women activists, she found that one difference between the pro-life and pro-choice groups was in the structure of their narratives, including "both the substance of the turning points and the way they were sequenced" (Riessman, 1993, p. 33). Although their reproductive experiences were thematically similar, the stories of those on one side of the abortion issue made sense of their stories differently than those on the other.

Narrative analysis adapts to this wide variety of narrative material because it emphasizes the role of form in conveying meaning. This allows narrative structures to be studied from a broad range of analytic perspectives. Although it is beyond the scope of this chapter to describe any in detail, a brief overview is offered to demonstrate the diversity of approaches that are available for studying visual narrative. Propp's (1970) typology of narrative functions has been useful in classification and cultural interpretation of formal literary texts. Wright (1975) adapted it in his study of Westerns, for example, showing how variations in plot structure relate to changing ways of dealing with the tension between the individual and society in American culture. Other popular approaches for analyzing formal texts as well as the discourse of personal narrative include van Dijk's (1980) rules of discourse analysis for summarizing a story, Labov's (1972, 1982, Labov & Waletzky, 1967) typology of structural elements, Burke's (1945) dramatistic pentad, and Gee's (1991, 1986) structure of poetic devices. Others, who focus on personal narrative as a form of identify formation, use typologies that link social and personal identity with such generic structures as comedy and romance (Murray, 1989).

None of these typologies was developed with the notion of an independently meaningful pictorial narrative plot structure in mind, however. Their usefulness to visual communication theory depends on finding equivalencies for pictorial structures in the concepts and terms that have been developed from a theoretical understanding of language structure. As an example, van Dijk's (1980) rules for summarizing the discursive structure of a story deal with propositional structures. For visual communication scholars, the first challenge in adapting an analytic structure such as this is in theorizing pictorial propositional structures in a way that does not arbitrarily impose verbal constructs on them. Similarly, analysis using Labov's (1972) method involves parsing languaged utterances and then organizing them according to their narrative function. Employing this approach with pictorial material would involve parsing the images of a visual structure and then determining their structural functions that Labov describes as abstract, orientation, complication, evaluation, resolution, and coda. Using Burke's (1945) dramatistic approach to analyze a visual narrative structure dictates identifying a pictorial grammar of act (what was done), scene (where or when was it done), agent (who did it), agency (how was it done), and purpose (why was it done). Although van Dijk, Labov, and Burke all work with text-based written language structure, Gee's (1986) approach focuses on the oral structures of how a story is told. Taking a similar poetic structural approach to analyzing visual narrative would include theorizing such poetic features of pictorial expression as framing metaphors, stanzas, and summarizing couplets. Any of these approaches provides a useful analytic tool for understanding how the pictorial syntax of a photograph, a film, a Web site, or any of the images we craft in our personal narratives organizes thought.

Theorizing *visual* narrative, in short, we pose questions about pictorial storytelling that narrative scholars since the time of Aristotle have asked: What is a pictorial story? Why do we need pictorial stories? Why do we need the "same" pictorial stories over and over? And finally, why is our need for more pictorial stories never satisfied? (Miller, 1990, p. 68). Do they, in the end, give a narrative form to a logically insolvable problem? If this is the case, as narrative theorists assert, then the issue for visual narrative, and especially the ambiguously "transparent" mediation of film and television narrative, is compelling (Gross, 1985, p. 3). The challenge is to theorize, study, and create visual narrative in ways that we appreciate its sense-making function as a way to better understand disordered, raw experience; as a powerful way of constituting reality and not a way of merely recording it. The notion of "pictorial narrative" as a way of "structuring thought" provides a useful tool for meeting that challenge.

ENDNOTES

[1] In *Poetics* Aristotle wrote: "The Plot, then, is the first principle, and, as it were, the soul of a tragedy: Character holds the second place. A similar fact is seen in painting. The more beautiful the colors, laid on confusedly, will not give as much pleasure as the chalk outline of a portrait. Thus Tragedy is the imitation of an action, and of the agents mainly with a view to the action" (Fergusson, 1961, p. 63).

[2] Because these "good" stories are made, not found, however, their good arguments are also inherently ideological. There are many ways to begin and end a story, and the choices a sense-maker makes in crafting one profoundly affects the good sense that it makes of reality.

[3] In his definition of a beginning, a middle, and an end, Aristotle identifies the causality inherent in a narrative structuring of events. "A beginning is that which does not itself follow anything by causal necessity, but after which something naturally is or comes to be. An end, on the contrary, is that which itself naturally follows some other thing, either by necessity, or as a rule, but has nothing following it. A middle is that which follows something as some other thing follows it. A well constructed plot must neither begin no end at haphazard" (Fergusson, 1961, p. 65).

[4] In the spirit suggested by Anderson, the interpretive claims made in this discussion are meant to be taken as "what ought to be" intended and not what is (1993, p. 216). Semantic or meaning-making properties are discussed in reference to a pictorial quality such as "scale," which is field of view and is operationally capable of composing various spatial relations of distance. The spatial organization of a pictorial composition inscribes meaning both literally and metaphorically. An operation of scale, for example, can show (or literally inscribe) spatial relations of "closeness," which are meant to be seen (or metaphorically inscribe) as "intimacy."

[5] The consequence of this perspective shift for the pictorial storytelling discourse is significant. Pictorial direct address simulates a camera-to-event encounter that engages the viewer as a participant in constructing the world of the text.

[6] Narrative analysis carries with it an understanding of language as deeply constitutive of reality. With the assumption that content is a function of form and meaning a product of a system of relationships, its use in the social sciences radically redefines the nature of documents into the notion of socially constructed "texts" that are meant to be read and interpreted. For the methodological implications of this change, see Manning and Cullum-Swan (1994).

[7] Riessman (1993) discussed this theoretical context of listening to, recording, and interpreting the voices of others in the shared production of a narrative. She described it in terms of five levels of representation, including attending to experience, telling about experience, transcribing experience, analyzing experience, and reading experience. Each successively moves the researcher further from the primary experience of talking and listening.

REFERENCES

Abraham, N. (1995). *Rhythms: On the work, translation and psychoanalysis.* B. Thigpen & N. Rand (Trans.). Stanford, CA: Stanford University Press.

Alasuutari, P. (1995). *Researching culture: Qualitative method and cultural studies.* London: Sage.

Anderson, J. (1993). The role of interpretation in communication theory. In N. Metallinos (Ed.), *Verbo-visual literacy: Understanding and applying new educational communication media technologies* (pp. 211–222). Delphi, Greece: International Symposium of the International Visual Literacy Association.

Bakhtin, M. (1981). *The dialogic imagination: Four essays.* C. Emerson & M. Holquist (Trans). Austin: University of Texas Press.

Barbatsis, G. (1996). "Look and I will show you something you will want to see": Viewer engagement with negative campaign commercials. *Journal of Argumentation and Advocacy, 32*(2), 69–80.

Barbatsis, G., & Guy, Y. (1991). Analyzing meaning in form: Soap opera's compositional construction of realness. *Journal of Broadcasting and Electronic Media, 35*(1), 59–74.

Barry, A. M. (1997). *Visual intelligence*. Albany: State University of New York Press.

Barthes, R. (1974). *S/Z*. R. Miller, Trans. New York: Farrar, Straus & Giroux.

Bateson, G. (1979). *Mind and nature: A necessary unity*. Toronto: Bantam Books.

Berger, J., & Mohr, J. (1982). *Another way of telling*. New York: Pantheon Books.

Blackmur, R. P. (1975). *New criticism in the United States*. Folcroft, PA: Folcroft Library Editions.

Boas, F. (1911). *The mind of primitive man*. New York: Macmillan.

Booth, W. (1961). *The rhetoric of fiction*. Chicago: University of Chicago Press.

Bruner, J. (1990). *Acts of meaning*. Cambridge, MA: Harvard University Press.

Burke, K. (1945). Introduction: The five key terms of dramatism. In K. Burke (Ed.), *A grammar of motives* (pp. xv–xxiii). New York: Prentice Hall.

Burke, K. (1970). *The rhetoric of religion: Studies in logology*. Berkeley: University of California Press.

Campbell, J. C. (1949). *The hero with a thousand faces*. New York: Bollingen Foundation, Inc.

Chatman, S. (1978). *Story and discourse: Narrative structure in fiction and film*. Ithaca, NY: Cornell University Press.

Crane, R. (1952). *Critics and criticism ancient and modern*. Chicago: University of Chicago Press.

Cronon, W. (1992). A place for stories: Nature, history and narrative. *Journal of American History, 78*(4), 1347–1376.

Derrida, J. (1980). The law of genre, *Critical Inquiry 7*, 55–81.

de Man, P. (1979). *Allegories of reading*. New Haven, NJ: Yale University Press.

Ferguson, F. (1961). *Aristotle's poetics*. New York: Hill & Wang.

Fisher, W. R. (1984). Narration as human communication paradigm: The case of public moral argument, *Communication Monographs, 51*, 1–22.

Fisher, W. R. (1985). The narrative paradigm: An elaboration. *Communication Monographs, 52*, 347–367.

Fisher, W. R. (1987). *Human communication as narration: Toward a philosophy of reason, value, and action*. Columbia: University of South Carolina Press.

Frazier, J. G. (1922). *The golden bough*. New York: Macmillan.

Freud, S. (1999). *The interpretation of dreams*. New York: Oxford University Press.

Frye, N. (1957). *Anatomy of criticism*. Princeton, NJ: Princeton University Press.

Gee, J. P. (1985). The narrativization of experience in the oral style. *Journal of Education, 167*(1), 9–35.

Gee, J. P. (1986). Units in production of narrative discourse. *Discourse Processes, 9*, 391–422.

Gee, J. P. (1991). A linguistic approach to narrative. *Journal of Narrative and Life History, 1*(1), 15–39.

Ginzberg, F. (1989). Dissonance and harmony: The sumbolic function of abortion activists' life stories. In Personal Narratives Group (Ed.), *Interpreting women's lives: Feminist theory and personal narratives* (pp. 69–84). Indianapolis: Indiana University Press.

Gleik, J. (1987). *Chaos: Making a new science*. New York: Penguin Books.

Goodman, N. (1976). *Languages of art: An approach to the theory of symbols*. Indianapolis: Hackett Publishing Company.

Greimas, A. J. (1987). *On meaning: Selected writings in semiotic theory*. P. Perron & F. Collins (Trans.). Minneapolis: University of Minnesota Press.

Griffin, M. (1991). Defining visual communication for a multi-media world. *Journalism Educator, 46*(1), 9–15.

Gross, L. (1985). Life vs. Art: The interpretation of visual narratives. *Studies in Visual Communication, 4*, 2–11.

Hall, E. (1982). *The hidden dimension*. New York: Anchor Books.

Ingarden, R. (1973). *The cognition of the literary work of art*. R. A. Crowley & K. R. Olson (Trans.). Evanston, IL: Northwestern University Press.

Iser, W. (1978). *The act of reading: A theory of aesthetic response*. Baltimore: Johns Hopkins Press.

Jameson, F. (1981). *The political unconscious: Narrative as a socially symbolic act*. Ithaca: Cornell University Press.

Kosko, B. (1993). *Fuzzy thinking*. New York: Hyperion.

Labov, W. (1972). The transformation of experience in narrative syntax. In W. Labov (Ed.), *Language in the inner city: Studies in the Black English vernacular* (pp. 354–396). Philadelphia: University of Pennsylvania Press.

Labov, W. (1982). Speech actions and reactions in personal narrative. In D. Tannen (Ed.), *Analyzing discourse: Text and talk* (pp. 219–247). Washington, D.C.: Georgetown University Press.

Labov, W., & Waletzky, J. (1967). Narrative analysis: Oral versions of personal experience. In J. Helm (Ed.), *Essays on the verbal and visual arts* (pp. 12–44). Seattle: University of Washington Press.

Lacan, J. (1977). *Ecrits: A selection*. New York: Norton.

Langellier, K. (1999). Personal narrative, performance, performativity: Two or three things I know for sure. *Text and Performance Quarterly, 19*, 125–144.

Levi-Strauss, C. (1976–83). *Structural anthropology*. Chicago: University of Chicago Press.

Lukacs, G. (1971). *History and class consciousness: Studies in Marxist Dialectics*. R. Livingstone (Trans.) Cambridge: MIT Press.

MacIntyre, A. (1981). *After virtue: A study in moral theory*. Notre Dame, IN: University of Notre Dame Press.

Manning, P., & Cullum-Swan, B. (1994). Narrative, content and semiotic analysis. In N. Denzin and Y. Lincoln (Eds.), *Handbook of Qualitative Research* (pp. 463–477). Thousand Oaks, CA: Sage.

McCrone, J. (1994, August 20). Quantum states of mind. *New Scientist*, 35–37.

Metallinos, N. (1992). Visual Literacy: Suggested theories for the study of television pictures perception. *Journal of Visual Literacy, 12*(1), 57–72.

Miller, J. H. (1990). Narrative. In F. Lentricchia and T. McLaughlin (Eds.), *Critical terms for literary study* (pp. 66–79). Chicago: University of Chicago Press.

Mishler, E. G. (1986). *Research and interviewing: Context and narrative*. Cambridge, MA: Harvard University Press.

Moriarty, S. (1996). Abduction A theory of visual interpretation. *Communication Theory, 6*(2), 167–187.

Murray, K. (1989). The construction of identity in the narratives of romance and comedy. In J. Shotter and K. Gregen (Eds.), *Texts of identity* (pp. 176–205).

Neiva, E. (1999). Redefining the image: Mimesis, convention and semiotics. *Communication Theory, 9*(1), 75–91.

Polking, K., Bloss, J., & Cannon, C. (Eds.). (1983). *Writer's Encyclopedia*. Cincinnati, OH: Writer's Digest Books.

Poulet, G. (1996). *The metamorphoses of the circle*. C. Dawson & E. Coleman (Trans.). Baltimore, MD: Johns Hopkins Press.

Propp, V. (1970). *The morphology of the folktale*. L. Scott (Trans.). Austin: University of Texas Press.

Rabiger, M. (1998). *Directing the documentary* (3rd Ed.). Boston, MA: Focal Press.

Ricoeur, P. (1984–88). *Time and narrative*. Vols 1–3. K. McLaughlin & D. Pellauer (Trans). Chicago: University of Chicago Press.

Riessman, C. (1993). *Narrative analysis*. Newbury Park, CA: Sage.

Schrag, C. (1991). Interpretation, narrative and rationality. *Research in Phenomenology, 21*, 98–115.

Schrag, R. (1991). Sugar and spice and everything nice versus snakes and snails and puppy dogs' tails: Selling social stereotypes on Saturday morning television. In L. Vande Berg & L. Wenner (Eds.), *Television criticism: Approaches and applications* (pp. 220–232). New York: Longman.

Stafford, B. (1996). *Good looking: Essays on the virtue of images*. Cambridge, MA: MIT Press.

Stephens, M. (1998). *The rise of the image the fall of the word*. New York: Oxford University Press.

Todorov, T. (1977). *The poetics of prose*. R. Howard (Trans.). Ithaca, NY: Cornell University Press.

Turkle, S., & Papert, S. (1993). Epistemological pluralism and the revaluation of the concrete. In I. Harel & S. Papert (Eds.), *Constructivism* (pp. 161–192). Norwood, NJ: Ablex.

Turner, V. (1980). Social dramas and stories about them. *Critical Inquiry 7*, 141–168.

van Dijk, T. (1980). *Macrostructures: An interdisciplinary study of global discourse, interaction, and cognition*. Hillsdale, NJ: Lawrence Erlbaum Associates.

Wartofsky, M. (1980, April 8). Camera can't see: Representation, photography, and human vision Afterimage.

White, H. (1973). *Metahistory*. Baltimore, MD: Johns Hopkins Press.

White, R. (1989, July). Visual thinking in the Ice Age. *Scientific American, 261*(1), 92–99.

Worth, S. (1981). *Studying visual communication*. In L. Gross (Ed.), Philadelphia: University of Pennsylvania Press.

Wright, W. (1975). *Sixguns and society: A structural study of the Western*. Berkeley: University of California Press.

Zettl, H. (1999). *Sight, sound, motion: Applied media aesthetics*. Belmont, CA: Wadsworth.

Using Narrative Theory to Understand the Power of News Photographs

TRISCHA GOODNOW
Oregon State University

How do we come to know the things that we know? Walter Fisher (1984) suggested that we learn things through the stories that we tell. If we think back to grade school and our first formal learning experiences, they were steeped in stories. From the "See Spot" books to the word problems in mathematics, narratives or stories are primary teaching tools. However, it is not just the fundamentals of education we learn through stories, we also learn the goals and values that guide a particular culture and how to live in that society. Phillipsen called these cultural myths and said that they are "a great symbolic narrative which holds together the imagination of a people and provides bases of harmonious thought and action" (1987, p. 251).

An additional way that we come to know things is by observing them. We take in information visually and assess that information via the adage that seeing is believing. Often this visual information comes in the form of the photograph. We know that the Great Wall of China exists because we have heard stories and seen photographs. Without the photograph, however, we could believe the Great Wall a myth. With the evidence in the photograph we have a believable proof that it is a tangible thing.[1]

The idea that society is guided by cultural myths that are not tangible things brings us to the question that guides this study. How do we know cultural myths are valid? I suggest here that, in part, we look for tangible evidence that either supports or challenges those myths. This tangible evidence can come in the form of the news photograph. These photos have the power to shock a society into challenging its cultural myths.

A few scholars have theorized about the narrative power of the photo image. A narrative is a story with a beginning, a middle, and an end, for example, and Maurice Berger (1992) argued that photographs are traumatic precisely because they lack the beginning and the end. The viewer has no recourse to prevent the events leading up to those in the photograph and can do nothing to stop the unfolding of events alluded to in the photo. Similarly, Vicki Goldberg in *The Power of Photography: How Photographs Changed Our Lives* suggested that "Photographs are tiny moments sliced from the flow of time" (1991, p. 223).

Using Walter Fisher's concept of the narrative paradigm, I illustrate how news photographs can challenge, affirm, or reaffirm cultural myths. I do this by first exploring the narrative paradigm and giving consideration to the idea of news photographs and cultural myths. Next, I examine three famous news images and consider how they challenged, affirmed, or reconfirmed publicly held beliefs. Finally, I draw implications from this analysis.

THE NARRATIVE PARADIGM AND THE NATURE OF THE NEWS PHOTOGRAPH

Fisher (1984) contended that humans are essentially storytellers; we come to know things through the stories we hear and tell. He also suggested, "the narrative paradigm insists that human communication should be viewed as historical as well as situational, as stories competing with other stories constituted by good reasons, as being rational when they satisfy the demands of narrative probability and narrative fidelity" (1984, p. 2). Narrative probability is the story's internal consistency; does the story make sense on its own? Narrative fidelity tests the story's external consistency; does the story ring true with what we know to be true in the real world? By judging the story's narrative probability and fidelity, we can make judgments about the story and whether we should believe that the story is true and rational. Accordingly, stories are compared to determine which is the story to be believed.

As a nation, we hold certain truths about how we live and how our nation survives to be inviolable. Fisher (1984) considered these truths narratives, and they are what Phillipsen (1987) called cultural myths. These are the stories against which governmental and personal actions are evaluated. For example, as Americans, we understand that the United States is the land of opportunity. If you work hard, you can achieve success. This is the Horatio Alger story and it is a driving force in life in the United States. Certain factions of society have come to realize that this story isn't true for everyone; other factors interfere with the opportunity. The cultural myth is questioned when evidence proves otherwise.

That evidence sometimes comes in the form of the news photograph. Barthes (1977) argued, for example, that the photograph itself is purely denotative, relaying the reality of the scene it portrays. As the public sees the photograph, it interprets the elements of the photograph to discern its meaning. Kobre argued that "multiple pictures, likewise, remain individual images unless they are integrated into a cohesive narrative" (2000, p. 12). With the news photograph, there is always a caption that frames the photograph and places it into a larger context. This larger context creates the narrative of the photograph. Berger (1992) contended that the caption reinterprets the space of the photograph providing clues as to the before and after of the photograph. Consequently, the photograph becomes part of the relaying of the narrative and can be judged along with the rest of the narrative for its rationality and the rationality of the larger narrative.

Most Americans conduct their daily lives certain of the safety and stability of life in the United States. Why do we feel that way? Probably because we are told in a variety of different ways on a daily basis that the United States is the best nation on earth. We are told in stories on the news about neighbors helping each other, commercials that espouse the abundance of the good life through convenience and goods, and movies that tell stories about our leaders conquering our foes. If we learn things through stories then American popular culture tells us to not worry, we've got the good life. So, we live our lives buying into that story. Why would we ever stop believing the story? If we had sufficient evidence to prove otherwise, we might start to believe a different story, to rewrite the original story. News photographs and the accompanying captions often provide that evidence.

Fisher's (1984) notions of narrative probability and narrative fidelity provide a theoretical grounds for understanding, in part, the power of the news photograph to challenge, affirm, or reconfirm the narratives of which they are part. First, a photograph must meet the standard of narrative probability or internal consistency. For a photograph, this translates into the believability of the photograph as an image of reality. Barthes contended, we remember, that the photograph can be taken as "the pure and simple denotation of reality" (1977, p. 28). At the same time, if we were to see a photograph of an adult Tom Hanks shaking hands with President Kennedy (as he did as Forrest Gump in the movie of the same name), we would understand that photograph not to be believable because Kennedy was dead long before Hanks reached adulthood. Narrative fidelity tests the photograph's syncopation with what we know to be true of the world. A tabloid photograph of George W. Bush shaking hands with a two-headed alien would be deemed to have low narrative fidelity as such an occurrence would probably make more than just tabloid headlines were it true. In this sense, photographs can be judged for their narrative rationality in much the same way that linguistic stories can be judged.

Photographs are different from linguistic narratives, however. The author of a verbal story chooses words that comprise the story. As a result, verbal stories necessarily leave something out as words can only highlight elements of the story. In this leaving out, verbal stories are subject to a much greater degree of manipulation yet still retain their narrative probability and narrative fidelity. Photographs, on the other hand, highlight in total one element of the story, usually its key event. We assume the photograph provides the truth of the moment. The caption frames this moment and reduces the before and after facts of the narrative to one line. Berger asserted, "The caption provides a handle, a means by which language, in the act of constructing a logical narrative, may reenter the space of the photograph" (1992, p. 14). The reduction of the narrative is there except in the moment of the photograph.

I argue here that it is precisely because we make these judgments about the narrative probability and narrative rationality of news photographs that these photographs have the power to challenge, affirm, or reconfirm our own societal narratives that guide much of our living. Because photographs provide evidence of their own narrative probability and narrative fidelity, they can raise doubts about previously held beliefs and, thus, challenge a cultural myth. In other words, if society believes one thing and a photograph clearly shows that another belief is possible, society must question the authenticity of the original belief. In addition, when society at large starts to challenge the cultural myth but cannot be sure whether the original cultural myth or the new narrative should be believed, photographs may provide evidence to affirm the new beliefs. Finally, when cultural myths are shaken with incontrovertible proof, the public may search for some evidence to reaffirm the original narrative and restore faith in the society's core beliefs. Berger (1992) called this "nostalgia for the norm." He cites, for example, photographs by Matthew Brady and George Barnard during the Civil War that are absent of corpses, clearly not an accurate portrayal as the casualties from that war were the greatest in American history. Trachtenberg suggested of this absence, "By memorializing, celebrating, remembering as sacred, [these] images participate in the process of making whole again, restoring American society to its familiar place in the bosom of nature" (1989, p. 23). Certain photographs, then, can restore the cultural myth to which people are accustomed. News photographs, because of their high narrative probability, can help the public to adjust their beliefs about cultural myths accordingly.

We can test these ideas by examining the power of three news photographs and the narratives they force the public to challenge, affirm, or reaffirm.

NEWS PHOTOGRAPHS

Oklahoma City Bombing

On the morning of April 19, 1995, Timothy McVeigh and coconspirators ignited a fertilizer bomb outside the Alfred P. Murrah Federal Building in Oklahoma City. The explosion killed 168 people including several children who had been at a day-care center in the building. A bank clerk and amateur photographer, Charles H. Porter IV, heard the explosion from his office a few blocks away and grabbed his camera to take photos of what he thought was a building being demolished. Instead, he saw a fireman carrying a baby from the ruins of the federal building. He snapped several shots and took the roll of film to a one-hour developing store. The baby was later identified as one-year-old Baylee Almon, who was pronounced dead at the scene. Porter sold the rights to the Associated Press who circulated the photo worldwide where it appeared on newspaper and magazine covers as the image to represent the Oklahoma City bombing. In 1996, Porter was awarded the Pulitzer Prize for Spot News Reporting.

Narrative Probability

The photograph of the firefighter holding a bloodied child has high narrative probability because it is a firefighter's duty to offer aid to those in distress. Although the photo is tragic, it is unfortunately believable without any further contextualization. No further information is necessary to make the photo a narrative by itself.

Narrative Fidelity

Narrative fidelity can be judged by a piece of rhetoric's believability against what is thought to be known of the real world. In this case study, we can judge a news photograph against what is thought to be true in everyday life. In the United States, in spite of evidence to the contrary, Americans feel that they are safe in the execution of their normal routines. Indeed, we feel safe in our homeland; we believe that terrorist attacks only happen elsewhere. Prior to the Oklahoma City Bombing, the United States had been relatively immune from citizens terrorizing both other citizens and the government, at least on such a grand scale.

Although the United States had been victim to terrorist attacks, especially in light of the Civil War and the Civil Rights Movement, those attacks were deemed to be targeted toward specific groups intent on upsetting daily life for a specific purpose. Attacks against the union and on minority populations were said to be the product of home-bred dissatisfaction with specific governmental policies. With the Oklahoma City bombing, however, citizens were confronted with the idea that fellow citizens would take drastic actions to announce to the public their dissatisfaction with those governmental policies. Indeed, news reports in the days and weeks following the bombing reported widespread disbelief that such an event could happen and that the perpetrator was a U.S. citizen. In fact, early reports after the bombing drew the conclusion that this was an act of international terrorism. Still, Americans were caught up in the belief that terrorism only happens elsewhere and that American citizens would never perpetrate such evil. *The Toronto Sun* speculated that "Americans could not accept that it was quite possible such a cowardly and horrible act against innocent people could have been committed by one or more of their own" (Raynier, 1995, p. 12).

Analysis

At nearly the same time that Porter snapped his shot, a gas company employee for Oklahoma National Gas, Lester LaRue, heard the explosion and grabbed his camera, capturing a nearly identical photo to Porter's. LaRue sold his photograph to *Newsweek* and it, too, appeared in countless newspapers and magazines. LaRue was involved in a lengthy court battle with Oklahoma Natural Gas as to the rights to the photograph. The photographs are nearly identical.

The primary differences between the photographs are two: first, the angles are slightly different with LaRue's photo to the right of Porter's (this is discernable by shadow placement and background images), and second, Porter's photo has a person in the bottom right corner of the frame, though the person is sometimes cropped out of the photo. The pose of the central figures in the picture, the firefighter with the child in his arms, is identical. At first glance, the photos seem interchangeable. Hence, the mainstream public would only perceive there to be a singular photo. This is important to note because my interest here is in how news photographs challenge cultural myths. The fact that there are two photographs that have both been widely viewed implies that it is the meaning behind the image rather than the image itself that creates the power of the photograph. Hence, when officials refer to "the photograph" the public understands that it is the firefighter's photo but not whether it is Porter's or LaRue's version.

Consequently, commentary on "the photograph" doesn't specify whether it is Porter's or LaRue's photograph. The broad image itself is what captured people's attention. With two photographs substantially the same and both widely circulated, it was the meaning behind the photograph that became important, not which photograph people meant. Tommy Almon, Baylee Almon's grandfather, said, "It was the photo felt around the world" (Strupp, 1995). David Longstreath (1995), Associated Press state photo editor, says the photo was everything that was indicative of the bombing—one of those rare shots that gives the entire story in a way that words cannot. Oklahoma Governor Frank Keating explained that the photo was "a metaphor for what's happened here" (People, 1995, p. 35). All of these comments assumed one photograph. We can consider now what the meaning behind both photographs implied in light of narrative theory.

When the Oklahoma City bombing occurred, Americans had to readjust and reevaluate the narrative that they believed about domestic tranquility and safety. The United States has been subject to both domestic and foreign terrorist attacks virtually from its beginnings. However, the Oklahoma City bombing was the first large-scale bombing that took place in the United States without any immediately revealing material as to why the attack took place or who did it. "The killer stole a fortune that day—lives, love, hope and our disbelief that a thing like that could ever happen here" (Mathis, 1997, p. 6). This reevaluation was due primarily to the fact that the narrative no longer had narrative fidelity or external consistency. What Americans thought to be true was violently shattered. The evidence of the new possible narrative was evident in the photograph of the firefighter holding the lifeless body of Baylee Almon. The photograph had become a symbol of what Americans were capable of doing to one another. Without the visual evidence, supported by the verbal contextualization, the original narrative could have been restored with a dismissive notion of "it wasn't that bad," "it was just a government building." However, the image of the firefighter and child made the horror of the tragedy impossible to deny. The original narrative was then left in doubt; if it could happen in Oklahoma City then it could happen anywhere in the United States. The claim here is not that the shift in narrative reality is because of the photograph. Rather, the photograph provides incontrovertible proof that the public narrative must be questioned.

If the firefighter photo from Oklahoma City illustrates how an image can make us question our beliefs about our nation, an analysis of another photograph may provide evidence that such questioning is justified.

The My Lai Massacre

On March 16, 1968, the men of Charlie Company, under the leadership of Captain Ernest Medina, with First Lieutenant William L. Calley Jr., expected to meet great opposition from the Vietcong during the Vietnam War. However, on this day they did not meet enemy soldiers. Instead, they encountered women, children, and the elderly; the U.S. soldiers murdered many of the residents of a nearby village. This event became known as the My Lai Massacre. When first reported, American newspapers only reported military casualties, no civilians. On the day of the massacre, however, an army photographer, Ron Haberle, had accompanied the troops. The official photographs he had taken were in black and white, the subject matter benign. He also had his own camera with color film. These photos he kept and the photographs showed evidence of the brutal massacre of civilians, including children.

Stories of the civilian casualties made the rounds, and they eventually led to a military investigation in which, Lieutenant Calley was charged with murder, the attack garnered passing but little news attention. When Haberle saw the brief news reports, he decided to go public with his photographs in November 1968 and contacted a *Cleveland Plain Dealer* reporter, Joe Eszterhas. When Eszterhas told his editor that he had world exclusive photographs, the editor reportedly said to forget the scoop because a moonwalk was scheduled the next day. After seeing the photographs, he said to forget the moonwalk because it was just a routine moonwalk (Hersch, 1970). The photograph that was printed first on *The Plain Dealer*'s front page on November 20 and then on the cover of almost every American newspaper was a pile of bodies in the middle of a road, including dead babies and small children. Television news programs showed the still photos on their broadcasts the night *The Plain Dealer* published the photos. With the widespread dissemination of the photographs, the story was clearly in the news and led to investigations of the photographs and the events that led to the massacre.

Narrative Probability

The photograph of a pile of bodies including babies and small children is, at first, misleading. At first glance, the bodies do not stand out. Rather, there appears to be a pile of clothes in the road. However, a closer examination reveals the bloody corpses including partially clothed children and babies. The shocking subject matter alerts the viewer to the possibility of its authenticity and begs the question, "How did this happen?" With the probability that the photograph depicted a real situation, the narrative fidelity of the photograph to American perceptions about the war in Vietnam was called into question.

Narrative Fidelity

Americans believe that the United States holds the values of justice and human life as supreme values. When the United States enters into war it is to uphold these values. During the Vietnam War, many Americans felt that the purposes behind the war not only did not uphold justice but also cost American lives. Consequently, the United States being in war did not fit the paradigm that some Americans believed justified war. As a result, some could not support the war. These strongly held beliefs are changed only when we have good evidence to prove that the narrative no longer fits. The My Lai photograph provided that proof.

Goldberg asserted about the My Lai photograph and other photos from the same incident, "The effect of these pictures depended on their power as evidence of a brutal event" (1991, p. 233). *Newsweek* reported, "It was only after photographs purporting to show the alleged massacre had appeared in *The Cleveland Plain Dealer*—and had been snapped up by *Life* magazine—that editors and readers began to feel reasonably convinced that the episode had occurred at all" (1969, p. 35). Although American sentiment toward the war had been suspect for a time, the My Lai Massacre photo gave credence to the brutal acts that some American soldiers were committing. This, in turn, forced Americans to reevaluate the noble motives of America's involvement in Vietnam. Americans could no longer deny the rumors of the atrocities that some American soldiers committed.

Analysis

Although the emotions and beliefs of Americans surrounding the Vietnam War are more complex than can be explicated here or by the analysis of a single photograph, the narrative probability of the photograph asked viewers to question the narrative to which the photographs' fidelity would be compared. That the photograph was believable forced Americans to reevaluate the narrative of a just war and give credence to the opposing opinion that Vietnam was not fought honorably. This photograph was but one piece of evidence in the onslaught of information about American motives and actions in Vietnam. But this one piece of evidence was a powerful force in reasserting a different narrative about war.

The photo from the My Lai Massacre enabled citizens to affirm doubts about the nation's motives in Vietnam, sparking further speculation and investigation. Other photos help to reaffirm the original narrative when faced with doubt about the veracity of a long held narrative.

The World Trade Center

September 11, 2001, is a day that most Americans will never forget. Four planes were hijacked by terrorists. The first plane crashed into the North Tower of the World Trade Center and then the second plane crashed into the South Tower. A third plane hit the Pentagon in Washington, D.C. The final plane crashed into a field in Pennsylvania. Within an hour and a half, both towers of the World Trade Center collapsed, killing thousands of office workers and rescue personnel.

At five in the afternoon of September 11, a photographer for the Bergen County *The Record*, Thomas Franklin, was finishing shooting photos of the destruction of Ground Zero for the day. He was on a pedestrian foot bridge when he saw three firefighters raising a flag from a yacht in the nearby harbor. The firefighters were raising a 5 foot by 3 foot flag onto the remains of a flagpole with the rubble of the World Trade Centers in the background. Franklin took the photo that reminded him of the flag raising at Iwo Jima from World War II (Hampson, 2001). Within a few hours the photograph was transmitted around the world by the Associated Press and was a finalist for the 2002 Pulitzer Prize for Breaking News Photography.

The images from September 11 are indelibly seared into the minds of most Americans, few of them positive. The flag-raising photo is surely not the only image that comes to mind of the terrorist attacks but it is clearly one of the most powerful images to surface. An examination of the narrative power of this photograph may help explain its power.

Narrative Probability

The main image in the flag-raising photo, the firemen raising a flag, is not particularly startling. As with the Oklahoma City bombing photo, firemen are caught doing an action to which the public is accustomed, raising flags. It is only a close examination that reveals the rubble amidst which the flag is being raised that creates the unusual setting for a standard activity. However, that firefighters would raise a flag is itself believable. Only when the photograph is tested within the cultural myths that were being questioned does the photo take on significant proportions.

Narrative Fidelity

The images of the planes hitting the towers were unbelievable. Even more unbelievable was the fact that the United States was so vulnerable to such a massive terrorist attack within our own borders. Most business and action stopped as Americans and people around the world watched as the reality of what happened sank in. The Federal Aviation Administration shut down airports for several days. Most sporting events were canceled until the following week. That Americans were frightened is undeniable; the airline industry is still trying to recover from the attacks. The idea that U.S. citizens were safe in their own country had been shattered.

The flag-raising photo offered hope in a hopeless situation, reasserting that the United States would survive this attack and triumph in the face of adversity. This affirmed the previously held belief that the United States could surmount its troubles. *USA Today* asserts that the photo is "a vision of defiance and courage at a moment of fear and retreat" (Hampson, 2001, p. 1A). Mary Panzer, a cultural historian, says that the composition of the photo allows the viewer "to get a sense of the firemen's accomplishment" (Hampson, 2001, p. 1A). Frankin, the photographer, noted the symbolism in the photograph and "the tremendous courage of these guys in the face of such destruction" (Torpey-Kemph, 2001, p. 36). The mayor of New York City at the time of the attacks, Rudolf Giuliani, claimed that the photograph "proved the terrorists did not achieve their ultimate goal of breaking the nation's spirit" (Robin, 2001, p. A06). Clearly, at this time, Americans needed reassurance that the country would survive, and could be that place of safety and stability. The flag-raising photograph provided that reassurance.

Analysis

The evidence in the photograph, or its narrative probability, allowed viewers to reaffirm their belief in what they thought to be true of the world, the narrative fidelity of the photograph. In this instance what viewers thought to be true in the real world was shaken. The photograph reaffirmed for viewers that their beliefs were justified.

The unmistakable similarity to the Iwo Jima flag-raising photo from World War II provided in part this reassurance. Fussell said of the Pulitzer Prize–winning photograph by Joe Rosenthal that it is a successful "emblem of the common will triumphant" (1982, p. 232). And, Goldberg suggested the photo "has endured as an icon of American patriotism" (1991, p. 147). Given the resemblance of the New York firefighter's photo to the Iwo Jima photo and the same need for the American public to feel reassured about

American survivability, it is not surprising that the New York photo could fulfill this function. Franklin's photo will most likely attain a similar place in history as the Iwo Jima photo because a postage stamp bearing the photo's image has been issued and a statue in its likeness was proposed.[2] In addition, the photo has been replicated on T-shirts and mugs, and editorialized in cartoons and countless other venues. Perhaps the potential for the endurance of this photo confirms the function that the subject of the photo fills for its viewers: reaffirming the idea that the United States is strong and will triumph.

IMPLICATIONS

News photographs are often taken as a record of an event by both their viewers and their creators. They provide proof of a narrative of the events that led to the subject of the photograph. However, to understand why certain images become part of a public consciousness, we need to understand the roll that certain news photographs play in a greater cultural myth. Although it is not my purpose to justify why certain photographs remain icons while others fade away, it is my contention that we can help to explain the power of certain photographs when they challenge, affirm, or reconfirm ingrained cultural myths.

Some photographs tell a complete story on their own, such as the Oklahoma City firefighter photo. The uniform on the firefighter implies some type of disaster and the lifeless child relays the depths of the tragedy. Although we don't know the specifics of that particular tragedy, we know that a tragic story has occurred. Were that photograph from a house fire caused by faulty wiring, the photo would have made the front page but would have faded from public memory relatively soon. However, when that photograph becomes part of the story of the Oklahoma City bombing, it starts to have a longer shelf life. Indeed, when it starts to represent a challenge to deeply held social beliefs about our safety from domestic terrorists, it becomes an icon set to remind us of a new reality. Only when we view this photo as part of the cultural myth do we start to understand the power of the photograph.

The fact that news photographs play into a larger cultural myth alone does not convince us of their power. The incontrovertible proof of news photographs of their own truth, their narrative probability, forces a reexamination of the cultural myths that surround the photograph. When we judge the narrative fidelity of the news photo, we are left to question the story against which the photo is judged. In doing so, the cultural myth may be challenged, affirmed, or reconfirmed.

CONCLUSION

The purpose of this chapter is to assert, in part, the power of the news photograph. I contend that this power lies in the positioning of the news photograph in the greater cultural myth of which it is part. News photographs do not relay elements only in the immediate context in which they are found; rather they are also elements of the cultural myth. Because they provide proof of their own veracity they have the power to challenge, affirm, or reconfirm that larger narrative. When viewers consider why news photographs disturb us, we should consider the photographs and the cultural myth of which they are part. We hold cultural myths to be inviolate, except when we are given reason to challenge them. News photographs often give us reason to do just that.

ENDNOTES

[1] I assume here that we are talking of unaltered photographs; photographs that have not been altered in terms of subject matter. Photographers may adjust lighting, perspective and framing. However, cropping subjects, adding subjects or joining subjects to purposefully mislead is not the intended subject of the current essay as other works deal in great length with photomanipulation. See, for example, Brugioni (1999) *Photo Fakery.*

[2] A statue based on Franklin's photograph was proposed to commemorate the terrorist attacks. However, the commission planning the statue wanted to change the race of the original three white firefighters to include one African-American and one Hispanic firefighter to represent the diversity of people who lost their lives trying to rescue victims of the attacks. The proposed changes caused great controversy and plans for the statue were scrapped.

REFERENCES

Barthes, R. (1977). *Image, music, text*. London: Fontana / Collins.

Berger, J., & Mohr, J. (1982). *Another way of telling*. New York: Pantheon.

Berger, M. (1992). *How art becomes history: Essays on art, society, and culture in post-New Deal America*. New York: HarperCollins.

Brugioni, D. A. (1999). *Photo fakery: The history and techniques of photographic deception and manipulation*. Dulles, VA: Brassey's.

Fisher, W. R. (1984). Narration as a human communication paradigm: The case of the public moral argument. *Communication Monographs, 51*, 1–22.

Fussell, P. (1982). *The boy scout handbook and other observations*. New York: Oxford University Press.

Goldberg, V. (1991). *The power of photography: How photographs changed our lives*. New York: Abbeville Publishing Group.

Hampson, R. (2001, December 27). The photo no one will forget. *USA Today*, p. 1A.

Hersh, S. (1970). *My Lai 4: A report on the massacre and its aftermath*. New York: Random House.

Kobre, K. (2000, January). Narrative storytelling. *Visual Communication Quarterly, 55*, 12–13.

Mathis, D. (1997, June 8). McVeigh's senseless bomb blew nation's doubts away. *The Houston Chronicle*, 6.

Newsweek. (1969, December 1). Song My: A U.S. atrocity?, 35.

People. (1995, May 8). Tiny symbol of life and death, 56.

Phillipsen, G. (1987). The prospect for cultural communication. In D. Kincaid (Ed.), *Communication theory: Eastern and Western perspectives* (pp. 245–254). New York: Academic Press.

Raynier, M. (1995, April 29). Objective reporting lost in hysteria. *The Toronto Sun*, 12.

Robin, J. (2001, December 22). "Flag-raising" statue unveiled; Model inspired by Sept. 11 photo. *Newsday*, A06.

Strupp, J. (1995, May 13). The photo felt around the world. [online source] *Editor & Publisher, 128*, 12–14.

Torpey-Kemph, A. (2001, September 24). Franklin's firemen: The shot seen 'round the world. *Media Week, 11*, 36.

Trachtenberg, A. (1989). *Reading American photographs: Images as history, Matthew Brady to Walker Evans*. New York: Hill & Wang.

Media Aesthetics

Aesthetics Theory

HERBERT ZETTL
San Francisco State University

INTRODUCTION

When reading film and television reviews, we are usually told by the critics whether the characters and their actions are believable or not, whether the plot has a logical development, whether it is too simple or too complex, and whether the setting is befitting the story. Occasionally, we learn about the director's skill or lack of it, or the creative or unimaginative camera work. But rarely, if ever, do these critics mention the specifics of lighting, picture composition, the continuity of shots, and the role of sound effects. This is understandable, because such media-aesthetic factors work mostly underground. In fact, one of the criteria for good editing is that it is seamless, and for effective film music, that it remains largely unnoticed by the audience. However, such meta-messages are crucial for the clarification and intensification of the various messages, and for how we finally interpret and feel about a particular television show or film. Even the creators of such media fare are often unaware of the perceptual effect a specific type of lighting or sound effect will produce, at least not until such an effect has been applied. What we obviously need for a more precise analysis and synthesis—production—of video, film, and computer presentations is a system that allows a closer look at the various aesthetic media factors, how they function, and how they interact. Applied media aesthetics is such a system.[1]

WHAT IS APPLIED MEDIA AESTHETICS?

Applied media aesthetics differs from traditional aesthetics in several fundamental ways. (a) Whereas traditional aesthetics deals principally with the question of what is beautiful and what is not, how we derive pleasure from it, and what art is and why we have it, applied media aesthetics deals primarily with how static and moving-screen images and sound are structured for maximally effective communication. (b) Traditional aesthetics and even the established methods of textual media analysis are primarily intended and useful for the analysis of existing works. Media aesthetics, on the other hand, can be successfully applied not only to analysis, but also to synthesis—the creation of screen events, such as movies, television shows, and various forms of Web displays. In comparison to semiotics, which is useful but limited to the decoding of messages and deconstruction of texts, the theoretical concepts of media aesthetics enjoy a greatly expanded use—the encoding and construction of messages and media texts. (c) Prompted by the original meaning of the Greek *aisthetike*, sense perception, and *aisthanomai*, perceiving, or more accurately, "I perceive," applied media aesthetics examines the various basic image elements of screen events, such as light, screen space, and sound, and how they can be structured for optimal clarification, intensification, and intended perception of media events. (d) The medium is no longer considered as a neutral channel for the convenient distribution of content, but as an essential component in the decoding (analysis) and encoding (production) processes.

Fundamental Elements and Structural Fields

Specifically, media aesthetics examines five basic aesthetic image elements that provide the aesthetic *materia*—the raw material—of television, film, and computer-generated images: (a) light and color, (b) two-dimensional space, (c) three-dimensional space, (d) time-motion, and (e) sound. A close examination of these elements shows their inherent properties, their basic functions, and their potential use.

The five corresponding aesthetic fields provide a theoretical setting in which these elements are analyzed or structured according to the technical and production requirements of various media. These aesthetic fields also promote the contextual use of the basic elements so that their combined aesthetic effect, their meta-messages, can be more readily detected and, at least to some extent, predicted in the preproduction and production stages. The aesthetic fields, rather than their specific elements, ultimately determine the degree of clarification and intensification of the screen event and the resulting meta-messages that establish the context for their interpretation by the audience.

Meta-Messages

Meta-messages set the perceptual agenda for the viewers. They are created not by explicit narrative, but by the more elusive aesthetic production variables. They are primarily responsible for providing the all-important background against which we tend to interpret all literal aspects of the event. Nonverbal meta-messages function similar to our first impressions when meeting somebody. We readily embrace the statements and actions of the person that fit into our first impression and tend to ignore the ones that go against it. In most cases, we have a hard time abandoning the initial frame of reference to hear without bias what the person is actually saying and doing. Indeed, our everyday perception of the world is never free of a perceptual bias. This bias is inevitably dictated by a variety of contextual meta-messages (Festinger, 1957). If possible at all, it takes great effort and skill to isolate an event from our perceptual prejudices (Spinelli, 1989; Zettl, 1998). Some philosophers claim that the really real is simply unknowable (Kant, 1956).[2]

Even if the contextual clues are relatively extant and obvious, we have a hard time not falling under their spell.

Let's visualize a man walking along the edge of a bluff above the ocean beach. In the first scene, he is happy and about to join his wife and children playing on the beach. In the second scene, he is extremely depressed. He has just lost his job, his wife and children have left him, and he feels that the world has come to a stop. We probably visualize the two scenes quite differently. But let's for a moment assume that we are required to use the identical footage of the man walking in both scenes and generate the difference in feeling simply by changing a few of the contextual aesthetic elements, such as lighting, color, and sound. In the first scene, we could show the bright colors of a sunny day and use the sounds of a gentle surf and laughter of children playing. For the second scene, we do away with colors and render the entire event in black and white. The sky is now covered with dark clouds. The surf is much louder and crashing against the rocks and, instead of the children's laughter, we hear the penetrating cries of seagulls. Whereas the main action remains exactly the same, the different aesthetic variables provide different contexts for opposite meta-messages—one of a joyful reunion with the children, the other of despair and anguish.[3]

The Russian film theorist Lev Kuleshov demonstrated the effect of creating meta-messages through a specific editing montage over 80 years ago. In one of his experiments, he juxtaposed expressionless close-ups of the famous actor Mosjukhin with shots of a bowl of soup, a dead woman in a coffin, and a little girl playing with her toy bear. According to his colleague Pudovkin:

> The public raved about the acting of the artist. They pointed out the heavy pensiveness of his mood over the forgotten soup, were touched and moved by the deep sorrow with which he looked on the dead, and admired the the light, happy smile with which he surveyed the girl at play. (1960, p. 168)

Such montage effects, in which various seemingly unrelated events are juxtaposed, are designed to create specific meta-messages. Meaning is induced not by the actual content of either of the two event elements, but by their juxtaposition. In effect, the meaning is not told, but generated in the viewer's head (Husserl, 1973; McLuhan, 1964).[4] But how do we know just what cognitive and affective effects the specific media-aesthetic elements and their combinations will have on the viewer? Let's take a look at the functions of the major elements and their structural fields.

THE FIRST AESTHETIC FIELD: LIGHTING

The electronic screen images of television and computers are, like film images, basically light shows. They all display their images as continual variations of colors and brightness (light and dark values). The control of light and shadows, commonly called lighting, is therefore one of the major aesthetic components.

Lighting Purposes and Functions

Lighting articulates our outer environment and the things in it. It shows what objects look like and where they are located relative to their surroundings. Lighting has also a direct influence on inner environment, our emotions. Like music, it seems to bypass our rational faculties and has us perceive its contextual meta-messages without first subjecting them to critical judgment. In creating specific lighting effects, we frequently need to pay much more attention to shadow control than to basic illumination. Attached shadows, which lie on the opposite side of the principal light source and are seen as property of the lighted object, define the basic shape of the object. Through the proper control of attached shadows, we can make a ball look round or more like a disc, emphasize the wrinkles in a face, or practically eliminate them.

Cast shadows, which can be seen independent of the object that causes them, can tell us where the object is located relative to its surroundings, roughly indicate the time of the day, and create interesting patterns. Despite their omnipresence on a sunny day, such as the cast shadows of trees, traffic lights, and utility poles, we are largely unaware of them. Yet they are a powerful and reliable agent for altering our inner orientation and for creating a specific mood.

A brightly lighted street corner with a minimum of shadows makes us feel relatively safe, even if past midnight. We can see quite well what is going on around us. But if the same street corner is sparsely illuminated, the lack of sufficient illumination and the preponderance of long cast shadows make us inevitably feel less comfortable. Lighting a person from below eye level results in the well-worn, yet effective, horror lighting cliché. We instinctively perceive the person not simply in a different light, but as the villain. Why? Because this lighting technique reverses the resulting attached and cast shadows and makes them fall upward, against our everyday experiences.

The manipulation of light and shadows is especially important in creating lighting effects synthetically through computer programs. The simulated light source does not automatically place the resulting attached and cast shadows on the opposite side. In fact, their direction, length, density (solid or transparent), and falloff (how quickly the lighted side turns into the shadow side) must be carefully programmed. For example, when an object is obviously lighted from directly above, it can't simultaneously cast a long shadow. Simulating a moving light source in which the shadows change accordingly makes the programming all the more complicated.

Chiaroscuro Lighting and Flat Lighting

The two principal lighting types are chiaroscuro and flat. Chiaroscuro lighting (from the Italian *chiaro* = light, and *oscuro* = dark) is a direct copy of the way two famous chiaroscuro painters, Caravaggio and Rembrandt, distributed the light and dark areas in their pictures. Like their paintings, chiaroscuro lighting usually shows a dark background, specific areas that are illuminated while others are kept dark, and fast-falloff attached and cast shadows. Because of its selectivity, this type of lighting, also called low-key lighting, can be highly dramatic (Millerson, 1991). We can readily observe the predominance of chiaroscuro lighting in soap operas, dramas, and crime and science fiction shows.

Flat lighting is just the opposite. Instead of using lighting instruments that throw a highly directional light beam, flat lighting uses flood lights, such as fluorescent light banks, that produce a highly diffused, practically shadowless illumination. It provides maximum visibility, but lacks the spatial definition that attached and cast shadows provide. Instead of the stark dramatic character of chiaroscuro, flat lighting suggests efficiency and cleanliness. Department stores, high-tech factories, and hospitals all have flat lighting. But it can also signal mechanization and depersonalization. Because flat lighting practically eliminates attached shadows, or at lest renders them highly transparent, it is a favorable lighting technique for commercials, news, and interviews.

High-key lighting is a form of flat lighting. It usually shows an overabundance of omnidirectional light, slow falloff, transparent shadows, and a light background. High-key lighting is used in the more high-energy, up-beat and cheerful situation comedies and game shows.

Recall the man walking along the bluff above the beach. The high-key lighting in the first beach scene supported the meta-message of joy; the low-key lighting (dark clouds) underscored the ominous mood.

THE EXTENDED FIRST FIELD: COLOR

Color fulfills three major functions: (a) It gives us more information about objects and events and lets us distinguish among them, (b) it can contribute to the visual balance of a screen image, and (c) it can express the essential quality of things, add excitement to an event, and help establish a mood.

Traffic signals operate on the informational function of color: Red and yellow mean stop (although many drivers seem to interpret yellow as "step-on-it"), and green means go. As in real life, the informational function is important in all screen events.

The weather map in television and on Web pages operates on certain agreed on color codes. When the script of a chase scene requests to "Follow the red car!" we obviously can't shoot in black and white. Any monochrome rendering of a screen event eradicates the informational function of color.

The problem of using colors to achieve screen balance is difficult in television and film because everything moves. Rather than applying the traditional canons of color balance, it is often better to set off high-energy colors (colors with high saturation that are loud and active, such a fire-engine red) against a low-energy background (colors with low saturation, such as beige, light green, or off-white). A high-energy dance number, in which the dancers wear colorful costumes would certainly lose some of its impact if performed in front of an equally high-energy color background. On the other hand, a more neutral background would certainly emphasize the color of the dancers' costumes and, in turn, intensify the whole dance number. Lighting helps in this color-energy balancing. By keeping the background relatively dark, the background colors become desaturated. Set off against a lower-energy background, the foreground colors in the brightly lighted action areas are intensified.

The expressive function of color is closely associated with the relative color energy. A child picks a red ball because it looks more active and promises more fun than a gray one. If we were now to imagine a new Corvette racing through tight curves, what color does it have? Probably red. Do we now visualize the Rolls Royce that is standing in front of an elegant mansion also in red? Probably not. We more prefer it to be silver, white, or black. But why? Media aesthetics can give a more precise answer. The high-energy red stresses external events, such as a high-powered sports car tearing up the road. The red color is, therefore, more suited to intensify the raw energy of the Corvette than the quiet luxury of the Rolls Royce. Silver or black is more appropriate because both colors are maximally desaturated and, therefore, low energy. Silver aptly reflects and reinforces the meta-message of style, wealth, and elegance.

The second beach scene previously mentioned was purposely shot in black and white to reinforce its meta-message of dread. Many of the highly internal, soul-wrenching movies, as Bergman's *Persona* or Spielberg's *Schindler's List*, are rendered in black and white to direct our view away from an external "looking at" the event to a more internal "looking-into" perception. The more generalized desaturation theory claims that the more a color is desaturated (making the color lose its hue), the more we turn from an external, psychological "landscape" view of an event to a more introspective "inscape" one (Zettl, 2005).

THE TWO-DIMENSIONAL FIELD: TWO-DIMENSIONAL SPACE

Just like the painter and photographer, in the screen arts—television, film, and computer imaging—we must display the world around us in a strictly defined two-dimensional space: the television, movie, and computer screens. Unlike the painters and photographers, who can stretch their frames horizontally as high or as wide as their subject demands, in the screen arts, we must work within a fixed-aspect ratio.

Aspect Ratio

Aspect ratio is the relation between picture width and height. Standard television screens and computer monitors have an aspect ratio of 4 × 3, which means that the screen is 4 units wide and 3 units high. DTV (digital television) screens and motion picture screens are considerably wider than the standard TV and classical movie screens, with aspect ratios of 16 × 9, or 5.3 × 3 for DTV and even wider (5.6 × 3) for movies.

The advantage of the classic 4 × 3 aspect ratio is that neither of these two dimensions is overpowering. Although the screen is horizontally oriented, this aspect ratio frames horizontal or vertical views equally well, and frame close-ups and extreme close-ups of people's heads without wasted space (see Fig. 23.1).

The wider DTV and movie screens can accommodate impressive vistas but have problems with framing tall objects, such as a tower or skyscraper. To squeeze it into such wide aspect ratios, we must either tilt the camera and look up at the building, or cant the camera and have the building lean along the screen diagonal. Framing a close-up of a person's face leaves empty, isolating screen space on either side of the screen (Fig. 23.2), unless the sides of the screen are filled with other event details (Katz, 1991).

A similar problem exists when wide-screen movies are shown on standard television. Moving close enough to make the picture fill the screen height, we inevitably lose the

FIG. 23.1. 4″ × 3″ Aspect Ratio (Source: Zettl, *Sight sound motion: Applied media aesthetics* (Wadsworth, 4th edition 2005). Used with permission).

FIG. 23.2. 16″ × 9″ Aspect Ratio (Source: Zettl, *Sight sound motion: Applied media aesthetics* (Wadsworth, 4th edition 2005). Used with permission).

information on both sides of the screen. Trying to show the whole width of the movie images creates dead zones at the screen top and bottom of the screen. Some enterprising producers consider these dead zones an asset rather than an aesthetic handicap. Even if the screen event was videotaped in the conventional 4 × 3 aspect ratio, the top and bottom dead zones are later added to pretend that the footage was originally shot for the high-end, wide-screen motion picture format.

Screen Size

Despite the craze of making television screens larger and larger, its relatively small size is actually one of its true aesthetic assets. To show things clearly on the small screen and to establish and maintain a certain aesthetic energy level, we need to use predominantly close-ups and inductive sequencing of close-up detail. Inductive sequencing means that we show an event not as a sequence that moves from an overview to progressively tighter shots, but rather in a series of close-ups. The overview, if shown at all, happens at the end of the sequence or, most often, in the head of the viewer. This mental composing of a whole from a series of parts, called *psychological closure*, requires an active, though subconscious, participation of the viewer (Köhler, 1947; McLuhan, 1964).[5]

When watching normal-sized television, we need to sit relatively close to the set. This physical closeness to the televised event and the watching of close-up sequences on the small screen establishes rather close video proxemics, a personal communication space that promotes intimacy and tends to make the television set a virtual conversation partner. In contrast, the large screen forces us to sit farther away and to look "at" rather "into" the event. In general, large screens are more suited to watching a high-energy spectacle rather than participating in a relatively private, and occasionally even introspective, small-screen communication act. The large screen is ideal for watching a football game; the small one for sharing the grief of a mother who is pleading for the return of her abducted child.

Structuring the Vector Field

Unlike the images of paintings and photographs, which are immobile within their frame, television and film images are almost always in motion and in constant change. The long established rules of composition are, therefore, only partially applicable in structuring effective television and film shots. We must distinguish, therefore, between picture *composition*, which connotes the structuring of static images within a frame, and the *framing* of shots that contain moving images. If computer images are relatively static, they yield to the traditional rules of composition (Arnheim, 1982). If they consist primarily of full-screen moving images, their structuring is quite similar to video and film framing. But renaming a process does not make it necessarily more useful. What we need is a system that can cope with the continual change of video and film images when framing shots. I suggest to look at effective framing not as balancing various graphic elements in a picture frame, but rather as structuring vector fields.

In media aesthetics, *vectors* are forces with a direction and magnitude (relative strength). Dominant lines, such as the edges of your table or the television screen, or the line created by people queued up at a bus stop, form *graphic vectors*. *Index vectors* are created by somebody or something pointing unquestionably in a specific direction. A person staring or pointing at the door generates an index vector, as does a one-way sign. A parked automobile also forms an index vector, but when moving, a motion vector. *Motion vectors* trace things moving (Zettl, 2005). When index and motion vectors point or move in the same direction, the vectors are continuing, regardless of whether we see them in the same shot or in succeeding shots. When they point or move toward each other, the vectors are converging. If they look or move away from each other, the vectors are diverging. To maintain their principal direction over a series of shots is the purpose of continuity editing. I return to vector continuity in the discussion of the four-dimensional field.

A specific vector field can influence, however subtly, the relative aesthetic energy of a shot. A predominantly horizontal vector field suggests calmness and stability. Vertical lines seem to defy gravity and suggest boldness. The graphic vectors of a tall skyscraper underline the dynamic spirit of contemporary people.

Tilting the horizontal plane by canting the camera has an immediate effect on how we perceive the whole scene. It renders the whole scene labile, which we intuitively interpret as high energy. Recall for a moment the brief mention of the Corvette roaring through tight turns and the Rolls Royce parked in front of the elegant mansion. Would a tilted horizon line intensify the precariousness of the speeding Corvette? By all means. On the other hand, the level plane of the elegant mansion implies stability, as does the parked Rolls on the driveway. Tilting the horizon would probably hint that all is not well

FIG. 23.3. Zero-Magnitude Index Vector (Source: Zettl, *Sight sound motion: Applied media aesthetics* (Wadsworth, 4th edition 2005). Used with permission).

FIG. 23.4. High Magnitude Index Vector (Source: Zettl, *Sight sound motion: Applied media aesthetics* (Wadsworth, 4th edition 2005). Used with permission).

and that disaster is about to strike. MTV capitalizes on the tilted horizon line. It tilts the shot even when the talent is merely saying good morning. Apparently, the in-the-face aesthetic intensifiers of the hard-rock beat, the harsh lighting and distorted colors, and the incessant zooming in and out are still not enough to satisfy the high-energy hunger of its audience.

Index vectors have a direct influence on how to frame a shot. When somebody looks straight into the camera (and, therefore, at the viewer), it creates an index vector of zero magnitude (minimal directional strength). The person is, therefore, best placed screen-center (Fig. 23.3).

But as soon as the person turns to look either left or right, the vector magnitude increases. It reaches its maximum strength in the profile position (see Fig. 23.4). Here the space in front of the person, often called *noseroom*, compensates for the increasing vector magnitude and also guides the index vector into the left or right off-screen space. If the shot sequence now cuts to the off-screen conversation partner, it needs to show this person looking into the opposite direction. All subsequent shots need to keep the two index vectors converging, whether we see them in a two-shot or in individual close-ups. As you can see, the vector field extends into structuring the off-screen space as well (Fig. 23.5).

FIG. 23.5. Converging Index Vectors (Source: Zettl, *Sight sound motion: Applied media aesthetics* (Wadsworth, 4th edition 2005). Used with permission).

THE THREE-DIMENSIONAL FIELD: THREE-DIMENSIONAL SPACE

We are fortunate that the painters and architects of the Renaissance have carefully documented the major ways of creating the illusion of depth on a two-dimensional surface (Arnheim, 1974). And, we are even more fortunate that, in the photographic arts, such an illusion is created almost automatically by the camera lens. In fact, the choice of a particular lens (specifically its focal length) has a great influence on how we perceive picture depth, how close a view we get of an object, how crowded or far apart we perceive objects that are lined up along the z-axis, the virtual axis that extends from camera to horizon, and how fast or slow we perceive their motion along the z-axis.

Wide-Angle and Telephoto Lenses

As we may know from operating a camcorder, zooming out puts the lens into the wide-angle (short focal length) position and provides a wider vista. Zooming in narrows the angle of the zoom lens and puts it in a telephoto (long focal length) position. We get a drastically reduced vista, but what is left in the viewfinder is greatly magnified. Perceptually, we interpret this magnification as bringing the object closer to the screen.

The wide-angle lens distorts scale. An object that is close to the camera appears much larger in the viewfinder than a similar-sized object that is located on the z-axis just a few feet behind the camera-near object. Our perceptual mechanism automatically translates this reduction in object size into distance. The camera-far object seems much farther away from the camera-near object than it really is. Shooting a tennis match along the z-axis from ground level with a wide-angle lens makes the court look as though it has the length of a football field.

The narrow-angle, or telephoto, lens does just the opposite. Because it magnifies distant objects, the two objects positioned along the z-axis look similar in size and, therefore, seem to be right behind each other. When shot with a telephoto lens, the tennis court shrinks and the two players at their base lines appear to be standing close to the net. In computer graphics, such visual distortions must be individually programmed. Because we are so used to seeing wide-angle and narrow-angle lens distortions, we readily accept the ones simulated by the computer artist.

Z-Axis Blocking and Z-Axis Motion

When blocking for the film screen, that is, arranging people and their movements, we have a relatively large x-axis space to position them along the screen width. In fact, many film directors make extensive use of converging motion vectors that intensify people and things moving toward each other from both sides of the screen. Such horizontal blocking is difficult to achieve on the small electronic television or computer screen. Even four or five people standing side-by-side along the x-axis fill the width of the screen, unless shown in an extreme long shot. As impressive x-axis motion can look on the big screen, it loses its punch when seen on the small electronic screen.

A better way of blocking objects and motion is along the z-axis, the virtual line from camera to horizon. Because the z-axis is such an accommodating dimension, it has become the trademark of effective small-screen framing (Zettl, 2005). When blocking along the z-axis, we can easily include a great number of people in a single shot (Fig. 23.6). In contrast to x-axis motion, z-axis motion (object moving toward or away from the camera) is equally easy to capture on camera, even if the movement is quite fast. More so, z-axis motion vectors pack more aesthetic energy and look more dramatic than even high-magnitude lateral motion.

Generally, computer screens simulate some form of screen depth through overlapping planes. If one screen portion is overlapping another, the one that is doing the overlapping is perceived to be in front of the one that is overlapped (Zettl, 2005; Barbatsis, 1999). When simulating z-axis motion in cartoons or programming for the computer screen, we continuously increase the size or the object that is doing the traveling. We interpret the increasing size as the object coming toward us (the camera). When it gets smaller, we perceive it as receding. The faster the size of the object changes, the faster we perceive its virtual z-axis speed (Kipper, 1989; Zettl, 2005).

THE FOUR-DIMENSIONAL FIELD: TIME-MOTION

Like music, dance, or stage presentations, video and film are time arts. Time is also essential to affect screen motion. Neither medium can exist without motion and is dependent on duration to unfold its sequences. Time and motion are also the principal factors that constitute the fundamental ontological differences between video and film.

Ontological Difference

Regardless of whether the televised event was previously recorded or not, analog or digital, the ontological, basic structural time-motion difference between video and film remains intact. Video in this context includes computer images, as well as any other displays that are electronically generated. The basic unit of video—the video frame—is

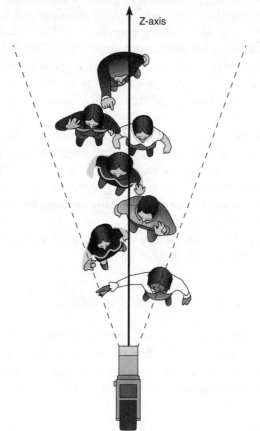

FIG. 23.6.   Z-Axis Blocking (Source: Zettl, *Sight sound motion: Applied media aesthetics* (Wadsworth, 4th edition 2005). Used with permission).

always in motion, even if it shows an object at rest. Created by constantly moving scanning beams, the video image is by its very nature evanescent, in constant flux, and always in a process of becoming. The film frame, on the other hand, exists as a complete picture that shows the object at rest regardless of whether the object is in motion or not. The film frame has existential permanence and is always in a state of being. Even when film is projected, its frames remain at rest. We perceive event motion on the screen only because each frames shows the moving object in a slightly different position. In contrast, the video image has no permanence even if it shows an object at rest. The constant creation and simultaneous decay of its image, its evanescence, suggests an isomorphic relationship between its image and the fleeting "now" of the present.

In this context, shooting television "reality" shows on film is a total contradiction. Because film calls inevitably for a restructuring of the actual event, its reality is by its very nature artificial and contrived. Such reality-show postproduction steps as inserting reaction close-ups of contestants to reveal their emotions might be stimulating to the audience, but are a long way from giving the viewers a slice of reality (Kipper, 2001).

Electronic Cinema

Electronic cinema, in which all postproduction and projection processes in the capture of images are done electronically, is somewhat of a paradox. The arguments of traditional film artists and critics that the high-definition, large electronic video displays in movie theaters still lack the elusive and subtle "film look" seem justified.

Even if the electronic images come close in definition and contrast range to those of film, their ontological structure is still video and not film. Instead of having a series of complete pictures projected, with each one separated by a brief period of black, we are now subjected to a barrage of always incomplete, restless images that decay as fast as they are updated. Video images also seem harsher than film. I argue that the mysterious "film look" is primarily caused by the periods of black screen that occur each time a new film frame is pulled up for projection. Such temporary blackouts are missing in electronic video projection. But film, even in its electronic form, cannot be live. Live video is the most significant unique feature of television and computer streaming.

Live Television and Film

Television and computer video are the only audiovisual media that can capture an event, clarify and intensify it, and distribute it while the event is still in the process of becoming. Film, even as electronic cinema, is by its very nature an historic medium. By this I mean that it can only play back previously recorded or synthetically constructed images. Almost always, film's screen events are constructs of careful postproduction processes. As such, a film event is always medium-dependent. Live video, on the other hand, is always event-dependent. This means that we cannot manipulate the duration of the actual event or its development during the live pickup. We simply cannot show the end of the event before its beginning. In a live pickup, the televised or computer-streamed event has the same "open future" as the actual event. This feature is especially prominent in events that are unpredictable in their very structure, such as football games, unrehearsed interviews, downtown fires, or game shows. This time affinity of real event to televised event allows us not only to witness such events, but to participate in their very creation.

But there is no virtue in doing a live telecast or computer-streaming of program material that is a priori deterministic. Putting on a live television drama does not make it more immediate for the audience, however exciting and demanding it may for the production crew. After all, a fully scripted play has no longer an open future; all of its moments—the dialogue, and the movements of actors and cameras—are carefully scripted and plotted. Any deviation from the script, including the time line itself, is considered a mistake. The possibility of an actor forgetting lines or the wrong camera being punched does not generate an open future; all it does is make everybody nervous and, more often than not, compromise the production quality.

Film, on the other hand, substitutes its lack of immediacy with a carefully crafted dramaturgy that moves from conflict to conflict, and finally to a not always predictable conclusion. That the fate of the characters in the play is predetermined and often known to the audience before watching the film does not seem to be a deterrent to the degree of *Einfühlung*, of sharing their destiny. As in a theater play, this type of feeling can readily lead to an emotional release in the audience, a "cleansing of the soul," as Aristotle defines catharsis (Aristotle, 1967).

Recorded Television

What about the majority of television that is not live, but recorded from a live show or carefully edited in the postproduction phase? If it is a live-on-tape recording, our perception of an open future depends on whether or not we are aware of how the event ends. If we know the final score of a football game at the beginning of the televised game, the future is closed for us. We will certainly approach watching the game with a different attitude and look for different details than if we were to believe that the game is actually live. In the latter case, our assumption of an open future makes our experience quite similar to watching a live game. Nevertheless, in a time context, we are cajoled into a pseudo experience. Even the fastest replay is not the actual moment. Such a pretense of the presence is considered by the television industry a major deception, although similar media manipulations through lenses are virtually ignored. The replay of a previously live show is usually clearly identified as such. However, once the television show is constructed in postproduction editing, time manipulations are readily accepted.

Mental Maps

A well-edited sequence appears seamless. We generally perceive it as though it were created by a single shot, although it may actually contain various shots that show a series of close-ups and medium and long shots. We perceive such sequences as continuous and make sense of them because they fit the mental map we established while watching them. Similar to the meta-messages that make us create a context in which to interpret what we see, mental maps establish a context for how we see. The mental maps register automatically the major object positions and vectors—where things are on the screen and where they should be in subsequent shots. If we first see a man on screen-left and a woman on screen-right looking at each other, they should, as previously shown in Fig. 23.5, continue looking at each other in subsequent close-ups. This means that their relative positions (man screen-left and the woman screen-right) and their converging index vectors must be maintained in subsequent close-ups. A reversal of positions or vector direction in the close-ups would certainly disturb our mental map and inhibit the intended communication. If, for example, you had the woman look screen-right instead of screen-left in the close-up, we would assume that both the man and the woman are now looking at something or somebody else in the right off-screen space. Our mental map obviously extends into off-screen space and helps structure it (Zettl, 1998).

Sometimes, such rules of continuity editing are deliberately violated to jolt us out of our perceptual complacency and to reveal the complexity and intensity of an event or feeling. Such complexity editing requires that we know the rules before we break them. Otherwise, the desired intensification may, more often than not, turn into painfully conspicuous editing mistakes.

Yet even widely differing, seemingly unrelated, events can be combined. For instance, shots can combine the colliding images of homeless people sleeping on park benches with those of elegantly dressed people rushing through the same park section to an open-air concert, which conjures up quite readily the meta-message of social injustice (Arnheim, 1957). Even if the vector structures of the two shots do not match very well, we perceive such montage elements as part of a larger "dialectic structure" if they are made part of the same time frame (Burch 1973). Husserl (1973), commenting on an intuitive perception through association, asserted that we can bring together different objects by juxtaposing them in an apparent space-time field. He wrote:

> We can say: we bring objects [or events] which belong to different fields of presence together by transporting them to *one temporal field*; we move the first objects to the intuitive temporal field of the others. In this way, we bring them into one intuitive coexistence (that is, into a unity of simultaneous duration). (1973, p. 181)

Computer Display

Such a unifying temporal field seems to be missing when looking at the various bits of written information and small graphic icons scattered over the computer screen. This information is often too fragmented to permit, or even encourage, any kind of unifying association. In fact, the need for scrolling up and down renders information discontinuous even if it hangs together thematically. Such scrolling takes the information sequences out of an intuitive temporal field and, with it, its apparent coexistence. Such fragmentation may well be an extension of the binary structure of computers that does not allow, nor cares about, any organic association. The rather chaotic assemblage of information on the Internet is the most striking example of such fragmentation.

However, when information is streamed, whereby the content is displayed in a specific screen space and continually updated while being transmitted, it regains the unified temporal plane that helps establish continuity.

If the images consist of video or film clips, or are synthetically computer-generated, they pretty much follow the canons of general media aesthetics. For example, a computer-generated weather map still needs to obey the general aesthetic rules of attached and cast shadow continuity, or the various video techniques of creating the illusions of three-dimensional space, even if the graphic appears on the computer screen rather than on television (Kipper, 1989). If the computer shows full-screen, real-time moving images, its media-aesthetic requirements are identical to those of any other video production.

The new and unique aesthetic potential of computer displays, which Barbatsis calls the "aesthetics of the newest communication art" (1999, p. 280), is its interactivity. A well-thought-out interface design should make it easy for the user to choose from a number of available hyperlinks (event modules), call them up, and sequence them according to his or her needs and desires. However, such links convert into an interconnected and functional chain only, if each of them is structured so that it facilitates closure. This means that each module must somehow relate to the others through subject matter, event detail, dialogue, narrative progression, or the more abstract aesthetic qualities as field of view (how close the object appears in the frame), point of view (from where the object is seen), or various vector fields. In effect, the user of the interactive program becomes the editor. But as any editor knows, the final event will be only as good as the available source footage. If the individual links are totally independent, they will not connect and transcend into a good gestalt (Barbatsis, 1999). It becomes quite apparent that the designers of interactive programs must not only be computer experts, but also, if not especially, good editors.[6]

THE FIVE-DIMENSIONAL FIELD: SOUND

Sound fulfills several key outer and inner orientation functions. The major outer orientation functions are to (a) communicate specific information, (b) orient us in space and time, and (c) describe a particular situation. The inner orientation functions are to create mood, add energy to a scene, and supply or reinforce structure.

Outer and Inner Orientation Functions

Television, more so than film, relies heavily on someone talking. Without sound, television would have lost its very existence. Because of the small size of the television screen and the importance the television set has gained as a conversation partner in almost everybody's home, we quite readily accept to be talked to by the television performer. In the movie theater, such direct-address techniques are rarely successful. Through literal sounds, which immediately call up in us a visual image of the sound-producing source, we can indicate what time it is (church bells, factory whistle, cricket sounds for night), where an event is occurring (traffic sounds suggesting a downtown intersection), and what the event is all about (baby crying, crash sounds followed by police sirens).

Music is one of the most effective means to fulfill a variety of inner orientation functions. It can readily create a happy or sad mood and add to the aesthetic energy of a scene. Even the most skillfully edited chase sequence would look rather flat without the typical dissonant, pounding chase music.

Let us go back to the two beach scenes we mentioned in the beginning of this chapter. The sounds are probably the most direct aesthetic device to set the different moods.

Combined with the upbeat lighting and color, the happy music, the sounds of the gentle surf, and the laughter of children provide the affective context of fun and happiness. We are bound to transfer, however subconsciously, the happy mood to the man walking on the bluff as well. Similarly, the dissonant music in the second scene, the sounds of the heavy surf and the crying of seagulls are the primary agent for the new meta-message. Although the action of the man walking along the bluff is identical to the first scene, he now appears to be deeply troubled. George Burt called this the "associative power of music," explaining that "the quality and language of music are vital aids in breaking down the objective explicitness of certain pictures where there is a need to redefine them in a way that is consistent with the intentions of the story" (1994, p. 10).

Structural Function and Matching of Vector Fields

One of the most important, though least conspicuous, functions of music is structural. A strong rhythmic piece of music or drum beat will inevitably superimpose a tight structure even on a rather loose, irregularly edited picture sequence. In this type of audiovisual matching, we seem to structure the video according to the audio rhythms, and not vice versa. In fact, even if we had a tightly edited metric video montage, in which shots of equal lengths create an editing rhythm, an erratic, irregular sound beat can fragment the visual structure (Eisenstein, 1957; Zettl, 2005).

When asking editors how they choose music for their edited video, most will probably answer that they don't use specific criteria for matching audio to video. They usually go by what "feels right," or by whatever "works well with the video." What these people instinctively do is match the general vector field of the audio with that of the video. If, for example, the video sequence has an especially complex visual vector field, they probably choose music that has several melodic and harmonic layers and a syncopated beat. If the video shows a rather simple and straightforward vector pattern, the choice for traditional matching should be music with a simple melody and a clear and direct harmony and beat. Fast action and rather quick cuts obviously need faster music than tranquil scenes and long takes.[7] Even if the video editing is rhythmically quite uneven, a music track with a strong beat will most likely make us perceive the editing as tightly structured. We have a tendency to adjust the video to the audio structure and not the other way around.

Although sound is far less important in computer presentation than in television, one of its more important use of sound is what I call cybernetic dialogue. So far, the majority of interactive programs use narrative or written instructions to direct the user what to do. I would prefer to have the computer engage me in a dialogue, however one-sided and predetermined it may be. Through Socratic-like questioning, the computer could gently steer the user to do find the right hyperlink or find the answer to a missed quiz question. This means that the designers of interactive programs must begin to pay special attention to the art of dialogue writing (Hicks, 1999; McKee, 1997).[8]

Ethics

As I have argued throughout this chapter, applied media aesthetics can be successfully used to detect meta-messages and their possible effect on the viewer (Potter, 1998; Messaris, 1997; Barry, 1997). Unfortunately, any media analysis is by definition ex post facto, after the communication has taken place. If there were irresponsible meta-messages embedded, the damage has been done. Although the knowledge of how we are manipulated may be some deterrent against future unethical manipulation, it is in the encoding stage where responsibility must be exercised.

The most blatant manipulative use of media aesthetics is in advertising. Every television commercial has as its ultimate goal to make us buy something we didn't know we needed, or, more insidiously, to influence choice (Messaris, 1994). The deliberate manipulation of our perceptions and emotions is not intrinsically bad; in fact it is, to a certain extent, the goal of every art form. When done in an ethical framework, it can help us give vision significant form and share this insight with a great number of our fellow human beings.

The only real safeguards we have is to shield ourselves from unethical manipulation is to remind the producers of such media fare to act with prudence and responsibility, and to hold in high esteem the trust the audience has put in them.

To emphasize this responsibility, I would like to quote part of my prologue to *Sight Sound Motion* as prologue:

> Irrespective of the scope of your communication—be it a brief news story, an advertisement, or a major dramatic production—your overriding aim should be to help people attain a higher degree of emotional literacy, the ability to see the world with heightened awareness and joy. All your aesthetic decisions must ultimately be made within an ethical context, a moral framework that holds supreme the dignity and well-being of humankind. (Zettl, 2005, p. 1)

CONCLUSION

Applied media aesthetics gives us the tools to make aesthetic analysis consistent and reliable, and aesthetic synthesis—production—maximally effective and efficient. Our knowledge of the major media-aesthetic factors, their potential, and their contextual interaction within their respective aesthetic fields will help predict, at least to some extent, their effect on the viewers' perception. We need to keep in mind that applied media aesthetics as a system is centered primarily on the use of nonverbal elements, such as light and color, two- and three-dimensional space, time-motion, and sound. Any valid analysis of the effect of a specific television, film, or computer presentation must necessarily include other vital contextual factors, such as what the event is all about, where it takes place, and who says what to whom.

As I see it, the convergence of video, film, and computer communication opens up a large and rich research area in media aesthetics. For example, perception psychologists and scholars of media aesthetics must continue their efforts to determine the thresholds of information complexity, that is, at which point television news and Web pages switch from information complexity to information overload. Each minute of CNN Headline News displays offers a plethora of research topics. A periodic investigation of meta-messages in television and Internet commercial spots could disclose not only interesting stylistic trends, but also specific techniques of persuasion and aesthetic manipulation.

On the production end, we could experiment with complex information presented simultaneously or sequentially on a single screen in comparison with the use of divided screens or separate multiscreens. Such "screens-within-screen" research is especially needed to make computer displays optimally effective.

Another fertile research field concerns the tendency in film to borrow television's inductive sequencing—the telling of a story exclusively through a series of tight close-ups. More and more, such high-energy presentation techniques are accompanied by high-volume soundtracks. What are the aesthetic limits of such intensification effects? At what point are inclined to tune out instead of in?

It is high time that we, as scholars of media analysis and synthesis—as students of media aesthetics—learn not only the techniques of production, but production theory as well.

ENDNOTES

[1] This system is developed in detail in Zettl. (2005). This chapter is based primarily on the key concepts of *Sight-Sound-Motion*.

[2] To get a closer look at the essence of an event, Husserl advocated the application of *epoché*, which means that we should "bracket," that is limit, the context so that we concentrate as objectively as possible on the actual data of an event (see Spinelli, 1989, p. 17). Kant (1956, p. 83) in his influential work *Kritik der reinen Vernunft* [Critique of Pure Reason] asserted that the *Ding an sich*—the thing in itself—is perceptually unknowable, because during the act of perceiving, the "thing" (observed event) is inevitably distorted by space and time.

[3] J. S. Douglass and G. P. Harnden (1996, pp. 71–94) give many examples from well-known motion pictures of how various aesthetic variables contribute to mood.

[4] Husserl (1973) explained why montage works. He said that there is "a *connection which is instituted between arbitrarily different presences*, of which one is actual, the other submerged," and that "The submerged is reawakened by association . . . and intuitively unified with the awakening of a new presence" (1973, p. 180). The various montage categories and montage as visual dialectic are explained in Zettl (2005, pp. 311–323).

[5] Köhler (1947) examined in great detail certain types of our hard-wired perceptions. As one of the major gestalt psychologists, he advocates that we inevitably try to pattern random elements into simple and stable configurations—a *gestalt* (German for shape, figure) (see Goldstein, 1999, pp. 178–191). Any successful montage operates on the gestalt principle. We combine the montage elements into a more encompassing whole, the resulting *tertium quid*. McLuhan (1964, pp. 311–315) asserted that low-definition images (standard TV pictures, newspaper photos) force the viewers to "subjective completion," by automatically filling in mentally the missing parts. By doing so, we participate, however involuntarily, in the very creation of the gestalt. This process is customarily called psychological closure.

[6] At the present, the interactivity through hyperlinks is basically determined by the available choice. Thus, the user is limited to choosing the right modules, but plays no role in their creation. I still think that true interactivity should not only offer the users a wide choice of hyperlinks, but also make it possible to actually influence the original message. As I see it, offering the user a choice among three or four endings to a story does not qualify as true interactivity. True interactivity should let the user write his or her own ending (or any other plot change) and see it materialize on the screen.

[7] An excellent example of sensitive structural matching is Michael Wanger's videotapes *Wildlife* and *Nature's Symphony*, published by Reader's Digest. These videotapes reveal a careful structural analysis of the sound vectors of various pieces of classical music and the video sequences with which they are brilliantly matched.

[8] There are many books on how to write for television and film, but few elaborate on the fine art of writing dialogue. Perhaps the best teacher of dialogue writing is a good ear, the ability to listen to what people say and how they say it. But good dialogue goes beyond imitating a conversation we may hear on

the telephone or in the supermarket; it is carefully crafted, but natural sounding. Good dialogue should not dazzle with a large vocabulary, but should compel us to say: "I wish I had said that!"

REFERENCES

Aristotle (1967). *Aristotle: Poetics* (G. F. Else, Trans.). Ann Arbor: University of Michigan Press.

Arnheim, R. (1957). *Film as art*. Berkeley: University of California Press.

Arnheim, R. (1974). *Art and visual perception: The new version*. Berkeley: University of California Press.

Arnheim, R. (1982). *The power of the center*. Berkeley: University of California Press.

Barbatsis, G. S. (1999). Hypermediated telepresence: Sensemaking aesthetics of the newest communication art. *Journal of Broadcasting & Electronic Media, 43*(2), 280–298.

Barry, A. M. (1997). *Visual intelligence*. New York: State University of New York Press.

Burch, N. (1973). *Theory of film practice*. New York: Praeger.

Burt, G. (1994). *The art of film music*. Boston: Northeastern University Press.

Douglass, J. S., & Harnden, G. P. (1996). *The art of technique*. Boston: Allyn & Bacon.

Eisenstein, S. (1957). *Film form and film sense* (J. Leyda, Ed. and Trans.). New York: World Publishing.

Festinger, L. A. (1957). *A theory of cognitive dissonance*. Stanford, CA: Stanford University Press.

Gibson, J. J. (1987). *The ecological approach to visual perception*. Hillsdale, NJ: Lawrence Erlbaum Associates.

Goldstein, E. B. (1999). *Sensation and perception* (5th ed.). Pacific Grove, CA: Brooks/Cole Publishing Co.

Harrison, C., & Wood, P. (Eds.). (1993). *Art in theory*. Cambridge, MA: Blackwell.

Hicks, N. D. (1999). *Screen writing 101*. Studio City, CA: Michael Wiese Productions.

Husserl, E. (1973). *Experience and judgment* (J. S. Churchill and K. Ameriks, Trans.). Evanston, IL: Northwestern University Press. (Original work published 1948)

Kant, I. (1956). *Kritik der reinen Vernunft (Critique of Pure Reason)*. Hamburg: Felix Meiner Verlag. (Originally published 1781)

Katz, S. (1991). *Film directing shot by shot*. Woburn, MA: Focal Press.

Kipper, P. (1989, February). *Television's computer imagery and a new spatial aesthetic*. Paper presented at the Convention of the Western Speech Communication Association, Spokane, Washington.

Kipper, P. (2001, April). *Call it show biz or call it artifice, but don't call it reality*. Paper presented at the Convention of the Broadcast Education Association, Las Vegas, Nevada.

Köhler, W. (1947). *Gestalt psychology*. New York: Mentor Books.

Levaco, R. (1974). *Kuleshov on film: Writings by Lev Kuleshov* (Selected by R. Levaco, Trans.). Berkeley: University of California Press.

McKee, R. (1997). *Story: Substance, structure, style, and the principles of screenwriting*. New York: Regan Books.

McLuhan, M. (1964). *Understanding media: The extensions of man*. New York: McGraw-Hill.

Messaris, P. (1994). *Visual literacy*. Boulder, CO: Westview Press.

Messaris, P. (1997). *Visual persuasion*. Thousand Oaks, CA: Sage.

Metallinos, N. (1996). *Television aesthetics*. Mahwah, NJ: Lawrence Erlbaum Associates.

Millerson, G. (1991). *Lighting for television and film* (3rd ed.). Woburn, MA: Focal Press.

Potter, J. W. (1998). *Media literacy*. Thousand Oaks, CA: Sage.

Pudovkin, V. I. (1960). *Film technique and film acting*. Ivor Montagu Ed. and Trans., New York: Grove Press. (Original work published 1928)

Spinelli, E. (1989). *The interpreted world: An introduction to phenomenological psychology*. London: Sage Publications Ltd.

Wanger, M. (Prod. and Ed.). (1991). *Nature's serenade*. New York: The Reader's Digest Association.

Zettl, H. (1988). The hidden message: Some aspects of television aesthetics. In A. A. Berger (Ed.), *Media USA* (pp. 207–224). New York: Longman.

Zettl, H. (1998). Contextual media aesthetics as the basis for media literacy. *Journal of Communication, 48*(1), 81–85.

Zettl, H. (2005). *Sight sound motion: Applied media aesthetics* (4th ed.). Belmont, CA: Wadsworth.

24

A Content Analysis of Political Speeches on Television

ROBERT TIEMENS
University of Utah

Although objectivity is considered a cornerstone of contemporary journalism, media aesthetics sometimes confounds that objectivity. Herbert Zettl, in a preceding chapter, has argued that the elements of media aesthetics can have a subjective impact on the audience's interpretation of televised news. This chapter utilizes a content analysis of 1,509 camera shots to examine how five news organizations, in covering the same event, might have produced different portrayals of the event based on differences in shot selection and production techniques. The event was Jesse Jackson's speech to the 1988 Democratic National Convention.[1] The results are then compared to those from a study that examined his speech to the 1984 convention.

Jesse Jackson's speech in 1988 was the culmination of a hard-fought campaign to gain the party's nomination for President of the United States. Jackson's chances of winning the nomination were out of reach long before the Democrats convened in Atlanta, Georgia, but the momentum of his campaign thrust him into the spotlight as the key figure of the convention. Columnist James Kilpatrick noted that, in observing 17 national conventions, "I can't recall anything exactly like it where the runner-up so dominates questions, news coverage, and everything else at this point. Every question here has to do with Jesse Jackson" (1988, p. A11).

It was not the first time Jesse Louis Jackson held the spotlight of the Democratic National Convention. In 1984 he addressed 30,000 delegates, guests, and media personnel at the San Francisco convention, a speech that was delivered via television to 23.9 million households, the largest television audience of the 1984 convention. The significance of that speech was noted, by television commentators Dan Rather and David Brinkley as "historic."

Jackson's appearance before the 1988 convention was no different. It was historic, and it was the highlight of the convention. Although the television audience was smaller in 1988[2] there was no doubt that Jackson's speech was the "main event" of the Atlanta convention. Two factors made Jackson's speech important. The first was the broad context for the speech established by the media themselves. Before the convention started, preconvention meetings between Jackson and Michael Dukakis were held in Atlanta to reconcile differences of opinion over issues of the party platform and party leadership. Media coverage of these meetings began to develop a scenario that depicted a "rift" between Dukakis and Jackson, a rift that threatened the unity of the party. Despite denials of a rift by both candidates, stories and reports coming out of the convention continued to focus on Jesse Jackson as a potential troublemaker. It was as though the media were preparing the script for a melodrama, and the night of Jackson's speech was to become "the moment of truth."

The second factor that made his speech important was Jackson's racial heritage. Throughout the 1988 campaign, Jackson drew unusual attention and commentary— not so much for what he said, but because he had established himself as the first serious presidential candidate in the United States who was African American.

A similar situation occurred in 1984 when even Walter Cronkite commented that Jackson's appearance before that convention was a "black event," and that it was the television coverage that made it so. Jackson's appearance in 1984 was the basis for a previous study that examined how television news sources covered his speech (Tiemens, Sillars, Alexander, & Werling, 1988). That study showed, through a detailed visual analysis, that differences in coverage by five news sources (ABC, CBS, NBC, CNN, and C-SPAN) could lead to very different interpretations of Jackson's speech by television viewers, depending on which version of the speech they saw. That premise guided the present study as well.

The impact of Jesse Jackson's speech went far beyond the 17,000 delegates, guests, and media personnel assembled in the Omni on the night of July 19, 1988. Through the medium of television Jackson was seen and heard in an additional 19.7 million households across the United States. Five television news sources transmitted the pictures and sounds of the event taking place that night. But those news sources were more than mere conduits of information. In addition to transmitting Jackson's speech to millions of viewers, the images selected by those news sources modified and reshaped the event so that five potentially different interpretations of Jackson's speech were possible. Television critic Phil Kloer observed in covering the events of the convention, that "television present[ed] its own reality to viewers" (1988, p. C11).

Despite his dynamic oratorical style, Jesse Jackson's televised speech was more than just words. The visual images that accompanied the transmission of those words into millions of households created a context for the speech that transformed it into a unique event. As Zettl has explained:

> Frequently, the camera reveals more than we could see merely by looking at the event. But the medium can also create an event. The camera, then, uses the actual event strictly as raw material for its creation. The new event created by the camera exists only on the screen—nowhere else. (1973, p. 226)

VISUAL ELEMENTS OF THE PRODUCTION PROCESS

This analysis considers three major elements of television production that potentially shaped and re-created the visual context of Jackson's speech: *selectivity*, *emphasis*, and *reconstruction*.

Selectivity

By using multiple cameras with telephoto lenses, the television production process allows a viewer to see elements of detail that cannot otherwise be seen because of time and space restrictions. For example, when the viewer sees a medium shot of Jesse Jackson speaking from the podium and, within a split second, witnesses the reaction of a person in the audience hundreds of yards away, that image represents a privileged point of view not seen by any member of the audience viewing the speech firsthand. The expanse of a public arena, such as the one in which Jackson spoke, prohibits the close-up views that the television audience sees.

The viewer has no choice in how these images are selected, however. Unlike the firsthand observer, who is free to select from a infinite number of alternatives what he or she will look at, the television viewer is given only one choice—those visual images that have been selected through the production process. The camera person and director dictate what the viewer is allowed to see, thereby narrowing the viewer's alternatives for interpreting the shot. The selectivity of the camera dictates what the viewer will interpret.

Emphasis

The production process emphasizes or intensifies visual information in two ways: (a) by altering the relative size of the image within the limits of the television frame (e.g., close-up versus long shot), and (b) through repetition of visual content. Close-ups direct the viewer's attention to visual detail and give greater emphasis to the visual content, whereas wide-angle shots, though they provide a greater visual array, minimize the visual detail in the shot. Also, as Kindem has suggested, a close-up will draw the audience's attention to an event. "Close-ups focus and direct attention and create dramatic emphasis" (1987, p. 106). Repetition of visual information can also be used to emphasize detail. By showing similar visual content over and over again, the television director can give greater emphasis to that content.

Reconstruction

The basic tenant of visual montage is that new meanings or interpretations can be conveyed through the juxtaposition of images. The viewer's interpretation of a shot is not based on the visual content of that shot alone. More often, it is the visual *context* of that shot that provides the basis for interpreting its content. Just as verbal language is interpreted by the order and combination of words, so is the interpretation of visual content influenced by the order in which the visual images are presented. The impact of visual images on the viewer is enjoined by the context in which they are shown and their juxtaposition to other images. Also, the visual images have the potential to either reinforce or alter the interpretation of what is being said. The speaker's message can be enhanced by showing images that reinforce what the speaker is saying. Contrarily, the speaker's message can be diminished by showing irrelevant or contradictory visual information. And, as with other elements of the production process, the viewer has no control over how the visual and aural messages are combined. The viewer must rely on the visual context established by the television director.

The elements of selectivity, emphasis, and reconstruction are not independent from one another. Selection of shots, for example, are directly tied to how the visual content is emphasized through repetition of similar shots. Similarly, selectivity governs the degree to which the event is visually reconstructed and how the visual images establish a context for the aural message. Thus, to separate these elements is not a useful approach in analyzing the visual content of a televised event, because it is the interaction of these elements that creates the richness and strength of the visual message.

How the television production process uses the elements of selectivity, emphasis, and reconstruction to re-create an event constitutes the basis for the central question of this chapter: How did the visual context of Jackson's televised speech, as constructed by five different news sources, provide the basis for common and/or differing interpretations of that event? A secondary question addressed by this study is how television's coverage of Jackson's speech to the 1988 Democratic National Convention differed from the coverage of his speech to the 1984 convention.

METHOD

Videotape recordings were made for each version (i.e., each news source) of Jackson's speech. A typed transcript of the speech was then used to prepare a production script for each of the five sources, showing shot changes and the times at which these changes occurred. Each version covered 50 minutes and 45 seconds of the speech, beginning with Jackson's opening "Thank you," and ending with him saying, "I love you very much."

Visualization of Jackson's speech by all five news sources included shots in which changes in the visual content or changes in camera framing resulted from camera movement or subject movement within the frame. These changes were noted on each production script and were treated as separate shots for purposes of this analysis.[3] In addition, four of the five news sources used very slow dissolves throughout the speech, which often resulted in a superimposition of two images. For example, one of the dissolves used by NBC lasted 16 seconds between the two images. Juxtaposition of images through the use of a long dissolve potentially heightens the viewer's perceived association between the two images. Because these superimposed images had the potential of conveying a special meaning, dissolves that had a duration of 1.5 seconds or more were coded as separate shots in the analysis. Using this method of classification, a total of 1,509 shots from all five news sources were used as the basis for the analysis.

A computer program was developed to facilitate the coding of data for each shot. For each shot 15 variables were coded (not including optional comments or written descriptions entered as notations), which resulted in the coding of 22,635 data points. The computer program presented a series of screens calling for input of data for each variable. As the code for one variable was entered (by a single key stroke), the program proceeded immediately to the next screen. When the coded information was confirmed as being correct, the data for each shot was written to a data file thus eliminating the need to code the data by hand or in written form.

Table 24.1 shows the categories of information that were coded for each shot. In the final analyses, some of the data were collapsed into fewer categories to make reporting of the results less cumbersome.

Two persons working together coded the data for each shot. Differences in judgment regarding such things as camera framing or camera position were discussed prior to entering the code into the computer program. This method of arriving at a consensual judgment had been used successfully in doing a visual analysis of Jackson's 1984 convention speech (see Tiemens et al., 1988), and rare instances where judgments differed were easily resolved.

ANALYSIS

The five news sources analyzed in this study (ABC, CBS, NBC, CNN, and C-SPAN) used a combined 1,509 shots to cover the 50 minutes and 45 seconds of Jesse Jackson's speech. This number is exclusive of the several hundred shots shown during the crowd demonstrations that preceded and followed the speech. Throughout the speech, cheering and applause of an enthusiastic audience interrupted Jackson's speech several times, though not for sustained periods of time. Most often, Jackson continued to speak as the crowd shouted and clapped its approval. It is noteworthy to mention, however, that those periods of interruption, especially when Jackson stopped talking, represent a sharp contrast, visually, to periods of time that the audience remained quiet. Thus, shots that coincided with these differing periods of reaction are treated separately in the analyses when appropriate to understanding the nature of the coverage of Jackson's speech.

GENERAL PRODUCTION TREATMENT

Shot Length and Cutting Rate

Table 24.2 shows the frequency and average length of shots used by the five news sources throughout Jackson's speech. NBC used a total of 443 shots, far more than any other source, and more than twice the number of shots used by C-SPAN (201).

The average shot length for all news sources was 10.1 seconds; but shots taken during periods of crowd interruptions when Jackson was not speaking averaged less than half that length (4.4 seconds), a pattern that was consistent across all sources. Compared with other news sources, ABC used a greater number of shots during periods of crowd interruptions (87) resulting in a faster cutting rate (3.5 seconds per shot). C-SPAN, on the other hand, used only 54 shots during those segments, which resulted in an average shot length of 5.6 seconds, a much slower cutting rate.

TABLE 24.1
Information Coded for Each Shot

1. Network (news source):
    1 ABC
    2 CBS
    3 NBC
    4 CNN
    5 C-SPAN

2. Time at beginning of shot: (mm:ss)

3. Type of transition:
    1 Cut
    2 Dissolve
    3 Superimposition or long dissolve
    4 Zoom in
    5 Zoom out
    6 Pan
    7 Movement of subject or object

4. Camera framing:
    1 Cover shot (faces or details not distinguishable)
    2 Wide angle (generally, more than six persons, signs, etc.)
    3 Medium shot (framed at about the waist)
    4 Close-up (shot shows shoulders)
    5 Extreme close-up (showing face only)
    6 Close-up foreground, medium shot background

5. Shot content:
    1 Jackson
    2 Delegates/floor audience
    3 Guest (unknown identity)
    4 National political figure (Carter, Cuomo, etc.)
    5 Celebrity (Ed Asner, Mike Farrel, etc.)
    6 News media personnel (Rather, Stahl, etc.)
    7 Objects (signs, balloons, etc.)
    8 Symbolic visual expression (hands, gestures, etc.)

6. Number of persons shown in the shot
    (medium and close-up shots only)

7. Demographics of audience (Race):
    1 White
    2 Black
    3 Mixed White and Black
    4 Hispanic
    5 Asian and Pacific
    6 Native American
    7 Undetermined Ethnic
    8 Mixed

8. Demographics of the audience (sex):
    1 Male
    2 Female
    3 Male and female

9. Demographics of the audience (age):
    1 35 years and younger
    2 35 to 60 years
    3 60 years and older
    4 Mixed-age group

10. Vertical camera angle:
    1 High camera angle (camera looking down at subject)
    2 Medium camera angle (camera positioned at eye level)
    3 Low camera angle (camera looking up at subject)
    4 Camera angle not applicable

(Continued)

TABLE 24.1
(*Continued*)

11. Camera position (relative to subject shown on camera):	1 Front
	2 Left front
	3 Left side
	4 Left rear
	5 Rear (back of head)
	6 Right rear
	7 Right side
	8 Right front
12. Audience reaction:	1 Serious/attentive
	2 Cheering
	3 Applauding
	4 Interactive dialogue (affirmation)
	5 Smiling
	6 Laughing
	7 Crying
	8 Indifference/nonattentive
	9 Unrelated activity (e.g., media interview)
13. Does the shot make a *semantic connection* to the speech? (Y/N)	
14. Verbal context of the shot:	1 Jackson speaking/audience quiet
	2 Jackson speaking/audience cheering
	3 Audience cheering/Jackson not speaking
15. Time at end of shot: (mm:ss)	

The rate at which these changes in the visual images flashed across the screen suggests two important considerations for how the production process may have influenced the audience's perception of Jackson's speech. First, the greater frequency of shots allowed for more repetition of similar visual content, thereby giving greater emphasis to what that content suggested. In other words, by repeating several shots that showed the audience cheering wildly, the director gave greater emphasis to that reaction. Second, the faster cutting rate, resulting from a greater frequency of shots over a constant time period, contributed to what Zettl (1990) has referred to as "tertiary motion." According to Zettl, tertiary motion intensifies the visual message and influences the viewer's perception of whether the event is fast or slow. Thus, in Zettl's terms, the fast cutting rate can heighten the dynamic quality of the event. This phenomenon is exceptionally relevant to how Jackson's speech was covered.

NBC used a relatively high number of shots (222) during periods when Jackson was speaking and the audience was quiet. In fact, the cutting rate for NBC during these segments was faster than periods in which Jackson was speaking and the audience was cheering. The increased cutting rate while Jackson was speaking had the potential to heighten the dynamic quality of Jackson's speech, depending on the visual content of the images shown.

TABLE 24.2
Frequency and Average Length of Shots

	ABC	CBS	NBC	CNN	C-SPAN	*All Sources*
Total number of shots	247	299	443	319	201	1509
Average shot length (in seconds)	12.3	10.2	6.9	9.6	15.1	10.1
Periods of Jackson speaking (audience quiet)						
Number of shots	58	118	222	120	109	627
Percent of total shots	23.5	39.5	50.1	37.6	54.2	41.5
Average shot length	13.3	14.9	6.3	11.6	22.0	12.3
Periods of Jackson speaking (audience cheering)						
Number of shots	102	101	165	138	38	544
Percent of total shots	41.3	33.8	37.3	43.3	18.9	36.1
Average shot length	19.4	9.8	8.4	9.6	9.2	11.1
Periods of crowd interruptions (Jackson not speaking)						
Number of shots	87	80	56	61	54	338
Percent of total shots	35.2	26.7	12.6	19.1	26.9	22.4
Average shot length	3.5	3.7	4.6	5.5	5.6	4.4

The shot length for all news sources averaged 10.1 seconds in duration and ranged from one second (the shortest unit of time measured) to 1 minute and 51 seconds. Shots of long duration were those that concentrated on Jackson; and shots that were longer than 90 seconds appeared only on ABC and CBS. Table 24.3 shows the relative distribution of shot lengths across the five news sources. As the table shows, about half of the shots appearing on ABC, CBS, and NBC were fewer than 5 seconds, whereas shots of this length on CNN and C-SPAN accounted for less than one fourth of the shots seen on these sources. In other words, coverage on CNN and C-SPAN tended to be more slowly paced.

Shot Transitions

Visual transitions, like shot length, influence the visual rhythm or pacing of a televised event. Cutting from one shot to the next generally results in a fast and abrupt change in the visual image and increases the production's visual pace. Dissolves, on the other hand, have a more fluid quality than do cuts. Dissolves can slow the pace of the event and convey a more relaxed mood.

As might be expected, the predominant use of transitions in covering Jackson's speech was the straight cut. The use of cuts by all five news sources accounted for 89.1% of all transitions used. With the exception of CBS, the news sources also used dissolves

TABLE 24.3
Distribution of Shots by Length (Percent of Total Shots)

Shot Length (in seconds)	ABC	CBS	NBC	CNN	C-SPAN
2 or fewer	19.4	20.1	18.7	9.1	7.5
3–4	28.3	33.8	35.2	13.5	14.4
5–10	25.1	23.1	32.3	51.1	36.8
11–20	10.5	8.0	7.0	18.5	17.9
21–30	6.1	6.7	3.6	3.5	9.0
31–40	2.0	4.0	1.8	2.8	4.0
41–60	4.5	2.7	1.1	1.6	7.5
61–90	2.4	1.0	0.2	0.0	3.0
over 90	1.6	0.7	0.0	0.0	0.0

throughout their coverage of the speech; and in several instances these dissolves were of such long duration that the images appeared as a superimposition on the screen. The use of these superimpositions or long dissolves is noteworthy because they tend to strengthen the connection or visual association between the two shots. As one shot slowly blends into the next, the visual images become one, emphasizing the relationship between the two. To allow for closer analysis of this occurrence, dissolves that were longer than 1.5 seconds were treated as a separate category.

Table 24.4 shows the frequency and percentage of cuts, dissolves, and long dissolves used by each news source. NBC's coverage included 72 dissolves throughout the speech, 70 of which were longer than 1.5 seconds, resulting in a momentary superimposition of two images. The longest of these superimpositions on NBC was held on the screen for 16 seconds.

Closer observation of how these long dissolves were used shows several differences among the four news sources (CBS used none). With the exception of ABC, most of the long dissolves were used in the early part of Jackson's speech, with 70% or more occurring before the half-way mark of 25 minutes. ABC, on the other hand, didn't use any long dissolves until Jackson was 25 minutes and 51 seconds into his speech. This had the tendency to slow the pace toward the end of Jackson's speech on ABC; and the fusing together of shots of Jackson and his audience gave greater emphasis to how Jackson related to his audience. C-SPAN was the only source to superimpose objects (banners or signs) over other images (4 of the 15 instances on C-SPAN). All other instances involved shots of Jackson, shots of the audience, or cover shots. ABC and NBC used superimpositions primarily to juxtapose images of Jackson with images of his audience. Long dissolves connecting images of Jackson with the audience were used in 6 out of 7 cases on ABC and in 42 out of 70 cases on NBC. Superimpositions of Jackson and his audience were shown only four times on C-SPAN and only once on CNN.

TABLE 24.4
Frequency of Shot Transitions

Type of Transition	ABC	CBS	NBC	CNN	C-SPAN	All Sources
Cut	189	254	276	254	145	1118
	(90.0)	(100.0)	(79.3)	(91.7)	(87.4)	(89.1)
Dissolve	14	0	2	11	5	32
	(6.7)	(0.0)	(0.6)	(4.0)	(3.0)	(2.6)
Long Dissolve	7	0	70	12	16	105
(2 seconds or more)	(3.3)	(0.0)	(20.1)	(4.3)	(9.6)	(8.4)

Note: Figures in parenthesis indicate column percents.

Camera Framing

Visual emphasis or intensity is achieved primarily through camera framing, the relative size of the image within the borders of the television frame. Wide-angle camera shots provide a greater array of visual information; but because the relative size of objects within the frame is reduced, visual detail is deemphasized. Close-ups, on the other hand, tend to direct the viewer's attention to eventful detail and give the image greater importance.

Camera framing is particularly relevant in the coverage of public-speaking events because of the way in which it directs the viewer's attention to the speaker or to pertinent details of the event (such as the audience's reaction). Using close-ups to increase the size of the speaker's image on the screen commands greater attention from the viewer and intensifies the speaker's remarks. Contrarily, wide-angle shots diminish the size of the speaker's image and commands less attention.

Table 24.5 shows how differences in camera framing were distributed among the five news sources during Jackson's speech. All of the news sources concentrated more heavily on medium shots and close-ups throughout Jackson's speech. This was particularly true of NBC, which generously used close-ups and extreme close-ups throughout its coverage. However, the distribution of camera framing for each news source differed with respect to shots of Jackson and shots of the audience. As Table 24.5 shows, with the exception of ABC and C-SPAN, close-ups and extreme close-ups were concentrated more on the audience than on Jackson.

Table 24.6 shows the relative length of time devoted to various levels of camera framing and illustrates how medium and close-up shots were used to visualize Jackson and his audience. All of the news sources concentrated on using medium and close-up shots of Jackson and his audience by devoting a greater number of shots and a greater percentage of time to this type of camera framing. By using tight camera framing such as this, the television news sources portrayed the event not so much as a public speech but something more akin to an intimate communicative dialogue between Jackson and

TABLE 24.5
Camera Framing

	ABC	CBS	NBC	CNN	C-SPAN	All Sources
All Shots*						
Cover shot	7.5	13.0	3.2	7.5	10.2	7.9
Wide angle	11.7	10.4	8.9	15.3	22.0	12.8
Medium shot	31.7	33.1	15.6	20.9	18.3	23.6
Close-up	37.5	32.4	38.7	42.4	45.2	38.8
Extreme close-up	11.7	11.0	33.6	14.0	4.3	16.9
Shots of Jackson*						
Wide angle	9.2	17.2	12.2	13.3	6.5	11.9
Medium shot	41.3	27.6	22.6	23.5	11.3	26.5
Close-up	42.2	49.4	53.9	55.1	74.2	53.3
Extreme close-up	7.3	5.8	11.3	8.1	8.1	8.3
Shots of Audience*						
Wide angle	11.5	6.0	7.8	14.9	34.0	12.8
Medium shot	29.8	46.0	13.2	23.2	27.7	25.9
Close-up	39.4	30.0	32.9	42.3	35.1	35.6
Extreme close-up	19.2	18.0	46.1	11.1	3.2	25.7

*Figures shown represent percentage of shots within each category.
Table excludes superimpositions and long dissolves.

his audience. ABC was particularly effective in this regard, by devoting more time to medium and close-up shots (92.4%) and concentrating its coverage on shots of Jackson. Medium and close-up shots of Jackson accounted for 41.3% of all shots shown on ABC and represented 80.2% of the total time devoted to those shots. In contrast to ABCs coverage, NBC and CNN concentrated more on the audience by devoting a greater percentage of shots and more time to medium and close-up shots of the audience. CBS and C-SPAN used proportionately more cover shots than the other news sources and devoted more time to the use of cover shots, thereby making Jackson's speech more of an auditorium event for viewers of those networks.

Camera Movement

When the camera zooms in or out on the image, the change in camera framing becomes even more important. A zoom-in on the speaker makes the change in size more compelling and demands greater attention from the viewer. A zoom-out, on the other hand, disengages the viewer's attention and diminishes the impact of the speaker's remarks.

As noted earlier, occurrences of camera movement or subject movement that significantly altered the camera framing or visual content shown within the frame were treated as separate shots. Visual transitions that resulted from camera or subject movement

TABLE 24.6
Frequency and Average Length of Shots

	ABC	CBS	NBC	CNN	C-SPAN	All Sources
Cover Shots	27	62	15	41	30	175
Percent of total shots	11.3	20.7	4.0	13.4	16.2	12.5
Total duration (seconds)	127	408	73	266	272	1146
Percent of total time	4.2	13.4	2.7	8.8	9.1	7.7
Average shot length	4.7	6.6	4.9	6.5	9.1	6.5
Wide-Angle Shots of Jackson	10	15	14	13	4	56
Percent of total shots	4.2	5.0	3.8	4.2	2.2	4.0
Total duration (seconds)	67	130	71	161	110	539
Percent of total time	2.2	4.3	2.6	5.3	3.7	3.6
Average shot length	6.7	8.7	5.1	12.4	27.5	9.6
Wide-Angle Shots of Audience	12	9	19	25	32	97
Percent of total shots	5.0	3.0	5.1	8.1	17.3	6.9
Total duration (seconds)	37	43	85	131	326	622
Percent of total time	1.2	1.4	3.1	4.3	10.9	4.2
Average shot length	3.1	4.8	4.5	5.2	10.2	6.4
Medium and Close-up Shots of Jackson	99	72	101	85	57	414
Percent of total shots	41.3	24.1	27.1	27.7	30.8	29.5
Total duration (seconds)	2430	1967	1532	1473	1814	9216
Percent of total time	80.2	64.6	56.8	48.6	60.8	62.3
Average shot length	24.5	27.3	15.2	17.3	31.8	22.3
Medium and Close-up Shots of Audience	92	141	224	143	62	662
Percent of total shots	38.3	47.2	60.1	46.6	33.5	47.2
Total duration (seconds)	369	499	938	997	463	3266
Percent of total time	12.2	16.4	34.8	32.9	15.5	22.1
Average shot length	4.0	3.5	4.2	7.0	7.5	4.9
Total Shots	240	299	373	307	185	1404
Total Length	3030	3047	2699	3028	2985	14789

Note: Table does not include superimpositions and long dissolves.

accounted for 149 (9.9%) of the shots from all news sources. The frequency of these transitions is so small that further analysis is not very useful. However, one point is noteworthy. CBS and NBC used more zoom-in shots than all other sources combined (23 for CBS, 12 for NBC, 14 for all other sources). Of those zoom-in shots that occurred on CBS, 20 of the 23 were shots of Jackson. Of those on NBC, 10 of the 12 were shots of the audience. In other words, CBS, by zooming-in on Jackson, more likely directed the viewers' attention to the speaker, whereas NBC gave greater emphasis to the audience in its use of zoom-in shots.

Camera Angle

Armer has described how vertical camera placement, relative to the subject being photographed, influences our perception of the person shown on the screen:

> When we look down on someone, figuratively as well as literally, we place him or her in an inferior position. He or she becomes subordinate, recessive, smaller than we.... We look up to people we respect, who occupy a higher position in society, who tower above us intellectually or professionally. Similarly, when a director places the camera below eye level, looking up at a character, that character assumes a position of dominance, of strength, of importance. (1986, pp. 183–184)

This phenomenon is exceedingly relevant in photographing a political figure, in that it can reinforce or contradict the person's intellectual persona. It can depict the person as a viable leader or as a person of less importance. Camera angle appears to have had little influence in how Jesse Jackson was shown, however. The relative distribution of medium and close-up shots for high, medium, and low camera angles is shown in Table 24.7. Almost all medium and close-up shots of Jackson were taken from eye level probably because the pool cameras that photographed Jackson in a head-on shot (full front) were positioned on a platform directly in front and at the same height as the podium. There were some exceptions, however; and the most striking deviation was in

TABLE 24.7
Vertical Camera Angle

	ABC	CBS	NBC	CNN	C-SPAN	All Sources
Medium and Close-up Shots of Jackson						
High	8	9	0	1	1	19
	(8.1)	(12.5)	(0.0)	(1.2)	(1.7)	(4.6)
Medium	89	60	100	81	42	372
	(89.9)	(83.3)	(99.0)	(95.3)	(72.4)	(89.7)
Low	1	3	1	3	25	23
	(1.0)	(4.2)	(1.0)	(3.5)	(25.9)	(5.5)
Not applicable	1	0	0	0	0	1
	(1.0)	(0.0)	(0.0)	(0.0)	(0.0)	(0.2)
Medium and Close-up Shots of Audience						
High	55	79	99	111	52	396
	(59.8)	(56.0)	(44.2)	(77.6)	(83.9)	(59.8)
Medium	22	42	82	25	7	178
	(23.9)	(29.8)	(36.6)	(17.5)	(11.3)	(26.9)
Low	15	20	43	7	3	88
	(16.3)	(14.2)	(19.2)	(4.9)	(4.8)	(13.3)

C-SPAN's coverage. C-SPAN used a camera positioned below eye level in 25.9% of the medium and close-ups of Jackson. ABC and CBS, on the other hand, used relatively more shots taken from a high camera angle; but the proportion of these shots is relatively small (8.1% and 12.5% respectively).

Vertical camera angle of shots taken of the audience were a different matter. Medium and close-up shots of the audience were predominantly from high camera angles, ranging from 44.2% on NBC to 83.9% of such shots on C-SPAN. However, ABC, CBS, and NBC also used a considerable number of low-angle shots in photographing the audience; the percentage of low-angle shots ranged from 14.2% (CBS) to 19.2% (NBC) of all medium and close-up shots of the audience. A possible reason for this higher proportion among these networks could be because of the number of remote camera units that they had on the convention floor.

AUDIENCE DEMOGRAPHICS

In the analysis of Jackson's 1984 speech, Tiemens and colleagues (1988) showed how television depicted his speech as a black event by concentrating heavily on visual coverage of African American delegates and audience members. A repetitive and frequent showing of African Americans was a consistent pattern across all news sources in 1984 and was particularly dominant in CBS's coverage.

The question of how news sources depicted Jackson's 1988 audience is equally germane. Throughout the campaign the news media were unremitting in reminding the public that Jackson is an African American and that he was the candidate for African American voters and other racial minorities across America. The prominent question seemed to be whether he could be a candidate for white voters. Thus, the identity of Jackson's audience as portrayed through the visual images of network news sources is significant.

Demographic statistics released by the Democratic National Committee in 1988 showed that 67.3% of the convention delegates and alternates were white, 22.9% were African American, and the remainder made up other racial minorities. Table 24.8 compares these figures with the percentage of medium and close-up shots showing delegates on the convention floor during Jackson's speech.

The percentage of reaction shots that showed African Americans ranged from 40.0% on ABC to 50.4% on CNN. These ratios are considerably higher than the 22.9% that were estimated to be in attendance. It is quite feasible that the percentage of African American delegates and alternates in attendance for Jackson's speech was higher than the official statistics would indicate. But it is unlikely that the percentages would be more than double those official figures. The distribution of reaction shots and the percentage of African Americans shown suggests that the news sources, as they did in 1984, emphasized Jackson's speech as a black event.

Also, the raw frequencies of these shots should not be overlooked, because the repetition of these shots further emphasized their visual content. NBC devoted 90 medium and close-up shots to African American members of the audience, a far greater number than those shown on the other networks (26 on C-SPAN, 30 on ABC, 50 on CBS, and 63

TABLE 24.8
Demographics of the Audience as Depicted in Medium and Close-up Shots

		DNC Stats	ABC	CBS	NBC	CNN	C-SPAN	All Sources
Race:	White	67.3	48.0	40.2	43.2	38.4	38.9	41.8
	Black	22.9	40.0	41.0	42.3	50.4	48.2	44.0
	Both Black and White		5.3	11.5	5.6	4.8	11.1	7.1
	Other	9.8	6.7	7.4	8.9	6.4	1.8	7.1
Sex:	Male	51.2	36.0	18.9	34.3	24.0	29.6	28.7
	Female	48.8	49.3	63.1	58.2	62.4	55.6	58.7
	Both		14.7	18.0	7.5	13.6	14.8	12.6
Age:	Under 35		25.3	27.0	40.4	33.6	31.5	33.4
	35–60		61.3	51.6	47.9	52.8	57.4	52.3
	Over 60		5.3	6.6	5.2	3.2	0.0	4.6
	Mixed-age Groups		8.0	14.8	6.6	10.4	11.1	9.7

on CNN). The repetitive and frequent showing of African Americans by NBC could have given the impression that proportionately more African Americans were in attendance.

In addition to concentrating on African Americans in the audience, all of the networks tended to focus on women more than men. The proportion of medium and close-up shots showing women for all sources (58.7%) is far greater than the actual 48.8% who were in attendance, based on the figures of the Democratic National Committee. And as noted before, the frequency with which shots of women were shown is an important consideration. The repetition of these shots created and reinforced the impressions that Jackson was addressing an audience made up mostly of African Americans and women.

VISUAL UNITY AND THE SPEECH TEXT

Visual Continuity

The space and time of a televised event takes on a quality that is unique to the medium. The physical space and real time during which the event takes place are no longer relevant, because the medium creates a space and time of its own. The physical constraint of viewing the event from only one vantage point (as does the firsthand observer) no longer exists when that event is visually re-created by the television medium. The television viewer sees the event from several vantage points as a result of instant changes from one camera shot to the next. And, the order and sequencing of those shots determine the extent to which the *televised* event maintains a meaningful coherence and unity.

The degree to which television coverage depicted Jackson's speech as a unified event relates to how well the medium preserved a visual continuity and spatial coherence between the speaker and his audience. This continuity can be analyzed by looking at the consistency of index vector orientations in shots of Jackson and shots of his audience. The "index vector orientation" of a shot is the screen direction in which the person shown is facing (for a more complete discussion of this concept see Zettl, 1990, p. 309). For example, when Jackson was photographed from a viewpoint that showed him facing to the left, a subsequent shot of someone in the audience should have shown that person facing to the right. The juxtaposition of these two shots would then establish that the person in the audience was looking at Jackson. If both Jackson and the audience member where shown facing the same direction on the screen, the juxtaposition of shots would suggest that the person in the audience was looking away from Jackson. In cases where Jackson was directly facing the camera, the index vector would be neutral, thus allowing for a subsequent shot that showed the audience facing either screen-right or screen-left.

The visual continuity of Jackson's speech was analyzed by looking at the degree to which each news source maintained appropriate index vector orientations in juxtaposing shots of Jackson with shots of his audience. Among all the news sources, 113 shot combinations showed medium and close-up shots of Jackson juxtaposed with medium and close-up shots of his audience. Of these combinations all but three maintained an appropriate vector orientation (i.e., visual continuity between the shots was correct), which is remarkable given the circumstances of covering a live event such as the Jackson speech.

Semantic Connections

Semantic connections refer to those instances in which the visual images are linked to the verbal text of the speech. A printed text of Jackson's speech was made available to the press prior to his appearance at the podium. Thus, production personnel had the opportunity to choose visual images that would match or reinforce verbal references in the text. Tiemens and colleagues (1988) found only 12 instances, out of more than 700 reaction shots in Jackson's 1984 speech, where the visual images made a semantic connection to the verbal text. In 1988 the five news sources were more proficient in choosing visual images to reinforce Jackson's oral comments. Of the 662 medium and close-up reaction shots used by all news sources, 88 were classified as semantic connections. Shots that were considered semantic connections fell into three broad categories: shots of celebrities or political figures (38.6 %), shots of delegates (36.4%), and shots of signs, banners, or objects (25%).

Only a few images, coded as semantic connections, were selected in common by the five news sources. When Jackson proffered a "special salute to President Jimmy Carter" all five sources showed Carter and his family seated in the Omni. Another semantic connection used by all sources except ABC was the shot of a sign proclaiming "Lesbians/Gays for Jackson" that was shown on the screen when Jackson encouraged lesbians and gays to fight against discrimination. And when Jackson shouted (as he did in 1984) "I would rather have Roosevelt in a wheelchair than Reagan and Bush on a horse," all news sources except C-SPAN focused their cameras on delegates who were seated in wheelchairs at the base of the podium.

Other semantic connections included shots of a quilt (in reference to Jackson's "patch-work quilt" metaphor), a multicolored flag (the "rainbow coalition"), and signs that read "ERA YES," "GENDER GAP," and "PAY EQUITY" (used to visually reinforce several of Jackson's many references to women). In contrast to the coverage of Jackson's 1984 speech, the news sources seemed to be more attuned in 1988 to selecting visual images that corresponded to the verbal text of Jackson's speech.

AUDIENCE REACTIONS

Jesse Jackson's long-awaited speech was the climactic highlight that everyone anticipated. An estimated 17,000 delegates, guests and media personnel jammed the relatively small Omni center leaving an additional 1,000 delegates and reporters locked out of the over-crowded hall. All delegate seats were filled and the aisles of the convention floor were so crowded with guests and media personnel that movement through the aisles was nearly impossible.[4]

The response of individual members in the audience was uniform and synchronous throughout Jackson's speech. Their cheers and applause were often prompted by a sudden brightening of the house lights, and their chants were instigated by Jackson "whips" using electronic megaphones. Despite the fact that the audience response was orchestrated, it seemed genuine and sincere.

The intensely crowded conditions and the large expanse of the arena limited firsthand observations to the responses of individuals who were in close proximity. That limitation was not imposed on the television observer, however. The multiple cameras used by each news source made it possible to observe, in close detail, the reactions of individuals spread throughout the arena.

The Immediate Audience

Newspaper accounts of Jackson's speech reported an enthusiastic and emotional audience noting that many individuals were crying. Reporters for the *Boston Herald* covering the speech in Atlanta noted that Jackson's speech "evoked tears, standing ovations and rapt attention from a packed Omni Center" (Woodlief, Miga, and Battenfeld, 1988, p. 1). Similarly, the *Dallas Times Herald* reported that the delegates "listened in rapt attention, many moved to tears by the power of his remarks" (1988, p. 1), and Richard Benedetto reporting for *USA Today* wrote that "thunderous cheers for the fiery civil rights leader shook the rafters and tears rolled down the cheeks of delegates jamming the Omni Coliseum" (1988, p. 1). The visual detail of these reports is interesting, given the limits of observing such detail on a firsthand basis. Reference to specific facial expressions and emotions suggests that the reporters relied on television images to observe the reactions of Jackson's audience. This raises the question of whether newspaper reports of Jackson's speech are a valid representation. If reporters relied on television to watch the event, their method of observation was no different from what the television viewer was engaged in.

Interestingly, newspaper reporters' accounts suggest that the audience's reaction was an odd mixture of cheers and tears; but objective analysis of the visual data leads to a different interpretation. Of 706 shots showing the audience's reaction, 366 or 51.8% showed individuals who were serious and attentive; 264 (37.4%) were shots of individuals cheering or applauding; 53 (7.5%) showed audience members smiling; and only 13 (1.8%) of the shots showed individuals who were crying. The distribution of these proportions was uniform across all five news sources.

Contrary to what reporters observed, the data reveal only a scant number of shots that showed people crying (none was shown on C-SPAN). One explanation for this discrepancy can be found by looking at the point during the speech when those few shots appeared on the screen. Of the 13 shots that showed audience members crying, 10 were shown during the last 3 minutes of Jackson's speech (one on ABC, three each on CBS, CNN, and NBC). Thus, the salience of this reaction to newspaper reporters, as well as to other television viewers, was likely because these images were a principal element in portraying the final moments of Jackson's speech.

The Extended Media Audience

How individuals in the television audience responded to Jackson's speech is a matter of speculation. The experience of immediate presence, surrounded by an enthusiastic and emotional crowd cannot be duplicated for television viewing. On the other hand, the privileged view provided by television's coverage offers visual detail and emotion that the immediate audience can't see. The only indication of what impact the speech may have had on television viewers must be gleaned from the published written reports and commentary. As noted, there is consensus among newspaper reports that Jackson delivered a fiery and emotional speech, arousing the delegates who were present in the Omni Center. The extent to which the television audience shared this perception, and indeed shared the emotions of the immediate audience, remains an unanswerable question.

An even more intriguing question is how those who were *not* present, and who did *not* watch the speech on television, reacted to Jackson's appearance before the National Democratic Convention. Based on a limited examination of newspaper reports, it seems apparent that those accounts of the speech were also subject to the filtering of the television medium. Newspaper reports that were based on the images of television are shaped by how the medium selects, emphasizes, and reconstructs the event, and by the perceptions of the reporter in assembling and conveying that information to readers.

CONCLUSION

Television critic Phil Kloer, noting that television's coverage frequently ignored what was really going on at the convention, suggested that the television audience got a flavor of the "real event" when Jackson spoke:

> The two roads of reality finally became one as Jackson's family arrived on the podium. The commercials and the cutaways were put away, and for the next hour, as Jackson spoke,

viewers at home were able to experience as closely as possible the same reality that those in the Omni perceived. (1988, p. C1.)

Kloer's comment provokes the critical question that this study addresses: What was the true "reality" of Jackson's speech? Was it the speech that convention delegates heard through the resonant sound system in the jammed Omni area? Or was the reality in one of the five televised versions of Jackson's speech that showed intimate and close-up images of Jackson and his audience?

Television's portrayal of events, such as the Jackson speech, is governed by how the medium selects, emphasizes, and reconstructs the visual images that represent the original event. Furthermore, the variability in how different news sources select and reconstruct those images, can lead to differing interpretations of the event that is portrayed. In the case of Jackson's speech to the 1988 National Democratic Convention, at least six interpretations were possible based on which version was observed.

The extent of television's influence on audiences' perceptions extends beyond what viewers see on their private 21-inch windows to the world. Based on limited evidence from newspaper accounts of Jackson's speech, it is apparent that the medium also influences how the event gets reported to those who are not privy to the firsthand television experience. Even those who saw the event on television likely had their impressions reinforced or altered by subsequent accounts reported in the press. It is important to recognize that those accounts were also based on observations that were filtered through the selectivity of the television medium.

ENDNOTES

[1] This research was supported, in part, by a grant from the Annenberg Washington Program. An earlier version of this study was presented to the 1991 convention of the National Communication Association (Tiemens, 1991).

[2] An estimated 19.7 million households tuned in to the 1988 coverage of the speech, compared to 23.7 million households that watched the 1984 speech. The difference in audience size was probably because of the lateness of the hour during which the 1988 speech was presented (10:57 P.M. EDT). The 1984 speech started at 10:04 P.M. EDT.

[3] Thus, the unit of measurement for this study, which is referred to as a *shot*, is defined as *a visual segment within which spatial and temporal continuity is preserved* (after Spottiswoode, 1970, p. 462). To avoid confusion, and for ease of readability, the term shot will be used throughout this chapter.

[4] The author was on the convention floor during the entire period of Jackson's speech. Firsthand observations are based on his presence in the Omni Center.

REFERENCES

Armer, A. (1986). *Directing television and film*. Belmont, CA: Wadsworth.
Arvidson, C. (1988, July 20). Jackson sets stage with electric speech. *Dallas Times Herald*, p. A20.
Benedetto, R. (1988, July 20). Jackson's big hurrah: HOPE. *USA Today*, p. A1.
Buchwald, A. (1988, July 19). Just a boring squabble fed by the media. *USA Today*, p. A11.
Kilpatrick, J. (1988, July 19). Jackson is the main topic. *USA Today*, p. A11.

Kindem, G. (1987). *The moving image: Production principles and practices*. Glenview, IL: Scott Foresman & Co.

Kloer, P. (1988, July 21). What networks' viewers see is not always what Omni gets. *Atlanta Journal and Atlanta Constitution*, p. C11.

Locker, R. (1988, July 19). Dukakis, Jackson join forces. *Tampa Tribune*.

Spottiswoode, R. (1970). *Film and its techniques*. Berkeley: University of California Press.

Tiemens, R. K. (1991). *Television's coverage of Jesse Jackson's speech to the 1988 National Democratic Convention*. Paper presented to the 77th annual convention of the National Communication Association.

Tiemens, R. K., Sillars, M. O., Alexander, D. A., & Werling, D. S. (1988). Television coverage of Jesse Jackson's speech to the 1984 Democratic national convention. *Journal of Broadcasting & Electronic Media, 32*, 1–22.

Warner, J. (1988, July 20). Jesse! *Atlanta Journal and Atlanta Constitution*, p. C1.

Woodlief, W., Miga, A., & Battenfeld, J. (1988, July 20). Jesse lights the fire. *Boston Herald*, pp. 1–5.

Zettl, H. (1973). *Sight sound motion: Applied media aesthetics*. Belmont, CA: Wadsworth.

Zettl, H. (1990). *Sight sound motion: Applied media aesthetics* (2nd Ed.). Belmont, CA: Wadsworth.

Examining Documentary Photography Using the Creative Method

CRAIG DENTON
University of Utah

When it comes to applied media aesthetics, theory and methodology are less visible and more pragmatic than in traditional visual communication research. The reason? The artifacts that aestheticians create are generally for mass consumption. They must use mass media to distribute their knowledge, so in order to realize their ideas, practitioners have to be aware of the exigencies of marketing communication. The aura of scholarship must yield to practices that attract and hold attention.

Still, the productions of applied media aesthetics are no less valuable as expressions of knowledge. Whether the mode of recording is a written investigative report or a filmed account, and no matter if the form of presentation is a book, film, or video, such artifacts represent epistemological ways of knowing. Although theory and methodology may be less visible and less openly expressed than in traditional academic inquiry, and although aesthetics might seem equally important as facts in media presentations, those twin companions of ideation and problem solving are embedded in applications in mass media.

This chapter focuses on one of those ways of discovering and organizing knowledge in mass media: documentary photography. Documentary photography is the process of using pictures and supplementary written text to record information, tell a story, or reveal a condition. Documentary photography resides in the realm of applied media aesthetics because it employs two of the aesthetic fields developed by Zettl, light and color and two-dimensional space, and because it is concerned with encoding and decoding meta-messages. It is a methodological way of knowing because the documentary photographer is an investigator who tries to apply a systematic approach in generating evidence and in analyzing those visual phenomena.

Although most people will think of the word *document* as a noun, it is derived from the Latin word *docere*, which means to teach (Coles, 1997). In the 18th century the word *document* took on its current verb definition when it came to mean furnishing evidence. Inevitably, then, the documentary and documentary photography have long been entwined with producing knowledge and understanding.

AESTHETICS IN DOCUMENTARY WORK

The documentarian faces an eternal quandary. Although he or she is in the business of providing factual evidence and is committed to truth-telling, the documentary is perceived in mass media as a form of personal expression. Often, the documentarian is identified as the sole author or at least part of a group of collaborators who claim authorship and whose names are printed on the page or rolled in the credits. Inevitably, there is a tension between truth-telling and the aesthetics of personal vision and statement (Gross, Katz, & Ruby, 1988). On one hand, docmentarians make an implied contract with both the subject(s) and the audience that what they present is true to what James Agee called "human actuality." They are charged with accurately representing what is there with a minimum of personal interference. Yet the documentarian is a person with an ego and is perceived as being a creator, so the creation of a personal vision and artistic statement are part of the motivation and reason for creating a documentary.

The aesthetics of documentary work can become confounded over time, too, and meta-messages can be created at any time in the creative process, from preproduction through production to postproduction. For instance, whereas a photographer might capture an image and originally intend it to be part of a larger presentation of many images on a page, each providing an additive element to the construction of a larger truth composed of all images, that single image might become larger than itself if it captures the serendipitous blend of content, form and composition. It is lifted above the rest of the images. Then, it might find itself in a new context, framed and hung on the wall of a museum, signaling a new expression: an art photograph, a new meta-message.

Although the photographic documentarian is trained to see and articulate visual fact, he or she also hopes that the gestalt of the image will be more than a simple sum of data. The social documentary photographer, for instance, hopes that the audience will be so touched by the revelation of a social injustice that it will be moved to action and lobby government or business to apply resources to correct the problem.

Ultimately, however, content is more important than artistry in documentary photography, and the expression of a coherent, engaging narrative is more important than self-expression. Aesthetic principles primarily are used to inform rather than to make or evaluate art. Applied media aesthetics are a form of pragmatics, with aesthetics being a way to operationalize vision, to make it articulate and comprehensible. For example, lighting reveals content, although it also might evoke a mood. Lens focal lengths provide means of organizing space in different ways, to capture more or less detail, while also possibly magnifying emotion. Composition is a tool for emphasis and subordination, establishing a hierarchy of meaning by saying to the audience, "This thing in your defined field of view is the most important part of the image and the other supplementary details reinforce that importance." Zettl refers to it as "clarification and intensification" in Chapter 23.

ETHNOGRAPHY AND ETHNOGRAPHIC METHODOLOGY

Although it might not be immediately apparent, documentary photography is a form of research because it follows much of the scientific method of traditional research. A documentary begins with questions, a curiosity on the part of the documentarian to learn about a culture or a social condition. Next, a plan is devised that would enable the documentarian to accumulate visual evidence that would reveal the culture or social condition and that might prove or disprove the original questions. After photographing that information, the documentarian looks at the results and tries to extrapolate themes that grow out of the original questions. Only after that systematic investigation does the documentarian begin to produce the documentary. The difference from traditonal research is that, while documentary photography sometimes finds its way into traditional research books or journals, it more often must speak to broader audiences through mass-mediated productions.

Research plans in documentary photography are typically field practices that are borrowed from ethnographic methodology. Ethnography is a form of social research that uses qualitative means of investigation and analysis. It looks at "the routine ways that people make sense of their world in everyday life" (Hammersley & Atkinson, 1995, p. 2). Ethnographic methodology refers to systematic ways that ethnographers apply social science techniques to their looking, analyzing, and reporting.

Ethnography requires that the investigator learns the culture being studied. Hence, ethnography often is associated with the study of anthropology. The ethnographer assumes that, when faced with some stimuli, people will try to interpret that stimuli and that that interpretation is in constant flux (Hammersley, 1995). To the ethnographer, those interpretations are of paramount importance because they hold meaning. Meaning, in turn, resides in human experience, because ethnography maintains that human beings have choices. When they exercise a choice, they do so for a meaningful reason (Lindlof, 1995).

Ethnographic methodology grew out of frustrations that social scientists had with physical science inquiry, which relies on a positivist model whereby scientific objectivity is the mantra. Social scientists found fault with that type of investigation because by adapting that model, the researcher was bound to limit the observation to phenomena and data that fell within the scope of the model. The model would necessarily color what was seen, because everything outside the model would have to be labeled extraneous and invalid (Jackson, 1987). There would be no room for field expedience and adapting to information as it unfolded. But social scientists felt that phenomena should be observed in their natural state, and that carefully controlled experiments in the laboratory wouldn't fit the investigation of human interaction and meaning because that would place the thing being observed in an artificial setting, devoid of surrounding context. Moreover, researchers doubted they could discover immutable laws of human behavior, because human behavior changes depending on the context.

Instead, social scientists initially stressed naturalism, observing social phenomena in the field, in place. A trained observer would adopt an antiseptic stance whereby he or she would become a "fly on the wall," an omniscient observer seeing everything but who would be unseen by the subjects being observed. Remaining essentially outside the action would lessen the subjectivity of the naturalistic inquiry.

But this stance came to be questioned, as social scientists began to acknowledge that there can be no such thing as a neutral observer. No matter how hard he or she might try, a person can't divorce the process of his or her looking from the personal attitudes and values that are a part of the investigator's psychological makeup. An observer brings that baggage to the site of observation, so it must be recognized. Instead of being a neutral observer, the social scientist should become the "participant-observer," and subjectivity would have to be accounted for in the report. The observer would be recognized as part of the context of what was being observed.

Participant observation recognizes the Heisenberg Principle in physics. Essentially, that theory says that an observer can't avoid affecting the thing being observed. To be sure, ethnographic fieldwork tries to minimize the intrusion by the observer and the per-forming by the subjects for the observer, but the methodology is necessarily introspective. Indeed, documentary photography, like all ethnography must be self-reflexive (Lindlof, 1995; Hammersley, 1995). Ethnography is part of the social world it studies. The observer shares in the "constraints, motivations, emotions and meanings" (Lindlof, 1995, p. 4) of the group's experiences. Because of that shared experience, the participant-observer is qualified to report on them.

All the while, however, the ethnographer must scrutinize the placement of the self in the observation (Coles, 1997). The participant-observer must take into consideration personal schemas developed over a lifetime that necessarily shape and color what is seen. "We learn to see only what we pragmatically need to see" (Collier & Collier, 1986, p. 6), and we become personally blind to the rest.

The notion of "seeing" is complex, too, because that seeing must take place at different points in the ethnographic process. It becomes part of the eternal problem of subjectivity and selection, as Coles pointed out:

> Who we are, to some variable extent, determines what we notice and, at another level of intellectual activity, what we regard as worthy of notice, what we find significant. . . . I face the matter of looking *and* overlooking, paying instant heed *and* letting slip by; and I face the matter of sorting out what I *have* noticed, or arranging it for emphasis—the matter, really, of *composition*, be it verbal or visual, the matter of re-presenting; and here that all-important word *narration* enters. Stories heard or seen now have to turn into stories put together with some guiding intelligence and discrimination: I must select *what* ought to be present; decide on the *tone* of that presentation, its *atmosphere* or *mood*. These words can be seen as elusive and they are compelling to an essay, an exhibition of pictures, or a film. (Coles, 1997, p. 89, italics his)

Fortunately, participant observation encourages field expedience and the application of common sense. Fieldwork must be adaptive and not overformalized or overrationalized. The participant-observer must be willing to modify the design when possibilities change (Jackson, 1987). That does not mean, however, that ethnographic methodology is devoid of theory. Becker (1974) suggested that the best social documentary photography work happens when the observers are well-versed in the culture and have a sufficiently rich theory that makes them aware of complexity. A theory in documentary photography is nothing more than a set of ideas with which you can make sense of a situation while you photograph it.

Inevitably, ethnography is about contexts, because behavior is a response to stimuli that is part of a larger context of time, place, and complex human interaction. Zettl applies context to aesthetics, too, when he states in his chapter that aesthetic fields are a product of specialized production techniques used in specific film frames or sequences, and that the creative choice of certain visual elements at certain times in the creation of visual artifacts by human beings produces aesthetic effects or meta-messages.

Coles (1997) pointed out that the notion of contexts in ethnographic research is confounding. Recording data in the field places the investigator in one context, but when it comes time to analyze the data, the researcher is often in another context: at home or the office. Placed outside the original location of recording, a new set of influences inevitably begins to work on the thought processes of the analyst, because the researcher is physically removed from the field and isolated from the human interactions that he or she was necessarily a part of when recording. The pressures of anticipated peer or audience review begin to work on the investigator, bringing in a new set of pressures. The context changes, too, when the investigator attempts to report the findings. Then, he or she faces the problem of trying to get published or aired, and that places the science within an uneasy economic context, which can influence meanings, perhaps transforming the original meanings gleaned from immediate field experience into something else.

The context of publication also influences how people "read" an image (Becker, 1995). A particular publication is a stimulus with a history and culture of perception of its own. Moreover, Becker points out that a single documentary image could be published in a variety of media. A single image could have photojournalistic elements and be published in a newspaper or magazine or it could have social documentary overtones and be part of a photography exhibit at a social service agency. It could be rich in social data or ritualistic nuance and find itself published in journals devoted to visual sociology or visual anthropology.

GETTING ACCESS

Once the documentary photographer has identified the subject matter to record, he or she must gain access to the culture. Typically, that means identifying opinion leaders within the community by first talking to people intimate with the community but outside it, a form of triangulation, and then by asking those first contacts within the community to identify others with responsibilities, special insights, or unique talents. Often, communities have already designated someone to act as the spokesperson and public liaison. Usually, several meetings with community leaders are necessary before some measure of trust can be established and the work of observation and photographic documentation can begin.

Getting and maintaining access is a negotiation between the documentarian and the subject(s). The documentary photographer is a performer in this process of inquiry and constantly needs to be aware of the dynamics of human interaction and apply common sense. For instance, the investigator relies on an understanding of the investigator's place in the interaction and the ways that that presence can influence interaction, both positively and negatively. What is said and meant in initial or subsequent interviews is a product of interpersonal interaction. The investigator must constantly monitor the state and status of the self to the other (Lindlof, 1995). The documentarian's performance is both for self-definition and for expression to the other.

When appearing on the stage to begin performing by observing, the documentarian adopts "normal appearances," wearing clothing that is appropriate for the situation but natural (Henderson, 1988). The participant-observer already will have been identified to the community and the reason for his or her presence will be common knowledge, so there is no point in acting otherwise. Clandestine activities or appearances arouse suspicion. In fact, the documentary photographer can rely on "stranger value" (Jackson, 1987) in the initial information-gathering interactions. Because the players have no prior experiences, there are no assumptions and the subjects often will be more open, just as they would with a stranger in an airport, whom they never expect to see again. But that stranger value won't be accessible at the next meeting, because by then, familiarity will be established and then proprieties will be erected. After the first meeting, people might feel they've said or revealed too much and tend to become inhibited.

The documentary photographer's strength as a participant-observer is in his or her marginalization. Not a part of the community, and therefore innocent and inexperienced in its ways, the subjects often will see the documentarian as a callow youth, eager and anxious to learn but not threatening, someone to take under a wing and offer intimacy and confidence. If a documentary photographer encounters resistance from the subject, he or she must either gracefully acknowledge that unwillingness to participate and withdraw, or if the documentarian senses the reluctance is not permanent, then he or she must engage in remedial work to reestablish access. That might mean offering more explanation for the intrusion into personal space, more elaboration of the intent or expected outcomes, more justification for the reasons why the work is important, some flattery or perhaps trivialization, making the encounter seem less important and less a threat to the subject's ego (Henderson, 1988).

MAINTAINING RAPPORT

Because successful documentary work must happen over time and repeated exposure, it's important for the documentarian to establish rapport with the subjects in the community being photographed. Maintaining that rapport is no different than the tactics that acquaintances and friends employ in personal interactions. Simply offering legitimate, honest interest in their lives is all important. It means being able to ask pertinent questions and offer informed responses at the right times. Of course, this means that the documentary photographer must be widely experienced and well-read, able to draw on an abundant set of life experiences that enable the observer to empathize.

Sometimes, the documentarian will employ different styles of conversation in interactions, depending on the demographic parameters of the audience, but without seeming forced or phony. Contrivance will put off people. Sometimes, the documentarian will provide some kind of reward to the subjects for sharing their time and expertise, if it is appropriate and if it would not likely affect future interactions.

The camera is a maddening necessity in the documentary photographic process. The documentarian relies on it because it acts like memory, capturing information, pattern, and proxemics and storing them in great detail and complexity. It allows the photographer to accurately view phenomena that he or she might not recognize at first glance but only come to understand when looking at the image through the lens of extended time, distance and experience.

Nevertheless, the camera is a third person in any interaction. It has its own kind of cachet, giving the documentarian access and legitimacy and an aura of public confidence, if he or she seems to know how to use the technology. It provides authority with its presence. It can be a conduit to understanding and intimacy, because it says to the subject that what you are doing is important enough that it should be recorded for posterity. But at the same time, it can be a barrier to fluid interaction if the subject is too sensitive to its presence. It signifies the documentarian as a person who is attempting to reveal, yet the camera can be perceived as a mask. It also can become a signal to the subject that it's time to perform, either legitimately and honestly or to promote self-interest. The charge of the documentary photographer is to sense and control all these multiple personalities that the camera brings to the encounter.

THE ETHICAL STANCE

The fact that the documentary photographer intrudes into the lives of others brings with it an ethical responsibility to behave in a moral fashion. The documentarian often is placed in the moral thicket of trying to balance personal needs against the rights of the subjects, who sometimes might not be aware of their rights, nor have a complete understanding of the documentary process and its pressures and outcomes. Gross (1988) calls these "moral imperatives."

In order to deal with the moral quandary, the documentarian relies on informed consent from the subject(s). Informed consent means that the documentarian discloses to the subject(s) the reasons for the documentary, what will be required of the subject(s), and the likely venues of public display for the images. The documentarian must tell subjects that they do not have to participate and that privacy laws prevent the documentarian from indulging in unwelcome physical intrusion, revealing embarrassing facts that aren't germane, putting the subject in a false light, or using the subject's image for advertising purposes without his or her permission.

Sometimes, subjects are media savvy and know their rights and the boundaries of the interaction, having become "exotic" for the media and having been interviewed or photographed before. Besides disclosing all the documentarian's motives, informed consent also means that the motives of the subjects need to be articulated so that there is no misunderstanding as to mutual expectations.

The ethical stance must be carried beyond the personal encounters and photographing on site. The documentary photographer is faced with a new set of ethical choices and moral imperatives when it comes time to analyze the visual data, edit the photographs and write the captions or the report. Already, photographic choices born of personal schema have been made in the framing of images. Later, the documentary photographer must honor the moral imperative of representing actuality when it comes time to crop images for printing, select images for their interactive, additive meta-messages, and create a narrative that weaves the experiences together under the mantle of authenticity.

PHOTO ELICITATION

The visual anthropologist John Collier is largely responsible for developing a technique called *photo elicitation*. This ethnographic method uses photographs to elicit new, extended responses from subjects in a documentary so that the narrative is enriched by increased breadth and density. Documentary photography is concerned with complex layering of evidence, and photo elicitation adds to the layering and helps ensure its clarity. Moreover, photo elicitation supports the ethical stance by empowering subjects, providing them a central role in the telling of their own stories.

In this technique the photographer literally uses photographs to interview the subjects. He or she will bring work prints of a previous photographic shoot to the subjects and ask them to comment on the images, prompting them with a set of questions that are designed to bring out significant detail, ritualistic nuance, or confusion.

In photo elicitation the subject becomes the teacher, often sharpening memories, thus helping to forge bridges between the subject and the documentarian. The dialogue taps into the subject's field of expertise and magnifies and legitimizes that personal authority. The technique allows for open expression while providing concrete talking points. Photos and their content become the focus of discussion, not the subjects themselves. Often, this triggers confidences and subjects reveal their values as well as attitudes.

Photo elicitation functions like a projective interview in psychology. Subjects project their feelings, as they talk "not so much to the photographer as to their own reflected images, a dialogue with themselves" (Collier & Collier, 1986, p. 118). The key for the documentary photographer is to find the appropriate respondents, to be able to return for the interviews, and to have established enough rapport that the process is welcomed and constructive.

THE VISUAL-VERBAL INTERFACE

Despite the fact that the documentary photographer works primarily in a visual medium, he or she also must work with words. For one thing, when it comes time to analyze and discuss photographs, words are the medium for those processes. One can't think or talk about images without putting those thoughts into words. Moreover, it's the documentary photographer's charge to provide captions for photographs, if not a full-blown written report or narrative. Consequently, documentary photographic method is also about the careful use of the visual and verbal so that the information they provide is integrative but not repetitive. Written text is not considered an "add-on." Rather the photographer uses the tactical strengths of images and words to construct that complex layering of meaning that is possible and desired in documentary work, when the two modes of communication work in concert to create a sum that is greater than the individual parts.

A caption must provide all background information, usually in a complete sentence, if not a paragraph, that isn't visually manifest in the image; in other words, the context in which an image can be understood. The caption can point out significant detail, that narrative information that might be small or hidden but that is necessary to be able to "read" the image correctly. The caption can point out potentially misleading information, too.

When it comes time to write captions, the documentary photographer can take several points of view. The documentarian can be a meditative onlooker thinking about what might be going on in an image and reconstruct that meaning. The writer can help control the emotions that the viewer might receive through the image. The analyst can adopt the persona of the scientist dissecting what is seen. He or she can be an historian remembering a distant past that is important for unlocking the meaning of the immediate past of an image. The caption writer can be a poet creating metaphor that resonates with the mood of the image, or the documentarian can be a verbal cropper who limits the boundaries of meaning possible when a person looks at an image. Finally, the documentarian can be a juxtaposer and contrast the content and actuality of an image with public myth and common beliefs or misconceptions. Irony is a form of additive meaning that often is forged in the juxtaposition of visual and verbal (Hunter, 1987).

PEOPLE OF THE WEST DESERT

In the early 1990s I began a photographic documentary that culminated in the book *People of the West Desert*. It looks at the lifestyles and self-perceptions of people who live in what is the least densely populated area of the lower 48 United States, rural areas of the Basin and Range province in Utah and Nevada. It was arguably the last frontier, at least a place where the distant frontier is a real, working image in the lives of the people. It is a hard landscape of scant rainfall that only can support a limited population, yet that is home to a complex culture of diverse communities: Native Americans, ranchers, hard-rock miners, back-to-the land utopians, migrant workers, social activists, land managers, and boom-or-bust dreamers living shy of the edge of success.

I conceived of the documentary as a multiyear project, investing a sabbatical leave in the field, as well as a year prior to that in planning, and several more years after the fieldwork and image-gathering in return trips, picture editing, crafting a book-length narrative to supplement the photographs, and last, finding a publisher. I visited some communities three or more times, being willing to invest that amount of time so as to add complexity and informed insight to the documentary. Luxury of time is something that traditional journalists crave but usually lack, but it takes that kind of time to glean perspective and establish trust between the participants and the documentarian. The knotted thread of community reveals itself only over time.

I decided to upset some tenets of traditional journalistic objectivity in the project. Because many of the communities I documented were radically dissimilar in philosophies and lifestyles, I could have adopted the perspective of being the naturalistic observer, recording the human actuality and posing one community against its polar opposite, assuming meaning would be forged somewhere between the extremes of the philosophical continuum. This often is how a newspaper report is written. The reporter listens to both sides and carefully tries to balance point with counterpoint within the same story. Instead, I attempted to act as a conduit. I tried to let each person or group speak for itself and reveal itself through images with minimum third-person intervention. When I approached each community, I told members that I was there to help them tell their own stories, that I would be acting "as a chronicler but not as a publicist." Everyone understood that I would not be there to promote their interests or viewpoints, but that I would represent them fairly and within context. I feared I could become a shill for self-promoters, but I did not want to purposely deflate a person or group's beliefs by coyly interjecting and juxtaposing a fact or countervailing opinion that would call a belief or position into question. Instead, I recognized the subjectivity of passive observation but hoped that some measure of objectivity, breadth, depth—and meaning—would become present in the collection of all stories, when all voices were heard and all their images recorded. I reasoned that, given enough information, the audience should be able to sort things out and provide its own interpretation. Last, I informed subjects that the images would likely be part of a public exhibition of all stories from the West Desert, but that if I developed enough material and could find a publisher, I hoped I could turn the documentary into a book.

For the sake of space, I want to limit my discussion of this exemplar study to one group, the Walker River Paiutes, largely because their Native American experiences are so different from my own that it required careful control of personal schema in the self-reflexive process of documentation. It was important, too, that I use photo elicitation with the community to make sure my perspective was not substituted for theirs.

The Walker River Paiutes are a tribe whose reservation is on the eastern slope of the Sierra Nevada Mountains in Nevada. The Walker River Paiutes were used to the media and the documentary process because they tend to be a politically activist tribe and were leaders in the Native American environmental movement at the time. Moreover, the tribe holds a yearly Pinenut Festival, open to all people, which made them more potentially accessible to an Anglo male documentary photographer, when other Indian tribes tend to be more guarded, some requiring Anglos to stay off their reservations.

Walker River Paiutes

I first visited the Walker River Paiutes in September 1992, after reading about their Pinenut Festival in *Native Peoples* magazine. It sounded like a good lead, as I had been concerned about getting any access into Indian culture.

I began tracking down the times and arrangements for the next festival. I first called Don Hague, the director of the Utah Museum of Natural History, whom I noticed was on the editorial board of the magazine. He had not heard of the festival, but gave me a list of people to contact, including Will Numkena, then director of Utah's Office of Indian Affairs. When I called Numkena, he also was not aware of the festival, but he did have the telephone number of the Walker River Paiute tribe and suggested I call the public relations person.

I had some Anglo preconceptions before I picked up the phone to call the tribe. I first expected no one to answer. If someone did, I assumed that it would only be after ten rings, and then that person would have no idea who the PR person was and suggested I call back in a few days when so-and-so would be there.

Yet when I called the tribal office, the telephone was picked up on the second ring. "Walker River Tribal office," was the energetic, fresh address. I explained who I was and my documentary project, and then somewhat sheepishly asked for the public relations person, expecting to get a blank silence or a hearty laugh. "That's Charlie Emm. Just a moment and I'll transfer you," the receptionist said. I expected to wait in Indian time telephone limbo, but within a few seconds, Charlie picked up the phone. She gave me a detailed description of the festival, reading from a well-prepared script.

When I arrived at the tribal headquarters, I found Emm. She quickly introduced me to Anita Collins, the tribal chairperson, and explained my project. Collins took me under her wing and showed me around the headquarters building, stopping by the trophy case to show me the artifacts of the community's history and pride. Then, she walked me to the park grounds where the tribe was beginning to separate the nuts from the pine cones for gift packaging.

I was accepted easily into the group, perhaps because I was introduced to them by the tribal chairperson. Yet I got the feeling that I would have been welcomed even without that introduction. It was obviously a time of good will and sharing, and that extended to the brotherhood of humankind. Or perhaps it was simply because there were a lot of pine cones to clean and nuts to harvest, and any set of hands was welcomed. I volunteered to help, and did so over two days prior to the start of the festival. I camped on the tribe's parade grounds and used the showers at the tribe's truck stop to clean up, besides eating my meals there. Of course, I was also becoming more visible and less of a distraction.

Most of the pine cone cleaners were women, and in fact, most of my contacts over my five days in Schurz, Nevada, were with women of the tribe. The topics of conversation at the cleaning tables ranged from families to drinking to health, but for the most part, the conversation always came back to sex. Almost any statement someone made became the substance for a double entendre by someone else. I couldn't tell if I was being teased, seduced, or that being white and helping with cleaning pine cones made me a eunuch.

After two days of cleaning cones, I slowly broke away from the group and began taking pictures of the festival preparations. By the time the festival started, all my attentions were focused on visually recording the events and talking to the participants to get their insights into strategies at such activities as handgame, the preferred method of gambling at most Indian gatherings.

When I returned in March 1993, I brought work prints with me for photo elicitation. I said that I wanted to get together the same group of women with whom I most associated the previous fall to get their comments on some of the images. I did not bring all images with me that I had shot. Rather, I did some preliminary picture editing and selected some images that either provoked questions in my mind that needed clarification, or photographs that I felt had a strong narrative element, rich detail or a visually compelling composition that potentially would be strong selections for a photographic documentary.

Four women commented on the photographs: Elveda Martinez, Viola Kennison, Charlie Emm, and Marlene Begay. Later, two teenage girls came into the room and were asked to make comments, too. All comments were tape recorded, and at the end of the session, I told the commentators to identify any prints they'd like for the tribe's use. Before the photo elicitation session began, I read the following script to the members of the commentary group:

> The photographs I'm about to show you are black-and-white work prints. That means that they are kind of rough. There has been no cropping to get rid of detail or to minimize confusion. There has only been one exposure for the print, so some might be too dark or too light. There will be some dust spots, but all these things can be corrected later.
>
> What I'm interested in now are your reactions to seeing these pictures. Often, your first reaction might be the most illuminating for us.
>
> I might show you a set of pictures on one subject or a single photograph. I'll also occasionally ask you specific questions regarding a group of photographs or a single photograph. But, in general, I'd like to you to consider the following questions when they apply as you go through these pictures:
> 1. How do you feel about seeing yourself performing this action?
> 2. Is the picture confusing? If so, why? How do you think the action should be captured to tell an accurate story?
> 3. Which photographs appear to be the most accurate or true to life?
> 4. What detail seems to capture your eye?
> 5. What detail perhaps should be explained or highlighted in a caption for a person not familiar with what goes on at this place?

After reading the prepared script, I told the commentators that I would use their input in my final selection of images for an exhibit or book. I said if there was universal agreement regarding a picture, I would follow those wishes. If there was not a shared perspective, I reserved the right to make final choices of images used.

All of the images provoked a rich dialogue that I was able to incorporate into the later book, either as captions or as chapter text. Several of them revealed the psychology of the tribe. One image in particular, a photograph from the Indian Car Contest, where participants show off their quintessential, beat-up cars (Fig. 25.1), demonstrated the subtle, wry, sophisticated humor of Native Americans. The session began with hearty, communal laughs when looking at the cars:

> **Begay**—Hey, is that my car? [more laughs]
> **Martinez**—At the beginning when we first started this, just about a couple of years ago, we thought, "Who's going to do this? Who wants to get in it?" We didn't think we'd get hardly anybody. Now it's like this is a big event. We've got people coming from out of town, now, with their Indian cars. Some of them fix their cars up, or mess them up, for the parade. Some of them are just typical cars that people use every day.
> **Emm**—Yeah.
> **Kennison**—If you want to see one, my husband will bring it when he comes to pick up the kids. It only opens on the back door. It used to open from the front door. If you rolled down the windows, you could open it from the inside, but it doesn't do that anymore.

FIG. 25.1. Indian Car Contest—In typically wry Indian humor, one of the events at the Walker River Paiute Pinenut Festival is the tongue-in-cheek Indian Car Parade and Contest. The object is to show off the perfect reservation car. That's typically one whose paint has largely faded, whose door has to be opened with a screwdriver and whose tires are as bald as a baby's head. But a car that is too obviously junk misses the spirit of the contest and is disqualified. The car has to run.

Begay—That's how my car looks. It's got a cracked windshield and a "For Sale" sign.

Denton—Well, I see a lot of new cars parked out there [in the parking lot].

Martinez—People have their town cars and but then there's a lot of Indian people, too, who have their around-here cars. Now like Marlene's had her van for how many years now?

Begay—About five years. I bought it for like about one thousand dollars when it had about 60,000 miles on it. Now it has 100,000 and it's still going.

Emm—That's like mine. I've had that Oldsmobile for like seven years. I paid, I think it was about a thousand or eight hundred for it, and I still don't have the title [a lot of laughs].

Begay—And, then once the cars give out, they just sit in people's yards. There's one new house up there that has three old cars sitting by it.

Martinez—We always laugh around here about Indian landscaping. We say, "Shoot, all you've got to do is, you don't need grass. All you've got to do is drag three old cars and you're done with it."

Kennison—No watering either.
[Big belly laughs here]

Martinez—It's really funny, but that's the way it is. A lot of people have cracked windshields because of the dirt roads.

Kennison—My husband's always trying to get me to get rid of my old Volkswagen. I like that old car, even though it's not running.

Martinez—Sentimental value. A lot of these people with these old cars, they have
            names for them. So, it's like they're part of your family.
Kennison—Like your little sister.
Begay—What about the bug [VW]?
Kennison—That's a Rabbit. A jack rabbit car.

Handgame is a sleight-of-hand game that is popular at all Indian festivals. Besides
playing for bragging rights and a team trophy and cash, individual Indians will make side
bets on the outcomes. The game calls for one team to select a member to hide two bones
in either or both hands. The other team then must choose a member to guess which
hand or hands the bones are in. It sounds simple enough, but the feinting and distraction
strategies are complex, as brought out in this conversation regarding a photograph of
handgame (Fig. 25.2):

Martinez—It kinda shows how, again even though it's team play, it's kinda individual
            play because the money is all bet in different spots on the ground. So, that
            this guy might just be betting him and they've got their money there. So,
            whoever wins, they can just collect their money.
Kennison—They are like side bets. You put your money out and you see if someone
            matches it from the other side.

FIG. 25.2.   Handgame—Gambling is an honored pastime when Native Americans gather to celebrate life, not tinged with moral weakness as in the Judeo-Christian ethic. Handgame is often the
game of choice, and it's one tradition that isn't in danger of fading away from lack of practice and
practitioners. In fact, young adults are as common on handgame teams as Indian elders. It's also a
cross-cultural tradition, with Anglos sometimes becoming part of a team when they join the culture
through marriage.

Martinez—So, this old guy might not be playing but he might have ten dollars right here. Anybody can go up and say, "I'm going to bet on this team here." I can get behind them and wave my money around and hopefully someone over there will match my bet. But it's only a 50-50 bet.

But, even though you can watch it, there are a lot of secrets to the game. There's a lot of sign language. They have ways of rubbing you on the back on which way to guess. Your teammates help you out too, help you to think. It's a psychological thinking game.

Denton—It's like telepathy?

Kennison—That's what they call "medicine," though. They use what they call medicine. Some people do. Some of them might have telepathy.

Denton—Are there major players who, in sense, rent themselves out to teams because they are proven winners?

Begay—No. They probably will lead a team.

Martinez—A lot of this guessing. You look into a person's eyes to see what they are doing. That's why they are wearing sunglasses.

But, few of them are going to look at you. When they are hiding the bones, they aren't even going to give you any sign looking into your eyes. They are going to look down.

Begay—Some of them will hide it [bones] behind a big blanket, while others, like this one, he just had a little thing on his lap and does that and then he drops it down. But, they have to drop it down before the people can guess.

Martinez—The captain of the team will give the bones to whoever they want to guess. He can hide them himself or pass them on.

Denton—But, if they do pass them on, the other team gets to know who's got them?

Martinez—Yeah. They do it right away. They might rub the bones around and then give them to Viola.

Begay—They don't just give it to 'em and guess. It's give it to 'em and then this, and this and this [gesturing]. So all types of psychological things.

Denton—Like taunting?

Begay—Yeah.

Denton—Part of the fun is the taunting afterward too.

Martinez—Yeah. Like if you missed em, and whoever has the bones goes, "Yoop! Yoop! Yoop!"

Denton—And the songs get louder.

Martinez—I like to watch that big guy from Warm Springs. What's his name? Big Wilson? And see him dance around in the middle.

Cradleboards are an ancient device that Indian mothers use to carry around their infants. At the Pinenut Festival there is a contest for the best cradleboards, although few of them are being made today. Two images of cradleboards provoked a rich description of their heritage and their use in contemporary child-rearing (Figs. 25.3 and 25.4):

Begay—Well, this guy's too big for his cradle [followed by much laughter. Begay clarified that he is still the right size for a cradleboard, but that he's just a big kid.]

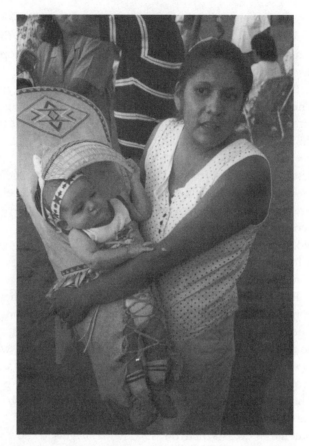

FIG. 25.3.   Cradleboard—Indian mothers report that fussy infants become strangely at peace when they are strapped into cradleboards. Beadwork symbolizes both the sex of the child and the origin of the maker.

Martinez—He probably got thrown in this cradleboard for his nap. He gets tied up when he's cranky. It's a restraint.

Kennison—They get used to it. They look forward to it. Secure.

Martinez—It's like someone holding them all the time.

Begay—They go right to sleep.

Martinez—People will tie them up in their cradleboard and rock them just a bit and then they're out. Sometimes, little babies won't go to sleep until they're all tied up, once they get used to their cradleboard.

Denton—Would every child have a cradleboard, or would it be only those who have a cradleboard in the family?

Begay—Pretty much around here everybody has one.

Kennison—They're passed on.

Emm—Whoever has one in a family that doesn't have one gets it.

Denton—Who makes them now? Does everybody have the ability and experience to make them or is that kind of a dying art?

Martinez—It's really a dying art. In Schurz does anyone make them?

FIG. 25.4. Cradleboard—Usually cradleboards are handed down from one generation to the next. The ones in this photograph are three generations old and of dramatically increasing value because fewer young women are learning the craft.

[The reply was basically no.]

> Probably two older ladies make them today, or they can. But, it's not like they make them like they used to make them. These are in demand. You wouldn't pay any less for one like this one with the buckskin for less than $700.

Denton—Is that what families typically do now? If they don't have one they go out and buy one?

Martinez—Yeah. It's just really different. The quality of work is not as good as it used to be.

Denton—What about the materials. Are there still willows around?

Begay—With this drought for the past seven years and with all the pesticides, is killing off the willows. Viola would know. She works with willows. [Viola has gone to answer the telephone.] You have to go higher [in the drainages].

Martinez—I like this one. Really what this shows is the reason why they are in the cradleboard contest is to show off all the baskets as well as their basket. A lot of these baskets, they could be 50 years old or more, whereas some of them could be only eight or ten years old. But, again, they are probably passed down. Even these mothers are all young mothers.

Kennison—This is Laurie. Her grandmother made that one. Edna made that basket.

Martinez—So that could be 80 years old.

Kennison—I don't know. I don't know how old she is.

Begay—Here. That looks like an Edna Jones basket too.

Denton—How long would these willows hold up? There are some in that cabinet
over there [headquarters building] that must be very old.

Martinez—They last hundreds of years. We have basketry that people made in this
area that are hundreds of years old in museums.

Begay

(to me)—Do you mean that can still hold a baby and be serviceable?

Denton—Yeah.

Begay—I think about 50 years old. After that they get kind of brittle.

Denton—So, willow makes the best material?

Martinez—That's all they use in this area. Like different tribes have different types of
cradleboards and make them out of different materials.

Kennison—The frames they usually make out of chokecherry because it's harder. But,
the hood and all the back part is all willow.

Denton—You have to be able to bend it? How did they do that? Did they heat it or
soak it?

Kennison—The chokecherry, they heat it.

Martinez—See it's like a barrier. It's like this all the way around the frame. And then
on the baskets, the hood here usually has a little design on it. It will have
either a boy design or a girl design. Like this one here is a boy design.

Denton—How can you tell?

Martinez—Because it's not crossed.

Begay—It's open. A girl's would be closed. Like a diamond or a cross. Is that right?
[There is some doubt in the group as to which is which.]

Martinez—Yeah, a lot of people around here, like Viola's mom or my mom, they can
look at a basket and look at this design up here and say, 'Oh, yeah. Edna
Jones made that or Avis Done made that one,' just by their design. These
people, once they had a design, it seems like that was their design.

Denton—Kind of like a family coat of arms?

Martinez—Yeah, some that way. For some reason they kept the design and that was
the way it was.

While I visited the tribe later in March for the first photo elicitation, I also took more
photographs. I was unable to return in person for a second photo elicitation session,
but because of the first experience, I trusted the commentators to run a session in my
absence. I shipped them a new set of numbered images and a blank tape, besides including
gift prints from the first session that they had requested.

One of the images I sent them for the second session was a problem for me. I didn't
know whether to include it in a later public presentation. It showed a new teacher in the
reservation school trying to lead a lesson, while students blatantly misbehaved in front of
her (Fig. 25.5). It posed a negative image, but it was a truthful account of the problems in
an underfunded reservation school where students felt the county school system ignored
them.

Elveda Martinez prefaced the second photo elicitation session by telling the group that
I had a tough time at the school. She said that I only was able to go into the seventh and
eighth grade, "And, they were terrible." Some asked Elveda why I went in there, alluding

FIG. 25.5. Passing note in school—The Walker River Paiute tribe was thrilled when Marlo Steel returned to the reservation to teach the seventh and eighth graders, as she would be a Native American role model for the youngsters. But the first-year teacher was discouraged when her bright energy was met with a lack of respect from some of the students.

to the shared knowledge that that was a problem grade. Martinez said, "I don't know. Because, I sent him in there because I told him we had a young Indian teacher in there." There seemed to be mumblings around the table that these weren't flattering pictures. I could hear comments on the tape like, "This one isn't a good one either."

After most of the generic comments were made, Colleen Bearcloud-Sides, a new participant, began the discussion—and community soul-searching:

> **Bearcloud-Sides**—We have five pictures here and there's only one of them, well two, that appear positive about the class. We know how these kids are, and we know that these other pictures are accurate. But, in Marlo's [the teacher pictured] favorite one, it [another image] shows what she's *trying* to accomplish.
>
> These ought to be xeroxed and posted somewhere, as a kind of public warning announcement.
>
> **Kennison**—Especially to the parents of the kids.
>
> **Begay**—I'd show them to my kids.
>
> **Martinez (directed to me on the tape)**—Craig, I think the consensus here is to give us copies of all the seventh and eighth grade class pictures. Because, Marlo still is a very young teacher, first-year teacher, and it's indicative of what has happened. The local people have really tried to get local

Indian teachers back to the reservation and it's kind of sad when our own Indian children won't appreciate that.

Kennison—I think the education system that our young teachers go through doesn't prepare them for the realities of teaching reservation students.

Martinez—I think [Fig. 25.5] just shows probably just a typical day on the reservation school where a teacher is trying, making herself physically attractive and presentable, trying to do a good job. And yet, there's still the disruption of the class or the inattentiveness. And it also shows that the people who really are willing to learn are in the front seats of the classroom.

Finally, another image caused me concern, because of its emotional and possibly stereotyping content. It was an image of two crosses driven into the macadam outside the tribal headquarters building (Fig. 25.6). The memorial was for a young couple from the tribe, who were to be married, but who were killed in an automobile accident caused by a drunk driver. The accident happened on the reservation and the other driver was also a tribal member. She survived. I wanted the tribe's feedback because the image would strike a raw nerve, deeply wounding the tribe, which was organizing a healing ceremony for the community in response to the tragedy, and because it played into stereotypes of drunken Indians.

FIG. 25.6.   Crosses—While the Walker River tribe has lost many of its people to alcohol-related traffic accidents off the reservation, the physical and emotional carnage seldom has hit home. When two teenagers died in front of tribal headquarters, Monty Williams, the tribe's drug and alcohol abuse counselor, sensed that for the first time the tribe was coming out of self-denial. He organized an alcohol-awareness intervention and healing ceremony, the Cry Dance, for the tribe.

Martinez—My favorite too, because it shows a tragedy that probably happens a lot on Indian reservations. And, the way I see it's almost like a love story tragedy because the two people killed in this were going to be married. Now, all we've got to see of that is two crosses and young lives when they were only 17 and 24 years old. I think this would really hit the spot on Indian reservations.

Again, it shows the cluster housing in the background. But, the one thing it really shows is that there is beauty on our reservation with the mountains and the snow. Because, we haven't seen a snow like that in eight years. It's really something.

Kennison (after hearing Martinez)—I think another thing to add to that is that those two young people will never see the winter of their lives, their old age.

Bearcloud-Sides—I like this one because it shows we still give respect to the people that have passed away. It's something that everyone will remember, because we all know it happened there.

This image generated the greatest number of requests for prints. I obliged as much I could, periodically sending prints I personally made in my darkroom as the requests came in. But when I received an order of approximately 120, enough for everyone in the tribe, time and expenses precluded me from fulfilling that wish.

CONCLUSION

Documentary photography has a history, through 19th-century photojournalism and social documentary photography born of the Progressive Era, that predates the argument between positivist objectivity and the recognition that subjectivity is necessary in participant observation. Still, the desire to use a camera to record environmental detail for later analysis and tell stories places documentary photography firmly within the realm of ethnographic methodology that includes visual sociology, visual anthropology, social documentary advocacy and photojournalism. In fact, documentary photography is an umbrella term that encompasses all these uses of a camera to record human actuality and draws them together.

In documentary photography, theory and methodology play their roles in the background. They are less visible because documentary photography must communicate in a world where the economics and mechanics of reproduction rely upon larger audiences. Complicating, and invigorating, documentary photography as a research method is the corollary fact that aesthetics must be a commanding presence in the document along with information.

Still, documentary photography represents a way of knowing. The documentary photographer generates visual evidence and employs methods of creating more density, reliability and ethically grounded layering of evidence through the use of such techniques as photo elicitation. Ultimately, the documentary photographer is a performer in the process of inquiry, and documentary photography's outcome is the reflection of interpersonal negotiation.

REFERENCES

Becker, H. S. (1974). Photography and sociology. *Studies in the Anthropology of Visual Communication, 1*, 3–26.

Becker, H. S. (1995). Visual sociology, documentary photography, and photojournalism: It's (almost) all a matter of context. *Visual Sociology, 10*, 5–14.

Coles, R. (1997). *Doing documentary work*. New York: Oxford University Press.

Collier, J. Jr., & Collier, M. (1986). *Visual anthropology: Photography as a research method*. Albuquerque: University of New Mexico Press.

Denton, C. (1999). *People of the west desert*. Logan: Utah State University Press.

Gross, L. (1988). The ethics of (mis)representation. In L. Gross, J. S. Katz, & J. Ruby (Eds.), *Image ethics: The moral rights of subjects in photographs, film and television* (pp. 188–202). New York: Oxford University Press.

Gross, L., Katz, J. S., & Ruby, J. (1995). Introduction: A moral pause. In L. Gross, J. S. Katz & J. Ruby (Eds.), *Image ethics: The moral rights of subjects in photographs, film and television* (pp. 3–33). New York: Oxford University Press.

Hammersley, M., & Atkinson, P. (1995). *Ethnography: Principles in practice*. London: Tavistock Publications.

Harper, D. (1987). *Working knowledge: Skill and community in a small shop*. Chicago: University of Chicago Press.

Henderson, L. (1988). Access and consent in public photography. In L. Gross, J. S. Katz, & J. Ruby (Eds.), *Image ethics: The moral rights of subjects in photographs, film and television* (pp. 91–107). New York: Oxford University Press.

Hunter, J. (1987). *Image and words: The interaction of twentieth-century photographs and text*. Cambridge, MA: Harvard University Press.

Jackson, B. (1987). *Fieldwork*. Urbana: University of Illinois Press.

Johnson, J. M. (1975). *Doing field research*. New York: The Free Press.

Lindlof, T. R. (1995). *Qualitative communication research methods*. Thousand Oaks, CA: Sage.

Lofland, J. (1976). *Doing social life: The qualitative study of human interaction in natural settings*. New York: Wiley.

Ethics

Visual Ethics Theory

JULIANNE H. NEWTON
University of Oregon

Mere purposive rationality unaided by such phenomena as art, religion, dream, and the like, is necessarily pathogenic and destructive of life. . . . Love can survive only if wisdom . . . has an effective voice.

—Bateson (1972, p. 146)

The visual has long been an issue in the study of philosophy. Consider Plato's exploration of humankind's preference for shadow illusions over near-blinding reality. Or Aristotle's explication of the cathartic potential of viewing a theatrical performance. One of the most influential explorations of visual perception during the Enlightenment centuries was the philosopher Bishop George Berkeley's *Essay Towards a New Theory of Vision* (1910). Berkeley based his argument for the existence of God on observation.

Particularly interesting for our topic here is that philosophers have so often linked the visual with the study of the ethical—sometimes positively, sometimes negatively. Nineteenth-century philosopher and cultural critic Friedrich Nietzsche, for example, argued that art facilitated the emergence of a "higher humanity" and a "higher morality." Twentieth-century postmodernists, on the other hand, targeted the visual as the evil-incarnate source of a host of societal ills, ranging from the misguided belief in objective reality to the procreator of spectator culture and government surveillance. I do not propose to offer you a synthesis of such multisided discussions here, nor do I believe I have the answers to the questions two millennia of thinkers have posed. I do, however, believe that we can articulate central concerns of visual theory that relate to ethics under the appellation *Visual Ethics*. These concerns warrant exploration within their own sphere.

First, I explore traditional and contemporary literature that sheds especially bright light on visual ethics as a field of study. Second, I suggest a theoretical approach through which we might anchor the study of visual ethics. I hope to answer the following specific questions within the necessarily limited confines of this chapter:

- Is there an ethic unique to the visual?
- If so, what is it and how does it operate?
- How can we study it?
- How can we use what we learn to improve the ways people use the visual to make meaning and interact?

TRADITIONAL AND CONTEMPORARY ETHICAL THOUGHT

Ethical systems derive from the central concerns of living entities and have profound implications for life. Human beings tend to believe that most of our ethical systems are based on reason. We believe our ethics are logic based. Those who live within an ethical system usually think the system is universal. Those who live outside an ethical system often can relate principles of that system to cultural norms, rather than universals.

Traditional literature of Western ethics is grounded in classical philosophy originating with the Greek Golden Age. As a core branch of classical philosophy, ethics focuses on the study of morality, which overlaps with issues of existence, reality, and knowledge. Traditional Western ethics might pose the questions: How does a person decide what is right and what is wrong? and How do we define right and wrong? These questions are exemplified in Socrates' famous assertion that "the unexamined life is not worth living." Contemporary ethicist Bernard Williams stressed an important corollary, "The only serious enterprise is living, and we have to live after the reflection; moreover . . . we have to live during it as well" (1985, p. 117), grounding the pursuit of ethical wisdom in the reality of everyday existence. At the same time, Western ethics have been rooted in religious practice stemming from various branches of Judeo-Christian beliefs. Their goal is to guide behavior in directions that will result in transcendence into eternal beneficence.

In contemporary ethical theory, we have applied classical philosophy and theology to the creation of a specific field known as *media ethics*. Media ethics explores a range of issues related to the mass media, such as free expression in print publications and regulation of violent content in films, television programming, and the Internet. Recent theory has led to work in representational issues, stereotyping, manipulative advertising, and altering images of photojournalism.

Philosophers and media ethicists think about such issues through years of study, contemplation, reflection, writing, arguing, and reasoning. They may put ethics into two categories, teleological (or goal oriented) or deontological (or rule oriented). They may argue such positions as the greater good for the greatest number (utilitarianism) or absolute right or wrong (Kantian categorical imperative). Media ethicists might pose such questions as: Does the media-conveyed message mislead or deceive? Does the message bring harm to someone? Does viewing violent imagery make someone more violent? Media scholars explore those questions through qualitative and quantitative research, as well as through the logic of traditional ethics.

Were humans prone to live and interact in reasoned ways, ethical explorations based on logical arguments would suffice. We can conclude quickly, however, that there is no reason people with light-colored skin should have more power in some societies than people with dark-colored skin. We can reason that representing women only as objects of sexual desire harms women, subjugating them to the aggression of those who gaze. The problem is that ethics as practiced in daily life are often based on responses that lie beyond reason. Those responses can range from reaction to human differences through reflexive fear for one's well-being. The responses are as variable as the living entities who experience them.

Yet the mythology of reason, promoted by the majority of serious thinkers during the 20th century, enveloped nonrational response within a web of irrationality deemed inferior and primitive. Scholarly and popular wisdom alike relegated the visual, long associated with artistic expression and emotion, to a position beneath and in opposition to the verbal, and to a marginalized status in regard to human needs. As a consequence, the visual became de facto undesirable, and, by extension, not trustworthy—by further extension associated with the unethical.

The visual was not so easily subsumed, however. Ironically, the 19th century, which McLuhan and Powers (1989) labeled the Visual Age, had bred visual inventions that would revolutionize humankind's abilities to extend the mind and heart beyond the body. Building on the invention of photography and then the motion picture, the visual pulsed forward, extending our perceptual capacities around and beyond the earth. The ultimate manifestation of this extension of sight is the virtual, a form of the visual that projects outward through holography and other computer-generated imagery—as well as inward through digitally enhanced visualization.

By the late 20th century, neuroscientists had determined that humans operate from perceptual bases that are more often unconsciously or intuitively oriented than rationally discerned. Contrary to popular and scholarly wisdom engendered by the mythology of reason, the assumed superiority of rational thinking processes over intuitive processes is shifting into a recognition of the need for both (Williams, 1999). Neuroscientists Antonio Damasio (1994, 1996; Bechara, Damasio, Tranel, & Damasio, 1997) and Joseph LeDoux (1986, 1996), for example, discovered evidence that the human "feeling-based" response system of unconscious cognitive processing and emotion is integral to good decision making, whether conscious or unconscious. We are learning how information discerned through our eyes—through vision—is a major source of information for decision making and for determining how to act, or react, to stimuli. Furthermore, new research on dreaming, an intrapersonal visual activity, indicates that humans use dreams to explore the problems of the previous day and to work out strategies for living. Most of this visual information is processed cognitively on unconscious levels and influences behavior prior to rational cognition or awareness. Evidence supporting strong links among the visual, human action, and ethics is mounting.

Most important for our current discussion is the work visual scholars are doing to determine the role vision plays in these rational and intuitive processing systems. Key themes include:

- Visual communication as a primary way of knowing—visual processing of information is at least as important as verbal processing (Moriarty, 1994).
- Visual intelligence—we can cultivate sophisticated understanding of the ways visual media manipulate us (Barry, 1997).

- Cognitive balance—we can learn to balance years of rational training in contempoary educational systems by accessing our intuitive processing abilities through integration of multiple literacies (Williams, 1999, 2003).

Traditional Western approaches to discussions of ethics typically draw on only a small part of the brain—and they typically focus on anthropocentric concerns. Such bases for ethical systems ignore millennia of life philosophies set forth by such Eastern thinkers as Confucius and the Buddha, by African and South American traditions, and by indigenous peoples throughout the world. An interesting contemporary development in ethical theory is recent work by Western scholars who locate their arguments in the nonhuman but living "other" of the earth's environment. Furthermore, the upheaval of thought manifested in postmodernism rearranged the ways we think about many ethical inquiries regarding such concepts as: self, other, reality, truth, representations.

Another especially relevant 20th-century theoretical development in the social sciences grew in tandem with theoretical physics. Heisenberg demonstrated in 1927 that the very act of measuring location of subatomic particles affected their velocity, and vice versa. In *Observing Ourselves*, social scientist Earl Babbie noted, "Since Heisenberg's contribution of the uncertainty principle, researchers in subatomic physics have increasingly attempted to include the observer in their understanding of the observed" (1986, p. 101). Although social scientists acknowledged similar issues through the Hawthorne effect, or the idea that observing a person affects that person's behavior, it would be the 1970s before they would incorporate that concept into their work. Mead and Bateson (1977) set the stage with their seminal work shifting understanding of the camera eye from non-neutral mechanism to purposive extension of individual perception. Visual sociologist Douglas Harper (1982) was among the first to turn the tables on that proposition, asking whether participant-observers even had the right to take a camera into their fieldwork. Newton (1984) combined concern for subject rights with concern for representing reality in her investigation of using photography in fieldwork. In *Image Ethics*, Gross, Katz, and Ruby (1988) applied such concerns to media representation. In the same year, John Tagg (1988) published his exploration of the social implications of photography's use in public institutions. In 1991, Paul Lester would articulate a growing concern for the ethics of photojournalism practice. And in 1995, Sheila Reaves published her empirical investigations into digital photojournalism.

Each strand of thought contributes a nugget of understanding to the complex system of moral study we term visual ethics. This background into the development of visual ethics sets the stage for defining terms more specifically.

DEFINITIONS

We can define *ethics* in a number of ways. In common, everyday use, when we say someone is highly ethical, we usually mean that person consistently makes choices based on discerning what is right and good, rather than on what is wrong and bad. Right usually means what is correct. Good usually means beneficent. But the problem is that "what is correct" and "what is good" must be judged against a standard. And who sets that standard? We know, for example, that by a Catholic's standard, personal confession through a priest is a primary route to forgiveness and redemption. By a Protestant's standard, personal confession directly to God is necessary. Does that mean that one or the other is unethical, simply because he or she follows different rituals of self-confrontation? Consider another example. To some Americans voting Republican is the ethical choice. To others voting Democratic is the ethical choice. Many individuals would argue, however, that the choice regarding for whom to vote is not a matter of ethics, but rather one of political conservatism or liberalism, or of states' rights versus strong federal government, or of a reasoned evaluation of candidates. In those instances, ethics are determined by cultural and social mores that have become interpreted as right or wrong by groups of individuals. Many believe ethics are highly personal, best determined through one's own process. Yet ethics also are highly public in that they affect and are affected by other people and activities.

The term *visual* typically refers to observable stimuli, either the process of seeing or the external something that can be seen by the eyes. We define light itself as the visible part of the electromagnetic spectrum. However, it is estimated that visual processing is only 10% ocular; 90% is cognitive. We also know that individuals who do not see light create visual worlds in their minds. For our discussion here then, visual refers to images of all kinds—dreams, imagination, art, self, handwriting, cyberspace, even the letterforms you are reading at this moment—and to all forms of image making, physical and metaphysical. Visual media therefore range from print through virtual (which includes imaginary) forms.

Visual ethics refers to a bright, purple umbrella, huge in breadth and depth—bright because of its necessary luminance in human life, purple because purple often is associated with nobility and eternity, broad in order to encompass all the ways we image, deep in order to focus our attention below surface reality. The umbrella covers such familiar topics as media ethics, image ethics, photojournalism ethics, truth in advertising, and stereotyping. Visual ethics also includes a number of areas less commonly associated with an ethic of the visual: self-image, interpersonal and intrapersonal communication, reality construction, virtual reality, perception, postmodernism, psychology, feminism, critical theory, political communication, social and physical science. Just as we can find an ethical component to just about any area of thought or action in life, we can find a visual component to just about anything—and an ethical component to anything visual.

To summarize, by *visual* I mean images and imaging. By *ethics* I refer to the study of right and wrong and to the human pursuit of a beneficent life. By *visual ethics* I mean the study of right and wrong uses of images and imaging. However, the central concerns of visual ethics go deeper than those simple definitions might lead you to believe.

Visual ethics is *the study of how images and imaging affect the ways we think, feel, behave, and create, use, and interpret meaning, for good or for bad.* Visual ethics includes the study of how we create and use images in communicating with others and ourselves. Visual ethics is not just digital ethics, or truth in advertising, public relations or TV journalism. It is not just avoiding imagery that stereotypes or imagery that subjugates others. Visual ethics is about the soul of communication, in the manner of the classic metaphor "the eyes are the windows to the soul." By *soul* I mean that immaterial entity that makes something what it is. So, the soul of communication refers to an almost indescribable, yet knowable, aspect of meaning making, conveying, and interpreting that makes it possible for one living thing to sense what another living thing is about and to act on that knowledge. In this way, cells composing the body make it known what their purpose is, what they are supposed to do in relation to one another. One cell communicating solely within itself can transform into a cancer cell, eventually spreading its maleficent, transformative action to other cells until the body they compose succumbs to their aggression. In visual communication, then, ethics addresses everyday murders of the spirit (Gornick, 1976) through countless acts of visual violence, domination, and manipulation. Yet in the same way that cells can regenerate parts of a wounded body, visual ethics also is about everyday births of the spirit through countless acts of visual beauty, harmony and authenticity. It is about the visual search for beneficence within a world that is too often maleficent—or at least for a balance of the two ends of the continuum of human behavior.

WHAT'S AT STAKE

The ethics of the visual begins and ends with *power*, for power can determine whether something or someone is visible or invisible, and how something or someone who is visible is likely to be viewed. In everyday life, if we cannot see something, we can easily deny its existence, or, at the very least, its significance. Keeping impoverished people on a certain side of town is one way to minimize their visibility, for example. Drawing a map so that one country appears larger than it physically is in relation to other countries has the effect of assigning social power to that country. Using the color of a person's skin to determine where she can sit on a bus exemplifies using visually discerned information to control a group of human beings by assigning value to the color of one's skin. By *power*, then, I mean an entity's ability to control or influence another entity, whether that entity be a living organism, such as a plant or human, or a resource, such as physical strength or authority. This context shifts our definition of ethics to the appropriate use of power in regard to self and others. Visual ethics then is *the appropriate use of imaging power in regard to self and others*. Must visual ethics be beneficent in order to be appropriate? As a minimum standard, visual ethics involves using imaging power in ways that do not harm.

A THEORETICAL SUGGESTION

So, the processes of imaging—and therefore the process of seeing itself—can be ethical or unethical. Taking the visual beyond seeing, that is, a step further, to include how people will use seeing to judge—or image—someone illustrates the potentially profound implications of an ethic of the visual. I want to suggest that we conceptualize visual ethics within a system of human living that I call an *Ecology of the Visual*. Thinking of visual ethics in terms of ecological theory focuses attention on the dynamic processes of making meaning in visual ways. The emphasis is placed on the process, the action, the behavior, rather than on the manifestation of that process as a product or medium. For example, if we think of visual ethics in traditional philosophical ways, we might examine what a photograph of a nude man symbolizes in any number of public forums, such as the discourse of art or the discourse of pornography. The analytical emphasis in such a framework is the image itself and whether it is fine art or something to be censored. Examining the same photograph as part of a human behavioral ecology focuses analysis holistically and systemically, facilitating study of synergistic, interdependent human behaviors. Extending our example through a visual ecology framework, then, leads us to consider the man who reflected light to create the image, how and why he posed, who took the photograph and why it was taken, how it relates to photographs of nude women or of children, what was the context of image making, what is the context of viewing, what does it say about men in general, how does it extend or inhibit our understanding of the human form, and so forth.

Ecological theory avoids analysis of hierarchies or discrete actions in favor of nested, dynamic series of shifts, each leading to other shifts in an unending flow of activity (Golley, 1998). Consider several layers, or nests, of behaviors in which a human organism participates. First is a *surface layer*, which includes attending and perceiving. Second is an *interpretative layer*, which includes recognizing, translating, recording. Third is an *interactive layer*, in which we construct, create, conceptualize, manipulate. In this layer we image self, other, group, world. We leave our individual minds to interact with other minds in some way, either interpersonally or in a group way. Finally, in a fourth layer, we achieve, mesh with, succumb to, or overtake the *power* of other entities' layers of behavior. In this way we engage in an ecology of the visual, in which the conscious and unconscious, overt and covert, individual and collective, local and universal, physical and cultural, nest through a continual, dynamic process of being, interacting, and meaning making.

Human Visual Behavior

I want to clarify that I am not arguing for a strictly behavioral approach to interpreting the visual in the classic use of the term stimulus-response *behaviorism*. Recent developments in ecological theory have led to the recognition that complexity and chaos are key components of any system, rather than purely predictable, deterministic stasis. With this in mind, I want to locate this discussion within the realm of the present, rather than the realm of what might be or has been. To me, that means focusing my attention on what is, or on the ways that I can choose to live and to interact with others. It is by definition a fleeting spot, a constantly shifting moment of awareness in which I can momentarily, consciously observe myself, as well as others, and adjust my responses as I become more aware of them and of their effects on me and others.

Acknowledging this existential continuum in which each of us, as one living organism among many, participates, focuses the current discussion in important ways. First, we have only moments in which to be aware of the fact that we are doing something. For example, if I look at a photograph of someone and think derisive thoughts about her, at that moment I am engaged in an act with ethical consequences. The consequences may never reach the person imaged in the photo, unless I know or encounter that individual and my derisive memories affect how I interact with that person or influence others to interact with her in certain ways. The consequences do touch me, however, because, at some level, I know what I thought. That thought, in and of itself, has an effect on me, either positively or negatively, rightly or wrongly. That effect can be minuscule, a fleeting moment of derisiveness that will, nevertheless, return to affect my perceptions, either consciously or unconsciously. On the other hand, that effect can be major. The derisive thoughts malign the person in the photo and through that process malign me, their creator, as well as other life forms to which they are transferred. In that way my behavior of viewing and deriding the person in the photograph has rippled outward from my momentary action and back again.

Not long ago I was involved in a media ethics seminar organized around the topic "Ethics in Virtual Reality." The first question we had to answer was, (a) Are there ethics in virtual reality? The second question: (b) Do they matter? My colleague Tom Bivins and I wrote an article, "The Real, the Moral and the Virtual" (2003). We concluded that anything we do in an immaterial realm, such as cyberspace, necessarily affects what we do in the material realm of physical existence. As Alluqerere Roseanne Stone noted, it's not a matter of cause and effect but rather a matter of "mutual emergence" (1995, p. 21). The shift can be so subtle, as in the changing of a tadpole into a frog (see "sorites paradox" in Audi, 1995), that we cannot visualize that moment between "before" and "then." The very act of seeing then is, in effect, a moment of "mutual emergence." When we view someone walking down the street, for example, that person is walking in a manner in which he or she has determined, based on physical ability and social learning (also based on seeing). The ocular stimuli we receive from that person's movements are gathered into our brains via the eye to merge with nonocular stimuli and memory of what we already know about people walking. That merger simultaneously influences our interpretation of that particular person who is walking, shifting or confirming what we know, as well as what we might think about walking in general. And as we see, we also emerge, in a continual ecology of the visual.

One way to conceptualize this process is to consider all of those activities (the walking, learning, being of the observed, and the seeing, interpreting, knowing of the observer) forms of *human visual behavior*. Although I am, by necessity because of the limited space of a chapter, focusing my discussion here on *human* behavior specifically, I want to qualify the discussion by noting that I am not arguing for the supremacy of human over other entities in the universe. Human is but a place to start, because human is what we who are writing and reading this book know best.

We can conceptualize human visual behavior in a number of ways. Most obvious is observable action, those movements by parts of the body that we can see as they occur. Note that it does a disservice to visual behavior to call gestures and body movements *nonverbal behavior*, in that it posits the visual in negative relationship to the verbal. Less obvious are incidents observable only in the mind of the seer, such as thinking of one's own childhood while watching a 9-year-old girl run through a meadow. Into this category fall dreaming, visualization, meditation, unconscious visual cognition and memory, and creative thinking. These activities occur through intuitive, or preconscious, processing in the brain, as well as through rational, or conscious processing in the brain. Einstein's initial observations, intuitive insights, and the subsequent conscious processing of the insights into his rational theory of relativity, all were forms of visual behavior.

Process and Meaning

Conceptualizing visual ethics as an ecological system of human behavior helps explain two aspects of visual knowing: the ethics of *process* and the ethics of *meaning. Ethics of process* refers to how the visual was made, created, constructed. In other words, did a photographer psychologically harm a grieving mother by making an image of her at her child's funeral? Or did a politician purposefully deceive the public by agreeing to a campaign ad that falsely maligned his opponent? In the first instance, ethics of process involved how the photographer approached a sensitive situation, how the photographer decided to photograph the grieving mother, whether the mother has agreed to the photograph, whether the public really needed to see a picture of that particular mother in a state of deep despair. In the second instance, ethics of process involved a candidate, campaign manager, and an advertiser deciding to create 30 seconds of video that would lead potential voters to believe something negative about another political candidate. To what extent did the campaigners try to determine the veracity of the negative material? To what extent did they rationalize their decision to use false material based on their belief that their candidacy was better for society? To what extent did they want to get their candidate elected, regardless of their methods?

We can use the same examples to describe *ethics of meaning*. In the grieving mother example, what does the photograph of her crying mean? Does it mean, "Look at her . . . everyone can understand her sorrow"? Does it mean, "Look at her . . . see how well this photographer covers difficult events"? Does it mean, "Parents, please don't let this happen to your child"? Does it mean, "Look at this . . . so you'll buy this magazine"? In the political ad example, ethics of meaning are partially determined by whether the ad is truthful, false, or misleading. The two modes of analyzing a visual usually overlap. For example, in the campaign ad example, did the ad creators edit out balancing material or segue material (ethics of process) that leads a viewer to discern a different meaning than they would were they to view the whole, original videotape (ethics of meaning)?

In the *ethics of process*, the harm can be done to the image-maker, to any individual involved in the process, to the message itself, to the viewer, and/or to society at large. In the *ethics of meaning*, the harm can be done to the image-maker, to any individual involved in the process, to the message itself, to the viewer, and/or to society at large. Unethical processes can produce either ethical or unethical messages, as can ethical processes. Unethical messages can, in turn, produce either ethical or unethical processes, as can ethical messages.

Ethical Process/ Ethical Meaning	Unethical Process/ Ethical Meaning
Ethical Process/ Unethical Meaning	Unethical Process/ Unethical Meaning

The above matrix appears to cover the range of possible combinations of process and meaning in terms of ethics. The problem is that ethics seldom is so easily categorized, but rather flows along a continuum of possibilities. An ecology, which can be visualized as a Mobius strip, can encompass that continuum. What if, for example, a visual behavior is ethic neutral, that is, neither ethical nor unethical, yet simultaneously catalyzes an ethical or unethical "emergence," or consequence? One way to explain this is to visualize the ethics of visual behavior as an ecology of the visual in the form of the tetrad graphic created for *The Global Village* (McLuhan & Powers, 1989). The graphic, designed by Blair P. Schrecongost working with Marshall McLuhan and Bruce Powers, "accompanied a four-part analysis to predict cultural change revealed by media effects" (Powers, private communication, June 14, 2004):

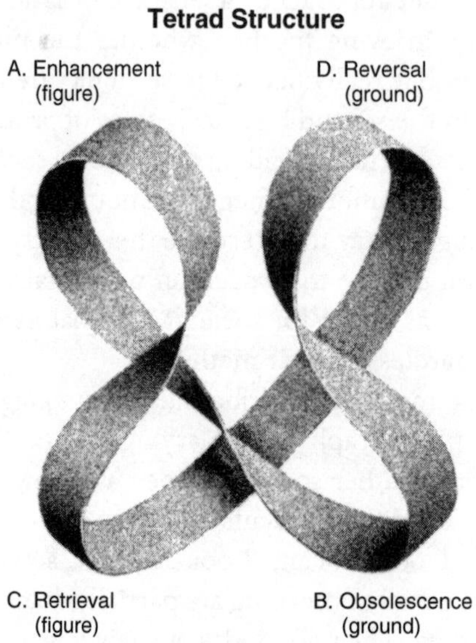

Tetrad Structure

A. Enhancement (figure)

D. Reversal (ground)

C. Retrieval (figure)

B. Obsolescence (ground)

FIG. 26.1.   Tetrad Structure.[1]

If we apply the tetrad structure to the concept of a constantly shifting, emerging ecology of the visual (Fig. 26.1), we can conceptualize the (A) foregrounding of a visual behavior, (B) backgrounding another behavior, (C) retrieving a behavior into the foreground, and (D) reversing into still another behavior (backgrounding, and so on), as shown in Figure 26.2.

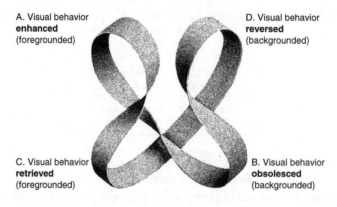

A. Visual behavior **enhanced** (foregrounded)

D. Visual behavior **reversed** (backgrounded)

C. Visual behavior **retrieved** (foregrounded)

B. Visual behavior **obsolesced** (backgrounded)

FIG. 26.2.   Ecology of the Visual expressed in Tetradic form.[2]

The original intent of the tetrad graphic was that it represent "simultaneous, constantly moving, connected cultural phenomena, a continual process," Powers explains (personal communication, June 14, 2004). Applications of the tetrad as an analytical aid vary according to individual interpretation of phenomena and cannot represent all phenomena. Although the activity appears to be sequential, linear and reactive, it occurs in a fleeting, timeless, mutually emergent instant.[2] Adapted to human visual behavior, which often, but not necessarily, occurs in response to other behavior or external stimuli, the tetrad structure incorporates phenomena that may be simultaneous and mutually emerging or occur in sequences of milliseconds—or millennia. Also important to applying the tetrad is to note that the tetrad does not flow neatly from A to B to C to D, but in a flurry of initial insights, the tetrad might vault from A to D and, at the same time leap from B to C, incorporating momentary chaos, or spontaneity. Nevertheless, a maturely developed Tetrad will eventually reflect a balance of complementarity—A : B as C : D (Powers, private communication, June 24, 2004).

To apply the tetrad in visual ethics, let us argue, for the sake of example, that when power in a visual interaction is exchanged equally, the ecology of the visual is maintained. Very important to note is that maintenance does not mean stasis or even that a behavior is necessarily predictable or enforced. It means, rather, that a dynamic ethic of process and meaning continues as part of a mutually beneficial network of interactions. When more of the power in the interaction shifts to one entity than the other, the potential for non-ethical disruption occurs.

For example, consider the visual behavior of one person extending his hand to another person (see Fig. 26.3). The extension enhances, or foregrounds, the power of the extender. The person observing the action is momentarily backgrounded until she makes an intuitive, instantaneous judgment of the intention of the hand extender. If she determines the extension to be friendly, her power is retrieved, or foregrounded, she extends her hand, reversing the behavior into one that backgrounds, or reverses, the power of the extender. Then the process of the visual behavior continues.

We can extend the discussion to *media imagery* by acknowledging that all human visual behavior between humans is, to some extent, mediated activity, negotiated through a mutually dependent, mutually emerging process. We cannot see or directly experience

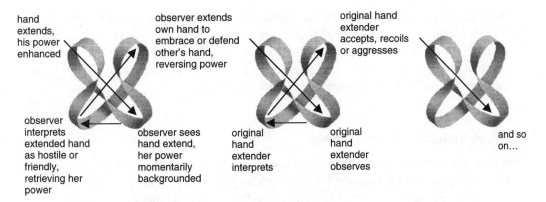

hand extends, his power enhanced

observer extends own hand to embrace or defend other's hand, reversing power

original hand extender accepts, recoils or aggresses

observer interprets extended hand as hostile or friendly, retrieving her power

observer sees hand extend, her power momentarily backgrounded

original hand extender interprets

original hand extender observes

and so on...

FIG. 26.3. Tetrad chain applied to moments of human visual behavior.[3]

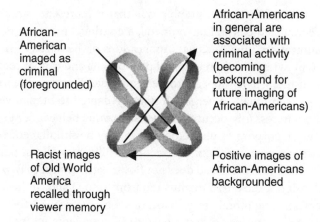

FIG. 26.4. Example of using the tetrad in a visual ecology framework to interpret the visual ethics of media stereotyping of African-Americans.

the inner workings of another person's mind. We respond to external indicators of those inner workings. Yet, at the same time, the manifestations are part of the behavior, part of the process and continually shifting meaning construction. Through the process and meaning of visual behavior, we exert personal and group power in the creation and use of imagery, internally and externally. That power can dominate or uplift, stereotype or enrich, deceive or validate. As an example, consider an act of stereotyping, which is generally accepted as a negative and unethical, but nevertheless, recurring behavior in mass media (see Fig. 26.4).

In conclusion, I want to try to answer the questions I set forth in the introduction to this chapter.

QUESTIONS

Is there an ethic unique to the visual?

Our visual system of knowing and communicating is fundamental to our survival, and any discussion of human survival necessarily involves power, which in turn involves ethics. The way we create visual messages, consume visual information, and store visual information affects the way we live, interact, and conceive of ourselves in unique ways. Determining the best way to live is a core concern of ethics.

If so, what is it and how does it operate?

In everyday terms, we speak of the visual as being very powerful: the Power of the Visual. What is the source of the power? Visual stimuli are powerful because they are arbiters of the reality we perceive, which necessarily affects the way we live that reality. Seventy-five percent of all information entering the brain is visual. If most of what we know is derived from the visual, the visual operates as the major source of stimuli on which we rely to form our perception of reality that subsequently guides our behavior.

How can we study it?

One way to grasp the complexity of an ethic of the visual is to conceptualize it in ecological terms as a synergistic, interdependent system of human behavior exemplifying a dynamic process of meaning making. Through that process, we live a continuum of empowerment and disempowerment, a continuum of ethical and unethical interaction. The tetrad structure offers one way to visually plot various continua for study.

How can we use what we learn to improve the ways people use images to make meaning and interact?

Each image is a part of the whole within the context of human image making. Examining visual behavior through an ecological lens can help us grasp as a gestalt the whole process, while at the same time offering a means for concentrating on specific aspects of the activity. One can study a variety of topics in this manner: digital manipulation of news photographs, political posturing for media stakeouts, stereotyping men of Middle Eastern descent, framing global warming as media hype, portraying children as sexualized associations with products, visualizing oneself looking like airbrushed models in fashion advertisements, and so on.

CONCLUSION

An image is not the result of but part of the ecology of the visual, part of the process of meaning making. The power of the visual is that it makes visible in some way that which has been invisible. The power of visual media is that—as does light—they make visible the previously invisible—the ideas, expressions, judgments, and stories that would otherwise remain beyond the realm of collective consciousness. In a similar manner, visual media background those who have little power via a kind of global unconscious composed of ignorance, a global ignoring of the possibility of pain other than our own, and a global consciousness composed of desire for power, a global collusion of those in control to oppress those who are not.

We live and interact in ways that are profoundly affected by the visual. How and what we see, gesture, imagine, dream, express, and remember affect how we respond to one another as mutually dependent, mutually emerging organisms in the dynamic process of meaning making we call life.

ACKNOWLEDGMENT

The author would like to thank Sheila Reaves and Rick Williams for their insightful comments on earlier versions of this chapter, and Bruce Powers, Eric McLuhan and the family of the late Blair Schrecongost for their discussions and allowing use of the tetrad.

ENDNOTES

[1] Tetrad Graphic © 1986 by Blair P. Schrecongost Artwork, Buffalo, NY, and Bruce R. Powers, co-author of *The Global Village*, 1989, p. 10, used with permission.

[2] See McLuhan and Powers (1989), pp. 180–181, for a full explication of the tetrad as envisioned in the original use of the graphic. See McLuhan and McLuhan (1988) for another explication of the tetrad as a conceptual tool. Note that Eric McLuhan envisions the four aspects of the tetrad process as a simultaneously occurring "pattern of resonances" (private communication, February 16, 2004).

[3] Please note that the arrows are added here simply as an aid to understanding the application of the tetrad in a chain.

REFERENCES

Audi, R. (Ed.). (1995). *Dictionary of philosophy*. Melbourne: Cambridge University Press.

Babbie, E. (1986). *Observing ourselves, essays in social research*. Belmont, CA: Wadsworth.

Barry, A. M. (1997). *Visual intelligence: Perception, image, and manipulation in visual communication*. Albany: State University of New York.

Bateson, G. (1972). *Steps to an ecology of mind*. New York: Ballantine.

Bechara, A., Damasio, H., Tranel, D., & Damasio, A. (1997). Deciding advantageously before knowing the advantageous strategy. *Science, 275*, 1293–1295.

Berkeley, G. (1910). A new theory of vision and other select philosophical writings. London: Dutton. Original published in 1790.

Bivins, T., & Newton, J. H. (2003). The real, the moral and the virtual: Ethics at the intersection of consciousness. *Journal of Mass Media Ethics, 18*(3–4), 213–229.

Damasio, A. (1994). *Descartes' error*. New York: Putnam.

Damasio, A. (1999). *The feeling of what happens*. New York: Harcourt Brace.

Golley, F. (1998). *A primer for environmental literacy*. New Haven: Yale University Press.

Gornick, V. (1976). Introduction. In E. Goffman (Ed.), *Gender advertisements*, pp. *vii–ix*. New York: Harper Colophon.

Gross, L., Katz, J. S., & Ruby, J. (Eds.). (1988). *Image ethics, the moral rights of subjects in photographs, film, and television*. New York: Oxford University Press.

Harper, D. A. (1982). *Good company*. Chicago: University of Chicago Press.

LeDoux, J. (1986). Sensory systems and emotion. *Integrative Psychiatry, 4*, 237–243.

LeDoux, J. (1996). *The emotional brain*. New York: Simon & Schuster.

Lester, P. M. (1991). *Photojournalism, the ethical approach*. Hillsdale, NJ: Lawrence Erlbaum Associations.

Mead, M., & Bateson, G. (1977). Margaret Mead and Gregory Bateson on the use of the camera in anthropology. *Studies in the Anthropology of Visual Communication, 4*, 78–80.

McLuhan, M., & McLuhan, E. (1988). *Laws of media: The new science*. Toronto: University of Toronto Press.

McLuhan, M., & Powers, B. (1989). *The global village: Transformations in world life and media in the 21st century*. New York: Oxford University Press.

Moriarty, S. (1994). Visual communication as a primary system. *Journal of Visual Literacy, 14*(2), 11–21.

Newton, J. H. (1984, Spring). Photography and reality: A matter of ethics. *Photo-Letter, 5*, 36–44.

Newton, J. H. (2001). *The burden of visual truth: The role of photojournalism in mediating reality*. Mahwah, NJ: Lawrence Erlbaum Associates.

Reaves, S. (1995, Winter). Magazines vs. newspapers: Editors have different ethical standards on the digital manipulation of photographs. *Visual Communication Quarterly*, 4–7.

Sargent, S. L., & Zillmann, D. (1999, May). *Image effects on selective exposure to news stories*. Paper presented to the International Communication Association annual convention, San Francisco.

Stone, A. R. (1995). *The war of desire and technology at the close of the mechanical age*. Cambridge: MIT Press.

Tagg, J. (1988). *The burden of representation: Essays on photographies and histories*. Basingstoke: Macmillan Education.

Williams, B. (1985). *Ethics and the limits of philosophy*. Cambridge, MA: Harvard University Press.

Williams, R. (1999). Beyond visual literacy: Omniphasism, A theory of balance (part one of three). *Journal of Visual Literacy, 19*(2), 159–178.

Williams, R. (2003). Transforming intuitive illiteracy: Understanding the effects of the unconscious mind on image meaning, image consumption, and behavior. *EME, 2*(2), 119–134.

27

A Survey of Reactions to Photographic Manipulation

SHIELA REAVES
University of Wisconsin–Madison

THEORETICAL BACKGROUND

Ethics is in the mind. It is not in the tools you use.

—Buell (1989, p. 1)

The *Los Angeles Times* war photo from Iraq was so arresting that picture editors from the *Chicago Tribune* and the *Hartford Courant* published it prominently. Unfortunately, the photographer lost his job over it. Maybe it was the fog of war, but the 5-year veteran of the *Los Angeles Times* had digitally cut and pasted together two similar images, and it fooled several news editors (Irby, 2003). In this war montage, truth was the first casualty, and the photographer's job was the second.

The mechanics of photography have always held secrets. The earliest secrets were also photomontages, where artists spliced together negatives, primarily to overcome the limitations of the primitive camera and its finicky film. As early as 1858, Henry Peach Robinson offended Victorian tastes with his photomontage "Fading Away" because the death scene of a young woman was considered too morbid. In fact, the death scene was fake, a montage of five negatives from healthy models and Robinson's understanding of perspective (Robinson, 1980). Visual deception was nothing new in 1980, but it required the time-consuming craftsmanship of a master technician with an artist's eye. Montages were labor-intensive, an alchemy of blunt tools and slow, exacting chemicals.

However, during the 1980s the computer revolution replaced blunt tools with a digital scalpel, and for many, a sense of magic. Digital alterations could improve reality and visual impact. This computer artistry was so seamless it could fool experts. One *National Geographic* photo editor admitted he tried to hire the photographer of a cover photo depicting three military jets flying over New York's Chrysler Building. When he contacted the magazine's art director, she revealed that the cover photo was her montage idea using three negatives (Reaves, 1991).

The mechanics of photography now digitizes its secrets. Ethics may reside in the mind, as Hall Buell of the Associated Press (1989) correctly asserted, but for over 20 years, digital technology has spawned ethical tempests, from *National Geographic*'s moving of a pyramid in 1981 to a growing unease over digital alterations of fashion models (Hitchon & Reaves, 1999; Reaves, Bush Hitchon, Park, & Yun, 2004a).

In Chapter 26, "Ethics Theory" in this volume, Newton distinguishes between the *ethics of process* and the *ethics of meaning*. Digital manipulation embraces both. In the ethics of process, digital alteration undermines what the photographer originally witnessed at the scene. In the ethics of meaning, readers usually believe what they see. And as Newton (2001) reminded us, we believe even when, cognitively, we know that seeing is suspect. Perhaps the most troubling aspect of digital manipulation, according to Wheeler (2002), is that small retouching can seem so trivial, so unimportant. At what point does digital retouching turn into an ethical quagmire?

Elliott and Lester (2000) teased apart aesthetics from ethics by using the metaphor of "the slippery slope": small transgressions do add up. Certain changes are not part of this slippery slope, such as intensifying colors for reproduction, eliminating "red eye" from electronic flash, or blurring offensive body parts. These are harmless aesthetic or etiquette decisions, they reason. However, tampering with seemingly small objects— such as removing a Diet Coke can or inserting a face into a background—can have profound ramifications of what constitutes visual truth (e.g., Kramer, 1989). As Elliott and Lester warned, "If you lie to your audience, if you perform acts that lead them to a false conclusion, if you create images rather than take them, you slide into the muck of unethical behavior" (2000, p. 19).

It seems so straightforward. Don't alter photographs; keep them as real as if your reader could somehow look over your shoulder and into your camera's viewfinder to see the same picture. Then why does the same problem continue to crop up among news and media professionals? Why did a sleep-deprived combat photographer digitally alter an Iraqi war photo?

Visual communication is highly interdisciplinary, and an ethical inquiry into digital manipulation is no exception. Several theories can help explain digital misuse, such as schema theory, semiotics, and organizational theory. Of course, this is just a beginning; scholars will expand theoretical analysis as they look at different effects of digital manipulation and new technology (e.g., Huang, 2001; Newton, 2001; Wheeler, 2002).

Schema theory can elucidate the inherent problems of digital manipulation. Words create the mental models to help us think about, and navigate, through our world (Moriarty, 1996). We have models in our mind—"cat," not "dog"—and we make sense by comparing the reality before us with the mental abstractions we store in memory. Schema theory argues that the use of categories is highly efficient. The human brain's ability to quickly process new information is based on prior knowledge stored in categories (Rosch, 1978; Smith & Meadin, 1981). Editorial categories serve the media by prescribing responses to certain categories of news. "Status-quo reporting" and "pack journalism" are part of the media's reliance on categorization and media routine of labeling people and framing events (Graber, 1990).

We now understand some of the underlying attitudes behind the media's routine of categorizing photographs (e.g., Kobre, 1980; Reaves, 1995b). Editors learn the mental categories, or schemas, of each photograph that crosses the news desk. This editing process is an example of organizational theory: Editors learn the norms of their newsroom. Editors group together news photographs that report breaking news events; they group together feature photographs that are *more evergreen timeless* like scenics or portraiture; they group together photo illustrations used for highly abstract or difficult topics. When there is no "human face" for a news story, then editors often consider a photo illustration (e.g., Kobre, 1980).

The digital scalpel allows editors to more easily mix up categories of photographs. In 1994, *Time* magazine editors transformed O. J. Simpson's police mug shot, considered a news photograph, into a photo illustration with the headline, "An American Tragedy." *Time* magazine's error was not overt racism, as many critics charged, but one of confusing categories, or schemas, of photographs. Once O. J. Simpson's mug shot was deemed a photo illustration—and not a news photo—the lights turned green for digital manipulation sanctioned by art directors and *Time's* news editors. The unintended effect of this new technology was, for *Time* magazine, a loss in credibility (Reaves, 1995a).

However, many digital manipulations involve feature photographs altered by media practitioners outside of the newsroom. Within public relations, an editor from the University of Wisconsin–Madison evoked national coverage over its admissions brochure when he digitally inserted the face of an African American into an all-white football crowd. *News Photographer* magazine (2000) sized up the public relations debacle with the headline "With Photoshop, Wisconsin Achieves Racial Diversity." Within the fashion media, Kate Winslet complained that Britain's *GQ* magazine excessively slimmed down her legs and torso using what the fashion media calls "cosmetic retouching" (Betts, 2003).

When does digital editing turn into a slide down the slippery slope? We can construct a continuum that delineates the edges of the slippery slope by using semiotic theory. Worth and Gross (1974) theorized that pictures, or sign events, fall into certain groups (or categories) that elicit different responses from viewers. If a picture is perceived as "natural," then it is regarded as informative much like a hidden camera recording an interview. A news photo is a "natural" sign event that purports to inform and educate. In contrast, a picture perceived as "symbolic," such as a cinematic film, invokes cultural codes to infer meaning. A photographic illustration is "symbolic," and viewers use cultural cues to construe meaning.

However, it is Worth and Gross' third group that is interesting for ethical decision making. Worth and Gross identified a third category of sign events they described as having "ambiguous meaning." These are images that do not readily fall into "natural/real" events or "symbolic/invented" categories. [Confronting this ambiguous image, the viewer pauses.] How to attribute this ambiguous sign? It is this pause that is significant for ethicists. The viewer must assess the ambiguous image: "*where* to place it—*how* do I respond?" Editors who casually attend to the ambiguous image might find themselves at the center of another digital controversy.

Nothing is new about using photographic categories; however, in the 1980s and 1990s, old values were unexamined in a *changed* technological context. Professionals don't always question *why* they do *what* they do; they're too busy meeting deadlines (Anderson & Ross, 2002; Shoemaker & Reese, 1991). Yet if these practices are juxtaposed with sudden technological change, these transparent practices can yield new understanding in ethical decision making.

Ethics is part of moral philosophy, but in practice it is also about recognizing choices. In media ethics these choices are often made under deadline. Media ethics often study the criteria underpinning editorial judgments of right or wrong actions. But how do researchers tease apart the attitudes that influence editors using digital technology?

A main assumption behind ethical decision making is that attitudes influence behavior and media routines. If we can isolate attitudes, we might be able to understand the complex decisions behind when—and when not—to digitally alter a photograph. New technology had outpaced our understanding of the photographic editing process. A national survey was one way to try and catch up with the computer revolution.

WHEN TO USE SURVEY METHOD FOR ASSESSING ETHICAL DECISION MAKING

Survey method might reveal editorial attitudes that could predict the slippery slope of digital manipulation. However, survey method is not a panacea. In visual communication, the interdisciplinary approach often works best. It's like picking up a jewel and considering the light emanating from each facet. In visual communication, qualitative methods inform the efficient use of quantitative methodology, especially the labor-intensive process behind national surveys.

For many researchers, qualitative research is the first fertile ground for asking the initial difficult questions. It is most efficient when sudden technological change is not widely understood by early adopters or educators. Using systematic interviews, an inquiry into the first adopters of the elite digital technology of Scitex (a 2-million-dollar investment during the 1980s) revealed differences in attitudes across the print media toward the digital manipulation of photographs (Reaves, 1987, 1991). The findings were intriguing because there was disagreement within the mass media. Experienced newspaper editors, known for their articulation of visual editing standards, were adamant about not altering a news photograph. And yet newspapers often found themselves in digital controversy. In contrast, consumer magazine editors considered a photograph a starting point for creating imaginative covers and illustrations.

Qualitative research yields rich perspectives of individual attitudes and behavior; however, there are limitations. Regardless of rigor, a qualitative sample is small, often elite and certainly not random. A small selection of individual opinions from a convenience sample cannot be generalized to the larger group.

In contrast, the survey method can create a national snapshot. Questionnaires applied to a probabilistic sample can adequately capture attitudes across large groups of editors that might predict possible media behavior. Survey method allows researchers to describe industry change and ascertain its rate of familiarity and adoption of new technology. It can also accurately describe what practitioners view as important by eliciting the ranking of items researchers consider to be influential.

Another advantage of survey method is that it can compare differences of attitudes within groups. Demographics are easily gathered within a random sample of a given population and are often important independent variables: age, education, gender, or circulation size. These independent variables can help explain the constellation of attitudes and behaviors in adopting new technology.

Perhaps most important, a survey can more easily compare differences across the media. Media practices, part of organizational theory, differ among newspaper, magazines, and television, and questionnaires can easily reach these larger groups.

Yet researchers must also understand the limits of survey method. It is a self-report from a sample of respondents. Becker (1998) contended that, for social scientists, attitudes can be tricky to assess. Because attitudes are self-reported, subjects are not always reliable: *saying* and *doing* are two different things. Moreover, subjects are notorious for wanting to please a researcher or give what they perceive to be a "correct" or "prestigious" answer. If questions contain bias, confusing noise or phrases that suggest the research hypothesis, then these design errors will invalidate conclusions.

Questions like these have plagued social scientists. Thomas Kuhn asserted that science can only make progress when scientists agree on conventionalized categories about what a problem is and what its solutions looks like. If there is no reliability (such as consistent answers) or validity (such as measuring what it purports to measure) then Kuhn said there is a situation where "you have plenty of scientists but no science" (Becker, 1998, p. 85) Pretests can lower the possibility of launching a major survey with faulty questions. Critiques from colleagues are another form of pretest.

Visual communication research can exacerbate traditional survey method. Telephone surveys ensure a higher response rate because of increased attempts to contact subjects, but naturally, responses are oral. In contrast, mail surveys traditionally elicit lower response rates. For example, Hesterman (1987) surveyed magazine editors for their use of written ethical guidelines—an important issue in any medium—yet she contended with hostile responses in addition to low rates of return. This in itself was interesting to report: Magazine editors didn't respond well to questions about their ethical practices.

Despite limitations to any investigation, the following study used survey method to explore the attitudes of newspaper and magazine editors regarding the ethics of digital manipulation. Survey method can adequately identify attitudes that may influence the tolerance levels toward digital manipulation. The following survey is a case study in grappling with the problems of survey method for visual research.

USING SURVEY METHOD: ATTITUDES AND USE OF DIGITAL ALTERATIONS AMONG MAGAZINE AND NEWSPAPER EDITORS

Are categories of photographs important to the ethical use of digital alterations? There was only anecdotal evidence that suggested editors should not alter news photos, and yet could alter photo illustrations. This suggested a continuum of choices, such as Worth and Gross (1974) semiotic theory. An untested possibility within the newsroom was that feature photographs, the timeless, non-news events, constituted "ambiguous" signs. The viewer/editor pauses to assess the ambiguous feature photograph. Editors might be more willing to digitally alter the feature photograph, deemed less ethically important than news photos. If they did, then educators could argue that the continuum was actually a slippery slope.

There was comparatively little published empirical data regarding digital manipulation (e.g., Kelly & Nace, 1994). However, an Ameritech grant allowed for a national survey of 670 magazine visual editors and 677 newspaper visual editors. The questionnaire examined attitudes and editing behaviors that influence or predict ethical decision making of digital alterations.

This national survey contained several hypotheses and research questions; however, for simplicity this chapter discusses the primary research question and hypothesis. A research question can clarify what is often a muddle of opinions, most often from elite editors who are the most vocal within the news industry. The primary research for this survey explored attitudes toward digital manipulation across the magazine and newspaper industries.

Research Question
What are the differences in attitudes toward digital manipulation between newspaper and magazine editors?

In contrast, a hypothesis attempts to predict responses based on theory, and therefore strengthens the assumptions and arguments underlying communication theory. The primary hypothesis tested categorization theory from semiotic theorists Worth and Gross (1974) and their theory of natural, symbolic, and ambiguous sign events.

Hypothesis
Newspaper editors will be least tolerant of the digital manipulation of spot news pictures, but find the most agreement with the digital manipulation of photo illustrations. However, their attitude toward feature photos will fall somewhere in between and constitute the "ambiguous sign event."

Designing a Questionnaire That Answers What You Are Asking

This survey had many concerns and potential traps: would visual editors accept the notion of photographic categories—and if so, would they be consistent in their attitudes? In other words, did categories of photographs make sense? Professionals might talk about feature, news, or photo illustrations. But did categories have any impact on how editors actually edited photographs? Again, digital technology had outpaced knowledge.

Surveys require producing a robust database that is both random and large enough for analysis. A random sample of visual editors from newspapers was acquired through the membership list of the National Press Photographers Association (NPPA), with an additional letter from the NPPA president encouraging respondents to complete the questionnaire. To reach magazine editors, a random sample of visual editors was obtained from the magazine resource Standard Rates and Data Service (SRDS). In turn, a letter from the president of the American Society of Magazine Photographers encouraged visual editors to complete the questionnaire.

Technically, the biggest problem was creating a questionnaire that appealed to professional visual editors. It was decided that a visual investigation into digital manipulation demanded visual stimuli in full color with glossy production values. Therefore, a separate visual insert provided visual stimuli that editors could keep after they returned the questionnaire. Some editors reported photocopying the visual insert and passing it around to their staff to generate internal ethical discussions (Reaves, 1993, p. 134).

This survey was testing editors' attitudes of digital manipulation—not their ability to perceive digital changes. Accordingly, editors did not have to guess what was digitally altered for each of the 15 visual samples. The majority of questions contained a clearly-marked original image next to its altered image with a brief description of which elements were altered. Editors were told the nature of the change plus a brief reason in order to give some editorial context. The editor was then asked a neutral question, "Do you agree with the computer editing change?" A five-point Likert scale recorded their reaction from "Strongly Agree" to "Strongly Disagree."

However, this survey would be seriously incomplete if it used 15 photo examples of digital manipulation. The largest limitation to using only visual stimuli is that researchers cannot generalize about future actions, which predicts possible behavior. A photograph is limited to its specific context. Researchers cannot extrapolate about future attitudes toward digital manipulations. Therefore the 15 visual stimuli were not useful in testing the hypothesis using schema theory or for predicting how categories of photographs might influence editorial decisions.

Consequently, the questionnaire had a verbal component for testing its hypothesis. To test categorization theory, a second crucial part contained nine verbal, hypothetical questions. These questions had no accompanying photographs and specifically asked about three categories of photographs: news, feature, and photo illustration. Yet this was another potential methodological trap.

How do researchers hide their hypothesis from savvy respondents? The hypothesis demanded a direct comparison of its independent variable, the different categories of photos. If you ask about altering a news photograph, how do you ask the *same* question about altering a feature or photo illustration? Clearly, the survey design was very vulnerable. Editors could not be tipped off about types of photographs.

Therefore, an experimental method was embedded into the survey. Newspaper and magazine editors were randomly divided into three groups. The three groups were sent different versions of the same nine questions. The independent variable, category of photograph, changed with each version of the questionnaire. Version 1 asked nine questions about particular computer editing manipulations for "spot news" photographs. Version 2 asked the same questions about "feature photographs," and version 3 asked the same questions regarding "photo illustrations." Therefore, a given editor would receive questions about only one category of photo. This prevented editors from deducing the hypothesis about categorization as they considered their responses.

In designing questionnaires, order effect is another inherent concern. Questions must be able to stand alone and be free of any internal relationships. Order effect addresses this possible internal conflict. Two versions of the questionnaire, A and B, reversed the order of the nine hypothetical questions. Tests were run to see whether order of questions had any effect on mean scores (there was no difference between versions A and B; hence, no order effect).

Operational definitions—"How do you define what you are measuring?"—also require rigor. Two well-known sources provided the definitions of the three categories of photos: spot news, feature, photo illustration. The NPPA defined photo categories for its national contests. NPPA defined spot news as "pictures of unscheduled events for which no advance planning was possible." Features were defined as "usually a found situation with strong human interest—a fresh view of the commonplace." Kobre's textbook provided the basis of a definition for photo illustration: "conceptual photos that combine the limitless possibilities of the drawing with the realism of the photograph. Includes editorial, food, and fashion illustrations" (1980, pp. 108–109).

In each version of the questionnaire, the category of photo was defined immediately preceding the nine questions. The questions asked editors to agree or disagree over when "it is generally OK to . . . " use such digital alterations as: removing telephone wires; moving people closer together to fit a layout; changing the color of a wall; stretching pixels to lengthen the depth of a photo; creating photographic montages; blurring backgrounds to emphasize a subject; cloning a border to lengthen a photo to fit a layout; electronically removing a background; removing distracting people in the background.

Researchers also need reality checks in designing questionnaires. Therefore, several pretests were given to professional photographers (not part of the sample group because they were not editors) to ascertain the importance and clarity of each of the nine hypothetical questions. The questions presented serious, real-world situations for professionals grappling with digital manipulation.

After pretests and subsequent editing changes, a survey was ready to launch. In addition to the first mailing, there were follow-up postcards asking respondents to answer the questionnaire. After several weeks, a second mailing was sent to nonrespondents. This is the time period during which researchers qualitatively test the power of prayer.

Results

An external grant allowed for a robust sample of media professionals. Of the 1,347 visual editors surveyed who regularly edit photographs for either consumer magazines or daily newspapers, 821 responded for an overall response rate of 65%. As suspected, there were differences in response rates between magazine editors and newspaper editors. Of the 677 newspaper editors surveyed, 511 responded for a response rate of 75%. Of the 670 magazine editors surveyed, 310 returned questionnaires for a response rate of 46%.

Differences in attitudes between magazines and newspaper editors were largely measured with t-tests. Multiple regression was used to test whether certain factors, such as publication type or education in photojournalism, were influential in predicting tolerance toward digital manipulation.

Newspaper Editors and the Visual Stimuli

The visual insert of 15 illustrated questions probing the primary research question was analyzed first. It was important to divide newspaper responses from magazine responses within the print media because newspaper editors constituted the largest media group actively concerned with digital technology. Therefore, the first analysis considered the responses of only newspaper photographic editors (Reaves, 1993).

In general, newspaper editors responding to the 15 visual examples were very critical of any kind of digital manipulation. Except for the traditional practices of printing (burning and dodging), they were strongly intolerant of digital manipulation of the visual insert. At least 50% consistently "strongly disagreed" with altering 14 of the 15 examples of digital manipulation.

But were there patterns within this technologically conservative group of newspaper editors? Demographic characteristics of respondents are often a rich source of analysis for survey research. Some newspaper editors did agree to computer alterations. Did they have anything in common besides their opinions? What demographics, or independent variables, could explain differences in attitudes among newspaper editors?

Analysis of total mean scores revealed that editors differed in attitudes depending on size of circulation, familiarity with technology, and education (Reaves, 1993). Editors of newspapers with circulations over 100,000, and editors who had a strong familiarity with new technology were less tolerant of digital alterations. Newspaper editors who possessed a college degree or who were active in professional developments, such as attendance at National Press Photographers Association seminars, were less tolerant of digital manipulation. Gender was not a factor.

Across the Print Media: Newspaper Versus Magazines

However, it was important to compare attitudes across the newspaper and magazine media of the 15 visual questions. The summed score of these 15 questions gave an index of tolerance level toward digital manipulation. T-tests revealed that there was a significant difference in attitudes between the visual editors at magazines and newspapers in their responses to 15 visual situations. Magazine editors were significantly more tolerant of digital alterations across 15 of the 15 visually-based questions (Reaves, 1995c).

Which editors were more likely to tolerate digital manipulation? Statistical analysis can tease apart variables and examine which independent variables (such as demographics) might predict a score (such as tolerance toward digital manipulation). A hierarchical multiple regression was used to see whether education in photojournalism might predict tolerance levels. The following variables were identified as possible predictors of increased tolerance: type of publication (magazine or newspaper), attendance at photographic seminars, photojournalism background. The dependent variable was the visual editor's summed score for all 15 illustrated questions.

Results were mixed. Multiple regression analysis indicated that publication type was the single strongest predictor of an editor's tolerance, accounting for 34% of the variance. Attendance at photographic seminars accounted for an additional 5%. However, the third was not significant among visual editors.

Surprisingly, a background in photojournalism accounted for only a minor change across newspaper and magazine professionals. Instead, professional development in the print media is a stronger predictor of tolerance levels than photojournalism experience. In light of the *Los Angeles Times* photographer who lost his job because of a composite war photograph, this finding on photojournalism background may interest visual communication educators. Professional development appears to matter more than photojournalism background.

Categorization Theory and Newspaper Editors

Could categorization theory predict an entry onto the slippery slope? As suspected, newspaper editors were the least tolerant of digital manipulation involving 15 visual examples. Analysis of the nine verbally based, hypothetical questions provided guideposts in ethical decision making.

Editors acknowledged the usefulness of photo categories for the nine verbal, hypothetical questions digital manipulation. Their answers were consistent. Analysis of the nine questions revealed a satisfactory level of reliability for the questionnaire's three versions: feature photos (alpha = .88); spot news photo (alpha = .89); photo illustration (alpha = .94) (Reaves, 1995b).

Category of photo matters, even for digitally conservative newspaper editors. Tests revealed that category of photo does suggest a continuum of attitudes, and therefore the contours of a slippery slope. Analysis of variance (ANOVA) compared the three versions of the nine verbally based questions that probed categorization. The group of editors who were least tolerant of digital alterations had received the survey version that contained the independent variable, "spot news photo." In contrast, the group of newspaper editors who were most tolerant of digital manipulation had received the version containing the independent variable, "photo illustration." Within-group difference between spot news and photo illustration was significant at the p < .05 level.

The feature photograph, however, was distinctly vulnerable to increased digital manipulation. This category of photo elicited more equivocal responses. A third, distinct group of editors responded to the survey version using "feature photo," and they differed by falling between news and illustration. Within-group difference between spot news and feature was significant at the p < .05 level; and within-group difference between feature and photo illustration was significant at the p < .05 level.

These tests supports the concept of a continuum of natural and symbolic sign events. The feature photo falls in between the two polar photos, spot news and photo illustration. The feature photo is the vulnerable image, the ambiguous sign event. Therefore the slippery slope has a predictable shape.

DISCUSSION AND CONCLUSION

Survey method can elucidate the slippery slope regarding digital technology. Quantitative research can provide data and support for ethical frameworks within decision making. For example, the continuum of natural and symbolic sign events offers support for discussing ethical philosophy.

In visual ethics, Rivers and Schramm (1969) first articulated the notion of a continuum of ethical practices for photojournalists. They asked a group of graduate students studying media ethics, when does "posing" a picture become "faking" a picture? Rivers and Schramm presented ethical cases and created a continuum whereby the ethics of posing became increasingly more troublesome to students. At one end of the continuum were the harmless scenes, such as rearranging leaves in a scenic. At the other end of the continuum were photographers who pulled out stuffed birds from their car trunks for adding "pictorial interest." When does a photojournalist stop posing? Rivers and

Schramm argued a categorical imperative: The time to stop posing is in the beginning, with the innocuous little scene with the leaves.

The spot news photo is part of the media's categorical imperative. The most exacting branch of deontological ethics, Kant's categorical imperative states that a virtue that is deemed good becomes a moral end in itself. Therefore, upholding the categorical imperative—such as news photos—regardless of circumstances, becomes the correct action for a news photographer (e.g., Lester, 2003). It is a hard path; absolutists who defend the First Amendment regardless of circumstances are upholders of the categorical imperative. Perhaps that is why the Los Angeles Times photographer lost his job so quickly.

At the other end of the slippery slope lies the digital illusion. The photo illustration captures the imagination of both art director and reader, and creative imagination is valued. Aristipus' principle of intellectual pleasure gives permission for editors to freely invent dramatic photo montages. Hedonism, as Lester (2003) described it, is the modern-day version of "Eat, drink, and be merry." The ethical dilemma arises when readers do not understand that a photo illustration's intent is, above all, blatantly illusory (Wheeler & Gleason, 1995). When the digital routines used to create photo illustrations are combined with glamorous advertising and fashion photography, there might be more unintended effects among some readers.

Visual communicators must keep examining the adage "Seeing is believing." For example, new research into digital manipulation looks at the connection between readers of fashion magazines and the rise in eating disorders. Female readers who are vulnerable to the "drive for thinness," the precursor to eating disorders, are also known to be heavy readers of women's fashion magazines. Sufferers of anorexia often use photographs of ultra-thin models to support their determination to get thinner (Harrison & Cantor, 1997; Hitchon & Reaves, 1999). Does the digital manipulation of fashion models have a public health impact? (Reaves et al., 2004b).

New technology often outpaces our understanding of its effects. Because survey method gives us a national snapshot, it can support scholars who argue for what Newton calls the "ethics of process and the ethics of meaning": a continued professional development of students, educators, and media professionals in ethical dialogues. The Iraqi war photo of April 2003 did not remain a digital secret for long, and the Los Angeles Times responded quickly to keep its news credibility. The digital scalpel has changed the ethical query "What's wrong with this picture?" to a more cynical question: "What's wrong with this *perfect* picture?"

REFERENCES

Anderson, R., & Ross, V. (2002). *Questions of communication: A practical introduction to theory.* Boston: Bedord/St. Martin's.

Barthes, R. (1977). *Image, music, text.* New York: Hill & Wang.

Becker, H. S. (1998). *The Tricks of the trade: How to think about your research while you're doing it.* Chicago: University of Chicago Press.

Berger, J. (1980). Understanding a photograph. In A. Trachtenberg (Ed.), *Classic Essays on Photography* (pp. 290–299). New Haven, CT: Leete's Island Books.

Betts, K. (2003, February 2). The man who makes the pictures perfect. *The New York Times,* section 9, pp. 1, 8.

Boorstin, D. (1972). From news-gathering to news-making: A flood of pseudo-events. In W. Schramm and D. Roberts, (Eds.), *The process and effects of mass communication* (pp. 116–150). Urbana: University of Illinois Press.

Boorstin, D. (1961). *The image: A guide to pseudo-events in America.* New York: Harper & Row.

Buell, H. (1989, September 11). TV Guide composite not without precedent. *AP World,* p. 1.

David, P., & Kang, J. (1998). Pictures, high-imagery news language and news recall. *Newspaper Research Journal, 19,* 21–29.

Elliott, D., & Lester, P. M. (2000, October). They should not tell a lie: Do minor touch-ups foretell a slide down the slippery slope? *News Photographer,* 18–20.

Elliott, D., & Lester, P. M. (2002, January). All that sparkles may be too bold: Small effects speak to larger issues. *News Photographer,* 16–17.

Graber, D. (1990). Seeing is remembering: How visuals contribute to learning from television news. *Journal of Communication, 40,* 134–155.

Harrison, K., & Cantor, J. (1997). The relationship between media consumption and eating disorders. *Journal of Communication, 47,* 40–63.

Hesterman, V. (1987). Consumer magazines and ethical guidelines. *Journal of Mass Media Ethics, 2,* 93–101.

Hitchon, J., & Reaves, S. (1999). Media mirage: The thin ideal as digital manipulation. In M. Carstarphen and S. Zavoina (Eds.), *Sexual rhetoric: Media perspectives on sexuality, gender and identity* (pp. 65–76). Westport, CT: Greenwood.

Huang, S. H. (2001). Readers' perceptions of digital alteration in photojournalism. *Journalism & Mass Communication Monographs, 3,* 149–182.

Irby, K. (2003, April 2). L. A. Times photographer fired over altered image. Poynter Online, at http://poynter.org/content/content_view.asp?id=28082.

Kelly, J. E., & Nace, D. (1994). Digital imaging and believing photos. *Visual Communication Quarterly, 1,* 4–7.

Kobre, K. (1980). *Photojournalism: The professional's approach.* Boston: Focal Press.

Kramer, S. (1989, April 29). The case of the missing coke can: Electronically altered photo creates a stir. *Editor & Publisher,* p. 18.

Lester, P. M. (2003). *Visual communication: Images with messages* (pp. 63–65). Wadsworth/Thomson Learning Belmont, California.

Moriarty, S. E. (1996). Abduction: A theory of visual interpretation. *Communication Theory, 6,* 167–187.

News Photographer. (2000, October). Caught: With photoshop, Wisconsin achieves racial diversity, 19.

Newton, J. (2001). *The burden of visual truth: The role of photojournalism in mediating reality.* Mahwah, NJ: Lawrence Erlbaum Associates.

Pavio, A. (1986). *Mental representations: A dual coding approach.* New York: Oxford University Press.

Reaves, S. (1987). Digital retouching in newspapers. *Journal of Mass Media Ethics, 2,* 40–48.

Reaves, S. (1991). Digital alteration of photographs in consumer magazines. *Journal of Mass Media Ethics, 6,* 175–181.

Reaves, S. (1993). "What's wrong with this picture?: Daily newspaper photo editors' attitudes and their tolerance toward digital manipulation. *Newspaper Research Journal, 13 & 14,* 131–155.

Reaves, S. (1995a). The unintended effects of new technology (and why we can expect more). *Visual Communication Quarterly, 2,* 11–15.

Reaves, S. (1995b). The vulnerable image: Categories of photos as predictor of digital manipulation. *Journalism and Mass Communication Quarterly, 72,* 706–715.

Reaves, S. (1995c). Magazines vs. newspapers: Editor have different ethical standards on the digital manipulation of photographs. *Visual Communication Quarterly, 2,* 4–7.

Reaves, S., Bush Hitchon, J., Park, S., & Yun, G. W. (2004a). You can never be too thin—or can you?: A pilot study on the effects of digital manipulation of fashion models' body size, leg length and skin color. *Race, Gender and Class, 11*(2), 140–155.

Reaves, S., Bush Hitchon, J., Park, S., & Yun, G. W. (2004b). If looks could kill: Digital manipulation of fashion models. *Journal of Mass Media Ethics, 19*(1), 56–71.

Rivers, W., & Schramm, W. (1969). *Responsibility in mass communication.* New York: Harper & Row.

Robinson, H. Peach. (1980). Idealism, realism, expressionism. In A. Trachtenberg (Ed.), *Classic essays on photography* (pp. 91–97). New Haven, CT: Leete's Island Books.

Rosch, E. (1978). Principles of categorization. In E. Rosch and B. Lloyd (Eds.), *Cognition and Categorization* (pp. 7–21). Hillsdale, NJ: Lawrence Erlbaum Associates.

Russial, J., & Wanta, W. (1998). Digital imaging skills and the hiring and training of photojournalists. *Journalism and Mass Communication Quarterly, 75,* 593–605.

Shoemaker, P., & Reese, S. (1991). Mediating the message: Theories of influences on mass media content. White Plains, NY: Longman.

Smith, E., & Meadin, D. (1981). *Categories and Concepts.* Cambridge, MA: Harvard University Press.

Wheeler, T. (2002). *Phototruth or photofiction?: Ethics and media imagery in the digital age.* Mahwah, NJ: Lawrence Erlbaum Associates.

Wheeler, T., & Gleason, T. (1995). Photography or photofiction: An ethical protocol for the digital age. *Visual Communication Quarterly, 2,* 8–12.

Wimmer, R., & Dominick, J. (1991). *Mass media research: An introduction* (3rd ed.). Belmont, CA: Wadsworth.

Worth, S., & Gross, L. (1974). Symbolic strategies. *Journal of Communication, 24,* 27–39.

Studying Visual Ethics by Applying a Typology of Visual Behavior

JULIANNE H. NEWTON
University of Oregon

We need to look at the subtle, the hidden, and the unspoken.

—Gladwell (2000, p. 80)

One of the most perplexing problems in doing visual research is the lack of reliable and valid methods for understanding, evaluating, and reporting visual data. The potential consequences inherently are a matter of ethical concern: Are we indeed measuring what we think we are? Are we interpreting and reporting our results in authentic and effective ways? Are we facilitating the study of visual communication practices in ways that promote ethical human behavior?

This chapter demonstrates a typology of visual behavior as a method for studying the ethical dynamics that arise when we create and interpret images. The typology addresses visual research in two ways: (a) It relocates the discussion from presentation issues to the image-making act[1] as the fundamental ethical unit for visual analysis, and (b) it offers an integrated visual and verbal symbol system for evaluating visual behavior. *Visual behavior* refers to what people do to communicate with imaging: nonverbal behavior (such as gesturing and facial expressions), using a camera to make a photograph or video, drawing, surfing the Web, and even dreaming, which is communicating visually with oneself. I use the term *behavior* because it grounds visual activity in the physical world and because it includes activity that can result from conscious or unconscious mental processing. If we see a spider and recoil, for example, we are operating on the basis of an external stimulus (seeing the spider) but with an unconscious response (protect myself by moving away). This chapter explains the typology of visual behavior and how it works by applying it as a method for analyzing the kind of still photographs made in photojournalism or documentary work. However, the typology can be used to examine other forms of visual communication as well.

The *typology of visual behavior* works on two levels. On one level, the typology verbally names and classifies visual actions and interactions of photographers, subjects and viewers, as well as their resulting artifacts—such as photographs, print publications, electronic media, personal and public memory, and modeled patterns of how to go about one's life. On another level, the typology visualizes those actions, interactions, and artifacts via image symbols that convey visual communication codes in a manner beyond words. The goal is to simplify and improve through both rational and intuitive synthesis[2] the complex stimuli and responses that occur when individuals communicate visually. It is important to remember that the rationale underlying the typology is inherently ethical: How we behave, whether in a personal or professional capacity, has consequences.

The typology ranges from visual embrace to visual murder and suicide. Categories are neither mutually exclusive nor exhaustive. The typology is designed to be expandable and to encompass the situational and psychophysiological relativity of human communication patterns. *Visual embrace*, for example, can refer to the public communication between a photographer and subject whose eyes meet for a brief but meaningful moment, or it can refer to the way someone viewing a photograph is drawn to stare into the eyes of a person imaged in the photograph. As with other forms of human communication, interactions vary according to situation or context, as well as according to such individual differences as personality characteristics, gender roles, photographic experiences, perceived authority, professional protocol. The typology facilitates analysis of the visual behavior that has immediate effects on those who are creating the images, on the content of those images, and on the ultimate uses and viewer responses to those images.

BASIS OF THE TYPOLOGY

The typology grew out of my own interactions with photographic subjects and my subsequent study of imaging, viewer responses, and ethical concerns.[3] For example, while documenting a teacher at work in her classroom in Mexico for a period of months, I noticed various influences on how she responded to my camera and to me. Among the influences were whether the classroom was warm enough on a cold day, whether she was ill, how she was dressed, how the children were interacting with her, how unobtrusive I made myself, how much the children noticed me, whether I used flash, whether I was close to her or standing on a chair in the back of the room, whether other teachers were watching us, whether her personality type was uptight or relaxed, whether she felt good about the way she looked. These factors seem intuitively obvious when we list them here: of course, they will affect how the teacher acts. As visual social scientists and visual journalists, we seldom pause to consider such factors, however, and they may not be obvious at all when we look at the photograph. The photograph may not communicate all of those details in an obvious manner. The photograph can, however, communicate more than we realize, just as human gestures can communicate powerfully on levels beyond our conscious awareness. Visual communication operates on such intricately sophisticated and subconscious levels that it is extremely difficult, if not impossible, for anyone to note and describe all of its effects in words. That is, in fact, precisely why visual communication is effective: The visual taps directly into primal mental processing that short-circuits rational, or more logical and verbal, processing (Barry, 1997; Bechara, Damasio, Tranel, & Damasio, 1997; Moriarty, 1994, 1996). Malcolm Gladwell (2000) used a variety of stories of visual activity to explain how "little things" can make the difference in how people behave. For example, psychologists (Mullen et al., 1986) found that subtle shifts in facial expression by news anchors affected the way viewers voted for candidates on which the anchors reported. Even though the anchor who most influenced viewers, Peter Jennings, asserted his reportage was neutral, careful research concluded that he used significant, noticeable facial expressions favoring then presidential candidate Ronald Reagan. Mullen stressed that nonverbal cues can be insidious. In another study, psychologists (Wells & Petty, 1980) found that asking audience members to move their heads up and down for seemingly unrelated reasons influenced the way they responded to an advertisement. In still another study, a social psychologist (Condon, 1982) spent a year and a half watching a 4.5-second segment of video before he became consciously aware of subtle visual cues communicated among a mother, father, and son while talking. The researcher was able to determine, via a visual method—long-term watching—that minute visual communication patterns affected when, what, and how people conversed with one another.[4]

Exciting new discoveries in neuroscience underscore the need to develop better methods for studying visual communication that acknowledge both the intuitive, which occurs below conscious awareness, and rational bases of human communication. Researchers are looking to our visual processing system (Crick, 1994) for primary cues about how our feelings affect how we think and behave (Damasio, 1992, 1999), how our bodies respond to the external world without our having to think in words (LeDoux, 1986, 2002), and how we learn strategies for living and everyday decision making (Bechara et al., 1997). Neuroscientist Antonio Damasio wrote that a "multimedia mind-show occurs constantly as the brain processes external and internal sensory events. As the brain answers the unasked question of who is experiencing the mind-show, the sense of self emerges" (2002, p. 4).

What does all of this have to do with imaging ethics? Everything. How we go about creating, using, and reading an image inherently requires decision making, and the decisions we make usually have consequences that result in ethical or unethical behavior. For example, are we trying to tell the truth when we make a photograph, or are we consciously or unconsciously trying to validate a point of view? Have we manipulated someone into an unrepresentative frame of mind before we photograph him or her? Are we aware of the extent to which our presence affects people's behavior while we photograph them? Do we believe what we, the photojournalists, see is true to the exclusion of other ways of seeing the same situation—or perhaps a little "more true" than the way someone else sees? Those questions reflect *ethics of process*, or how we go about making an image. A second set of questions reflects *ethics of meaning*, or how we use an image, what we say it means, and, on the other side of communication, how we view an image and how we remember it. Those questions include: Does the image represent the story authentically, or does it highlight one unrepresentative moment? Does the image unnecessarily intrude on a vulnerable individual? Do the caption and headlines that direct interpretation of the image mislead us or guide us to a considered viewing? Did we crop something out of the photo that is key to its authentic meaning? Did we digitally alter the photograph?

So, how do we begin to investigate the ethics of such a complex system as *The Visual*? I believe we often go about the business of visual research in the wrong way. Far too often, we try to translate visual communication into verbal communication while not fully considering that the visual communicates in fundamentally different ways than the verbal. If someone is trying to translate a poem originally written in Spanish—say a poem by Pablo Neruda, for example—into English, the translation will be only as good as the translator's ability to communicate in *both* Spanish and English—and the translator's ability to comprehend and execute the nuances of poetic communication in both languages. Even then, the poem most likely loses something, or at the very least changes somewhat, through the translation because the rhythms and sounds and words of the Spanish language express thoughts and emotions in ways that are different from the ways English expresses thoughts and emotions. We perceive the meanings differently— so, in effect, the meanings *are* different. This does not mean we should forego attempts to translate a poem from one language into another. But it is important to recognize that the translation will be only as good as the translator and cannot convey precisely the same meaning in precisely the same way as the original. I believe the same is true in visual communication—perhaps even more so because so much of the visual occurs beyond conscious awareness.

That line of thinking has convinced me that we need to devise unique visual methods to research visual questions. How else can we claim to measure what we say we are measuring—in other words, conducting *valid* research? Focusing on the translation of visuals into words or numbers, which is what qualitative and quantitative research often does, too easily directs attention away from the uniquely visual component of the communication we want to study. I am not advocating that we abandon words and numbers, but rather that we look for ways to make our methods of study correspond more closely to the form of the communication we study. We can think of many ways visuals are used as tools of research, or as part of the methods of conducting a study: visual social science, experimental designs using images, surveys that refer to imaging, historical analysis involving images as data, and analyses of visual content. In most cases, however, the methods used determine that the resulting information must be interpreted in words or numbers. When graphs, charts, and models are used to help us visualize the data and theoretical implications, our understanding of complex ideas can deepen substantially. A postmodern critique of traditional research methods offers further motivation for devising new methods. Articulated earlier by Marshall McLuhan (1967) as the now-classic "the medium is the message," the postmodern critique of traditional methods stresses the fundamental influence a particular *form* of research has on resulting data "found" in the course of employing the method. In this way method becomes theory and theory becomes method.

Typology as Method

This analysis focuses on photojournalism, a mass-media practice that often originates with interaction between two individuals. It also refers to documentary photography and visual social science, processes through which an image-maker studies an issue or individual in depth and which typically result in a large body of work, such as a book or video. Conventionally, we name those individuals *photographer* and *subject*. Yet both terms convey established roles in relation to power and affect the key concepts underlying our discussion. Consider, for example, that the term *photographer* comprises an active individual who holds the recording instrument, decides where to point it, and decides when and how to use it. In this traditionally conceived scenario, the photographer is assumed to hold the power. Further, his or her assignment often is to catch the subject in a vulnerable, unmasked, revealing moment, a special moment when the photographer supposedly sees the "true self" or "true action" of the individual. When the photographic context involves a number of visual elements, such as several people walking in and out of a frame backgrounded by a wall of geometric shapes, the photographer watches for "the decisive moment," Henri Cartier-Bresson's (1952) term for the essential, defining instant when elements come together before the photographer's lens. The subject, on the other hand, is viewed as someone who moves into the viewing frame, or, in more aggressive photographic terms, someone to hunt, to shoot, to woo, to coax, or even to trick into what the photographer sees as a self-revelation.

Consider another scenario, however. A politician experienced in projecting his best self turns his head just right, smiles just enough to get a bit of endearing twinkle in his eye, and subtly caters to a favorite press photographer. The politician, with his presumed celebrity status, assumes an air of authority that embues the photographic moment with the practiced charisma of a strong personality accustomed to being in the public eye. Power resides with this subject, who has learned to manipulate his own image at will in order to elicit particular interpretations.

What happens with the viewer of the photographs resulting from the above scenarios? Reception studies stress that the viewer brings her own power and history to the reading of the image, projecting meaning based on her individual responses to visual stimuli in the frame (Hagen & Wasko, 2000; Staiger, 1992). In the earlier "decisive moment" scenario, in which the photographer is assumed to hold the image-forming power, the resulting image might move a viewer to contemplate the countenance of a subject revealed in such intimacy—or the viewer might just as well merely glance at the image, rejecting possible connection with another human being out of her own inability to relate intimately—or maybe the viewer is simply in a hurry. In the second, political, scenario, a viewer might look quickly at the photograph as published with a story on the front page of a newspaper and believe the photo's contents to be authentic and unmanipulated. Another viewer, on the other hand, might glance at the photo with skepticism, using previous visual experiences with politicians to interpret the moment as a stage-managed "photo op."

At any given moment, the power between the person who is observing, or looking at someone or an image, and the person who is observed, either firsthand or via an image, can shift. Power can be exchanged through a gaze, subverted through inauthentic communication, or held in a kind of breathless, tenuous balance known only to individuals who are able and willing to open themselves to such an intimate revelation. Power is the heart of ethics—power to choose what is moral, to choose not to be moral, to exploit, to expose, to manipulate, to share, to reveal, to give, and to savor. My hope is that the

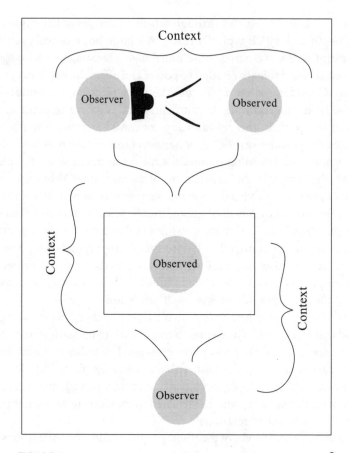

FIG. 28.1.   The interactive model of photographic communication.[5]

typology of visual behavior offers a way to examine those highly variable choices, which can occur almost instantly without words or overt gestures, and to understand the power dynamic communicated visually among photographer, subject and viewer.

Understanding how to apply the typology of visual behavior begins with studying a model I call the Interactive Model of Photographic Communication (see Fig. 28.1).

The first level of the model, which indicates observer and observed at the top of the frame, portrays a photographer (observer) and subject (observed) in a shooting situation (context), such as a public sidewalk or a park. Each brings his or her own personality characteristics, physiological makeup, and personal experiences to the context. The two interact and the result is a photograph. The photograph (represented in the model by a rectangle) then carries an image of the observed person as recorded through the interactive filter of that unique scenario. In photojournalism the photograph quickly will enter another context, probably a newsroom, where it is selected or discarded, altered or used as is in a publication. The photograph has then entered another context, perhaps a newspaper page, in which it can be seen by the next level of observer, the person reading the newspaper. At that point, the viewer (the circle at the bottom of the model) has replaced the photographer as observer as he or she interacts with the observed (subject) via the photographic image.

At each level, visual ethics is a factor. How the photographer and subject interacted, for example, affected every subtle facet of the final image, including whether the photograph would be seen as authentic or staged. How the editor interacted with the content in the photo affected whether its meaning remained as originally framed or if it was shifted via digital manipulation, cropping, or juxtaposition with words. How the reader/viewer interacts with the photograph affects whether and how she connects with the image: Does she stare into the eyes of the imaged person or does she glance at the photo and move on to the comics? Each stage involves ethics of process (how the image was made and used) and meaning (what the image will communicate).

Now consider another version of the interactive model (see Fig. 28.2). The observed in the frame looks different than the original observed, having taken on aspects of both

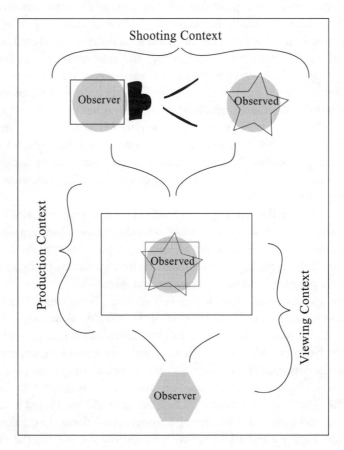

FIG. 28.2.   Revised model of photographic communication.

the Observed and Observer during their interaction. The viewer-observer also is different than the original photographer observer. Note, also, that the contexts for each level of the model have been designated as shooting context, production context, and viewing context. These slight changes in the model illustrate the fundamental variables typical of the photographic communication process. Thinking of each component as a kind of shifting shape or entity visually reflects the interactivity and shift of power, as well as meaning. Consider, for example, how the model shifts if we change shooting context to imaging context. An aggressive event becomes a more creative event simply through word choice.

We are now ready to introduce the typology. Consider the following simplified visual symbols:

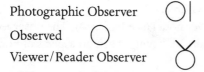

By adding arms in different positions, we can quickly illustrate emotive, expressive communication conveyed visually. For example, \\o/ can stand for a person who is open to being photographed, whereas <o> can stand for a resisting, or closed subject. Using these basic symbols, which are simple to draw by hand or by using even a word-processing software's drawing tool, we can construct a normative continuum for noting an array of visual behaviors affecting the production and interpretation of meanings that result from an interaction, whether on the level of photographer-subject, or on the level of subject-viewer. The verbal terms come from a variety of sources ranging from scholarly literature (i.e., hooks, 1995) to casual conversations to my own invention. As noted earlier, the typology does not list all possible categories, but rather a list of categories I have found especially useful when studying images and imaging behavior. One version of the typology is illustrated in Fig. 28.3.

Now, how do we use the typology as a method for studying ethical issues in photographic communication? As a demonstration, we examine two photographs—one posed shot and one unposed shot. In addition to looking at the photographs in terms of the basic categories of the typology, we will examine four attributes of the visual behavior involved in each: *perspective, intensity, intention,* and *effect*.

I want to begin the analysis with one of my own photographs (Fig. 28.4) for an important reason: I know the circumstances of the imaging situation, which gives me good insight into the visual behavior. "Leti" was taken in 1978, a year when I lived in a small town in Northern Mexico. A colleague and I were conducting an ethnographic study of life in the community. His work focused on verbal analysis of people's attitudes toward education.[6] My work focused on documenting photographically key aspects of community life. The "Leti" photograph came about while we visited a family. People often invited us to dinner, and in turn, I photographed them. Leti asked if I would take her picture. I agreed and asked her where and how she wanted the picture taken. My intent was to give her as much power over the image as possible. Leti said she thought the couch would make a good setting. As I began to take out my camera gear

FIG. 28.3. Typology of visual behavior.

and set up the tripod and flash, Leti scurried around the house gathering her dolls and stuffed animals. She arranged them carefully. Then she climbed in their midst. I was delighted. Leti had built a stage set full of props, thereby facilitating a photograph I would never have seen on my own and that I would not have set up had I thought about it.

This *photographic event* (Milgram, 1977) falls into several typological categories. One is *visual gift*. Leti clearly gave me this picture—she envisioned it, she planned it and she participated fully in it. In those ways, the power behind the image resided with her and I became something of a mechanism for operating the camera. In that way the image we produced authentically represents Leti's view of how she wanted to be

FIG. 28.4.   Leti. Photo © by Julianne Newton.

seen. We could also term this photograph *visual theater*. Using the term theater does not necessarily mean the photo is inauthentic, but rather acknowledges the performative aspects of everyday interactions (Goffman, 1973). Leti performed for my camera and for me, and I watched, participated with, and recorded her performance. But something else also occurred—a *visual embrace*. As our eyes met, the two of us interacted and connected via visual behavior. We also could term the image a *visual document*, in that I consciously worked to position my camera in relation to Leti and her dolls in the least controlling manner possible. I could have chosen, for example, to move in close with a super wide-angle lens in order to exaggerate Leti's doll-like eyes and cheeks. I was trying, however, to *visually quote* the moment as authentically as possible yet with sufficient self engagement with Leti to create a document, possessing evocative timelessness, rather than a simple quote that recorded a fact of time, person, and place. Most interpersonal theorists call the visual components of this one-on-one interaction "nonverbal behavior." I prefer the term *visual behavior* because it emphasizes the key aspect of the activity, rather than activity in negative relation to verbal communication (Streeck & Knapp, 1992).

In addition to applying the basic categories of the typology, we can probe the ethics of the photograph of Leti more deeply by considering four attributes of *visual behavior*: perspective, intensity, intention, and effect. I consider the *intensity* of the photograph to be moderate—there is an energy in the child's pose and flowing between us that was recorded in the photograph. My visual *perspective* was somewhat above Leti's, though she directly confronts the camera. I am tall, but one can see via the photo that I had squatted down a bit to get more on the child's-eye level—an equalizing gesture on my part. Leti had gathered her dolls around her in a kind of fortifying gesture that made her less vulnerable, another visual behavior that helped to equalize our interaction. My *intention* was ethical: to create a portrait of and with this child to give to her and her family and to create a photograph that was more than a snapshot, that communicated something beyond the superficial in a manner that would draw viewers to interact with this child via the photograph. Known *effects* of the photo are that Leti and her family liked the image and recognized they had a visual gift from me, a moment of Leti's life that was unique. I was pleased with the photograph and appreciated Leti's gift. People who view the photo usually smile, indicating pleasure, and they often say something such as, "A little doll among dolls."

Over time I have come to interpret the photograph through a wider lens than I did when consciously taking the image. I see a girl child, one with the beauty of a carefully crafted doll, who had already learned to identify herself with female beauty and perhaps even had an intuitive sense of her symbolic value in the community as a pleasing object of observation. As I write at this point, I return to considering the photograph via two categories of the typology. I return to *visual quote*—I have not altered the visual statement Leti made except via a translation from the full dimension and color of the material world into the two dimensions of a black-and-white frame (that alone is a substantive translation). In terms of moment and framing area, the image also is a direct quote taken from the context of a more complex situation. Other family members milled around the house at the time, and Leti's sister was donning her *quinceañera* dress for her own portrait. Yet the frame of the photo excludes that activity, focusing instead on a quoted moment and space taken from the whole, much as a word quote is lifted from a larger speech. Finally, the image is a *visual document*. I worked carefully in the community to record activities authentically and to impact them as little as possible. Even if one argues that Leti created this moment, one nevertheless must agree that the photograph documents how she wanted to be seen.[7]

How does this analysis, in which we considered various ways to interpret the photograph by translating our understanding into verbal terms expressing visual behaviors or artifacts, play out in visual form? This is the point where the typology becomes more visually enlightening, and, I argue, more valid. I will note visually each of the categories discussed above, using symbols from the typology.

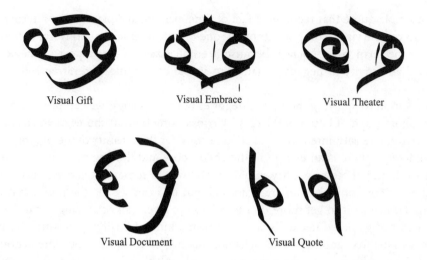

Visual Gift   Visual Embrace   Visual Theater

Visual Document   Visual Quote

As a visual person, I relate more directly to the symbolic figures than I do to the verbal analysis. It took me several hours to translate into words the visual behavior underlying the photograph. That exercise was useful in that it helped me consider a number of approaches to interpreting the photo and gave me a distinct vocabulary for classifying ethical issues of visual behaviors. The process was largely rational and wholly dependent on my ability to express what I saw in words. My key argument with this chapter is that verbal analysis at best deals with parts of visual information. By using visual symbols of visual behaviors underlying the photograph, we can retain intuitive aspects of the behavior in a manner that is more true to the original behavior. In a few seconds, I can visually scan the photo and begin drawing the symbols that will help me synthesize the ethical dynamics of this photograph. Both subject and photographer participated in creating the image through their visual embrace. Each gave something to the other. And though the photograph recorded a theatrical moment (Leti's pose with her dolls), it nevertheless authentically records the way Leti wanted to be seen. In terms of ethics of process, the photograph was made in an ethical manner, without coercion or harm to the subject, without inappropriate manipulation by the photographer, and with full awareness of the subject and her family. In terms of the ethics of meaning, the typology helps us understand different ways the same visual elements can communicate, thereby increasing validity of our reading. We can at once become aware of the photograph's potential ambiguity, of our own interpretive filters, and of other possible interpretations.

Now let's move on to a photograph taken by photojournalist Kurt Jensen (see Fig. 28.5). I do not have information about Jensen's intentions in creating the photograph, and I know little of the context of the photographic event.

The first element I see when I look at this photograph is the woman's face. I read her as female because of her bangs and long hair. I note she is pressed to the ground and that it appears her arms and hands must be to her side or behind her back. I respond to her apparent anger and frustration with empathy and curiosity. What is happening?

FIG. 28.5. More than 600 demonstrators were arrested in the days surrounding the World Trade Organization meetings in Seattle in late November and early December 1999. Most were charged with disorderly conduct. All charges were later dropped. Photo © Kurt Jensen, used with permission.

The caption tells me more than 600 people were arrested during WTO demonstrations in Seattle. It does not tell me her name or if or why she is being arrested, although the caption and photo imply so. Next, I see the person who is kneeling over her. The person—I cannot tell whether the person is male or female—wears a helmet, gloves, and knee protector and has something sticking out of her or his holster or belt. The officer (assumed by the "costume") appears to be holding the woman down and restraining her hands, perhaps with loops similar to the ones on the ground. In the background I see a number of people seated close together on the ground and a few others standing behind them. Those standing may be members of the press—a conclusion I reach because one individual is holding a camera and has what could be a press tag hanging from his neck. It appears to be cold and perhaps rainy because everyone wears jackets and the woman being arrested appears to be wearing a jacket with a hood or wide collar up. The ground could be a sidewalk or an area outside a building. The large, rectangular sections of concrete or brick indicate that the activities are occurring on a sidewalk or an area near a building. In the background I see barren trees, another indication that it is cold, and the windows of what looks like an office building. I interpret the photo to mean that a woman is being forcefully apprehended while other people sit quietly behind her. The fact that I can see her face clearly leads me to focus on her, with the person in riot gear (presumed) quickly read as an anonymous, authoritative force. The key visual behavior appears to be one of domination and resistance—a police officer exerting power over a woman who appears to be attempting to resist the officer's power.

Now, let's apply the typology to the photograph. I see the following categories:

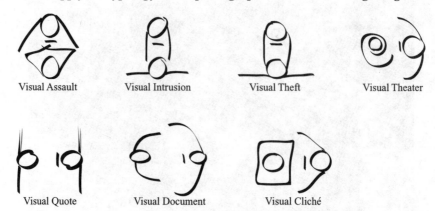

Visual Assault   Visual Intrusion   Visual Theft   Visual Theater

Visual Quote   Visual Document   Visual Cliché

Where was the photographer when he took this photograph? I read that he was directly in front of the action, which places my viewer *perspective* directly in front of the action. The moment is *intense*, primarily because there is physical contact between the officer and the woman, she is on the ground, and she is grimacing or shouting. Although I don't assume the photographer intended to assault this woman visually or to steal her image visually, one could argue that he contributed to her discomfort by making the image. I would not term this a visual assault because I do not feel the photographer nor I as the viewer are attacking the woman. One might argue that the photographer is visually intruding on the woman and officer by getting right in front of them and on their level in order to take the picture. One might argue the photograph is visual theft: Did either the woman or the officer give consent to be photographed? We need more information: Did the photographer know the woman? Who is she in relation to the protests? What had she just done or not done that warranted police action? That kind of information provided in a caption would greatly help us interpret the photograph. I determine the photographer was close because the photograph has good depth of field, or near-to-far sharpness of detail, indicating use of a wide-angle lens. An easier shot would have been from standing above the wrestling pair, which would have given us more of the officer's perspective, or from a safe distance with a telephoto lens. The soft shadows in the photo would likely indicate it was an overcast day. As an image of photojournalism, I read the photograph as a visual quote, an image taken from the scene, bound by time and frame. The photograph also is a visual document because of several factors: the significance of the event in U.S. and world history, the evidentiary power of the photograph (it clearly shows how an officer handled one person and it clearly identifies her), and the storytelling power of the photo enhanced by inclusion of background information. Sadly, I also view the photograph as a visual cliché because I have seen so many other photographs like it—photos of grimacing people being forcefully restrained by police in riot gear. One factor that makes this photograph stand out, however, is the photographer's perspective. To have such access, to be so close to the action of such activity is somewhat unusual. Often photographs of events such as this are taken from a standing position and rarely show faces clearly. As I write this, the term visual theater comes to mind. Was the woman purposefully exaggerating her facial expressions for the benefit of the camera? Did the photographer's presence actually comfort the woman because she knew her efforts would be seen by a wide audience? Was the officer purposefully restraining the force he would have used had no camera been present? Undoubtedly, both individuals were aware they were being observed—the presence of other people, as well as more members of the press, are too obviously part of the scenario. One can argue that protests are inherently theatrical in that they are public demonstrations—visual behavior—of group opinion, planned events meant to be seen and photographed. I want more information from the caption. How many arrests involved physical confrontation? Why was this woman seemingly fighting the officer while other individuals were seated peacefully behind her? Why are people protesting? The police must have anticipated potential violence because of their riot gear. The newspaper sticking out of the woman's backpack also draws my eye. I want to see the photograph on the front page, but I cannot make it out. I conclude that at the very least, I am witnessing an act of power of one authoritative individual over one struggling individual.

Okay, now let's take the typological analysis a step further and apply it to the viewer's side of the behavior. Returning to the photograph of Leti, application results in increased understanding of the complexity of imaging behavior. Consider just one of the categories, visual embrace. When we consider the photographer and subject, we come up with the following:

Add a symbol for the photograph of the subject:

Or, should the symbol of the photograph look like this, in order to note the fact that the photograph is the result of the subject-photographer interaction?

Now, let's add the viewer. Does the viewer look at the photograph in the same spirit in which the photographer and subject created the image, as a visual embrace?

Or does the viewer glance at the photo, experiencing a visual encounter in which he quickly decides the image is the result of visual theater?

So, what do we learn by using the typology to analyze the photographs? One crucial factor is that the typology requires establishing the location of the photographer, and in so doing establishes a likely perspective of a viewer of a photo. The typology also requires a researcher to consider a continuum of possible interactions that resulted in the photograph, as well as possible responses to the photograph, expanding the interpretive aspects of viewing the photograph beyond initial response. In the case of the photo of the arrest of a protester, I found that applying the typology changed my initial response, which was somewhat emotional and immediately empathetic with the woman being restrained but is now tempered by other possibilities. Most important, however, applying the typology facilitates understanding of the many possible visual behaviors related to the creation and interpretation of an artifact of human behavior—a photograph.

CONCLUSION

Is using the typology different than doing a qualitative content analysis of the photograph? It is indeed a qualitative content analysis. Yet the method takes us beyond both individual subjective interpretations and rational, word-based interpretation to reveal possible meanings with varying ethical implications of which we might not otherwise be aware. The method clarifies photographer and viewer perspective, possible intentions in creating the photo and potential levels of intensity viewers might sense via the photo. With the photo of Leti, the effects are relatively simple to interpret. In the photo of the arrest, we can envision effects ranging from viewer demands that arrests be less violent to police use of the photo as evidence that the individual resisted arrest. Applying the typology can help a researcher think through possible interpretations and articulate ethical categories of visual behavior related to a photograph. But more important, the typology can retain basic visual communication related to the photograph via simple visual symbols, which can be used for interpretive work and to report results. For example, by considering the photographer's point of view, we can note that a viewer of the photograph is looking through the photographer's eyes at the instant the photograph was taken, drawing the viewer more viscerally into the photo. We step into the scene. Although this is what happens when we are drawn to a photograph, we often do not become aware of our visceral responses through verbal analysis. Using a visual symbol system is more likely to produce valid interpretations of the complex interplay of visual behavior that resulted in the photograph and that is evoked by the photograph.

Studying visual communication requires using visual research methods. We need careful methods that track the visual through the entire communication process, from creation to recontextualization via medium, through perception, interpretation, and effects. We need methods that call attention to the dynamic nature of the behavior at each state of the process and at the same time help us grasp the ethics of the communication in a holistic manner consistent with the original process. In fact, using the term *dynamic moment* may be more appropriate for analyzing issues of visual ethics than the *decisive moment*. For the making of a photograph, which is only one form of visual behavior, is both complex and a momentary fraction of a second. Paradoxically, at the same time, one characteristic of the visual is its ability to synthesize, to globalize, and to view a complex problem holistically. Applying the typology of visual behavior is one way to study both complex and holistic aspects of forms of visual communication. Anecdotal evidence from my own observations of people using the typology lead me to believe it can evoke thorough and valid interpretations of the ethics of visual behavior. The method needs to be tested systematically. At this point, I hope the typology at least illustrates the need to integrate visual synthesis with verbal analysis in order to analyze "the visual" with valid methods.

ENDNOTES

[1] See Bakewell (1998) for an excellent discussion of "image acts."

[2] See Williams (1999) for clarification of rational and intuitive.

[3] This chapter focuses on applying the typology as a *method* of analysis. For the *theoretical* foundations underlying the typology, see Newton (1998, 2001).

[4] See Gladwell (2000) for more examples supporting this point.

[5] See Newton (2001).

[6] See Newton (1981).

[7] For a discussion of this controversial idea, see Stott (1973).

REFERENCES

Bakewell, L. (1998). Image acts. *American Anthropologist, 100*(1), 22–32.

Barry, A. M. (1997). *Visual intelligence: Perception, image, and manipulation in visual communication*. Albany: State University of New York Press.

Bechara, A., Damasio, H., Tranel, D., & Damasio, A. (1997). Deciding advantageously before knowing the advantageous strategy. *Science, 275*, 1293–1295.

Berger, J., & Mohr, J. (1982). *Another way of telling*. New York: Pantheon.

Cartier-Bresson, H. (1952). *The decisive moment*. New York: Simon & Schuster in collaboration with Éditions Verve of Paris.

Collier, J. Jr., & Collier, M. (1986). *Visual anthropology: Photography as a research method*. Albuquerque: University of New Mexico Press.

Condon, W. S. (1982). Cultural microrhythms. In M. Davis (Ed.), *Interaction rhythms: Periodicity in communicative behavior* (pp. 53–76). New York: Human Sciences Press.

Crick, F. (1994). *The astonishing hypothesis: The scientific search for the human soul*. New York: Scribner.

Damasio, A. R. (1994). *Descartes' error: Emotion, reason, and the human brain*. New York: Putnam.

Damasio, A. R. (1999). *The feeling of what happens: Body and emotion in the making of consciousness*. New York: Harcourt Brace.

Damasio, A. R. (2002). How the brain creates the mind. *Scientific American*, Special Edition, *12*(1), 4–9.

Gladwell, M. (2000). *The tipping point: How little things can make a big difference*. Boston: Little, Brown.

Goffman, E. (1973). *The presentation of self in everyday life*. Woodstock, NY: The Overlook Press. (Original work published 1959).

Graber, D. A. (1990). Seeing is remembering: How visuals contribute to learning from television news. *Journal of Communication, 40*(3), 134–155.

Hagen, I., & Wasko, J. (Eds.). (2000). *Consuming audiences? Production and reception in media research*. Cresskill, NJ: Hampton Press.

Harper, D. (1993). On the authority of the image: Visual methods at the crossroads. In N. K. Denzin & Y. S. Lincoln (Eds.), *Handbook of qualitative research* (pp. 403–412). Thousand Oaks, CA: Sage.

Hartley, C. (1981). *The reactions of photojournalists and the public to hypothetical ethical dilemmas confronting press photographers*. Unpublished master's thesis, University of Texas, Austin.

Hartley, C. (1990). Ethics in photojournalism: Past, present and future. In P. M. Lester (Ed.), *NPPA Special report: The ethics of photojournalism* (pp. 16–19). Durham, NC: National Press Photographers Association.

Hartley, P. (1993). *Interpersonal communication*. London: Routledge.

Henderson, L. (1988). A selected annotated bibliography. In L. Gross, J. S. Katz, & J. Ruby (Eds.), *Image ethics, the moral rights of subjects in photographs, film, and television* (pp. 273–379). New York: Oxford University Press.

Hooks, B. (1995). *Art on my mind: Visual politics*. New York: New Press.

Knapp, M. L., & Hall, J. A. (1997). *Nonverbal communication in human interaction* (4th ed.). Fort Worth, TX: Harcourt Brace.

LeDoux, J. (1986). Sensory systems and emotion. *Integrative Psychiatry, 4*, 237–243.

LeDoux, J. E. (2002). Emotion, memory and the brain. *Scientific American*, Special Edition, *12*(1), 62–71.

Lester, P. M. (Ed.). (1996). *Images that injure: Pictorial stereotypes in the media*. New York: Praeger.

Lutz, C. A., & Collins, J. L. (1993). *Reading national geographic*. Chicago: University of Chicago Press.

McLuhan, M., & Fiore, Q. (1967). *The medium is the massage*. New York: Random House.

Milgram, S. (1977). *The individual in a social world, essays and experiments*. Reading, MA: Addison-Wesley.

Moriarty, S. (1994). Visual communication as a primary system. *Journal of Visual Literacy, 14*(2), 11–21.

Moriarty, S. (1996). Abduction: A theory of visual interpretation. *Communication Theory, 6*(2), 167–187.

Mullen, B. et al. (1986). Newscasters' facial expressions and voting behavior of viewers: Can a smile elect a President? *Journal of Personality and Social Psychology, 51*, 291–295.

Newton, J. H. (1986, Spring). Photography and reality: A matter of ethics. *Photo-Letter, 5*, 36–44.

Newton, J. H. (1991). *In front of the camera: Ethical issues of subject response in photography*. Unpublished doctoral dissertation, University of Texas, Austin.

Newton, J. H. (1998). Beyond representation: Toward a typology of visual ethics. *Visual Anthropology Review, 14*(1), 58–72.

Newton, J. H. (2001). *The burden of visual truth: The role of photojournalism in mediating reality*. Mahwah, NJ: Lawrence Erlbaum Associates.

Newton, P. T. (1981). *School and society: A small town in Northern Mexico*. Unpublished Ph.D. dissertation, University of Texas at Austin.

Potter, R. F., Bolls, P. D., & Dent, D. R. (1997, May). *Something for nothing: Is visual encoding automatic?* Paper presented to the annual meeting of the International Communication Association, Montreal.

Reaves, S. (1995a, Winter). Magazines vs. newspapers: Editors have different ethical standards on the digital manipulation of photographs. *Visual Communication Quarterly*, 4–7.

Reaves, S. (1995b). The vulnerable image: Categories of photos as predictor of digital manipulation. *Journalism & Mass Communication Quarterly*, 706–715.

Ruby, J. (1987). The ethics of image making. In A. Rosenthal (Ed.), *Documentary challenge* (pp. 7–13). Berkeley: University of California Press.

Sargent, S. L., & Zillmann, D. (1999). *Image effects on selective exposure to news stories.* Paper presented to the International Communication Association annual convention, San Francisco.

Schultz, M. (1993). *The effect of visual presentation, story complexity and story familiarity on recall and comprehension of television news*. Unpublished doctoral dissertation, Indiana University, Bloomington.

Sherer, M. (1990). Bibliography of grief, Ethical issues in photographing private moments, and Photographic invasion of privacy: Pictures that can be painful. In P. M. Lester (Ed.), *NPPA special report: The ethics of photojournalism* (pp. 10–15, 23–27, 35–41). Durham, NC: National Press Photographers Association.

Shoemaker, P. J. (1996). Hard-wired for news: Using biological and cultural evolution to explain the news. *Journal of Communication, 46*, 32–47.

Staiger, J. (1992). *Interpreting films: Studies in the historical reception of American cinema*. Princeton, NJ: Princeton University Press.

Stott, W. (1973). *Documentary expression and thirties America*. London: Oxford University Press.

Streeck, J., & Knapp, M. L. (1992). The interaction of visual and verbal features in human communication. In F. Poyatos (Ed.), *Non-verbal communication* (pp. 3–23). Amsterdam: Benjamins.

Wells, G. L., & Petty, R. E. (1980). The effects of overt head movements on persuasion. *Basic and Applied Social Psychology, 1*(3), 219–230.

Williams, R. (1999). Beyond visual literacy: Omniphasism, a theory of balance. *Journal of Visual Literacy, 19*(2), 159–178.

Visual Literacy

Visual Literacy Theory

PAUL MESSARIS
University of Pennsylvania

SANDRA MORIARTY
University of Colorado

Like many other people who write about visual communication, we find it convenient to use the term visual *literacy* as a label for an important concept, namely, the viewer's awareness of the conventions through which the meanings of visual images are created and understood. Although the linguistic analogy implied by the word literacy may be inappropriate and potentially misleading because it suggests that visual messages operate similarly to verbal messages, we can think of no existing, commonly employed alternative to this usage. Rather than resorting to neologism, then, we will stay with the term visual literacy in this chapter.

WHAT IS VISUAL LITERACY?

Visual literacy has been defined variously as a hierarchy of skills (Fransecky & Debes, 1972), a set of competencies (Debes, 1969), elements and strategies of communication (Dondis, 1973), a set of components or dimensions (Seels, 1994), a set of skills-oriented learning objectives (Schamber, 1987), and an aptitude for visual communication, visual thinking, and visual learning (Seels, 1994). A common factor in these definitions is the view of visual literacy as a learned skill. This approach is apparent in the first edition of the pioneering textbook *Instructional Media and the New Technologies of Instruction*, in which the authors said, "Visual literacy is the learned ability to interpret visual messages accurately and to create such messages" (Heinich, Molenda, & Russell, 1982. p. 62). That definition, as well as one from the same year by Braden and Hortin, emphasizes both the comprehension and the creation or use of visual messages: "Visual literacy is the ability to understand and use images, including the ability to think, learn, and express oneself in terms of images" (1982, p. 169). In a more elaborate statement of a similar position, Deborah Curtiss emphasized the important role of culture and aesthetics:

> Visual literacy is the ability to understand the communication of a visual statement in any medium and the ability to express oneself with at least one visual discipline. It entails the ability to: understand the subject matter and meaning within the context of the culture that produced the work, analyze the syntax—compositional and stylistic principles of the work, evaluate the disciplinary and aesthetic merits of the work, and grasp intuitively the Gestalt, the interactive and synergistic quality of the work. (1987, p. 3)

In all of these approaches, then, visual literacy is defined in terms of two constant components—first, the ability to understand visual images and, second, the ability to create or use images as means of expression and communication. This distinction parallels the read and write characteristics of print literacy.

But on another level, there is more to visual literacy than the comprehension and articulation of visual meaning. In terms of broad educational goals, visual literacy can be seen as promoting greater experience in the workings of visual media coupled with a *heightened conscious* awareness of those workings. Seels equated this critical viewing competency to the larger meaning of literacy: "A literate person today is an educated person, a person who has learned the fundamentals needed to function as a responsible citizen" (1994, p. 98). This critical thinking dimension of visual literacy was described eloquently by Paul Lester who poses the following challenge to student readers of his visual communication textbook:

> If you learn to analyze visual messages in terms of your personal reaction, their historical context, how they are made, the moral responsibilities of the producer, and their impact on society, you will be able to create and use memorable pictures. (2000, p. 351)

As these comments and definitions suggest, there are a number of reasons for the considerable concern over visual literacy that has been evident in both scholarly and more popular writing in recent years. One source of concern is the notion that, in a world in which picture-based media are playing an increasingly prominent role, it may be incumbent on the system of formal education to pay more attention to students' abilities to both comprehend and create messages for these media (e.g., see Burmark, 2002; Lohr, 2002; Wilde & Wilde, 2000). A related motivation for the advocacy of visual literacy has to do with the aesthetic appreciation of images and stems from the assumption that a conscious understanding of the conventions of any medium enhances one's capacity for the appreciation of artistry (e.g., Tucker, 2001). At the same time, visual literacy can also be seen as a potential antidote to attempted manipulation of the viewer in TV, print, and Web-based advertising; visual journalism; and other forms of pictorial entertainment, information, or persuasion (Messaris, 1998). In our following discussion, we group these various considerations into two, very broad (and, of course, nonmutually exclusive) ways of looking at the benefits of visual literacy: first, proactively, as a gateway to cognitive enrichment; second, reactively, as critical viewing, which is a defensive necessity in a world of potentially manipulative or harmful media.

VISUAL LITERACY AND COGNITIVE ENRICHMENT

Learning to communicate visually involves a unique set of mental skills that are important not only in themselves but also as stimuli for more general cognitive growth. Referred to as visualization, this ability to construct a mental image and manipulate it is a basic skill for graphic designers and artists, as well as photographers and filmmakers. Nowhere is this more apparent than in situations in which students (or anyone else, for that matter) encounter the intricacies of actual creative work in visual media. For someone who has not worked in visual media before, the process of learning how to compose individual shots and how to edit those shots together entails a genuinely new way of thinking.

Thinking in Pictures

One of the most important things that novice visual artists need to learn is to go beyond the literal content of images. The meaning of an image is not just a matter of the people or places that appear in it, or the action that it depicts. How those people or places or actions are portrayed—in close-up or long shot, in balanced or asymmetrical compositions, in high-key or low-key lighting, and so on—are essential ingredients of the creation of visual meaning. To learn to think in pictures is to learn how to use these ingredients effectively as elements of one's overall message. Among inexperienced film- or video-makers there is a very strong tendency to compose every image as if it were a snapshot: If there is a singe person in the image, he or she is framed dead center; if there are two people, they are framed symmetrically and at equal distances from the viewer. It could be argued that this type of composition is based on the way in which people tend to orient themselves toward each other in real life. However, as a quick glance at almost any professionally produced movie or TV show will demonstrate, this is not the way most images are framed by professional directors and cinematographers.

As an illustration of this difference, consider a brief scene from a feature-length film (*Grad-School B-Movie*) produced by students in Messaris' Visual Communication Laboratory at the University of Pennsylvania. In this scene, Natasha, one of the movie's protagonists, is talking to her officemate, Elsa. As the scene progresses, Natasha learns that she has made a mistake that may have very serious consequences for her. When this scene was being rehearsed, the two women were placed at equal distances from the camera, and Natasha, who is working on her computer at the beginning of the scene, was filmed facing away from the viewer (Fig. 29.1). However, in the version that actually appears in the movie, this composition was altered radically. Natasha, who was now shown working on a laptop, was placed much closer to the viewer, and facing forward rather than backward (Fig. 29.2). So, although the dialogue remained exactly the same, the new visual composition produced a fairly substantial shift in emphasis: The fact that Natasha's image is now much larger highlights her status as the principal character and

FIG. 29.1.   *Grad-School B-Movie:* Rehearsal.

FIG. 29.2.   *Grad-School B-Movie:* Revised composition.

focuses the viewer's attention on her reactions. These two ingredients—image size and orientation—were also used, together with color, to underscore Natasha's plight at the end of the scene. As Natasha realizes her mistake, Elsa moves forward and casually sits on the edge of her desk, facing away from the viewer and blocking much of the image with her body (Fig. 29.3). Natasha's face is confined to a small section of the frame, between the black laptop and Elsa's black-clad figure—graphic representations of the fact that Natasha may have stepped into a trap.

FIG. 29.3.   *Grad-School B-Movie:* End of Scene.

From Scene to Shot Sequence

To anyone who has grown up with television—that is, to almost all people in almost all parts of today's world—nothing could appear more natural than the division of scenes into shots. Indeed, there is some intriguing evidence that the ability to make sense of shot sequences may come naturally even to inexperienced movie viewers. In a one-of-a-kind experiment conducted some 20 years ago in rural Kenya, people with almost no prior exposure to movies were shown two versions of a short video narrative. One version was filmed continuously, with no cuts. For the other version, the story line was broken down into several distinct shots. In tests of narrative comprehension, the division into shots did not prevent these inexperienced viewers from being able to follow the basic story line (Hobbs, Frost, Davis, & Stauffer, et al., 1988). This finding fits in with the arguments of writers who believe that shot sequences in movies may mimic the succession of visual impressions that our eyes focus on as they look back and forth among the objects of the real world (see Carroll, 1996).

With these points in mind, we might expect that inexperienced movie-makers would have a natural inclination to break scenes down into shots. However, judging from some of the student projects in Messaris' lab, it would appear that the ability to organize a shoot in terms of shifting views and partial actions cannot be taken for granted. More often than not, these novice media creators exhibited a tendency to plan and shoot each action as a continuous, unbroken scene. This tendency was reflected in the shot lists that many of them used to previsualize their shoots, such as the following example, taken from a longer list for a bulimia-awareness public service announcement (PSA):

Shot # 3: The two girls are sitting at a table talking and "eating" (possibly at Cosi). When her friend looks away, the girl slips a piece of the cake inside a napkin and then she hides the napkin between her legs under the table. . . .

Shot # 4: Then we see her in the gym, putting her books down, and exercising again.

Shot # 5. When she returns home, her roommate is having dinner . . . offers her some of it, it looks good, but she looks and says (or gestures) "No, it's okay, thank you, I ate a lot on the way home. . . ."

Shot # 6: In her room, closes door behind her . . . then we see her looking at mirror and/or stepping on scale.

It is tempting to draw a parallel between this style of movie making and the stylistic conventions of early cinema. Narrative filmmakers began to use editing to assemble one scene after another within 2 or 3 years of the birth of the medium in the late 19th century. However, it was not until several years later that directors went beyond that, subdividing scenes into shots. Indeed, the ability to visualize scenes in terms of close-ups, reverse-angle shots, and the like, is commonly considered one of the major achievements in the history of cinema. D. W. Griffith, who is erroneously credited (by himself and, often, by subsequent writers) with having invented the language of narrative editing, liked to boast about what a momentous intellectual leap had been involved in cutting to a closer view in the middle of a scene (Griffith, 1972). Although the first film to employ this device was shot several years before Griffith began to make movies, it does seem to be true that the ability to "parse" continuous actions into sequences of partial views is a genuine creative achievement—in short, an important step in the acquisition of visual literacy.

It would be fascinating to study how exactly movie-makers learn to take this step. The student who created the shot list we have just quoted ended up making one significant change when she actually shot her video. As she was taking shot # 5, which was supposed to be a long shot of two roommates having a brief discussion, she realized that the camera lens did not have a wide enough angle to include both girls in a single view. So, on the spot, she decided to subdivide the scene into two complementary shots: one of the central character, the other of her friend. In other words, she employed reverse-angle editing. But this incident is not very similar to the situation of early filmmakers. They were starting from scratch, whereas the student had seen reverse-angle editing before, even if she had not employed it herself.

A closer analogy to the original invention of editing can be found in Sol Worth's classic study of Navajo filmmaking (Worth & Adair, 1972). At the time of Worth's study, it was possible to find Navajos who had little or no prior exposure to movies. Worth taught a group of young Navajos the technical aspects of 16 mm film, including how to cut and splice celluloid, but he did not give them any instruction in the formal conventions of Hollywood storytelling. He was thus able to observe how they went about exploring the medium on their own. On one memorable occasion, Worth was watching a young man preparing to film a horse. Suddenly the man began to cast tentative sideways glances at Worth, and eventually he asked the following question: If I take shots of parts of the horse—the head, the legs, the tail, and so on—and stick them together, one after another, will people know that it's all one horse? Stifling his excitement, Worth managed to answer in the neutral tones of the social scientist: How do *you* think people will react to that? Cautiously, the man replied that he thought viewers would indeed realize they were seeing a single animal (Worth & Adair, 1972, pp. 97–98). And so it was that the close-up was reborn in this first-time filmmaker's acquisition of visual literacy.

Editing and Spatial Intelligence

Although the acquisition of a visual vocabulary is valuable in and of itself, it is worth noting that the intellectual benefits of a visual education often extend beyond the realm of visual media as such. As students become more fluent in creating, framing, and combining images, they also develop certain broader mental aptitudes that these activities bring into play. This connection between visual creativity and general cognition has been explored in the well-known work of Howard Gardner (1999), who has used the term *spatial intelligence* as an encompassing label for the kinds of mental skills that are cultivated by working in visual media. Spatial intelligence is the process of forming mental representations of three-dimensional reality as a basis for understanding one's environment and interacting with it effectively. It is a type of intelligence that is crucial for success in professions such as architecture or carpentry, but is also a vital ingredient of any person's everyday physical activities. Spatial intelligence also happens to be a vital ingredient in the perception of visual images, as well as their creation.

In photography and graphic design, spatial intelligence is exhibited in the way the elements in a visual display are composed or framed and in the way elements in a layout are arranged. In this two-dimensional form, sensitivity to space is exhibited through an understanding of the basic elements of composition, such as the frame, the figure against its ground, the shapes, lighting, scale and dimension, focal point, and texture. Similarly graphic design principles guide designers who are laying out the various elements in an advertisement, brochure, or magazine page based on sensitivity to such visual concepts as unity, direction, dominance and contrast, balance, simplicity, proportion, harmony, and tension. In addition to their use as the tools of production, viewers also respond to these principles depending on their visual literacy or specific training in photography or layout. These principles are aesthetic guidelines, but they also function as meaning cues. For example, a cluttered, busy layout in an advertisement usually denotes a store or company that has a multitude of lower-priced offerings, such as a discount store. A simple design with proportionately fewer items and more white space framing the central image will suggest a more upscale store or brand.

One of the clearest examples of spatial intelligence is the ability of movies to conjure up a coherent sense of place and action out of a succession of fragmentary views. As any budding editor soon learns, there are some ways of putting shots together that make sense, and others that viewers find obscure or confusing. Learning what works and what does not is not just a case of acquiring a set of artistic conventions. It is also a process of cognitive exploration of the relationship between vision and space. Here is how one group of students in Messaris' lab encountered the workings of one of the most basic rules of editing, the so-called eye-line match. In a scene from another feature-length movie shot in the lab, a hit man comes up behind one of the central characters and aims a gun at his back. When this scene was originally filmed, the camera was placed on the left side of the intended victim (Fig. 29.4) but on the right side of the hit man (Fig. 29.5). A preliminary edit quickly revealed what had not been evident when the shots were taken—namely,

FIG. 29.4.   Eye-Line Match: 1st Shot.

FIG. 29.5.   Eye-Line Match: 2nd Shot-Wrong Version.

that the composition of these two shots gave the misleading impression that the two men were facing each other, whereas the hit man was actually supposed to be several paces in back of the main character. The only way of correcting this misimpression was to reshoot part of the scene with the camera on the other side (Fig. 29.6).

The general rule that was initially violated and then obeyed in this little episode is very simple: always keep the camera on one side of an imaginary line between the two characters in the scene. However, learning to construct spatially coherent visual sequences is not simply a matter of blindly following such rules. In fact, cases in which

FIG. 29.6. Eye-Line Match: 2nd Shot-Correct Version.

this particular rule has been ignored with seeming impunity can be found in the work of some of the most celebrated figures in the history of filmmaking, such as John Ford (e.g., *Stagecoach*, 1939), Stanley Kubrick (e.g., *A Clockwork Orange*, 1971), and Akira Kurosawa (e.g., *Throne of Blood*, 1957). Knowing when the rules can be broken and when they must be obeyed requires a sophisticated understanding of how viewers construct mental representations of space on the basis of a movie's visual and narrative cues—in short, it requires spatial intelligence, not memorization of a rule book. Indeed, in research on the relationship between film production experience and cognitive skills, it is editing in particular that appears to lead to the most substantial gains in spatial intelligence (Tidhar, 1984).

Visual Literacy and Analogical Thinking

In his discussion of spatial intelligence, Howard Gardner (1999) also made reference to the intellectual activity of "analogical thinking," which he subsumed under spatial intelligence but which is, in certain respects, the broader of the two terms. Analogical thinking is the ability to discern similarities between superficially disparate aspects of reality and to derive insight from those similarities (see Stafford, 1999). It is often claimed that analogical thinking is the basis of scientific creativity (Boden, 1991; John-Steiner, 1985). Analogical connections are also a pervasive feature of visual media. When a filmmaker uses a close-up to enhance the dramatic impact of an image, she or he is relying on an analogical connection between visual size and emotional significance. When an editor speeds up a scene's cutting rate to make it more exciting, she or he is drawing on an analogical connection between fast pace and visceral impact. Low versus high angles, dark versus bright lighting, slow versus fast camera movement—these and many other visual conventions are all examples of visual analogies.

Indeed it could be argued that the most obvious sense in which visual images can be called analogical is illustrated by any clear, full-color photograph of a recognizable object. Here there is a more or less close analogy between the shapes, colors, and overall structure of the image, on the one hand, and the corresponding features of the real world, on the other. (See Messaris, 1994, for a detailed examination of this contention, which is sometimes considered controversial in the world of visual scholarship.) However, the analogical quality of visual representations is by no means confined to representational realism. Consider the case of quantitative graphics (bar graphs, pie charts, etc.)—a ubiquitous, but often taken-for-granted, type of visual display. Here, too, analogical meaning plays a central role. When a quantitative relationship is represented in graphic form, there is a precise analogical relationship between the dimensions of the visual representation and the corresponding physical quantities. This aspect of visual language has been explored extensively by Edward Tufte (1990, 1997, 2001) in a series of books that make a compelling case for the significance of visual literacy in this area.

Related uses of analogical image making occur in the area of scientific visualization. Among scholars interested in the nature of creative thought, analogical thinking is commonly regarded as crucial not only to artistic creativity, but also to scientific reasoning and discovery (Hargittai & Hargittai, 1994; Vosniadou & Ortony, 1989). In fact, it is sometimes seen as *the* basic component of creativity (Mitchell, 1993). In the area of science, the classic illustration of this point is the story of the discovery of the structure of the benzene molecule (Kemp, 2000, p. 124). The scientist responsible for this discovery had been assuming that benzene's six carbon and six hydrogen atoms were lined up in a row. Then one night he saw in a dream strings of atoms metamorphosing into a snake holding its own tail in its mouth. Subsequent research confirmed that the structure of benzene is indeed based on atoms arranged in a circle. The broader point of this story is that creativity is often—or, perhaps, always—a matter of proceeding by analogy from a familiar situation (the properties of snakes) to an unfamiliar one (the properties of a string of atoms). In this sense, the interplay between visual literacy and analogical thinking can be seen, optimistically, as a broader enhancement of one's creative capabilities.

Visual Analogies in Editing

As far as the more artistic uses of visual analogy are concerned, a practice that is of particular interest in the present context is the creation of what might be called visual "simile" or "metaphor" in editing. A textbook case of this type of visual analogy occurs in a Madonna video from 1994 (*Take a Bow*, directed by Michael Haussman). The video starts out with Madonna watching a bull fight and continues with a sex scene between her and the bullfighter. But the timeline on the screen is not linear. Instead, the director cuts back and forth between the sex scene and the bullfight, both of which climax simultaneously. The intercutting between the two events creates a clear analogy between them.

This kind of editing has a long history, dating back at least as far the films of Sergei Eisenstein and other directors working in the early years of Soviet cinema. One of the best-known examples from Eisenstein's films occurs in a scene from *Strike* (1925), in which striking workers are massacred by government troops: At the climax of the massacre, Eisenstein edits into the scene a number of shots of animals being butchered in a slaughterhouse. This cross-cutting between the two sets of images can be seen as the equivalent of a simile. It explicitly juxtaposes two events and implies an analogical connection between them. For several years, this kind of device was also popular in Hollywood, where Charlie Chaplin's notorious comparison between factory workers and sheep (*Modern Times*, 1936) was one of many direct imitations of Soviet-style editing. Eventually, though, such juxtapositions became a rarity in fictional movies. As film critic Andre Bazin (1967) argued, the interruption of a movie's story line by the insertion of an extraneous image may have been incompatible with Hollywood cinema's increasing tendency towards unobtrusive narration. Consequently, when such an interruption is encountered in more recent movies—for example, the juxtaposition of a sex scene and a rocket blasting off in *The Naked Gun 21/2* (1991)—it is almost invariably a deliberate parody.

Whereas editing that is based only on analogy, without a narrative component, is now quite rare in mainstream fiction film and television, it is much more frequent in music videos and, especially, in advertising, including political ads in the United States (see Morreale, 1991; Prince, 1990). Juxtaposition based on visual or conceptual analogy between two images is also very common in print advertising. For example, automotive advertisers have featured their products in association with lions (a Toyota ad emphasizing power and dominance over the competition), ice skaters (an Oldsmobile ad emphasizing smooth performance and elegant styling), jet airplanes (a Dodge ad emphasizing speed and power), eagles (a General Motors ad emphasizing speed and ease of travel), and tigers (appearing in ads for Exxon gasoline).

In all of these ways, then, creative engagement with visual media entails the development of a set of mental skills that find expression in the myriad conventions of visual communication: conventions of pictorial composition, camera placement, editing rhythm, montage, and the like. Furthermore, as we have seen, there are intriguing areas of overlap between these visual-media skills and the operations of scientific creativity. Becoming a visual "literate" person involves the acquisition of such skills and the broader cognitive enhancement that flows from exercising them. However, as we noted in the introduction of this chapter, visual literacy can also be viewed from a more critical perspective, as a tool for effectively encountering the moral or political challenges posed by contemporary mass media. This aspect of visual literacy will be our focus in the pages that follow.

HOW DOES VISUAL LITERACY CONTRIBUTE TO CRITICAL VIEWING?

A critical viewer should be able to analyze the rhetorical aims of a visual message and, in particular, see through visual falsehood—faked or staged or manipulated images that are passed off as authentic representations. Moreover, as some of the definitions at the beginning of this chapter suggest, critical viewing can also be regarded as a broader awareness of the potential influence of images, even when that influence does not entail any kind of falsification. What can visual literacy contribute to these two aspects of critical viewing?

Visual Literacy and Visual Lies

For the past 20 years or so, visual deception has been one of the central topics in academic and journalistic writing about images (e.g., Newton, 2000; Wheeler, 2003). To a great extent, this literature is a response to the large-scale adoption of digital-imaging technology by the media industry. The digital manipulation of photographs first became a public issue in 1982, in the well-known case of the *National Geographic* cover photograph that was recomposed by computer because the original composition was too wide to fit the magazine's cover. Since then, the digital creation and alteration of images have become major preoccupations of visual scholars and critics. Their writings have served to deepen our understanding of visual truth and deception, even though it seems fair to say that by no means have we reached any consensus on these issues.

Two contradictory tendencies recur in this body of writing (Rosler, 1991). On the one side are those writers who worry that digital manipulation can be used to mislead or to lie. Paul Lester put it bluntly: "Journalism manipulation, especially by amateurs with access to inexpensive software, is a serious threat to the integrity of the profession because it distorts the historical record of a culture. . . . Of equal concern is the fact that many media organizations are willing to publish or broadcast questionable images" (2000, p. 327). As an example of the latter point, Lester cites the *TV Guide* cover in which Oprah Winfrey's head was superimposed (without acknowledgment) on a photograph of Ann-Margaret (Lester, 2000, p. 329).

In seeming opposition to such worries, other writers have argued that the idea of photographic truth has always been an illusion and that concerns about digital lying are misplaced (Kember, 2003). According to the authors of a theoretical treatise on new media, "Digital photography poses a . . . threat for those who believe that the traditional photograph has a special relationship to reality. . . . But in any case photographic 'truth' was not unassailable even in the nineteenth and early twentieth centuries" (Bolter & Grusin, 1999, p. 106). Along somewhat similar lines, a recent textbook discusses the "myth of photographic truth" and refers to a time when still photography was "regarded as a more objective practice than, say, painting or drawing" (Sturken & Cartwright, 2001, p. 16). By implication, the authors appear to be distancing themselves from such beliefs.

These two positions point to two different ways in which visual literacy could potentially contribute to a critical perspective on digital manipulation: on the one hand, it could help a viewer discern *when* he or she is being lied to; on the other hand, it could lead to a realization that, in a sense, he or she is *always* being lied to. In principle, the latter point may seem to be the more penetrating stimulus to critical viewing, and visual scholars commonly treat this point as one of their major contributions to public enlightenment about the nature of visual communication. In practice, however, we might want to question just how unenlightened the public is to begin with. How many people really do believe in the "myth of photographic truth?" How much of a need is there for visual education aimed at countering this myth?

In thinking about these questions, it is worth noting that many writers who worry about photographic fakes are hardly naive with regard to the broader issue of photography's relationship to reality. Some of the most forceful condemnations of digital manipulation in photography have come from professional photographers with an unusually sophisticated understanding of the many layers of subjectivity that any photograph inevitably imposes on its subject. Lester, whose concerns about digital manipulation in photojournalism we have just encountered, spoke elsewhere about photojournalistic subjectivity using his own work as one example (Lester, 1996). One of the most sustained assaults on digital fakery has come from Kenneth Brower, a distinguished photo editor who has also provided a nuanced account of everyday fakery in traditional photography (Brower, 1998). As a young man, Brower had worked as an assistant for Ansel Adams, whose celebrated images of the American wilderness are not usually associated with notions of photographic trickery or deception. Nonetheless, as Brower points out, Adams routinely altered the appearance of his images through such darkroom techniques as "burning" or "dodging," selectively over- or underexposing portions of a photographic print so as to emphasize certain features and suppress others.

Although conceding the challenge that such examples pose to any idea of a direct connection between photography and reality, Brower still insists that a meaningful distinction can be drawn between unobjectionable and fraudulent manipulations of photographs. In his view—and, we suspect, in the view of many other lovers of landscape photography—Adams's dodging and burning do not rise to the level of outright falsehood. As an example of imagery that did violate his sense of photographic truthfulness, Brower cites the work of another well-known nature photographer, Art Wolfe. In the mid-1990s, Wolfe was the cause of a major controversy in photographic circles when it was revealed that his book *Migrations* (1994) had involved digital copying, repositioning, and multiplication of animals in scenes of mass migration. To Wolfe, these changes were matters of aesthetics, motivated by the need to correct those parts of the image that had been "disrupting the pattern [he] was trying to achieve" (cited in Brower, 1998, p. 4). But Brower strongly objected to this reasoning: "Whose patterns is the nature photographer supposed to celebrate—nature's or his own?" (1998, p. 4).

What makes one kind of manipulation acceptable and the other a lie? Although the difference may appear intuitively obvious to some people, it can be surprisingly difficult to articulate explicit criteria that are capable of withstanding logical analysis. However, the issue can be approached from a somewhat different angle that bypasses the need for a priori definitions. As a postscript to his discussion of *Migrations*, Brower briefly comments on a follow-up volume by Wolfe, in which, once again, several images contained digital effects. This time around, though, there was no controversy. What had changed? According to Wolfe himself, the new book's digital illustrations "were labeled as such, and no one objected. So we figured out that people were upset less because we used the technology than because we did not always say we had" (cited in Brower, 1998, p. 2). To put it a little differently, we could say that visual deception occurs when a digital effect violates the implicit contract between photographer and viewer.

This line of reasoning brings us back to the question of what the broad public knows about digital imaging, and what people's expectations are regarding the use of this technology. At the time that this chapter is being written (summer 2003), the mass media are paying a great deal of attention to the computer-generated (CG) imagery in *The Matrix Reloaded* and other movies featuring digital effects. In that respect, then, it seems reasonable to assume a general public awareness of the extent to which computers have infiltrated into the world of picture making. In fact, in a *Time* magazine article on movie car scenes, *Charlie's Angels* director McG makes the following point: "Audiences have a built-in CG detector. So you need to be slippery. You use a lot of real elements so you can get away with the CG" (quoted in Corliss, 2003, p. 3). If this assertion is accurate, we can conclude that the existence and basic capabilities of digital imaging have indeed become common knowledge.

If people already possess this level of knowledge, what more can visual literacy contribute toward the development of critical viewing? We would like to outline three, relatively distinct possibilities. First, even if it is true that movie viewers "have a built-in CG detector," we can't take it for granted that this detector works equally well outside of the movies. McG's remarks were about complicated stunt sequences, in which, by his own admission, computer-generated imagery can sometimes look "cartoonish" (Corliss, 2003, p. 3). The work of digital animators and compositors keeps getting better, but it has not yet reached the ultimate goal of complete photorealism in all circumstances, especially when complex movement is involved. On the other hand, there are many circumstances, particularly in still photography, in which digital manipulation can fool any ordinary viewer. We know, because we ourselves have been fooled on occasion. In such circumstances, it may still be possible to detect the manipulation through closer scrutiny, and some critics have developed systematic procedures for analyzing the kinds of details that betray the presence of visual fabrication. A notable compendium of such procedures is contained in a recent book by Brugioni (1999, Chapter 5). For example, Brugioni discussed the analysis of lights and shadows (are they consistent across the image?), sharpness of detail (does it vary consistently with the type of lens that appears to have been used?), and a variety of other procedures that he developed during his years as a photography expert at the CIA.

Somewhere between the professional expertise of specialists such as Brugioni and the everyday viewer's "CG detector" envisioned by McG, there is a level of visual literacy that can add a sharper critical edge to our encounters with images. In addition to knowledge about technique, though, critical viewing also needs to encompass a heightened sense of the ramifications of context. If (as we noted earlier) viewers' expectations are a prime criterion regarding the truth or falsehood of photographic manipulation, those expectations deserve critical scrutiny just as much as pictures do. In the United States at the moment, the mainstream media and their audiences appear to be operating on the basis of a strict contract with regard to one kind of image, namely, "straight news." In the presence of such an image, viewers have been led to expect a complete absence of certain types of manipulations (e.g., adding, deleting, or repositioning objects, etc.), and violations of this contract are subject to substantial penalties, as in the case of an *Los Angeles Times* photographer who was fired after it was discovered that he had altered the position of a soldier in a photograph of the U.S. war in Iraq. However, outside the area of noneditorial journalism, the implicit rules as to what constitutes acceptable manipulation are much more fluid. Consider the following two cases.

First, a familiar situation with a somewhat new twist: A photo editor working on a fashion spread lengthens the legs of a model by cutting them at the thigh, moving them over, and filling in the gap with cloned flesh. Second, a publicist for an institution of higher learning inserts the image of an African American student in a photograph depicting campus life. (Some readers may recognize the latter incident, which received considerable attention a few years ago.) Both of these images are essentially advertisements, and, in a sense, both changes can be seen as accomplishing the same goal, namely, enhancing a desirable quality of the thing being sold—in one case clothes, in the other a school.

However, the implicit social standards regarding these two kinds of changes appear to differ considerably. Whereas the digital insertion of the African American student was considered a major transgression when the case became public, the "enhancement" of fashion images is a routine practice without any evident negative consequences for its practitioners, despite the protests of feminists and other critics. In other words, the former incident was judged by the kind of strict standard that applies to news images, whereas the latter appears to enjoy the greater latitude afforded to pictures which are not thought of as being primarily informational.

This implicit logic is understandable. The image of the African American student could certainly be considered a statement of fact not only about that particular student's presence when the picture was taken but also—and more importantly—about the degree of diversity of the school's student body. It can be argued, on the other hand, that fashion images are seen mainly as fantasies, without any substantial factual content. However, suppose we were to turn this distinction around. Is there a sense in which the picture of the student could also be seen as an aspirational image—what the school would like to be or is trying to be—rather than a straightforward statement of fact? And isn't it true that in some viewers' eyes fashion images are real enough as standards against which to judge oneself? From this reverse perspective, it is much less clear that one type of visual manipulation is more fraudulent or objectionable than the other one. What this comparison should make clearer, though, is the extent to which critical assessment of digital manipulation must be based on an understanding of viewers' expectations and responses. Visual literacy must encompass this kind of knowledge just as much as knowledge of the formal properties of images.

To conclude our discussion of visual lies, let us consider a variation on the image of the African American student discussed earlier. This time, there is no digital manipulation. Instead, the image is chosen by itself to represent the school on the cover of a brochure. The intent is presumably the same, but the means have changed. Because the photograph has not been altered, is the issue of deception now completely irrelevant? What if the actual proportion of African American students in that institution's student body is actually minuscule? In terms of their effects on viewers' expectations, perhaps the altered image and the stand-alone image are not as different as might appear on the surface. This example illustrates a broader point, namely, the fact that visual misrepresentation can very often be accomplished through the simple act of selection. By choosing a misleading image in place of a more representative one, a picture editor can create a false impression just as surely as through alteration of the image itself. This point was demonstrated by Kurt and Gladys Engel Lang (1971) in what may be the earliest published research on visual manipulation, their study of the televised presentation of General Douglas MacArthur's visit to Chicago in 1951, after he was relieved of his command in Korea. The well-known finding was that viewers who saw the events of the day on television were given a selective view of enthusiastic crowd response that was at considerable variance from the impressions of trained observers at the scene.

Awareness of the potential consequences of image selection is a crucial feature of visual literacy—more important, arguably, than awareness of digital manipulation, because selection is ubiquitous and inevitable, and it is always a product of a particular point of view. Anyone who compared U.S. media with their foreign counterparts during the

U.S. war in Iraq received a dramatic demonstration of how radically two sets of images can diverge in their representations of the "same" events. This fact was noted both in the United States and abroad, often in the form of side-by-side comparisons between CNN and Al-Jazeera (e.g., Harman, 2003; Slaney, 2003). Commenting on the differences between these two sources, a writer for Arab News complains that CNN is biased in favor of the official U.S. attitude toward the war: "CNN tries to tell you exactly what the American administration wants you to hear" (Qusti, 2003). However, the lesson we would draw from this kind of comparison is somewhat different. As this man's own one-sided response demonstrates, one of the most difficult things to accomplish when one is faced with competing representations is an informed synthesis of their versions of reality. The temptation to adopt a single perspective is extremely powerful, and it is this temptation that the visually literate viewer should be most aware of.

Visual Literacy and the Power of Images

We have devoted considerable space to the topic of visual lies because of its central place in recent visual scholarship. However, as far as the broader issue of critical viewing is concerned, the role of visual literacy can be just as important in situations in which truth or falsehood are not really at stake or not even relevant. In such situations, visual literacy can sharpen the viewer's critical faculties by making her or him more aware of the many ways in which images can engage a viewer's attention, emotions, or allegiances. In this discussion, we give a brief overview of four major principles accounting for the power of images, but we do not attempt an exhaustive survey of all such principles.

Analogy to Everyday Experience

We have already discussed the topic of visual analogies in the previous section of this chapter. Here we extend the discussion to the area of visual influence and critical viewing. Analogy to everyday experience is the underlying principle in a considerable variety of superficially unrelated conventions through which visual images affect their viewers (Messaris, 1997). For example, many TV ads are built around a discussion between two people, one of whom recommends the product to the other. The director has to decide whether to view the action "objectively" (i.e., from a point of view other than those of the characters in the ad) or "subjectively" (i.e., as if through the eyes of one of the characters, or of both in succession). Directors in this kind of situation often shoot a good part of the ad from a subjective perspective, and it is typically assumed that this camera angle in and of itself is an enhancement of the ad's persuasive appeal. The reason for its apparent effectiveness is that it parallels an aspect of most viewers' everyday experience, namely, the fact that, in a wide variety of cultures, a direct angle of interpersonal interaction tends to elicit a more intense level of engagement (other things being equal) than a less direct angle.

If this is, even partially, the correct explanation for the effectiveness of the subjective camera in this kind of situation, then what we have here is not simply an instance of a particular persuasive device, but also an example of the more general principle of visual influence based on analogy with everyday viewing experiences. In this case, the image's replication of the direct orientation of certain everyday interactions is a means of evoking the emotional tone of such interactions. This particular analogy is relatively concrete, in the sense that the image reproduces not just the abstract feature of directness of orientation, but also the actual situation, a two-person conversation. It is not difficult, however, to find instances of more abstract relationships between symbol and referent.

For example, in an early study of the formal characteristics of TV commercials aimed at children, Welch, Huston-Stein, Wright, & Plehal (1979) argued—with strongly supportive empirical evidence—that the appeal to conventional conceptions of masculinity in commercials aimed at boys should be evident in such stylistic devices as fast editing and the use of straight cuts, while commercials for girls should be characterized by slower editing and relatively greater use of fades and dissolves. Here the features reproduced in the images—speed and abruptness versus smoothness and a more even pace—are mere abstractions, without any necessary embodiment in the person of a fast-moving male or a gentle female. In a follow-up study, Huston, Greer, Wright, Welch, & Ross (1984) found that even quite young children were able to infer the gender orientation of an ad on the basis of the kinds of abstract features mentioned earlier. However, there is a question that this study does not answer: Was the ability to tell the boys' ads apart from the girls' ads also accompanied by an understanding of what features were responsible for this difference? It seems reasonable to assume that critically inclined viewers—of whatever age—may be better equipped to discern and assess the underlying values if they are aware of the devices through which those values are expressed.

Manipulation of Point of View

Although such uses of editing are extremely common, in our estimation it is not editing but composition in which analogy is most often in evidence as an instrument for the manipulation of viewers' perceptions and responses. In particular, analogical composition appears to play a major role in affecting viewers' emotional engagement by means of point of view. This topic has already been introduced in our earlier examination of the specific case of directness of orientation in TV advertising. The more general principle here is as follows: By controlling the viewer's positioning vis-à-vis the characters, objects, or events in an image (including the image sequences of film or television), the image's producer can elicit responses that have been conditioned by the viewer's experience of equivalent interrelationships with real-life people, things, and actions. This kind of analogical connection is probably most clearly evident in the well-worn cliché of filming someone from a low angle to make her or him appear more imposing; but the most frequent use of camera positioning as an analogical device is undoubtedly that which occurs when the distance (real or apparent) between the camera and its subject is employed as a means of modulating the viewer's identification or involvement with the characters or events on the screen.

This variable is one of the principal visual means for such effects as heightening the intensity of a scene as it moves toward its climax, maintaining the viewer's sympathy with the hero and emotional distance from secondary characters, releasing the tension of a scene or of the movie as a whole following the resolution of the action, and so on. Because of the analogy between the role of camera-to-subject distance in such instances and the function of interpersonal distance as a regulator of intimacy and involvement in real-life social interactions, Meyrowitz (1986) labeled this aspect of visual manipulation "paraproxemics." It might seem that such devices—dramatic close-ups, zoom-ins to a significant object, camera pull-backs as a movie ends, and so forth—must be obvious to mature viewers, but in fact there is evidence that even highly educated people with an interest in visual media are generally unaware of these manipulation devices (Galan, 1986). Furthermore, there are certain broader, ideologically oriented arguments for focusing on this area. A major tenet of much feminist film criticism is that camera positioning in mainstream cinema has consistently served to ally the viewer with a male point of view and to objectify the female presence (see Mulvey, 1989).

Implicit Argumentation

In advertising, visual analogies and metaphors are part of a broader visual language, whose aim is to make a claim or an argument in favor of whatever it is the ad is selling. In ads featuring analogies, the argument consists of comparing the product to some other desirable object or situation. Other common visual arguments in advertising entail contrast (the advertiser's desirable product versus the competitor's undesirable product) or causality (the product juxtaposed with various desirable outcomes: sex, social status, good health, etc.), to name just two familiar types of ads. Because visual advertising is such a pervasive feature of our lives, we rarely need to think twice about the meanings of the visual arguments we encounter on TV, in magazines, or in other mass media. Nevertheless, there is a sense in which a creative leap is involved every time we interpret such ads, even if we do so without any conscious reflection. This has to do with one of the fundamental differences between images and words. Whereas verbal language contains an explicit vocabulary for indicating how one object is related to another ("a is like b," "c leads to d," "e is different from f," etc.), visual language has no such indicators. Unless they are spelled out through captions or voice-over, the meanings of visual arguments are always implied. One image is placed next to another image, and it is up to the viewer to infer the connection (Witkowski, 2003).

The lack of explicitness of arguments that are made visually, and the consequent fact that one can use images to put forth propositions that might appear false or ridiculous if stated in words, has long been recognized as a central characteristic of advertising (Marchand, 1985). This characteristic allows advertisers to make claims or arguments without explicitly taking responsibility for them. A telling example of this possibility was demonstrated in a TV expose about nutritional supplements for body builders. According to this program, there is a substantial market for these products, but nutritional analysis reveals that they confer no special benefits to their users. Armed with this information, the producers of the TV program confronted one of the manufacturers of these supplements with a print ad for his products. The ad featured an extremely muscular man juxtaposed with a large picture of the product. The manufacturer was asked: Since the product will not produce the dramatic results illustrated here, isn't this a misleading ad? Not at all, he replied. Nowhere in the ad was it stated verbally that this product could produce these results. If the viewer made such an inference from the images, that was his or her own subjective interpretation, for which the manufacturer could not be held accountable. One suspects that similar positions might have been taken by liquor advertisers confronted with ads linking their products to sex, or cigarette advertisers asked to explain the juxtaposition of their products with images of cartoon characters.

Associational Juxtaposition

The general strategy of pairing images in order to bring about an unconscious association between them—whether or not an implied causal link or other kind of logical connection is also intended—may be referred to as "associational juxtaposition." There is considerable evidence that this kind of manipulation of response is effective for both human and animal subjects, and, within this larger body of evidence, there is also some research that specifically supports the notion that Pavlovian conditioning can work with pictorial stimuli—most notably, perhaps, a pair of studies in which subjects were turned into boot fetishists through repeated exposure to sexual images paired with pictures of boots (see Rachman, 1966; Rachman & Hodgson, 1968). In the area of advertising, evidence of the effectiveness of associational juxtaposition comes from a study by Zuckerman (1990), who found that high school students' responses to certain products appeared to have been conditioned by the imagery paired with those products in magazine ads. The use of conditioned learning, as well as cognitive strategies, is discussed in advertising textbooks, but most notably in "How Advertising Works," Chapter 4 in *Advertising Principles and Practices* (Wells, Burnett, & Moriarty, 2003, p. 169).

Although the conventions of mass advertising are obviously designed to appeal to a specified target audience, it is entirely conceivable, of course, that any given viewer may not, in fact, see the causal or other type of link in these kinds of juxtapositions. Should we conclude that this juxtaposition was wasted on these viewers? A different perspective on the effects of visual juxtaposition suggests otherwise. As Stout (1984) noted, advertising of the kind described here, in which a picture of the product is paired with a picture of a desirable situation, is typically designed to work through repetition. Even if the viewer doesn't make a conscious connection between the two images, it is assumed that, over time, the connection will establish itself in viewers' minds according to the standard principles of conditioning. That is why this kind of advertising can referred to as "Pavlovian."

CONCLUSION

The study of visual literacy touches many disciplines from communication to psychology, education, aesthetics, and cultural studies, among others. Literacy implies learning, and the various theories of learning certainly provide a foundation for any investigation in this area. A central question has to do with how people learn from visual images—how they understand what they see. But understanding is more than simply perception, and current scholarship in the area of visual literacy recognizes the impact that images can have on attitudes and emotions, as well as knowledge. Understanding a visual image occurs on two levels. On a more fundamental level, understanding involves applying a constellation of basic perceptual principles to the acquisition of meaning from what we see, whether it be a sign, an image, or a graphic representation. On a different, perhaps higher, level, understanding involves deconstructing the intended meaning in terms of techniques used by the producer of the image to stimulate or manipulate certain responses. The latter type of understanding corresponds to critical viewing.

In addition to exploring the process of understanding images, the study of visual literacy also focuses on the production of visual meaning through various forms and media. Visualization, the ability to construct a mental image and manipulate it, is basic to the production or creative dimension of visual literacy. So, parallel to understanding visual images is the development of the ability to create messages that are communicated visually. In other words, understanding how images work feeds into the process of creating them. By analogy to reading and writing, both aspects of visual literacy—the production as well as the perception of meaning presented through images—are important to visual literacy scholars.

Through training in critical viewing, visual literacy can be a tool for better understanding the power of images, particularly as they are used in the mass media and advertising. In this discussion we have reviewed several sources of that power, including the creation of analogies to everyday experience, the manipulating of point of view, the presentation of arguments by implication rather than overtly, and the creation of associational juxtapositions. These visual devices tend to operate below the level of conscious reaction, unless a viewer is trained in visual literacy and has developed skills of seeing that go beyond the act of superficial perception.

This discussion also looked at visual literacy as a form of cognitive enrichment. As novice creators working in visual media become more fluent in producing, framing, and combining images, they also develop certain broader mental aptitudes that these activities bring into play, including spatial intelligence and analogical thinking. Rudolf Arnheim once complained that some psychologists believe "there can be no thinking except in words" (1989, p. 142)—a notion that denies the richness of other forms of cognition, particularly visual intelligence. Visual literacy, with its capacity for cognitive enrichment, opens up new forms of thinking, analyzing, and reasoning that can work in tandem with the reading and writing skills of traditional literacy.

REFERENCES

Arnheim, R. (1989). *Visual thinking*. Berkeley: University of California Press.

Bazin, Andre. (1967). *What is cinema?* (Hugh Gray, Trans.). Berkeley: University of California Press.

Boden, M. (1991). *The creative mind: Myths and mechanisms*. New York: Basic Books.

Bolter, J. D., & Grusin, R. (1999). *Remediation: Understanding new media*. Cambridge, MA: MIT Press.

Braden, R., & Hortin, J. (1982). Identifying the theoretical foundations of visual literacy. *Journal of Visual Verbal Languaging, 2*(2): 37–51.

Brower, Kenneth. (1998, May). Photography in the age of falsification. *The Atlantic* Online. Available at www.theatlantic.com.

Brugioni, D. A. (1999). Photo fakery: The history and techniques of photographic deception and manipulation. Herndon, VA: Brasseys.

Burmark, L. (2002). *Visual literacy: Learn to see, see to learn*. Alexandria, VA: Association for Supervision & Curriculum Development.

Carroll, N. (1996). *Theorizing the moving image*. Cambridge, UK: Cambridge University Press.

Corliss, R. (2003, June 16). Summer of vroooom. *Time* Online Edition. Available at: www.time.com.

Curtiss, D. (1987). *Introduction to visual literacy*. Englewood Cliffs, NJ: Prentice-Hall.

Debes, J. (1969). The loom of visual literacy. *Audiovisual Instruction, 14*(8), 25–27.

Dondis, D. (1973). *A primer of visual literacy.* Cambridge, MA: MIT Press.

Franck, F. (1979). *The awakened eye.* New York: First Vintage Books Edition.

Francesky, R. B., & Debes, J. (1972). *Visual literacy: A way to learn—A way to teach.* Washington, DC: Association for Educational Communication and Technology.

Galan, L. S. (1986). The use of subjective point of view in persuasive communication. M.A. thesis, Annenberg School for Communication, University of Pennsylvania.

Gardner, H. (1999). *Intelligence reframed: Multiple intelligences for the 21st century.* New York: Basic Books.

Griffith, D. W. (1972). *The man who invented Hollywood: The autobiography of D. W. Griffith* (James Hart, Ed.). Louisville, KY: Touchstone Publishing.

Hargittai, I., & Hargittai, M. (1994). The use of artistic analogies in chemical research and education. *Leonardo, 27*(1), 223–226.

Harman, D. (2003, March 25). CNN vs. Al Jazeera: Seeing is often believing. Available at. www.csmonitor.com/2003/0325/p01s04-woiq.htm.

Heinich, R., Molenda, M., & Russell, J. (1982). *Instructional media and the new technologies of instruction.* New York: Wiley.

Hobbs, R., Frost, R., Davis, A., & Stauffer, J. (1988). How first-time viewers comprehend editing conventions. *Journal of Communication, 38*(4), 50–60.

Huston, A. C., Greer, D., Wright, J. C., Welch, R., & Ross, R. (1984). Children's comprehension of televised formal features with masculine and feminine connotations. *Developmental Psychology, 20*(4), 707–716.

John-Steiner, V. (1985). *Notebooks of the mind: Explorations of thinking.* Albuquerque: University of New Mexico Press.

Kember, S. (2003). The shadow of the object: Photography and realism. In Liz Wells (Ed.), *The photography reader* (pp. 202–217). New York: Routledge.

Kemp, M. (2000). *Visualizations: The Nature book of art and science.* Berkeley: University of California Press.

Lang, K., & Lang, G. E. (1971). The unique perspective of television and its effect: A pilot study. In W. Schramm & D. F. Roberts, (Eds.), *The process and effects of mass communication,* Rev. ed., (pp. 169–188). Urbana: University of Illinois Press.

Lester, P. M. (Ed.). (1996). *Images that injure: Pictorial stereotypes in the media.* New York: Praeger.

Lester, P. M. (2000). *Visual communication* (2nd ed.). Belmont, CA: Wadsworth.

Lohr, Linda L. (2002). *Creating graphics for learning and performance: Lessons in visual literacy.* New York: Prentice-Hall.

Marchand, R. (1985). *Advertising the American dream.* Berkeley: University of California Press.

Messaris, P. (1994). *Visual literacy: Image, mind & reality.* Boulder, CO: Westview Press.

Messaris, P. (1997). *Visual persuasion: The role of images in advertising.* Thousand Oaks, CA: Sage.

Messaris, P. (1998, Winter). Visual aspects of media literacy. *Journal of Communication,* 70–80.

Meyrowitz, J. (1986). Television and interpersonal behavior: Codes of perception and response. In G. Gumpert & R. Cathcart (Eds.), *Inter/media* (pp. 253–272). New York: Oxford University Press.

Mitchell, M. (1993). *Analogy-making as perception: A computer model.* Cambridge, MA: MIT Press.

Moriarty, S., & Shaw, D. (1995, Spring). An antiseptic war. *Visual Communication Quarterly,* 4–8.

Morreale, J. (1991). *A New Beginning: A textual frame analysis of the political campaign film.* Albany: State University of New York Press.

Mulvey, L. (1989). *Visual and other pleasures.* Bloomington: Indiana University Press.

Newton, J. (2000). *The burden of visual truth: The role of photojournalism in mediating reality.* Hillsdale, NJ: Lawrence Erlbaum Associates.

Paivio, A. On exploring visual knowledge. In B. S. Randhawa & W. E. Coffman (Eds.), *Visual learning, thinking, and communication* (pp. 113–131). New York: Academic Press.

Prince, S. (1990). Are there Bolsheviks in your breakfast cereal? In Sari Thomas & William A. Evans (Eds.), *Communication and culture: Language, performance, technology, and media* (pp. 180–184). Norwood, NJ: Ablex.

Qusti, R. (2003, March 26). Study in contrast: CNN vs. Al-Jazeera. Arab News. Available at: Foi.missouri.edu/jourwarcoverage/studyincontrasts.html.

Rachman, S. (1966). Sexual fetishism: An experimental analogue. *Psychological Record, 16,* 293–296.

Rachman, S., & Hodgson, R. J. (1968). Experimentally-induced "sexual fetishism": Replication and development. *Psychological Record, 18*, 25–27.

Rosler, M. (1991). Image simulations, computer manipulations: Some considerations. *Ten, 8*, 2(2).

Schamber, L. (1987). Visual literacy in mass communications: A proposal for educators. San Antonio, TX: Annual Conference of the Visual Communication Division of the Association for Education in Journalism and Mass Communication.

Seels, B. A. (1994). Visual literacy: The definition problem. In David M. (Mike) Moore and Francis M. Dwyer (Eds.), *Visual literacy: A spectrum of visual learning* (pp. 97–112). Englewood Cliffs, NJ: Educational Technology Publications.

Slaney, C. (2003). CNN vs Al Jazeera—Whose war will you watch? Middle East Times. Available at: www.metimes.com/2K3/issue2003-8/reg/cnn_vs_al.html.

Stafford, B. M. (1999). *Visual analogy: Consciousness as the art of connecting.* Cambridge, MA: MIT Press.

Stout, R. (1984). Pavlov founded advertising because he showed that imagery could be transferred. *Television/Radio Age* (31), 160.

Sturken, M., & Cartwright, L. (2001). *Practices of looking: An introduction to visual culture.* New York: Oxford University Press.

Tidhar, C. E. (1984). Children communicating in cinematic codes: Effects on cognitive skills. *Journal of Educational Psychology, 76*, 957–965.

Tucker, A. (2001). *Visual literacy: Writing about art.* New York: McGraw-Hill.

Tufte, E. R. (1990). *Envisioning information.* Cheshire, CT: Graphics Press.

Tufte, E. R. (1997). *Visual explanations: Images and quantities, evidence and narrative.* Cheshire, CT: Graphics Press.

Tufte, E. R. (2001). *The visual display of quantitative information* (2d. ed.). Cheshire, CT: Graphics Press.

Vosniadou, S., & Ortony, A. (1989). *Similarity and analogical reasoning.* Cambridge, England: Cambridge University Press.

Welch, R., Huston-Stein, A., Wright, J., & Plehal, R. (1979). Subtle sex-role cues in children's commercials. *Journal of Communication, 29*(3), 202–209.

Wells, B., Burnett, J., & Moriarty, S. (2003). *Advertising principles & practices* (6th ed.). Upper Saddle River, NJ: Prentice Hall.

Wheeler, T. (2003). *Phototruth or photofiction? Ethics and media imagery in the digital age.* Hillsdale, NJ: Lawrence Erlbaum Associates.

Wilde, J., & Wilde, R. (2000). *Visual literacy: A conceptual approach to graphic problem solving.* New York: Watson-Guptill.

Witkowski, M. (2003). The bottle that isn't there and the duck that can't be heard: The "subjective correlative" in commercial messages. *Studies in Media & Information Literacy Education, 3*(3).

Wolfe, A., & Sleeper, B. (1994). *Migrations: Wildlife in motion.* Hillsboro, OR: Beyond words Publishing.

Worth, S. & Adair, J. (1972). *Through Navajo eyes: An exploration in film communication and anthropology.* Bloomington: Indiana University Press.

Zuckerman, C. (1990). Rugged cigarettes and sexy soap: Brand images and the acquisition of meaning through associational juxtaposition of visual imagery. M.A. thesis, the Annenberg School for Communication, University of Pennsylvania.

Media Literacy, Aesthetics, and Culture

ELIZABETH BURCH
Sonoma State

Television production textbooks instruct students on the "right way" to produce programs, but is there really a wrong way to make TV? And who gets to decide the rules? When more and more U.S. programming is exported to other countries through new communication technologies, the implications of this right way/wrong way approach for international television becomes troubling. Is television around the world beginning to look alike? If not, what does it look like? And what explains the differences? To explore these questions, this chapter investigates how culture informs television production. It analyzes aesthetic conventions applied to one highly successful television soap opera in India in order to assess how the visual syntax perhaps differs from the professional norms of American TV. By examining television within a Third World context, a key methodological aspect of media literacy is explored: How aesthetics are bound, in part, by culture.

Research on media literacy examines the interpretation and creation of media texts (Potter, 2001; Lewis & Jhally 2000). According to Messaris and Moriarty, the link between culture and aesthetics is critical in studies on visual literacy since it provides a context in which to base meaning. Culture refers to all "socially transmitted and shared ways of thinking and acting" (Goonasekera, 1987, p. 7). In its most basic sense, visual literacy deals with the shared meaning of the creators and consumers of visual messages. Thus, the concepts of *connotational meaning* and *analogical connection* that Messaris and Moriarty discuss are highly relevant to the study of cultural aesthetics in visual literacy. Analysis of these visual cues (or clues) helps to develop the skill of "spatial intelligence."[1] In order to elicit analogical connections—such as the use of a production element to produce an intended emotion—producers should be aware of message comprehension. To do so, they must also access the message's connotational meanings (metonymy), "by going beyond the literal content of images." Both processes are informed by culture-rich codes.

As Messaris and Moriarty state, the benefits of culture-based aesthetic studies are dual-purpose, providing cognitive enrichment in the pursuit of visual literacy while teaching skills to evaluate and produce media. Analytical skills help viewers defend against the negative effects of potentially manipulative messages, such as advertising (Lewis & Jhally, 2000; DeBenediittus, 2001). Equally important for producers in developing countries is the awareness of the harm that a highly Westernized media can have on international cultural diversity. Communication scholars refer to the problem of Westernization as "media imperialism." Media imperialism is described as a one-way flow of cultural products from Western countries to nations in the developing world, which result in a dependency for cultural goods and the homogenization of culture (Nordenstreng & Varis, 1974; Nordenstreng & Schiller, 1979; Tomlinson, 1991). A homogenized or globalized culture would begin to all look the same, and, some argue, that sameness would look American (Tunstall, 1977). In terms of visual literacy, this means that a uniformity of aesthetics would prevail, despite the backgrounds of those creating or interpreting a message.

VISUAL LITERACY WITHIN A CULTURAL CONTEXT: DECODING MEANING

Culture does create difference in society and the use of its cultural products. In the examination of visual literacy, audience reception studies show that the decoding process (Fiske & Hartley, 1978; Hall, 1980) can be discussed in terms of culture because symbolic associations are culturally learned (Zettl, 1973). For instance, Katz and Liebes' (1984) groundbreaking study of the American serial *Dallas* showed that varying cultural groups differed in their interpretation of the media texts (Liebes, 1988). This and other studies examining media imperialism suggest a countermodel to the threat of Western dominance. Research into the regional success of Latin American soap operas (*telenovelas*), for example, provide evidence that developing countries produce programs that are competitive with Western media (Straubhaar, 1991, 1997; Straubhaar, Burch, Duarte, & Sheffer, 2002).

Understanding the decoding process is important for those trying to create successful TV programs in developing countries, especially in parts of the world where television penetration is still relatively low. TV producers whose viewers are new to the medium say interpretation should not be taken for granted. Hobbs, Frost, Davis, and Stauffer (1988) wrote that systematic efforts to examine the comprehension skills of television-naive viewers is essential if broadcasting is to be used to communicate information about agriculture, sanitation, nutrition, and health care. McFee (1978) suggested examining comprehension of users of one-dimensional visual media to understand how visual literacy is developed by television viewers. Seeing objects in reality is not the same as perceiving them in pictures and pictorial object recognition often depends on prior experience. If people have already learned that a flat picture can represent three-dimensional objects, then they will be better able to understand that the images in those pictures connect with reality. Familiarity with a topic also helps with recognition. In this way, culture seems to play a factor. When Scottish and Zambian youth were compared in their recognition of motor vehicles and animals, it was found that the Scottish children could more readily separate the vehicles from the animals. They were better equipped to interpret the information because those in First World countries had more prior experience with machines, and also more experience with seeing pictures of animals (McFee, 1978).

CONTEXTUALISM AS METHOD: VISUAL LITERACY AND THE ENCODING PROCESS

Another approach to examine what is decoded in visual literacy is aesthetic analysis, or *contextualism*, which analyzes how texts are encoded. The term *aesthetic* derives from the Greek word meaning "through the senses." Hegal wrote, "Aesthetics means, precisely, the science of sensation of feeling" (1979, p. 1). Zettl defined aesthetics through a method of analysis called, "contextualism" (1973, 1990, 1998). Contextualism is, "the study of certain sense perceptions and how these perceptions can be most effectively clarified, intensified, and interpreted through a medium, such as television or film, for a specific recipient" (Zettl, 1973, p. 2). The method facilitates the analysis of production elements in a narrative. Contextualism is also a useful analytic tool in understanding how audiences read television by examining encoding (Zettl, 1990, 1998; Barker, 2000; Lang, Zhou, Schwartz, Bolls, & Potter, 2000). Likewise, the method provides new insights into cross-cultural research because classification and comparison of visual codes clarify how meaning is generated through media in other societies.

TV AESTHETICS ACROSS CULTURES

Aesthetics can be examined in terms of its relationship to information retrieval. In a UNESCO report on cross-cultural broadcasting (1976), Contreras discusses a community development project in Peru in which a film on hygiene was shown to villagers. The study reveals that the visual aid had failed to convey its intended message. The problem was that the audience perceived each scene (and in some cases even each discrete shot) as complete and separate incidents. When cutaways (separate close-up images) of lice under a microscope were shown, people concluded that what they were seeing was an animal, not a bug that could get on a person's body. Most importantly, villagers did not infer that the information related to their own bodies.

In India's neighboring country of Nepal, one exploratory study found that an understanding of local viewpoints on comprehension can serve television producers who hope to use the medium for educational purposes (Ogden-Gurung, 1987). Health information in villages in Nepal is usually disseminated via visits by health workers because most people in the country do not have access to television. Villagers were shown a video on how to make rehydration solution. It was found that comprehension of the information in the video was low, primarily because the Western editing conventions used in the program confused viewers. Viewers were to learn that they needed to put three handfuls of sugar into a glass of water with salt in order to make the solution. Western aesthetic standards demand that the scene be edited down into a number of shots, such as close-ups and medium shots of the health worker, which provide various perspectives on the action. When the narration said: "Now add three handfuls of sugar," editors cut at least one of the shots of the hands actually pouring the sugar into the glass. The expectation is that the viewer will fill in the missing information. This is referred to as *psychological closure*, according to contextualism. Yet the audience was unaccustomed to such television techniques. Consequently, viewers did not learn the correct information from the video. It became clear that the program should show the information in one complete segment without any cuts (a cut is the most common form of editing transition). Continuity editing typically entails cutting shots together to maintain continuous action within a scene, which preserves the illusion of reality. Often, much is cut out. To those more bound by Western aesthetic standards of continuity editing, this scene might "feel" excruciatingly slow or boring. Yet understanding that the intended viewers would not be able to read the picture information otherwise, the non-Western aesthetic choice would be the more successful communication route.

One seminal study assessed how Native American producers create texts finding limited evidence that even in the United States, non-Western filmmakers sometimes make aesthetic choices that differ with traditional Western production techniques (Worth & Adair, 1972). Anthropologists Worth and Adair taught one group of Navajo Native Americans how to make films while trying not to impart too many rules of cinematography based on Hollywood film standards (such as headroom in framing, etc.). The question was, if left to make their own choices, would Navajo producers create films that expressed themselves through unique aesthetic codes? Producers did sometimes edit narratives using a different set of conventions. For instance, as in the Nepal study, what is perceived as boring in one culture may simply represent a passage of time in another. Within the Navajo community, much of people's day-to-day transportation was conducted by foot rather than moving vehicle. More importantly, there is a "mythic quality of walking as an 'act'" (Worth & Adair, 1972, p. 146). Consequently, many of the Navajo producers edited their films using long walking scenes with a slow pace. This is in contrast to Hollywood editing style, which, for the most part, demands the removal of such detailed moments of reality (even today in so-called reality TV shows). Therefore, how time and timing is constructed relates to a normative expectation of audience members within a given culture.

AESTHETICS AND INDIAN SOAP OPERAS

In order to identify how aesthetics are regionally bound by culture, one can limit a study to specific genres and production elements within a society. Communication scholars in the West, such as Allen (1995) and others, have focused considerable attention on the television soap opera genre. Examining soap operas within a Third World context, Singhal and Rogers (1989) discussed the "edutainment-value" of the genre in developing countries, such as India, in their evaluation of shows like *Hum Log* (We People) and others.[2] Edutainment refers to entertainment-education programs that intentionally place educational content in entertainment messages (Singhal and Rogers, 2002). The approach is an attempt to introduce development messages in ways that would draw viewer interest. Another very successful spin on the television soap opera model in developing countries is religious soap operas. The first of its kind, called *Ramayan*, was produced in India. The serial was aired to Indian and Nepalese TV audiences in 1987. Although not meant for educational entertainment, the show's estimated following of over 70 million regular viewers in India was instructive on the Hindu religion.[3] As Sherry (2002) pointed out about educational soap operas aired in the 1980s, options for program choice were limited for viewers at the time. However, a strong measure of a program's success is its appearance in reruns. *Ramayan* was aired again in 1999, and with the diffusion of satellite TV technology viewers in countries with Hindu Diasporic populations watched the program as well (Sagar, 1987).[4] *Ramayan* and other Hindu soap operas that it spawned such as *Mahabharat* are very successful, not only in India, but also regionally and beyond (Bhatia, 1989; Mitra, 1993). Today, religious soap operas are widely available in Indian video stores in the United States.

The program was produced by Ramanand Sagar, a famous Indian film director from the school of Hindi Cinema based in the Western city of Mumbai (formerly called Bombay). Said to be the Hollywood of the East, "Bollywood" films are a highly commercialized genre that incorporate song and dance sequences as a matter of formula.[5] *Ramayan* is obviously influenced by Hindi film style but with a twist: fantasy creates a suprareality that incorporates the Hindu religion into the soap opera form. The story of *Ramayan* chronicles the life of a Hindu hero, Rama, a human incarnation of Vishnu (the god of preservation). Rama is born on earth to restore the balance of good and evil in the world.[6] A rich body of research on aesthetics within India offers insight into the popularity of religious television. Sukla (2001) referenced the ideas of the father of Indian aesthetics, Bharata (1967), to assess scholarly views on the conception and use of dramas, like *Ramayan*. Bharata discusses Hindu mythology, which he says incorporates drama as a form of prayer. In this sense, shows like *Ramayan* perhaps serve as a way for religious Hindus to worship while being entertained.

RESEARCH QUESTIONS: AESTHETIC ANALYSIS

In order to explore visual literacy in light of a culture-based televisual aesthetic, I asked three questions:

Q1. What visual production elements of Indian religious soap operas like *Ramayan* are aesthetically different from the so-called professional standards most widely taught to TV producers within the United States?

Q2. Does *Ramayan* serve as a counterexample to the charge that media around the world is beginning to look the same no matter who produces it?

Q3. What new insights can be provided through explication of non-Western analogical connections and connotational meanings to continue to develop the spatial intelligence of all producers of pro-development programming?

METHOD

I conducted a qualitative, aesthetic analysis of the text of the first episode of *Ramayan*. This show was chosen based on the assumption that the beginnings of TV serials include the highest production values in order to attract a large, loyal audience base. Zettl's *Sight, Sound, Motion: Applied Media Aesthetics* has been required reading for many university students of television production in the United States (1973, 1990). Analysis of Indian television aesthetics using Zettl's rules (based on the first edition because *Ramayan* was produced before the second one) provided a vehicle for a cross-cultural comparison between Indian and U.S. television. Aesthetic levels of analysis ("fields") that were clarified and intensified in the production were explored in order to reveal patterns in the encoding process. These fields encompass the variables most widely manipulated by directors of television productions around the world even today. The visual conventions discussed are examples of analogy and denotation to connotation (the literal to the perceived). The four aesthetic fields included: (a) conventional usage of light and color, (b) two-dimensional space (area and vectors or directional forces on the screen), (c) three-dimensional space (screen volume through articulation of X and Z axes; and visualization of field of view, camera angles and subjective camera), and (d) time and motion (through motion vectors and editing) (Zettl, 1998). Definitions of these terms were presented in the context of the analysis because their complexities warrant immediate illustration. Field five, which deals with sound, is an extremely important element of Indian television and was examined but excluded from this chapter in order to focus on the visual elements of the production. An attempt was then made to analyze the analogical connections and the connotational meanings of the work as viewers might decode them. As stated earlier, the core concern of this study is how visual literacy can help identify the diversity of production devices, or the lack thereof, and how that awareness informs us as creators and consumers of media content within a cultural context.

WESTERN BIAS

This methodology brings into question the objectivity of the author. As a researcher, I have extensive fieldwork experience in South Asia and consider myself sensitive to concerns about paternalism. Nonetheless, ignorance of aspects of Indian culture could bias the results. Therefore, special effort was made to incorporate feedback on the findings from Indian colleagues in communications (Pendakur, personal communication, May 20, 2001). Another concern is that, as an American television producer, my biases about professional standards could affect interpretations. Rather than shy away from this problem, however, this study attempts to explicate it. Zettl likely never intended his television production textbook to be used to imply a Western aesthetic was right while all others were wrong. The analysis simply compares the non-Western syntax of *Ramayan* with the rules presented in Zettl's educational materials because they are widely used and respected by television departments throughout the United States. Still, these findings are meant to be exploratory in nature and would benefit from further validity checks, such as audience effects research, in-depth interviews with producers about program elements and contextual analyses conducted by researchers within the culture.

STRUCTURING THE FIRST AESTHETIC FIELD

The following discussion highlights a few of the differences between the four aesthetic fields represented in Zettl's television production textbook and the aesthetic standards encoded in *Ramayan* (Burch, 2002). Of course, decoding by viewers of these elements requires an understanding of some of the aesthetic conventions in television. Miscommunications could result without these skills. Thus, assessments of perceptions are not generalizable without audience feedback. To begin, the study examines the effectiveness of communicating the narrative of *Ramayan*'s text. According to Zettl's rules of television production, the first aesthetic field that should be investigated deals with light and color. Painters and sculptors have always understood the importance of light in their work. Most of the scenes to be analyzed in the first episode of *Ramayan* used the typical television flat lighting technique known as "Notan." Notan lighting provides basic illumination, as opposed to "Chiaroscuro" lighting that uses light and dark contrasts to emphasize volume and mood. Notan lighting is a fairly typical lighting technique in U.S. soap operas, thus many of the scenes in *Ramayan* are lit as they would be in U.S. soaps. What is different in *Ramayan* is the use of internal lighting effects, such as chromakey (or matting effects).

With chromakey, one picture is electronically cut into another picture through the use of a switcher (the technique is still used in television newscasts today during weather reports). In *Ramayan*, the first scene and many subsequent scenes depict conversations between the Hindu gods and goddesses, which are set in heaven where they are said to reside. The chromakey effect in *Ramayan* is used to make those scenes seem painted, as in a painting on a stage for a play. The real actors in the scenes are electronically cut into the sets. The aesthetic is familiar to Hindi audiences in the sense that it re-creates a simulation of a live, theatrical condition that is the norm in the performance of religious festivals in villages and urban centers throughout India.

Scene one of *Ramayan* depicts a conversation between the three gods—Vishnu, Shiva, and Bramha. The three together form an important religious trinity. Shiva and Brahma convince Vishnu, the god of preservation, that he must be reborn on earth as the son of a king in order to save the world from a demon's destruction. A split screen is a visual effect that shows two or more different images placed in separate parts of the frame at the same time. Filmed in split screen, the lower half of the frame is filled with a shot of the ocean with the upper portion of the screen depicting the sun. The characters, including their followers, seem to float suspended, electronically imposed against a dense background that is "painted" to be shimmering. The shimmering may have been created by a key effect in the switcher. The technical aspects of the scene relate to the religious narrative and audiences must know the story of *Ramayan* to understand that. Vishnu is to be interpreted as the ocean (*Nara*), which was spread everywhere before the creation of the universe. He is also called "moving in the waters" (*Narayana*). In *Ramayan*, Vishnu is represented in human form in the upper portion of the screen with the other gods.

Internal lighting effects are used in one more shot in scene one. The shot depicts the demon king's reign of terror over the earth. The devil's laughing face is chromakeyed behind a foreground of fighting warriors. Because of the size relationship (the face large and the warriors small), one can tell that he is inciting war among the humans. To those familiar with *Ramayan* the scene also means the destruction of human kind and the imbalance of evil over good. Chromakey effectively creates a representation of a Hindu spirit-reality in *Ramayan* quite acceptable to Indian audiences. However, as a production technique, Western television aesthetisists might view its use in this way as more theaterlike than the norm for television. Today, current computer animation techniques are widely in use in India.

The interpretations of color provide an interesting study of culture-based aesthetics. In exploring the first aesthetic field, light and color, Arnheim remarked that, "studies of color preference are likely to yield a reliable picture of the cultural setting" (1969, p. 335). Color can function in three principal ways. It can either be informational, expressive, or compositional. Zettl (1973) wrote that color associations are learned, typically grounded in ones cultural experience.

Color plays a peripheral informational role in *Ramayan*. Costume colors, prop colors, and in some cases even skin colors are used to conjure associations in viewers' minds (Ions, 1967). Without prior exposure to Hindu mythology, viewers of *Ramayan* probably would not be able to identify many of the characters in the narrative. For instance, in terms of the many supreme beings said to exist in Hinduism, the god Vishnu in *Ramayan* is depicted as having blue skin. Although Vishnu is not always represented this way, those familiar with Hinduism would know who he is exactly by who he is not if he is blue (note the other gods described later).

Other factors work along with color's simple informational or cueing role because characters can also be identified by their mythologized costumes and the props that surround them. In the first scene of *Ramayan*, viewers can also tell who blue Vishnu is because he has four arms and is shown reclining on a coiled serpent, which is a kind of boat for him. He is accompanied by his noted mistress, the revered goddess Lakshmi. The god of creation is Brahma. Though usually seen with red skin and riding a goose, in *Ramayan*, Brahma cannot be so easily recognized. Instead, he is dressed as his "other self" for prayer and sacrifice in austere white robes. White is one of the colors traditionally associated with prayer in Hinduism. Brahma floats on a pink lotus petal. His followers are angels, spirit-priests and even Mother Earth herself. Their identity is clear to local viewers because most of the characters are dressed in white or orange robes like real Hindu priests. The third god in the scene is Shiva, the god of destruction. Shiva is clothed in a black and orange spotted tiger cloth and has matted hair in which rests on a white crescent moon. A dangerous looking cobra is draped around his neck. Shiva represents the end of time and completes the cycle of creation, preservation, and destruction in Hindu mythology. Out of the end is said to come the beginning. Culturally fluent viewers are the most likely to know that the image of Shiva is also associated with fertility.

Finally, on color that cues information to viewers, although Vishnu's skin is blue in these scenes, it should be noted that skin tone is an issue that factors into the Hindu caste system (a religious hierarchy that predetermines the greatest privilege to those on the top). It is no surprise that the gods, high priests, and royal family have light skin while many of the villagers are dark. As Bista's 1991 often-cited study *Fatalism in Development* noted, light skin communicates status, and that is even so in some parts of the Hindu world today. These informational visual cues help viewers well versed with the religion to know to whom the characters in this complex narrative refer.

A more instrumental role for color in *Ramayan* is its expressiveness, which functions to establish mood. Zettl (1973) said the more intimate or introspective an event becomes, the more one can treat outer reality as low definition. In terms of color, this means that a subdued color scheme would be used to depict spirituality, because it would not distract viewers from the latent narrative. Thus, the more introverted an event is, the less important color becomes. In some ways, this rule does apply in the representations of Hinduism. When people in the region mourn a death, they wear white (versus black in the United States). Still, the aesthetic rule is broken in *Ramayan* as it is in real life in India. For instance, high-energy colors are used to portray the gods and priests. Likewise, in *Ramayan*'s religious festival scene, characters wear the traditional red powder "tikas" (a red spot on the forehead where the so-called third eye is said to be). These colors represent holiness and a spiritual "inner reality" in Indian culture. Yet these high-energy colors emphasize external reality by American TV aesthetic standards.

Another point can be made about color throughout *Ramayan*. Zettl wrote that the compositional function of color is to help establish form. Colors can define, emphasize, and deemphasize certain screen areas, "in order to bring the energies of the pictorial elements into a balanced, yet dynamic, interplay" (1973, p. 97). This concept of balance, however, is highly subjective. By American aesthetic standards, *Ramayan*'s color combinations are often highly saturated. Under the Western rule of compositional balance, color combinations throughout the episode might be considered too dynamic to be harmonious. Yet, Indian viewers see it differently. Therefore, what is a so-called dissonant or unbalanced color combination in one culture, may not be viewed as such in another.

STRUCTURING THE SECOND, THIRD, AND FOURTH AESTHETIC FIELDS

Regarding the second, third, and fourth aesthetic fields, the visual principles examined in the shooting of *Ramayan* involve several units of analysis that the Hindi producers manipulated to elicit viewer satisfaction with the production. Most pronounced are those shown within a celebration scene. Upon the announcement of the birth of Ram to his father the King, a festival occurs in which multiple dancers display their prowess. In this case, one can examine the cinematography of *Ramayan*'s dance scenes. There are three types of motion discussed in contextualism: primary (event motion in front of the camera), secondary (camera motion), and tertiary (editing). Dance is "primary" motion in aesthetic terms. Indian dancers are typically classically trained, although Indian folk dancing also has a strong tradition. Dance is said to be like a prayer to many religious Hindus. Each gesture of a dance can have a signification as precise as a word. The dancers use their bodies to recount complicated legends. The gestures are familiar only to the well-versed Hindu spectator. In this way, the total experience of viewing *Ramayan* may mirror the active forms of Hindu worship for those practicing the religion.

In an examination of the cultural influence of Hindi films on Indian television, Agrawal wrote that the Indian cinema is "uniquely Indian" (1998, p. 126). No more is this so than in the examination of the song and dance numbers that are standard formula in the genre. Because *Ramayan* borrows heavily from the Hindi cinema school, the dance scenes are similar to those found in many Indian commercial films. For instance, aside from the technical and religious aspects of the gestures in the dances, culture-specific gestures are included. They are sometimes performed in an exaggerated style, which is meant to add humor. Translation to those outside of the culture is necessary for complete comprehension. Likewise, as in the production of most Hindi cinema, "play back singing" is performed in *Ramayan*. The technique demands that songs be recorded and then played back over the action with actors lip-synching the songs on screen. This lip-syncing requires great visual precision by the actors and editors. However, the norm in Hindi Cinema is that the performances have a clear look of being dubbed. As a rule, U.S. audiences generally reject lip-synching if it is in the least bit perceivable, responding negatively to the production technique. But within India, *Ramayan*'s use of playback singing is quite acceptable primary motion to local audiences because it is the filmic precept in that culture.

Several aspects of the shooting of *Ramayan* are different than typical commercial television in the United States. First, visualization, which deals with the building of screen space, varies in terms of field of view and editing. Field of view involves how much of an image the shot includes and how far way the event is from the viewer's vantage point. As Messaris and Moriarty discuss, composition (as in point of view) can manipulate viewers eliciting analogical symbolism. In some of the beginnings of scenes in *Ramayan*, producers do not provide establishing shots (a wide shot that typically appears in Hollywood films in the first shot of a new scene to orient viewers to the location and time). This breaks a basic rule applied in most U.S. TV programs. For example, the dance scenes start with medium close-up shots instead of wide shots. Why this is so and how viewers deal with this symbolic disorientation is not exactly clear but the device is in contrast to American TV. The second point on the festival dance relates to all of the three types of motion discussed in contextualism: primary, secondary, and tertiary. As most dance scenes are constructed on TV around the world, the festival dance is blocked, shot, and edited to intensify screen space. In doing so, producers may have elicited a kind of cognitive and affective viewer participation. Images are placed together to provide a seemingly endless perspective of the scene (based on multiple fields of view and camera angles). This kind of editing incorporates countless camera angles, which serve as a visual metaphor to increase the energy of the dance scenes. Vectors are directional forces on the screen that make us look one way or another. A motion vector is created by an object moving in a specific direction on the screen. In *Ramayan*, viewers have to follow the dancers around the set through fast paced camera movements such as pans and zooms (types of "secondary motion"). A pan involves camera motion that moves from side to side ("X-axis motion vectors") while a zoom is camera motion toward or away from an object on the screen providing a sense of depth ("Z-axis motion vectors"). Also in *Ramayan*, "swish pans and zooms" (very fast pans/zooms) are used a number of times. They are often accompanied by an abrupt cut during either the pan or the zoom. Zettl (1973) explicitly warned against repeated use of swish pans and zooms, or cuts during them, because the devices are said to annoy viewers (making them feel dizzy). Yet the warning is ignored in *Ramayan*. Although used regularly in music videos today, swish pans and zooms were once considered "amateurish," according to so-called Western aesthetics. Apparently, *Ramayan*'s producers adopted the technique long before it became an established professional expression in the United States and the program's viewers did not react negatively to it.

Another element of secondary camera movement different about *Ramayan* is the repeated technique related to framing, angles, and vectors. Many shots begin above or below the actors and then pan to a centered position within their eye line. Often, shots then immediately zoom in or out avoiding any stagnation of the image. Like the swish pans and zooms, this technique was not encouraged by production books in the West (it was seen as too busy and distracting). It is not clear what this motif meant to local viewers but it clearly was acceptable. In the United States, shows like *Hill Street Blues* began to incorporate a somewhat similar cinema verite style of shooting despite what the books said (but not the same as *Ramayan*), with MTV, AT& T commercials, and *NYPD Blue* making them the norm today. This movement, albeit subtle, again requires fuller audience participation and is employed to attract viewers to the visuals. With so much visual (and aural) stimulus that one can encounter in India (even in watching television with others in ones home), perhaps the approach helped viewers to focus on the images.

Particularly unique in *Ramayan* is the repeated practice of combining the off-centered camera movement with using shots of the feet of actors before showing their faces. This fits in with the lack of establishing shots at the beginnings of some of the scenes. In *Ramayan*, the characters' feet are sometimes shown in this style when they are barefoot. This may be meant to be a statement on the representation of Hindu spirituality. The simplicity of the bare feet connotes humility. This is illustrated in the scene when the king makes a barefoot pilgrimage to his priest to conduct a sacrifice that will bring fertility to his wives. Accordingly, index vectors are used in a culture-specific way in *Ramayan*. Index vectors are directional forces that point unquestionably in a specific direction on the screen. Eyes are excellent index vectors because they look in one direction or another, which causes viewers to look those ways as well. Eyes are also very effective communicators within and across cultures. In *Ramayan*, many shots show actors looking down or away from the expected directions during conversations. Within the story line, this makes sense since it would be viewed as disrespectful for peasants to look directly at kings or gods. It is a subtle aspect of the culture that viewers could know relates to religious caste and class differences as well.

Another aesthetic element that was used in *Ramayan* but is rarely seen in U.S. television is the mix of film and video within the scenery of the episode. Interior shots are videoed while exteriors are filmed. When narratives alternate between two or more lines of action, they suggest that the different actions are occurring simultaneously or are thematically related (Blandford, Grant, & Hillier, 2001). Through this parallel editing, the indoor images of the kingdom are juxtaposed against a village location. The effect is one in which nature is depicted with a lower resolution image. The graininess of the exterior shots portrays a sense of reality in that the images look like they belong in a documentary. Why this is done is not explained (perhaps stock footage was incorporated as a matter of budget constraints) but the aesthetic brings India's reality to the surface. The motif of "the village" is a social construction of reality that exists in developing countries today, yet there is little that is similar to the experience in the developed world. According to the 2001 Indian census, there is a 52% literacy rate within the country.[7] In the absence of high levels of literacy in parts of the nation, much of Hindu mythology is passed along through festival songs and dances often depicted in rural settings. Through the use of this kind of open set, there is a shared meaning among *Ramayan*'s viewers not only of the story of the myth and its ancient nonurbanized time, but also of the importance of agriculture and survival in nature. Likewise, even highly literate urban audiences are encouraged to feel a reminiscent bond to village life upon viewing the performance. The image is a subtle frame of reference focused on the joy of tradition, which carries an undertone deeper than the obvious happy emotions portrayed through smiling faces in the dance scenes, for example.

Other elements in *Ramayan* that vary from U.S. productions seem incidental to the narrative, thus their meaning is unclear. For instance, some of the action is presented more as a live performance than a pretaped show, because blocking includes inaccuracies. This may be meant to add to its charm (i.e., a child moving one way, then correcting his actions during the scene is left in the final edit). Further, jump cuts, which are a break in the continuity of a shot or between two shots caused by removing a portion and placing together what remains, appear in a few of the scenes (Blandford et al., 2001). A couple of the superimpositions (two images displayed at once) during the festival contain jump cuts, as does one of the monologues of the God Shiva. Finally, the episode ends very abruptly with a title and music suddenly replacing one of the god's commentaries on the events. Overall, it is unknown whether these aspects of the visual vocabulary created in Ramayan were calculated or unplanned, but a producer of Ramayand Sagar's stature is likely to incorporate preferred production standards. Still, budget constraints may have affected production and local artists know that Third World audiences are more accepting of these kinds of "inconveniences" than those in the West.

One final point can be made about the style of shooting of Hindi films that likely influenced production of programs like *Ramayan*, though not the first episode of the show itself. The rapid editing in Hindi song and dance scenes include many complete changes of set and costume. This is constructed through parallel editing. For example, the same two dancers will be depicted in a given song against several backgrounds and wearing numerous costumes (particularly on the female of the duo). This is entertaining, perhaps especially for audience members constrained to less affluent fashions and surroundings. Although standard fare in some Western music videos today, these kinds of visuals in *Ramayan* have been part of a common lexicon of Hindi films long before MTV performers ever incorporated it.

CONCLUSION

Question one examined what visual production elements of Indian religious soap operas like *Ramayan* are aesthetically different from the so-called professional standards most widely taught to TV producers within the United States. Television producers know that choice of aesthetic codes is driven not only by technological innovation but also by formulas firmly grounded in culture. In the case of *Ramayan*, traditional Western technical standards were not always applied to the four levels of production examined.[8] Through question two, one can hypothesize that *Ramayan* serves to counter charges that worldwide television is essentially similar. Of course, Indian television programs have evolved dramatically since *Ramayan*'s first showing in 1987. Continued research of this kind may show that Western professional television conventions are becoming more universal across cultures. Still, traditional Hindi films have not changed that much and the powerful industry's influence on television is evident.

In a sense, *Ramayan* promoted an aesthetic revival in the region. By creating a demand for the imagery, television producers have reached back into the pool of ancient

Hindu art treasures and recreated Hindu culture for television. Given the opportunity to be creative, perhaps Indian producers already resist the trend toward Westernization of aesthetics of visual media, such as television. It is a subtle aspect of the problem to measure and for some, perhaps, a minor issue. Marxist influenced critics noted that the commercialization of the over 100 episodes of *Ramayan* made the program, "the opium of the masses" (sic) (Bhatia, 1989, p. 75). They argued that audience obsession with religious soap operas distract the nation from addressing the needs of the poor and help to maintain an oppressive religious caste system (Bista, 1989). Likewise, feminist scholars could argue that programs like it maintain outdated gender roles (note the lines in the script that say the queens are "empty" if not mothers and have "increased their worth" upon childbirth). Still, it is likely the trend to serialize religious mythologies on television will continue in the region because of their popularity and wide commercial sponsorship (Thussu, 2000). In either case, exploring the processing of televisual codes in non-Western genres is illustrative from a cross-cultural perspective.

Question three was meant to offer insights specifically into issues of visual literacy that might help producers of pro-development programming better discern non-Western analogical connections and connotational meanings of their potential viewers. After many years of research on "entertainment-education" relying mainly on audience surveys (along with some content analyses and audience letter feedback), Singhal and Rogers (2002) urged methodological pluralism. Media literacy applied through the examination of the contextual aesthetics of soap operas in developing countries does provide an innovative framework in which to know what goes into creating such a popular genre within a given culture. Understanding "what works and what does not" (according to Messaris and Moriarty) within a cultural context may bring producers one step closer to creating better media campaigns as a tool for education and national development in countries like India. For instance, identifying what visual cues in religious soaps promote consumerism or classism (multiple costume changes, lack of eye contact between rich and poor) versus *dharma* (humility and humane action—religious or otherwise—through images connected to nature, like walking through forests in bare feet, etc.) is inherently useful to those concerned with the preservation of indigenous art forms and the improvement of life for the impoverished in the Third World. Hopefully, what we learn about television production through the study of visual communication and culture in popular religious soap operas like India's *Ramayan* can add to the overall success of less commercial prodevelopment television programs in the future.

ENDNOTES

[1] Messaris and Moriarty define Howard Gardner's concept of *spatial intelligence* as the process producers need to undergo to form a mental representation of three-dimensional reality.

[2] The first of its kind, *Simplemente Maria*, appeared on television in 1969.

[3] *Ramayan* is by no means meant to be defined as edutainment.

[4] *Ramayan* aired in many countries besides India, including Nepal, Sri Lanka, Malaysia, Indonesia, and Surinam.

[5] The Indian film industry is the world's largest producer of feature films (Thussu, 2000).

⁶ Hinduism is known to have arisen in the Ganges Valley in Asia in the second half of the first millennium BC. Approximately 82% of Indians are Hindus (2001 Indian Census).

⁷ See http://millenniumindicators.un.org/unsd/methods/inter-natlinks/sd_natstat.htm.

⁸ For a detailed discussion on musical ragas and Hindi film songs, see Burch (2002).

REFERENCES

Abbs, P. (1989). Aesthetic education: A small manifesto. *Journal of Aesthetic Education, 23*(4), 75–85.

Agrawal, B. C. (1998). Cultural influence of Indian cinema on Indian television. In Shrinivas R. Melkote, Peter Shields, & Binod C. Agrawal (Eds.), *International satellite broadcasting in South Asia: Political, economic and cultural implications* (pp. 123–130). Oxford: University Press of America.

Allen, R. C. (1995). *To be continued: Soap operas around the world.* New York: Routledge.

Arnheim, R. (1969). *Art and visual perception.* Berkeley: University of California Press.

Barker, D. (2000). Television production techniques as communication. In Horace Newcomb (Ed.), *Television: The critical view* (pp. 169–182). New York: Oxford University Press.

Bharata, M. (1967). *The Natyasastra: A treatise on ancient Indian dramaturgy and histrionics.* Calcutta, India: Manisha Granthalaya.

Bhatia, J. (1989, March). War by another means. *Far Eastern Economic Review,* 76–77.

Bista, D. B. (1989, September/October). Ramayana, ramayana, ramayana. *Himal, 1*(4), 30.

Bista, D. B. (1991). *Fatalism and development: Nepal's struggle for modernization.* Calcutta, India: Orient Longman Limited.

Blandford, S., Grant, B., & Hillier, J. (2001). *The film studies dictionary.* New York: Oxford University Press.

Burch, E. A. (2002). Media literacy, cultural proximity and TV aesthetics: Why Indian soap operas work in Nepal and the Hindu Diaspora. *Media, Culture & Society, 24*(4), 569–577.

DeBenediittus, P. (2001). Available at: www.medialiteracy.net.

Fiske, J., & Hartley, J. (1978). *Reading television.* London: Methuen.

Goonasekera, A. (1987). The influence of television on cultural values: With special reference to third world countries. *Media Asia, 14*(1), 7–11.

Hall, S. (1980). Encoding/decoding. In Stuart Hall, Dorothy Hobson, Andrew Lowe, & Paul Willis (Eds.), *Culture, media, language* (pp. 128–138). London: Hutchinson.

Hegal, G. W. F. (1979). *Hegal's introduction to aesthetics.* M. Knox, Trans. New York: Oxford University Press.

Hobbs, R., Frost, R., Davis, A., & Stauffer, J. (1988). How first time viewers comprehend editing conventions. *Journal of Communication, 38*(4), 33–44.

Ions, V. (1967). *Indian mythology.* London: Hamlyn.

Katz, E., & Liebes, T. (1984). Once upon a time in *Dallas. Intermedia, 12*(3), 28–32.

Lang, A., Zhou, S., Schwartz, N., Bolls, P. D., & Potter, R. F. (2000). The effects of edits on arousal, attention and memory for television messages: When an edit is an edit can an edit be too much? *Journal of Broadcasting and Electronic Media, 44*(1), 94–109.

Lewis, J., & Jhally, S. (2000). The struggle over media literacy. In Horace Newcomb (Ed.), *Television: The critical view* (pp. 439–450). New York: Oxford University Press.

Liebes, T. (1988). Cultural differences in the retelling of television fiction. *Critical Studies in Mass Communication, 5*(4), 277–292.

McFee, J. K. (1978). Cultural influences on aesthetic experience. In Jack Condous, Janferie Howlett, & John Skull (Eds.), *Arts in cultural Diversity* (pp. 45–52). Australia: INSEA World Congress.

Mitra, A. (1993). *Television and popular culture in India: A study of the Mahabharat.* New Delhi, India: Sage.

Nordenstreng, K., & Schiller, H. I. (1979). *National sovereignty and international communications.* Norwood, NJ: Ablex.

Nordenstreng, K., & Varis, T. (1974). *Television traffic: A one-way street.* UNESCO: Paris.

Ogden-Gurung, S. (Producer). (1987). *Video in Dhoko* [Video].

Potter, J. W. (2001). *Media literacy.* Thousand Oaks, CA: Sage.

Sagar, R. (Producer). (1987). *Ramayan* [Video].

Sherry, J. L. (2002). Media saturation and entertainment-education. *Communication Theory, 12*(2), 206–224.

Singhal, A., & Rogers, E. M. (1989). Prosocial television for development in India. In Ronald E. Rice & Charles Atkins (Eds.), *Public communication campaign* (pp. 331–350). Thousand Oaks, CA: Sage.

Singhal, A., & Rogers, E. M. (2002). A theoretical agenda for entertainment-education. *Communication Theory, 12*(2), 117–135.

Straubhaar, J. D. (1991). Beyond media imperialism: Asymmetrical interdependence and cultural proximity. *Critical Studies in Mass Communication, 8*(1), 1–11.

Straubhaar, J. D. (1997). Distinguishing the global, regional and national levels of world television. In Annabelle Sreberny-Mohammadi, Dwayne Winseck, Jim McKenna, & Oliver Boyd-Barrett (Eds.), *Media in global context: A reader* (pp. 284–298). New York: Oxford University Press.

Straubhaar, J. D., Burch, E. A., Duarte, L. G., & Sheffer, P. (2002). International satellite television networks: Gazing at the global village or looking for "home video?" In Carolyn A. Lin & David J. Atkin (Eds.), *Communication, technology and society: Audience adoption and uses* (pp. 307–327). Cresskill, NJ: Hampton Press.

Sukla, A. C. (2001). *Art and representation: Contributions to contemporary aesthetics.* New York: Praeger.

Thussu, D. K. (2000). *International communication: Continuity and change.* New York: Oxford University Press.

Tomlinson, J. (1991). *Cultural imperialism: A critical introduction.* Baltimore: Johns Hopkins University Press.

Tunstall, J. (1977). *The media are American.* New York: Columbia University Press.

World Development Indicators Database. (2002). World Bank. Available at: http://devdata.worldbank.org.

Worth, S., & Adair, J. (1972). *Through Navajo eyes.* Bloomington: University of Indiana Press.

Zettl, H. (1973). *Sight, sound, motion: Applied media aesthetics.* California: Wadsworth.

Zettl, H. (1990). *Sight, sound, motion: Applied media aesthetics* (2nd ed.). California: Wadsworth.

Zettl, H. (1998). Contextual media aesthetics as the basis for media literacy. *Journal of Communication, 48*(1), 81–95.

Cultural Studies

31

Cultural Studies Theory

VICTORIA O'DONNELL
Montana State University

INTRODUCTION

In a recent episode of *ER*, the long-running television drama about a Chicago hospital emergency room, two African American surgeons, Dr. Peter Benton and Dr. Cleo Finch, are seen attending to a patient while nearby on the other side of the room, a group of five medical students, four men and one woman, are getting a tour of the emergency facilities. Dr. Finch, who is very light in color, says, "What is wrong with this picture?" Dr. Benton, who has much darker skin, is focusing on his patient and says, "Hmm?" Dr. Finch then says, "Those medical students—not a black face in the bunch. Getting no response from him, Dr. Finch says, "That doesn't concern you?" Dr. Benton looks up at the students and replies, "I see five. Not exactly a representative sample." She responds with, "I'm glad you take such an interest." He chuckles and nothing else is said, but the look that is exchanged between these two doctors, who are also lovers, is probably meant to imply that Dr. Benton is not going to make an issue of racial diversity and that he can be quite patronizing when it come to logic. This is consistent with his character on the series, for he is a brilliant, competent, and ambitious but arrogant surgeon.

A cultural studies analysis would ask what meaning could viewers make of this brief scene? One viewer might agree with Dr. Finch that there should be better racial representation. Another might agree with Dr. Benton's logic, concluding that you cannot generalize from a small sample. Another might conclude that practicing good medicine is an African American doctor's only concern. Someone else might say that both positions are fairly represented and that is all right. There could be other meanings. For example, one could dispute the untypical representation of race in an elitist profession that required years of study at great financial cost because such circumstances are unavailable to those without opportunity. Although Dr. Benton, professionally acted by Eric La Salle, is an extremely competent surgeon, he is also very arrogant and moody, thus another viewer might say that he is "uppity" and erudite and no longer in touch with people of his race.

Michael Michele, who plays Dr. Finch, is tall, model-thin, and beautiful. Another viewer might see her as nonrepresentative of women in general or black women in particular and therefore be unable to identify with her or her attitude at all. For others, she could be a role model of what other women want to become. Someone else could observe that Dr. Finch did not say anything about the disproportionate ratio of men to women in the group of five medical students. Still another might note that because the Chief of Staff, Dr. Romano, and the Chief Attending Emergency Room doctor, Dr. Green, are white males, they represent white male dominance over the African American doctors.

These various meanings are some of the possible responses of several viewers on seeing a brief scene on television. Cultural studies theorists understand that many meanings can be made from a single scene because viewers observe and interpret images and supporting dialogue through the lens of their own cultural experiences. A cultural studies analyst focuses on both the visual image and the verbal discourse, for they may converge into meaning or perhaps incite observers to perceive contradictory meanings if the image and the discourse are at odds with one another. In visual media such as film, television, and advertising, the visual communication is likely to be prominent and central in provoking viewer-meaning. Nevertheless, the verbal communication is usually inherent in the medium and likewise subject to interpretation of meaning. This chapter highlights visual imagery in cultural studies whenever possible without compromising the ideas in cultural studies.

One collection of readings in cultural studies that isolates the visual is *Visual Culture*, edited by Jessica Evans and Stuart Hall, who remind us that the meaning of an image, whether in a photograph, a painting or drawing, a film, or on television or a computer screen, is "not in the visual sign itself as a self-sufficient entity, nor exclusively in the sociological positions and identities of the audience, but in the articulation between viewer and viewed, between the power of the image to signify and the viewer's capacity to interpret meaning" (1999, p. 4) The presence of a viewer as the necessary other and whose conduct an image provokes makes meaning possible. The spectator, the image, and the meaning are not in a relationship of cause and effect; rather the relationship is a complex one in which various elements interact and lead to an outcome that is dependent on one's culture and the cultural practices of looking and seeing. Consequently, the possibility of multiple meanings, *polysemy*, exists depending on the interpretations of various spectators who bring their own subjectivities to the image and take up various positions of identification in relation to its meaning. Furthermore, whatever meaning is derived is not necessarily fixed or stable across time. It is also important that multiple meanings of various subjects not be reduced to a common mean or median, for the recognition and understanding of the encoding and individual decoding of representations is at the heart of cultural studies.

CULTURE AND CULTURAL STUDIES

Cultural studies theory and methodology are not monolithic. Cultural studies has genealogical connections with several academic areas of study, including anthropology, literary criticism, social history, semiotics, political economics, psychoanalysis, and feminist criticism. It has included many theoretical pathways and crosscuts, some of them in contention. The theories of Karl Marx, Antonio Gramsci, Louis Althusser, Michel Foucault, Roland Barthes, Jacques Derrida, Raymond Williams, Stuart Hall, Lawrence Grossberg, and others have constituted foundations for the derivation of cultural studies. Furthermore, cultural studies practitioners have responded to changing historical and political conditions. The emergence of social movements in the 1960s and 1970s and subsequent changes in legal and social conditions related to equality for blacks, women, ethnic groups, and gays also changed the nature of academic inquiry into literature and popular culture. Consequently, there are many ways to conduct a cultural study.[1] It is not the purpose of this chapter to chronicle the history and various theories behind cultural studies, but rather this chapter offers selected theories from some of the most influential figures in contemporary cultural studies that can be merged in order to set forth a clear and workable method for conducting an analysis. Although it is impossible to separate cultural theoretical inquiry into written discourse and visual image, this chapter attempts to focus on the visual image by emphasizing cultural theoretical concerns with image, representation, and viewer response.

The notion of *culture*, of course, is inherent in most intellectual endeavors, but it can be a confusing term. Culture is sometimes thought of as high and low, or, in other words, elite culture such as art, classical music, literature, theater, and the like, and popular culture such as film, television, popular music, cartoons, magazines, computer games, and so on. Culture is also what anthropologists study to learn the folkways of various human societies. For the purpose of this chapter, culture is defined as *the actual practices and customs, languages, beliefs, forms of representation, and system of formal and informal rules that tell people how to behave most of the time.* Culture produces shared social meanings (i.e., the ways that we make sense of the world). Our social practices can, in turn, alter the culture by creating new meanings to be shared (Jowett & O'Donnell, 1999). James Carey, an important writer on communication and culture, pointed out, "Culture as a system of construed meanings changes in relation to other cultural objects such as technologies and economic practices or other social processes such as conflict and accommodation, such changes are transformations on a given cultural tradition, a tradition that insists on reasserting itself" (1988, p. 11).

BRITISH CULTURAL STUDIES

Cultural studies, as we have come to know it, grew out of the British cultural studies movement, primarily from the vision of Raymond Williams, a fellow at Jesus College, Cambridge, who wrote in 1961 that there was no academic subject that allowed him to ask the question concerning how culture and society, democracy and the individual voice interrelate (Couldry, 2000, p. 1). In a 1958 essay "Culture is Ordinary," Williams (in Gray & McGuigan, 1993) emphasized that culture concerns everyone. Culture is not just Shakespeare or Beethoven; rather it is the symbolic life of peoples, and for Williams, it was especially the customs of working-class life. I attended a tribute to Williams at the National Film Theater in London in October 1988 where several of his BBC videos were shown posthumously. In one he talked about the 18th-century paintings of England's great estates that depicted beautiful land and domestic animals. One painting had sheep peacefully grazing on a meadow with a little girl "dressed up" in shepherd's clothes sitting against a tree. Williams asked, "Where are the real shepherds?" His point was that the workers on whom the running of the state depended were all but invisible. Williams insisted on thinking about an 18th-century painting or a 19th-century novel from a much broader range of cultural practice. He spoke of cultural formation, emphasizing that "cultural texts should never be seen as isolated but always as part of a shared practice of making meaning involving everyone in a particular culture" (Couldry, 2000, p. 24). Williams went beyond an elitist definition of culture as high culture, and he was aware of the anthropological definition of culture, but he wanted to develop a way to analyze works of high or popular culture from a new perspective, as specific works and as an ongoing life process. He asked questions such as:

1. How does a work (any work) relate to the shared living conditions of the time?
2. What meanings does a work have when it is absorbed into the lives of its audiences?

For Williams, cultural studies filled a gap as a distinctive approach to culture that values each person's voice and reflections. Although he concerned himself with local practices, especially in the Welsh working-class community, his notion of community as a space where each person has the right to be heard (or seen) is a basic tenet of cultural studies.

Writing in 2000, Nick Couldry claimed that actual culture as practiced is still a concentration, not a dispersal, of voices that prevents us from speaking directly in our own voice because we are represented by others. He said that speech and image are closed and commodified, that is, turned into a market commodity. He advocated complete openness of representation. This is why he says that "culture" is a paradoxical term, a paradox that each of us as individuals may feel (2000, p. 2).

Perhaps the most influential and prominent British cultural studies scholar is Stuart Hall, whose work has made an international impact. He began his work at the Center for Contemporary Cultural Studies at the University of Birmingham and continued it at the Open University in Milton Keynes. Today he is a professor emeritus at the Open University and a Visiting Professor at Goldsmiths College, University of London. Hall broadened the scope of Williams' inquiries to include matters of race and immigration in the United Kingdom. Hall's theories include the study of both discourse and images. Two major premises are theorized by Hall: (a) Images are always associated with power, and (b) Images have different meanings or no meaning at all. There is no guarantee that viewers will interpret the images in the way that they are intended. The second premise is the basis for Hall's famous model of encoding/decoding meanings, which is explained in a later section of this chapter.

IMAGES AND POWER

That images (and discourse) are always associated with power relations is the one premise that all cultural studies practitioners agree on. Power relations, whether driven by economics, politics, or social discrimination, are said to determine who is represented and who is not, who speaks and who is silent, which issues are important and which ones are not. Power is related to dominance and/or superiority of ideology, another central concept in cultural studies. Ideology is a conceptual framework that includes

> a set of beliefs, values, attitudes, and behaviors, as well as ways of perceiving and thinking that are agreed on to the point that they constitute a set of norms for a society that dictate what is desirable and what should be done.... Ideology contains concepts about what the society in which it exists is actually like. It states or denies, for example, that there are classes and that certain conditions are desirable or more desirable than others. An ideology is also a form of consent to a particular kind of social order and conformity to the rules within a specific set of social, economic, and political structures. It often assigns roles of dominance or subordination to gender, race, sexuality, religion, age, and social groups." (Jowett & O'Donnell, 1999, p. 281)

Another related term that important is *hegemony*, defined as the power or dominance that one group holds over another. Antonio Gramsci, an Italian political theorist in the 1920s whose work was primarily written while he was in prison and was translated into English in the 1970s, said that hegemony is "forceful but not automatic persuasion emanating from the dominant controllers of culture to the less powerful masses of society. Consent rather than coercion persuades the marginalized people to accept the status quo" (Real, 1996, p. 29). Cultural hegemony occurs when a strand of meanings tends to be dominant, producing, maintaining, and reproducing authoritative sets of meanings and practices (Barker, 2000, p. 260). In other words, there is a power to shape the ways things look and what they would seem to mean. Yet people have power also to struggle against and change ideology and to alter hegemony.

The early work in British cultural studies was a critique of contemporary society, critiques of ideological domination and political power that tended to show how hegemony or the dominant ideology reproduced itself invisibly and inevitably. The media seemed to position viewers within images and discourse as subjects living and thinking under specific conditions of domination by authority. Williams explained, however, that although those who were assimilated into the dominant ideology "*do* think; if they do not speak, it may be because we have taken their speech away from them, deprived them of the means of enunciation, not because they have nothing to say" (Grossberg, p. 140). Hall (1997) recognized that the audience is not passive, rather they are active consumers who decode images and make their own meanings. This was a turning point in cultural studies, bringing the recognition that images and discourses did not have a single meaning, but they are open texts, capable of being interpreted in different ways by different people, thus the term "polysemy," a multiplicity of meaning.

POLYSEMY AND ARTICULATION

Working within the framework of Gramsci's concept of hegemony, Hall developed a theory of "articulation" in order to explain how receivers used a produced message and derived meaning from it. The word articulation is commonly defined as some kind of joining of parts to make a unity, including dentistry and medical procedures. Common use of articulation in speech suggests the clinging together of sounds. Hall said that articulation is

> the form of the connection that can make a unity of two different elements, under certain conditions. It is a linkage which is not necessary, determined, absolute and essential for all time. You have to ask, *under what circumstances can a connection be forged or made?* (italics are mine)... the "unity" which matters is a linkage between the articulated discourse and the social forces with which it can, under certain historical conditions, but need not necessarily be connected. (Slack in Morley & Chen, 1996, p. 115)

The theory is called articulation because meaning has to be expressed and joined to a context of some kind. An image, for example, is produced within a specific context, a specific time in history, and, in a medium, for example, a television program, a magazine, cartoon, a film, or a computer site. Hall offered the metaphor of a trailer truck to help explain his theory: the front (cab) and back (trailer) can but need not necessarily be connected to one another. The two parts are connected to each other but through a specific linkage that can be broken. He said, "the theory of articulation... enables us to think how an ideology empowers people, enabling them to make some sense or intelligiblity of their historical situation, without reducing those forms of intelligibility to their socio-economic or class location or social position" (Grossberg in Morley and Chen, 1996, pp. 141–142). Thus articulation suggests the expression or representation of an image, a reception of it, and a link to other cultural domains. In an interview at the University of Massachusetts in 1989, Hall said that articulation is

> an understanding of the circuits of capital as an articulation of the moments of production with the moments of consumption, with the moments of realization, with the moments of reproduction.... Production, consumption, realization, reproduction-the expanding circuit.... You have to know, analytically, why consumption and production are different in order to talk about how they're articulating. (Cruz & Lewis, 1990, pp. 255–257)

Later in the interview, Hall clarified that although there is a continuous process of signification of the cultural/ideological world, his encoding/decoding model is about the specific practice of making and responding to television programs or a literary text or a bureaucratic paper or any other kind of recodification. A specific practice may have a specific ideology that opposes the dominant cultural ideology that exists in the world. In other words, Hall said that he takes the cultural/ideological world as something which always exists, and within that world, he analyzes what is specific about the activity of a certain practice and response to it (Cruz & Lewis, 1990, pp. 259–163). This process is not the same as deconstruction, which Hall feels has been made into a kind of intellectual playground. Every moment of deconstruction, to Hall, is also a moment of reconstruction, the production of a new meaning.

HALL'S ENCODING/DECODING MODEL

Hall's theory of encoding/decoding is thus based on the premise that there is a correlation between a person's social situation and the meanings that person decodes from an encoded image or discourse. There is no single meaning for a message. If the decoded meaning is the same as the encoded meaning, then there would be perfect hegemony. However, if the image/discourse is representative of the dominant ideology and the viewer's social situation is not, then there is tension resulting in a negotiation between the viewer and the image/discourse. In other words, the viewer does not necessarily passively accept the dominant meaning unless it is preferred by the viewer. The choice of the word *preferred* is deliberate because it indicates that the viewer has some power in interpreting meaning, yet it is important also to remember that the viewer's decoding takes place *within* the encoding process.

According to Hall, an image/discourse "hails" a viewer as it were hailing a taxi. In other words, it calls to the viewer. To answer the "hailing," the viewer must recognize that it is she or he, and not someone else, being hailed. To respond to the hailing, a viewer recognizes the social position that has been constructed in encoding the image/discourse, and if the response is cooperative, the meaning is adopted. Thus, returning to the example of the scene from *ER* at the beginning of this chapter, if the viewers are hailed as nonracist, equal opportunists, and they accept that position, then they constitute themselves as *subjects* in an ideological definition that the television program proposes. A subject is a social construction who recognizes one's social position, thus a hail is created by the encoding process through which a viewer is addressed, summoned, questioned, or challenged. If the viewer accepts the position in the program, then that person accepts the subject position that has been encoded and decodes it accordingly. The program hails the viewer who, if recognizing oneself as being spoken to, constitutes the self as being addressed in the ideological definition of subject that the program proposes.

Initially, Hall's model had three social positions: dominant, oppositional, and negotiated, although Hall speculated that there could be other positions. The dominant position is accepted when the viewer accepts the dominant or intended meaning; whereas the oppositional position is in direct opposition to the dominant meaning or an acceptance of an opposite point of view. The negotiated position is a completely open category for viewers who primarily fit into the dominant ideology but need to resist certain elements of it. Negotiated positions are popular with various social groups who question their relationship to the dominant ideology. Negotiated meanings are what most people get out of messages most of the time. Cultural studies analysts may examine audience decoding through ethnographic methods, using in-depth interviews, often over time, to determine how people actively make sense of media images and discourse, social experience, and themselves. Cultural studies analysts also work in a manner similar to literary critics, but the "texts" they examine are media discourse and visual images. In the latter instance, the critic attempts to make sense of a meaning from personal experience or attempt to derive multiple meanings as the result of analysis. As in the example of the scene from *ER*, the decoded meanings are hypothetical based on the framework of my assumptions. We decode by interpreting, said Hall, "from the family in which you were

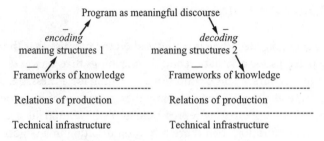

FIG. 31.1.   Stuart Hall's Encoding/Decoding Model.

brought up, the places of work, the institutions you belong to, the other practices you do" (Cruz & Lewis, 1990, p. 270). When we belong to the same communities, we may share the meanings we derive. Fig. 31.1 depicts Hall's model (Hall in During, 1993, p. 510), which he developed for television originally in 1973 but modified, as shown, in 1980: Meaning structures 1 and 2 may not be the same, for encoding and decoding are not likely to be symmetrical. Meaning intended by producing certain codes is not necessarily meaning received based on interpretation of codes.[2]

Television images are complex because they are based on visual representation. Television images are mediated images; three-dimensional places, people, and objects viewed on a two-dimensional plane; not life-size; and produced by technical means controlled by cameras and camera angles and movement, directing, lighting, computer manipulation, and editing. As images, they are representations, that is, commonly considered to be production attempts to duplicate, although they are not duplications because they have been constructed to represent or imitate the real. The real is a thing in the world in its own right. Representation is a construction that tries to be recognizable as the real; it is a substitute, an imitation that attempts to evoke a response as if to the real thing. A representation is, thus, a "constructed, artificial character of forms of life, in contrast to the organic, biological connotations of 'culture'" (Mitchell, 1995, p. 423).

Of course, a representation can also be a symbol, something that stands for something else. Understanding of symbols requires learning the connections between symbols and what they stand for. There need not be any verisimilitude between a symbolic image and what the image is about. The heart-shaped symbol ♡ tends to stand for love in our culture, but a connection had to be learned between the image and its meaning. In a culture where the heart-shaped symbol has no known meaning, it is unlikely to get a response, or it may get a different response. On the other hand, an anatomical drawing of a human heart should be a representation of a real human heart to anyone anywhere in the world who has adequate knowledge of human anatomy.

Hall has two important works on representation, a book (Hall, 1997), and a video (Jhally, 1996), in which he questions representation as a reflection of the real, that is, depicting something, a singular and fixed meaning, that is already there. Consistent with his encoding/decoding model (Fig. 31.1), Hall said that representation constitutes multiple meanings because reality itself has multiple meanings. There is no one thing that is so fixed that it will always be represented in a certain way. True meanings depend on the meanings that different people derive from a representation. Furthermore, a representation does not exist after the event because it is in the context of the event. He recommended that we "go inside the image itself" to ask:

- What is present and what is absent?
- What is at stake in a representation?
- How does the meaning that we derive implicate us in the production of that meaning?
- How are we limited in our ways of seeing?
- Can we place ourselves inside the image, identifying with it?
- What do we get out of the image if we identify ourselves in relationship to the image?
- Is there meaning that is different from what we expected to find in a representation?
- Are there new meanings, new identities, new knowledge?

There is no guarantee that the viewer can answer all of these questions, for the image can touch levels of a person's experience "beyond the purely rational level of awareness, and disturb by the very way in which they exceed meaning. The cultural practices of looking and seeing, then, . . . rest on complex conditions of existence, some of which have psychic and unconscious dimensions"(Evans & Hall, 1999, p. 312). Yet Hall believed that we can discover and play with identifications of ourselves and observe how we are imagined in representations. We may even discover something of ourselves for the first time. What is important to Hall is openness to understanding that what a person thinks one week may change the next. Although Hall made significant contributions to cultural studies theory, he insisted that the practice of studying culture be open-ended: "Cultural studies has to be open to external influences, for example, to the rise of new social movements, to psychoanalysis, to feminism, to cultural differences" (Morley & Chen, 1996, p. 150). John Fiske, an Australian academic who teaches at the University of Wisconsin, praised Hall for making us aware that "people are neither cultural dupes nor silenced victims, but are vital, resilient, varied, contradictory, and as a source of constant contestations of dominance, are a vital social resource, the only one that can fuel social change" (Fiske in Morley & Chen, 1996, p. 220). Fiske amplified Hall's model by delineating the encoding process, specifically in a television production, in his book *Television Culture*, thus providing the cultural studies analyst with a set of categories to examine.

THE CODES OF TELEVISION PRODUCTION

Fiske regards television as the bearer, provoker, and circulator of meanings and, like Hall, believes that television is replete with potential meanings. He also believes that through the means of television production, a preferred meaning is attempted. To encode a preferred meaning, recognition of the codes is helpful. Fiske defined "code" semiotically as "a rule- governed system of signs, whose rules and conventions are shared amongst members of a culture, and which is used to generate and circulate meanings in and for that culture" (1987, p. 4). In television, codes link the programs and the audiences by utilizing the conventional codes of our culture. In other words, according to Fiske, "reality is encoded, or rather the only way we can perceive and make sense of reality is by the codes of our culture" (1987, p. 4). A casting director for television, Fiske says, uses these codes most conventionally and subsequently stereotypically. Fiske organized the categories of codes into three levels: Reality, Representation, and Ideology.

Reality

Reality, as noted, is already encoded by certain *social codes* that relate to appearance, behavior, speech, sound, and setting. Appearance includes skin color, clothing, hair, makeup, speech, facial expressions, and gestures. Speech includes spoken language, accent, dialect, formal or vernacular style, and paralanguage, such as pitch, rate, and inarticulate utterances. Sound includes natural sounds, such as wind or rain, and artificial sounds, such as sirens or music. Indoor settings may denote place, such as an office, a living room, or a hospital. Objects in the place may denote taste, social class, and could promote certain feelings such as comfort or tension. Outdoor settings may suggest peace and tranquility or fear and danger. Obviously, much depends on other codes to encode certain preferred meanings. Some physical behaviors, for example, dancing, kissing, shaking hands, playing sports, fighting, and so on, may be easily recognized as such. Others require more contextual information and supplemental codes to provoke meaning. Makeup can be dramatic or subtle, and certain personality qualities can be conveyed with it. The appearance of little makeup on a woman may convey "naturalness" to some viewers; whereas heavy application of makeup may be a sign of falseness or poor taste to others. Once again, much depends on the other codes as they are put together to form a whole. Hair is similar and depends on other codes as well; however, it is a conventional code that short hair on a man is considered more common; whereas long hair on a man may suggest that he is a nonconformist in some way, for example, a rock musician or an artist. Obviously, more information is necessary before one can draw conclusions about social codes, and, furthermore, different people will interpret these codes in different ways. Social codes, once chosen for a television program, are encoded by representation.

Representation

Representation on television is encoded by technical codes with the camera, lighting, sound, music, and editing in order to transmit conventional representational codes in order to convey the narrative, conflict, character, action, dialogue, setting, casting, and so forth. The following technical codes, as indicated by Fiske, have not been explained in all their technical complexity, nor could they be in a single chapter. They are, however, vital to representation on television and are suggested here as types of technical codes that function to encode meaning together with other codes used in television production.

Camera use (placement angle, distance, movement, framing, and focus) like other technical codes can be specified by the director in order to achieve desired effects. A close-up, for example, may be used to represent intimacy on one hand or to reveal anxiety by emphasizing a person's furrowed brow or tears. *Lighting* changes the way we look at people by the way it is placed, for example, to create shadows across a person's face or to provide a certain color for special effect. *Editing* is a powerful way to provide continuity when none exists or to transform time, interaction, and other elements and rhythms. For example, I was on a public television forum on television violence and children with eight other panelists. The moderator spoke at the beginning and then not again for 2 hours during which the nine panelists discussed the topic while being videotaped. When we finished, the moderator was videotaped, speaking into the camera for about 10 minutes. The final program was edited to appear that the moderator would ask a question and two or three of the panelists would respond to it. The moderator appeared to be chairing a panel discussion. The responses had been carefully edited to fit the moderator's questions. *Sound and music* create mood, attitude, and other various emotions. Music is also thematic and can suggest a program and various characters. This is a cursory discussion of technical codes, which deserve a much more thorough treatment than can be given in this chapter. It is important, however, to recognize the role that technical codes play in encoding meaning.

Representational codes have to work together to encode a preferred meaning and to appear natural at the same time. A script provides the setting, narrative, conflict, action, dialogue, and characters, but the actors who are cast in various roles bring the characters and the plot to life. Casting of characters is complex because actors are real people whom viewers may know in other contexts, for example, films, talk shows, magazines, and so on. Certain actors bring with them other intertextual meanings. Robert Downey Jr.'s character, Larry, on *Ally McBeal*, for example, has nothing to do with the actor's real-life problems of being arrested for drug use, but because he has received so much publicity, viewers may add the residue of social meaning to meanings conveyed by his character on television.

The social codes play a large part in conveying conventional representational codes. Appearance, speech, sound, facial expressions, and gestures in a contemporary setting have to be consistent with what viewers know in their own culture. Narratives that are set in other cultures or time periods also have to convey a sense of naturalness, but even in these instances social codes are usually adapted to the culture of the present. For example, on American television, a program set in France will most likely have the dialogue spoken in English. Other cultural codes may be more deeply embedded in representation. Fiske refers to these in the third level, Ideology.

Ideology

Representational codes are organized into coherence and social acceptability by ideological codes, such as individualism, patriarchy, class, materialism, capitalism, and so on. All of the codes come together to encode a preferred meaning that supports a certain ideology. Fiske said that a partriarchal code is embedded in the dialogue when a woman asks questions and a man answers them, seemingly because the man is supposed to be more knowledgeable than a woman. He used the example of the dialogue between two jewelry thieves in a *Hart to Hart* episode as embodying a capitalist ideology when one of the thieves says he will hold onto an expensive necklace that he wants to steal as an "investment" for his "retirement fund." There is no guarantee that a different cultural analyst will make the same meanings or even find ideology at all. Viewers who occupy different social positions may interpret the representation as something altogether different.

Pleasure

Fiske said that a viewer not only makes meanings but also derives pleasure from the process. Pleasure can be derived from opposing the preferred meaning or negotiating an individual meaning or accepting the preferred or dominant meaning. Experiencing pleasure in one of these ways frees the viewers from ideological dominance and gives them a sense of control over meanings. Fiske wrote:

> Pleasure for the subordinate is produced by the assertion of one's social identity in resistance to, in independence of, or in negotiation with, the structure of domination. There is . . . real pleasure to be found in, for example, soap operas that assert the legitimacy of feminine meanings and identities within and against patriarchy. Pleasure results from the production of meanings of the world and of self that are felt to serve the interests of the viewer rather than those of the dominant. . . . Pleasure requires a sense of control over meanings and an active participation in the cultural process. (1987, p. 19)

Another writer who has examined the concept of pleasure within cultural studies is John Corner, professor of politics and communication studies at the University of Liverpool in England. Corner developed a typology of pleasure that viewers may derive from television:

1. Visual pleasure gained from looking at an event as if the viewer were present, pleasure from images that appeal to the eye, and pleasure from watching things happen. Some of this pleasure is related to aesthetic appreciation of an image.
2. Pleasure from observing enactments, whether real or fictional. Such enactments often have high intensity and cultural portrayal.
3. Pleasure from gaining knowledge of public affairs, factual information (such as the correct answers in a quiz show), and insight into human behavior as observed in drama.
4. Pleasure gained from the humor in comedy. Corner said, "the themes of the comic is an important part of the cultural pattern, particularly of public values and the desires and fears of private life. Factors of social division and social change across class, gender, race, age group, and region are strongly present in comic expression" (1999, p. 97).
5. Pleasure gained from fantasy, that which stimulates the viewer toward scenarios which are highly improbable for them. Fantasy, then, could be both fiction and realistic depictions of lifestyles that some viewers could never obtain (Corner, 1999, pp. 93–100).

The concept of pleasure, originally coined by Roland Barthes in relationship to literary experience, has been adapted to television and cultural studies by both Fiske and Corner. In French, Barthes' language, pleasure has two meanings: *plaisir*, pleasure that is essentially cultural in origin, and *jouissance*, physical pleasure. Fiske adds a third meaning of pleasure that relates to the social structure and practices of the people who experience them. This is the pleasure gained when the viewer has some control over the production of meaning. A viewer may experience validation of one's social identity from accepting the dominant meaning. There may also be a form of pleasure in negotiating meaning in a person's own terms. Pleasure can even be derived from resisting the dominant meaning, as Fiske said, "by maintaining one's social identity in opposition to that proposed by the dominant ideology, [for] there is a power in asserting one's own subcultural values against the dominant ones" (1987, p. 19).

The concept of pleasure is another indicator that viewers make active choices regarding the meanings they decode. People make their own sense out of what they see, and the sense they make is related to a pattern of choices about their own social identities. This is one of the reasons for television's popularity, said Fiske, because it offers "such a variety of pleasures to such a heterogeneity of viewers," enabling them to actively participate in culture which has a social system that can only be held in place by the meanings that people make of it (1987, pp. 19–20). For example, I once tested students' reactions to the film *The Long Good Friday* that had a scene of extreme violence in a gay bathhouse. My students, who had read Fiske's *Television Culture* as one of their texts, were asked to indicate on hand-held computers as they watched the film their own sense of pleasure on a continuum from none to strong while a computer monitor at my seat compiled their responses by gender. The opening of the scene depicted a nude male couple embracing in the shower, and the compiled result was that males in my class did *not* take pleasure in this scene; whereas the women's response was neutral. One of the men in the scene was actually an IRA agent masquerading as a gay man in order to murder the other man who was an Irish informer. That the victim was gay had nothing to do with the plot. During the murder on the screen, the computer registered strong pleasure from the males in the class and none from the females. It was not possible to determine if anyone in the class derived pleasure from negotiating meaning or resisting it. Theoretically viewers could have gained pleasure from resisting the violence. That the men in the film's scene were gay made drawing a conclusion more difficult. Did the males in my class take pleasure in the violence alone or because it was violence against a gay man? That could only be determined by a more specific instrument to measure their responses or by an ethnographic method known as reception studies that was initially developed in the late 1980s for cultural studies.

RECEPTION STUDIES

Reception studies focused on the domestic context of television reception within a household and television viewing habits tracked over time in order to examine the social uses of television, that is, how television is used within different families and how television material is interpreted by its audience. David Morley (1988), the most cited researcher in this area, was critical of the ways in which cultural studies analysts exclusively engaged with questions of representation at the level of the media text. In order to provide empirical data about how audiences made meaning, he interviewed in depth members of families in the United Kingdom from different social backgrounds. He theorized that "talk" about television would sustain the viewers' involvement and identification with what was on the screen as well as maintain the families' interactions with one another. He found that part of the pleasure that people gained from television was its incorporation into their everyday domestic life. The difficulties that Morley faced in trying to correlate social class with types of decoding indicated that viewer interpretation is quite complicated and difficult to determine. However, he found that television viewing practices significantly correlated with gender. Men, both fathers and sons, had control over program choices; planned their television watching by selecting programs ahead of time from the television schedule; preferred news, current affairs, documentaries, and comedy shows; were more attentive when they watched; and watched television for greater amounts of time. Women, mothers and daughters, enjoyed watching drama, especially "weepies," alone, preferred fiction television, disliked comedy, and were much more willing to talk to friends and coworkers about what they watched on television. Other reception studies have raised issues about how people understand fictional stories about romance (Radway, 1984) and how television promotes discourse in the home (Spigel, 1992). These studies were considered to be on the fringe of cultural studies and have since become an independent theoretical and methodological area of study.

CULTURAL STUDIES AND THE CYBORG MANIFESTO

As Hall has indicated, cultural studies needs to be open to external influences, such as feminist studies. Another work to be discussed in this chapter is "A Cyborg Manifesto" by Donna Haraway (1993), who takes a feminist/cultural look at technology and its control over work and leisure and scientific developments that have enhanced our ability to alter the course of nature, including the genetic development of the human species. Haraway's work is included because it tackles the complex arena of the current technological revolution and how it is impacting culture. Also, the following exemplary essay, "Monitor Head: We Eat, Drink, and Sleep This Stuff," represents the image of the cyborg.

The cyborg is a hybrid of machine and organism, a coupling between an electronic or mechanical apparatus and a human being, both a creature of social reality as well as a creature of fiction. Both the signs of the human and the signs of the machine mark the dual nature of the cyborg that is neither purely human nor purely machine. The cyborg is dualistically human and artificial. The cyborg sets the natural body in opposition to the technologically recrafted body and may reform how we think about the social and cultural body including its gender and race. Haraway wrote, "We are all chimeras, theorized and fabricated hybrids of machine and organism; in short we are cyborgs . . . the condensed image of both imagination and material reality" (in During, 1993, p. 272). The cyborg transgresses boundaries, is potently fused, and has dangerous possibilities. She means that cyborgs are the plants that humans have created by biotechnology, artificial intelligence, "smart" missiles used in warfare, and artificial body parts. The cyborg is the "illegitimate offspring of militarism and patriarchal capitalism" (p. 273). The cyborg is, of course, a metaphor for the relationships between humans and machines, or between and among human beings who are not unified or complete. The cyborg has the potential for a more egalitarian consciousness, for it is liberated from the limitations that culture imposes on gender, race, and sexual orientation. Technology in our culture has fostered inequality through the concentration of power in scientific and informational institutions. Women,

Haraway claimed, in their crisis to achieve equality, have split apart and have failed to achieve unity, remaining different, and are seen as the "other." Furthermore, within race, for example, women may be considered black or chicano but not black women or chicanas. In other words, woman does not exist as a subject. Women have been integrated and exploited "into a world system of production/reproduction and communication called the informatics of domination. The home, workplace, market, public arena, the body itself–all can be dispersed and interfaced in nearly infinite, polymorphous ways, with large consequences for women and others" (During, 1993, p. 283). Haraway issues a call for women to code their own selves and to resist patriarchal control. She said, "We can learn from our fusions with animals and machines how not to be Man, . . . From the point of view of pleasure in these potent and taboo fusions, made inevitable by the social relations of science and technology, there might indeed be a feminist science" (in During, 1993, p. 291). Digital technology has the capability to enhance human neurological systems without regard to gender. By assimilating characteristics that are sustaining and generative without regard to gender, a new social order can be formed.

CONCLUSION

Cultural studies develops a critique that is concerned with making meanings about the roles and practices of different people and the way that culture interacts with their lives. Culture is the actual practices and customs, languages, beliefs, forms of representation, and system of formal and informal rules that tell people how to behave most of the time. Culture is about the production and exchange of meanings between and among the members of society. Cultural studies analysis is interdisciplinary and has methodological fluidity. This chapter focuses on the cultural studies methods that focus on the meanings that various people make from representations, especially in images. Cultural studies has a demystifying role in our attempts to discern what attitudes, beliefs, values, preferred forms of conduct, and ideologies are embedded and reinforced in images and supporting discourse. A representation can have multiple meanings (polysemy) that are dependent on the viewers who make the meanings by the process of decoding. Viewers may accept the dominant meaning, negotiate a meaning, or resist and oppose a meaning. Representations give viewers pleasure in viewing them, but pleasure is also derived from validating one's social identity by accepting the dominant meaning or by negotiating a meaning on one's own terms or by resisting the dominant meaning and maintaining one's social identity by opposing it.

A cultural studies analyst values what all members of a culture have to say in their own voices and images. One asks about the process through which the voices and images have been formed and the conditions under which they are seen and heard. One also asks about inclusions and exclusions, hierarchies, power relations, and the ways in which they interact with our lives.

Many cultural studies analysts have an affection for localized critiques and situated analyses. Lawrence Grossberg wrote, "Cultural studies always and only exists in con-textually specific theoretical and institutional formations. Such formations are always a response to a particular political project based on the available theoretical and historical resources. In that sense, in every particular instance, cultural studies has to be made up as it goes along" (cited in Couldry, 2000, p. 9). Couldry, on the other hand, said, "Cultural studies risks becoming merely reactive, at the mercy of changing historical and political events" (2000, p. 9). The theorists represented in this chapter have given us guidelines for completing a cultural studies analysis that incorporates the specific institutional formations and, at the same time, keeps us from being merely reactive.

A METHODOLOGY FOR CULTURAL STUDIES IN VISUAL COMMUNICATION

The following are questions to be asked in doing a cultural studies analysis in visual communication. Although one would concentrate on images in visual communication, it is also useful to pay heed to discourse in film and television. I have used the term *work* to represent the object of our criticism whether it is a painting, a cartoon, a computer graphic, a poster, a film, a television program, or something else.

1. How does a work relate to the shared living condition of the time?
2. What is present and what is absent? How are we limited in our ways of seeing?
3. Can we place ourselves inside the image, identifying with it? What do we get out of the image if we identify ourselves in relationship to the image? How does the work position the viewer as a subject? When the work "hails" you, do you answer?
4. What meanings are preferred by the work? (In other words, what is the dominant ideology (hegemony) that is embedded in the work?)
5. Examine the codes of the work: What are the realistic, representative, and ideological codes?
    a. How is the work encoded in social codes, such as appearance, behavior, speech, sound, and setting?
    b. How do the technical codes, camera use, lighting, editing, sound, and music, convey the conventional representational codes (narrative, conflict, character, action, dialogue, setting, and casting)?
    c. How do the representative codes work together to encode a preferred meaning that supports and ideology? What is the ideology?
6. What meanings can different viewers make of the work? What is the dominant meaning? What meanings are possible from negotiation? What meanings might be resisted or opposed?
7. How might the decoded meanings give the viewer a sense of power? How might they provide pleasure? How is this related to the viewer's sense of identity?
8. How does the work help the subject make sense of social experience?
9. In what ways does the work seem natural, that is, accepted as real? How is the naturalness articulated? What is at stake in the representation?
10. How do the meanings that we derive implicate us in the production of the meanings?
11. What meanings does a work have when it is absorbed into the lives of its viewers? Might they take on new meanings, new identities, new knowledge?

These questions will enable the viewer to "play" a work as if it were a piece of music—interpreting it, activating it, giving it a living presence. They will also enable you to go into the work to understand the cultural implications in it.

Cultural studies analyses allow us to reflect on the ideals and contradictions of our culture, to examine issues of power in and among groups of people, and to realize how very complex responses to images are.

ENDNOTES

[1] Three recent books (Barker [2000], Couldry [2000], and Lewis [2002]) provide useful background for understanding the contributions of the various academic areas and foundational theories of cultural studies. Cultural studies readers edited by Grossberg, Nelson, and Treichler (1992), Grossberg (1997) and During (1993) include a variety of theoretical approaches and analyses.

[2] The codes of television production as defined by John Fiske are discussed later in this chapter.

REFERENCES

Barker, C. (2000). *Cultural studies; Theory and practice.* Thousand Oaks, CA: Sage.

Carey, J. (1988). *Media, myths, and narratives.* Newbury Park, CA: Sage.

Corner, J. (1999). *Critical ideas in television studies.* New York: Oxford University Press.

Couldry, N. (2000). *Inside culture: Re-Imagining the method of cultural studies.* London: Sage.

Cruz, J., & Lewis, J. (Eds.). (1990). *Viewing, reading, listening: Audiences and cultural reception.* Boulder, CO: Westview Press.

During, S. (Ed.). (1993). *The cultural studies reader.* London: Routledge.

Evans, J., & Hall, S. (Eds.). (1999). *Visual culture: The reader.* London: Sage.

Fiske, J. (1987). *Television culture.* London: Metheun.

Gray, A., & McGuigan, J. (Eds.). (1993). *Studying Culture: An Introductory Reader* (2nd. ed.). London: Arnold.

Grossberg, L. (1997). *Bringing it all back home: Essays on cultural studies.* Durham, NC: Duke University Press.

Grossberg, L., Nelson, C., & Treichler, P. (1992). (Eds.). *Cultural studies.* New York: Routledge.

Hall, S. (1997). *Representation.* Thousand Oaks, CA: Sage.

Haraway, D. (1993). A cyborg manifesto. In S. During (Ed.), *The cultural studies reader* (pp. 271–291). London: Routledge.

Jhally, S. (Producer). (1996). *Representation and the media* [videorecording]. Northampton, MA: Media Education Foundation.

Jowett, G., & O'Donnell, V. (1999). *Propaganda and persuasion.* Thousand Oaks, CA: Sage.

Lewis, J. (2002). *Cultural studies: The basics.* Thousand Oaks, CA: Sage.

Mitchell, W. J. T. (1995). *Picture theory: Essays on verbal and visual representation.* Chicago: University of Chicago Press.

Morley, D. (1988). *Family television: Cultural power and domestic leisure.* London: Routledge.

Morley, D., & Chen, K.-H. (1996). *Stuart Hall: Critical dialogues in cultural studies.* London: Routledge.

Radway, J. (1984). *Reading the Romance.* Chapel Hill: University of North Carolina Press.

Real, M. R. (1996). *Exploring media culture.* Thousand Oaks, CA: Sage.

Spigel, L. (1992). *Make Room for TV: Television and the Family Ideal in Postwar America.* Chicago: University of Chicago Press.

Williams, R. (1958). Culture is ordinary. In A. Gray & J. McGuigan (Eds.), *Studying culture: An introductory reader* (pp. 5–14) (2nd ed.). London: Arnold.

32

A Burkean Analysis of a Television Promotional Advertisement

JOSEPH C. HARRY

Slippery Rock University

In cultural studies research, the goal is to study the meaning of things. The analyst attempts to understand the meaning of one or many cultural texts—books, songs, paintings, cartoons, movies, TV shows, advertisements, films, newspaper articles, fast-food restaurants, museum installations, carnivals, human organizations, or any other part of our social world that can be studied as *text*—and through various forms of interpretation. The main elements of a cultural studies perspective (Grossberg, 1995, 1993; Grossberg, Nelson, & Treichler, 1992) include a commitment to observing, understanding, and explaining human action through language and imagery; the acceptance of conflict and contradiction as a central condition of human societies; an interpretive focus on popular texts such as music, movies, and television; the notion that textual meaning is in many ways structured (encoded) within the imagery and language of a given text, but that viewers, listeners, or readers are the final arbiters of textual meaning (Hall, 1980); an interdisciplinary interest in interpreting texts by borrowing and combining theories and methods from various academic disciplines such as communication, linguistics, history, philosophy, literary theory, sociology, economics, political science, and anthropology; and a belief that a given popular culture text is typically based on familiar, culture-specific stories, norms, scenarios, themes, myths, or ideals that can be interpreted critically within the political, historical, economic, and social *contexts* that shape a text's meaning. Accordingly, meaning is partly in the text, partly in the culture at large, and partly in the viewer, listener, or reader.

Within a cultural studies framework, this chapter uses a multidisciplinary method to analyze television network promotional ads, or promos. The analysis incorporates rhetorical-visual criticism that draws on the methods of Kenneth Burke, financial analysis common to a political-economy perspective, and an ideological interpretation of underlying cultural themes and myths. This multimethod approach helps us understand how program promos do their ideological work by situating the TV networks' *material mode of production*, which is a political-economic reality, within the key images, themes, and major visual, verbal, and auditory meanings that form their *symbolic mode of reproduction*, which is an ideological reality. Burke's (1969, 1966) dramatistic-pentadic method of focusing on key symbolic elements in the text, when coupled with an analysis of economic factors associated with the production of a text, invites a close reading of program promos in which political-economic themes, as well as dramatic stories and, finally, ideological norms or worldviews emerge.

The program promos examined in this study were broadcast by ABC, CBS, and NBC in the summer 1996 to introduce their new fall line-up of situation comedies and drama series. A sample of 34 promos was drawn from those aired in the prime-time hours when most viewers watch television (*TV Dimensions*, 1996). The sample, totaling 11 minutes, 47 seconds, has an estimated value, in commercial airtime, of $2.27 million, or $3,244 per each second of promo time.

Discussion focusing on a single, 30-second promo for the CBS situation-comedy *Pearl* demonstrates each component of the multimethod approach and its use in analyzing how visual elements contribute to meaning making in a televisual text. At the same time, the analysis shows how this method can be applied to any number of other promos that would comprise part of a larger research project and, by making interpretive links between the promo for *Pearl* and the 33 other promos studied, demonstrates how valid interpretive connections can be made by finding common thematic patterns.

Network program promos play a significant part in our contemporary televisual culture and are ideal vehicles for examining the visual confluence of art, commerce, and ideology. They comprise a significant part of the daily television schedule, account for millions of dollars of commercial airtime, and are seen by tens of millions of viewers. Like the commercial whose airtime it displaces, a network promo is an audience-targeted, distinctly visual-rhetorical communicative format, which encodes two levels of meaning. First, at the network level, where the goal is to draw the largest possible number of viewers and, consequently, significant advertising revenues, there are meanings associated with a text's *material mode of production*. Concurrently, at the storytelling level, where viewers experience promos as dramatic, individual slices of visual culture, there are meanings associated with its *symbolic mode of reproduction*. These two interconnected levels of meaning will be identified throughout the analysis of the program promo for *Pearl*.

BURKE'S METHOD OF PENTADIC-DRAMATISTIC CRITICISM

Burke's dramatistic-rhetorical analysis is an interpretive method accompanied by a theory of meaning, which holds that human language and symbol making are essentially social, dramatic, and philosophical in nature. Dramatistic analysis studies key elements within the "grammar" of a text to explain what Burke called "attitudes" or "motives," which are interpreted as textual meaning (Burke, 1969, 1966). The method is ideal for visually rich texts like the promo because of its reliance on the visual to carry out its persuasive strategy (Mitchell, 1995).

The three components of Burkean rhetorical criticism used in this discussion are the *representative anecdote, pentadic (5-term) analysis*, and *ratio analysis*. Though the three elements function as an integrated method of interpretation, each will be defined and illustrated separately with examples from the visual text of the promo for *Pearl*. The setting for the story portrayed in the promo is a traditional college lecture hall and the lead character is Rhea Perlman, who viewers would undoubtedly recognize from *Cheers*. The fact that her name is Pearl and that she portrays a middle-aged, working-class woman promotes instant identification with the new show. As she climbs over chairs, tables, and other students in an attempt to claim her place in this new world of higher learning, the words Rhea Perlman and New Series appear on the screen along with the CBS logo and "Wednesdays this Fall." The image is composed as a wide shot of medium scale, which creates an objective, scene-setting perspective.

REPRESENTATIVE ANECDOTE

As a first step toward framing an interpretation, the textual critic identifies an underlying plot, tale, or story line that represents the essence of a text (Burke, 1969; Brummett, 1984). This basic plot line is the representative anecdote and it is demonstrated by fleshing out and interpreting dramatic elements that make up the tale. As Burke (1969) characterized it, the representative anecdote implicitly contains what is explicitly "drawn out" in close analysis of key and secondary textual elements and their dramatic relationships. Accordingly, the representative anecdote in the promo for *Pearl* can be identified as: *A working-class woman struggles to better herself through acquiring higher learning, by returning to school to earn a college degree, thereby raising herself up to a higher level of knowledge and social standing. The struggle entails her steady adjustment to a more refined, learned environment unlike the everyday blue-collar world, the central conflict depicting a clash between competing forms of knowledge and different kinds of social standing.*

In the program content, the most telling evidence for the representative anecdote is the depiction of Pearl as a nervous, uncertain, insecure, and even bumbling new student who makes a spectacle of herself. We can contrast the confident professor with the scatterbrained new student: his confidence, knowledge, and power to ask serious questions, with her comical but well-intended responses, his begrudging and superior chuckle with her sheepish expression, his serious and stonelike presence with, in the final shot, her smile of only slightly innocent self-satisfaction.

At the level of the network-message, the representative anecdote is supported by a graphic that first appears as the letters CBS and then morphs into three R's. In association with an image of Pearl in the classroom, two of the Rs form the words Reading and 'Riting, and the third, after a pause, becomes Rhea. With this visual move, CBS as network-rhetor makes a connection between the new show and what we already know of the star and her previous character from *Cheers*. The network message—as representative anecdote—invites us to watch a show about a well-known actress playing *yet another* working-class woman struggling to enter an uncommon and challenging environment.

Pentadic Elements

As the analysis proceeds, we look for a collective of five interacting components of visual and verbal elements that make up the text, and that Burke (1969, 1966) called the *pentad*. They include: the *act* (what is happening), the *agent*[s] (who is involved as main actor or actors), the *agency* (how, or through what means, things are happening or accomplished), the *scene* (where, or in what kind of environment, things are happening), and the *purpose* (why, or for what larger reasons, things occur in the text in the way they do).

The *scene* component in the *Pearl* text is both the college classroom and a scene or place of higher learning. The *agents* are Pearl, other students, and a professor. Often one agent will emerge as central to the drama, however, and in this case it is Pearl. In the short, 30-second text, we see images of her sitting at a desk, walking into a classroom, standing up to answer the professor's question, and, in a close-up smile of satisfaction at having mastered that day.

The *act* centers on Pearl in the process of getting an education, as act and agent, in this case, merge closely. Though we see her stumbling into class, the intense demeanor captured by a close-up indicates her intention of being taken seriously, even though the response of the professor, again captured in close-up, is one of chuckling bemusement.

The *agency* is the educational process itself, represented by the professor's lecture about *Moby Dick* and Socrates. Agency explains how important dramatic action occurs or is accomplished and, symbolic of higher education as a means to elite knowledge, the agency through which education occurs is the professor's lecture.

Finally, we turn to the *purpose*, the most philosophical of the five terms of the pentad. It typically relates to intellectual, moral, ethical, or spiritual aims. Pearl's main purpose is to improve upon her working-class life by returning to college for a higher education. The *purpose* is conveyed graphically: three red letter Rs spin into focus and two of the three quickly spell out Reading and 'Riting. But what of the third R? The implication is obvious, though when a voice-over completes the triad with her name, it is in the form of a question: *Rhea?*

At the same time, there is also a story of the network embedded within this narrative. It is expressed as visual direct address by the words and accompanying graphics on the screen. In this story, the *scene*, an electronic place of routinized activity characterized by a program schedule, is the most prominent element. This place of the network-as-rhetor (communicator) is set with the CBS logo. These letters then morph into RRR, which become Reading and 'Riting. After images of Pearl in the classroom, the words Rhea Perlman appear on the screen. As the third R is connected to the first two, it serves to announce that Perlman is now on the CBS scene.

The *agent* is the network as central communicator. It announces its aims in terms of who is presenting this new show (CBS) and when to tune in (Wednesdays this Fall). The *act* or action on the part of the network is the promo itself. With the words New Series appearing on the screen along with images of the back-to-school Pearl, the promo is an active attempt to induce us to imagine watching the real show when it premieres. The *agency* is the show itself as the means or tool through which the audience can experience this drama as the appearance of the words Rhea Perlman on the screen indicate. Finally, the *purpose*, from the network frame of reference, is to remind us that CBS will bring us this thoughtfully comical piece of weekly entertainment. Here the purpose is evoked by the promo redundantly informing us who and where (CBS), when (Wednesdays this Fall), and what to watch (Rhea Perlman as Pearl), each of these graphic messages accompanied by images from the upcoming show. In this sense, the promo as visual message veers back and forth—as any promo does in varying degrees—between presenting the rhetoric of the show and the rhetoric of the network.

Ratio Analysis

The above exercise demonstrates how one can link various elements of a text (and even the same elements of the text) with different terms of the pentad, though the five terms (act, agent, agency, scene, purpose) should be understood as analytic, not reductive, categories—each one offering its own route to interpretation. Burke's method calls for somewhat more than this, however. Interpretation of the symbolic work going on in the visual text proceeds by identifying dramatic relationships emerging when these elements are paired as key and secondary, or *controlling* and *controlled* terms. This is what Burke calls the ratio analysis, which allows us to more strictly assess the meanings in a text (Cragan & Shields, 1995, p. 79). It is conducted by the rhetorical critic choosing, through a careful examination of all dramatic elements, what appears to be the single-most-important term among the five, the one that most reasonably seems to be a controlling term structuring the drama, and through which everything else happens. This key term is then related to a secondary or *controlled* term, selected from one of the remaining four terms of the pentad. This controlled term is viewed as the one most logically suggested by the primary term as its most reasonable match. These two terms form the symbolic ratio, or *ratio analysis*, which provides a narrowed lens through which the drama can be most thoroughly understood. Various related or "clustered" symbolic elements such as the visuals, words, and sounds scattered throughout the text serve as evidence. In actual practice, the real work of interpretation truly emerges through ratio analysis.

On close inspection, the classroom story line of the promo for *Pearl* seems most strongly to evoke an *agent/purpose* pairing. *Agent* (Pearl) is the controlling or key element, the main character in the dramatic story line, and her ambition, her overarching goal or *purpose*, is to complete her college education. In other words, the purpose of higher education can only be understood in relation first to Pearl as determining agent with a purpose. An agent-centered ratio, according to Burke (1969), indicates an idealistic, individual philosophy, the notion that individuals can surmount all barriers before them. This particularly American ideological concept, according to Campbell and Burkholder (1997), is likely to resonate with many TV viewers.

Narrowing our focus toward a ratio analysis requires an interpretive process, which shifts back and forth between the controlling and controlled pentadic elements to bring out their symbolic interaction. In the promo's opening shot, using a midrange, midlevel camera angle, Pearl is seen sitting at her new classroom desk, smiling broadly, clearly happy to be at school. Superimposed on the screen are the already-mentioned three Rs, subsequently spelling out Reading, 'Riting, and, in a voice-over, *Rhea*. This completes the reading, 'riting, 'rithmatic theme of education, which indicates Pearl's main purpose. The subsequent image is a wide-angle view of the classroom and a full shot of Pearl as she stands to answer the professor's question. At this point her purpose is woven into the visual text by virtue of a quick cut to the lecturing professor, against whom Pearl is cast. She remains standing in her next shot, intently poised to answer yet another question. Images of the lecturing professor include the model of a human skeleton, connoting scientific investigation, a hallmark of elite, college-bred knowledge. This itself serves as a reminder of the agent (Pearl) and her goal (purpose) of understanding, learning, questioning, and rising up to a higher level of knowledge. A close-up shot of the professor shows him responding negatively to an incorrect answer from Pearl. But in the promo's final shot, Pearl is framed from the desktop up, sitting once again, and smiling with a clear look of satisfaction. This final glimpse of the agent evokes in the viewer a sense of the agent's (Pearl's) own satisfaction at having made some progress in her goal (purpose) of actively learning.

A ratio analysis for the network-centered story line is somewhat simpler to construct. Because this promo is framed more from the perspective of a program-centered drama than from a network-focused drama (the network's own message about itself and its show), CBS seems most directly to cast itself as the agency, the tool or means through which the audience will experience Perlman as Pearl. Accordingly, a case can be made most strongly for an *agency/agent* pairing. Returning to the promo, we recall that the opening shot showing Pearl at her desk is superimposed with the letters CBS in big red letters, including the CBS oval-shaped logo. This is followed by these letters spinning toward us, and morphing into the three Rs, representing Reading, 'Riting, and Rhea. In this way, the network emerges as *agency* simultaneously with Perlman's introduction as the star (*agent*) of the new show. She is first introduced with her real first name (Rhea), to remind viewers that CBS is the means through which we will see this established sitcom star. Of course, the name of the show, as well as that of its main character, is the root word of Perlman's last name, further commingling the network's desire to instill in us Perlman's star power.

During the shot where Pearl climbs frantically over classroom furniture and students to get to her seat, the phrase New Series is superimposed in large letters. In the final shot, showing Pearl sitting and smiling contently at her desk, the name of the show is superimposed, alongside the familiar yellow CBS logo and the phrase "Wednesdays this Fall." Though the network chose to attract viewers by focusing on the dramatic content of the show itself, the network-as-agency was keen to remind viewers of the show's star character and to name the show after her as a way to draw attention to the network's ability to bring us a big-name star.

We can now move to consideration of two important contextual factors that help broaden this interpretation—political economy, and ideological criticism.

POLITICAL ECONOMY

A political-economy analysis of television promos can look at a broad range of factors, such as audience ratings, advertising revenues, distributional considerations, legal restrictions, and institutional or political constraints that bear on the production and consumption of mediated messages. The most thorough political-economic analysis examines the largest possible number of factors of production, distribution, and consumption of cultural products (Meehan, Mosco, & Wasko, 1993) in an effort to complement textual analysis by providing important background knowledge and contextual understanding of the factors influencing the production (encoding) of a text. This level of analysis can precede textual interpretation or be woven into an interpretation at appropriate points. In the multimethod approach used here, only financial and audience-ratings factors are considered, and this information is then used to provide insight into the economic reality behind the production of television promos and the interests of the network-as-rhetor.

Because promos are a form of advertising, one indication of their relative worth as a commodity is their dollar value in the buying market. Obtaining actual network financial information for this kind of data is difficult. A reasonable estimate can be made by calculating the advertising revenue that could have been gained by selling commercial airtime, but that was used instead to run a network promo. To determine the value of this "opportunity cost," a fairly simple calculation is made by multiplying total air time by a standardized advertising rate of Cost Per Thousand (CPM) viewers (*TV Dimensions*, 1996) and then multiplying this by the estimated number of viewing households during a scheduled program slot. This method of calculation shows, for example, that CBS invested an opportunity cost of nearly $96,000 in the 30-second promo we have been discussing, plus another $96,000 for the two additional 15-second promos for the show that it ran in one evening. By understanding the high cost the network places in even a single promo, we can better understand an important aspect of the rhetorical motive behind the network-as-rhetor: The network's strategy is one in which an economic calculus (the need to attract the highest possible advertising revenues) drives the search for culturally acceptable storylines (new shows), with promos serving as the lure for those shows. What is reproduced, ultimately, as saleable commodities for popular consumption, is an endless stream of relatively conventional and usually middle-of-the-road, politically unthreatening but enduring cultural myths, stories, sagas, societal norms, and ideological visions—the "sociocultural truisms" (Gronbeck, 1984) common to an American television mindset.

Within the *Pearl* promo, at the symbolic level of reproduction, we might enjoy and identify with the fairly conventional story line about an everyday, working-class woman being cast into a challenging but familiar and ultimately safe cultural environment (the university), an environment where a comedic take on social power and cultural dominance will metaphorically be played out. But in understanding this same promo in terms of the network's material mode of production, we also witness television logic at work, in the form of a slickly crafted 30-second product ad with a network price tag of nearly $100,000. Recall that this was just one of 34 promos aired during one primetime evening for 18 new shows, the promos collectively accounting for just under 12 minutes of air time worth just over $2.2 million.

Understood as part of a daily flock of television ads, the rhetorically engaging and high-priced promo for *Pearl* becomes just a blip in the network's weekly display of its symbolic self. Contemplating both the rhetorical and political-economic sides of the network promo helps bring into focus the ideological reality of our televisual culture.

IDEOLOGY

Ideology is one of the more significant terms in cultural studies analysis because culture has a close affinity with ideology. As O'Donnell (in Chapter 33) describes it, culture is "practices and customs, languages, beliefs, forms of representation, and the system of formal and informal rules that tell people how to behave most of the time." Ideology operates at an abstract level as a set of group or community beliefs and assumptions (implicit or explicit) that inform cultural practices. It may be thought of as a precon-structed worldview, a norm-based, overarching way of seeing and understanding the world from a certain group's perspective and interests (van Dijk, 1998), but always artic-ulated in visual, verbal, and other kinds of signifying practices.

As a method, ideological analysis functions as an interpretive activity founded in look-ing beyond the immediate surface structure of a visual, verbal, or any other kind of text for broad, abstract beliefs and assumptions suggested by that surface structure. From the stance of someone doing textual-ideological analysis, ideological worldviews should be seen as posed from a partial, therefore contestable, contradictory, self-interested, and imaginary vantage point (Althusser, 1971; Eagleton, 1971). This is what Althusser means by saying ideology is a process of constructing one's imaginary relations to "lived" (i.e., actual, real) conditions of existence (Althusser, 1971; see also Hall, 1991). Barthes (1972) construed ideologies as cultural myths, everyday fictions in which the brute actualities of history are almost magically transformed into naturalized, depoliticized common sense. Making the connection between rhetoric and the cultural myths it embodies, Barthes construes rhetoric as "the signifying aspect of ideology" (1977, p. 49), while Eco (1972), also from a linguistic perspective, sees ideology as preexisting any mes-sage. Because ideological worldviews are also rooted in and therefore influenced by conflictual, hegemonic, societal relations of power, authority, conflict, and dominance (Thompson, 1990), an ideological analysis searches for a dialectic, for inherent textual contradictions, the analysis of which offers a deeper understanding of the text-producer's motives.

To attract commercial sponsors, television networks must present programs that will be ideologically satisfying and not seen as excessively offensive, disturbing, or difficult to understand by viewers. As a result, television engages in ideological work through its use of conventional ideas and images that tend to offer commonsense, generally acceptable definitions of middle-class reality or social-cultural truisms (Gronbeck, 1984). Having examined the promo for *Pearl* by means of Burkean criticism and political-economy analysis, we could consider it as simply an economic calculus devoted to selling viewers a specific story line. Ultimately, however, any story can be seen to have an ideological meaning in the form of foundational cultural themes that resonate with or question commonsense beliefs, norms, and values. Considering the classroom story portrayed in the promo for *Pearl*, for example, we experience an ideological divide between the well-schooled, higher-status professor, sipping tea and confident in his standing, on the one hand, and his new charge, the working-class woman stumbling over chairs and other students, on the other; between the "reading and writing" (the two Rs) *versus* Rhea (the third R), on the one hand, and the reading, 'riting, and 'rithmatic, on the other. Images of the professor show him fully in control and secure in his superiority, allowing himself a chuckle at Pearl's erroneous answers. We associate him with the skeleton propped behind him, both of them evocative of higher learning itself, and dialectically reminding us of his student who is so distant from that world, but who so diligently wants to possess what it has to offer. A quickly interspersed, wide-perspective shot of the professor, occurring just after a shot of him lecturing, shows him bounding up concrete steps toward a university building. The steps physically symbolize the notion of higher learning as a literal pathway up toward the actual place of aspiration, the college classroom. But the next shot shows Pearl standing in class, responding erroneously to the professor's lecture question (having to do with Socrates' advice about the greatest thing a man or woman can achieve, followed by Pearl's answer relating, irrelevantly, to an old TV commercial). The dialectic is clear: The confident professor is the model, the insecure but willful student merely the clay to be shaped in his image. Higher knowledge and elite social standing meet their opposite—everyday knowledge and working-class status. When ideology is understood as relations of dominance at work in any social structure (Thompson, 1990; van Dijk, 1998), there is little question which character is dominant and which is dominated in this promo, even though the relationship is, dialectically, called into question by Pearl's struggle to remain herself in the new and domineering environment.

At another level of meaning (the *network* frame), the dialectic involves the big, swirling red letters spelling out CBS, and the accompanying three Rs—Reading, 'Riting, and Rhea—reminding us of both who's presenting the show (CBS) and what it's about, as opposed to who's starring in it. In the classroom story, the ideological message, though delivered as comedy, valorizes academic knowledge as a culturally superior way of knowing. Yet it is clear that this way of knowing will be ideologically challenged by Pearl's. Although the text pokes fun at this superior knowledge through its characterization of the stuffy professor, it dialectically invites us to empathize more with Pearl and her aspiration to become college-educated. In this way the promo actually provides the viewer some means of resistive power (Fiske, 1987), a way to call into question the supposed superiority of higher learning, and to perhaps contemplate more favorably the value of everyday knowledge. By representing working-class knowledge, the text invites us to identify with Pearl as embodying a subordinate, resistant, common knowledge that, ironically, is both desirous of, but resistant to higher learning in the form of the university, and represented by the professor.

CULTURAL-IDEOLOGICAL PATTERNS AND THEMES

The multimethod analysis described here provides a rich cultural text of texts in which one finds that the promo for *Pearl* encodes art, commerce, and ideology in a 30-second text that shows interesting similarities, as well as distinctive differences, with other program promos broadcast during the same evening.

Because a cultural studies perspective examines popular texts that routinely draw on culture-specific plots, scenarios, stories, myths, norms, and ideals, the major story or plot line (as representative anecdote) that emerges from a Burkean textual analysis of one promo might be expected to reveal itself in promos that are part of a larger grouping, or even in different kinds of generic texts (Brummett, 1984). In this way we can see how conventional stories, especially in the mass media, recur throughout a culture, presenting tried-and-true themes that can also be interpreted ideologically, for the worldviews or cultural myths (Barthes, 1972) they embody. Finally, then, let us briefly consider such connections between the promo for *Pearl* and others aired that evening.

A promo on NBC for *Mr. Rhodes*—a sitcom about a hip young man teaching in a rowdy high school—projected essentially the same ideological theme as did the promo for *Pearl*. Though each of these two promoted shows contained their own fairly distinct representative anecdotes, at the ideological level both depicted essentially the same underlying ideology: a struggle between competing forms of knowledge, between higher and lower forms. The fact that two different networks (CBS and NBC) planned to air shows pertaining to essentially the same ideological message shows us this is a theme reflective of an enduring cultural ideology.

Other more prevalent ideological themes emerging in this multimethod analysis of visual texts included a Savior-Hero myth, characterizing three shows on three different networks; an Order-versus-Chaos myth, characterizing two shows on two networks; a War-of-the-Sexes myth, characterizing three shows on three networks; and a Middle-Class-Life-and-Problems myth, characterizing three shows from three different networks. The Savior-Hero ideology, which plays out the idea that a human with superior or even supernatural powers will save everyday humans from various dilemmas, occurred in promos for dramas having to do with supernatural plot lines. Similarly, the Order-versus-Chaos theme, portraying the restoration of order and sanity by human and superhuman forces, was associated with supernatural and, interestingly, police dramas. The War-of-the-Sexes theme, centering on gender, social, cultural, and everyday domestic differences, was linked to situation comedies. Finally, the Middle-Class-Life-and-Problems theme, portraying the daily struggles of domestic family life, was another ideology connected with comedy rather than more serious fare.

It is clear from this analysis that certain cultural ideologies tend to be connected with specific televisual storytelling genres. We also learn that despite the proliferation of different rhetorical storylines in any single promo, underlying ideological worldviews, read as culturally enduring themes, collapse into a much smaller number. Finding common patterns among all promos in this manner provides insight into the types of dramas and ideological perspectives that are relied upon as common story forms by various networks. This is an important dimension to the overall interpretation.

CONCLUSIONS

While focusing on the visual elements of the television promo for this analysis, it is important to recognize that any electronically mediated text contains several layers of interrelated meanings created not only by images, but also by words and sounds (Barbatsis & Guy, 1991; Barbatsis, 1996). The ideological work achieved in the promo for *Pearl* is a complex relationship between multiple symbol systems. A viewer does not experience the visual separately from the verbal text, or the linguistic separately from the pictorial (Mitchell, 1995). The spoken words in the promo for *Pearl* create their own representational drama of confrontation between high and popular cultural knowledge, and as the script shows, this text also encodes the confrontation in two story lines. One story, centered on the show itself, is created by the two fictional characters that interact within the television's story-world space. The other story, centered on the network, takes place on either side of the screen through the mode of visual-verbal direct address. Keeping in mind the earlier visual-centered analysis of the promo for *Pearl*, we can now finally link that knowledge to the verbal information, including what the characters say to each other and what the network says to viewers.

Voice-over:	*This Fall CBS puts a new spin on the 3 Rs: Reading, Riting, Rhea?*
Pearl:	*So here I am, back and ready to go!*
Professor:	*I'm sorry, have we met?*
Voice-Over:	*Rhea Perlman's going back to school.*
Professor:	*Moby Dick represents evil. What does Ahab represent?*
Pearl:	*Charlie the Tuna?*
Voice-Over:	*Taking higher learning to new heights.*
Professor:	*What did Socrates say was the greatest thing a man or woman could do?*
Pearl:	*Raise children?*
Professor:	*No, any idiot can raise children—Look around you!*
Voice-Over:	*Pearl—CBS Wednesdays this Fall.*

With the words spoken by Pearl and the professor, we're presented with the contrast between Herman Melville's high-culture novel *Moby Dick* and the low- or popular-culture message in a commercial for tuna fish, as well as the contrasting views of Socrates and a working-class mother. In the voice speaking directly to viewers, we're presented with a more personalized contrast between the viewers and the network, where, as viewers, we have a place to regularly experience this funny new show. The representative anecdote identified in the visual text of the promo for *Pearl*—blue-collar, low-status knowledge and social standing confronts higher-status knowledge and professorial social class—is made even more clear when we read the verbal-vocal text in relation to it. *Moby Dick*, one of the great symbols in modern high-brow literature, confronts Charlie the Tuna, a cartoon character in television commercials from decades ago, and representing probably the lowest form of popular culture. We're never told the correct answer to the professor's second question—what Socrates said was the greatest thing a man or woman could do. But Pearl takes a comical stab at it by allowing that it may be "raising children," to which the professor disdainfully suggests that she scan the classroom to see all of the children raised by idiots. In this putdown of everyone in the class, a dialectic emerges between elite and everyday knowledge. In these ways, the verbal text brings into even clearer focus what the televisual imagery has already accomplished, although even without the promo's accompanying spoken text, we still understand a great deal about the comedy being played out on the screen.

Of course all methods are open to critique, and the one outlined here is no exception. For example, having calculated advertising rates for the promos, there remains the practical problem of where best to place this information, and of presenting it in a way that will contextually broaden but not overwhelm the more qualitative aspects of a textual-ideological interpretation. One partial solution is to develop a chart listing promos and offering individual and total ad rates as summary information. In this way readers can review the summated information as an overall context for the textual interpretations. The brief network financial analysis in this discussion is offered to suggest the contours of a more detailed one.

Second, Burke's dramatistic framework is open to much flexibility and even ambiguity, as the author himself acknowledged (Burke, 1969, 1966). Much care and thought is required in analyzing textual material of any kind to ensure that the analyst makes a reasoned interpretation based on key textual elements both explicit and implicit. Qualitative methods, of which Burkean rhetorical criticism is a part, are to varying degrees devised after repeated interactions with textual matter, and are open to the discovery of patterns that can emerge only from repeated analysis.

Finally, ideological criticism is sometimes a freestanding interpretive activity, which allows for several ways to conceptualize ideology (see Althusser, 1971; Hall, 1991; Billig et al., 1988; Eagleton, 1991; Kervin, 1991; Thompson, 1990; van Dijk, 1998; White, 1992). The perspective one takes is always defined in part by the position of the analyst and in part by the particularities and contexts of the text or texts at hand. In the present case, which takes a critically oriented cultural studies approach, ideology is grounded in an awareness of power and dominance and a communicator's attempt to reproduce social norms, preferred ways of seeing and being, and convenient cultural myths. Still, it should be understood that the analyst's interpretations, however well-grounded, are always open to potentially different interpretations from audience members, and that the meanings anyone makes of a text may differ, as well, from those meanings that seem most clearly intended by the message creator (see Hall, 1991, 1980; Condit, 1991; Moffitt, 1993; Steiner, 1991).

With this in mind, it is hoped the present chapter offers a flexible methodological guide for studying televisual promotional messages from an interdisciplinary interpretive approach, or for analyzing virtually any other aspect of our mass-mediated, visually rich culture.

REFERENCES

Althusser, L. (1971). *Lenin and philosophy and other essays* (B. Brewster, Trans.). London: New Left Books.

Barbatsis, G. (1996). Look and I will show you something you will want to see: Pictorial engagement in negative campaign commercials. *Journal of Argumentation and Advocacy, 33,* 2.

Barbatsis, G. S., & Guy, Y. (1991). Analyzing meaning in form: Soap opera's compositional construction of "realness." *Journal of Broadcasting & Electronic Media, 35*(1), 59–74.

Barthes, R. (1972). *Mythologies.* New York: Hill & Wang.

Billig, M., Condor, S., Edwards, D., Gane, M., Middleton, D., & Radley, A. (1988). *Ideological dilemmas: A social psychology of everyday thinking.* London: Sage.

Broadcasting & Cable. (1996, September 2). *126*(37), 29.

Brummett, B. (1984). Burke's representative anecdote as a method in media criticism. *Critical Studies in Mass Communication 1,* 161–176.

Burke, K. (1966). *Language as symbolic action: Essays on life, literature, and method.* Berkeley: University of California Press.

Burke, K. (1969). *A grammar of motives.* Berkeley: University of California Press. (Originally published 1945)

Campbell, K. K., & Burkholder, T. R. (1997). *Critiques of contemporary rhetoric* (2nd ed.). Boston: Wadsworth.

Condit, C. M. (1991). The rhetorical limits of polysemy. In R. K. Avery & D. Eason (Eds.), *Critical perspectives on media and society* (pp. 365–386). New York: Guilford.

Cragan, J. F., & Shields, D. C. (1995). *Symbolic theories in applied communication research: Bormann, Burke and Fisher.* Cresskill, NJ: Hampton Press.

Eagleton, T. (1991). *Ideology: An introduction.* London: Verso.

Eco, U. (1972). Towards a semiotic inquiry into the television message. *Working papers in cultural studies, 3*, 103–121.

Fiske, J. (1987). *Television culture*. London: Metheun.

Gronbeck, B. E. (1984). Audience engagement in "Family." In M. J. Medhurst & T. W. Benson (Eds.), *Rhetorical dimensions in media: A critical casebook* (pp. 4–32). Dubuque, IA: Kendall/Hunt Publishing Company.

Grossberg, L. (1993). Can cultural studies find true happiness in communication? *Journal of Communication, 43*(4), 89–97.

Grossberg, L. (1995). Cultural studies vs. political economy: Is anyone else bored with this debate? *Critical Studies in Mass Communication, 12*(1), 72–81.

Grossberg, L., Nelson, C., & Treichler, P. (Eds.). (1992). *Cultural studies*. New York: Routledge.

Hall, S. (1991). Signification, representation, ideology: Althusser and the post-structuralist debates. In R. K. Avery & D. Eason (Eds.), *Critical perspectives on media and society* (pp. 88–113). New York: Guilford.

Hall, S. (1980). Encoding/decoding in the television discourse. In S. Hall, D. Hobson, & P. Lowe (Eds.), *Culture, media, language* (pp. 128–139). London: Hutchinson.

Kervin, D. (1991). Gender ideology in television commercials. In L. R. Vande Berg & L. A. Wenner (Eds.), *Television criticism: Approaches and applications* (pp. 235–253). New York: Longman.

Meehan, E. R., Mosco, V., & Wasko, J. (1993). Rethinking political economy: Change and continuity. *Journal of Communication, 43*(4), 105–116.

Mitchell, W. J. T. (1995). *Picture theory: Essays on verbal and visual representation*. Chicago: University of Chicago Press.

Moffitt, M. A. (1993). Articulating meaning: Reconceptions of the meaning process, fantasy/reality, and identity in leisure activities. *Communication Theory, 3*(3), 231–251.

Steiner, L. (1991). Oppositional decoding as an act of resistance. In R. K. Avery & D. Eason (Eds.), *Critical perspectives on media and society* (pp. 329–345). New York: Guilford.

Thompson, J. B. (1990). *Ideology and modern culture: Critical social theory in the era of mass communication*. Stanford, CA: Stanford University Press.

TV Dimensions. (1996). New York: Media Dynamics, Inc.

Van Dijk, T. A. (1998). *Ideology: A multidisciplinary approach*. London: Sage.

White, M. (1992). Ideological analysis and television. In R. C. Allen (Ed.), *Channels of discourse* (pp. 161–202). Chapel Hill: University of North Carolina Press.

A Cultural Analysis of the Unisys "Monitor Head" Television Commercial

VICTORIA O'DONNELL
Montana State University

INTRODUCTION

Television commercials are a mainstay of network and cable television because television production and distribution is a business that is sustained by advertising with the purpose of delivering viewers to advertisers and advertisers to viewers. Name-brand recognition is one of the primary goals of advertising, thus many commercials will have somewhat irrelevant content, but emphasis on the brand name is nearly always a major part of the commercial. Viewers may find television commercials annoying interruptions, use them to take breaks, or perhaps enjoy their slick content and production techniques. Because computers and the Internet have become cultural mainstays in our lives, television commercials that advertise these products and services have become more commonplace.

In 1998–1999, Unisys, "an e-business company that provides technical expertise and consulting skills to help customers operate confidently in the Internet economy,"[1] sponsored an excellent CNN series of 24 weekly episodes about the Cold War. Just as the end of the Cold War brought freedom to Eastern Europe and hope for global peace to the world, the end of the millennium signaled a new age of information and technology. Computers and the Internet had widespread usage, changing and challenging the workplace. Unisys was featured in two commercials entitled "Monitor Head: We Eat, Sleep and Drink This Stuff" repeatedly throughout the series. Both commercials featured a human body with a computer monitor for a head. One was a man playing golf; the other was a woman dancing at a party. This cultural analysis investigates the latter.

Unisys is a company based in Bluebell, Pennsylvania, with offices in 100 countries and 37,000 employees worldwide. It has several slogans, including "We help you transform" and "We have a head for e-business." Its Web pages depicted men and women at the top of the page with one of them on each page having a flashing computer monitor for a head. Obviously, this is a favored image for this company. The commercials that were featured during the CNN Cold War series were designed to illustrate that the Unisys employees never stop working until they solve their client's problems. Unisys also wanted the ad to reinforce its company shift to information services from computer hardware. Their research indicated that people remembered the ad and that their own employees had positive attitudes toward them.

There are many methodologies that could be used to analyze and criticize this commercial, but a cultural analysis reveals that it is emblematic of the complicated and contradictory nature of representation through visual images. It has symptomatic images of women, race, ethnicity, and the human body; it visually represents the female body as a spectacle; it emphasizes the current age of technological advancement and globalization; it stresses the blurring of work and leisure; it relies on viewer familiarity with certain aspects of popular culture; it perpetuates the image of the cyborg[2]; and it is consistent with the dominant ideology of our culture although it is also capable of polysemy, a multiplicity of meanings. This analysis examines how the Unisys commercial attempts to hail viewers and create a subject position for them within its ideological worldview.

CULTURAL STUDIES THEORY

An image such as the Unisys commercial is produced within a social context, a certain period in history, and in a medium. With the Unisys commercial, the medium is television, the historical period is the present, a time of technological advancement, and the social context is a combination of the world of work and the world of leisure as well as popular culture represented by dress, music, and dance. These elements are important aspects of culture, *defined as the actual practices and customs, languages, beliefs, forms of representation, and system of formal and informal rules that tell people how to behave most of the time.* Because of culture, we are able to make sense of our world through a certain amount of shared meanings and recognition of differing meanings. Viewers bring to their understanding of an image other aspects of their culture that link the image to a recognizable context. This enables each viewer to make his or her own sense of an expression or a representation.

According to Stuart Hall, images are associated with power relations because they determine who is and is not represented and what issues are or are not important. A power-related term is "hegemony," the power or dominance that one group holds over another. Hall's 1980 encoding/decoding model (see Chapter 31, Fig. 31.1) enables us to see that a viewer may prefer the intended or dominant meaning and thus become the subject within the cultural hegemony, the dominant strands of meaning. However, if a viewer resists the dominant meaning, then the viewer also has the power to oppose it and find a meaning contradictory to the intended one. Some viewers may primarily fit into the dominant ideology but will tend to resist certain elements of the intended meaning; therefore, they will negotiate their own meanings according to the ways in which they question their relationship to the dominant ideology. When viewers have some control over the production of meaning, they are likely to experience pleasure because they have maintained their own social identity even when they resist the dominant meaning of an image. There is also a certain kind of pleasure in the recognition of and understanding of the elements of one's culture.

Cultural studies analysis investigates the production and exchange of meaning between a visual image and its viewer and recognizes that many meanings can be made by different viewers. The meaning of a television commercial is not just a plea to buy certain goods and services but rather to create a recognition of a need, a problem, a lack, or a desire. If the viewer identifies with the images in the commercial, she or he may be able to realize that the need, problem, lack, or desire actually exists. The commercial will subsequently offer its product or services to fulfill the need, solve the problem, supply what is lacking, or fulfill a desire. In order for the viewer to derive meaning from the commercial, "articulation" or a connection is made that unifies the different elements within the given context "between the viewer and the viewed, between the power of the image to signify and the viewer's capacity to interpret meaning" (Evans & Hall, 1999, p. 4) and link it to other aspects of his/her culture. A television commercial "hails" or summons us, and if we recognize that it is speaking to us, we respond to it, thus acknowledging the social position that is encoded within it and within us. We thus become its subjects.

THE UNISYS COMMERCIAL

The commercial opens with music, three beats of a bongo drum and coronet, signifying a Latino type of music. A 20-something man with dark hair, dressed in a black suit and blue shirt with an open collar says, "Earth to Stephanie," and, as music continues, we see that he is dancing a sort of salsa dance with Stephanie, his dance partner. In the highly lit background, a brown-skinned man in a white shirt with big ruffled sleeves plays the bongo drums. There is a close-up on his hands. Another brown-skinned man, with a shaved head, dressed in a tan suit with a long white scarf, plays the coronet and dances to the salsa beat while playing. Stephanie, dressed in a red camisole top, short black skirt, and red high-heeled sandals, has a computer monitor for a head. Her partner takes no notice of this and continues dancing with her. The images on her monitor are not clear at first. In the background, there are other dancers—a white, dark-haired man in a suit dancing with a tall woman, whose ethnicity may be Asian, in a white camisole top and black slacks, a long-haired blonde woman in a red slip dress dancing with a dark-haired white man in a grey leisure shirt. Stephanie, who has rotated away, returns to her partner, and in the background is a dark-skinned woman in a low-cut black dress with lots of cleavage showing. She has long dark curly hair and appears to be Hispanic. Passing behind this couple is an older, heavy-set, bald man carrying a tray and a towel on his arm. He is apparently a waiter.

The color images on Stephanie's monitor head become very clear in several close shots as she continues dancing—a large office with computers and people working there, a group of people around a long table appear to be having a meeting, three Asian women working at a desk, a satellite dish seen from various distances and angles, and then an image of many satellite dishes. Stephanie's partner, who is never named nor spoken to by Stephanie or anyone else, says, "Is there something you want to talk about?" As they dance there are rapid sequential close-ups on Stephanie's torso, arm, breasts, and feet. A male voice-over says, "At Unisys our people can't stop working until they've figured out ways to solve our clients' problems." There is a pause in the voice-over as they continue to dance. Then the voice-over says, "And even then she's still thinking about a network solution for a bank in Hong Kong." The image on Stephanie's monitor shows a diagram of circuits. Suddenly, she says, "Of course," and the monitor disappears. For the first time we see Stephanie's face. She is also 20-something, fair with black hair pulled back in a twist. Her ethnic origins are ambiguous. She could be Anglo or she could be Hispanic. The voice-over continues, "Because when we set out to do something we really get into it." Stephanie moves away from her partner and the other dancers, grinning and twirling, hair falling in her face as she turns, smiles, and then becomes a tiny figure still dancing and smiling in the lower right corner under the words "UNISYS" in red lettering and "We eat, sleep and drink this stuff" in black lettering. At the bottom of the frame is the UNISYS web address.

THE GENERAL METHODOLOGY OF CULTURAL ANALYSIS AND ITS USEFULNESS FOR INVESTIGATING A TELEVISION COMMERCIAL

The analysis of a commercial for Unisys presented here demonstrates how a cultural studies methodology enables us to interpret and go inside its visual text to understand its cultural implications. Cultural analysis is well suited to the analysis of television images because they are based on visual representation. Produced for television transmission, these images are determined by technical means controlled by cameras, camera angles, camera movement, direction, lighting, computer manipulation, and editing. Television images are production attempts to construct images that resemble the real, therefore they are representations. Just as reality has the possibility of different meanings, so does the representation of reality. The practice of looking and seeing television rests on complex conditions of existence. Viewers may discover and think about their own identification and imagine themselves in the televised representations. Furthermore, viewers may have their perceptions changed within a short period of time. The recognition of the self in an image, whether the viewer accepts or resists the representation of the image, is an indicator that viewers make active choices of the meanings they decode and thus gain pleasure from the experience. This is one reason for the popularity of television because it offers a variety of pleasures to different viewers.

The following are questions to be asked in doing a cultural studies analysis in visual communication. Although one concentrates on images in visual communication, it is also useful to pay heed to discourse in television.

1. How does a television commercial relate to the shared living condition of the time?
2. What is present and what is absent? How are we limited in our ways of seeing?
3. Can we place ourselves inside the image, identifying with it? What do we get out of the image if we identify ourselves in relationship to the image? How does the

television commercial position the viewer as a subject? When it "hails" you, do you answer?

4. What meanings are preferred by the television commercial? (In other words, what is the embedded dominant ideology (hegemony[3]).
5. Examine the codes of the television commercial:
   a. Realistic Codes: How is the television commercial encoded in social codes, such as appearance, behavior, speech, sound, and setting?
   b. Representative Codes: How do the technical codes (camera use, lighting, editing, sound, and music) convey the conventional representational codes (narrative, conflict, character, action, dialogue, setting, and casting)?
   c. Ideological Codes: How do the representative codes work together to encode a preferred meaning that supports and ideology? What is the ideology?
6. What meanings can different viewers make of the television commercial? What is the dominant meaning? What meanings are possible from negotiation? What meanings might be resisted or opposed?
7. How might the decoded meanings give the viewer a sense of power? How might they provide pleasure? How is this related to the viewer's sense of identity?
8. How does the television commercial help the subject make sense of social experience?
9. In what ways does the television commercial seem natural, accepted as real? How is the naturalness articulated? What is at stake in the representation?
10. How do the meanings that we derive implicate us in the production of the meanings?
11. What meanings does a television commercial have when it is absorbed into the lives of its viewers? Might they take on new meanings, new identities, new knowledge?

Question #5 is derived from John Fiske's breakdown of the codes of television,[4] codes being the "rule-governed system of signs, whose rules and conventions are shared amongst members of a culture, and which are used to generate and circulate meanings in and for that culture" (Fiske, 1987, p. 4). Decoding analysis relies upon the context in which the images are represented. Television images are complex for they are mediated images. Three-dimensional places, people, and objects are viewed on a two-dimensional plane that is not life-sized. The actual visual context of a television image is controlled by artistic and technical means determined by the television producers. Television images are produced by technical means controlled by cameras, camera angles, movement, directing, lighting, computer manipulation, and editing. The production efforts attempt to duplicate, but the images are not duplications because they have been constructed to re-present or imitate the real. The real is a thing in the world in its own right. Representation is a construction that tries to be recognizable as the real; it is an imitation that attempts to evoke a response as if to the real thing. The production results are regarded as "codes" through which images are encoded and include the social codes that encode realistic images, the representational codes that make television production possible, and the ideological codes that give consent to a particular kind of social order, assigning roles of dominance or subordination to gender, race, sexuality, religion, age, or social groups. Because television is viewed by a mass audience, the codes need to be conventional and shared among members of a culture. For this reason, the codes are often stereotypical. Because television commercials seek brand recognition and a positive response from the viewer, the viewer who answers the "hail" does so by recognizing the social position that has been constructed in encoding the image and is likely to accept the intended meaning, decoding it accordingly.

The questions for analysis enable the viewer to "play" a television commercial as if it were a piece of music—interpreting it, activating it, giving it a living presence. The answers to the questions are determined by the content of the television commercial *and* the analyst's knowledge of the cultural context in which it was made. The analyst must be a student of culture, understanding not only hegemony but also resistance to it. As Hall has insisted, cultural analysis "has to be open to external influences, for example, to the rise of new social movements, to psychoanalysis, to feminism, to cultural differences" (Morley and Chen, 1996, p. 150). In conducting a cultural analysis, meaning is determined by both production and reception of images in a context. It is therefore possible that the meaning that one analyst may derive could be different from that of another analyst. After examining the television commercial, the analyst determines how the answers to the questions fit together to form clusters of analysis. This helps avoid repetition in the written analysis, and the clusters help focus on the significant findings of the analysis. The resulting clusters enable the analyst to understand and report the cultural implications of the television commercial. Cultural studies analyses allow us to reflect upon the ideals and contradictions of our culture, to examine issues of power in and among groups of people, and to realize how very complex responses to images are.

CULTURAL ANALYSIS OF THE UNISYS COMMERCIAL

In this analysis, the 11 methodological questions were adapted to the specific elements of the Unisys commercial and four major clusters emerged from the analysis: (a) Visual codes and Representation, (b) The Dominant Ideology and the Preferred Meaning, (c) Articulation, Positioning Viewers as Subjects and Pleasure Derived from Viewing, and (d) Making Sense of Social Experience.

VISUAL CODES AND REPRESENTATION

This analysis begins with the obvious, the visual codes within the television commercial. The first code, *realistic*, has to do with how social codes (appearance, behavior, speech, sound, and setting) are used to represent reality. For the most part, this is straightforward description of what you perceive in the images. The clothing, music, and behavior of the people in the Unisys commercial are conventionally coded to represent a social setting such as a party or a club. The women are dressed in evening clothes that tightly skim their slender idealized bodies—camisole tops, slip dresses, low-cut tops and dresses, high heeled sandals. The men wear leisure shirts and suits. The musicians' attire includes a ruffled-sleeved shirt and a long scarf worn with a suit. All of the dancers are youthful, probably in their 20s. A waiter, the only older person there, has a tray, but no one is drinking or eating. The music is festive; everyone but the waiter is dancing. Salsa music, an appropriation of Latino culture, was very popular for dancing in 1998 and 1999. The setting, however, is inconsistent with a party or club atmosphere. The set has a stark, highly lit background. There is nothing on the walls, and there is no furniture. It looks like what it is, a bare television set that does not give a sense of reality. Of course, the other unrealistic code is the monitor as a substitute for Stephanie's head. Here the commercial presents us with a cyborg—part woman, part computer. This is a signification of woman as career-driven and unable to separate work and leisure. The cyborg image sets the natural body in opposition to the technologically recrafted body and may reform how we think about the social and cultural body. This will be more apparent in the discussion of the ideological codes.

Gender, race, and ethnicity are obvious except in the case of Stephanie. The other dancers are white males and white, Hispanic, and Asian women. The musicians have dark skin. They may be representations of African Americans, or they may be from island countries, such as Cuba or Jamaica. Stephanie's ethnicity is ambiguous, for her light skin and dark hair suggest that she could be Anglo or Hispanic or a mixture of both. Everyone except the waiter is slender, well-built, and represented as physically attractive according to cultural ideals. Stephanie has a waifish quality, for she is small, curvaceous, perky, and energetic. This is consistent with the idealized female body in the media.

There is little spoken dialogue, but what is spoken is a reflection of conventional popular culture. Stephanie's dancing partner says, "Earth to Stephanie," an intertextual reference to science-fiction films and television programs. It is also colloquial language that generally means, "You're not paying attention to me." Later the same man says, "Is there something you want to talk about?" This is also popularized jargon recognized as a form of psychological talk.

The second code, *representational*, includes *technical* codes (camera, lighting, sound, music, and editing) that are used to transmit conventional *representational* codes (narrative, conflict, character, action, dialogue, setting, and casting). Camera use and editing are of particular interest in this commercial. Stephanie, still wearing her monitor head and lacking a solution to her work problem, is represented by close-up shots of her body parts—her torso, arm, breasts, and feet, that represent her as an object presented to the viewer in rapidly edited shots. Likewise, the images on her computer head change from close-ups of people in offices to long shots of satellite dishes. When she finds the solution to her problem, her monitor head disappears and the camera focuses on her entire body. She has become a complete woman, dancing away from her partner and the others while, at the same time, becoming smaller and smaller until in the last shot, she is a tiny figure dominated by the Unisys logo. The editing is rapid, allowing the viewer quick and brief glances at the others in the commercial. The focus is clearly on Stephanie, a woman as spectacle. The male voice-over with its explanations of the mission of the Unisys Company ("At Unisys our people can't stop working until they've figured out ways to solve our clients' problems.") contrasts with the ultra-brief dialogue of the actors. This defines the narrative, a problem-solution set-up in which the capabilities of the computer have been combined with Stephanie who "can't stop working" while she is dancing. As a cyborg, Stephanie is controlled by her work and the narrator, who not so incidentally is male.

As stated before, race and ethnicity are represented in this commercial. All of the male dancers and the waiter are white, but the women are white, Asian, and Hispanic. Although there is diversity in the mix of the couples, the dark-skinned musicians dance alone. The disembodied hands of the man playing the bongo drums are seen in one close-up shot as if to signify his hands as performing objects. The realistic, technical, and representational codes combine to reveal the dominant *ideological* codes.

THE DOMINANT IDEOLOGY AND THE PREFERRED MEANING

The third code, *ideological*, is derived from the analysis of the first two codes and is recognizable in the culture embedded in the Unisys commercial. An ideology is a set of beliefs, values, attitudes, and behaviors that are agreed on to the point that they constitute a set of desirable norms for society. Ideology is a form of consent to a particular kind of social or economic order, for example, equality and capitalism. Because the Unisys commercial blurs the distinction between work and leisure, features ethnic diversity in attractive and youthful actors, emphasizes images of technology and globalization, and uses the gimmick of a cyborg-woman, the following ideologies are present in the commercial: (a) a work ethic leading to success, (b) technological advancement and globalization, (c) ethnic diversity that is limited to attractive young women and men, and (d) woman driven and controlled by her career.

The work ethic is extended to a blurring of work and leisure, and round-the-clock work is rewarding to both employee and employer. It is not difficult for the viewer to articulate this meaning, for longer hours at work and extensions of the work week into the weekend have become common practice in commercial America. Energy and enthusiasm for work are also important commercial values. Stephanie embodies energy and enthusiasm, especially when she finds a solution for the client's problem, thus sending her into ecstasy at the end of the commercial. Success is an important American value, and success is achieved by Unisys because, as the voice-over says, "Our people can't stop working until they've figured out ways to solve our client's problems." The company's corporate ideology is stated outright in the voice over as well as in the slogan, "We eat, sleep, and drink this stuff."

Technological advancement and globalization are considered crucial to today's market-place. This meaning is embedded in the images on Stephanie's monitor head. Not only do we see computers and satellite dishes, but we also see a variety of international settings and people, especially Asians, and these images together with the voice-over mentioning "a client in Hong Cong," suggest that business in the Far East is an important feature of Unisys. Stephanie's computer head may signify that technology is such an integral part of our lives that we have corporeally incorporated it. She would not be a success without technology to aid her in solving problems for the corporation. Her computer gives her power, but finding the solution to a client's problem releases her to her own complete body. The male voice-over, however, controls the narrative and defines Stephanie's work. That she does not have a human woman's head until the very end may suggest woman is defined by both the disembodied male voice as well as the technology that replaces her head.

Other meanings include an emphasis on ethnic diversity that seems to be restricted to young and attractive men and women. Its articulation depends on transferring what is seen in the commercial to assumptions about the company's hiring practices. The commercial suggests that whites, Hispanics, and Asians are treated equally in the Unisys corporation; however, the representation of the dark-skinned musicians as happily servile seems to mean that they may not be considered as important. Because the music's origins are Latino, it is puzzling that the musicians would appear to be African American or from the Carribean islands as opposed to being Hispanic. All of the dancers are youthful, slender, and attractive. They have slender, idealized bodies that emphasize a preference for being thin. The waiter, however, is middle-aged, fat, and bald. Does this representation mean that someone like him would not be a typical Unisys employee?

Further, the treatment of woman as spectacle derived from the objectification of Stephanie's body parts suggests a rewriting of the career woman's body. She wears a monitor for a head while she is trying to solve the problem, but she becomes a complete woman when she solves it. Is she a postfeminist woman, effective in her career but also successful in her appearance and social life? Or is she so obsessed with work that she neglects her partner? He has no name, Stephanie completely ignores him, does not answer his questions, and twirls away from him when she finds the solution to her client's problem. Does this suggest that today's career woman no longer needs nor wants a man?

The analyst interprets possible viewer responses to the television commercial according to an understanding of a heterogeneous cultural audience. The preferred meaning is the intent of the commercial and is thus targeted to the majority of its viewing audience. This commercial "hails" potential clients who want young, energetic, and attractive women and men of ethnic diversity who are willing to work overtime until they solve a problem, and it hails young, energetic, and conventionally attractive women and men in today's workforce. These people would probably accept the ideology of the commercial—rewarding work above leisure, success through solving problems, technological advancement, and globalization in a capitalist marketplace, and career-driven women—and constitute themselves as subjects because they recognize their social position and that they are being spoken to because they accept the dominant ideology.

Some viewers could become subjects *if* they could negotiate and modify the ideology, tweaking it to fit their own identities. A negotiated position might include acceptance of a capitalist marketplace, free enterprise, technological advancement, and globalization but rejection of longer working hours and the extension of work into leisure time. Another negotiated position might accept all of the above, including the blurring of work and leisure, but would possibly reject the emphasis on ethnic diversity or gender equality. Another might reject the representation of women as objects or dark-skinned men as musicians or older, overweight, bald men as waiters rather than computer technicians.

Oppositional meanings could also be derived from the above observations. In addition to the opposing the representative images of gender, race, and ethnicity, opposition could also be made against advancement in technology because of the fear of its dominance over people skills. There is much concern today about artificial intelligence and its role in our lives. People want what technology has to offer but fear the possibility of its superiority or dominance. Also, opposition might be made toward globalization or even to capitalism itself. As Hall said, we decode meaning by interpreting "from the family in which you were brought up, the places of work, the institutions you belong to, the other practices you do." (Evans & Hall, 1999, p. 312).

That the Unisys commercial was shown repeatedly during the Cold War series is important, because the television programs celebrated the defeat of communism and the victory of the free world along with free enterprise and international capitalism. It is most likely that viewers accepted the preferred meaning and the dominant political ideology of the commercial or negotiated their own meanings of it.

ARTICULATION, POSITIONING VIEWERS AS SUBJECTS, AND PLEASURE DERIVED FROM VIEWING

In order for a viewer to derive meaning from a television commercial, articulation or a connection has to be made that unifies the different elements within the cultural context of the viewer and the viewed, between the signification of the image and the viewer's ability to interpret meaning. Because of the cultural context, viewers are capable of making the connection between the elements of the commercial and the derived meaning. In other words, articulation is possible, enabling viewers to make sense of the commercial and their contemporary situation. In the Unisys commercial, the images and sounds "hail" the viewers with culturally identifiable music, a heterosexual social situation, evening dress codes, and salsa dancing. It gets viewer attention with a cyborg gimmick, a monitor head on a dancing woman. This is a variation of the live television commercials of nearly 50 years ago when dancing girls in live television commercials had cigarette packs covering their head and torsos. Mary Tyler Moore got her start in television as a dancing cigarette pack. The notion of the cyborg, part woman/part machine, is also familiar in media, especially in science-fiction films and television programs. The monitor head can be recognized as a cultural gimmick appropriate for an e-business advertising technical expertise and computer systems consulting skills. Computer programs and hardware are not just commonplace in the business world, they are essential. Internet communication has aided the global economy. Computer technology is an essential part of contemporary culture. Viewer recognition of and identification with the images in the commercial empowers them, giving them pleasure through understanding the preferred meaning or negotiating an individual meaning or from opposing the dominant ideology. Furthermore, some viewers may gain pleasure from looking at the players in the commercial, observing their pleasure and leisure behavior. The commercial gives the viewers the opportunities to make their own connections, articulating individual meaning.

Cultural diversity has become a norm as Hispanic and Asian populations increase in the United States, thus it is not unusual to see diversity in a television commercial. The youthfulness of the actors in the commercial may also be appropriate because diversity has become a norm in colleges, universities and the high-technology workplaces. The ambiguity of Stephanie's ethnicity may enable both white and Hispanic women to identify with her. Whichever ethnic background she represents, she is obviously bright, successful, and attractive according to contemporary ideals for female bodies. The images are shown in rapid succession, thus requiring multiple viewing to see them all. This, too, is consistent with a culture that emphasizes quick studies, sound bites, MTV, and other forms of rapid information flow.

The commercial is upbeat, easy to understand, and emphasizes success, happiness, and enthusiasm, all of which are common American values. Further, it stresses problem solving, a key paradigm in western civilization's preference for linear thinking. It probably appealed to most viewers.

Viewers of television are used to seeing youthful and physically attractive actors in programs and commercials, thus the absence of older or less attractive persons in positions of power may not present a problem. Yet feminist viewers are likely to be disturbed by the close-up shots of Stephanie's torso, breasts, and feet as well as the tight clothing on all of the women that emphasizes their sexuality rather than their accomplishments. Male viewers may experience difficulty articulating the message when the only man who speaks is Stephanie's partner, a man without a name who is disregarded by the successful woman. Dark-skinned or black men and women may reject the images of the musicians whose only roles are to provide music. This harkens back to the days of early film when the only appearance that black people made in mainstream films was as entertainers. Finally, middle-aged men may resent being represented as overweight, bald waiters. There are many possible ways to connect to this commercial, but to articulate the preferred meaning, the viewer has to accept the dominant ideology and objective of the Unisys corporation.

Making Sense of Social Experience

Because the analyst understands the nuances of the culture and uses them upon to explain the television commercial, sense is made according to the context of social experience in the culture. Cultural analysis of a brief television commercial also can enable viewers to make sense of their own social experience because television commercials reflect a national culture. Whether viewers approve of technological advancement, globalization, the blurring of work and leisure, successful but driven career women, and cultural diversity or not, these values are part of our culture today. Even though presented through frivolous content in the commercial, these cultural norms represent American business and corporate life. They are also present in other institutions—educational, nonprofit, government, and service industries. Life is lived at a fast pace, and those who succeed in a capitalist society are rewarded.

It is important to notice who and what are represented and who and what are not. A cultural analysis gives us an opportunity to challenge power ratios, to protest the ways in which groups of people—old, young, male, female, white, black, Hispanic, Asian, and so on—are represented or omitted, and to question the norms of our culture.

CONCLUSION

This cultural studies analysis was based on finding answers to the 11 methodological questions within a television commercial made for Unisys. Through description, analysis, and interpretation of the visual codes that brought forth representations of women and men dancing at a party, ideology was determined and a preferred meaning became apparent. Through recognition and understanding of the cultural context in which the television commercial was shown, other meanings and resistance to the ideology could be speculated upon. A cultural analysis of a television commercial reveals what is emblematic of the complicated and contradictory nature of representation through visual images.

ENDNOTES

[1] www.unisys.com

[2] In an age in which technology has permeated our culture, cyborg images abound. A cyborg is a hybrid of machine and an organism, a coupling between an electronic or mechanical apparatus and a human being. Both the signs of the human and signs of the machine mark the dual nature of the cyborg that is neither purely human nor purely machine. The cyborg is dualistically human and artificial, articulating a human body with certain cultural formations. A cyborg may be Frankenstein's monster or Hal, the talking computer in *2001: A Space Odyssey*. Culture has advanced to the point where it dominates nature with replaceable body parts from hips to hearts, aesthetic surgery, cloning, stem cell research, biotechnology, and "bots" that perform assembly-line factory work. The theoretical conception of the cyborg is that it is a metaphor for the relationships between humans and machines in which we both value and fear the power of technology.

[3] Hegemony occurs when images convey a strand of dominant meanings associated with cultural power.

[4] Fiske (1987, pp. 4–13).

REFERENCES

Evans, J., & Hall, S. (1999). *Visual Culture: The Reader*. London: Sage.

Fiske, J. (1987). *Television culture*. London: Metheun.

Morley, D., & Chen, Kuan-Hsing. (1996). *Stuart Hall: Critical dialogues in cultural studies*. London: Routledge.

Unisys. Retrieved, February 1999, from: www.unisys.com.

A Historical Approach to Understanding Documentary Photographs: Dialogue, Interpretation, and Method

GERALD DAVEY
San Antonio College

Although some scholars, such as Joseph Turow (1992), argue that fields such as cultural studies fail to give adequate consideration to other well-established perspectives, such as his own industrial perspective, there can be little doubt that the explanatory power of cultural studies can prove invaluable in the interpretation and explication of media productions as salient and influential cultural creations and in discovering the range of interplay between viewers and media through the new cultural meanings that are created.

As O'Donnell points out in Chapter 31, the range of methodological perspectives among cultural studies practitioners is wide. What all share, however, is critically important, and it is only by contrasting the work of cultural studies practitioners with representatives of other interpretive traditions that both its breadth and its fundamentally identifying characteristics can be discerned. Thus, in this chapter, the goal is to concentrate on a fundamental feature of cultural studies approaches—its emphasis on ideology critique—used within an actual field of interpretation—the interpretation and understanding of historically significant documentary photographs—and then contrast it with other interpretive approaches, notably the aesthetic approach common to photographic criticism. By contrasting these approaches, some of the practical advantages as well as potential perils involved in undertaking such interpretative work become apparent.

APPROACHES TO UNDERSTANDING PHOTOGRAPHS

Contemporary and historic approaches to understanding and interpreting photographs broadly fall into three categories: those that emphasize the inherently objective nature of the photographic medium (it's *"transparency"*) and tie its communicative capacity primarily to objective presentation; those that emphasize the capacity of the photograph—exercised to varying degrees—as a vehicle for unique artistic expression—the aesthetic approach noted earlier; and those that deemphasize both and argue that social, economic, and political forces shape and ultimately account for the existence, nature, distribution, and use of photographs as well as other media—a position (critique of ideology) linked with cultural studies.

This latter position is one of the basic commitments that distinguishes cultural studies as a disciplinary field. Cultural studies theorists are united, as O'Donnell pointed out, by little except their commitment to the assertion that relations of power within society are embedded in and reproduced through cultural creation. From this perspective, media-generated cultural productions are critical to the maintenance of power relations in modern Western societies. Hence, regardless of the particular methodological technique used, which can range broadly across the entire spectrum of the humanities and the social sciences, there is a fundamental commitment to what may be called a "critical edge" (Thompson, 1990).

In other words, although the role of media may vary enormously and its uses be equally open to a panoply of creative attempts to generate a variety of meanings—not all by any means serving dominant social interests—nevertheless, the concept of ideology, like hegemony, remains fundamental. As O'Donnell notes in her discussion of Fiske, there are preferred meanings, meanings of resistance and negotiated meanings, created through the interplay of media and its audience, but the underlying reality of the "preferred meaning" is a given in cultural studies. Indeed, the concept of ideology has great explanatory power. It is uniquely suited to interpreting patterns of sameness or difference in analyzing media products. It helps us understand the interrelationship between media and other social, economic, and political institutions and the relative stability of modern societies. Although the term has undergone substantial revision since its reintroduction in the writings of Marx, it remains critical to any real understanding of the function of mass media in society and its relations of power.

Advocates of each of the above-mentioned approaches have successfully presented largely coherent and yet strikingly different, often mutually exclusive, interpretations of photographs, their nature, and communicative potential. The focus here is on the latter two—aesthetic and cultural—both of which admit to and originate within an attempt to understand the nature of the fundamental transformation implicit in the photographic process itself. A few examples of the interpretive power of each will here have to suffice to understand their most fundamental characteristics and their contrasting strengths and weaknesses.

John Szarkowski, who succeeded Edward Steichen in 1954 as director of the Department of Photography at the Museum of Modern Art, is widely regarded as the dominant influence in bringing photographic works into the world of art museums and galleries. As Richard Woodward wrote: "No one has done more to uncover important new work, expand and redefine tradition, and foster an appreciation of the unique contributions of photography to art history" (Woodward, 1998).

In *Looking at Photographs: 100 Pictures from the Collection of the Museum of Modern Art*, one of Szarkowski's most enduring works, his skill at the aesthetic interpretation of individual photographs is demonstrated in the analysis of more than 50 photographic images (Szarkowski, 1973). As Szarkowski noted in the preface:

In 1929, when the acquisition of a painting by Cezanne was still considered adventurous, the proposition that photography deserved serious critical study would have been simply unintelligible to the leaders of most art museums. (p. 9)

Against this background, and the continuing resistance to the inclusion of photography in collections and discussions of art, the need for an intensive defense of the aesthetic potential of the photograph was widely felt within the photographic community. Szarkowski, himself a professional photographer, when called—much to his surprise—to the museum post, took up the challenge.

That the medium itself has a unique capacity for artistic and meaningful expression is the basic proposition of Szarkowski's work. This accounts for his unusual inclusion in *Looking at Photographs* of such a broad spectrum of photographers over the entire history of photography, with content varying from news photos to aerial reconnaissance, with no more than one photograph per photographer represented.

It is important to note, however, that this emphasis does not reduce the central importance of the creative artist to Szarkowski's aesthetic approach. While Szarkowski noted that his work includes photographs from a wide range of "known and unknown" photographers, 47 of the 50 photographs included were made by widely collected and well-known photographers. These are the masters of the craft, here presented and discussed typically through one of their lesser known works, a demonstration of their abiding aesthetic, expressive genius.

Among the better known photographers presented in this work is Bill Brandt whose work is represented by the inclusion of his "Young Housewife in Bethnal Greene, 1937" (Szarkowski, 1973, p. 122). In this photograph, a young woman in heavily soiled and stained clothing is on her knees and appears to be rinsing out a cloth or sponge, which she is using to clean an entryway floor. The woman's face is downcast and she is crouched down. The lighting is overhead which accentuates the woman's face, shoulders, arms, and knees. The bucket is in the low center of the composition. The woman is framed by that part of the doorway, which is visible in the photograph and she is placed toward the upper right of the photograph. Within the frame, only the doorknob of the entry door is visible. There is no discernible detail of the interior of the house, only a suggestion of darkness and a flat, closed-in space.

Szarkowski's begins his commentary on the photograph with a general discussion of the nature of artistic tradition, which he holds "exists in the minds of artists, and consists of their collective memory of what has been accomplished so far. . . . Its function is to mark the starting point for each day's work." Szarkowski then goes on to note Brandt's early study with Man Ray, his exposure to Atget and "the French Surrealist film-makers." He wrote, Brandt's "own work already possessed a strongly surreal character," which he characterizes as a "mordant, poetic romanticism suggestive of de Chirico and Dore" (1973, p. 121).

Szarkowski noted Brandt's relative isolation from contemporary photographers and argues that for some "of the most independent talents" such isolation can constitute "a sanctuary where radical visions can develop undisturbed" (1973, p. 121).

In commenting on Brandt's corpus of work, Szarkowski noted: "In the years following his return to England, Brandt concentrated on photographing his countrymen, of all classes and conditions." Further, he wrote: "These pictures are moving and strange; they express both sympathy and tranquil detachment, as though Brandt were photographing something that existed long ago." Finally, he asserted: "Though unsparingly frank, his pictures seem to refer less to the moment described than to the issues of role, tenacity, courage, and survival" (1973, p. 121). Szarkowski's emphases reveal some of the most salient features of the aesthetic approach to understanding photographs. First, the discussion ties Brandt directly to his position within an artistic tradition and in spite of the fact that the subject matter of Brandt's photographs concentrates so heavily on "his countrymen, of all classes and conditions," Szarkowski said nothing about Brandt's *own* social, political and economic status in English society. Indeed, it is as if Brandt's whole identity were that of *artist* and in photographing "his countrymen, of all classes and conditions," he was not so situated within that range that his position influenced or contextualized his vantage point—at least not sufficiently so to be essential to understanding the photograph itself.

Here, then, is a special genius whose work can be understood without reference to his own historicity (except in so far as it lies at a specific point within the history of art) and, indeed, by interpreters whose special expertise allows them the same privilege. Both, it seems, stand ensconced in a tradition that cuts through the broader forces of history like a knife. Szarkowski's commentary on Russell Lee's "Son of a Sharecropper Combing Hair in Bedroom of Shack, Missouri" (1938) illustrates other characteristics of modern aesthetics. In commenting on this photograph, Szarkowski contextualizes the image within the pictorial tradition of the toilette "an important subject for artists since the Egyptians." His only comment on the surroundings in which the young boy's grooming takes place is that "the nature of his surroundings make the moment no less private or ceremonial" (1973, p. 134).

No other mention is made of the poverty in which the boy lives, or the documentary aim of those photographers, of which Lee was one of the most productive, who produced photographs such as this for the Farm Security Administration during the Roosevelt administration in an effort to make known the widespread rural poverty within the United States, which FDR's political agenda hoped to address.

Szarkowski himself was intimately and fully aware of this context, but here found it consonant with a viewpoint which he was struggling against, namely the factual, "objective" tradition of photographic meaning. Here, only an appreciation of the universal and transcendental traditions of aesthetic creation were essential to appreciate the *art* of this man's work. Even the seemingly sad, disheartened expression on the boys face–reflected in a broken mirror—fails to warrant the attention of Szarkowski's interpretive gaze.

As a result, it seems, the material circumstances become merely the occasion, the accidental accompaniment to the universal, the thematic in art history. Thus, Szarkowski focuses on an activity that transcends the individual moment, one in which the boy himself is actor but not truly subject.

Contemporary cultural studies perspectives, on the other hand, constitute some of the more coherent, systematic expressions of societal viewpoints (i.e., those see the photograph as "used" and even created by a social framework that it serves). The emphasis on ideology now associated with cultural studies originated with the Frankfurt School at the Institute for Social Research where, in a 1937 essay by Max Horkheimer, the term *critical theory* first appeared (Ingram, 1990). Dissatisfied with the failure of the positivistic social sciences to produce substantial change in Western capitalist society, concerned with the rise of fascism and the dire results of communism under Stalin, the founding members of the Frankfurt school produced a unique synthesis of critical social philosophy consisting of an amalgam of insights from Marx's political economy and Kant's critical philosophy, psychoanalysis and social science (Jay, 1973).

Stuart Hall, one of the leading figures in contemporary British cultural studies, a movement informed by the Frankfurt School, characterized the problem of ideology as "to give an account, within a materialist theory, of how social ideas arise" and noted further "[ideology] has especially to do with the concepts and the languages of practical thought which stabilize a particular form of power and domination; or which reconcile and accommodate the mass of the people to their subordinate place in the social formation" (Hall, 1986). John B. Thompson, in *Ideology and Modern Culture* (1990), wrote similarly:

> The analysis of ideology . . . is primarily concerned with the ways in which symbolic forms intersect with relations of power. It is concerned with the ways in which meaning is mobilized in the social world and serves thereby to bolster up individuals and groups who occupy positions of power. Let me define this focus more sharply: *to study ideology is to study the ways in which meaning serves to establish and sustain relations of domination.* [emphasis original] (p. 56)

And as the philosopher Paul Ricoeur (1981) put it succinctly, ideology is "the systematic distortion of communication by the hidden exercise of force" (p. 301).

This, then, is the beginning point toward understanding the critique of ideology and its central role in cultural studies. Although objectivist traditions tend to focus on the photographic process per se and aesthetic approaches focus on the "formable" characteristics of the medium subjected to the creative force, most typically, of individual artists, *critique of ideology argues that all must be seen within the larger social and cultural world within which they form an integral part and through which their particular characteristics and actions gain actual, historical meaning.* Thus, one well-known philosopher and cultural theorist, Janet Wolff (1983), explained that fundamentally: "Ideas and beliefs are *not* transparent, but always originate in and conceal social structures and processes" (p. 105). Photographic creations, such as those discussed here, do not stand apart from the broader society and its interests, but serve a key function within it (i.e., an ideological function).

Ideology critique, then, like aesthetic consciousness, militates against any primarily "objectivist" approach to understanding the photograph. The individual artist, his or her status as giving material expression to his or her uniquely inspired genius is here rejected or at the very least, subsumed. Indeed, from this perspective, as John Tagg (1988) noted, the aesthetic tradition is not somehow isolated form the larger and perhaps, more mundane, forces of its time, but to the contrary, ideology is "mediated by the aesthetic code" (p. 120). So, too, the artist is here imbedded within the fullness of history and indeed, rather than a unique genius standing outside those lesser souls around her, she provides "the personal mediation of a group consciousness." For here, "individuals are always subjects, and, as subjects, are constituted in ideology. There is no 'subjective essence' which escapes this constitution" (p. 131).

Tagg's (1988) text *The Burden of Representation: Essays on Photographies and Histories* is an especially noteworthy and well-received work devoted wholly to photography and photographic history from this perspective and will here serve as an important example of work in this tradition. Fundamental to Tagg's analysis is the assertion of a radical distinction between the photograph and the "world," which it purports to present objectively:

> At every stage, chance effects, purposeful interventions, choices and variations produce meaning, whatever skill is applied and whatever division of labour the process is subject to. This is not the inflection of a prior (though irretrievable) reality . . . but the production of a new and specific reality, the photograph, which becomes meaningful in certain transactions and has real effects, *but which cannot refer or be referred to a pre-photographic reality as to a truth.* (p. 3) [emphasis added]

Although the aesthetic perspective presented above shares the view that there lies a key distinction between the photograph and any prior reality, the precise nature of that distance is here sharply different. Rather than resorting to the explanatory power of the "genius" of the artist/creator, we have what to traditional aesthetics would seem an altogether new descriptive language with references to "chance," "division of labour," "transactions," and even "production" as here understood. Further, Tagg continued, "we have to see that every photograph is the result of specific and, in every sense, *significant distortions* which render its relation to any prior reality deeply problematic" (p. 2) [emphasis added]. What has hitherto been seen as the fruitful culmination of an artist's creative efforts, an ontological *transformation*, the creation of a newly inspired reality, is here recast as a *"distortion"* of any prior reality designed to further the material interests of a societal system, a production that serves to imbed and promulgate a constrained perception of reality.

For Tagg, the photograph (i.e., *photographs actually produced in history*), is broadly the result of ideological constraints that develop and maintain dominating social, cultural, political, and economic structures and practices and, thus, present a "distorted" relation between man and world throughout. Indeed, according to Tagg, the act of picturing, framing the subject, is inherently an ideological imposition upon the "world."

Thus, the photograph, for Tagg, is an artifact which reflects the institutional interests of a dominant social order empowered in a certain historical moment. *Any attempt to understand the photograph apart from such structures, the traditional province of both the aesthetic and objective traditions, results in a fundamental failure to grasp its meaning.*

It might seem to some readers that it would be difficult to apply two such opposed readings to the same photograph. Surely, scholars from each persuasion have their favorite images, those which seem more conducive to their individual readings. However, scholars from all perspectives find it necessary to address certain well-known photographs. Such photographs constitute a battleground on which the different interpretive forces and their underlying world views come into sharp relief. Here, one such photograph will serve to bring those differences to conscious attention.

FIG. 34.1.   Russell Lee's "Hidalgo County, Texas," 1939.

Analysis of a Russell Lee Photograph

In an analysis of Russell Lee's 1939 photograph "Hidalgo County, Texas," Tagg's cultural analysis draws our attention to the image as a whole and the interrelation of each element within it, characteristics shared with the aesthetic approach (Fig. 34.1). It is what is necessarily a part of any view of the photograph as in some sense a "statement" or a presentation of a point of view, distinguishing both from the objectivist tradition. Tagg's ideological reading, however, characterized Lee's photograph as

> dense with connotations, as every detail-of flesh, clothes, posture, of fabric, furniture and decoration—is brought fully lit, to the surface and presented . . . so we see every object both singly and coming together to form an ensemble: an apparently *seamless ideological structure* called a home. (p. 159) [emphasis added]

Then he continued

> On the one hand, the ideological construction put on the objects and events concretizes a general mythical scheme by incorporating it in the reality of these specific historical moments. At the same time, however, the very conjuncture of the objects and events and the mythical schema dehistoricizes the same objects and events by displacing the ideological connection to the archetypal level of the *natural and universal* in order to conceal its specifically *ideological nature*. (p. 160) [emphasis added]

Here, Tagg's reading revealed key emphases shared by the critique of ideology. First, the photograph is seen as "a construction," here understood as "put on" the objects and events depicted in the photograph. This is a kind of ideological overlay that "concretizes" (i.e., makes "real" a "general mythical scheme"). The latter, as Tagg showed earlier, is "the apparently seamless ideological structure called a home." That newly created structure, in turn, "dehistoricizes" the persons and objects depicted by "displacing" the ideological connection (i.e., the real, historical basis in the forces that shape this communication), "to the archetypal level" (i.e., the level of that which seems to us "natural and universal" and thus, beyond our questioning). In so doing, it serves to "conceal its specifically ideological nature." It draws a veil over our eyes in such a way that the ideology here being constructed escapes our critical awareness and so leads us to confuse that which is ideologically constructed, a manipulation designed to serve actual historical interests, with reality itself.

Janet Malcolm (1980), on the other hand, in her well-known book of essays *Diana and Nikon: Essays on the Aesthetic of Photography*, took an aesthetic approach to understanding the same photograph. Malcolm described the photograph thus:

> sitting in respectful symmetry around their magnificent floor-model studio of Aztec modern design, she sewing and he leafing through a magazine. . . . Over the enormous radio (which had taken the place of the hearth in 1939, with people warming themselves around its songs and comedies and romances) hangs a machine-art tapestry printed on black cloth and depicting a scene from a French rococo court, with aristocrats in powdered wigs graciously gathered about a harpsichord. The stout, swarthy American woman's head is covered with a black hairnet, to keep her pincurls in place, and her stockingless feet are comfortably encased in disreputable laceless shoes. The husband's right sock has an enormous hole at the ankle, about which he is equally unconcerned. His picture's life- "its action"-comes out of the contrast between Art Deco and life plain (and homely and poor), but its irony is gentle and good humored. (pp. 159–160)

The details in Malcolm's description seem to bring the picture to life as a narrative. She concentrated on the absolute particulars that constitute the image, though she organized her reading around a series of traditional aesthetic and design concepts, "respectful *symmetry*," genre ("which had taken the place of the hearth in 1939, with people warming themselves around its songs and comedies and romances"), a "machine art tapestry," "printed on black cloth," "depicting a scene," and ultimately saw "the life" of Lee's picture as that which "comes out of the contrast between Art Deco and life plain (and homely and poor,)" utilizing an "irony . . . gentle and good humored" to make his point.

What a stunning contrast! Malcolm drew attention to details of the photograph that concern Tagg secondarily, if at all. Utilizing her aesthetic repertoire, she seemed able to weave a narrative for her readers of how the different elements go well beyond any mere "ideology of the home" and so constitute a unique work, a work that apparently reveals extraordinary, creative contributions by the individual photographer himself. Here, one cannot escape the photographer's *unique* choice of that particular composition and Malcolm *alone* provided a coherent explanation of one of the photograph's most striking features, the man's left sock and the woman's hairnet and shoes, details not at least obviously necessary or even appropriate to Tagg's "ideology construction . . . of the home."

Malcolm, however, like Sarkowski, provided no significant contextualization in the historical events of which the photograph was an integral part. Indeed, she seemed comfortable with the presumption that the mind of the photographer is preoccupied with "art deco and the plain, homey and poor life" of the couple. Her reading of the photograph, of course, supported that conclusion, and her attention to details suggested that she has provided a reasonably compelling case for an aesthetic reading.

But, Malcolm left no reference whatsoever to the undeniable, contemporary ideological purposes that had placed Lee in Hidalgo County, Texas, in 1939, which shaped his mission as a whole and which constituted the basis on which his work was judged. Indeed, her interpretation appears to place Lee and his concerns—with his enthusiasm for the "contrast between Art Deco and life plain (and homely and poor)"—at the periphery of the broader task at hand. This makes problematic the assertion that this interpretation could have any broader explanatory power in the interpretation of Lee's massive photographic contribution to the FSA project.

Tagg's ideology critique, on the other hand, pointed to the fundamental importance of the institutional function of the photograph. As Tagg wrote, there is a "power to bestow authority and privilege on photographic representations" held by "certain ideological apparatuses, such as scientific establishment, government departments, the police and law courts" (p. 160). Yet Tagg left little, if any, room for the specific and unique qualities of the photograph. Indeed both are ultimately *reducible* to the ideological content and function of the photograph:

> What I am trying to stress here is the absolute continuity of the photographs' ideological existence with their existence as material objects whose "currency" and "value" arise in certain distinct and historically specific social practices and are *ultimately a function of the state*. [emphasis added] (p.165)

Thus, Tagg tends to reduce the photographer to a functionary, if not a cipher, with no clearly distinguishable, singular communicative intent and the photograph itself is reduced to an essentially featureless "type."

DISCUSSION

In an attempt to move past this impasse, we must first understand that despite these basic and indeed, ultimately irreconcilable differences, Tagg and Malcolm, and indeed, Szarkowski as well, hold to a fundamental, even if unstated, assumption that an objectively true meaning of the photograph can ultimately be determined, discerned by the piercing vision of a methodologically competent interpreter. This faith is implicit in the objectivist view as well (not discussed here), where the photograph in some basic sense is a window on the world, a window through which the viewer (subject) sees and understands the world (object).

And it is that faith, however ill-placed, that remains at least implicitly central to contemporary scholarship in the humanities generally and leads, inexorably, to a failure to fully appreciate the ineluctable and ever present need for radically open dialogue across methodological, philosophical and other boundaries. Indeed, does it not seem odd that there is no mention, no direct confrontation of Malcolm's interpretation of this photograph in the first printing of Tagg's text seven years later? And, similarly, when Malcolm published a second edition of her text in 1997, why is there no dispute of Tagg's interpretation of 1988, republished in 1992? It is very much as if the two were written in two different languages, with readerships in two different "worlds."

Method here, then, is contingent, penultimate, and always subject to revision. The multiplicity of methodological perspective in cultural studies is one of its strengths, rather than a weakness. Yet it is not only method itself, but also the underlying conceptual framework from which it derives that must be brought to conscious reflection, made open to radically dialogical debate and subject to inexhaustible scrutiny.

It is here that Tagg's reach has exceeded his grasp. For method and the conceptual framework from which it stems can lead one astray as well as lead one forward. Tagg's account earlier attempts to move to an understanding that is more inclusive of contemporary historical forces and their role in determining the character of photographs than Malcolm's approach ever could.

Yet Tagg's ideological insights, although coherent, do not appear to lead us deeply into the photograph, they scarcely seem to penetrate it's surface. Tagg has here reduced the object of study, the picture, to nothing more than an illustration, lacking any uniqueness, any depth, any individuality or nuance. This is *no* dialogical encounter. It is domination, not too unlike that which Tagg aims to uncover in the work of others.

Malcolm, on the other hand, has taken us deeper into *an* appreciation of some of the details of the individual photograph than Tagg was able, or even interested, in doing. Yet in the process, she disposes of the larger historical forces of which it was a part and her methodology draws our attention to aspects of the image, which may or may not be compelling to others (Curtis, 1989), and she fails utterly to place the image within the broader context of imagery of which it was a part. Her encounter seems incomplete, at best, and the coherence is dangerously limited—as is its fecundity.

These differences, then, call into question the completeness of both interpretations, as well as their underlying worldviews. And neither shows a significant concern for the historical actuality of the people who are in a very real and basic sense still the apparent subjects of the photograph, as an objectivist approach would allow.

Methods can open new understandings, more complete and compelling visions of meaning. They can close them off as well. An underlying and typically only cursorily examined commitment to particular worldviews can do the same. They can, as in Tagg's treatment of this image, lead us down a relatively barren, yet far from meaningless, path. Insights drawn from an endless array of fields of human endeavor have at least the potential to provide unique insights that may reveal a different yet compelling reading of the text and it is critical to accept that reality along with the radical finitude, historicity, and hence fallibility of one's own insights and contributions. Interpretation and meaning are fluid, neither arbitrary nor relative. Understanding is always tentative, incomplete, ready to be radically challenged and even overturned. And as H. G. Gadamer (1989) noted, although "All that is asked is that we remain open to the meaning of the other person or text," it remains true that "this openness always includes our situating the other meaning in relation to the whole of our own meanings or ourselves in relation to the whole of our own" (p. 268).

REFERENCES

Cutis, J. (1989). *Minds eye, mind's truth*. Philadelphia: Temple University Press. Note: James Curtis writes, in part: (Lee placed the object [the radio] at the center of his composition not to suggest that it was an extravagant purchase, but to show the important role radio played in promoting the family unit. The shiny console is the only hint of affluence in an otherwise spare interior" (p. 103).

Eaglton, T. (1991). *Ideology: an introduction*. London: Verso.

Gadamer, H.-G. (1989). *Truth and method*. 2nd Rev ed. J. Weinsheimer & D. G. Marshall (Eds.). New York: Crossroad Publishing.

Grossberg, L. (1984). Strategies of Marxist cultural interpretation. *Critical Studies in Mass Communication, 1*, 392–421.

Guimond, J. (1991). *American photography and the American dream*. Chapel Hill, University of North Carolina. Note: Guimond offers that "the couple's own effort to look more prosperous and middle class than they really are makes them seem pathetic and a little comic" (p. 125).

Hall, S. (1986, summer). The problem of idealogy-marxism without guarantees. *The Journal of Communication Inquiry, 10*(2), 29.

Hardt, H. (1992). *Critical communication studies: Communication, history, and theory in America*. London: Routledge.

Ingram, D. (1990). In *Critical theory and philosophy* (p. 1). New York: Paragon.

Jay, M. (1973). *The dialectical imagination: A history of the Frankfurt school and the Institute of Social Research 1923–1950*. Boston: Little Brown, 1973. Note: For a contemporary perspective on mass-media research in America from a viewpoint informed by critical theory, see Hardt (1982), Grossberg (1984) provided a brief introduction, and see Douglass Kellner (1990). Terry Engleton presents its status in postmodernist academic circles including a strong defense of its conceptual value. See also Ingram's work cited in this chapter.

Kellner, D. (1990). Critical theory and ideology critique, In R. Robin (Ed.), *the Aesthetic of the Critical Theorists: Studies on Benjamin, Adorno, Marcuse, and Habermas* (pp. 85–123). Lewiston, NY: Edwin Mellen Press.

Malcom, J. (1980). *Diana and Nikon: Essays on the aesthetic of photography*. Boston: David R. Godine.

Ricoeur, P. (1981). *Hermeneutics and the human sciences: essays on language, action, and interpretation* (p. 301.). J. B. Thompson (Ed. & Trans.). Cambridge: Cambridge University Press; Paris: Maison des Sciences de l'homme.

Szarkowski, J. (1973). *Looking at photographs: 100 pictures from the collection of the Museum of Modern Art*. New York: the Museum of Modern Art.

Tagg, J. (1988). *The burden of representation: essays on photographies and histories* (p. 120). Amherst: The University of Massachusetts Press.

Thompson, J. B. (1990). *Ideology and modern culture: Critical social theory in the era of mass communication*. Stanford, CA: Stanford University Press.

Turow, J. (1992). *Media system in society: Understanding industries, strategies, and power* (pp. 5–7). White Plains, NY: Longman. Note: Turow does not mention cultural studies theorists directly. Rather, he referred to "a contingent" of scholars who see mass media technological systems and advancement as likely to "*diminish* the chance for organized democratic consciousness and actions" [Emphasis original]. This position is readily associated with the critique of ideology. At the same time, Turow is critical of scholars who take the opposing view that mass media and media technology will "bring sweeping economic, political, social, and cultural changes." Turow argued in sum, that it is the industrial, structural internal struggle over leverage and resources that is primary in the shaping and distribution of media products.

Wolff, J. (1983). *Aesthetics and the sociology of art* (p. 105). London: George Allen and Unwin.

Woodward, R. B. (1988, March). Picture Prefect. *Art News, 97*, 168.

Author Index

Numbers in *italics* indicate pages with complete bibliographic information.

A

Abbs, P., *516*
Abdullah, H., 186, *189*
Abraham, N., 332, *347*
Adair, J., 486, 487, *502*, 506, *517*
Agrawal, B. C., 511, *516*
Alasuutari, P., 345, *347*
Aldrich, V. C., 167, *176*
Alexander, D. A., 386, 389, 400, *404*
Allen, C., *22*, *43*
Allen, N. W., *115*
Allen, R. C., 109, *112*, 271, *291*, 317, *325*, 506, *516*
Althusser, L., 546, *550*
Anderson, D., 214, *222*
Anderson, J. A., 232, 234, 240, 276, 279, 282, *291*, *293*, *312*, *347*
Anderson, R., 448, *455*
Andrews, C. L., *266*, *267*
Ang, I., 281, *291*
Ansolabehere, S., *295*, *313*
Antes, J., *43*
Aristotle, 155, *165*, 378, *384*
Armer, A., 397, *403*
Armstrong, M., *22*, *44*
Arnheim, R., 7, *20*, *42*, 82, *95*, 101, *112*, 307, *313*, 372, 374, 379, *384*, *500*, 510, *516*
Arrell, D., 109, *112*
Arvidson, C., *403*
Astington, J., 216, *222*
Atkinson, P., 407, 408, *426*
Audigier, J. Y., 143, *151*

B

Baarda, B., 214, *222*
Babbie, E., 432, *441*
Back, K. W., 109, *112*, 167, *176*
Bain, C., 81, *95*
Bakewell, L., 475, *475*
Bakhtin, M., 332, *347*
Barbatsis, G. S., xi, xxi, 236, *241*, 290, *291*, 291, 296, 312, *313*, 339, 344, *347*, 375, 380, *384*, 548, *550*
Barker, C., 525, 537, *537*
Barker, D., 505, *516*
Barnette, B. D., 64, *79*
Barnhurst, K., *291*, 291, 312, *313*
Barry, A. M., *xxi*, 82, *95*, 197, 200, 202, *209*, 235, 240, 288, 289, *291*, 303, 307, 309, 312, *313*, 334, 337, *348*, 381, *384*, 431, *441*, 461, *475*
Barthes, R., 230, 231, 234, 237, 238, *240*, 245, *255*, *267*, 332, *348*, 352, 353, *361*, *455*, 546, 547, *550*
Bass, E., 186, *189*
Bateson, G., 17, *20*, 331, *348*, 429, 432, *441*, *442*
Battenfeld, J., 401, *404*
Baudrillard, J., *267*
Bazin, A., 101, *112*, 491, *500*
Beardsley, M., 109, *112*
Bechara, A., 195, 196, 198, 199, 201, *209*, 431, *441*, 461, *475*
Becker, H. S., 280, *291*, 408, 409, 449, *455*
Begun, B., 159, *165*
Beilin, H., 8, *22*, *44*
Benedetto, R., *403*
Benjamin, W., *267*

Subject Index

Numbers followed by an *italic f* indicate a page with a figure. Numbers followed by an *italic t* indicate a page with a table.

I

Iconic signs, archive/image interrelate as, 258–259
Ideological analysis, of television promotional
    advertisement, 545–547
Ideology, as code of television production, 531–532
Illusions theories, 109–110
Illustration
    as art, 319–320
    as astronomy, 320–323
Image bank
    in cross cultural communication, 121–122
    in visual cross-cultural analysis, 120
Images
    power relations and, 525
    visual literacy and, 496–499
Implicit aesthetic relationships, 8–11, 9f, 10f, 11f
Indexical relationship, 100
Indexical signs, archive/image interrelate as, 258
India study
    of cross cultural communication, 124
    of soap operas
        aesthetics, 506–508
        lighting, 508–511
        western bias, 508
Intelligence(s)
    cognition and, 199–201, 201t
    multiple, 212–213
    spatial, 487–489, 488f, 489f
    televiewing experience and, 213–214
Interdisciplinary perspective, of visual
    communication, 5–6
Internet advertising, eye movement research and,
    64–65
Internet banner ads, eye tracking and, 65, 66
Internet pages advertising, eye tracking on, 63–65
Interpretation, in semiotic theory, 238–239
Intuitive cognitive system, 194
Isomorphism, perception of, 84–85, 85f

J

JIU. *See* Jones International University
Jones International University (JIU), in visual
    rhetorical study, 157

K

Knowing, parallel ways of, 204t
Korean student study, in cross cultural
    communication, 124–125

L

Latin-square design, 68, 68t
Layered aesthetic meaning, 35, 37, 39–41
    man in mayhem, 39f
    self-portrait, 38f
Layering
    in aesthetic relationships, 41
    process of, 24
    in visual aesthetics, 18
Lee, Russell, Hildago County, Texas photograph by,
    571f
    analysis of, 571–573
Left brain, 197–199
Lesbian and bisexual women's study, of cross
    cultural communication, 126
Lighting
    in applied media aesthetics, 367–369
    as code of television production, 530–531
    in Indian soap operas, 508–511
Linguistic metaphors,
    visual metaphors and, 168–171
Linguistic sign, 99
Literal structure, in narrative theory, 336–338, 338f
Live film, in applied media aesthetics, 378
Live television, in applied media aesthetics,
    377–378
Logic
    narrative, 333–334
    in narrative theory, 331–333
    pictorial, 333–334
    of visual aesthetics, 15–18

M

Madonna and the Floursack photograph, analysis
    of, 261f, 261–262
Magazine editors, photographic manipulation
    among, 449–454
Magazines versus newspapers, in photographic
    manipulation, 453
Magnetic resonance imaging (MRI), visual
    communication and, 52
Majority culture images, in visual
    cross-cultural analysis, 119–120
Make-believe theories, 110–111
Manipulation. *See also* Photographic manipulation
    of point of view, 497–498
    in visual literacy theory, 497–498
MANOVA. *See* Multiple analysis of variance
Market segment study, of cross cultural
    communication, 125–126